Jefferson Davis: Tragic Hero

BOOKS BY HUDSON STRODE

JEFFERSON DAVIS: AMERICAN PATRIOT

JEFFERSON DAVIS: CONFEDERATE PRESIDENT

DENMARK IS A LOVELY LAND

SWEDEN: MODEL FOR A WORLD

NOW IN MEXICO

TIMELESS MEXICO

FINLAND FOREVER

SOUTH BY THUNDERBIRD

THE PAGEANT OF CUBA

THE STORY OF BERMUDA

IMMORTAL LYRICS: *An Anthology of English Lyrics*

SPRING HARVEST: *An Anthology of Alabama Stories*

Cameo portrait of Jefferson Davis made in Washington, D.C., in 1851, as a remembrance for his eldest sister, Anna Davis Smith

JEFFERSON DAVIS

TRAGIC HERO

THE LAST TWENTY-FIVE YEARS

1864–1889

———◆———

BY HUDSON STRODE

———◆———

Harcourt, Brace & World, Inc.

NEW YORK

For
Jonathan W. Warner
and
Prewitt Semmes, Jr.

"Show me a hero and I will write you a tragedy."

—F. SCOTT FITZGERALD

"It is our duty to keep the memory of our heroes green. Yet they belong not to us alone; they belong to the whole country; they belong to America."

—JEFFERSON DAVIS, *April, 1882*

CONTENTS

INTRODUCTION

IN THE SECOND century, Lucian, the Greek satirist, declared: "A writer of history ought in his writings to be a foreigner, without country, living under his own law only, subject to no King, nor caring what any man may like or dislike, but laying out the matter as it is." In today's world with its changing alignments and shifting passions it is not easy for a historian or a biographer to meet the test of Lucian's dictum.

Thirteen years ago I approached the subject of Jefferson Davis almost as a stranger. From college days my historical affections had always lain abroad, and my previous books were all written about foreign lands and peoples. I had now to study the whole period of the War Between the States from the beginning. I had never been, nor am I now, what in the vernacular is called a Civil War "buff." I had no theory to advance. I did not know what I would find. So, in a partial sense, I fit the requirements of Lucian. In this biography I have endeavored to "lay out the matter as it is."

When I began this life of Jefferson Davis in 1951, I had expected to produce a one-volume work. But as I proceeded with research and discovered quantities of essential material that had never been in the public domain, the plan of the book grew. What I had originally thought to do in four years has turned out to be a thirteen-year task and a three-volume work.

This third and final volume begins on New Year's Day, 1864, when the war was about to enter its final stages. It ends with the death of Jefferson Davis twenty-five years later.

For the sake of authenticity I have followed Davis's postwar footsteps into his prison cell, to Canada, where he sought refuge after his release from Fort Monroe in 1867, and to Europe, to which he

made five trips between 1868 and 1881. With the guidance of Edgar
Collard, editor of the Montreal *Gazette,* I saw all the places where
Davis lived and the Canadian streets on which he walked. In 1962
I traced him in his 1868 travels across Scotland, through the Robert
Burns country, and down the river from Glasgow to Greenock. I
have made use of contemporary Scottish newspaper accounts of this
trip as well as the Davis letters. In London, while reading in the
British Museum, I visited the Davis haunts. I went to Karlsruhe,
Germany, where his younger daughter attended school for five years
and where he visited her in October, 1876. Most important of all,
I spent parts of two summers in Colorado Springs, where resides
the Confederate President's only living grandson, who gave me access to almost a thousand private letters that no other historian or
biographer has as yet seen.

To penetrate into the unknown being of a man separated from
us by a long stretch of years, wrote Marc Bloch, the French historian,
"one must almost cast off one's own self," and the biographer should
be on guard not to drown his subject's voice with his own. In the
text of this trilogy I have tried to keep my voice as low as possible,
to let Jefferson Davis speak for himself in letters, in official papers,
and in recorded conversations.

By presenting Davis in times of rural quiet as well as high emergencies, I have endeavored to create a sense of actuality: to show
him "in his habit as he lived," in the intimacy of the family circle,
in the heat of battle, on the statesman's dais, in prison chains, and in
his last decade on the Mississippi Gulf Coast blessedly "chequered
with solitude."

For the sake of clarity I have followed a rather strict chronology.
And because I have portrayed events as largely seen or known by
the subject of this biography, I have presented the Southern view-
point, as Bruce Catton in his splendid volumes on the Civil War
frankly admits that he writes from the Union point of view.

Dunbar Rowland, the Mississippi author, spent nine years (1913-
1922) collecting Davis material, copying letters and documents,
while preparing to write a definitive life of the Confederate President. Finally, he relinquished his purpose, because, he declared, in
the process of research, he had become a hero worshiper. When confronted with this possibility myself, though in the beginning it
seemed extremely unlikely because I had not been attracted to the
Davis coldly portrayed in history books, I recalled Boswell and two

of the most popular American biographies of our time: Sandburg's *Abraham Lincoln* and Freeman's *R. E. Lee.* Delving into the mind and heart of Jefferson Davis these past dozen years, and refusing to accept the stereotypes of former commentators, I have come to have such enormous respect and admiration for this misunderstood man that I may appear at times to lack objectivity. But I have sought to reveal the plainness and solidity of truth and yet hint at what Virginia Woolf calls "the rainbow-like intangibility of personality."

As Davis's Ohio biographer, Landon Knight, pointed out in 1905, few men in history have ever had to withstand such measures of malign misrepresentation as Jefferson Davis. Do the American chronicles reveal any other man who faced such fierce and sweeping blasts of false indictment and malice and yet stood erect? Jefferson Davis had to drink perhaps the bitterest cup in our history; yet he survived, with his principles consistent to the end.

Like Thomas Jefferson, for whom he was named, Davis never participated in public life from personal choice. He was first a soldier and then a planter. He was thrust into the political arena by his eldest brother, Joseph, who stood as a father to him, and by the clamoring citizens of his state. The offices of United States Senator, Secretary of War, and President of the Confederacy were all handed to him. He accepted the latter two high positions without joy and in doing so sacrificed his own desires.

According to contemporary records, Jefferson Davis proved to be one of the great Senators of all times and as such had a pervading influence on constructive legislation. Even his opponents admitted that as Secretary of War he had not been surpassed. Before the birth of the Confederacy Davis had performed consummately patriotic deeds in the Black Hawk and Mexican wars and had reached political heights few men in this country ever attain. In 1861, he held the unique position of proven statesmanship and conspicuous service on the battlefield.

Most of Davis's critics agree that he ever maintained an unflagging idealism and an unfaltering courage. His chief political enemy, Vice-President Alexander Stephens, declared: "Mr. Davis was the bravest and most courageous man I ever knew. He was absolutely without fear. He was absolutely indifferent to danger."

Jefferson Davis was, first of all, a man of unusual common sense. He was remarkably free of crochets or foibles. His simplicity precluded the sentimentality that was general in the last half of the nineteenth century. After years of investigation I have concluded that one of Davis's most outstanding characteristics was his unselfishness, and it supported his integrity. Rather than deny his conscience he would break with powerful supporters. He was throughout upheld by his unwavering conviction of the righteousness of the cause to which he had become dedicated.

When Davis faced a sullen audience which had been disturbed by some newspaper's false charge of governmental negligence, he became the more resolute in proportion to the force of the opposition. With his unshakeable firmness and cool control, plus an indefinable mystical quality of leadership, he had the power "to move, control or electrify an audience." In adversity Davis's ability to stir soldiers and citizens alike was extraordinary. Almost invariably he sent men away from his public addresses, prepared or impromptu, with a higher opinion of the Confederacy, their President, and themselves.

Again and again during the writing of this biography, a speculation recurs: if Jefferson Davis could have had the benefit of radio, as did Franklin Roosevelt and Winston Churchill, if disheartened people in their homes and the hungry soldiers in the camps could have listened to his eloquence and felt his dauntless resolution, it is likely that the war would have ended differently. If Northerners could have seen and heard Davis on television, as the world later could see and hear John F. Kennedy, the one-fourth of the Northern people who were eager to stop the slaughter of brothers and who wished to prevent a centralization of Federal power might have been more effective and conceivably could have prevailed.

It should be remembered that though he believed firmly in the inherent right of secession, Davis was a most reluctant secessionist. Because of the South's defenseless situation he doubted the practicability of its success, and, for economic reasons, he feared that the North would coerce and crush the South. To him, Mr. Lincoln's election was "a fact of grave significance, as it was purely sectional," yet it was not a sufficient cause for the initial secession of South Carolina. Davis fervently hoped, and repeatedly urged, that sectional differences should be worked out within the framework of the Union, which he loved. As Bruce Catton writes, most of Davis's far-ranging activities in Washington had been "sincerely aimed at strengthening and unifying the country."

Though he was disinclined to accept the position of chief executive of the Confederacy—it was indeed thrust upon him—Jefferson

Davis became a President in a historical situation without a precedent. He was perhaps the only political chief in history who successfully organized a new nation in the course of pursuing a mighty war.

Whereas some commentators contend that Davis's very self-reliance and strong will contributed to the failure of the Confederate cause, others, including numerous Northern observers, are otherwise convinced that it was his personal ability and determined exercise of will that kept defeat off so long.

Woodrow Wilson, in the fourth volume of his *History of the American People,* speaks of "the masterful characteristics of Mr. Jefferson Davis."

He had the pride, the spirit of initiative, the capacity in business, which qualify men for leadership, and lacked nothing of the indomitable will and impervious purpose to make his leadership effective. He moved direct, undaunted by any peril, and heartened a whole people to hold steadfast to the end.

To amplify this appraisal by a noted historian I quote a simple comment by Davis's great-niece, Lucy Stamps Farrar, who as a young matron was at his deathbed. "Uncle Jeff," she wrote, "was a very appealing sort of man, very handsome, and with tremendous charm." Both summations, though derived from utterly different points of observation, I find true and not inconsistent.

A prime factor that Davis's biographers have largely failed to realize is the love he inspired among men in a man's world: in generals and soldiers, in bishops and clergymen, in a number of Cabinet officers like the urbane Judah P. Benjamin and the rough-hewn Texan, John Reagan, in President Franklin Pierce, in Negroes, slave or free. And his elder daughter, Margaret Hayes, set down in a letter to Dean Walter Fleming in 1907 a touching impression of the man as his family knew him. "I have a sketch of my father, as father and grandfather, partly written—it shows the sweetest, softest, most entirely lovable side of his, to me, perfect manhood." His younger daughter, Winnie, emphasized in a New York newspaper article his love and understanding of children.

We children always believed that there was no natural upheaval too stupendous not to be dominated by our father. Never did we feel that anything which annoyed or hurt us could be beneath his notice, for he was one of those delightful persons who seem always possessed of time to listen and endless store of sympathy to expend. His anger against one who frightened or abused a child was appalling.

Davis was as elegant in the drawing room as he was forceful and magnetic on the platform. Though extremely neat in his person, almost to the point of fastidiousness, he was never personally extravagant. (Once in New Orleans he bought better shirts for his colored servant, Robert Brown, than he did for himself.) As his daughter Margaret wrote to Fleming, he "talked but little of himself at any time." He minimized his exploits as he did his tribulations; he spoke little of his Mexican War wounds; and he bore the excruciating pain he suffered from facial neuralgia without imposing on others. His prison doctor at Fort Monroe deemed self-control to be his outstanding characteristic.

In regard to Davis's "flaws," many of his friends wrote that "being human, of course, he had his faults," but they did not specify what they were. His habit of command and his consciousness of intellectual superiority may on occasions have made him seem imperious, but never did they intrude on his attitude of a gentleman. His good manners seem to have been unfailing. He believed that a gentleman might be distressed by his own lack of capacity, but that he should never be disturbed by the failure of others to recognize his merits.

It was sometimes hard for Davis to delegate responsibility, because, like Thomas Jefferson, his genius for statesmanship lay in his ability "to sense fundamental issues in a maze of complexities." He was sensitive and somewhat thin-skinned, and he often made the mistake of answering some of his critics and thus wasting time. However, though he felt the sting of unjust criticism, he could "look with an obstinate eye on the Devil himself." He was loyal to honest men who were giving their all to the cause, even though he would have gained popular favor by getting rid of some of them.

Davis did not possess Lincoln's gift for practical politics. He was not always conciliatory, and he made enemies by letting his petitioners know his opinion or decision at once, not permitting them to go away still hoping and maneuvering. He lacked the saving evasiveness and fluidity of the politician. Davis was not formed of elements that would make of him a revolutionary dictator. He could not be ruthless. He was too much of a deep-dyed constitutionalist. Therein, in the view of some critics, he failed. Others believe that he should have muzzled inimical newspapers and jailed the editors, because of the dissension and distrust they created in the camps and on the home front. But to Davis, the right of free speech was fundamental.

After his final release from Federal custody, Jefferson Davis had years of struggle in trying to find employment to support his large family. Northern prejudice pursued him to England, where again and again he made business negotiations which were broken off after warnings of disapproval from Northern interests. He failed to secure desired executive posts with Southern railroads because they were financed by Northern capital. "Radical" Republicans in Congress prevented him—and him alone—from being allotted a meager Mexican War pension, though he had returned severely wounded from that conflict with a hero's triumph second only to that of Zachary Taylor. Through the demagoguery of James G. Blaine, his was the sole name scratched from the last general amnesty bill in the 1870's, which would have permitted him, if he had chosen, to reenter the United States Senate with the attendant emoluments.

When he was unable to find a suitable lucrative position, Davis perforce spent three years in writing *The Rise and Fall of the Confederate Government,* in which he defended his political philosophy and gave a full account of the Confederacy's activities. As he approached seventy, he was bequeathed "Beauvoir," a charming place on the Mississippi Gulf Coast, in which he spent his last years. Yet even in the eighth decade of his life, when he might have enjoyed rural occupations and reverie, he had on him the burden of his old Delta plantation, Brierfield, which was periodically inundated by the uncontrolled Mississippi River. And living in comparative solitude, disenfranchised, without citizenship, he suffered periodic attacks by a few Northern politicians and a monstrously false accusation by one of his generals. Yet in the last three years of his life, during triumphal tours, he was lauded as "The Uncrowned King of the South"; and at his death in December, 1889, he was given the greatest funeral the South has ever known.

Edward Channing, in Volume VI of his monumental *History of the United States,* concludes that "Davis's motives and actions are above reproach." And he asserts without equivocation: "Putting Davis on one side and those within the Confederacy who opposed him on the other, one is amazed in comparison with the littleness of his opponents."

Jefferson Davis remains one of the philosophically consistent figures of American history. The Constitution was to him a sacred compact, by which a number of sovereign states agreed to hold their possessions in common under strict limitations. He had learned his lessons of constitutional law in the school of Jefferson and Madison. With a singleness of purpose Davis gave his loyalty to the Government of the United States as it was originally constituted, for he regarded it as the most nearly perfect yet devised by man. He did not vary from this view of the nature of the Government under which he filled so many important positions with outstanding success before 1861. To the end, Davis felt that he was fighting for State Rights—for the North as well as the South. With the Greeks, he respected free government as something in the nature of a metaphysical manifestation, and he was, like Socrates, "compelled to survey the beauty that is in institutions and laws."

All through the war Davis took comfort in the fact that a goodly fourth of the Northern people believed in the justice of the Confederate cause. Edgar Lee Masters, the Illinois poet, was to write with conviction that the South "poured the flower of her youth from her colleges and academies into the cause of the Declaration of Independence." And in his opinion the Confederates fought "with a courage, manliness, and a devotion never perhaps equalled since the days when Athens inspired the noblest men to give up their lives for their city."

Jefferson Davis was a tragic hero in the Greek, rather than the Shakespearean, sense. After lifting him to the heights and decorating him with signal honors, fate seemed determined to destroy him, finally casting him into prison and stripping him of everything except what the Hellenes called "virtue." His private life was invaded by grievous calamities, including the deaths of all four of his sons. But doom did not break his spirit or even cause him to relinquish faith in a higher power. I can find no fatal "flaw" in the Davis character like to that which Shakespeare gives his heroes to bring about their own ruin, unless it be a passion he shared with the classic Greeks: an almost fanatical belief in freedom in government.

Ours is now one nation. All resolute and virtuous deeds that have been done in it are the shared heritage of the American character. Because the order of high merit rests on the breast of Jefferson Davis, his life cannot but add luster to the national aspect.

HUDSON STRODE

Cherokee Road
Tuscaloosa, Alabama
May 12, 1964

Jefferson Davis: Tragic Hero

CHAPTER I

THE NEW YEAR LULL BRINGS
NEW PROBLEMS

WHEN JEFFERSON DAVIS awakened on Saturday, January 2, 1864, the morning was bright and clear. Though the night had been excessively cold, the weather was definitely moderating. He was tired from six hours' standing and handshaking at the New Year's Day reception. But he was gratified to recall that the affair had been a success; as many declared, "the most brilliant party yet." After almost three years of devastating war, it was remarkable that the Southerners could be so gay. The capital's first ladies had worn their finest jewels and their most elegant costumes, however much refashioned. Outwardly, at least, the morale of the citizens was at a high level. And soldiers on leave had exhibited a heartiness and a dashing, devil-may-care attitude that scorned the terrible odds against them.

Later this Saturday morning, as the President sipped pungent sassafras tea, he was thankful that no aggressive activity threatened on any battlefront. True, the North was preparing another mighty offensive against Richmond, but this was not too alarming. Davis could recall that all the former Union attacks—led successively by McDowell, McClellan, Burnside, Hooker, and Pope—had failed. Though the Federals had obtained decisive success at Chattanooga in late November, the North was not overelated. Mr. Lincoln had admitted there was much fighting still to be done; and everyone knew that a large part of the Northern public was becoming restive under the prolonged hostilities. The peace party in the North and the so-called Copperheads were causing the Federal Administration considerable disquiet. Six months after Gettysburg, the Union Army of the Potomac, under General George Gordon Meade, was still more than fifty miles from Richmond.

3

Yet Davis reflected that the inequalities of the struggle had become more glaring as time passed. Every material advantage lay heavily on the side of the enemy. The North possessed overwhelming industrial power, together with well-functioning railroads, an ever increasing naval force, a world-ranging merchant marine, and a white population that outnumbered the South's by more than four to one and was increasing. The Federal Administration, despite the Pope's protest, continued to replenish its armed forces by shiploads of impoverished Irish Catholics and Germans, luring them by means of homesteads and cash bonuses, and using them to fight the South's diminishing ranks. The Confederacy's want of manpower was appalling, more serious than the shortages in meat, munitions, and railway equipment.

Rumors of scattered disaffection had been reaching President Davis since Gettysburg. Such signs of weakness were as disturbing as the fact that General Lee would most likely have to face his next would-be conqueror with half the enemy's force and half his armaments and rations.

On this first business day of 1864, the President of the Confederate States walked to his office with mixed feelings and perhaps as heavy a load on his thin shoulders as any public man in America ever bore. Few men in the annals of history had had to create a new nation within the cauldron of a great war. But Davis was fired by his resolve to fight aggression to the last hilltop. The chill January atmosphere gave his somewhat sunken cheeks a sanguine glow. By the time he entered his office, for all his extreme leanness, he looked remarkably well. Departmental officials marveled how he was able to keep going and, generally, in such good temper under the grueling pressures. In almost three years Davis had not taken a single day's real vacation. Such a strain, they said, might well have felled a man far more robust than the Chief, which was what Burton Harrison, his young Private Secretary, always called him.

This morning, after the accustomed exchange of pleasantries, it pained young Harrison to lay before the President a disquieting letter from Zebulon Vance, Governor of North Carolina. As Davis glanced swiftly over the missive, dated December 30, 1863, he sensed the menacing undertone of disaffection. The Raleigh *Press* had recently urged peace at any terms, declaring that the alternative was starvation, although North Carolina was better stocked with foodstuffs than any other state. Now Vance declared that if the

President did not initiate peace overtures, it might be "impossible to remove the discontent in North Carolina."

Like a few other politicians in high places, Vance did not grasp the enormity of Davis's problems, and was mainly concerned in pleasing his constituents. He knew perfectly well that before the war broke out Confederate emissaries had tried desperately to talk with President Lincoln and his Secretary of State, William Seward, to settle differences around a conference table instead of on a battlefield. Every Southerner was aware that as recently as July, Mr. Lincoln had refused to receive his one-time friend Alexander Stephens on a humane mission concerning prisoners' welfare. The Confederacy's Vice-President had been allowed to get no nearer to Washington than Fort Monroe, Virginia. How could the Confederate Government negotiate with President Lincoln, who refused to admit that the Confederate States even existed, although it was costing Northern taxpayers hundreds of millions to coerce this non-existing republic?

Reading Vance's letter over carefully, Davis discerned something more deadly to the Confederacy's cause than the blast of Union guns. If the South was finally defeated, the catastrophe might come from inner corrosion! He would have to answer with restraint and tact, but with such force and cogency that the baby snake might be destroyed before it developed fangs and venom. He would wait until he had cooled somewhat.

When Mary Chesnut heard from her husband, Colonel James Chesnut, Jr., one of the President's aides, of Vance's wavering attitude, she confided her dismay to her diary. "Mr. Chesnut came in and almost killed us with this piece of latest news. North Carolina wants to offer terms of peace! We need only a break of that kind to finish us. I shivered as one does when the first handful of earth comes rattling down on the coffin of one we cared for above all."

In the afternoon of January 7, snow, which had been falling all day, covered Richmond with a solid whiteness for the first time that winter of 1863-64. From his office windows the President beheld a transformed Richmond. The shabbiness of three years' disrepair and the accumulated grime from factory soot were obliterated. Gay music was in the air. The streets were animated with people on their way to the railway station to greet General John Hunt Morgan, the famous Kentucky raider. On a summer's raid into Indiana and Ohio, Morgan and several of his band had been captured on July

26. Incarcerated in the Columbus Penitentiary, they had been roughly treated, not as prisoners of war but as common criminals. The handsome Kentuckian had had his head completely shaved, as well as his distinguishing beard. By careful planning and exhausting labor Morgan and some of his officers had dug through the floor of a cell into an air chamber beneath and tunneled through a stout wall into the prison yard. They had then scaled the outer wall and escaped into hostile country in bleak November weather. Morgan had reached Georgia safely, and now, with some of his companions, he was arriving in Richmond for a hero's welcome.

The President was not going to the station; he would entertain Morgan later. He knew from the arranged program that the escaped General would have a tumultuous reception and that the ebullient "Jeb" Stuart was prepared to speak "with all his voice."

While Mrs. Chesnut, with some other ladies, stood "ankle-deep in snow," listening to the high-flown speeches lauding Morgan— "never did women enjoy a jollier tramp"—the President called for his horse and unaccompanied rode off with his problems. The observant war clerk, J. B. Jones, saw him pass his house alone, "to indulge his thoughts in solitude in the suburbs." As "Kentucky" trotted slowly through the silent part of town between shimmering rows of white-branched trees, his hoofbeats muted by the snow, the reply to Governor Vance began to take final shape in the President's mind.

The next day President Davis composed a lengthy letter to Vance. He recounted three distinct efforts he had made to communicate with the Federal Government, all "invariably unsuccessful."

To attempt again to send commissioners to propose peace, is to invite insult and calumny, without the slightest chance of being heard. No true citizen, no man who has our cause at heart can desire this. . . . Such course would receive the condemnation of those true patriots who have given their blood and their treasure to maintain freedom.

In almost every message he had sent to the Confederate Congress, Davis pointed out, he had reiterated that the Confederacy's desire was peace. "Contrary-wise," he declared, "I have seen no action of the Federal House of Representatives that does not indicate by a very decided majority the purpose of the enemy to refuse all terms to the South except absolute, unconditional subjugation or extermination."

It is with Lincoln alone that we ever could confer, and his own partisans at the North avow unequivocally that his purpose in his message and proclamation was to shut out all hope that he would *ever* treat with us on *any* terms. If we will break up our Government, dissolve the Confederacy, disband our armies, emancipate our slaves, take an oath of allegiance binding ourselves to obedience to him, and to disloyalty to our own States, he proposed to pardon us, and not to plunder us of anything more than the property already stolen from us.

"Peace," Davis affirmed, "on any other terms is now impossible. To obtain the sole terms to which you or I could listen, this struggle must continue until the enemy is beaten out of his vain confidence in our subjugation."

He warned Vance against the "bad men" in his own state who initiated movements to give aid and comfort to the enemy. "With your influence and position," he said in admonition and appeal, "the promoters of the unfounded discontent, now prevalent in your State, would be put down without the use of physical force, if you would abandon a policy of conciliation and set them at defiance. In this course frankly and firmly pursued, you would rally around you all that is noblest in your State, and your triumph would be bloodless."

It was a clear, forceful letter, calculated to make Vance see the light and rally him to patriotic duty, and at the same time not sting.

And now General Joseph Johnston, who had such difficulty in making up his own mind, wrote the President four times in five days. On January 12, from his headquarters at Dalton, Georgia, Johnston threatened to draw farther away from the inactive Federal forces because he was feuding with cantankerous Governor Joseph E. Brown over Georgia's railway facilities. He informed Davis that if he did not use his influence on Brown to give him the authority he needed over the railways, he would withdraw. "As the falling back of the Army," Davis telegraphed, "would be so seriously detrimental, both from military and political considerations, I trust you will not deem it necessary to adopt such a measure."

The repetitive pattern of Johnston's complaints and threats of withdrawal was already in evidence in this first month of 1864. The men close to Davis in Richmond wondered how his patience could hold out. Yet, on the slightest occasion, the editors of the Richmond *Examiner* sang the praises of Joseph E. Johnston and rarely missed a day criticizing the Confederate President.

While the Governors of Georgia and North Carolina were making difficulties for Davis, he felt nibbling disaffection close to his own chair. Mrs. Chesnut set down a list of the halfhearted ones: "Stephens, the Vice-President, is number one." Davis already had his hands full in managing a quarrelsome Congress, with obstructionists like Henry Foote, his perennial enemy, and Louis Wigfall, his one-time friend, concocting embarrassments to harass him. Yet, despite grumblings in Congress and displays of demagoguery, that undistinguished body, for the most part, supported the energetic measures of the President. Even many of those members who railed against him were constrained to vote as he wished. The first achievement of this new congressional session was the repeal of the "substitute law." By such legislation 70,000 more soldiers might be recruited.

"Our Congress is so demoralized, so confused, so depressed," wrote Mrs. Chesnut, "they have asked the President, whom they have so hated, so insulted, so crossed and opposed and prevented, in every way, to speak to them and advise them what to do."

In his speech to the Confederate Congress on February 3, the President had one dominant aim: to halt any treasonable designs within the Confederacy. And, strict constitutionalist that he was known to be, he had to persuade the politicians that in critical emergencies certain rights of states should be temporarily given up for the general good. First, he admitted that the original zeal that had animated the people to spring to the defense of their cause had in some parts of the Confederacy been impaired by the long continuance and magnitude of the struggle.

While brigade after brigade of our brave soldiers who have endured the trials of the camp and battlefield are testifying their patriotism by voluntary reenlistment, discontent, disaffection, and disloyalty are manifested among those who, through the sacrifices of others, have enjoyed quiet and safety at home. Public meetings have been held, in some of which a treasonable design is masked by a pretense of devotion to State sovereignty, and in others is openly avowed.

Dangerous citizens arrested for admitted disloyalty, Davis declared, had been set free by demand of the civil authorities for want of "competent legal testimony." "Twice," he announced, "the Government has received secret and confidential information of plots to release the prisoners confined in Richmond. I have satisfactory reasons for believing that spies are continually coming and going in our midst . . . important information of secret movement among the negroes fomented by base white men has been received from faithful servants, but no arrests of instigators could be made because there was no competent testimony."

Then he asked ironically, "Must the independence for which we are contending, the safety of the defenseless families of the men who have fallen in battle and of those who still confront the invader, be put in peril for the sake of conformity to the technicalities of the law of treason?"

Coming to his main objective, which he feared might be contested, he said, "Having thus presented some of the threatening evils which exist, it remains to suggest the remedy. And in my judgment that is to be found only in the suspension of the privilege of the writ of *habeas corpus.*" He conceded that it was a sharp remedy, but a necessary one: "A remedy plainly contemplated by the Constitution."

To temporize with disloyalty in the midst of war is but to quicken it to the growth of treason. I therefore respectfully recommend that the privilege of the writ of *habeas corpus* be suspended.

Before this logic, opposition melted. On February 11, Congress suspended *habeas corpus* throughout the Confederacy. The President had again got his way.

Down in Georgia, Vice-President Stephens quivered with outrage at "the unconstitutionality." Governor Brown expressed "horror" at the "wicked act." And Linton Stephens, Alexander's idolizing brother, who had already cried, "I would strike a thousand blows to pull down this infamous government rather than sustain it," boldly announced that "Jeff Davis should be impeached."

On February 3, the day the President's message was delivered to Congress, General William Tecumseh Sherman, with 20,000 men, moved from Vicksburg along the railroad to Jackson, wrecking and burning as he went. Speculations had it that he would head towards Mobile or go straight east to Selma, Alabama, to destroy the gun foundry there and to cut off Confederate food supplies in the Tombigbee River Valley. Sherman occupied Meridian and halted to await Brigadier General William Smith, who was coming from Memphis with reinforcing Union cavalry. But Nathan Bedford Forrest upset Smith's plans by whipping him at Okolona, Mississippi, and driving him back to Memphis.

As Sherman marched east General Leonidas Polk begged help

from Joseph Johnston at Dalton. President Davis directed General Johnston to give Polk all the aid in his power. On February 13, he wired Johnston asking what he could do to strike at the enemy in motion and "before he establishes a new base." When Johnston, apparently paralyzed at the thought of releasing any of his men, made no move whatever, Davis directly ordered him to detach General Hardee with the infantry of his corps to proceed with all possible dispatch to unite with Polk's force. But Johnston had delayed too long.

As General Smith failed to arrive, Sherman burned Meridian to the ground and turned towards Vicksburg again, trailed by "miles of negroes," who now looked to the bluecoats for succor. The Negroes were disappointed in their "deliverers," who had burned them out of house and home and now declared they had no rations for them. When some of the kindhearted Union soldiers wanted to help the exhausted mothers carry their hungry, fretting children, Sherman shook off the encumbrances by ordering a quick march. The baffled blacks were left languishing in despair all along the charred trail.

The letters that Davis received from his state about the Negroes' misery caused him distress and indignation. In regard to Sherman's aggressive march to Meridian, Davis felt that if Johnston had acted with dispatch, as Forrest had done, Sherman might have been so mangled that his future in the Federal forces would have been decidedly curtailed.

CHAPTER II

"LIKE SAILORS IN THE
SPIRIT CLOSET"

———◆———

THE NEW YEAR'S party having evoked such popular response, Jefferson Davis now consented to hold a reception at the Executive Mansion every week until spring activity started on the battlefronts. Opportunity was thus afforded soldiers on leave to greet their Commander-in-Chief in person. At these levées the President unbent. "Davis," T. C. De Leon wrote, "had that marvelous memory which locates instantly a man not seen for years, and his familiar inquiries pleased the visitors." Mrs. Davis, he said, received every man with a pleasant welcome, and she never differentiated among the guests, but "made the lowliest feel as if he were present by right."

For the first two months of 1864, while beneficent mud bogged down aggressive enemy moves, all Richmond took time out to entertain. The capital was crowded as never before with heroes to be cheered. And the President continually summoned general officers from various fields for consultation. While the dwindling Southern armies were being revivified with recruits, the citizens spent lavishly of their capital and assumed a bravura gaiety. The last of the good wines were brought up from old cellars.

Benefit charade parties became the vogue and the admission fees were turned over to committees to provide comforts for the wounded or succor for soldiers' widows. President Davis was persuaded to lend his presence to a benefit at the home of his Northern-born aide Colonel Joseph Ives and his wife, the former Cora Semmes, well-to-do niece of the Confederacy's foremost Admiral. Maggie Davis, his nine-year-old daughter, called "Pollie," was to perform, and she had coaxed her father to come to see her act.

The Ives house was one of the few private homes in which Jefferson Davis ever appeared. It was sometimes called "a detached segment of the White House"; for the Iveses continually entertained foreign guests and various dignitaries for the President.

A sofa of honor had been set "in front of all" like a kind of royal box for the President and his lady. Many of Davis's favorite young friends were on the program: among them, General J. E. B. Stuart, Burton Harrison, Cora Ives, and Constance Cary.

For this benefit Frank Vizetelly,* correspondent and illustrator of the London *Illustrated News,* who was "covering" the war in the South for his paper, had painted the sets. An exuberant, large man with a bushy red beard, Vizetelly added as much gaiety and energetic spirit to Richmond's social life as Stuart's Prussian Chief of Staff, the huge Heros von Borcke. Having traversed the world and seen foreign campaigns as a correspondent, he was full of good stories. He could sing, dance, design scenery; and often he acted a leading part in dramatic performances. This night in one scene the comedian Vizetelly was hilarious in dandling a "squalling baby," for which soldiers backstage made the infant howls.

The President himself had furnished the costume for Burton Harrison, who appeared as an Indian brave. It was a warrior's outfit, which in 1831 Wisconsin Indians had given to the "Little Chief," as they affectionately called tall Lieutenant Davis, then but twenty-one years of age. The costume, though complete, was remarkably scant. It revealed an extensive view of Harrison's athletic physique that had been improved on the playing fields of Yale. Burton had even shaved his cherished mustache for sweet charity's sake. Constance Cary, the beauty with the classic profile, whom he hoped to marry, appeared as a witty barmaid. Jefferson Davis was amused at parts of the show and impressed by the stage assurance of his little daughter. But much of the time he was preoccupied with the immense problems of his harassed country.

When supper was served in the dining room the President walked in alone. Seeing Mrs. Chesnut and two other ladies with his good friend Senator Benjamin Hill of Georgia, he offered her his arm. The couple turned and began walking up and down the long room. Their conversation was anything but gay. "Nobody knows so well as he does," Mrs. Chesnut wrote that night, "the difficulties which beset this hard-driven Confederacy."

* Vizetelly had arrived in New York in May, 1861, stayed in the North until the late summer of 1862, and had then slipped across the Potomac in the night. He had radically changed his opinion of the Confederates and he had written London of his astonishment "at the unanimity displayed in the South on the subject of separation."

He talked of things as they are now in a melancholy cadence; he has a voice that is perfectly modulated, a comfort in this loud and tough soldier world.

The benefit charades and parties in Richmond did not reflect complete insouciance. Mary Chesnut, who entertained continually because she could get supplies from her South Carolina plantation, confided in her diary a concern that fastened on her heart.

God help my country! I think we are like the sailors who break into the spirit closet when they find out the ship must sink. There seems to be for the first time a resolute determination to enjoy the brief hour, and never look beyond the day.

General A. R. Lawton, whom the President had made Quartermaster General just in time to help bring the Confederates victory at Chickamauga, held a gala dinner for John Hunt Morgan and his jolly Kentuckians. Later, at a supper at Mrs. Randolph's, he confessed to Mrs. Chesnut that his heart was heavy. "This seems too gay," he complained, "too careless for such terrible times. It is all out of place in battle-scarred Richmond."

Jefferson Davis really felt the same way, though the papers insisted that as head of the republic he should entertain often. And, of course, there was psychological value in Richmond's presenting to the world a gay and confident surface appearance six months after Gettysburg.

All did not run smoothly, however, with subsequent entertainments at the President's mansion. One reception in late January proved somewhat sensational. During the party the house was set on fire, and smoke billowed up from the basement. An arsonist had crawled through a window and set shavings and fagots afire against a huge woodpile. The flames were quenched without serious damage, but the evening was spoiled.

A sharp new worry was now added to the troubled President: the lives of his wife and children were endangered. As the Richmond *Examiner* "helpfully" pointed out, if the malefactor had only waited until the reception was over, when the Davises, fatigued from the activities, were sound asleep, a real disaster might have occurred. The attempted house-burning was reported to be part and parcel of a "Yankee scheme" to harass the President's private life.

One of the Negro houseboys absconded the next day and eventually slipped through to the Federal lines. Mrs. Davis's brown maid, Betsy, a hired servant, decamped. A few days earlier Mrs.

Davis had seen eighty dollars in gold in her possession—equivalent to some $2,400 in Confederate paper. The Davises were fond of Betsy and she had always seemed happy with them, but enemy gold had proved too tempting.

Faithful Robert, the butler, however, was to stay on, and to serve the Davises devotedly even in their misfortunes and poverty after the war. But this incorruptible Negro, through no fault of his own, created a scare at the final Presidential reception in January. With "half of Richmond" at the affair, Robert broke out all over with smallpox, and the guests stood not upon the order of their going.

Thus the President was plagued not only by the contrariness of Congressmen and civil authorities in various states, but by personal household annoyances and dangers.

Mrs. Davis gave her last memorable ladies' luncheon on the last Saturday of January, 1864. She made it as elegant as possible and served most of the delicacies she had stored up. The company feasted on gumbo, duck with olives, chicken in jelly, chocolate cream, jelly cake, claret, and champagne.

The daily Richmond *Examiner,* which found wrong whatever the Davises did, had often complained that the Chief Executive rarely entertained so that he might hoard his salary. Now the editor, John Daniel, excoriated Mrs. Davis's extravagance. He even frowned on the weekly receptions. He saw that they were making the President more popular, and he wanted everyone to hate Jefferson Davis.

With criticism hissing from the *Examiner,* Constance Cary and a committee of young ladies asked General Lee for advice. Did he approve of the partying? Did he frown on the dancing? "My dear," he said, "my boys need to be heartened up when they get their furloughs. Go on, look your prettiest, and be just as nice to them as ever you can be."

The *Examiner* and other enemies of Mrs. Davis remarked that Mrs. Lee never appeared conspicuously in society. But everyone knew that Mrs. Lee, a passionate Confederate, was confined by arthritis to a chair, where she sedulously knitted socks for soldiers. When, however, the General was in the city, he was pleased to go to parties of all kinds, and as Burton Harrison wrote, Lee "relished the little *on dits* of society."

A very few persons continued to entertain in style. Mrs. Stannard, the rich widow from Louisville, spent her fortune lavishly and attracted the cream of society and the intellectuals of the Administra-

tion, as well as soldiers on leave. Though she boasted that she had
never read a book in her life, she provided the nearest thing to a
salon in the capital, where Judah P. Benjamin, the Secretary of
State, would often give recitations.

In February, the President attended the last notable affair of
the Confederacy's social life. Virginia Clay, wife of the Senator
from Alabama, persuaded him to see her act the role of Mrs.
Malaprop in *The Rivals*. Again it was a soldiers' benefit performance in the Iveses's double drawing rooms. The capital had buzzed
with anticipation and the rehearsals had proceeded as rigorously
as if the cast were preparing for a major battle. The irresistible Mrs.
Clay had coaxed Mrs. Drew, the noted New York stage star, who was
playing at a local theater, to watch some rehearsals and give advice.

Along with the President and Mrs. Davis came Cabinet members, various Congressmen, and noted Generals. An audience of
three hundred was seated in the Iveses's "connecting colonial parlors." The Davises again occupied a sofa in front center.

Mrs. Clay, probably the best amateur actress in the South, was
"beyond wildest hopes" as Mrs. Malaprop. The ingenious lady had
achieved a marvelous high coiffure by putting a pair of her satin
boots on top of her head and piling her hair over them. She threw
herself into the part so heartily that when she pinched Lydia's
shoulder and called her "an antricate little huzzy," Constance Cary,
playing the part, half-screamed in pain. The President saw she was
really hurt, and the next day he heard that she was indeed black
and blue.

The performance, followed by supper, was regarded as the "most
ambitious social event ever in the life of the Confederate capital."
It was the climax and the end. The frolicking and the feasting
ceased shortly after February, 1864. By November, delicately
brought-up ladies would be "thanking God when they could get a
pitcher of sorghum molasses for their children and themselves."

Jefferson Davis felt personal relief at the curtailment of social
functions. The White House receptions had been an added strain
he had undergone for the morale of his people. General Lee now
came frequently to the Davis house for consultations. The President
would be closeted with Lee in his private study at all hours without
fear of interruption. One morning—February 22—when Lee came
to breakfast, the President invited a few friends to join them. During the meal a Mississippi Congressman undertook to tell the Gen-

eral just what he ought to do. While the gentleman outlined a campaign for him, Lee listened blandly. When he had finished, Davis was amused to hear the courteous Lee make a quiet reference to wise civilians who stayed away from the battlefields and "from afar arranged the movements of armies."

The escape of more than a hundred Union officers from Libby Prison in Richmond on February 9 was discussed. The President could say that by now most of them had been recaptured. On the fifteenth the Government had begun to send consignments of prisoners to a place called Andersonville down in Georgia, where escapees would have a difficult time getting back to Union lines.

On February 24 Davis made an appointment which he felt would initiate another burst of criticism against himself. He assigned General Braxton Bragg "to duty at the seat of the Government, under the direction of the President." General Lee had held the same position as the President's military adviser until June, 1862, when he was given the active command of the Army of Northern Virginia.

Some months before, Davis's good friend General Leonidas Polk had suggested that Bragg would prove highly valuable in Richmond. That Bragg's usefulness in the field was over, Davis knew, and, though he himself found him personally unattractive, there was no other man available with Bragg's military knowledge and experience. With the spring offensives coming on, Davis desperately needed help in Richmond.

As expected, the newspapers inimical to him derided the appointment and expressed high indignation. Davis ignored the jibes and barbs. He realized acutely that the "sole nepenthe for the national afflictions was military success." So to this end he devoted his energies as the only solution for his nation's sorrows and difficulties. Bragg settled down to work with a will. He relieved the President of much bothersome detail and proved highly efficient. Criticism of Bragg halted. A friendly Richmond journalist wrote: "Probably at no period of the war did the Confederate administration exhibit more energy and skill in the employment of its limited resources than in its preparations for the campaign of 1864."

CHAPTER III

DISCORD IN GEORGIA AND A
RAID ON RICHMOND

JEFFERSON DAVIS HAD now given up hope that official England would recognize his new republic. But he was counting heavily on the ironclad rams being built for the Confederacy in Great Britain. The President had every reason to believe that the English people in general were friendly to the Confederacy and had high respect for its legal position. A lobby of prominent Britishers continued to speak eloquently in behalf of the beleaguered South.

From the first, Lord Campbell (Stratheden) had been among the most ardent of the pro-Southern propagandists, who included such distinguished men as Alexander Beresford-Hope, the Marquess of Lothian, Lord Montagu, Lord Eustace Cecil, and Lord Robert Cecil. Campbell had early attacked Lord John Russell's position on the Federal blockade and had declared that it was by no means effective. On March 23, 1863, he had made a lengthy speech in Parliament in favor of recognition and criticized the Foreign Minister sharply for having failed to cooperate with Napoleon in November, 1862. Campbell had insisted that Britain's recognition would alone be sufficient to end the war and enable the North to withdraw from the conflict with self-respect. He had persisted in proclaiming his Confederate adherence and in keeping the cruelly unequal struggle before the public mind of Britain.

A copy of Lord Campbell's speech before the Southern Independence Association in Manchester in February, 1864, finally reached the President in Richmond. It was an eloquent tribute to himself, which he read with gratification.

No man of reflection, can, in my opinion, glance at the daily life of Mr. Davis without a sentiment which even passes admiration. (Immense cheering)

If an independent and despotic power had been granted to him, such as great men are apt to claim under such circumstances—still, to keep

17

the mind engaged upon every part of an almost interminable frontier, to divine the plans of a government whose movements it is difficult to calculate, to prepare for every possible event, to picture each imaginable difficulty, to plan campaigns upon a territory so extensive and under circumstances so unprecedented, would tax the very highest reach of military genius.

But this is not the whole of the burden that devolves upon Mr. Davis. This task he is called upon to perform, while at the same time he is accountable to a representative assembly, to a Senate, and to a Cabinet. (Hear)

But even that is not the limit of his trials. He had to face these difficulties, to aim at these results, with a free press to criticize and to reprimand him . . . and sometimes to reveal to distant armies much which in his opinion it would be more judicious to conceal from them. The liberty of that press he has not once attempted to control or wished to override. (Cheers) And yet to meet this threefold trial might well exhaust the wisdom of a ruler, the resources of a general, and the temper of an angel. (Cheers)

Come what may, gentlemen, you cannot be deprived of the reflection that, in your day, according to your power, although divided from him by the ocean, you have done something to uphold one of the bravest and noblest minds which Providence has formed!

While such exalted commendation from a high source across the seas warmed his heart, Jefferson Davis reflected sadly that Lord Campbell was not the Government of England. Though the British peer had a ready sense of the burdens under which he labored, certain Southerners seemed to take a diabolical zest in encumbering him with more impediments. In his own capital the editors of the *Examiner* continued to denigrate him, while down in Georgia his Vice-President and Governor Brown concocted procedures that smelled of something like treason.

Alexander Stephens had professed to discern a moral obstacle to conscription, and had declared openly that the war ought to be abandoned when conscription became necessary. On March 9, 1864, Governor Brown, aided by the Stephens brothers, drafted an anti-Administration message to the state legislature. Senator Benjamin Hill, General Howell Cobb, and L. Q. C. Lamar were in Georgia working in support of the President. From Richmond, Georgia's Herschel V. Johnson* tried to steady the wrought-up Vice-

---

* Johnson, who had been Stephen Douglas's running mate on a Democratic ticket in 1860, which Davis opposed, had not been completely friendly to the Confederate President.

President, who wanted Davis forced out of office. "You are evidently
in a towering passion," Johnson wrote his friend, and declared that
he himself would fight the war "according to the President's plan."

When the Georgia legislature met on March 10, Brown's firebrand
message was delivered. Though it seemed seditious, Alexander
Stephens did not hesitate to claim, "I advised it from stem to stern
and approve it." His brother Linton offered resolutions condemning
the suspension of *habeas corpus,* and presumptuously set forth
terms on which peace should be offered the North.

On March 16 the Vice-President addressed the Georgia legislature. With burning eyes, in a shrill voice, the little man spoke
hysterically for three hours. Over and over he declared that conscription was "radically wrong" and that suspension of *habeas corpus* was a menace to public liberty. "Liberty and life, together," he
shouted. "Not independence first and liberty later!" Stephens had
never quite understood that the brand-new Confederacy was fighting for the mere right to exist against a mighty foe that waxed in
strength as the conflict progressed. He did not seem to realize that
without the Confederacy's success there would be no real liberty.
He declared that if he must have a master, he did not care whether
he was Northern or Southern. It was a bitter speech, breathing
rancor against the Administration. Davis read the report with
amazement and indignation. His admiring young friend, L. Q. C.
Lamar, shocked to his marrow, made a stirring appeal to the
legislators to stop cantankerous opposition and support the Government. After three days of wrangling, an amendment to Linton
Stephens's resolutions was passed, expressing confidence in the President.

But Governor Brown, not to be stilled, had his anti-Administration message printed, together with Alexander Stephens's speech
and Linton's resolutions, and sent to Georgia soldiers throughout
the Confederate armies. Political Georgia was rent asunder. Howell
Cobb said he would be happy to see Brown hanged. Senator Hill
called the Governor and the Stephens brothers traitors. Many of the
soldiers agreed with Hill. Herschel Johnson wrote Alec sternly
from Richmond, "You have allowed your antipathy to Jefferson
Davis to mislead your judgment." This noisy discord in Georgia was
naturally sweet music to General W. T. Sherman, who had his eyes
on strategic Atlanta.

In 1946 Stephens's most scholarly biographer, Rudolph von Abele,
coolly adjudged: "There can be no palliation of his role in the

collapse of the Confederacy." And he pointed out with specific accusation that Stephens certainly "lent his name to the snivelings and evasions of men like Vance, Brown, Wigfall, and Foote, who out of blindness, spite, and envy did the best they could to ruin the government in whose councils they had thought to take a larger part than was assigned." On the other hand, the historian declared that Davis "wielded his vast powers for the most part with circum-spection and self command. . . . Without holding vast powers he could not have fought the war. Had he been permitted to wield them more effectively he might have won."

The prime excitement of the new year came shortly after General Bragg had assumed his new duties. On the last day of February an expedition of picked Union cavalrymen under twenty-two-year-old Colonel Ulric Dahlgren, who had lost a leg at Gettysburg, set out on a daring undertaking. The expedition had been conceived by a West Point graduate, General Judson Kilpatrick, who hoped to gain enough renown from it to be elected Governor of New Jersey. Dahlgren, who had volunteered as one of the leaders, had first moved within twenty-two miles of Richmond. Then, as he pro-ceeded, he began to destroy dwellings, mills, canal boats, grain and cattle.

On the gloomy, wet morning of March 1, President Davis was surprised to hear artillery fire to the north, uncomfortably close. Couriers, arriving in hot haste, announced that some 5,000 Union horsemen were within the capital's outer fortifications. A rumor reached Secretary of War James Seddon that his family had been captured at his country place twenty miles away.* Senator James Lyons came into Davis's office to say that the enemy was shelling his home, "Laburnum," outside Richmond. Brigadier General Custis Lee, the President's aide, rushed off to direct the city's defense. Local militia were mobilized. Alarm bells made a brazen din as horsemen galloped through the streets and wagons went rattling to the fray.

Despite the turbulence no great fear was outwardly manifest, for the mustered civilians were believed to be strong enough to de-fend the city, and Fitzhugh Lee's cavalry was not far away. But, wrote War Clerk Jones, the President was in bad humor "when

* Colonel Dahlgren did enter the Seddon home and Mrs. Seddon drank blackberry wine with him from her best silver goblets, reminding him that his father, the Union's Admiral Dahlgren, had once courted her and had married one of her schoolmates.

the enemy's guns were heard even in his office." Davis was trying to concentrate on how to reply to a contention of former Quartermaster Colonel A. C. Myers, whom he had removed from office in September just before the battle of Chickamauga and who now claimed that he still held his old position. Davis laid down his pen and called for Colonel Chesnut to ride with him to inspect the fortifications.

In her husband's absence Mrs. Davis and her sister Margaret Howell prepared for emergencies. "Though not at all frightened," they dressed themselves for flight in case they had to run. They had "no horses or carriages or any way to ride out or carry baggage"; so they put on all the clothes they could. Mrs. Davis wore "seven petticoats, 3 chemises, 2 pair of stockings on her legs and six pair buckled round her legs by her garter." Maggie had on quite as much "with the addition of two dresses and her cloth coat." Mrs. Davis wrote her youngest brother, Jeffy D. Howell, that the Yankees would have caught them surely for they were so heavy they could hardly walk—running would have been impossible.

The raiders were routed on March 3. On the retreat, the Union cavalry was ambushed by "furloughed soldiers, home guards and citizens." The Confederates captured about ninety prisoners and nearly a hundred horses, many small arms, and one Napoleon gun. Dahlgren was among the twenty killed. Some extraordinary memoranda were found on his body and in the pockets of captured raiders.

The purpose of the raid had presumably been threefold: to liberate the 22,000 Federal prisoners on Belle Isle and in other neighboring prisons; to burn the city of Richmond; and to assassinate the President and his Cabinet. The *Examiner* quoted from the memoranda:

We hope to release the prisoners from Belle Island first; and having seen them fairly started, we will cross the James River into Richmond, destroying the bridges after us, and exhorting the released prisoners to destroy and burn the hateful city; and do not allow the rebel leader, Davis, and his traitorous crew to escape.

Upon the dead Dahlgren's person was found a notebook containing a rough draft in pencil of his address to his soldiers, with instructions that the Confederate authorities be "killed on the spot."

General Fitzhugh Lee himself brought the papers to the President and assured him they had not been altered in the slightest way. When Davis was at first incredulous, Fitz Lee declared that he himself did not want to believe what was true. He had been an intimate friend of the young man's parents. "Once," he said, "Commodore Dahlgren brought the little fair-haired boy to show me how pretty he looked in his black velvet suit and Vandyke collar. I cannot reconcile the two Ulrics."

When the horrendous plan was released through the Richmond press the citizens were in such a fury that they demanded the execution of the prisoners whose evil purport was violative of the rules of war. The Cabinet united in urging that the prisoners draw lots and every tenth man be shot. The President refused to sanction such a measure; he would not shoot unarmed men. "Some Cabinet members," wrote Postmaster General John Reagan, "called attention to the monstrous purpose of burning the city and exposing the women and children to the infuriated mob of released prisoners and insisted on their recommendation being carried out." The President emphatically said No; he would not shoot unarmed men. And when Davis became emphatic the Cabinet rarely said more.

Though some of the captured Federals had been disguised in Confederate uniforms and by the usages of war they might legitimately have been hanged as spies, Davis insisted that their service was not voluntary, that they could not be held responsible for infamous instructions from above. Secretary of War Seddon said he did not want to divide the responsibility in which the Cabinet and Braxton Bragg had finally concurred with the President, but he asked General Lee's opinion to still mutterings among Lee's own men. Lee pointed out that the Federals had surrendered with arms in their hands and had been accepted as prisoners of war; they could not, in retaliation for the unexpected designs of their leaders, be treated otherwise. The conclusions of Davis and Lee did not please soldiers or citizens, and the Southern press was quite bitter.

General Lee sent photographic copies of the papers found on Dahlgren to General Meade with an inquiry as to whether such deeds were authorized by his Government. He said that if doubts were raised, the original documents would be submitted. Meade did not ask for the originals, and Lee accepted Meade's denial that neither the United States Government nor he himself "had authorized, sanctioned or approved the burning of the city of Richmond and the killing of Mr. Davis and Cabinet."

Ulric Dahlgren's body was brought to Richmond and decently buried in Oakwood Cemetery. In the North, the daring Dahlgren, who had had a meteoric rise from private at nineteen to cavalry colonel at twenty-two, became briefly a national hero. His cutthroat adventure evoked a paean of praise in some of the Northern papers, which chose to picture young Dahlgren as a hero who had been "assassinated" while on "a philanthropic mission." But many Northerners were deeply shocked by the young man's bloodthirsty designs.

Varina Davis had no compassionate feelings for the Swedish Yankee who had wanted to murder her husband. In a letter to her brother, she wrote: "The vile wretch was shot as he deserved and killed instantly; he had not time to ask for forgiveness. May God judge him more mildly than I can."

Jefferson Davis, who was not so stern in judgment as his wife, reflected on the influence of latitude and habitat. For Ulric Dahlgren's uncle, Charles G. Dahlgren, was a Confederate officer. Born in Philadelphia, he had been sent as a young man to Natchez as a cashier in the Bank of the United States. When the bank was dissolved, Charles Dahlgren, liking the Southern way of life, had decided to stay. He had bought a plantation, acquired slaves, and become rich. In 1861 he patriotically raised a regiment, the Third Mississippi, of which he was Colonel. Wounded at Vicksburg, he was back in service when his nephew, who had spent a pleasant summer vacation with him on the plantation in 1859, set out to perform his "deed of dreadful note." If the Admiral, John, had moved South, both American branches of the Swedish Dahlgrens might have been fighting on the Southern side.

The chief effect of Dahlgren's raid was the hastening of Union prisoners from Richmond to Andersonville, Georgia, where rescue would be more difficult, and where overcrowding caused misery.

On March 9, the anniversary of the *Monitor-Merrimac* stalemate, President Lincoln, who had summoned Ulysses S. Grant to Washington, presented him with a commission of Lieutenant General, the only one in the Federal army. It was the first time the two citizens of Illinois had ever met. Two days later Grant was put in command of all the Union armies. On March 18 the new army chief gave Sherman command of the military division of the Mississippi. Grant had a long secret conference with him on strategy. Then on March 26 he took up his headquarters at Culpeper, Virginia. There he began preparing work for an early campaign in which General Meade would continue in name to head the Army of the Potomac.

Grant's overall strategy, as Davis saw it, was patently simple.

While Grant hammered to pulverize Lee's columns, Sherman was to incapacitate Joseph Johnston's army in the West, seize strategic Atlanta, and bisect the Confederacy. Having won a series of victories, Grant's ability was obvious. Boldness, perseverance, and independence were the features of his generalship, though, of course, he had the good fortune to be backed by overwhelming numbers and vastly superior equipment. Lincoln had chosen the right general for the business of crushing Lee. Scorning the formulas of military colleges and great commanders of history, Grant would employ the maximum of force continually against a foe half his strength.

CHAPTER IV

THE NEXT MOST FATAL APRIL

———◈———

WHAT, JEFFERSON DAVIS wondered, would the fickle month of April hold for the Confederacy? It was in April, 1861, that President Lincoln had launched the ships for Sumter that brought on a shooting war. In the following April the battle of Shiloh had been won one day and lost the next, and the chivalrous Albert Sidney Johnston had needlessly died of a wound in the thigh. In April, 1863, General Hooker had put his Federals across the Rappahannock in a campaign which, though it ended in Southern victory at Chancellorsville, had brought death to the indispensable Stonewall Jackson. And at that same April's end, after months of prodigious maneuvering, General Grant had finally crossed the Mississippi below Vicksburg and begun his drive that was to end in the capitulation of the starved-out town.

So far, the Aprils in the Confederacy's life had meant special trouble for Davis and had brought him poignant griefs. Though the South was to suffer no cataclysmic defeat in arms this April of 1864, it was to be a peculiarly trying period to the President and to end with a personal tragedy that cut deeper than anything since the death of his bride, Sarah Knox Taylor, in 1835.

A blow potentially more disastrous than the defeat of battalions was struck on paper the very first day of the month. It was a communication from Lord Lyons, the British Minister to the United States.

President Davis read the letter with perturbation and dismay. His emotions changed to anger. Lord Lyons was transmitting the formal protest and remonstrance of Her Majesty's Government "against the efforts of the authorities of the so-called Confederate States to build war vessels within Her Majesty's dominions to be employed against the Government of the United States." Secretary of State Seward had put a new fear into the British Government and demanded that the cruisers and rams being built for the Confederacy not be allowed to sail, though the guns were to be installed in another country. England had tried to ignore the construction of the war vessels. But by the use of detectives the estimable United States Minister Charles Francis Adams and the vigilant Consul Thomas H. Dudley at Liverpool had collected significant evidence of their ultimate destination.

Though the matter was in litigation in the British courts, England's Government now said that the rams should not go to the Confederacy. Jefferson Davis and his Secretary of the Navy, Stephen R. Mallory, had had strong hope that if the virtually completed rams could be launched the South might yet win independence by destroying the Union ships blockading its ports. How could England, Davis exclaimed, callously withhold the last weapon by which the Confederacy might save its life?

Lord Russell's letter had not been addressed to President Davis, but sent to Lyons, "to be conveyed through such channel as shall be available." Lyons had forwarded "an extract" of Russell's dispatch by special messenger to Richmond on a flag-of-truce boat. The British Foreign Secretary suavely professed to rely "on the frankness, courtesy, and discernment which Mr. Davis has displayed in the difficult circumstances in which he has been placed during the past three years" for a recognition of "the correctness" of the position of Her Majesty's Government. Davis was able to disregard the undiplomatic manner of the procedure, but he highly resented Russell's use and repetition of the word "so-called" before "the Confederate States." He was, in fact, bitterly indignant. He felt that his admired England had struck his country a most unnecessary and cruel blow.

He did not deign to reply in person, but sent his answer through his Private Secretary. Into his dictation Davis poured his pent-up disappointment with Britain and the distress of three ghastly years. For he felt that England could have recognized the Confederacy after the battle of Manassas in 1861 with no danger to herself, and that most of the subsequent bloodshed might have been avoided. England, which was selling to the United States enormous quantities of guns, armaments, and woolen fabrics at huge profits, had now become the silent ally of the North against the back-to-the-wall South. As a foreboding clutched at the President's heart, in-

vective and contempt came easily to his lips. He dictated to Burton
Harrison:

The President desires me to say to your Lordship, that . . . it would be
inconsistent with the dignity of the position he fills, as Chief Magistrate
of a nation comprising a population of more than twelve millions, occupy-
ing a territory many times larger than the United Kingdom . . . , to allow the attempt of Earl Russell to ignore the actual existence of the Confederate States, and to contumeliously style them "so-called," to pass without a protest and a remonstrance. The President, therefore, does protest
and remonstrate against this studied insult; and he instructs me to say,
that in future any document in which it may be repeated will be returned
unanswered and unnoticed.

With respect to the subject of the extract from Earl Russell's dispatch,
the President desires me to state, that the plea of neutrality, which is used
to sustain the sinister course of Her Majesty's present Government against
the Government of the Confederate States, is so clearly contradicted by
their actions, that it is regarded by the world, not even excepting the
United States, as a mere cover for actual hostility. . . .

He cannot but feel, with the history and traditions of the Anglo-Saxon
race before him, that under a government faithfully representing the people of Great Britain, the whole weight and power of that nation would be
unhesitatingly thrown into the scale in favor of the principles of free government, on which these States were originally formed, and for which
alone the Confederate States are now struggling.

As Davis dictated, his anger mounted. He scorned any semblance
of diplomacy, and chose words bearing a sting.

He cannot but feel that a neutrality most cunningly, audaciously, fawn-
ingly, and insolently sought and urged, begged and demanded by one
belligerent, and repudiated by the other, must be seen by all impartial
men to be a mere pretext for aiding the cause of the one at the expense of
the other, while pretending to be impartial; to be, in short, but a cover
for treacherous, malignant hostility.

He then proceeded more coolly to the last paragraph:

As for the specious arguments on the subject of the rams, advanced by
Earl Russell, the President desires me to state that he is content to leave
the world and history to pronounce judgment upon this attempt to heap
injury upon insult, by declaring that Her Majesty's Government and law
officers are satisfied of the questions involved, while those questions are
still before the highest legal tribunal of the kingdom, composed of members of the Government and the highest law officers of the Crown, for
their decision. The President himself will not condescend to notice them.

The President's letter, signed "Burton N. Harrison, *Private Secretary,*" was that of an angry, proud man in a desperate situation. Davis was disgusted by what he regarded as Russell's lack of courage and at the spectacle of Her Majesty's Government in "the persistent persecution of the Confederate States at the beck and bidding of officers of the United States." *

Since the Confederacy could expect nothing from the British Government, Davis took satisfaction in throwing diplomacy to the winds. Although able Confederate agents were to remain in England, apparently the last bridge with Britain's Government was burned. The South would have to steel herself still further to endure the Federal onslaughts without the diversion that might have been created by Confederate ironclad rams.

As spring buds began to swell and daffodils to bloom, the enemy legions in Virginia readied themselves for the march on Richmond. On April 4, Grant put Major General Philip H. Sheridan in command of the Federal cavalry in Virginia, which had heretofore been outclassed in performance by the Confederate cavalry. This move was ominous for the South. Able, bandy-legged little Sheridan was a born scrapper, shanty Irish by inheritance and as tough as they came. He boasted his loathing for anything that smacked of aristocracy, and this no doubt helped to enforce his policy of fire and destruction through the beautiful Shenandoah.

Before Sheridan got into action, however, President Davis received word of a Confederate victory in the West. On April 12, Nathan Bedford Forrest made an attack on Fort Pillow, forty miles above Memphis. The fort was garrisoned by nineteen Union officers and 538 men, of whom 262 were Negroes. The rest were white Unionists from east Tennessee, "home-made Yankees" as they were called contemptuously. Forrest had offered to treat with the garrison upon its immediate surrender as prisoners of war. The garrison asked for an hour to consult, which was not granted. The officers then refused to surrender, and the Negroes "jeered obscenely" at Forrest's troops. In a half-hour's ferocious fight, the Southerners took the fort.

The President read Forrest's dispatch, which had been relayed through his commander, Lieutenant General Leonidas Polk.

---

* But in one important thing the President was wrong. Lord Russell, while fearful of angering the United States, was secretly in favor of the Confederacy, as some of his *Correspondence,* published in 1925, reveals. His sentiment was such a well-guarded secret, however, that his close friends did not realize the truth.

I attacked Fort Pillow on the morning of the 12th inst. . . . After a
short fight we drove the enemy into the fort, under cover of their gunboats, and demanded a surrender, which was declined. . . . I stormed
the fort, and after a contest of thirty minutes captured the entire garrison,
killing 500 and taking 100 prisoners,* and a large amount of quartermaster
stores. . . . I sustained a loss of 20 killed and 60 wounded. The Confederate flag now floats over the fort.

N. B. Forrest, Major-General

Again Forrest had proved himself a mighty fighter. Because seventy per cent of the Negro troops had been killed or wounded, a cry
went up in the North that an "atrocity" had been committed and
that the colored men had been massacred. Northern papers fed the
flames, and an investigating committee, led by Congressman Benjamin F. Wade of Ohio, whose son had chosen to command a Negro
regiment, denounced the affair as "an act of deliberate savages."
But certainly no massacre had been ordered by General Forrest.
The investigation unearthed no significant evidence. Subsequent
Northern historians, reading the official records, have concluded
that "it was just war and not slaughter." †

The capture of the river stronghold was a welcome, if minor, success. But closely on its heel, the President learned to his consterna-
tion and sorrow that on April 17 General Grant had announced his
refusal to exchange any more prisoners. In the North, as well as in
the South, his decision was extremely unpopular with both civilians
and soldiers. Northerners wanted their captured sons home, particularly those sick or wounded. But Grant, the stern realist, was
aware of the South's desperate lack of manpower, whereas the
North had fresh hundreds of thousands yet to draw upon and
"mercenaries" from abroad were arriving by almost every ship.
Grant knew, too, that the rations of Southern soldiers were drastically reduced, that every mouthful furnished to Federal prisoners
would be a drain on the Confederate economy. Even General Lee,
the papers proclaimed, was eating meat only twice a week; his chief
diet was cornpone and a head of cabbage boiled in salt water.
Whatever humane feelings for prisoners Grant may have had, under
a directive from Secretary of War Stanton, he would stifle for the
overall object of victory.

Since the exchange of prisoners had gone on with at least a semblance of orderliness for three years, Davis had not conceived that

---

* Forrest's figures are slightly exaggerated.
† The quotation is from *The Civil War* by Ralph Newman and E. B. Long.

such a harsh policy could ever be inaugurated. He knew Grant's decree was bound to cause harrowing distress on both sides. He
frankly declared it "contrary to the uses of civilized warfare."

On April 24 the President received a telegram from General Lee:
"Should the enemy remain quiet this week and the weather good,
will it be convenient for you to visit the army? . . . " He followed
his telegram with a letter, giving details of reconnoitering and making speculations on Grant's plan. He ended by pressing the President to visit him. "It would be very gratifying to the troops," he
said, "and I hope pleasing to Your Excellency."

"It was Lee's custom," Freeman wrote in *Lee's Dispatches,* "to
confer with the President before a campaign opened." The General
had always made Davis aware that he valued his military advice.
So it pained Davis to have to decline just now, but he was laboring
under terrific pressure. He had a series of scheduled appointments
in Richmond, and he was preparing his message for Congress,
which was to convene the next week. He hoped to see General Lee
at the beginning of May.

When the last morning of April, 1864, came, the President could
reflect that except for the crushing decision of England to withhold
the Confederate rams, no real disaster had befallen the Confederacy during the month. As to his immediate family, Varina was unusually well, though she was expecting another baby in late June.
The children were in exuberant good health. His refugee brother
Joseph and his great-niece Lise Mitchell were safely in Tuscaloosa,
Alabama, enjoying the hospitality of Robert Jemison, a member of
the Confederate Senate.

But Davis, concerned by lack of manpower, had had an almost
sleepless night. For General Sherman at Chattanooga had alerted
his 98,000 men for the move against Joseph Johnston's 60,000 in
Georgia. And Grant's army, twice the size of Lee's, was stretched
along the Rapidan ready to cross the river and blast its way to the
capital. All through the night regiments had been tramping through
Richmond on their way to strengthen Lee's thin lines. Davis expected the great battle to start almost immediately. He had heard
the public speculations that when this battle did come it would end
the war.

Washington was as tense as Richmond. Salmon Chase, the United
States Secretary of the Treasury, was openly saying that if Grant did
not speedily achieve success in the field, the nation's finances would

be ruined. Though Lee was still regarded in Virginia as invincible on his native soil, how long could his special genius withstand the enemy's two-to-one advantage? Whereas Secretary of War Stanton had denied troops to General McClellan, the Democrat, he now boasted that he could reinforce Grant at leisure, whenever he called for more. But Davis knew feelingly that when Lee's men were killed or incapacitated, there were no replacements to call upon.

Yet Davis had firm faith that the ill-equipped Army of Northern Virginia, inspired by Robert Lee, would put up as stout a fight as any soldiers in recorded history. He had seen them on the battle-field, talked with them in their log-and-tent cities. And he probably thought of them much as did one of Meade's staff officers, Colonel T. B. Lyman, who was to behold them in action a few days hence and write with a touch of awe: "These Rebels are not half-starved and ready to give up—a more sinewy, tawny, formidable set of men could not be."

When the Confederate President was fully roused from his fitful slumber on the morning of April 30, he saw that the morning had broken fair. The breeze was from the south, warm and balmy. Summer had virtually arrived. The gardens of Richmond were splashed with color. From his own window Davis could look down upon his cherry trees in full blossom. Before he was out of bed the children came dashing in to give their father a morning kiss, Pollie and Jeff, Jr., Joseph and toddling Billie. Davis enjoyed his children's high spirits, even though they were often too unrestrained, too noisy, and sometimes too self-willed. All except Joe, the four-year-old; Joe was the gentle child, the "confiding one." He was also the most promising of the boys, the most intelligent. It was Joe who came to him every night to say his prayers; with his hands clasped he would lean on his father's knees as if they formed a personal *prie-dieu*. "On Joe," Mrs. Davis wrote in her *Memoir*, her husband had "set his hope. This child was the greatest joy in his life."

At breakfast on this last day of April, Margaret Howell, Varina's young sister, was in an exhilarated mood. It was her birthday, and by way of celebration she had been invited on a picnic excursion with the Mallorys, the Oulds, and Mrs. Chesnut. They were going down the James to witness an exchange of prisoners, perhaps the last, because of Grant's recent decree. Despite the gladness of the day, the President scarcely touched breakfast. Mrs. Davis promised to take a basket luncheon to his office, as she often did when he had no appetite. As he left the dining room he could have noted the new lumber for some construction work that was being done on the balcony outside.

At his office he bade goodbye to Clement C. Clay, Jr., and Jacob Thompson, whom he was sending as commissioners to Canada to meet with friendly Northerners in an effort to bring about peace. Just before one o'clock he looked up from his desk to see his wife's full figure in the doorway. She bore a small basket covered with a white napkin. He smiled gratefully, for he knew she had prepared something to tempt his indifferent appetite. As she was setting out the dishes, a household servant rushed in, breathless, with terrible news. Little Joe had fallen from the side balcony onto the brick-paved court thirty feet below.

The parents reached the child's side just before he died; but he did not recognize them. His skull had been fractured and both legs broken. Jeff had found him and rushed to tell Catherine, the Irish nurse. To their neighbor Mrs. Semmes, wife of the Senator from Louisiana, who reached the house before the parents did, Jeff cried, "Mrs. Semmes, I have said all the prayers I know how, but God will not wake Joe."

Apparently the little boy had missed his footing in climbing over a connecting angle of the balustrade. But some thought he had walked up a plank left carelessly resting against the balustrade and jutting out, when the carpenters went to lunch. A piece of lumber lay mutely on the brick pavement beside him. Catherine was incoherent and hysterical. Since no one had witnessed the accident, no one knew anything for sure but that Joe had fallen and was dead.

Burton Harrison arrived with a doctor and took charge. Varina's uncontrolled grief was a most pitiable thing. But, as Burton told Constance Cary, "the terrible self-control" of the father was more heartbreaking to see. That afternoon a courier arrived with an urgent dispatch from General Lee at Orange Court House. It was marked: "Recd at Richmond Apl 30, 1864 at 3 o'clock 45 minutes." The President held the sheet in his hand for some moments. Then he looked at his wife fixedly and said, "Did you tell me what was in it?" She saw that his mind was temporarily paralyzed. At last, he tried to write an answer, but he gave up, and cried out, "I *must* have this one day with my little son."

Someone took the dispatch to General Cooper to answer. The parents were left alone with their dead child. Finally the President shut himself in his bedroom and walked the floor the rest of the afternoon and "the live-long night."

At dusk, Mrs. Davis sent her carriage to Drewry's Bluff to meet Margaret Howell and Mrs. Chesnut at the landing. As they approached the vehicle the two women were chatting about the mid-river exchange of prisoners. Mrs. Chesnut remarked that she was glad to have seen her first "genuine Yankee" prisoner; all those Union prisoners she had seen these three years "well or wounded, had been Germans, Irishmen, Scotchmen, and mostly Germans." Margaret, who was in front of her on the way up the incline, suddenly let out an agonizing scream. The coachman's voice, coming out of the darkness, had announced, "Little Joe has killed himself." The shock completely unnerved her. As the women drove the two miles to Richmond "the silence was broken only by Maggie's hysterical sobs."

When they arrived at the Executive Mansion Mrs. Chesnut was amazed to see the house lit up in every room, even the third story. All the windows were wide open and the curtains were blowing in the night breeze. Mrs. Semmes received them at the door and told them all she knew of what had occurred. After Margaret went upstairs, "the whole house was silent as death." Sitting alone in the drawing room, where the curtains flapped and the gas flames flared, Mary Chesnut could hear the President's ceaseless steps pacing back and forth in his room upstairs. There was no other sound. Burton Harrison had made all the funeral arrangements; the undertaker had come and gone. Before she left at midnight, Mrs. Chesnut went upstairs and saw Joe lying "white and beautiful as an angel, covered with flowers." Prone on the floor beside his bier lay Catherine, the Irishwoman, keening with grief and self-accusation. April ended at midnight and the new month was May.

The Chesnuts, who were to leave for South Carolina on May 1, postponed their departure to attend the funeral. An immense crowd gathered at Hollywood Cemetery above the James River, which swirled about its rocky islets and sparkled in the sun. "A thousand children" wound up the hill and around the monuments of Presidents James Monroe and John Tyler to Joe's new-dug grave. Each child clutched a bunch of spring flowers or a green spray to drop on the burial plot which was already massed with white flowers.

Before the open grave of his favorite son stood the bareheaded President, his hair quite gray now, looking older than his fifty-five years. But his figure, dominant against the blue sky, was straight as a spear. Constance Cary remarked the "mournful, dark eyes" of Mrs. Davis, as she stood slightly behind her husband, "her tall figure wrapped in black, drooped, heavy with her pregnancy."

Richmond had no remembrance of a more moving funeral. For days to come the townsfolk were to express their sympathy for the parents. Mrs. Davis could deal with her grief in private, but in his position as leader of his people, the President had to stifle his sorrow for his country's sake. His extraordinary will power sustained him, and on May 2, the day after his child's funeral, he went to his office. His message to the newly assembled Congress was delivered that day.

The next day Grant's mighty army began crossing the river into the Wilderness, not far from Chancellorsville where a year ago the Union forces had been beaten.

Though in an agony of grief and with military affairs at a crisis, Davis took time out for personal amenity and wrote a brief note of thanks to Senator Robert Jemison of Alabama. Jemison had left at his office the day before a letter from the President's aged brother for whom his dead son had been named.

Accept my thanks for the letter from my Brother which you left for me, with a kind message concerning his health. I regret not to have seen you and hope soon to do so. My Brother has informed me of your hospitable attention to him, and I am more grateful to you than I can express.

God forbid that you should ever be so circumstanced as to permit me to return your goodness in kind, but be assured of the gratification it will give me to prove in any way how much indebted to you I feel.

The next day firing began in the scrub oaks and junglelike thickets of the Wilderness. The final struggle for Richmond had begun.

CHAPTER V

THE WILDERNESS TO
SPOTSYLVANIA

————◆————

AS FIERCE FIGHTING between the North and South was about
to resume, the attitude of Jefferson Davis was somewhat like that of
General Lee, who now wrote his son Custis: "If victorious, we have
everything to hope for in the future. If defeated, nothing will be
left for us to live for. . . ."

On May 5, the President received a long letter from Lee. "You
will already have learned that the army of Gen. Meade is in motion and is crossing the Rapidan on our right. . . . It is apparent
that the long-threatened effort to take Richmond has begun." He
urged that troops in North Carolina be returned to him at once
and that General Beauregard "with all force available for the purpose" be brought without delay to Richmond.

Your opportunities of deciding this question are superior to my own, my
advice being based upon such light as I possess. It seems to me that the
great efforts of the enemy here and in Georgia have begun and that the
necessity of our concentration at both points is immediate and imperative.
I submit my views with great deference to the better judgment of Your
Excellency, and am satisfied that you will do what the best interests of
the country require.

The army was put in motion today, and our advance already occupies
our former position on Mine Run. . . .

The President was in full accord with Lee. He had already ordered concentration as quickly as practicable. Longstreet's corps,
which he had recalled from Tennessee, was encamped on the North
Anna, within a day's march of Lee. Davis had also anticipated Lee's
suggestion about Beauregard by more than a fortnight. Bragg had
sent him a telegram asking if he would come to Virginia to serve in
the field.

After active operations had been suspended in the winter of 1863-64, General P. G. T. Beauregard, in command of the Charleston defenses, brooded over the minor role he was playing in the war and nursed his corroding hatred of Jefferson Davis. He now regretted his precipitous departure from the top command of the Army in the West, without asking Richmond for leave of absence. Consistent in his inconsistency, at one moment he desired a big chance; at the next, he dreaded it. On December 8, 1863, he had written Pierre Soulé: "I hear that if Lee defeats the Federals he will go west and I will be sent to Virginia. I do not want to command an army where any job is to watch a defeated foe. My health is too bad for me to take the field, but if I have to, I desire the command of my former army." To Soulé, who had influence in Congress, he expounded his sixth grandiose plan for winning the war. It began: "Let the western army be reinforced from Virginia and other sources to a size of one hundred thousand." Characteristically, he disregarded the glaring want of Southern manpower and the faltering condition of the patched railroad.

On March 10, 1864, the Richmond *Whig*, Beauregard's mouthpiece since First Manassas, urged the President to restore him to his old command in the West, where the *Examiner's* "white knight," Joseph E. Johnston, held the commanding position. Many of Davis's friends suggested that because of the glittering image in the public mind of a dashing commander it would be politic to give Beauregard some special eminence, so that his clique in Congress would moderate opposition to the Administration. Davis had been ruminating on how to use the romantic Creole when the spring push came.

When Beauregard agreed to Bragg's request to come to southern Virginia to serve in the field, he was ordered to proceed to Weldon, North Carolina, close to Virginia's border, where he would receive instructions.

Beauregard reached Weldon on April 22. President Davis sent a staff officer to explain in person the military situation. Beauregard was to assume independent command of the Department of North Carolina and the part of Virginia south of the James. His chief duty would be to defend Petersburg, twenty-three miles south of Richmond and the strategic center of five railroads. Davis was relieved to hear from all reports that the volatile General was on his best behavior. And now that he himself was far from Charleston, he was willing to remove most of the troops from that region and add them to his new command.

On May 5, President Davis learned that at Grant's directive, General Benjamin F. Butler, commanding the district about Fort Monroe, had brought an army of 22,000 men in transports up the James and had taken City Point on the south bank, a bare eight miles from Petersburg. Major General George Pickett of Gettysburg fame had hardly more than a regiment to defend Petersburg and keep the railroads intact. Pickett sent frantic dispatches to the War Department and to Beauregard urging speediest help. In this hour of crisis, Beauregard wired the War Department that he was not well enough to travel. He advised that Pickett should keep command and withhold any Confederate troops passing through the town to join Lee, who was just then in the thick of his first conflict with Grant.*

General Bragg brought the disturbing news of Beauregard's indisposition to the President. Was the mercurial General trying to avoid responsibility? The President decided to try to spur him to action. On May 6 he telegraphed: "I hope you will be able at Petersburg to direct operations both before and behind you, so as to meet necessities." He was cautious not to give him precise instructions.

Lee had let Grant cross the Rapidan without interference on May 4. On the next day, when the enemy had got into the jungle of scrub oaks and vines known as the Wilderness, he had concentrated his forces and sprung at Grant with tigerlike swiftness. Though the numerically superior Federals had overwhelming artillery, the topography of the mazelike terrain was against them and they lost heavily.

The next morning the battle began shortly after dawn. At one period the Union forces were turning the Confederate right wing and the situation was critical, when Longstreet arrived in the nick of time. With furious assaults his battalions drove back the blue lines.

Near midmorning the Federals were swept with panic. Even the redoubtable General Hancock could not stop the pell-mell retreat. The situation was reminiscent of Chancellorsville the year before.

---

* On this same critical day of May 5, Beauregard sent a strange letter to General W. H. C. Whiting, who was now under his command: "I do not yet know whether I will take an active part in this Great Drama about to be enacted around Richmond. . . . I fear, however, to be 'a little too late.'"

Grant's army was on the verge of disaster. General Micah Jenkins of South Carolina paused to congratulate Longstreet on the effect of his crushing attack. He expected the enemy to be pushed across the Rapidan before nightfall and declared jovially, "We'll smash 'em now!" Longstreet was radiantly sanguine. He believed he had "another Bull Run on them." Just then a volley from the roadside underbrush rang out. Jenkins fell, fatally wounded. A heavy bullet tore through Longstreet's right shoulder and penetrated his throat. When he was taken from his horse and stretched on the ground he almost choked to death on his own blood. He had been shot by Virginians, who mistook his brand-new, very dark gray uniform for Union blue.

Jefferson Davis had hardly had time to rejoice at hearing of the successful Confederate advance, when a dispatch announced Jenkins' mortal wound and Longstreet's serious one. The tragic accident had occurred near the spot where Stonewall Jackson had been felled by Virginians almost exactly a year before. Fate was playing its old tricks with the Confederates, elating them in one hour and then dashing their spirits with some odd malevolence the next.

Lee's advance was halted when Longstreet was borne to the rear. Shortly after the lull the thickets between the opposing lines caught fire. In a roaring inferno that made the night like a scene from Dante, some of the dead were cremated on the spot, and a few of those too severely wounded to crawl away from the flames were burned alive as they futilely screamed for stretcher-bearers who could not reach them.

Though the Union casualties amounted to 17,666[*] and the Confederate less than half that number, President Davis was disappointed. For Grant did not pull back to the campsites across the Rapidan, but started sideslipping to the south towards Hanover and Spotsylvania Court House.

Lee, anticipating his move, had ordered a part of his force under General Richard H. Anderson, who had succeeded Longstreet, to intercept him. When Grant arrived he found Confederates entrenched across his path. The fighting was resumed, and the field was piled with more slaughtered bodies. On May 11 Grant sent a dispatch to Halleck in Washington which would become famous. "We have now ended the sixth day of very heavy fighting. . . . I propose to fight it out on this line if it takes all summer."

[*] The figures are from the *Century War Book* and are accepted by the historian James Ford Rhodes.

Few persons in the North dreamed that it was to take all summer, all fall, all winter, and half the following spring to break Lee's lines. For those Federal officers who questioned his generalship, Grant reiterated his purpose: "to hammer continuously against the armed force of the enemy and his resources until by mere attrition the South should be subdued." Davis understood Grant's attrition policy, which was sound enough, if in no sense brilliant, and he could only hope that while Lee endured, the Northern peace party would wax stronger and raise more powerful protests to stop the carnage.

Though Beauregard had telegraphed the President that he purposed to leave Weldon on May 7, he did not depart until the tenth, after receiving the news of Grant's losses in the Wilderness. Late that afternoon Bragg brought the President a telegram from Beauregard at Petersburg: "Have just arrived. Will take the offensive as soon as practicable." Since April 22, Beauregard's admirers had kept Richmond in a state of high expectancy of some brilliant feat on his part. But on Tuesday, May 10, General Gorgas noted in his diary, "Everybody complains of the tardiness of Beauregard's movement."

Fighting had occurred all that day in the direction of Drewry's Bluff and Petersburg. When dusk came the President could see the reflections of flickering flames on the horizon where the woods were afire. Now Davis noted that for the first time Richmond citizens began to look anxious. And "well they may," Gorgas wrote, "with 30,-000 Yankees close upon the city and not 12,000 troops to defend it." Reports came that Grant's entire cavalry under Sheridan was approaching Richmond from the direction of Ashland, nine miles north of the city, that Jeb Stuart was hot at their heels, but that the Federals had a good start.

In the excitement, Mrs. Davis sat down to answer a letter of the widow of Brigadier General Richard Griffith, the Philadelphia-born Confederate who had been killed at Savage's Station in June, 1862. She was now living precariously at Jackson, Mississippi. Mrs. Davis, still overcome by grief over the death of her son, hardly knew what day of the month it was.

Your letter found me in the deepest affliction. One week ago I should have been able to tell you of my most beautiful and promising child. Now I can tell you that I have three left—none so bright, none so beautiful, but all precious. . . . My youngest, William is an unusually fine boy . . . as

large at two years as other children at three. Very active and very good.
. . . While I write the alarm bells are ringing.

She spoke of her husband as being "in a state of anxiety, which
he does not express" but which she could not "fail to participate
in." "The enemy are pressing us everywhere, and Gen. Lee is fighting desperately alone, hopeful of preventing the seize of Richmond."

That night the President was kept awake by the ringing of bells
and the screeching of sirens. Next morning, according to the War
Clerk, J. B. Jones, Secretary of War Seddon seemed to believe that
the hours of the capital were numbered. Virtually all the executive
offices were emptied of clerks who had gone to the city's outer defenses. Business was suspended. No one was allowed to leave town.
Adding to the tension, a terrible storm swept Richmond and un-
roofed houses.

The morning of May 12, 1864, broke with thunder, lightning, and
rain. The date was to mark another disaster for the Confederacy
and another personal grief for Jefferson Davis. The day before, during the skirmishing six miles north of the capital, General Jeb Stuart
was mortally wounded.

According to Heros von Borcke, his Prussian Chief of Staff, Stuart had only 1,800 men to Sheridan's 8,000. To protect the capital,
he made a furious detour around Sheridan and intercepted his
forces at Yellow Tavern. A protracted contest ensued. Stuart, who
was "quite in advance," had fired the last charge in his pistol when
he discovered a dismounted bluecoat squatting by a roadside fence.
He ordered the man to surrender. The horseless cavalryman
promptly shot him in the abdomen. In terrible pain, the gallant Stuart kept in his saddle, urging his men on. Finally, he was lifted from
his horse and taken, dying, in an ambulance to Richmond. The
tragic news was brought to the President.

Because the Confederates were having a difficult time against
the larger Union forces, General Robert Ransom with two small
brigades of cavalry had hurried in the night from the vicinity of
Drewry's Bluff. Shortly after sunrise he was in position to confront
Sheridan. He found Jefferson Davis already upon the field. Ransom
wrote later, "He never appeared to greater advantage. Calm,
self-contained, hopeful, determined, he was an inspiration to every
soul who saw him. He did not once interfere, suggest, or order
anything, but he was there demonstrating his readiness, and I have

often thought his purpose, to assume control should the desperate moment arrive."

Davis remained on the field most of the morning. Sheridan's men had withdrawn and were now said to be miles away. When the President rode back into Richmond he went to see the wounded Stuart at the home of Dr. Brewer. He was told that the General's wife, who was in another town, had been sent for. This lovely, Virginia-born girl had already suffered more than most soldiers' wives, for while her husband was the most famous of the Confederate cavalrymen in the east, her father, Philip St. George Cooke, was a Major General in the Union army.

It was just before noon when Jefferson Davis entered Stuart's room. He could hardly believe that this splendid specimen of vital manhood, only thirty-one years old, could be in imminent danger; for, as he wrote later, "he was so calm, and physically so strong." But his physician said that the ball, which had entered the lower abdomen, had pierced the kidney and grazed the liver. The President sat by the soldier's bedside and tenderly took his hand. "General," he asked solicitously, "how do you feel?" With a faint smile Stuart replied, "Easy—but willing to die." With some comforting words, Davis, who still had hope, left his bedside. Out in the hall Dr. Brewer told him that the patient was bleeding inwardly, and that the end was quite near.

In the early afternoon Stuart took a turn for the worse. His fever rose and he became delirious. He spoke of battlefields, his absent wife, a child of his who was dead. His pain became agonizing. He asked if he were dying. At the doctor's nod, he said, "I am resigned, if it be God's will." At the dying man's request, Heros von Borcke and other intimate friends about the bedside sang, with scalding tears in their eyes, "Rock of Ages." For Stuart, like Jackson, who had died a year before on May 10, was an ardent believer. At sunset the end came.

When the expected death was announced to the President, he felt a despairing grief. He had been unusually fond of the gay-hearted horseman, who perhaps more than any other individual had been able to rally soldiers' drooping spirits. Indefatigable in cheerfulness, he brightened the camps with his banjo and his songs and made men forget their hardships. This rollicking, husky warrior needed no stimulation of liquor to elevate his mood. He never drank and he never smoked, and to men in uniform his manly virtues were like a walking sermon. The value of such a radiant spirit was beyond computation. And as a cavalry officer, Stuart was invaluable: alert, efficient, audacious, and tireless. Davis was to speak of him in *The Rise and Fall* as "our most distinguished cavalry commander— fearless, faithful Stuart." Lee said he never brought him a false piece of information. What would Lee do now without "the eyes of his army?"

The President reflected on the South's three irreplaceable losses: Sidney Johnston, Stonewall Jackson, and J. E. B. Stuart. Each death had come in the spring at a year's interval, and each had lost his life because of a courage that impelled him too far to the front. If this trio had been spared, would the South have won independence? Jefferson Davis always believed so.

Now Lee was in a more serious plight than ever. He had to face the determined might of Grant without Stuart, as well as minus Longstreet, his chief lieutenant, who was completely incapacitated. A. P. Hill was ailing, and the fatigued Dick Ewell, with a leg gone, was hardly able to carry on. The President was greatly troubled. But as far as Richmond was concerned, people breathed more freely. The enemy cavalry to the north had completely retired. Fitzhugh Lee had taken command of Stuart's men.

On May 12, when the Confederates faced disaster from Grant's terrific hammering at a place near Spotsylvania to be known as the "Bloody Angle," Lee himself rode to the head of a column and prepared to lead it in a charge that might save the day. The horrified troops refused to budge until Lee returned to the rear. Then they fought like demons. The President wrote Lee a strong letter imploring him not to expose himself.

I have been pained to hear of your exposure of your person in various conflicts. The country could not bear the loss of you, and my dear friend, though you are prone to forget yourself, you will not, I trust, again forget the public interest dependent on your life.

The reports of the casualties at Bloody Angle on the twelfth were sickening to the President. Some of the most ferocious fighting had been hand-to-hand. But the Confederates had held and repulsed each assault. In the battling from May 5 to May 12, according to Professor J. G. Randall, Grant "lost almost 26,000 men in killed, wounded, and missing." Yet he doggedly determined to fight it out his way. Stanton again assured him that he could replenish his army at will. President Lincoln, in his quaint, colloquial idiom, wired encouragement: "Keep a-peggin'!"

As the fighting persisted, with Federal forces maneuvering and making thrusts here and there, the dead and wounded piled up in macabre patterns outside the Confederate lines. General Grant would not ask a truce to bury his dead and remove his wounded to field hospitals. For two days Southerners watched one agonized boy in blue attempt to knock his brains out with the butt end of a musket, but he was too weak to give himself a mortal blow. Finally, on the third day, there was no more trying.

It was reported to President Davis that on the morning of the eighteenth, Grant, reinforced by 8,000 fresh troops, made another violent attack just where the bloody assault of May 12 had occurred. Grant himself supervised the mighty effort. Lieutenant General John B. Gordon, who proved his ability in this engagement, was to tell the story to Davis:

In superb style the Union army moved to the assault. The Confederates were ready for them and, as Hancock's and Wright's brave men climbed over the old abandoned works and debouched from the intervening bushes, a consuming fire of grape, canister and Minié balls was poured in incessant volleys upon them. Such a fire was too much for any troops. They first halted before it and staggered. Then they rallied, moved forward, halted again, wavered, bent into irregular zigzag lines, and at last broke in confusion and precipitate retreat. Again and again they renewed the charge, but each assault ended as the first, in repulse and heavy slaughter.

Thus near Spotsylvania Court House ended the second series of battles in which Grant had unsuccessfully tried to drive Lee from the field. After the ghastly slaughter of May 18, the Union Colonel Theodore Lyman paid the Southern fighters sincere compliments. Of Lee he wrote, "He is *not* retreating. He is a brave and skillful soldier and will fight while he has a division or a day's ration left." Of the Rebel privates, he wrote with peculiar discernment:

In education they are certainly inferior to our native-born people, but they are unusually quick-witted and they know enough to handle weapons with terrible effect. Their great characteristic is their stoical manliness; they never beg or whimper or complain, but look you straight in the face, with as little animosity as if they had never heard a gun fired.

The President had been in almost daily communication with Lee by telegraphic dispatches, and on May 19 he received a long detailed letter from the General in which Lee graphically explained the current situation and why he could not attack.

The enemy's artillery is superior in weight of metal and range to our own, and my object has been to engage him in motion and under circumstances that will not cause us to suffer from this disadvantage. . . . I shall continue to strike him whenever opportunity presents itself, but nothing at present indicates any purpose on his part to advance. . . . General Grant can, and if permitted will, repair the losses of the late battles, and be as strong as when he began operations.

I deem it my duty to present the actual situation of affairs to your Excellency, in order that your judgement may be guided in devising the means of opposing the force that is being arrayed against us.

The next day the President received a telegram that emphasized Lee's meaning.

The forces around Washington and the Northern cities are being stripped of troops. The question is whether we shall fight the battle here or around Richmond. If the troops are obliged to be retained at Richmond I may be forced back.

Davis promptly sent Lee every man possible, even to endangering the capital, for now Ben Butler was pushing closer.

How far the morale of your army would be affected by a retrograde movement no one can judge as well as yourself. It would certainly encourage the enemy, and if he wants time and opportunity to recruit, he would thus have it with absolute security. We should lose the Central railroad and all the supplies, together with the growing crops, in that portion of Northern Virginia. I am willing to leave the matter to your decision. You are better informed than any other can be of the necessities of your position . . . and I cannot do better than leave your judgement to reach its own conclusion.

On the twenty-second Lee reported to Davis that Grant was now withdrawing from his position and moving towards Bowling Green. "The enemy's whole force, with the exception of the 9th Corps, had left their former positions before dark yesterday."

While Lee was hastening to oppose any flanking movement of Grant, Davis was receiving discouraging reports from Georgia. General Johnston was falling back as hard as he could. He had placed himself behind the Etowah River with his headquarters at Altoona. Gorgas wrote in his diary:

Johnston will reach Macon in a few days at the rate he is retreating— I trust the country will sooner or later find out what sort of a general he is. I don't think he will suit the emergency.

Davis had all along had discomforting doubts about Johnston's will to fight. Though the State of Georgia was having conniption fits at each successive retreat, Johnston's newspaper champions in Virginia hailed his retrograde movements as remarkable strategy.

"Johnston verified all our predictions of him," Gorgas noted on May 25. "He is falling back as fast as his legs can carry him. . . . He is falling back behind the Chattahoochie and will, I fear, give up Atlanta. . . . Where he will stop Heaven only knows!"

As dispatches arrived, Davis, in his mind's eye, watched Johnston give up one strong entrenched position after another from which it seemed he might have given hardy battle to the oncoming Sherman. Though he had the mountains' protective arms to form natural barriers, he moved back nearer to the plains—after Dalton, to Rocky Face Ridge, Varnell's Station, Resaca, Turner's Ferry, Cassville. And he would give no indication whatever to the War Department as to where he intended to stop and fight.

The President had not had so many anxieties crowding upon him since his double worries at the time of Gettysburg and Vicksburg. In a letter of May 22 to her mother in Canada, Varina revealed some of the tension in the Davis household. Though still crushed by sorrow over little Joe, and with new calamities happening almost every day, she attempted to be philosophical: "I feel hourly how much I have to be thankful for, and am not rebellious, only grieved."

Jeff, as you surmise, has been forced from home constantly and in the various battles around Richmond has been pretty much exposed. A man's arm was taken off by a shell within five feet of him. . . . It was a very sanguinary battle, and the loss great and I fear is but the prelude to many in the ensuing summer.

I think I shall send Maggie to Mrs. Preston's and then to Mrs. Chesnut's for a visit, and it may be send the children also. . . . I shall not very much miss them, as it is my only comfort to sit alone.

Jeff is much worried by anxiety . . . and I hear the roar of artillery and crack of muskets it seems to me all the time.

There is an immense deal of suffering here now, so much so that they are impressing servants in the street to nurse the wounded. Erysipelas has appeared in some of the hospitals and there are many deaths from slight wounds.

CHAPTER VI

DISAPPOINTMENT AT DREWRY'S BLUFF AND HORROR AT COLD HARBOR

———<*>———

AS BEN BUTLER moved towards Richmond, Secretary of War Seddon telegraphed Beauregard that the capital was in "hot danger." He directed him to Drewry's Bluff below the city to join forces there with General Robert Ransom, who was in charge of Richmond's defenses. Beauregard, characteristically, tried to change the orders and suggested other strategy. Seddon insisted that he obey the first directive agreed on.

Bragg came into the President's office to tell him that now the Creole's feelings were hurt. Beauregard had written Bragg that he was serving in the field at great danger to his health, and if his conduct were not approved, could he please be relieved of his command.

The President, the Secretary of War, and General Bragg were all exasperated by Beauregard's dangerous delay and peevishness. Finally, however, on May 13, he arrived at Drewry House before dawn with reinforcements. In the afternoon of the fourteenth the President rode down to greet him.

Davis tells the story in his *Rise and Fall* :

Supposing his troops to be on the line of entrenchment, I passed Major Drewry's house to go thither, when someone by the roadside called to me and told me that the troops were not on the line of entrenchment, and that General Beauregard was at the house behind me.

My first question on meeting him was to learn why the entrenchments were abandoned. He answered that he thought it better to concentrate his troops. Upon my stating to him that there was nothing then to prevent Butler from turning his position, he said he would desire nothing more, as he would then fall upon him, cut him off from his base, etc.

According to my uniform practice never to do more than to make a sug-

46

gestion to a general commanding in the field, the subject was pressed no further. We then passed to the consideration of the operations to be undertaken against Butler, who had already advanced from his base at Bermuda Hundred. I offered, for the purpose of attacking Butler, to send Major General Ransom with the field force he had for the protection of Richmond. In addition to his high military capacity, his minute knowledge of the country in which they were to operate made him specially valuable.

General Whiting's force was holding a defensive position before Petersburg. Beauregard proposed that the main part of Whiting's force be advanced and united with his in attacking Butler *wherever he should be found between Drewry's Bluff and Petersburg.* To this the President was constrained to offer distinct objections "because of the hazard during a battle of attempting to make a junction of troops moving from opposite sides of the enemy." Davis proposed that Whiting's army should move at night by the Chesterfield road, where they would not be observed by Butler's advance. They would be united with Beauregard's troops, rest on Sunday, and be prepared to attack Butler on Monday. Beauregard apparently accepted the President's ideas, and said that he would prepare the order as soon as possible. Davis rose to take his leave, and the General courteously saw him down the stairs. But Beauregard secretly changed the plan.

Ransom, now under Beauregard's command, reported to him at noon the next day. Beauregard gave Ransom what he called "the moving part of the army" and asked him to take the initiative, as he knew the region.

By sunrise on Monday, though fighting in a dense fog, Ransom had captured several hundred prisoners and occupied three-quarters of a mile of the enemy's temporary breastworks. Then he sent a message to Beauregard urging that his own, Ransom's Brigade, be sent to him at once so that he could press his advantage. No answer. He begged a second time for his brigade. Instead, Beauregard sent him "two small regiments" and said that he was keeping Ransom's Brigade by his side, since it was the most seasoned and "could best avoid disaster."

Postmaster General Reagan rode down to the field where Beauregard was. Everyone was waiting for Whiting's guns. The general officers met at the Petersburg turnpike for consultation, and while talking an enemy bullet hit one of them in the back. The wound was not serious and the others joked with the wounded officer about a Confederate being shot in the back. Butler's artillery was keeping up an almost continuous fusillade.

A little later in the day, the President, this time accompanied by aides, went to Drewry's. He learned that the enemy had seized the Confederate line of entrenchment, which Beauregard had left unoccupied. A severe action had occurred with serious loss before Ransom could dislodge the enemy.

A shower of rain came as President Davis rode up to ask how the battle was going. He had not expected rain and was without a raincoat, so he guided his horse under the boughs of a leaning silver maple tree. A young officer approached solicitously and insisted on throwing his own waterproof cape about the President's shoulders. General Beauregard came up just then and suggested to Mr. Davis that they go into one of the shanties near-by to get out of the wet. Two of Davis's aides begged Reagan to try to persuade him to leave the field. Persons in the vicinity were getting hit occasionally and the President was as likely as anyone to get struck. Reagan urged him to withdraw. Davis smilingly disregarded his request and started with Beauregard for the shack. A shell burst, and a young soldier who accompanied them had an arm blown off near his shoulder. Beauregard remarked that the enemy seemed to have the range of the place, so he and the President went across the turnpike to open ground. As the shells continued to sweep the area they moved farther back. At last the Union rear-guard firing ceased. Butler had apparently retreated with little damage done him. Whiting had not yet begun his part in the battle.*

Later, in a monograph on the Battle of Drewry's Bluff, General Ransom explained his own actions move by move, dilating upon Beauregard's indecision and his waiting all afternoon to get into the fight, while Butler was moving off. Finally, worn by impatience, Ransom returned around three o'clock to headquarters to discover the cause of delay. He found President Davis there, disturbed that all this time Butler was marching away. "A little before five o'clock," Ransom wrote, "Beauregard seemed to have determined on some aggressive movement." Ransom was directed to have his troops ready to move at an instant's notice, and to await orders. "I galloped to my division and waited with impatience and disgust till after sundown when the order came: 'Bivouac for the night.'"

When the Union rear-guard firing ceased, Davis knew Butler had

* According to Reagan: "The reason General Whiting did not commence the attack, as expected, was because he was drunk."

escaped and that Beauregard had let slip an almost certain chance for significant victory. The President did not upbraid Beauregard for substituting the unwise plan for his. As dusk fell, Davis, perplexed and grave with disappointment, rode back to Richmond in silence.

Whiting had blacked out from drink, exhaustion, or mental confusion resulting from the changed orders. T. Harry Williams, Beauregard's most searching biographer, wrote, "the responsibility for Whiting's failure rests on Beauregard. . . . It was he who insisted that Whiting move to the field instead of to Drewry's Bluff," as Davis and Bragg had urged. "It was he who changed Whiting's orders."

The next day, the seventeenth, the Confederates were ordered down the river road, but by four in the afternoon they had not yet come upon the enemy. Butler had escaped into the safety of the peninsula known as Bermuda Hundred at the confluence of the James and the Appomattox.

Jefferson Davis smothered his discontent as well as he could, and years later wrote with moderation: "It would be neither pleasant nor profitable to dwell on the lost opportunity for a complete victory, or to recount the possible consequences which might have flowed from it." As it was, Butler's twenty-odd thousand were bottled up in Bermuda Hundred. At least "the back door to Richmond" was temporarily closed.

Not blaming himself for his irresolution or the escape of Butler, Beauregard, with a bold display of confidence in his own ideas of strategy, addressed a memorandum to General Bragg from "Hancock House, May 18, 1864, 9:30 P.M." It would be something for posterity, as well as for Beauregard's admirers, to chew upon. The first sentence was strong, vigorous—and highly ironic: "The crisis demands prompt and decisive action." Beauregard recommended that General Lee fall back behind the Chickahominy so as to be nearer him. He proposed that he be reinforced immediately by 10,000 men from General Lee's army and by 5,000 drawn from the scanty Richmond defenses. Then he would crush Butler in his entrenchments, rejoin Lee, overwhelm Grant, and "march to Washington." With a cavalier disregard for logistics, Beauregard estimated that all this could be accomplished in two or three days.

When this extraordinary document was handed to President Davis, he read it with astonishment. Before returning it, he endorsed on the back: "General Lee is best informed of his situation and his ability is too well established to incline me to adopt the pinion of anyone at a distance as to the movements which his army should make."

With Lee fighting for his very life, outnumbered two to one, the humblest clerk in the War Office could have seen glaring flaws in Beauregard's pretentious scheme. But out of courteous consideration, the President dutifully sent Beauregard's plan to Lee. On reading it, Lee promptly directed Beauregard to shorten his line so as to reduce the number of troops required to keep Butler bottled up and to send the balance to join him north of the James.

Bragg went in person to Beauregard's headquarters to reason with him. He told him frankly that he already had enough men under his own command to defeat Butler.* Then the President himself went down later in the day to meet with Beauregard. He thought Beauregard should attack Butler at once, and he promised to return to him Ransom's troops, which had been withdrawn north of the river to parry a Union cavalry attack. Beauregard looked solemn and temporized.

On May 20, in answer to a strong appeal from General Lee, the President wrote Beauregard:

Whenever it can be done with safety to our line of communication and the defense of the capital, I desire you to throw forward strong reinforcements to General Lee. I would be glad, as I am sure he would, that you should go forward and command them.

But Beauregard had no desire to join General Lee as a subordinate.

In a new sideslipping movement Grant reached the North Anna River on May 23. Again he found Lee entrenched. Wherever the Union line moved, Davis noted with gratification, there before it was a line of Confederates, "nothing showing but the bayonets and the battle flags stuck on top of the works." Davis remarked that it was Virginian earth that was saving lines for Lee. For whenever the Southerners halted they first made good rifle pits, then a regular infantry parapet with artillery in position, and then, if possible, a parapet with an abatis in front and entrenched batteries behind.

Davis had now reinforced Lee by six brigades from the Richmond defenses and by Breckinridge's division from the Shenandoah Val-

---

* Eleven years after Bragg had dropped dead while walking down a street in Galveston, Beauregard claimed that Bragg was in favor of his plan.

ley. "Whatever route he [Grant] pursues," General Lee wrote the President, "I am in a position to engage him while in motion."

> I shall be near enough Richmond, I think, to combine the operations of this army with that under General Beauregard. . . . General Grant's army will be in the field, strengthened by all available troops from the North, and it seems to me our best policy to unite upon it and endeavor to crush it. I shall be very glad to have the aid of General Beauregard in such a blow, and if possible to combine, I think it will succeed.

Lee's high confidence inspired Davis to expect a successful offensive action. Lee's concentrated, entrenched position in a V shape at the North Anna was now most fortuitous. His troops were wedged between the widely separated wings of the Federal army in such a position that neither wing could reinforce the other without twice crossing the river. According to Nicolay and Hay, "Grant was completely checkmated."

On the twenty-fourth, just when he had his first opportunity to hit one-half of Grant's forces, Lee was taken violently ill with bilious dysentery. He was confined to his bed, and fever prevented his giving sound orders. In his feverish agitation, however, he realized that the strategic moment he longed for had come. He kept repeating, "We must strike a blow! We must strike him now!"

The confidential news of Lee's illness caused Davis the gravest anxiety. With Lee incapacitated, how could the army that lived by his looks carry on? And if the illness should prove fatal? The idea was too dreadful to be thought on. In any case, unexpected misfortune had again struck the Confederacy at a critical hour.

Grant, realizing his perilous position, sidled southeast to safer ground. On May 27 the crisis of Lee's illness came. He rallied, and said to his physician, "If I can get one more pull at Grant, I will defeat him." Such an opportunity was not to come again. Instead, Lee shortly faced being overpowered.

On May 29, at the President's urgent request, Beauregard went to Lee's headquarters. In conference, he insisted that he could spare no men at all, although Butler was sending Grant troops by the thousands from his base at Bermuda Hundred. Lee became as exasperated with Beauregard as Davis and the War Department had been.

The next day Grant reached Cold Harbor, only nine miles from Richmond. In this critical situation, which thinned the Confederate line dangerously, Lee called directly on Beauregard for immediate reinforcements. Beauregard coolly answered, "War Department must determine when and what troops to order from here."

Lee telegraphed the President: "I think it very important to strengthen this army as much as possible. . . . If this army is unable to resist Grant the troops under Gen. Beauregard and in the city will be unable to defend it. . . . The result of this delay will be disaster."

Davis was himself forced to command the transfer of General R. F. Hoke's seasoned division from Beauregard to Lee. Four brigades with a battalion of artillery arrived just before Grant commenced his most furious assault of the war. But Lee, just up from his sickbed, had moved swiftly and strengthened his lines. His troops were entrenched opposite Grant's. His artillery had set guns in ambush to await the enemy's advance.

On May 31, War Clerk Jones wrote in capital letters: "The GREAT BATTLE is imminent."

Troops have been coming from the South side [Beauregard's] for twenty hours, and marching down Main Street towards the Williamsburg Road. . . .

All the local troops are ordered to be in readiness to march at a moment's warning this evening or morning.

At half past seven on June 1, Jefferson Davis heard cannon and musketry to the northeast. Around noon the noise receded. Lee had repulsed a series of heavy infantry attacks. As soon as he could finish some essential office business, the President rode out to the battlefield. He found General Lee sufficiently recovered to direct the battle. It had been only two years earlier that he had given Lee command of the Army of Northern Virginia and elicited a chorus of sarcastic protest. The world had long since accepted his own instinctive estimate of Lee. Now the soldiers, after weeks of grueling warfare, were in excellent spirits. Abundant rations had been coming in during the last four days; full stomachs made them eager for the fight.

The men he had ordered from Beauregard had arrived by late afternoon and were ready to hold against Grant's onslaught. The Federal lines extended from the Chickahominy above Grapevine Bridge past Gaines's Mill, much as McClellan's had done in June, 1862, though Grant had not penetrated so near to Richmond's spires as had "Little Mac." Grant's reinforcements had made up for his mounting casualties, and his men again outnumbered Lee's two to one. Grant had been promised still more troops by Washington. No imminent battle had yet had so much at stake. If the enemy broke through, Davis knew only too well, Lee had no reserves. The President returned to Richmond in a state of mingled tension and hope.

Few dispatches came to Richmond on the morning of June 2; both armies had spent most of the preceding day in perfecting their lines. In the afternoon, quick and heavy cannonading coming from the east could be heard in Richmond. It continued until dark, when heavy rain began to fall. It was raining when the President went home from his office, and it was still raining when he went to bed. The morrow would determine Richmond's fate.

That night the wakeful Davis might as well have been on the field. He could feel the alertness in Lee's camp as keenly as if he were lying among the troops. As early as five in the morning of the third he heard an incessant roar of artillery and felt slight tremors in his house. Then came great crashes of musket fire, "as if whole divisions were firing at a word of command."

Before seven, the three Davis children appeared in the doorway to wish their father "Happy Birthday." The President was now fifty-six. With a pang he became acutely aware of the absence of little Joe.

In his mail that morning Davis received a letter from the Board of Directors of the Hollywood Cemetery Company manifesting "sympathy and respect" and tendering "without cost, the lot in which your son Joseph is buried." If the Davises desired any other unsold lot instead of the one selected hurriedly under the trying circumstances of their bereavement, they were at liberty to exchange. How very kind and thoughtful Richmond people were!

This birthday of June 3, 1864, would be a day to remember; the battle that was being fought nine miles away would be called in history the Battle of Cold Harbor.

Shortly after one o'clock the President received a cheering dispatch from General Lee. "So far every attack of the enemy has been repulsed. His assaults began early this morning, and continued until about 9 o'clock." This extremely modest report had just been preceded by the return of Colonel William Preston Johnston, Davis's aide, with a personal report of the morning's amazing success. Grant had ordered a direct frontal attack against Lee's entrenchments. At half past four in the morning, the first advance, twenty-six men deep and extending the length of the lines, lasted hardly a quarter of an hour. Ten thousand men in blue dropped to the ground.

The President called for his horse and rode down to greet General Lee on the field. When he arrived at Lee's headquarters the dead covered more than five acres of ground "about as thickly as they could be laid." The shooting was all over. The worst carnage had come in the first hour.

William Swinton, the Union historian of the Army of the Potomac, wrote:

The loss on the Union side in this sanguinary battle was more than 13,000, while on the part of the Confederates it is doubtful whether it reached as many hundred. General Meade sent instructions to each corps commander to renew the attack . . . but no man stirred, and the immobile lines produced a verdict, silent, yet emphatic, against further slaughter.

At half past twelve Meade received a face-saving order from Grant, "You may direct a suspension of farther advance for the present."

On the battlefield, Davis found the Confederate troops victoriously relaxed, but still poised behind triple lines of breastworks. He recalled again how contemptuous Southern soldiers had been at first of "cowardly breastworks" and how the *Examiner* had derided Lee for the confidence he placed in "spade work." Lee's troops had learned to have a healthy respect for breastworks, and when they lacked spades they used bayonets and tin plates and even split canteens as implements to throw up protective dirt.

While the President was in conversation with General Lee, General Gorgas rode up, wearing a blue cape. Lee turned from the President, beckoned Gorgas courteously and warned him to go back; in his blue cloth he might be shot at by either side. Then he added smilingly that he would rather the Ordnance Chief would return to Richmond and send him ammunition.

From the open spaces between the lines the wounded writhed in agony under the scorching June sun, groaned and moaned in the most piteous way, and begged for "water, water, water!" The President returned sickened to Richmond.

For four days the awful chorus of agonized men lying in their own blood and excrement made night and day hideous. The torture of festering wounds and paralyzing thirst finally muted curses and supplications to quavering whimpers or to deathly stillness. Grant, out of earshot of the heartrending polyphony, stubbornly refused to ask for a truce to salvage his helpless wounded and bury his dead, whose putrefying stench almost suffocated the soldiers in the trenches, both the blue and the gray, depending upon which way the neutral wind blew. Against the searing summer heat the Northern wounded would half-burrow under some stinking neighbor cadaver. Sometimes they would beguile their misery by reading over and over the identification strip of paper pinned to the back of a dead man's jacket, so his folks back home would learn that he was killed.

As the press reported the Union losses, the North was shaken with horror. "Grant had lost almost as many men in the entire campaign as Lee's whole army." "Hero" Grant was now being called "the Butcher."*

With the cries of "shame" following Grant's last bloody fiasco, the peace party in the North was said to be augmenting. Four days after Cold Harbor, the Republican convention met at Baltimore. Davis's eyes had not only been on the military campaigns east and west, but on political movements in the North. President Lincoln was rumored to have doubts about his renomination. A powerful radical element in the Republican party was itching to shelve him and put in some "stronger" man who would be more relentless in his subjugation of the South.

Secretary of the Treasury Chase, pining for Lincoln's place, gave ready ear to the men of dubious character who solicited him. Circulars were broadcast declaring radical ideas were needed and a more vigorous prosecution of the war. Lincoln, they said, was hardly the man for this. Even Horace Greeley, in a letter to *The Independent,* suggested that Chase, Frémont, Butler, or Grant would make as good a President as Lincoln, and called the one-term principle "salutary."

Ben Butler, notorious for his ruthless rule in New Orleans, and now bottled up at Bermuda Hundred, seemed to Thaddeus Stevens, the Southern-hating House leader, to be an ideal choice of the "loyal" people of the United States. And dramatically Stevens had

---

* The losses of Grant from May 5 to June 12, when he withdrew from Lee's front and began sideslipping to the James, were 54,929, according to the historian Rhodes. "A number nearly equal to Lee's whole army at the commencement of the campaign."

And Rhodes points out that it was the flower of the Army of the Potomac (McClellan's great creation) that was decimated. For "the bounty-jumpers and the mercenaries skulked to the rear."

pointed in Congress to Representative Arnold of Chicago, a friend of Lincoln's, as the only one he knew who favored the Illinoisian's renomination.

But Lincoln's renomination on June 7 was really a foregone conclusion; his choice by state delegates would have been unanimous on the first ballot except for Missouri, which cast her votes for Grant. Davis had expected Lincoln to be the overwhelming choice of the Republicans, and certainly he was a far better choice than Grant or Chase, the fanatical Frémont or the corrupt Butler. However, the nomination of Andrew Johnson for Vice President astounded him. This able but ill-mannered man had been chosen because he was a Southerner and a stout Unionist. To insure Lincoln's election it seemed necessary to have a Democrat on the ticket of what was now called the Union Party.

Johnson, "home-made Yankee" from Tennessee, was more pleasing to the extreme radicals than was Lincoln. He was known as "Jeff Davis's most virulent hater" in Congress, and as one who detested everything connected with Southern "gentry." The Union party consisted of the Republicans and those Northern Democrats who favored continuing the war. It would be a powerful combination for the regular Northern Democratic party to beat. But if Lee could wreck Grant's army and if George B. McClellan were nominated by the Democrats!

Finally, on June 7, the day Lincoln was nominated, Grant relented and requested the customary truce for removing his wounded. The gruesome work proceeded. After four days of suffering the tortures of the damned, those helpless wounded men in blue had not much use for U. S. Grant.

For more than a week the opposing armies lay facing each other, barely nine miles from Richmond. On June 9 the President warned General Lee to be on his guard: "The indications are that Grant, despairing of a direct attack, is now seeking to embarrass you by flank movements." Speaking of the other major theater of war, he wrote: "Unless General Johnston strikes before the enemy has brought up all his reinforcements reported to be moving, his chances will be greatly diminished for the success which seemed attainable before he retreated and which still seems to be practicable."

CHAPTER VII

PETERSBURG

———◀◉▶———

THOUGH THE CRUSHING Union defeat at Cold Harbor brought some relief to the burdened Jefferson Davis, the situation in Virginia was still critical. If Grant had lost 60,000 men in a month, Lee had lost about a third of that number. Grant's forces could be replenished; Lee's could not. Lee now had only 45,000 effectives, including artillery and cavalry. Grant's forces still numbered more than 100,000 men. The Union troops in the Shenandoah were overpowering the Confederates and preparing to sweep the region. To meet the desperate situation in the Valley Lee agreed to detach Breckinridge and 2,000 men from his own depleted number.

In the middle of the night of June 11, President Davis, with many worries on his mind, rode down to the bivouacking troops near Bottom's Bridge, which crowned the Chickahominy eight miles from Richmond. Between two or three o'clock in the morning, General Robert Ransom, sleeping with his head on his saddle, felt a light hand on his shoulder. He started to get up when a voice spoke in low tones: "Do not rise." In the darkness he recognized it as the President's. Leaning closer, Davis spoke as if in apology. "I know you have but just fallen asleep. I give you an early call. Grant will not attempt to cross here. He is planning to do so below. Today you will be relieved here. I have to send you with General Early to meet Hunter, who is devastating the Valley. Your task will be hard. You will organize the wild cavalry which has just been defeated at Rock Fish Gap. . . . Make your arrangements. You will get the order today." Then, his mission done, the President disappeared into the night, treading softly among the sleeping soldiers.[*]

[*] The story is taken virtually verbatim from General Ransom's reminiscences of Jefferson Davis, as quoted in Mrs. Davis's *Memoir*.

On the thirteenth the President rode to Lee's camp, but the General was out. So he left him a note asking his opinion of the feasibility of Early's moving up the Valley towards Washington. The next day Davis received an answer from Lee.

I regret very much that I did not see you yesterday afternoon, and especially after your having taken so long a ride. If the movement of Early meets with your approval, I am sure it is the best that can be made, though I know how difficult it is with my limited knowledge to perceive the best.

I think the enemy must be preparing to move South of James River. Our scouts and pickets yesterday stated that Gen. Grant's whole army was in motion for the fords of the Chickahominy from Long Bridge down, from which I inferred that he was making his way to the James River as his new base.

Lee suspected that Grant intended to place his army within the fortifications around Harrison's Landing (as McClellan had done). There, with the aid of his gunboats, he could offer a strong defense. "I do not think it would be advantageous to attack him in that position."

Three hours later Davis received another dispatch from Lee.

I see no indications of his [Grant's] attacking me on this side of the River, though, of course, I cannot know positively. As his facilities for crossing the River and taking possession of Petersburg are great, and as I think it will more probably be his plan, I have sent Gen. Hoke with his command to a point above Drewry's Bluff. . . . He will execute any orders you may send him there.

On June 15 Davis received grievous news: General Leonidas Polk had been killed the day before. Davis had lost another friend, a man in whom he could put an absolute trust. Polk had been Albert Sidney Johnston's roommate at West Point, when Davis was a plebe. They had run together in the same "set" at the Academy. Later, as Episcopal Bishop, he had confirmed Jane Davis, the President's mother, at her home in Woodville, Mississippi, when she was eighty-two.

Polk had unnecessarily exposed himself on Pine Mountain in Georgia and a Union artilleryman had "sniped him with a field piece." General Sherman had seen some men in gray studying him through their field glasses. "They are saucy!" he said, and had given an order for three volleys to make them take cover. Captain Hubert Dilger, an expert Prussian artillerist, had sighted his gun and clapped his hands. As shells burst, the three central figures in gray separated. Two—Generals J. E. Johnston and W. J. Hardee— had scurried for cover. The third, Polk, departed with some dignity; "he did not want to appear too much hurried or cautious in the presence of his men." When he paused in the open to have another look at the enemy, a Union cannon ball caught the brave old man in the breast. General Hardee wept. So did many of the soldiers who had been with Polk since he occupied Columbus, Kentucky, on September 3, 1861.

Davis knew that Polk would be a sad loss to the Army of Tennessee. It was he who could keep peace between Johnston, who did not want to fight yet, and Hood, who was raring to. The preceding May he had baptized both Generals in camp. At midnight on May 11, in General Hood's headquarters at Resaca, the one-legged warrior had been baptized in the Episcopal faith with holy water from a tin basin. Six days later, after the twenty-three-mile retreat from Resaca to Adairsville, Joseph Johnston had confessed faith and been baptized by the good Bishop. The ceremony seemed to lift Johnston's spirits, for on May 19 he told his soldiers that they would now turn and "march to meet the enemy's advancing columns. . . . I will lead you to battle," he promised. "We may confidently trust that the Almighty Father will still reward the patriot's toil." But his exalted mood did not last long. The very next day he decided it would be better strategy to retreat another ten miles on a line between Kingston and Cassville, where he prepared a trap for Sherman; one which the wily Ohioan deftly avoided by a flanking movement that enfiladed Johnston's right and caused him to withdraw again.

With Polk, perhaps even more than with his young friend J. E. B. Stuart, Jefferson Davis felt a sharp personal loss. It came to his mind what some people had been saying since Sidney Johnston's death at Shiloh, that in the end "chivalry" might defeat the South. Chivalry could be another name for reckless valor.

But Davis had little time to spend on grief, for rumors ran that Grant was crossing to the south side of the James to attack Petersburg. And he had to find a successor to General Polk immediately. He sent Lee a list of officers, asking which he would advise for Polk's place.

Finding Generals to replace those killed or those who proved incompetent was one of the President's chief problems. Davis finally decided to give the promotion to Alexander P. Stewart, a raw-boned Tennessean and a West Pointer, who was commissioned Lieutenant General on June 23.

Late on June 15 Beauregard informed Lee, without warning, that he had fallen back from his advanced lines at Bermuda Neck to the trenches protecting Petersburg to the northeast. Lee was alarmed. Now Butler was "unbottled," though Beauregard had been specifically ordered to hold. In the town of Petersburg itself wiry ex-Governor Henry Wise commanded an oddly mixed force: grandfathers and beardless youths in civilian clothes mingled with a scattering of uniformed soldiers and were armed with primitive weapons including stakes and stones.

Davis was extremely anxious. Neither Lee nor Beauregard could tell Richmond precisely about Grant's movements and intentions. At the head of Pickett's division, however, Lee reached Drewry's Bluff on the south side of the James just before ten on the morning of the sixteenth.

On June 16 Lee sent three telegrams to Beauregard. In the first he said, "I do not know the position of Grant's army and cannot strip the north bank of James River." In the second he declared, "Have not heard of Grant's crossing James River." In the third he asked, "Has Grant been seen crossing James River?"

Grant was already across the river. His advance guard had reached Wilcox's Landing on the morning of June 13. A pontoon bridge had been constructed by midnight of the fourteenth, and the whole army had expeditiously crossed the river the next day. For the first time Grant's strategy had deceived Lee. Grant's movement from Cold Harbor to the James was made with extraordinary celerity and skill. Federal engineers worked hard at constructing roads and bridges, and the pontoniers had done master service at the wide expanse of river.

Grant had earlier dispatched a corps to Bermuda Hundred, and sent a conditional order to Butler on June 11 to "seize and hold Petersburg." Then he made a spurring visit to Butler, while the river crossing was in progress. He ordered Butler to capture Petersburg immediately, while he himself returned to speed the transfer of troops and artillery across the water.

On the sixteenth Union troops attacked Beauregard's thin line. After three hours of hard fighting, the Confederate extreme right was finally broken. More and more Federals had come up to back the Union attack. Beauregard had only some 10,000 to withstand 40,000 Union troops. He wired Lee for reinforcements. Lee could not leave Richmond unguarded. He was still ignorant of Grant's intention or position. The crux of his problem was Grant's whereabouts. And apparently both Lee and Beauregard had been ignorant of Grant's movements.

On the night of the sixteenth the worried President received a dispatch indicating Lee's uncertainty and sense of frustration.

I have not learned from General Beauregard what force is opposed to him in Petersburg or received any definite account of operations there, nor have I been able to learn whether any portion of Grant's army is opposed to him.

Earlier in that day Davis had been surprised to receive a long letter from Lee about the railroads.

For some few days back we have been only able to get sufficient corn for our animals from day to day—any accident to the railroads would cut short our supplies. . . . I think it is clear that the railroads are not working energetically and unless some improvement is made, I do not know what will become of us—I am therefore obliged to appeal to Your Excellency as reluctant as I am to trespass upon your time and attention. . . . Our existence depends upon everyone's exerting themselves at this time to the utmost.

This communication was nearer to admonitory than anything the President had ever received from General Lee. It struck him as somewhat extraordinary, particularly the timing. For Beauregard was even then in a desperate struggle against four-to-one odds to keep the Federals from destroying those very railroads and bringing famine to the army as well as to Richmond. Railroad transportation was a constant problem to Davis. With the worn-out facilities and with Federal raiders slashing lines wherever they could, the subject was ever present in his mind.

On the seventeenth Lee advanced a large part of his force nearer to the Bermuda Hundred line. That night at ten o'clock he received a desperate dispatch from Beauregard telling of the increasing Federal forces. "I may have to evacuate the city shortly." Lee sent Kershaw with 5,000 South Carolinians on the double-quick to Petersburg. A. P. Hill was ordered to the south side of the James to be within a day's march of the endangered town.

Friday, the seventeenth, was a day of terrific combat. Beauregard fought brilliantly. All his best martial qualities came to the fore. No theatrical posturing now, no moody doubts or fantastic theorizing, but bold, tenacious fighting. The Confederates contended stub-

bornly until eleven that night. Beauregard saw, however, that he
could no longer hope to hold the extended Petersburg line against
such odds, and before dawn he slipped back to a new position,
where his men began throwing up protective dirt with every possible digging tool and even with their bare hands. Fortunately,
Grant had still not arrived on the scene. By staying at the river to
hasten the crossing he had missed a golden chance for a smashing
victory.

After midnight Beauregard had sent Lee three frantic messages
by courier. At last Lee was convinced and grasped Petersburg's
peril. By half past three in the morning he was astir and ready to go
to Beauregard's rescue. Kershaw's men had already arrived to
meet the Federal onslaught.

Before he left, Lee took time to write a dispatch for the President,
marked "Confidential."

From information received last night it is pretty certain that Grant's
whole force has crossed to the South Side of the James River. I have ordered all the troops over towards Petersburg, leaving the outer defenses
of Richmond in charge of Gen. G. W. C. Lee. . . .

Davis received the message while the climactic battle was raging.

The big offensive by the Federals had started at dawn. Finally,
realizing that the old Confederate trenches had been abandoned,
they had stopped to reorganize. Just before Lee's arrival the major
attack was launched against Beauregard's new position. The Confederates now had 20,000 men, and more were coming up. The
Union assault was repulsed with heavy loss.

Just before noon Lee himself arrived at Petersburg astride Traveller. The townspeople flooded the streets to greet him. Ladies at
their front gates served cool water to the troops and what food they
had. In an overflow of joy they caressed the soldiers' grimy
hands. Lee sought out Beauregard, and they went together to inspect the lines. The keyed-up defender urged an attack upon the
enemy immediately. But Lee shook his head. The exhausted, tattered men who had saved the town were still greatly outnumbered.
The strain showed in their complexions, their drained expressions,
and their glazed eyes. They must have rest before they fought
again.

Lee's first message to Davis after his arrival at Petersburg was
calm and cool. He did not speak of Beauregard's valiant repulse of
the enemy, but simply wrote, "General Beauregard had felt con-

strained to contract his lines on the east side of Petersburg before my arrival, and I found his troops in their new position. . . . No attack has been made by the enemy since my arrival."

At night there was a complete lull. The surcease marked a setback for the North, success for the South. Petersburg was saved. Richmond was intact. The relieved President reckoned that Grant was now several miles farther away from the Confederate capital than he had been at Cold Harbor.

The successive Federal assaults ordered on June 16 and the two sequent days had ended in repulses and the loss of approximately 10,000 more Northern troops. Davis was puzzled as to why Grant with his masses had not overpowered the thin Confederate lines, swarmed into Petersburg, broken the five railways, and caused the evacuation of Richmond. Later, as Charles A. Dana wrote to Secretary of War Stanton, the work "was not equal to our previous fighting, owing to our heavy loss in superior officers."

The truth was that the mighty Army of the Potomac was tired out with Grant's "hammering." After forty-five days of fighting without victory and being forced to make long marches through the night, the men were exhausted and depressed. Though reinforcements had continually been sent to bolster Grant, they had not raised the morale. "The reinforcements," declared Rhodes, "were, for the most part, mercenaries, many of whom were diseased, immoral or cowardly." *

Wilkerson in his *Recollections of a Private* wrote that the men sat in the trenches at night and discussed the "disintegrating force which Grant commanded."

Enormous losses of prisoners were reported—losses that were incurred while charging earthworks . . . our troops surrendered rather than attempt to take them or to return to our line under the deadly accurate fire of the Confederate infantry. . . . Volunteers vehemently asserted that the bounty-paid recruits really deserted during action to seek safety in Confederate prison pens.

President Lincoln and the whole North were in gloom. "There was at this time," wrote the historian Swinton, "great danger of the collapse of the war."

More good news reached President Davis. General Wade Hamp-

* Other interesting opinions on the failure to take Petersburg before Lee arrived may be found in Porter's article in *The Century Magazine*, April, 1897; Nicolay and Hay, Vol. IV, p. 412; Walker, *Life of Hancock*, p. 246; Ropes, *Papers of the Massachusetts Historical Society*, Vol. X, p. 267.

ton battered Sheridan at Trevilian Station on June 11. Early drove Hunter into West Virginia a week later and was now heading for the Potomac. If only Joseph Johnston would make some telling attack on Sherman, or stand and fight!

CHAPTER VIII

EARLY SCARES WASHINGTON
AND JOHNSTON IS REMOVED

———— ‹◆› ————

ON JUNE 27 Varina Davis was delivered of a girl baby. The father had already chosen the name: Varina Anne. But she was almost never to be called by her christening name. As a baby the children would call her "Pie-cake"; as a schoolgirl and young lady she was to be known as "Winnie," Davis's own pet name for his wife. The delivery had gone without complications and the household tension was greatly relieved.

That day from Marietta, Georgia, where Joseph Johnston had his new headquarters, came the only really cheering dispatch President Davis ever received from the General.

The enemy advanced on the whole line today . . . they were repulsed. Their loss is supposed to be large. Ours is known to be small.

At Kennesaw Mountain Sherman had made a direct frontal attack on the Confederate entrenchments, and had lost 3,000 men in contrast to the Confederates' five hundred.

The same day more good news arrived: the men of Jubal Early's Second Corps, those who had shoes, marched north from Lynchburg towards Washington. On the preceding June 13, Early, heading the Second Corps of Lee's army, numbering slightly over 8,000 muskets and two battalions of artillery, had left Richmond secretly to strike at Major General David Hunter, who was raiding the upper Shenandoah. The plan was bold: to destroy Hunter's forces if possible, then to move down the Valley, cross the Potomac, and threaten the capital of the United States.

Because of the essential secrecy of Early's move, involving the daring withdrawal of almost a fifth of Lee's depleted forces, the President earnestly enjoined the Richmond papers not to allude to the movement. This time they kept silent.

65

The first reports of Early's progress had been gratifying. On the seventeenth he reached Lynchburg and quickly chased Hunter with considerable loss into West Virginia. After a two-day halt at Staunton "to lighten weight" for the dash to Washington and to try to procure shoes for those of his troops who were barefoot, the Confederate advance headed for the Potomac. Jefferson Davis followed the reports of Early's progress with the keenest interest. Though he did not think Early a phenomenal commander, he admired his rugged fighting quality and his audacity. A West Point graduate of 1837, later a lawyer and legislator, Early had voted against Virginia's secession. But he had led the Twenty-fourth Virginia Infantry at First Manassas, and had been active in all engagements of the Army of Northern Virginia. On May 31, 1864, when General Richard Ewell was temporarily retired from field duty, Lee had given Early command of his Second Corps, and the President had made him a Lieutenant General.

A fresh consignment of shoes arrived before Early reached Winchester on July 2, and there he drove General Franz Sigel to Maryland Heights. On July 4 the Confederates reached the Potomac at Shepherdstown above Harpers Ferry. Two days later all the units were in Maryland. Early levied $20,000 from Hagerstown, and on July 9 entered Frederick City, which he laid under contribution for $200,000. That same day he fought and routed General Lew Wallace's forces near Monocacy Bridge.

The defeat of Wallace threw Washington into great alarm. The entire North became apprehensive. Telegrams from affrighted committees of citizens began pouring into President Lincoln's office, such as "Baltimore is in great peril." Secretary of War Stanton called on the State Governors for urgent help. When the Southern cavalry struck at the railroads and cut communications between Washington and Northern cities, excitement in the capital mounted. Captain Gustavus Fox, Assistant Secretary of the Navy, readied a vessel to take Mr. Lincoln down the Potomac to safety.

Early's plan, Davis knew, comprised the release of 17,000 prisoners at Point Lookout. On June 26, Lee had written the President:

Great benefit might be drawn from the release of our prisoners at Point Lookout. . . . I have understood that most of the garrison there was composed of negroes. I should suppose that the commander of such troops would be poor and feeble.

Early intended to arm the prisoners and march them straight on the way to Washington. He sent ahead a detachment of cavalry to release them. But most of the prisoners had already been rushed to Elmira, New York.

On July 7, Davis received a communication from Lee commenting on Grant's aversion to reducing the army. "It is so repugnant to Grant's principle and practice to send troops from him that I had hoped, before resorting to it, he would have preferred attacking me." But Grant had already sent (July 6) the veterans of the Sixth Corps and some 3,000 cavalry.

On the morning of July 10 Early moved nearer Washington, taking the route by Rockville, and then turning to the left to get on the Seventh Street Pike. "The day was very hot, and the roads exceedingly dusty," but the Southerners marched thirty miles.*

On the tense Sunday of July 10 a worried President Lincoln wired Grant his hope that he could retain his hold at Petersburg "and bring the rest with you personally, and make a vigorous effort to destroy the enemy's force in this vicinity." Grant's veterans of the Sixth Corps arrived at the Washington wharf that noon, when Early was already reconnoitering in the suburbs. By four o'clock the Federals approached Fort Stevens. And the Nineteenth Corps from New Orleans, destined for Fort Monroe, had their orders changed and shortly debarked at Washington.

On July 11 Early and his dog-tired Confederates beheld the dome of the Capitol from the Seventh Street road north of Washington. They went through Silver Springs, Maryland, and approached the city, protected by formidable Fort Stevens.

The next day, after a sharp skirmish with advance Union forces, Early gave the signal for withdrawal. In Silver Springs his army passed the suburban house of Postmaster General Montgomery Blair, who had pressed Lincoln to launch the Sumter Expedition that brought on the war. In retaliation, the Confederate soldiers burned Blair's house.

Early's instructions had been merely to "threaten" Washington. But if his exhausted men could have got around the fortifications, he felt they might have seized the specie in the Treasury, taken large stores of arms and clothing, destroyed important government property, and escaped. Though Early could not have held the city with his slim forces, he would have seriously damaged Union prestige.

The Federal forces pursued the Confederates with little vigor,

* The reports from July 6 to July 12 in *Official Records*, Vol. xxxvii, Parts i and ii, make exciting reading.

and Early crossed back into Virginia with his army and spoils intact.

The relief Davis felt from Varina's good condition and the fine report of Jubal Early's successes was shortly clouded by very bad news from abroad. Captain Raphael Semmes, the South's foremost sailor, had met with disaster in the English Channel. The *Alabama,* the most noted ship in the war, had been sunk near Cherbourg, where she had been taken for docking and repairing, to land Union prisoners from the last two captured ships, and to load coal.

On June 19, 1864, the *Alabama* had left the harbor of Cherbourg to engage the *Kearsarge,* which was her superior in size, armaments, and strength of crew. Semmes had often fought brilliantly against odds, but he did not know that the sides of the *Kearsarge* had been cleverly covered with heavy chains concealed by superficial planking. So when he steamed out to fight a wooden ship, he found himself engaged with an ironclad. After battling for an hour and ten minutes, Semmes realized that the *Alabama* was sinking. He struck his colors and sent the wounded and those who could not swim off in the quarter boats to the *Kearsarge.* Then he instructed the others to jump overboard, each to save himself as he could. Semmes stood on the quarter-deck until the vessel began to go down. Then he threw his sword into the sea, to lie buried beside his ship, and leaped into the water. After swimming for some time, he was picked up, along with Mrs. Davis's brother Beckett and several of his crew, by an English gentleman named John Lancaster, who was cruising in his yacht, the *Deerhound.* The rescued Confederates were taken to Southampton. There Semmes's official report was written, dated June 21, 1864.

Davis grieved over the loss of the *Alabama,* which had played such a gallant part in helping the Confederacy win its independence. Within two years, as a ship-of-war, she had captured and destroyed sixty-two Federal merchantmen, and Semmes had won a name for himself as one of the great sea fighters of all times.

Before Semmes sailed for home five months later, officers of the British Army and Navy presented him with a new jeweled sword, and an English noblewoman gave him a large silk Confederate flag, which she had made herself. The President commissioned Semmes a Rear Admiral, and on his return put him in command of the Confederate gunboats on the upper James. It distressed Davis to have only this humble, restricted command to offer the naval hero who had ranged the seven seas.

While Early's footsore infantrymen were approaching Washington, Senator Benjamin Hill of Georgia arrived in Richmond on an important mission. A few minutes after leaving his luggage at his hotel on Sunday morning, July 10, he was closeted with the President in the Executive Mansion. Davis received him with special warmth. Hill was one of the nation's ablest legislators and a friend in whom he had implicit trust. As the Senator had recently talked with Joseph E. Johnston at his headquarters in Marietta, several days after Kennesaw, Davis was eager for Hill's opinion and advice. Hill found the President "looking quite well, but growing not only gray but white with his cares."

For three weeks one thought had been recurrent in Davis's mind: Would Johnston really fight? Or would he give up Atlanta without a struggle? The War Department had repeatedly urged him to reveal his plans. Johnston's replies were vague and inconclusive.

Atlanta was in grave danger of falling into Federal hands. As Sherman neared the city, the whole South was figuratively holding its breath. Atlanta was regarded as the back door to Richmond. It was not only the Confederacy's most important railway center, but with its rolling mills and foundries, its accumulation of military stores, and its factories for making essentials for civilians, its value was beyond calculation. If Johnston let Sherman into Atlanta, the spinal column of the Confederacy would be severed. Since the first of July the most intense anxiety had permeated Georgia and spread to the outermost ends of the Confederacy. Telegrams and letters poured into Richmond expressing doubt of Johnston's ability. The press had heretofore built up in the public mind an image of Johnston as a military man of profound and subtle sagacity. But now some of his most extravagant admirers had lost faith.

The President explained in detail to Hill that he had withheld nothing of men or materials at his disposal from Joseph Johnston. Batteries made for Lee's army had been diverted and sent to him. Absentees had been rapidly returned to the Army of Tennessee. Troops had been withdrawn from Mobile, Savannah, and Charleston to aid him. Cavalry from East Tennessee had reinforced him. The main army of Alabama and Mississippi under Leonidas Polk had been placed at his disposal. Johnston's was the largest Confederate army the West ever had. Notwithstanding his losses in infantry and artillery of approximately 22,000, Johnston's Return of July 10 to the War Department showed an aggregate force of 73,849 men.

From the first, Johnston had reiterated his complaints about the deficiencies of his force and the difficulties to be encountered in an offensive movement. Sherman had begun advancing in May with Johnston retreating. Sherman had successfully flanked him again and again. And in his flanking movements Sherman, who did not favor Grant's sledge-hammer tactics, had used "every advantage of strategy and combination." Except at Kennesaw, Sherman had approached with caution, saving the lives of his soldiers as much as he could. Johnston had lost one seemingly powerful position after another. He had allowed himself to be driven through "an entire district of mountain passes and defiles and across rivers" until he was now approaching the suburbs of Atlanta. Davis had been pained to watch from a distance the farm land rich with sustaining corn fall into enemy possession.

Since Grant had failed in his strategy against Richmond, Davis knew how fervently the Republicans looked to Sherman for a signal victory that would assure President Lincoln a second term. John Sherman, Senator from Ohio, wrote his brother William that his action before Atlanta "would probably decide the fate of the Union." Davis realized to the fullest the mighty boost the fall of Atlanta would give the disheartened North and how devastating it could be to Southern morale.

Hill now told the President that in the course of his conversation with General Johnston he had asked, "How long can you hold Sherman north of the Chattahoochee River?" This was important, because Morgan's cavalry, which Johnston had asked for, would have to move from Abingdon, Virginia, and everything had to be done before Sherman drove him into Atlanta. By the various data Johnston gave out, Hill concluded that Johnston could hold Sherman north of the Chattahoochee "at least fifty-four days, and perhaps sixty days." To this estimate Johnston agreed. General Hood, who was present, interposed: "Mr. Hill, when we leave our present line, we will in my judgment cross the Chattahoochee very rapidly." "Why, what makes you say that?" asked General Johnston with some interest. "Because," answered Hood, "this line of the Kennesaw is the strongest we can get in this country. If we surrender this to Sherman, he can reconnoiter from its summit the whole country between here and Atlanta, and there is no such line of defense in the distance." "I differ with your conclusion," said General Johnston. "I have two more strong lines between this and the river from which I can hold Sherman a long time."

Hill relayed this conversation to the President, as well as all the facts elicited from General Johnston, together with his request for troops from various other commands. Davis showed that Johnston had in every case exaggerated the number of men in different commands from which he wanted reinforcements.

Then looking at Hill steadily, Davis asked, "How long did you understand General Johnston to say he could hold Sherman north of the Chattahoochee?"

"From fifty-four to sixty days."

The President reached for a dispatch lying on his desk and handed it to him. Hill read with astonishment that Sherman had already crossed the Chattahoochee the day before, on July 9. Johnston's miscalculation was gross.

Next morning, Monday, July 11, the President wired General Johnston.

Senator Hill has arrived, and after conversation with him I have called for exact statements from the War Department, after the receipt of which I will endeavor to reply to the various propositions and reflections which have been presented to me.

The telegram had just been dispatched, when a somewhat frantic wire arrived from Johnston. He asked that a force be sent to him immediately to remove all the Federal prisoners from Andersonville. Davis was astounded. Andersonville was 150 miles to the southeast of Atlanta, half again as far as Richmond was from Washington. Did Johnston contemplate a fast and full retreat?

The President replied:

You have all the force which can be employed, to *distribute or guard prisoners*. Know the condition of the country and prospects of military operations. I must rely on you to advise Genl. Winder as to the proper and practicable action in relation to *U.S. Prisoners*.

Then he wired Lee at Petersburg:

Genl. Johnston has failed, and there are strong indications that he will abandon Atlanta. He urges that prisoners should be removed immediately *from Andersonville*. It seems necessary to *relieve him* at once. Who should succeed him? What think you of Hood for the position?

Lee wrote much as Davis had expected.

It is a grievous thing to change the commander of an army situated as is that of the Tennessee. Still, if necessary, it ought to be done. . . . If Johnston abandons Atlanta, I suppose he will fall back on Augusta. This

loses us Mississippi and communications with Trans-Mississippi. . . .
Hood is a good fighter, very industrious on the battlefield, careless off.
. . . I have a high opinion of his gallantry, earnestness and zeal. General
Hardee has more experience in managing an army. May God give you
wisdom to decide in this momentous matter.

General Lee had not been very helpful. Davis had gone through
these same arguments again and again with himself. In December,
1863, when Bragg resigned, he had sent William Preston Johnston
from Richmond to beg Hardee to take the top command of the
Army of Tennessee. Hardee had adamantly refused the responsibility when affairs were relatively quiet. So Davis could not conceive of his accepting a responsibility vastly greater when matters
were so critical.

On the thirteenth, the President telegraphed Lee that Bragg,
whom he had sent on July 9 to confer with Johnston, had arrived
in Atlanta. "It is a sad alternative, but the case seems hopeless in
present hands. The means are surely adequate, if properly employed, especially as the cavalry force is ample."

After a two-day visit at Johnston's headquarters, Bragg wired
the President.

He [Johnston] has not sought my advice, and it was not volunteered.
I cannot learn that he has any more plans in the future than he has had
in the past.

Davis now sent a telegram demanding that Johnston state his
plans for future operation. Johnston replied that he intended leaving Georgia state militia in charge of the Atlanta entrenchments,
while he moved his army into the field. The statement seemed conclusive that he would give up Atlanta without a battle. Davis saw
no possibility of Johnston's halting Sherman on the flat terrain before Macon, when he had failed to check the enemy's march
through a mountainous terrain studded with prime defensive positions.

Secretary of War Seddon, who had first pressed the President to
restore Johnston to command, now demanded his removal. Judah
Benjamin, who had never had faith in Johnston's fighting abilities
and who had opposed giving him any command since Seven Pines,
urged his removal. The rest of the Cabinet agreed. As telegrams
begging the President to change commanders poured in, Senator
Hill, speaking for Georgia, strongly pressed the issue.

On Sunday morning, July 17, the President called a Cabinet

meeting. As it was his custom to make an exhaustive study of a situation before reaching a final decision, he reviewed all the facts with his Cabinet. They were unanimous in urging Johnston's removal. Davis consented. Senator Hill dined *en famille* with James Lyons that day and informed him of the removal. He told him that the President had said with great feeling the day before, "Gentlemen, it is very easy to remove the General, but where will you find the man to fill the place?"

Davis was aware that he might be excoriated by papers like the *Examiner,* that it might even be absurdly claimed that he removed Johnston because of personal animosity. He also realized that by his action he might be saving Johnston's reputation. But there was never a moment in Davis's career when he did not put his country above any thought of his own popularity.

"That evening," Lyons wrote later, "the President rode out to my farm and took tea, as he often did, when visiting the Batteries on my farm, and told us of the removal—I expressed my regret of it and asked him why he did it. He replied, 'I could not help it—Hill urged it on behalf of the people of Georgia, and Benjamin and Seddon were so violent that they would listen to nothing. Suffice it to say,' Davis declared, 'I thought the injury consequent upon a change of commanders less than that of leaving General Johnston longer in command.'"

CHAPTER IX

A YANKEE EVALUATES THE
CONFEDERATE PRESIDENT

ON THE NIGHT of Saturday, July 16, while Jefferson Davis was gravely considering the change of commanders at Atlanta, two Northern gentlemen were being assigned Room No. 60 on the fourth floor of the Spotswood Hotel. They had been brought into Richmond in semisecrecy by Judge Robert Ould, head of the Confederate Exchange Commission. One, James F. Jaquess, who wore a long duster over his blue uniform of a Colonel of the Seventy-third Illinois, was in civilian life a Methodist clergyman. The other was a well-known journalist and lyceum lecturer, J. R. Gilmore, who wrote under the pen name of Edmund Kirke.* A husky Captain of the Richmond Provost Guard was their shadow and slept in the room with them. Though the circumstances of their being in Richmond were highly unusual, they were in no sense dangerous characters. They bore documents from President Lincoln, Ould himself, and a letter to Jefferson Davis from Mary Bradford Brodhead, a favorite niece, his sister Amanda's daughter, who was living in Pennsylvania. The men had come on a self-appointed peace mission, because many Northerners sincerely believed that "the revolted States" would return to the Union if assured the protection of their "peculiar institution." They wanted to ascertain from the Confederate President himself if peace could be arranged on this basis.

On Sunday morning after breakfast, at Judge Ould's suggestion, the Northerners drafted a note to Judah P. Benjamin, the Secretary of State.

---

* The material for this section is taken largely from *The Atlantic Monthly*, September, 1864, pp. 372-383, and from a fuller account of the midsummer journey to the "hot and dangerous latitude of Virginia" in Edmund Kirke's book *Down to Tennessee and Back by Way of Richmond*, 1864, pp. 252-282.

74

Dear Sir,—

The undersigned respectfully solicit an interview with President Davis.

They visit Richmond only as private citizens, and have no official character or authority; but they are acquainted with the views of the United States Government, and with the sentiments of the Northern people relative to an adjustment of the differences existing between the North and the South, and earnestly hope that a free interchange of views between President Davis and themselves may open the way to such *official* negotiations as will result in restoring PEACE to the two sections of our distracted country.

They, therefore, ask an interview with the President, and awaiting your reply, are

Truly and respectfully yours

Judge Ould took the letter to Benjamin, together with the commendatory letter from Davis's niece. At ten o'clock Benjamin received them cordially in the northwest corner of the old "United States" Custom House, where the words "State Department" were marked above his door. Colonel Jaquess admitted frankly that he had no "official" capacity. "We come as men and Christians—hoping in a frank talk with Mr. Davis to discover some way by which this war may be stopped."

The Secretary of State told them that, as it was Sunday, the President would be at church in the afternoon; "so, suppose you call here at nine this evening." He did not mention the important Cabinet meeting that was shortly to take place.

Jefferson Davis was touched to hear from "Malie" Brodhead. It was really because of him that she was now living on the Northern side of the war, though her heart was completely with the South. As a girl of nineteen, in December, 1845, she had been taken along to Washington to companion his nineteen-year-old bride Varina, when he took his seat in the House of Representatives; subsequently she had married Congressman Charles Brodhead from Pennsylvania. Though deeply troubled about Atlanta, Davis agreed with Benjamin that it would be well to receive the gentlemen from the North.

After a day spent in seclusion in their drab hotel room, they were escorted by Judge Ould and their guard to Benjamin's office at the appointed time of night.

Mr. Benjamin occupied his same seat at the table and on his right, so Gilmore wrote, "sat a spare, thin-featured man with iron-gray hair and beard, and a clear, gray eye full of life and vigor."

He had a broad, massive forehead, and a mouth and chin denoting great energy and strength of will. His face was emaciated, and much wrinkled, but his features were good, especially his eyes,—though one of them bore a scar, apparently made by some sharp instrument. He wore a suit of grayish-brown, evidently of foreign manufacture, and, as he rose, I saw that he was about five feet ten inches high. . . . His manners were simple, easy, and quite fascinating; and he threw an indescribable charm into his voice, as he extended his hand, and said: "I am glad to see you, Gentlemen. You are very welcome to Richmond."

"And this," Gilmore commented humorously, "was the man who was President of the United States under Franklin Pierce, and who is now the heart, soul, and brains of the Southern Confederacy! His manner put me entirely at my ease."

The Illinois soldier-clergyman, Colonel Jacquess, told the President that he and his companion had sought this interview in the hope that Davis, who was said to desire peace, might suggest some way by which this war could be stopped.

"In a very simple way," Davis replied quietly. "Withdraw your armies from our territory, and peace will come of itself. We do not seek to subjugate you. We are not waging an offensive war, except so far as it is offensive-defensive,—that is, so far as we are forced to invade you to prevent your invading us. Let us alone, and peace will come at once."

"But we cannot let you alone so long as you repudiate the Union. That is the one thing the Northern people will not surrender."

"I know. You would deny to us what you exact for yourselves,— the right of self-government."

"No, Sir," Gilmore put in. "We would deny you no natural right. But we think Union essential to peace; and, Mr. Davis, could two people, with the same language, separated by only an imaginary line, live at peace with each other? Would not disputes constantly arise?"

"Undoubtedly," Davis agreed, "with this generation. You have sown such bitterness at the South, you have put such an ocean of blood between the two sections, that I despair of seeing any harmony in my time. Our children may forget this war, but we cannot. How can we feel anything but bitterness towards men who deny us our rights? If you enter my house and drive me out of it, am I not your natural enemy?"

"You put the case strongly. But can you, Mr. Davis, as a Christian man, leave untried any means that may lead to peace?"

"No, I cannot," the President replied with fervor. "I desire peace as much as you do. I deplore bloodshed as much as you do; but I feel that not one drop of the blood shed in this war is on *my* hands, —I can look up to my God and say this. I tried all in my power to avert this war. I saw it coming, and for twelve years I worked night and day to prevent it, but I could not. And now it must go on till the last man of this generation falls in his tracks, and his children seize his musket and fight his battle, *unless you acknowledge our right to self-government.* We are not fighting for slavery. We are fighting for Independence,—and that, or extermination, we *will* have."

"We have no wish to exterminate you," Colonel Jaquess replied. "The North, I know, loves the South. It would now welcome you back, and forgive you all the loss and bloodshed you have caused. But we *must* crush your armies and exterminate your Government. And is not that already nearly done? You are wholly without money, and at the end of your resources. Grant has shut you up in Richmond. Sherman is before Atlanta. Had you not, then, better accept honorable terms while you can retain your prestige, and save the pride of the Southern people?"

Mr. Davis smiled, thinking that only a few days before Jubal Early's army had reached the suburbs of Washington and had given the North a terrible fright. "I respect your earnestness, Colonel, but you do not seem to understand the situation," he said. "We are not exactly shut up in Richmond. If your papers tell the truth, it is your capital that is in danger, not ours. Some weeks ago, Grant crossed the Rapidan to whip Lee and take Richmond. Lee drove him in the first battle, and then Grant executed what your people call a 'brilliant flank-movement,' and fought Lee again. Lee drove him a second time, and then Grant made another 'flank-movement'; and so they kept on,—Lee whipping, and Grant flanking,—until Grant has lost seventy-five to eighty thousand men,— *more than Lee had at the outset*,—and is no nearer taking Richmond than at first; and Lee, whose front has never been broken, holds him completely in check, and has men enough to spare to invade Maryland, and threaten Washington!" He paused for emphasis and then went on: "Sherman, to be sure, is before Atlanta; but suppose he *is*, and suppose he takes it? You know that the farther he goes from his base of supplies, the weaker he grows and the more disastrous defeat will be to him."

"As to money—" Davis made a slight gesture with his hands—

"we are richer than you are. You smile; but admit that our paper is worth nothing,—it answers as a circulating medium; and we hold it all ourselves. If every dollar of it were lost, we should, as we have no foreign debt, be none the poorer. But it *is* worth something; it has the solid basis of a large cotton-crop. As to resources: we do not lack for arms or ammunition, and we have still a wide territory from which to gather supplies. So, you see, we are not in extremities."

Then, as the surprised visitors could think of no rejoinder, the President leaned forward and put a feeling gravity into his words: "But if we were,—if we were without money, without food, without weapons,—if our whole country were devastated, and our armies crushed and disbanded,—could we, without giving up our manhood, give up our right to govern ourselves? Would *you* not rather die, and feel yourself a man, than live, and be subject to a foreign power?"

"From your standpoint," the Colonel replied at last, "there is force in what you say. But we came, hoping to find some honorable way to peace; and I am grieved to hear you say what you do."

"I know your motives, Colonel Jaquess," Davis said most kindly, "and I honor you for them; but what can I do more than I am doing? I would give my poor life, gladly, if it would bring peace and good will to the two countries; but it would not. It is *they* who desolate our homes, burn our wheatfields, break the wheels of wagons carrying away our women and children, and destroy supplies meant for our sick and wounded." He paused, and then said in summation, "At your door lies all the misery and the crime of this war,—and it is a fearful, fearful account."

Taken aback, the Illinoisian at length protested, "Not all of it, Mr. Davis. Elements of barbarism are entering the war on both sides, that should make us—you and me, as Christian men—shudder to think of. In God's name, then let us stop it. Let us do something, concede something, to bring about peace. You cannot expect, with only four and a half millions, as Mr. Benjamin says you have, to hold out forever against twenty millions."

Mr. Davis smiled, incredulous. "Do you suppose," he said, thinking of his personal friends in the North and that third of the Northern population he believed opposed the war, "there are twenty millions at the North determined to crush us?"

"I do,—to crush your *government*. Whoever is elected in November, he *must be* committed to a vigorous prosecution of the war."

"Mr. Lincoln, I know, is about to call out five hundred thousand more men," Gilmore interjected, "and I can't see how you *can* resist much longer; but if you do, you will only deepen the radical feeling of the Northern people. Let the Northern people once really *feel* the war and they will insist on hanging every one of your leaders."

Davis was silent for a few moments. "Well, admitting all you say, I can't see how it affects our position. There are some things worse than hanging or extermination. We reckon giving up the right of self-government one of those things."

"By self-government you mean disunion,—Southern Independence?"

"Yes."

"And slavery, you say, is no longer an element in the contest?"

"No, it is not," the President said firmly. "It never was an *essential* element. It was only a means of bringing other conflicting elements to an earlier culmination."

"Well, Sir, if I understand you, the dispute between your government and ours is narrowed down to this: Union or Disunion."

"Yes; or to put it in other words: Independence or Subjugation."

"Then," Gilmore said, "the two governments are irreconcilably apart . . . but suppose the two governments should agree to something like this: To go to the people with two propositions: say, Peace, with Disunion and Southern Independence, as your proposition,—and Peace, with Union, Emancipation, No Confiscation, and Universal Amnesty, as ours . . . the PEOPLE shall decide the question."

"That the *majority* shall decide it, you mean. We seceded to rid ourselves of the rule of the majority, and this would subject us to it again."

"But the majority must rule finally, either with bullets or ballots."

"I am not sure of that. Neither current events nor history shows that the majority rules." Davis fixed his gaze steadily on Gilmore, and then smiled good-humoredly. "Why, Sir, the man who shall come before the Southern people with such a proposition—with any proposition which implied that the North was to have a voice in determining the domestic relations of the South could not live here a day! He would be hanged to the first tree."

"But seriously, Sir," Gilmore said with an answering smile, "you let the majority rule in a single State; why not let it rule in the whole country?"

"Because the States are independent and sovereign. The country is not. It is only a confederation of States; or rather it *was:* it is now *two* confederations."

"Then we are not a *people*,—we are only a political partnership?"

"That is all."

"Your very name, Sir, '*United* States,' implies that," Benjamin interposed. "But, tell me, are the terms you have named—Emancipation, No Confiscation, and Universal Amnesty—the terms which Mr. Lincoln authorized you to offer us?"

"No, Sir," Jaquess said quickly. "Mr. Lincoln did not authorize me to offer you any terms. But I *think* both he and the Northern people, for the sake of peace, would assent to some such conditions."

"They are *very* generous," replied Davis, showing a trace of anger for the first time during the interview. "But Amnesty, Sir, applies to criminals. We have committed no crime. Confiscation is of no account, unless you can enforce it. And Emancipation! You have already emancipated nearly two millions of our slaves,—and if you will take care of them, you may emancipate the rest. I had a few when the war began. I was of some use to them; they never were of much use to me. You may 'emancipate' every negro in the Confederacy, but *we will be free!* We will govern ourselves. We will do it, if we have to see every Southern plantation sacked, and every Southern city in flames."

Jaquess shrugged. In the face of Davis's high resolve and undoubted sincerity, he gave up the argument and prepared to rise. "We love the old flag," he said, "and that must be our apology for intruding upon you at all."

"You have not intruded upon me," Davis assured him, resuming his cordial manner. "I am glad to have met you both. I once loved the old flag as well as you do; I would have died for it; but now it is to me only the emblem of oppression."

The visitors rose to go. The President gave Gilmore his hand, bade him a kindly goodbye and expressed the hope of seeing him again in Richmond in happier times. He would appreciate his taking a letter to Mrs. Brodhead, which he would send later to the hotel.

Then turning to the "fighting parson," and feeling the depth of his earnestness and his moral courage, Davis clasped Jaquess's hand in both of his. With a compassionate smile he said, "Colonel, I respect your character and your motives, and I wish you every good I can wish you consistent with the interests of the Confederacy."

As the visitors reached the door, Davis added, "Say to Mr. Lincoln from me that I shall at any time be pleased to receive proposals for peace on the basis of our Independence. It will be useless to approach me with any other."

As quickly as it was convenient, Gilmore wrote down the whole interview, reporting Davis's conversation as nearly as possible in his exact language, and "coloring nothing."

When he returned home, he prepared an article about the Richmond interview for *The Atlantic Monthly*. Towards the end of it he set down his candid, objective impression of Jefferson Davis: "He is a man of peculiar ability. Our interview with him explained to me why, with no money and no commerce, with nearly every one of their important cities in our hands, and with an army greatly inferior in numbers and equipment to ours, the Rebels have held out so long. It is because of the sagacity, energy, and indomitable will of Jefferson Davis. Without him the Rebellion would crumble to pieces in a day; with him it may continue to be, even in disaster, a power that will tax the whole energy and resources of the nation."

CHAPTER X

ATLANTA FALLS

———◆———

ON MONDAY MORNING, July 18, 1864, Adjutant General Samuel Cooper sent General Joseph E. Johnston one of the most significant telegrams dispatched during the war.

Lieutenant General J. B. Hood has been commissioned to the temporary rank of General under the law of Congress. I am directed by the Secretary of War to inform you that as you have failed to arrest the advance of the enemy to the vicinity of Atlanta and *express no confidence that you can defeat or repel him,* you are hereby relieved from the command of the Army and Department of Tennessee, which you will immediately turn over to General Hood.

Johnston, whose jealousy of Lee and hatred of Davis were widely commented upon, was the more embittered by his removal. In his reply to the War Office, he claimed that he had not been given as good a chance as Lee and yet had done better. And during the remainder of his long life he was to do all he could to blacken Jefferson Davis's reputation.

Down in Columbia, South Carolina, Sally "Buck" Preston was distressed to hear the news that General Hood, who wanted to marry her, had replaced Johnston. In a flowing white dressing gown she met Mary Chesnut at the head of the stairs, "her blue eyes wide open and shining black with excitement." "Things are so bad," she cried, "that they cannot be worse. So they have saved Johnston from the responsibility of his own blunders, and put Sam in. Poor Sam!" Sam was the name for Hood among his close friends.

Mrs. Chesnut, unprepared for her attitude, exclaimed, "Why, Buck, I thought you would be proud of it!"

"No," the girl protested. "Now they will blame Sam for Johnston's mistakes. I have prayed as I never prayed for him before. . . . And I went to the convent and asked the nuns to pray for him too."

On July 19 General Gorgas wrote in his diary: "Johnston has been relieved of his command and Hood placed in charge of the Army. This, of course, means fighting, and a battle must soon be the result. General J. will doubtless have a strong party who will condemn his removal." But at the time there was little outspoken criticism. A few days later Gorgas commented:

People are, I think, generally satisfied with the removal of General Johnston. They have praised him and waited for him to fight until he has lost all Georgia, and they have got tired of him. Nevertheless if Hood fights and is victorious, there will be plenty who will exclaim: "behold the fruits of Johnston's strategy," while if he is defeated these people will cry: "see the fruits of the removal of Johnston!" The Administration will gain nothing in the estimation of such in either case.

Johnston made lame excuses for himself to his friend Louis Wigfall, asserting he "dared not let the President know his plans, because there was a spy in the War Office who invariably warned the Yankees." But it seemed obvious after months of retreating that Johnston had no plan.

The indignant Mrs. Chesnut sarcastically wrote:

A misunderstanding between the President and one of his generals will serve the General to explain any disaster. But a general who is known to disdain obedience to any order, who refuses to give the President any information for fear the President will betray him to the enemy? If that is not the madness of self-conceit, what is? Seward's little bell would have lodged Joe Johnston within triple walls in the twinkling of an eye, years ago, if he were a Yankee.

She quoted her Charleston friend William Brewster, who was no staunch admirer of Davis, as likening Joe Johnston to "a snake blinded by its own venom."

Though Johnston's friends were later to make capital of the "terrible injustice" of his removal, a majority of thinking Southerners then believed that Davis had been too lenient and long-suffering with Johnston's retreats, delays, and muddy replies.

Sam Hood certainly did not want the command. With Generals Hardee and Stewart, he signed a telegram urging that Johnston be kept in command. The President replied: "A change of commanders under existing circumstances was regarded as so objectionable that I only accepted it as the alternative of continuance in a policy that has proved disastrous." He ended: "There can be but one question which you and I entertain, that is, what will best promote the public good, and to each of you I confidently look for the sacrifice of every personal consideration in conflict with that object."

After protesting to Richmond against taking command, Hood wrote "Buck" Preston that they had "left all the good fighting ground behind them, and that an army by constant retreating loses confidence in itself." But, on the whole, Joe Johnston's men still liked him and had faith in him, and some were shocked at his removal. Hood, however, immediately readied his army for combat. Hood fought the battle of Peach Tree Creek on July 20 and the battle of Atlanta on the twenty-second. His losses were slightly greater than Sherman's, but throughout the South the papers claimed victory. The cheering word circulated: "Sherman is checked before Atlanta." Though Hood was somewhat crippled by his attacks, the South was elated. President Davis felt that the morale value of Hood's successes exceeded any solid gain. It was evident that the Confederates had stopped retreating, and Hood was praised for his dauntless courage.

When Sherman shifted his line farther to the east and south, Hood gave battle again—at Ezra Church—on July 28. This time he gained only a little ground and lost many men. Sherman himself made no effort to attack, but, secure in a line of communication with his base, coolly sat down before Atlanta to await Hood's next move. George Stoneman and his Union cavalry tore up railroads, but were summarily halted before Macon on July 30.

The same day that the railroad to Macon was saved in Georgia, Davis received news from Petersburg of the most spectacular event of the war. When Grant found that all his efforts to break the Confederate lines had failed, he agreed to a scheme to blast his way through. For weeks men had laboriously dug a long shaft under a salient of Beauregard's fortifications and filled it with explosives. In the early morning of July 30 a man crawled cautiously down the tunnel and lit a fuse. At five minutes to five the earth split open. Dense volumes of smoke issued from fissures and sulphurous flame shot up as if from an erupting volcano. A deafening blast hurtled 275 Confederates into the air, amid tons of red dirt and broken guns and carriages. The resultant crater was approximately 170 feet long, 60 feet wide, and 30 feet deep. A wildly triumphant Federal division rushed into the smoking hole for a breakthrough. Re-

covering quickly from the initial shock, the Southerners pulled back
their lines. Brigadier General William Mahone energetically took
charge. He ordered the Confederates to face the yawning crater
and open fire on the mass of bluecoats struggling to cross the jagged
terrain. As more and more Union troops were rushed forward, they
became entangled with screaming, dying men and those struggling
to escape. Some of the Negro troops who had been drilled to lead
the assault reached the outer edge of the crater only to be driven by
withering Confederate fire down again into the jammed hole, where
three white divisions desperately milled about, unable to move forward or to escape. The frightful carnage was made the more ghastly
by hysteria. General Grant's maneuver resulted in a gaping cavity
and the loss of 4,000 Union men. Jefferson Davis had never known
a more striking application of Hamlet's phrase "hoist with his own
petar." For Mahone's brilliant action, Davis made him a Major
General.

The month of August opened with Richmond safe, Lee's forces
holding steadfast about Petersburg, Atlanta in Confederate hands,
and, in the words of J. G. Randall, the biographer of Lincoln, "no
obvious or striking result to show an angry North for the thousands
whom Grant had led to the slaughter."

In reply to a plan from Hood, Davis telegraphed him on August
5 that he hoped his "cavalry would be able to destroy railroad bridges and depots of the enemy on the line to Bridgeport
[Alabama] so as to compel the enemy to attack you in position or
retreat." Then he tactfully warned the impulsive commander.

The loss consequent upon attacking him [the enemy] in his entrenchments *requires you to avoid that if practicable.* The enemy have now
reached a country where supplies can be gathered by foraging expeditions, and a part of your cavalry will be required to prevent that. If he
can be forced to retreat for want of supplies, he will be in the worst condition to escape or resist your pursuing army. General Hardee's minute
knowledge of the country, and his extensive acquaintance with the officers and men of the command, must render his large professional knowledge and experience peculiarly valuable in such a campaign as I hope is
before you.

For a fortnight or more there was little action on any front to
report to the President. Then, on August 20, the phenomenal Forrest
boldly rode into Memphis, which had been held by the Federals
for over two years. With a thousand soldiers and a roar of musketry,

he fell upon the unsuspecting enemy. Forrest's secondary incentive was to take three Union generals prisoner; but only one was captured—in his nightshirt. His real purpose was to draw Union General A. J. Smith out of North Central Mississippi. This he quickly and effectively accomplished. Sherman was so exasperated at Forrest's galling success that he wired Secretary of War Stanton that he was ordering Smith "to go out and follow Forrest to the death, if it cost ten thousand lives and breaks the Treasury."

In late August, though President Davis did not know it, a kind of gloom hung over Washington. A depressed President Lincoln wrote on August 23, "This morning, as for some days past, it seems exceedingly probable that this administration will not be re-elected."

The same day of Lincoln's expressed discouragement, Admiral David Glasgow Farragut, with four ironclads and thirteen wooden ships, steamed up Mobile Bay and, despite the mines and torpedoes, captured Fort Morgan. The city itself remained in Confederate hands, but it was rendered useless as a port for blockade runners.

Except for Farragut's victory, as Davis read the news, confused though it was, it seemed good for the South: "Riots in New Orleans; Memphis retaken; two thousand Federal prisoners taken at Petersburg; a Union raid on Macon, Georgia, failed."

When the Democratic National Convention met in Chicago on Monday, August 29, Davis's one-time protégé, General George Brinton McClellan, was overwhelmingly nominated on the first ballot. The only other man who had been seriously considered for the nomination was Franklin Pierce, Davis's closest friend in the North; but the ex-President would not permit his name to be put up. Clement L. Vallandigham, most ardent of the peace advocates, moved that McClellan's nomination be made unanimous.

The convention declared that the war as conducted by the Lincoln Administration was a failure. One noisy Iowa Copperhead yelled: "With all his vast armies Lincoln has failed, failed, failed, and still the monster usurper wants more victims for his slaughter pens." Several peace-at-any-price delegates and State Rights men demanded that the prolonged carnage should be stopped at once, even if it meant Southern independence. But McClellan forthrightly stated his position: "The re-establishment of the Union in all its integrity is and must continue to be the indispensable condition in any settlement." He made it clear that he would defend and restore the Constitution, which he felt Mr. Lincoln had circumvented.

Jefferson Davis's special hopes were now centered in Hood's ability to hold Atlanta until the November election. If he could do so, Davis believed that Lincoln might be defeated. Though he knew McClellan to be a determined and loyal Unionist, he was a man with whom the Confederates could negotiate, and at least the war would be conducted on a more humane plane.

The Democrats' chances for victory, which seemed reasonably good on August 29, were utterly shattered four days later when Sherman occupied Atlanta. The Convention had ironically proclaimed the war lost by the North just as it was now seemingly won.

Fired with eagerness to clinch Lincoln's election, Sherman began the last of a series of maneuvers against Hood. On September 1, Hood came to the sad conclusion that he must evacuate the city or risk capture. He made a skillful withdrawal. Protected by Hardee's corps, he passed across the front of Sherman's victorious troops and marched south to Lovejoy's Station. The ordnance and ammunition that could not be carried off were fired at two o'clock in the morning of September 2. When Sherman was awakened by the explosions, he realized Atlanta was his. At daylight he made ready to move into the coveted city. Although he made no attempt to destroy Hood's army, it was a decisive victory for the North. Sherman had given Lincoln a second term in the White House.

Davis took what consolation he could from the fact that though Atlanta was lost, Hood's army was intact. Sherman, safe in the city, drew his troops into entrenched lines against any possible attack by Hood, who was now encamped thirty miles away. Hood telegraphed Richmond that he could not engage Sherman again until he was reinforced. The President, deeply troubled, knew there was little possibility of reinforcing Hood. It pained him to have to wire: "Every effort has been made to bring forward reserves, militia and detailed men for the purpose. No other source remains."

Secretary of War Seddon had made a futile effort to bring the Georgia militia into Confederate service. On August 30, he had written Governor Brown that Georgia was faced with a serious invasion; he requested 10,000 or more militia, "and such further force of militia to repel invasion as you may be able to organize for Confederate service." Instead of complying, at this critical juncture when Hood and the President needed all possible support, Governor Brown by proclamation had declared the emergency in Georgia over. He withdrew the State troops from Hood's command, and granted blanket furloughs for them "to return to their homes and look for a time after important interests." And, in the words of Rudolph von Abele, Brown "continued to spit froth at the Richmond authorities until Sherman drove him and his government out of Milledgeville in panic-stricken flight."

Sherman, deciding to make Atlanta a fortress and a supply center, directed, on September 5, that all white civilians living in Atlanta, male and female, should leave the city within five days of the order. This involved immediate expulsion from their homes and deprivation of the only means of subsistence of thousands of "unoffending women and children, whose husbands and fathers were either in the army, in Northern prisons or had died in battle." The Mayor of Atlanta pleaded with the Federal commander to modify his harsh order. Sherman replied in writing: "I give full credit to your statements of the distress that will be occasioned by it, and yet shall not revoke my order, because my orders are not designed to meet the humanities of the case."

Hood agreed to a truce to assist in the pitiable exodus. The women and children were expelled from their homes in near-panic, and before they reached the Southern lines they had been largely robbed of the few articles of value they had been allowed to carry away.

Davis's sensibilities recoiled at such uncivilized procedure. Thousands of helpless refugees crowding the roads, most of them penniless and all without shelter for the night, added to the fearful demoralization in Georgia.

In the grim situation that faced the President, a saddening dispatch from Tennessee seemed little more than an historical footnote. General John Hunt Morgan, the dashing raider, was surprised and killed on Sunday morning, September 4. With his staff he was sleeping in a private home at Greenville, in east Tennessee, and was betrayed to the enemy by a daughter of the house. As he attempted to escape he was killed while fighting in the garden; the spirited cavalryman had determined never to be a prisoner again.

The tension that followed Sherman's occupation of Atlanta now pressed in on Jefferson Davis increasingly from every side. General Lee wrote him that every man liable for military service should be enrolled at once; that cooks, mechanics, and teamsters should be employed as soldiers and their places filled by Negroes. "The necessity will never be more urgent." The President knew this necessity only too well. And Governor Brown was threatening to call back the Georgia regiments in Lee's army to save imperiled Georgia, though exaggerated reports came that in that state alone there were "no less than 40,000 exempts, details, and applications for detail." The Richmond *Sentinel* charged that the invasion of Georgia was due to the Governor's exempting 15,000 men for a service "which was performed in Virginia with 1,400; in Alabama with 1,000; and in Mississippi with 110." It was generally rumored that there were enough skulkers to destroy Sherman if they were added to Hood's lists.

Brown, a plaguing, stubborn critic of the conscription act, was extremely difficult to handle. Hoping to reach him through Herschel V. Johnson, Davis, in reply to a letter of Johnson's half-friendly, half-critical, wrote on September 18: "I think Atlanta can be recovered if the absentees from Hood's army can be sent back, and the men of Georgia, who by the operation of law are exempt from military service, will give temporary aid; that Sherman's army can be driven out of Georgia; perhaps utterly destroyed."

He went on to answer certain specific complaints in Johnson's letter:

You are no doubt right in your conclusion that General Johnston was not relieved soon enough, but the judgment is sustained upon evidence which was not possessed before the event. I did not anticipate the abandonment of the mountain region of Georgia. . . .

Charleston, Savannah, Mobile, Mississippi and North Alabama were stripped to give Johnston a force which would ensure success so speedily that the troops could return to those places in time to prevent disasters. . . .

The first effect of disaster is always to spread a deeper gloom than is due to the occasion. No one was more anxious than myself to prevent the fall of Atlanta. I was not among those who deemed the result inevitable as soon as the enemy had crossed the Chattahoochee, and I was not willing that it should be yielded before manly blows had been struck for its preservation.

He ended his letter with a manly plea. "We need the support of public opinion. With confidence I appeal to you for aid."

CHAPTER XI

THE PRESIDENT GOES TO
GEORGIA

———◆◈◆———

AFTER JOHNSTON'S REMOVAL, the President had received
quantities of letters from prominent men across the South heartily
applauding his action. Among those sending congratulations was
Alabama's Leroy Pope Walker, Davis's first Secretary of War, whose
frustrating dealings with Joe Johnston had been a motivating factor
in his early resignation. But now that Hood had been forced
to evacuate Atlanta, public opinion veered like a weather vane to
throw blame on the harassed President. A swelling chorus began to
call for Beauregard to save the West. While Davis had no great confidence in Beauregard's stability or in his capacity as a top commander, he recognized his romantic appeal to the populace and decided to act.

Beauregard had not been happy in Virginia in a secondary place,
and Lee had been none too happy with him. Lee had always got
rid of officers in his command with whom he did not feel comfortable. Recently, when Lee was absent in Richmond and Beauregard was in charge of Petersburg, the Federals had captured the
important Weldon Railroad. Though the loss was not really Beauregard's fault, he was criticized for lack of vigilance. Lee had tactfully asked Beauregard to inspect the defenses at strategic Wilmington, North Carolina. So the President had let Beauregard
stay on at Wilmington, and he was there when Atlanta fell.

Now, in an effort to still the rising discontent and please the public, the President asked Lee to ascertain if Beauregard would be
willing to serve in the West. Beauregard promptly replied that,
though he felt "unequal to the responsibility," he would obey any
order of the Government.

It was not Davis's intention to put Beauregard in direct charge of the Army of Tennessee. He would create a new Military Division of the West, embracing the vast territory from the Mississippi River to Georgia and from Kentucky to the Gulf. The command of General Richard Taylor in Alabama and Mississippi was also to come under Beauregard's supervision. The position, which carried enormous prestige, was to be largely an advisory one. Beauregard would be free to go wherever he felt he was needed at any time.

It was widely rumored in Richmond—and incidentally true—that Sherman had invited Vice-President Stephens and Governor Brown to confer with him on terms of peace: the return of Georgia to the Union. Sherman had even sent a messenger with a verbal message to Stephens at his plantation, Liberty Hall. In a scathing rebuke, Secretary of War Seddon wrote Brown of "the foreshadowing of a guilty purpose to array your State in armed antagonism against the Confederacy and so to betray the cause of herself and sister States. . . . Our enemies appear to have conceived that your State could be seduced or betrayed by treachery." Georgia's Governor and the Vice-President of the Confederacy apparently were ready to consider either that the current Confederate Government should be put out of office or that Georgia should secede. But Robert Toombs warned Stephens that under no circumstances should he meet with the Federal commander.

Because Davis had good reason to fear that Brown might actually negotiate with Sherman, he decided to go to Georgia at once and make personal appeals. His other important objectives were to inspect Hood's army, to confer with him on future plans, and to compose differences among the officers.

On the morning of September 20, the President wired General Lee in cipher:

I expect to start for the Southwest this afternoon at 4 P.M. by the Danville road, and if General Beauregard could meet me at Burkesville and go on with me, I would be glad to confer with him and have his company.

As Davis was preparing to take the train late that afternoon, he received Lee's message that Beauregard would serve in the West, but that he would be unable to join him en route; he would meet him later. In the evening the President left with Custis Lee and ex-Governor Lubbock of Texas, who had only recently arrived in Richmond to become a Presidential aide-de-camp.

At the station Davis learned that Jubal Early had been defeated the day before at the Fourth Battle of Winchester and had been pushed up the Valley by Phil Sheridan, who was reported to have 50,000 men to the Confederates' 15,000. Lee's difficulties, Davis feared, would now be greatly increased.

In the face of this latest dark news, the President began to consider what he could say to reanimate the spirit of Georgians who had been corrupted by the perverse course of the Governor. Not only had Brown paralyzed the energies of the State by legislative decree, but he had set his clique of malcontents and croakers to join in his splenetic assaults on the President. Chief among them was the defeatist Vice-President Stephens.

Davis was doubtful of his welcome in distracted Georgia. But no matter how disquieted he himself was about the military situation and the growing disaffection, he would try to stimulate a new confidence.

On Sunday, September 25, the President reached Hood's headquarters at Palmetto. He reviewed the whole army and spoke to the various commands. He addressed the depleted ranks with ringing words of encouragement. "Be of good cheer," he said to the downhearted troops from Tennessee, "for within a short while your faces will be turned homeward, and your feet pressing Tennessee soil." His promise of an advance northward was received with tremendous cheering.

After inspecting the troops, Davis went into conference with Hood and the division commanders. It was agreed that the only chance of success was to cut Sherman's communications with Chattanooga and Nashville and, if possible, raise a people's war in Georgia and Alabama. To attack Sherman's entrenchments in Atlanta, Davis insisted, was not to be considered. Hood would strike at the railroad north of Atlanta in the hope of drawing Sherman back for a battle on his line of communications or on the northeastern border of Alabama. If Sherman could be sufficiently beaten, Hood might then invade Tennessee. But if at any time Sherman moved south of Atlanta, Hood was to follow him and attack him in the rear. Davis emphasized that "no operation should be considered which would place Hood's army beyond striking distance of Sherman should the Union army move southward from Atlanta."

The President explained to Hood his intention of placing Beauregard in immediate command of a Department of the West, embracing Hood's army and that of General Richard Taylor. "Without relieving you of the responsibilities and powers of your especial commands," he stressed.

Despite the depletion of Hood's forces by Governor Brown's decree and by the thousands absent without leave, the President left the Army of Tennessee with hope.

From Palmetto the President went with General Howell Cobb, who had joined him at Hood's headquarters, to Cobb's home in Macon. They arrived quite unexpectedly on the 4:00 A.M. train. After breakfast a committee called on Davis with a formal invitation to speak at a meeting scheduled at the Baptist Church to devise means for relieving the destitute refugees from Atlanta.

When the President entered the hall and came down the aisle he was greeted with thunderous applause which continued after he had reached the platform, where Cobb was to introduce him. The enthusiastic response was greater than he had expected. And according to the papers, he "repeatedly bowed very low." He confessed that the State was in peril. Two-thirds of the men were absent from the army, he said, "some sick, some wounded, but most of them absent without leave."

He spoke of his father, who as a Georgian soldier had fought against the British for American Independence. He insisted that despite the defeats of the Confederates around Atlanta the cause was by no means lost. "Sherman cannot keep up his long line of communications; retreat, sooner or later, he must," he declared. "And when that day comes the fate that befell the army of the French Empire in its retreat from Moscow will be re-enacted." Many took this hope to mean that the people in Sherman's path, going or coming, should destroy everything that would give sustenance or comfort to the enemy. In the heat of the moment Davis had indeed exaggerated a possible development. The comparison was inept because of the difference in the winter climates of Russia and Georgia. But Davis was speaking inpromptu to a depressed citizenry.

The President fervently urged that every citizen of Georgia, women as well as men, should bring pressure to induce deserters to return to the ranks of the Army of Tennessee.

And will they not come? Can they see the banished exiles, can they hear the wail of their suffering countrywomen and children and not come? By what influence they are made to stay away it is not necessary to speak. If there is one who will stay away at this hour, he is unworthy of the name of Georgian.

Without mentioning by name Governor Brown or Alexander Stephens, Davis laid the blame where it belonged. He ended his half-hour address with a restatement of his plea to draw men back into the army.

If one half the men now absent without leave will return to the front, we can defeat the enemy. . . . I may not realize that hope, but I know there are men that have looked death in the face too often to despond now. Let no one despond.

"Let no one despond" was to be a theme of all his addresses on the Southern tour.

From Macon the President went to Montgomery to confer with General Richard Taylor. He spoke in the Capitol, where he had been inaugurated. Acknowledging the disasters of late, he pointed with pride to Virginia. He reminded the legislature that against tremendous odds the Confederates had beaten General Grant and still held the lines before Petersburg and Richmond. "That pure and noble patriot," he said eloquently, "that great soldier and Christian, General Lee, although largely outnumbered in front, largely outnumbered on his flanks, commands a body of men who have never known what it was to be whipped and never stopped to cipher."

He urged the South not to listen to whispers that a possible victory of a Democratic President in the North would bring overtures for peace. "Victory in the field," he proclaimed, "is the surest element of strength to the peace party. Let us win battles, and we shall have overtures soon enough."

"Is there a man in the South in favor of reconstruction?" he demanded. Then he drew a vivid and prophetic picture of the horrors and humiliations of "reconstruction," which meant only "utter subjugation." "The man who is in favor of this degradation," he declared, "is on the wrong side of the line of battle. There is but one duty for every Southern man. It is to go to the front."

There be some men who when they look at the sun can only see a speck upon it. I am of a more sanguine temperament perhaps. But I have striven to behold our affairs with a cool and candid temperance of heart, and applying to them the most rigid test, am most confident the longer I behold the progress of the war. We should all marvel and thank God for the great achievements which have crowned our efforts.

In this impromptu speech Davis had hit upon a felicitous phrase that was a keynote to his own character. For, with all his fire, Davis did possess a certain "cool and candid temperance of heart." His audience could immediately identify Stephens and Brown as politicians who saw sunspots and General Joseph Johnston as one given to retreat because he always "stopped to cipher."

That evening the President took General Dick Taylor back to his hotel room and they "spent the night in work." He explained the plan he had agreed on with Hood, and the position he was to offer Beauregard, with its powers and limitations. Taylor's hope, however, was waning. Reinforcements could not be brought over from the Trans-Mississippi, he said, because the river was patrolled by gunboats. Davis understood only too well. But before they retired he had raised his brother-in-law's drooping spirits.

General Beauregard met the President in Augusta on October 2. The meeting was cordial. Davis offered Beauregard the new post as Commander of the Department of the West. Beauregard was to advise and to go in person to either Hood's or Taylor's army when his presence was necessary. He seemed satisfied and sincerely reluctant to take on field command. He asked Davis if his presence with an army *imposed* on him the necessity of assuming command: "Should not my orders merely pass through the commanding general?" Davis answered that this was correct: he was not to assume command of an army, adding that if he did he "might not be able to leave it."

The plan of operation which the President had discussed with Hood was fully explained to Beauregard and he apparently approved. If Sherman started towards the seacoast, the militia, the local troops, and civilians should obstruct the roads and fords in his front by felling trees and burning bridges, thus delaying his progress until his provisions should be consumed and absolute want deplete his army.

CHAPTER XII

"IF EVERY MAN IN GEORGIA
COULD HAVE HEARD HIM!"

———◆———

A PATRIOTIC RALLY had been scheduled in Augusta for Monday, October 3. On the stage with the President sat impressively Generals Beauregard, Cobb, and Hardee, who at his own request had been transferred to command the forces at Charleston and Savannah. In his last speech in Georgia, Jefferson Davis assured the populace that he left the State with far more confidence than when he came. He declared the South was stronger that day than four years before, "better able to repulse the vandal who is seeking to overthrow us." The Confederacy, he pointed out, had commenced the fight without an army, a navy, arsenals, mechanics, money, or credit. "Now we have arms for all, and are begging men to bear them." "This city of Augusta alone," he declared, "produces more powder than the army can burn."

Again Davis repeated his theme of Macon and Montgomery in different words:

Every man able to bear arms must go to the front, and all others must devote themselves to the cause at home. There must be no pleading for exemptions. We are fighting for existence; and of fighting alone can independence be gained.

He praised the women for their courage and their sacrifices. "You have given up all," he said.

You have sent your husbands, your fathers, your sons to the army, but you must do more. You must use your influence to send all to the front and form a public opinion that shall make the skulker a marked man, and leave him no house wherein he can take shelter.

During a pause for tumultuous handclapping, a thick-brogued Irishman shouted, "Three cheers for the Confederacy." The cheers

96

were given with ringing enthusiasm. Davis quickly made capital of the incident; he said that from the accents of the man's voice he knew that he had come into this country from a land that had lost its liberty. "Upon the success of the Confederacy," he proclaimed, "now alone depends the existence of Constitutional liberty in the world. We are fighting for that principle. Upon us depends its last hope."

Ours is not a revolution. We are a free and independent people, in States that had the right to make a better government when they saw fit. They sought to infringe upon the rights we had; and we only instituted a new government on the basis of those rights.

Our struggle is for inherited rights; and who would surrender them? . . . From the grave of many a fallen hero the blood of the slain would cry out against such a peace with the murderers. The women of the land driven from their homes; the children lacking food; old age hobbling from the scenes of its youth. . . .

There is but one thing to which we can accede—separate State independence.

Davis waited for the applause to die down, and then went on coolly.

Who now looks for intervention? Who does not know that our friends abroad depend upon our strength at home?

Words will not now avail. You must consult your hearts, perform more than the law can exact, yield as much as free men can give and all will be well. With peace and freedom a glorious career opens for these Confederate States.

He seemed to have reached his climax, and vociferous handclapping made him pause for some time. But there was still one more emphatic message he had for the Georgians and especially for their Governor and his own Vice-President.

There are some I know who have looked upon Confederate legislation as needlessly harsh. I would that it could have been unnecessary. I would that goods could have been bought in market rather than impressed; that the armies could have been filled by volunteering rather than by conscription; and yet I look upon the latter as the more just. You force all men to make roads, pay taxes, serve on juries; why should not all men fight your battles? My opinion on this subject has not changed. I believed, and believe now, it is just; that it would have been better had it been the policy from the beginning of the war; and I endorse it in all its length and breadth and depth.

He ended with a homily. "Be of good cheer. In homely phrase, put your shoulder to the wheel, and work while it is day."

After thunderous applause for Davis, General Beauregard arose to great handclapping; he said he had fired the first gun at Sumter and hoped to live to fire the last of the war. Hardee declared that before he left the Army of Tennessee, Hood had said to him that he hoped to lay his claws on the state road in rear of Sherman, and having once fixed them there, it was not his intention to let them loose their hold.

The rally was a stirring success. Among those in the crowd profoundly moved by the President's magnetism and patriotic appeal was a planter from the interior named J. M. Clark, who happened to be in the river town. The next day, still under the spell of Jefferson Davis, he wrote his wife:

He is one of the finest speakers on the continent. Never in my life have I listened to a man who has such fine use of the language. He is a grave, dignified, and solemn speaker. Every word he utters is befitting the occasion & the man. There is nothing little, nothing comic, nothing theatrical about him. Take him all and in all, he is the greatest man I ever saw. While I had a high opinion of him before, I have a still higher one now. He is an honor to the Confederacy.

The people here are more hopeful than they were before the President's speech. There was so much heroism in what he said—so much patriotism, so much devotion to the cause that a new inspiration was breathed into the people. If every man in Ga. could have heard him, our cause would be in the ascendant in three weeks.*

In the middle of the night, after an exhausting day, Davis was roused to take a northbound train to Columbia, the capital of South Carolina. Affairs were not going harmoniously in the Palmetto State, although popular Brigadier General James Chesnut was doing his best to compose differences. State conscription laws had been recently passed which kept Lee from getting his proper quota of soldiers. While Robert Barnwell Rhett, the belligerent editor of the influential Charleston *Mercury*, was a red-hot patriot, as determined as Davis to resist the invaders, he was still maliciously trying to turn public opinion against the President, whose position he had coveted in 1861.

A little after daylight on Tuesday, October 4, the President, with his party including Custis Lee and Governor Lubbock, arrived at

---

* A photostatic copy of J. M. Clark's long, detailed letter of October 4, 1864, was sent to the author by his grandson, Leigh M. Clark, a prominent attorney of Birmingham, Alabama.

the Chesnut house in Columbia. Mrs. Chesnut received him at the front gate. Davis greeted her with a kiss. After breakfast General Chesnut and the aides rode off on business with Governor Milledge Bonham. The President and his hostess went out on the veranda for a chat. Some little boys passed on their way to school. Suddenly one cried out excitedly, "Hey, come and look! There's a man on Mrs. Chesnut's porch who looks just like Jeff Davis on the postage stamp." People began to gather. The President went inside.

After the news spread, flowers for the President began to arrive. Mrs. Cheeves McCord sent the first bouquet. "What a comfort it is in all this upsetting foolish talk," Mrs. Chesnut wrote that night, "that Mrs. John S. Preston, one of the most sensible women I know, and Mrs. McCord, the very cleverest, are both Jeff Davis's supporters and friends, heart and soul. Men may be selfish and self-seeking, but my noble female friends are purely patriotic." Mary Chesnut with her quick intuition had casually set down a sharp truth about Southern women. And in referring to self-seeking men—both politicians and certain high-ranking army officers—she had hit upon a prime cause of the Confederacy's decline and fall.

While the President was watching Mrs. Chesnut prepare a mint julep for Custis Lee, who had come in exhausted, someone announced that a great crowd had gathered and was calling for the President to speak to them. The Arsenal cadets were there in full, their band playing welcome tunes. Many of Columbia's foremost ladies were noted in the crowd. People began pushing in, even through the back door, until the house overflowed "upstairs, downstairs, and in my lady's chamber"—everywhere except in Mr. Davis's sacrosanct room, which opened onto the veranda. The Episcopal rector arrived, held his hands high over the President's head, and fervently blessed him. Theodore Stark, a family friend, went to the kitchen for a glass of brandy, and loudly announced his personal opinion: "Jeff Davis will do. I like that *game* look the fellow has."

Though physically weary from his week of travel and gravely concerned about the future of Hood's army, Davis rallied his strength to give encouragement to the South Carolinians. He walked out into the sunlight and spoke straight from his heart of his inflexible demand for victories. "There is but one means by which you can gain independence and an honorable peace," he declared, "and that is by uniting." Then, with clearest emphasis, especially for the Charleston newspaper correspondents, he said:

If there still be left any of those military critics who have never spoken of our generals but to show how much better things could have been managed, or of our Government but to find fault with it because it never took their advice—in mercy's name, let these wise ones go to the front and aid us in achieving our independence.

When the approving murmurs and applause died away, Davis went on: "A plan of negotiation has been offered for consideration." A tense silence gripped the crowd. "What are the terms offered?" he asked scornfully, his eyes flashing indignation.

If you will acknowledge your crime, lay down your arms, emancipate your slaves, and turn over your leaders to be punished, then you will have permission to vote together with your negroes, and Mr. Lincoln will be graciously pleased to allow you to live as a part of the nation over which he presides.

Davis paused, and then said with feeling:

If there be a man within the sound of my voice who contemplates such a proposition, I pity him from the bottom of my heart. His is not the spirit which animated our fathers in 1776, and he is not fit to exist among the men who are now imperilling their lives in the cause in which we are all engaged.

His manner changed. Color came into his cheeks; his whole countenance visibly brightened.

I have just returned from that army from which we have the saddest accounts—the Army of Tennessee, and I am glad to bring you words of cheer. That Army has risen in tone; its march is onward; its face, looking to the front. So far as I am able to judge, General Hood's strategy has been good and his conduct has been gallant. . . . He hopes soon to have his hand upon Sherman's line of communications. . . . I therefore say be of good cheer, for I hope that brighter intelligence will soon reach you.

With Georgia's bad example in mind, he spoke with subdued emotional fervor:

Is this a time to ask what the *law* demands of you, to ask if the magistrate will take you out of the enrolling office by a writ of *habeas corpus?* Rather is it the time for every man capable of bearing arms to say "My country needs my services, and my country shall have them!"

As the improvised speech drew to a climax, Mrs. Chesnut had a frosted mint julep ready for the President when he returned to his room. Because he had warmly defended General Hood in his speech, the ecstatic Buck Preston rushed up to kiss him. Holding the silver goblet in one hand and embracing the excited girl with the other, he "'smoothed her down the back from the shoulders as if she were a ruffled dove."

The dinner, at which Governor Bonham sat at the hostess's left, did credit to South Carolina hospitality. "Almost everyone" in Columbia had sent some delicacy for the President. Mrs. Preston had prepared a boned turkey stuffed with truffles. General Chesnut served sixty-year-old Madeira from Mulberry Plantation. It was the last fine food the President was to taste for many years.

When a crowd of boys came to pay their respects, the President knew just how to meet them and in a couple of minutes sent them away happy. At train-time a servant from Wade Hampton's plantation, "Millwood," arrived with a dozen bottles of wine for the party's homeward journey. Though Davis's mind was deeply troubled about Sherman's future movements and Alexander Stephens's disaffection, his heart had been warmed by his brief visit to South Carolina's capital.

The President had expended great energy during his arduous trip, but he had kept unusually well. He had even stood the strain better than his aides. Now in the cars he could let go and relax at least for some hours before he faced grave problems in Richmond. He was weary, but gratified. He had taken the people into his confidence. For, as a true democrat, Davis believed in keeping the public well informed, "without destroying the privacy essential to diplomatic negotiations or military maneuvers." He had explained the critical situation, how it got to be what it was, and the ensuing difficulties to be faced.

Stragglers and soldiers absent without leave had already begun to return by the hundreds to the Army of Tennessee. Hood was capturing Federal posts on the railroad between Chattanooga and Atlanta. Davis knew so well that in war the psychological factors are often decisive. He had tried to impress upon the Southern consciousness that "disunity within one's own ranks makes deeper wounds than the enemy's sword" and that internal dissension opens the door wide to the invader's attack.

The President's appearance on the Georgia scene had apparently quashed Governor Brown's scheme to treat with Sherman and take his State out of the Confederacy. Davis, like thousands of others, must have reflected that if fate had given the Confederacy a more normal Vice-President and a less cranky and stubborn Governor of Georgia, his country would not be in such peril. "The opposition of Georgia," as Dr. Rudolph von Abele rightly judged, "affected the outcome of the war in a degree scarcely to be underestimated." If Georgia had had Benjamin Hill or Howell Cobb in the Governor's chair, it is conceivable that Sherman would have been stopped and the South might have won its independence.

While in Augusta President Davis had received some unofficial sad news that touched him with uncommon sorrow. Rose Green-how, returning by blockade runner from a year of patriotic service abroad, had been drowned within sight of Fort Fisher, near Wil-mington. She was bringing to him and Secretary of the Navy Mal-lory valuable dispatches, and he had been looking forward to seeing her and hearing from her own lips a recountal of her personal ex-periences abroad, much of which he had gleaned from letters and English newspapers and periodicals.

The full details of the calamity Davis learned only on his return to Richmond. He did not know that Mrs. Greenhow had accepted a proposal of marriage from the widowed Earl of Granville, but had postponed the wedding until after she had reported by word of mouth to the President of the Confederacy. Rose had worked well with James Murray Mason and John Slidell and with Matthew Fon-taine Maury, whom Davis had sent to Europe in 1862 because of his international prestige, with the high expectancy that he would be able to secure for the Confederacy the rams and ships needful to smash the Federal blockade. In the spring of 1864, Commander Maury, disillusioned and frustrated by the dillydallying and timid-ity of the British Government, had crossed the dangerous seas to make a secret report to Jefferson Davis on the shipping situation and on Napoleon's maneuvering with Maximilian, who was a friend of Maury's. Then Maury had told him something of Rose's social success in London and Paris. She had been received at court by both Queen Victoria and the Empress Eugénie, who was strongly pro-Southern. She had had a long interview with Napoleon III him-self. She had talked with French bankers and diplomats. In Lon-don Rose published a book about her grimy imprisonment in Wash-ington, and it had sold well. She had been pressed into service as a lecturer and a writer of articles. She was an admired propagandist, not only in English shipping circles but in the best London drawing rooms, and she did her tactful utmost to counteract the rising pres-tige of the able and estimable Charles Francis Adams, the American Minister, who at first had been chilled by his reception by the

British. Rose had worked hard with the Society for Obtaining the Cessation of Hostilities in America, backed by men of the nobility, the purpose of which was to promote the cause of Southern independence.

Rose had also been accepted by the literary set presided over by Thomas Carlyle, and she had become an intimate friend of Florence Nightingale. Though a tremendous social success in London, she had never paused in her ardent championship of the South and in her intense hatred of the invading North. She did not say idly that she was willing to die for the Confederacy. And when she sailed on the *Condor,* a brand-new blockade runner, to report to President Davis, she had a mild premonition that she might do just that.

Along with her official dispatch bags, which the British commander kept in the ship's strongbox for her, Rose bore a leather reticule containing two thousand dollars in gold attached to her person by a long chain about her neck.

All went well with the voyage and the stopover in Halifax, until the ship approached the safety of Fort Fisher, when it was pursued by a Federal gunboat. In a tempestuous wind, the *Condor* was grounded with a terrific crash on a bar. In terror of being captured and not able to get her dispatches to Richmond, Rose demanded that she be sent to shore in a lifeboat. The ship's captain argued strenuously against the procedure because of the might of the waves. But the strong-willed Rose finally won the desperate argument. At dawn she entered the boat with two men and two rowers. A gigantic wave struck her boat broadside, turned it upside down, and Rose, weighted by her gold, sank. The dispatch case was lost. But the body of the impetuous patriot was washed up on the North Carolina sands, her heavy reticule still hanging about her neck, and a memo about her fiancé, Lord Granville, among the glittering golden coins. From St. Thomas's Episcopal Church in Wilmington, while Jefferson Davis was making his last rallying speech in Georgia, she was given a military funeral.

Davis could reflect that here was another luckless end to a glorious adventure, something like the unnecessary deaths of Stonewall Jackson and Sidney Johnston. He regarded Rose Greenhow as a prime heroine of the Confederacy. She had used all the opulent gifts with which she was endowed in the service of the South. While she might have enjoyed a life of luxury in England as Lady Granville, she had sacrificed herself for an ideal.

Southern women erected a marble cross to mark her grave. It

bore the simple inscription: "Mrs. Rose O'N. Greenhow, a bearer of dispatches to the Confederate Government." The London *Times* wrote an admiring column about her. Then it commented in some awe about the fury of the conflict.

The Americans are making war as no people ever made it before. Their campaigns combine the costliness of modern expeditions with the carnage of barbaric invasions. Grant squanders life like Attila, and money like Louis XIV.

Though Grant was pounding away at Lee's thin lines not many miles from Richmond, Davis was more worried about conditions in Atlanta.

CHAPTER XIII

"THE TRUE PATH TO PEACE"

THE DAY OF October 6 in Richmond was "bright and warm," as War Clerk J. B. Jones reported in his diary. "The President returned this morning, hastened hither by the perils environing the city." Davis found Richmond under a severe tension. The Federals had captured Fort Harrison within the Richmond defenses on September 29. Citizens were now bearing arms and wearing most anxious expressions. More and more governmental employees were being thrust into uniform. The soldiers in Virginia had become dispirited. Desertions were daily thinning Lee's ranks. "Harrowed and overworked," as Gorgas sadly remarked in his diary, "they were getting worn out with the campaign." They no longer had the energy to fight as they did at Spotsylvania. Because they were enlisted for the war's duration, many had begun to look upon themselves as doomed and saw little before them but inevitable death.

The President was acutely concerned about the Confederacy's perennial trouble: want of manpower. As Lee's army shrank, Grant was being reinforced by an estimated thousand men a day. Colonel R. H. Chilton, Lee's Chief of Staff, told Gorgas that General Lee had said to him, "If we can't get the men, all that is left for us is to make peace on the best terms we can." Gorgas wrote in secret, "I cannot think that he was serious, but I regret to hear such language from his mouth. I heard almost the same expression now attributed to him uttered by him in June, 1861."

Burton Harrison was to write later that Jefferson Davis, knowing the mighty odds against the South in the beginning, had not believed that the South could win until Lee's first great victories in 1862. Thereafter he never wavered—no matter what the outlook—but used every ounce of strength to keep his people up to the utmost courage and sacrifice.

105

Though Davis was now disturbed to hear talk of increasing discouragement in the ranks of the Army of Northern Virginia, he knew that there was no one like their idol, "Uncle Bob," as the soldiers affectionately called Lee, to uphold their morale.

Davis suffered acutely over the current miserable situation in the lower Valley. Sheridan was pillaging and burning the beautiful Shenandoah. Grant had recently met him at Charles Town and given him permission to destroy everything before him. "Acting under orders from Grant," Edward Channing wrote in a noted passage of his *History of the United States,* "he [Sheridan] destroyed everything eatable by man or beast, set fire to barns and hayricks, and left the Valley in such condition that a crow flying over it would have to carry his food with him." The tales of misery of the fleeing, foodless citizens sickened the compassionate Davis. And he was shocked to find that though Sheridan's manner of warfare caused extreme suffering on the part of the destitute civilians, the destruction was justified by the Northern Republican press.

But the Confederate President had no thought of giving up and submitting to the will of the aggressors. He called for a special session of Congress on November 7.

Varina Davis was too disconsolate to give comfort to her terribly burdened husband. In writing to Mrs. Chesnut to thank her for the "regal" entertainment of the President in Columbia, she revealed her downcast mood.

We are in a sad and anxious state here now. The dead come in, and the living do not go out so fast. . . . Strictly between us, things look very anxious here. . . . I am so constantly depressed that I dread writing, for penned lines betray our feelings despite every care.

In the fortnight following the President's return to the capital, though there were no climactic events, dispatches of mixed good and bad tidings came to his desk in rapid sequence. The Confederate raider *Florida* had been sunk at Bahia, Brazil, on October 7. The new cruiser C.S.N. *Shenandoah* had sailed from England on October 8. Aged Chief Justice Roger B. Taney, who had served under eight Presidents and had always been a Southern sympathizer, died on the twelfth in his eighty-eighth year. Salmon Chase, the South's inveterate foe, was given his place. Early's vigor was waning as he fought gamely against Sheridan's five-to-two advantage. He lost engagement after engagement, and, to the grief and dismay of Ordnance Chief Gorgas, at Cedar Creek "on the nineteenth, he lost nineteen guns!" It was the last big battle in the Shenandoah.

Hood had continued to take stations on the railroad between Chattanooga and Atlanta, and on October 13 captured Dalton, Georgia. He drew Sherman from his Atlanta stronghold, but neither Sherman nor he seemed eager for a full-scale battle. Hood crossed the Alabama line to replenish his supplies at Gadsden's supply depots and to ponder his next move. Beauregard joined him there and, without Davis's knowledge, encouraged Hood in his audacious new plan to invade Tennessee, capture Nashville, and head for the Ohio.*

In the midst of his anxieties Davis had gratifying evidence that his trip to Georgia was bearing fruit. Exactly a fortnight after his speech at Augusta, Governors of six Southern states, Virginia, North Carolina, South Carolina, Georgia, Alabama, and Mississippi, met in that town. Governor William Smith of Virginia presided over the meeting and led the discussions. After a "full, free, and harmonious consultation and interchange," resolutions were passed to let the people know that the state Governors were backing Richmond. On October 24 the President received a copy of the document with an accompanying letter from Governor Smith.

Davis was particularly pleased to read in the first of the eight resolutions:

There is nothing in the present aspect of public affairs to cause any abatement of our zeal in the prosecution of the war to the accomplishment of a peace based on the independence of the Confederate States. And to give encouragement to our brave soldiers in the field, and to strengthen the Confederate authorities in the pursuit of this desirable end, we will use our best exertions to increase the effective force of our armies.

The seventh resolution proclaimed what Davis hoped the Southern body politic would determine in its corporate heart:

And, lastly . . . to declare our firm and unalterable purpose . . . to maintain our right of self-government, to establish our independence, and

---

* Historians have quarreled over the pros and cons of Hood's advance into Tennessee. Some have flatly and falsely stated that this was one of Davis's chief military errors. In his *Advance and Retreat*, published in 1880, Hood completely absolves the President. He takes the entire blame, and declares that the plan originated with him. But Davis always believed that the change in the agreed strategy may have originated with Beauregard. He and the War Department had seen so many of the Creole's grandiose plans for winning the war quickly. The *Official Records* indicate that Beauregard thought Hood might succeed in his invasion of Tennessee.

to uphold the rights and sovereignty of the States, or to perish in the attempt.

The entire set of resolutions was infiltrated with echoes of the Confederate President. Yet the document was signed by the obstructionists Zebulon Vance and Joseph E. Brown as well as by the other Governors. Two days after the meeting, Brown began restoring to active duty the militia he had so "inopportunely furloughed" before Sherman took Atlanta.

Alexander Stephens now lapsed into moody silence. Davis had been remarkably forbearing with his Vice-President, but he did write him a reprimanding letter asking him if he did not think it would be more becoming for "such an able man, in so high a station" to return to his post at Richmond rather than remain away working up hostility against the Administration. Professor Dodd of Chicago expressed perhaps the best historical judgment on the Vice-President when he wrote in 1907: "If ever a man of mature years and high reputation talked and behaved like a child, it was Stephens in the autumn of 1864."

Davis paid little attention to the talk everywhere about the coming Federal election on November 8. He knew that the peace men in the Middle West called "Copperheads" were becoming more active. He heard that the Democrats were emphasizing that their candidate, General McClellan, who had once been the pride of the Army of the Potomac, had been shabbily treated by the Lincoln Administration. For, though Grant had been hammering away since the first of May and had lost more than 80,000 men in the process, he had not got as close to Richmond in 1864 as McClellan had in 1862. Davis read that McClellan had created an excellent impression by the few campaign speeches he did make. But he himself had no doubt that Lincoln would be re-elected. When Sherman occupied Atlanta, he had given up hope of a Democratic victory. He spent much of the first week of November preparing his message to Congress. He was trying to get into it something like Montaigne's dictum that "nothing noble is done without risk."

In the first week of November, Richmond felt winter's first sharp bite with "slow, cold, penetrating rains." The miserable weather corresponded with the sullen mood of the gathering anti-Davis legislators.

On November 7, the day the Confederate Congress convened, Davis was extremely perturbed by a dispatch from General Hood.

I hope to march for Middle Tennessee by the eighth or ninth. Should he [Sherman] move two or three corps south from Atlanta, I think it would be the best thing that could happen for our general good. General Beauregard agrees with me as to my plan of operation.

Hood had taken his army clear across the State of Alabama and was now at Tuscumbia in the northwest corner, virtually on the Tennessee border. Davis had expected Hood to break Sherman's communications and, if possible, to draw him out of Atlanta for battle. They had agreed that he was to pursue Sherman if the Federals moved south of Atlanta. With Beauregard's approval, Hood had steadily moved farther away from Atlanta on his own strategic objective of capturing Nashville. Beauregard remained with Hood two weeks at Tuscumbia, "during which interval"—the words are Hood's—"the inaugurated campaign was discussed at great length." While the President was averse to interfering with his commanding generals, particularly when they were two of such high rank as Hood and Beauregard, he wired cautiously:

The policy of taking advantage of the reported division of Sherman's forces by attacking him where (or *when*) he cannot reunite his army is too obvious to have been overlooked by you. . . . If you keep his communications broken he will probably seek to concentrate for an attack on you, but if, as reported to you, he has sent a large part of his force southward, you may first beat him in detail and *subsequently* without serious obstruction or danger to the country in your rear advance to the Ohio River.

In *Advance and Retreat* (on page 273) Hood was to write specifically:

The President was evidently under the impression that the Army should have been equal to battle by the time it had reached the Alabama line, and was averse to my going into Tennessee. He was not, as General Beauregard and myself, acquainted with its true condition. Therefore, a high regard for his views notwithstanding, I continued firm in the belief that the only means to checkmate Sherman, and co-operate with General Lee to save the Confederacy, lay in speedy success in Tennessee and Kentucky, and in my ability finally to attack Grant in rear with my entire force.*

* And in a footnote on the same page Hood states: "Almost every writer upon the subject of my campaign into Tennessee has fallen into the popular error that the President ordered me into that State; and, strange to say, General Taylor, brother-in-law of Mr. Davis, has also grossly erred in this regard, when he could have addressed a note to the Chief Executive of the Confederacy and have ascertained the truth."

In his address to Congress on November 7, President Davis gave no indication of weakening.

If we had been compelled to evacuate Richmond as well as Atlanta—the Confederacy would have remained as erect and defiant as ever. Nothing could have been changed in the valor of its troops, or in the unquenchable spirit of its people. . . .

There is no military success of the enemy which can accomplish its destruction. Not the fall of Richmond, or Wilmington, or Charleston, or of all combined, can save the enemy from the constant and exhaustive drain of blood and treasure which must continue until he shall discover that no peace is attainable unless based on the recognition of our indefeasible rights.

We know ourselves fully competent to maintain our own rights and independence against the invaders of our country, and we feel justified in asserting that without the aid derived from recruiting their armies from foreign countries the invaders would ere this have been driven from our soil.

It was a long address, covering everything from foreign relations, the War Department, and finances, to potential negotiations for peace. In regard to slaves in military service, Davis spoke cautiously. He did not want to stir up violent antagonism in rich Senators like Virginia's R. M. T. Hunter, who set great store on his slave property. He recommended the employment of 40,000 slaves in the various armies. Then, taking up certain contingencies, he came to this conclusion: "The policy of engaging to liberate the negro on his discharge after service faithfully rendered seems to me preferable to that of granting immediate manumission, or that of retaining him in service."

The President ended his address with an appeal to Congress and the South, "to devote our united and unimpaired energies to the defense of our homes, our lives, and our liberties. This is the true path to peace. Let us tread it with confidence in the assured result."

All in all, it was a valiant speech. Even the President's most bitter foes acknowledged his gameness and his power to stimulate confidence.

The next day Abraham Lincoln was re-elected President of the United States by a huge electoral majority. McClellan carried only three states. Yet the General had received forty-five out of every hundred popular votes cast in the North, and, of course, there were no Democratic votes in the South to be counted.

Lincoln now had a clear mandate to continue the war. "There is no use in disguising the fact," Gorgas ruminated in his diary, "that our subjugation is popular at the North, and that the War must go on until this hope is crushed out and replaced by desire for peace at any cost."

Sherman, who had really been responsible for Lincoln's election, now determined on a bold plan: to win the war by making it hell. Sending a third of his force under General George H. Thomas to protect Nashville against Hood, he boldly prepared to march through Georgia to the sea, burning and looting as he went. He would be cut off from his communications, and when the supplies were used up, his "bummers" "would live off the land." As he boasted, he would "make Georgia howl."

During the spring, summer, and fall of 1864, despite his other manifold duties and anxieties, Jefferson Davis had continued to work to effect an exchange of prisoners. He grieved over the miserable conditions of prison camps both in the North and the South, and especially in crowded Andersonville in Georgia. In February, 1864, the Richmond *Enquirer* had advised the Government to publish the facts about conditions in Northern prisons, declaring that "thousands of Confederate prisoners were scantily clothed on bleak prairies or by the shores of frozen lakes; and, starved in the midst of plenty, rot in their vile dungeons, and nothing is known to the outside world."

In his message to Congress, May 2, 1864, President Davis had openly deplored the Federal policy of refusing exchanges.

The prisoners held by us, in spite of humane care, are perishing from the inevitable effects of imprisonment and the homesickness produced by the hopelessness of release from confinement. The spectacle of their suffering augments our longing desire to relieve from similar trials our own brave men who have spent so many weary months in a cruel and useless imprisonment, endured with heroic constancy.

When Judge Robert Ould had failed in his efforts to persuade the Northern authorities to return to the usage of the July 22, 1862, cartel, Davis had sent General Lee himself to General Grant to try to effect an exchange in the name of humanity. When Lee reported a negative result, he had said to the bitterly disappointed President: "We have done everything in our power to mitigate the suffering of prisoners and there is no further responsibility on our part."

Sick and wounded Union men were dying in Southern camps because the Federal Government had declared all medicines contraband to the South. So Davis offered to buy medicines solely for Northern prisoners and to pay in cotton, tobacco, or gold, even at two or three times the regular price, if required, and, moreover, he stipulated that such drugs might be brought into the Southern lines and dispensed by Northern surgeons. Incredible as it appeared to Davis, this offer, too, was ignored.

In midsummer Davis had gladly allowed the captives at Andersonville to send three men of their choosing to Washington to plead with Lincoln for relief. They bore a petition signed by thousands of Federal prisoners. They saw Stanton, who, one of them wrote, treated them with contempt such as they had never received at Andersonville. When the President of the United States declined to receive them, they returned utterly disconsolate. And in August the prisoners, blackly discouraged and feeling abandoned by their Government, began dying daily by the hundreds.*

Davis knew that it was not starvation—for the Northern prisoners were getting the same corn meal rations as Lee's soldiers or their own Confederate guards—but despondency, overcrowding, and lack of medicines that caused the deaths from dysentery, scurvy, malaria, and gangrene.

Finally, to alleviate the worst of the suffering, Davis authorized his Agent of Exchange, Judge Ould, to offer to return ten to fifteen thousand sick and wounded Federal prisoners, *without requiring any equivalents*. Ould only asked the Agent of the United States to furnish transportation at the mouth of the Savannah River. Because of the increasing mortality Ould several times urged haste. But it was not until after the middle of November that the Federal authorities finally sent ships to collect some 13,000 Federal prisoners at Savannah. The hospital prisons had been searched for the most desperate cases and at the ships' arrival in Annapolis photographs were taken of the most emaciated returned prisoners and spread throughout the Northern newspapers as typical cases, though Ould had also sent 5,000 well prisoners among the lot. The

---

* "Men who had cheerfully faced death on many a battlefield," John W. Urban was to write in *Battlefield and Prison Pen*, "lay down and died broken-hearted as the terrible suspicion forced itself into their minds that the Government they loved so well and fought so hard to save, was indifferent to their sad fate."

Annapolis photographs, terrible indeed, proved effective propaganda in stirring up a new fury in the North.[*]

Although the terms of Ould's offer to deliver Federal prisoners required no equivalent, yet 3,000 sick and wounded Confederates were eventually delivered at the mouth of the Savannah. When Ould beheld the ghastly shipload, he termed it "a cargo of living death." And he called upon every Federal and Confederate officer and man who witnessed the character of both deliveries, to note that the misery the Confederate prisoners portrayed at Savannah surpassed that exhibited by the Annapolis photographs. The original rolls showed that some 3,500 had started from Northern prisons, but death had taken about 500 in transit, and "the mortality of those delivered alive was frightful in the months following."

As Christmas, 1864, approached, Jefferson Davis was heartsick over the plight of hapless prisoners in the North. Midwinter would go far worse with the Confederates in freezing Northern latitudes, where, from reports, many men in the Elmira, New York, prison existed without a single blanket in tents without a floor.[†] He knew that zero weather would take its terrible toll, even in a land of plenty, where there was deliberate malnutrition as well as inadequate covering. Though feeling helpless against Stanton's harsh decree of no more exchanges, Davis did not give up trying and hoping. Some potent Northern criticism finally had effect on Grant, and in February of 1865 he would be willing to resume some exchanges.

It would not be until July, 1866, when Davis himself was a prisoner at Fort Monroe, that Secretary of War Stanton would release a report on prison deaths. Although 50,000 more Union soldiers were held in Southern prisons, 26,436 Confederates died in Northern prisons as against 22,576 Federals in Southern prisons. Whereas 84 per 1,000 soldiers died in Southern prisons, 120 per 1,000 died in Northern prisons. The shocked North would then begin to reassess its judgment of the "inhumanities."

---

[*] In a long article letter to *The National Intelligencer* on the Exchange of Prisoners dated August 17, 1868, Robert Ould asked a bitter question: "But why was this delay between the summer and November in sending transportation for sick and wounded for whom no equivalents were asked? Were Union prisoners made to suffer in order to aid the photographs 'in firing the popular heart of the North'?"

[†] On pp. 161-162 of *Official Records,* Series II, Vol. VII, the report of B. F. Tracy, Colonel Commanding 127 New York Volunteers, reports the bad condition of the Elmira prison, where men slept on earth without blankets and "died unnecessarily from scurvy."

CHAPTER XIV

SHERMAN'S BRAND ON GEORGIA

————◆◉◆————

THE CONFEDERATE PRESIDENT had designated Wednesday, November 16, as a day of worship and prayer. The morning, bright and frosty, was like a Sabbath with all of Richmond's shops closed. Before Davis could go to Saint Paul's to the special service a dispatch reached him that Sherman had burned Atlanta in the night. It was an unexpected move. Hood's Army of Tennessee was some 275 miles away at Tuscumbia, Alabama. It had been held up there since October 30 while a supply railroad from Corinth, Mississippi, was being rebuilt.

When his army pulled out of the trenches around flaming Atlanta on November 16, Sherman sent all surplus stores and trains back to Tennessee. With plenty of ammunition but only a few days' supply of rations, Sherman cut his communications with the North and boldly set out for the sea to "live on the country" en route. To provide sustenance for men and beasts, he detailed thousands of foragers whom he designated "bummers." These men were chosen for their vigor and aggressiveness, and if they were tough or vicious so much the better. Georgia's recent crop had been the best in years, and more abundant because patriotic folk had obeyed the injunction of their President to plant foodstuffs instead of cotton. The crops had all been gathered. Barns, bins, cribs, hogsheads, and smokehouses were full.

From the dispatches that poured into the War Department Davis learned that Sherman had divided his army into two bodies, each about 30,000 strong; one was following the Georgia Railroad towards Augusta and the other heading towards Macon.

Hardee prepared to defend Macon with his small army of Georgia reserves under General Howell Cobb and the artillery which

114

had been sent there by Hood. But Sherman skirted Macon without giving battle. Looting and burning, he passed through central Georgia, pausing at Milledgeville, the capital, where he used for his headquarters the mansion from which Governor Brown had just fled.

Frantic appeals for help came to the President in Richmond. In the pillaging virtually no house was spared. Even the poorest white in his isolated cabin lost his slim store of sweet potatoes. Slaves lost their jugs of molasses, their tobacco, best clothes, quilts, and their meager savings as well. On whim arsonists applied their torches to humble dwellings as well as to columned mansions, country stores, and gin houses.

A vivid personal tale of distress was set down by a Maine-born widow, Dolly Sumner Lunt, who managed the family plantation near Covington, Georgia. A distant relation of Senator Charles Sumner, she had gone South to teach school and married a planter. Sherman's bummers swooped down on her estate on November 18. While her nerves still tingled from the terrifying experience with the vandals, she recorded details in her journal.

Like demons they rushed in, she wrote; to her smokehouse, her dairy, kitchen, and cellar, breaking locks and whatever was in their way. In a twinkling, the thousand pounds of meat in her smokehouse was gone, and her flour, lard, butter, eggs, pickles, and wine. All her jugs and jars were taken. Her eighteen fat turkeys, hens, chickens, and pigs were shot down in the yard and "hunted as if they had been rebels themselves." The invaders took the mules and the sheep, and, worst of all, they forced her Negro "boys" to go at bayonet's point, even a lame lad who had "crawled under the floor" to escape.

Mrs. Lunt saw Sherman himself and a great portion of his army pass her house, behind, as well as before. They made a road through her back yard, tore down her fences, and "wantonly devastated" her place "when there was no necessity." Dinnerless and supperless as she and her household were, they had the great fear of being "driven out homeless to the dreary woods," for they saw the heavens "lit with flames from burning buildings."

But Mrs. Lunt barely escaped conflagration. Her carriage house had in it eight bales of cotton with a hundred pounds of carded cotton rolls. Though a twist from the rolls was set on fire and thrown into "the boat" of her carriage, the cotton only burned over, and, "Thanks to my God," she wrote, "they went out."

Two Union guards came into her bedroom and laid themselves by the fire to watch for the night. They were Germans and she could not understand a word they said. Too agitated to close her eyes, she kept walking to and fro, fearing that the coming day might bring more men in blue uniforms and new horrors. *

Thousands of householders in the fifty-mile swath Sherman was scorching through Georgia were going through similar experiences, though most of them were not lucky enough to have the "cotton burn over" and go out.

While Lincoln, fearful of the fate of Sherman's army, paced the long White House corridors in Washington, the anxiety of Davis in Richmond was even more acute. Hood on the south side of the roiling Tennessee River was in a state of impatient frustration. Autumnal rains fell in torrents as his men fashioned pontoon bridges to cross the river at Tuscumbia. It was essential to get to Nashville before the able but ponderous General George Thomas consolidated his defensive force. At last, on November 20, in a sea of mud, Hood's men, drenched to the skin, plunged northward.

With Hood's army far away on the Tennessee River bank there was little to oppose Sherman's destructive march except state militia and General Joe Wheeler's small band of cavalry. Wheeler's fierce energy could do little more than prevent foraging parties from spreading far from the two main bodies. He alone was able to keep Richmond and the commanding Southern generals informed of Sherman's movements and whereabouts. Georgia's militia functioned feebly, and their harassments did the Union troops no serious damage. The bluecoats did not have much fighting to do. Their vigor could be poured into tearing up railroads, twisting the heated rails about tree trunks, looting, and burning. They destroyed the bridges after they had passed over them.

Sherman's orders had been to cover fifteen miles a day; then, "to enforce a devastation more or less relentless," he slowed the pace to ten miles a day. Directly before him the only opposition as yet was women, children, very old men, and confused Negroes.

The President telegraphed Colonel William M. Browne, his aide-de-camp, at Augusta:

You will convey to Generals Comdg. Armies or Posts in Southern Georgia my instructions that every effort will be made by destroying bridges,

* Dolly Lunt's *A Woman's Wartime Journal*, published by the Century Company in 1918, reveals the frequent happy relations between Negroes and plantation owners, as well as graphic experiences with Sherman's bummers.

felling trees, planting sub-terra shells and otherwise, to obstruct the advance of the enemy. All supplies which are likely to fall into the enemy's
hands will be destroyed.

Communicate with General Hardee, Comdg. forces in Southern Georgia, or with General Beauregard if he has arrived, to learn whether any
force has been sent from the Army of Tennessee to co-operate in the defense of South-eastern Georgia.

If it is not too late, I wish that Forrest with his cavalry should be sent
to impede the march of Sherman's army, and prevent it from foraging on
the country.

At the President's suggestion, patriotic appeals by prominent
Georgians were made to the citizens to move all provisions from the
two paths of the invader and to obstruct the roads in front of the
enemy's advance. From Richmond Senator Benjamin H. Hill telegraphed his Georgia constituents:

Let every man fly to arms. Every citizen with his gun and every negro
with his spade and ax, can do the work of a soldier.

Remove your negroes, horses, cattle and provisions and burn what you
cannot carry. Assail the invader.

The Augusta *Constitutionalist* urged the country folk: "Let the
invader find the desolation he would leave *behind,* staring him in
the face."

But the farmers in Sherman's destructive path would not heed the
President's call for sacrifice. Each one thought he himself might
escape the ravishment and in effect hoarded his supplies for Sherman's 62,000 gobbling men who went through the agricultural
regions like a plague of locusts. The bluecoats feasted on beefsteak,
broiled chicken, roast turkey, honey, sweet potatoes, and peanuts.
Looters poked into lawns and orchards with ramrods seeking buried
silver. They sniffed out horses secreted in deep woods. They ripped
open feather beds for hidden treasure, ransacked trunks and ward-
robes, and snatched jewelry off women. They tortured frightened
Negroes to make them tell where treasure was hidden. Southern
men were shot down at the doors of their homes for no offense other
than that of attempting to defend their property against the in-
truders.

As Sherman marched through an undefended country towards
the sea, he was impeded only by time out for the plunder. He
ordered hundreds of captured horses shot to discourage laziness in
his footsore soldiers who were riding in the rear. When marching by
night was commanded, riders galloped ahead to set fire to zigzag-

ging rail fences along the roads so that the troops could be guided, avoid ruts, and be cheered by the parallel illuminations.

The Confederate President feared the effect of Sherman's brutal march on the spirit of his people. And Sherman's fierce warfare against civilians did become a terror to the South. His scheme for ending the war seemed to be the policy of devastating property rather than life—in other words, wrecking citizen morale, rather than killing soldiers. The Richmond *Whig* noted shrewdly: "Sherman is simply a great raider. . . . He is conducting a novel military experiment and is testing the problem whether or not a great country can be conquered by raids."

No one South or North yet knew Sherman's destination. President Lincoln, immeasurably worried, could learn of his movements only through Southern papers. In reply to persistent questioners, he would say in his inimitable rustic way, "I know the hole he went in at, but I don't know the hole he will come out at."

On November 30, President Davis wrote General Beauregard in Augusta:

It is probable that the enemy, if short of supplies, may move directly for the Coast. When that is made manifest you will be able to concentrate your forces upon the one object and I hope if you cannot defeat his attempt that you may reduce his army to such condition as to be ineffective for further operations. Until Hood reaches the country proper of the enemy, he can scarcely change the plans for Sherman's or Grant's campaigns. They would, I think, regard the occupation of Tennessee and Kentucky as of minor importance.

Beauregard, whose command had been extended to the Atlantic seacoast, had control of Taylor's forces in Mississippi, Dabney Maury's small army at Mobile, and Hardee's army of 12,000, first at Macon and then at Savannah, and all troops scattered between. But as T. Harry Williams has pointed out, Beauregard, "the great advocate of concentration," did not concentrate.

In the midst of his terrible uncertainties, Davis learned that General Joseph E. Johnston called at the War Department in Richmond on November 29 and was warmly greeted by his friends. That night War Clerk Jones wrote:

If Sherman's campaign should be a success, Johnston will be a hero; if the reverse, he will sink to rise no more. A sad condition, for one's greatness to depend upon the calamity of his country.

Johnston's appearance was extremely well-timed for his own advantage, for on November 29 Hood lost a wonderful opportunity to defeat half of the Union army at Spring Hill, Tennessee. And the next day he plunged impetuously into a frontal attack against the Federals at Franklin. In one of the most sanguinary battles of the war six Confederate general officers were killed on the field, including that brilliant fighter Patrick Cleburne, for whom Davis had the highest admiration.

Hood's hazardous campaign was really lost in this battle at the little riverside town. But now angered and still more full of fight, he moved on to Nashville to attack Thomas's mighty army.

Davis distrusted the presence of Johnston in Richmond; he was a kind of nucleus for Virginia malcontents and the congressional enemies of the Administration. And now, after an absence of a year and several months, Vice-President Stephens also turned up in the capital. In a recent meeting of the Georgia Legislature Governor Brown had made another wild attack on the President; and Stephens's brother, Linton, had introduced resolutions calling for a state convention to consider making a separate peace with the Lincoln Administration. A strong letter from Davis had quashed any such idea, and the Legislature had ended by giving the Confederate President its vote of confidence.

Alexander Stephens, who was regarded by many as Davis's most dangerous enemy, had come especially to prevent the renewal of the act suspending the writ of *habeas corpus*, which had expired on August 1. Stephens, as was his right, presided over the Senate when it considered the *habeas corpus* bill. The meeting was tense. Davis knew that the vote would be close. He feared that the important matter might be resolved, not on merit or necessity, but on political consideration and personal prejudices. The result was a tie. Stephens gleefully prepared an address condemning Davis, which he purposed to deliver in the Senate when he cast his deciding ballot against the amendment. Then at the last moment one Senator changed his vote in favor of renewal. Stephens could not make his speech. In fuming fury, the little man left the Senate Chamber after announcing his intention to resign his high office.

Davis had got his way again, but these victories over his antagonists were wearying, particularly when he needed every ounce of energy for military deliberations. In the midst of his deep concern about Hood in the West and Sherman's scorching march through Georgia's heartland, Davis had continually to contend with plaguing political foes. On the streets Congressman Foote blatantly advocated that Davis be thrown out of office. When he

mentioned such a scheme to Robert Tyler, the son of the late President told Foote that he ran a great risk of being "arrested, tried
by drumhead court martial, and shot—before night."

In early December Governor William Smith, who was friendly to
the President, recommended in his message to the Virginia Legislature the employment of Negro troops in the army, even if it resulted in emancipation. War Clerk Jones reported the reaction in
his diary:

The rich men are generally indignant at the President and Gov. Smith
for proposing to bring a portion of negroes into the army. They have not
yet awakened to a consciousness that there is danger of losing all, and
of their being made to fight against us. . . . They abuse the government
for its impressments and yet repose in fancied security, holding the President responsible for the defense of the country without sufficient men and
adequate means.

In early December the whole South, as well as Davis, awaited
with keen interest Lincoln's message to the United States Congress.
When it appeared in the newspapers, it was quite disappointing to
Southerners. But the tenor of the message delivered on December 6
was more or less what Davis had expected. Lincoln announced
without equivocation: "They can, at any moment, have peace simply by laying down their arms and submitting to the national
authority." And he added significantly, "I retract nothing heretofore said about slavery. . . . I shall not attempt to retract or modify the Emancipation Proclamation."

General Gorgas summed up his opinion in his diary:

Lincoln's message spawns nothing but subjugation. He says the door
of conciliation is not yet closed, and we may lay down our arms and return
to the fold. I hope six months hence a different story will be popular at
the North, especially should we catch Sherman. . . .

Southerners, both civil and military, were still half-expecting
Sherman to be surrounded and cut to pieces by Confederates con-
verging from somewhere. Gorgas hoped "the roads and distances
would destroy Sherman if the Military did not."

Gorgas could manufacture ordnance with conspicuous success,
but Davis could not create manpower. His great *want*, as usual,
was *fighting men*. And as Gorgas conceded, "even genius avails not
much without resources." And resources of every kind, animate and
inanimate, Lincoln had in superabundance.

As in the concurrent climactic days of Gettysburg and Vicksburg in July, 1863, Davis's apprehensive thoughts now turned to Savannah and then to Nashville, to the east and to the west, in dread and in hope.

Davis received what purported to be an encouraging letter from Beauregard written at Augusta on December 6. The General felt assured that Sherman could be prevented from capturing Augusta, Savannah, and Charleston, and would lose heavily before reaching the coast. He defended himself for not countermanding Hood's advance into Tennessee after Sherman began his march from Atlanta. He pointed out that Hood could not possibly arrive in time to be effective. If Hood was victorious at Nashville Sherman would have to retreat.

The President was not much reassured by Beauregard's vague hopes. There was one big difference, however, Davis noted, between Beauregard and Joseph Johnston. Occasionally the Louisianian, for no visible reason, would send in cheering messages about looked-for victories. On the other hand, Johnston's reports had almost invariably seemed soaked in gloom, larded with complaints of deficiencies and threats of withdrawal, and bristling with self-justification and veiled contempt.

Contrary to Beauregard's sanguine forecast, Sherman was now not many miles from the sea. Within a few days Davis got climactic bad news: on December 13 Sherman captured stout Fort McAllister that guarded the approaches to Savannah. The stronghold had apparently been taken by surprise and the small garrison had put up feeble resistance. Now Sherman was in contact with the Federal fleet and he could forget about supply lines. What would happen to Savannah and Hardee's 12,000 men? Davis could only wonder. Could the city be saved? Would Hardee lose his army?

In the West, despite the freezing December weather, Hood assailed the fortifications of Nashville. General George Thomas, who was on the verge of being cashiered by Washington for his slowness, was now in prime readiness to meet the Confederate attack. His well-fed, warmly clothed, splendidly equipped army outnumbered Hood's by more than two to one.* Davis was worried in the extreme. He knew that Hood embodied the popular ideal of the soldier: fearless, dashing, chivalrous, gallant. Up to this ill-fated Tennessee campaign he had proved a skillful leader against heavy odds. And Davis had seen for himself that Hood had "a kind of

* The official figures list the Union forces engaged, not counting reserves, as 49,-773; Confederates: 23,207 engaged.

magnetic mastery over troops which gave the common soldiers an irresistible resolution." But could he be victorious against almost insuperable odds?

The answer came soon. On the evening of the sixteenth, after two days of terrific fighting, Hood's men were in full flight. The Federals had captured more than 4,000 prisoners.

Davis had not approved this move of Hood's and he had warned him that he should defeat Sherman in detail before advancing into Tennessee. But he had not countermanded Hood's risky campaign. And as he refused to clamp down on the press, inimical editors now did their utmost to shatter confidence in the Davis Administration. While Joe Johnston could take satisfaction in Hood's debacle, the President was in no position to defend himself.

Davis, whose taut nerves had been strained to the limit, became alarmingly ill. Wild rumors ran through Richmond that he might die. Some Cabinet ministers and heads of bureaus became more polite to Vice-President Stephens, who had felt decidedly uncomfortable in Richmond because of the general coolness to him. And, according to Jones, "when it was feared that the President was *in extremis,* Mr. Hunter, fat as he is, flew about right briskly."

In his diary Jones declared that the day of December 19, 1864, (when the news of Hood's disaster had become widely known) was "the darkest and most dismal day upon earth except one—the day of the Crucifixion. . . . There was no light when the usual hour came round, and later the sun refused to shine; there was fog, afterwards rain."

Under that same date General Gorgas recorded: "This is a gloomy day here—one of the gloomiest in our struggle. . . . The plan of campaign which was terminated so disastrously is due probably to Beauregard, whose favorite plan has been always to enter Kentucky and carry the war to the Ohio." Down in Columbia, South Carolina, Mary Chesnut wrote that day, "The deep waters are closing over us and we are in this house, like outsiders at the time of the flood."

Though the somber day accorded with the gloom in Southern hearts, the President suddenly rallied. General Lee, "looking robust, if weather-worn," came to see him on the twentieth. The President was resting on a couch in the little morning room where the Davises received only their most intimate friends. Lee apologized to Mrs. Davis for walking on the white carpet in his splashed boots. The two West Point collegemates plunged straight into talk about military matters. The outlook for the Southern army was almost as dark as the day before had been. In Mrs. Davis's words, "The two old friends talked in a circle until both were worn out." Then, abruptly, the General commented on the silver saucepan on the hearth. "That is a comfortable and pretty little thing," he said. "What do you use it for?" It gave Varina great pleasure to heat until steaming hot the *café au lait* it contained and hand the drink to the General in a Sèvres cup. When she rose to ring for a servant to bring luncheon, Lee stopped her. "Do not call a servant," he said. "It is very cozy here just so." He praised the *café au lait,* but declared he could not eat anything. Gazing at the delicate cup appreciatively, he remarked with a twinkle in his eye, "My cups in camp are thicker, but this is thinner than the coffee."

With his remarkable resilience, the President was able to return to his office much sooner than anyone expected. But the official reports spread before him held little enough cheer, except that Hardee had escaped from Savannah with his 12,000 men by the last wagon road, just before Sherman cut it. The Mayor surrendered the city. On December 21 Sherman took formal possession. In a telegram, he presented the seaport to President Lincoln as "a Christmas present," "with 150 heavy guns and plenty of ammunition and also about 25,000 bales of cotton."

On Christmas Eve Grant gave Sherman his sanction for a punitive raid on South Carolina. Sherman wrote Halleck that night: "To be sure Jeff Davis has his people under pretty good discipline, but I think faith in him is much shaken in Georgia; and before we get through with her, South Carolina will not be quite so tempestuous." To Halleck Sherman indicated his dire purpose:

The whole army is burning with an insatiable desire to wreak vengeance upon South Carolina. I almost tremble at her fate, but feel she deserves all that seems in store for her. . . . I look upon Columbia as quite as bad as Charleston, and I doubt if we shall spare her public buildings as we did at Milledgeville.

When Davis left his office on Christmas Eve and stepped out into the air, he could hear the dull boom of Grant's guns down the river more distinctly. He merely raised his head a trifle higher.

"Alas for President Davis's Government!" Jones wrote. "It is now in a painful strait." The Confederacy's back was really pressing against the wall.

. . .

Christmas in Richmond passed quietly. At the Executive Mansion the meager celebration was centered as usual about the children and their friends. Few were the goodies, and the presents were mostly homemade. But the house rang with childish laughter. Mrs. Howell, the President's mother-in-law, had helped his children compose Christmas notes to their father attesting to their love, prompted by each child's individual inclination and expression. Along with the affectionate missives, Davis received numerous gifts from strangers, among them a useful pair of chamois riding gauntlets with an embroidered monogram from someone living close to Fort Monroe. Mrs. Davis took gifts and food to the Episcopal Orphanage. The President, with most of his family, walked on the snow-covered sidewalks to a Christmas service at Saint Paul's. Though Union pickets were hardly more than an hour's march from Richmond, Davis noted smiling faces on the streets and an occasional holiday drunk. That night at a neighbor's house there was a "starvation party" with an orchestra for dancing. Young officers from nearby camps rode into town and defiantly made merry.

But the news was all cheerless. Pitiable tales came to the President of hungry Confederate prisoners in bleak Midwest prisons being frozen to death "in cold blood," their blankets having been taken from them. Two of these young men who died of cold and privation—a Boykin and a Venable—were personally known to him and came of the South's foremost families. From Georgia ghastly stories of homeless, half-starved women and children wandering miserably in the woods reached his ear. The plight of Negroes who had followed in the wake of Sherman's army was peculiarly distressing. After local foodstuffs had been appropriated or wantonly destroyed, thousands of slaves had trudged behind Sherman's forces for rations, as they had done after Meridian, some cherishing an expectancy of entering a new land of promise with no work. When the black followers became an embarrassing hindrance, Sherman would rid himself of them by destroying the bridges after his soldiers had crossed a stream, leaving the trusting people bemused and desolate in some wilderness miles from their old homes.

When Jefferson Davis contemplated the ravages in Georgia, he could recall nothing—as he later wrote—since the Duke of Alva's "atrocious cruelties to the noncombatant population of the Low Countries in the sixteenth century" that equaled Sherman's wanton destruction. Sherman himself was inclined to agree with Davis's opinion, for he was to write his wife from Savannah (January 5, 1865): "They regard us just as the Romans did the Goths and the parallel is not unjust."*

In all the dark manifestations of sad news there was one note of moderate relief. On December 27 Davis was informed that Forrest had managed to hold off Federal pursuers until the remnants of Hood's army had reached the Tennessee River and recrossed it the day after Christmas. Though the magnitude of Hood's disaster was apparent, he still had over 20,000 men left when he reached Tupelo to fight again, and he wired Beauregard for reinforcements, while Beauregard called desperately on Lee to help him save Charleston. But Davis knew only too well that there were no reinforcements to be sent anywhere. From his dwindling forces Lee could spare no troops without risking the loss of Richmond.

On his last visit to the front, the President had seen that Lee was holding works forty miles in length, with less than a thousand soldiers to the mile. But the tattered Army of Northern Virginia continued to repulse Grant's attacks, and the South still regarded Lee as invincible. The President, who was continually in direct communication with his great captain, believed in his extraordinary powers, and, in turn, he kept Lee buoyed up by his remarkable faith.

The tag end of 1864 was far more grim for Davis and the Confederacy than the last days of 1863 had been. The resources of the Confederacy were steadily being reduced; her coasts were blockaded; her armies were diminishing; discouragement was invading the hearts of the people. A critical and constant problem was transportation. The railroads were falling apart. Crossties were rotted. Engines and cars had been patched to the limit. Federal raiders often tore up tracks only hours after they were relaid. Colonel Lucius Northrop as Commissary General was roundly and constantly abused for delays and failures caused by transportation breakdowns.

At the very end of 1864 Davis received a hopeless letter from Governor A. G. Magrath of South Carolina, who was now expecting Sherman to devastate his state too. "It is not unwillingness to oppose the enemy, but a chilling apprehension of the futility of doing so which affects the people."

Davis foresaw that such terror would be Sherman's best ally in

* *Home Letters of General Sherman*, edited by De Wolfe Howe, are extraordinarily frank and revealing and show that Sherman had no regrets.

the new campaign. His aim, as he himself declared afresh, was "to whip the rebels, to humble their pride, to follow them to their inmost recesses, and make them fear and dread us." Davis knew it might be impossible for a citizen who had endured the Union march through Georgia ever again to feel assurance of an ultimate Confederate victory.

Adding to the President's crushing load of burdens, serious political troubles were brewing in Richmond. He read in the *Examiner* a malicious editorial designed to influence the people to demand his removal. Some Congressmen were muttering that General Lee should be given full control of all military affairs. A scheme was contrived to force Davis to restore Joseph Johnston to his old command. On December 31 Jones wrote: "There is supposed to be a conspiracy on foot to transfer some of the powers of the Executive and the overthrow of the Constitution."

Since he was human, it was not unnatural for Jefferson Davis to suffer hours of complexity and depression. But his courage in the face of multiple calamities evidenced his title deed to eminence. He could stand unjust criticism heaped upon him, and he was prepared to contend with Congress for everything he believed in. His white-hot fusion of principle and patriotism could take him into the new year of 1865 with heart undaunted, however saddened.

CHAPTER XV

NEW CONFLICTS WITH CONGRESS

———◆———

NEW YEAR'S DAY of 1865, a Sunday, was bright with winter sun in Richmond. Two inches of snow had fallen during the night, and the jaded city glistened with freshness. Because he was once again afflicted by facial neuralgia, President Davis went to Saint Paul's wearing a woolen cap his wife had knitted for him. He heard Dr. Minnegerode preach a sermon attacking the faint-hearted and the croakers. In spite of himself, he could not help but be amused when the German-born rector, "feeling a surge of revolutionary belliger- ence," would bleat loudly, "Oh, Lamp of God, I come, I come."

At the beginning of 1865, there were many "faint-hearted" South- erners who believed that the exhausting struggle would end in some sort of reconstruction. Would the South, they wondered, be ruthlessly subjugated or allowed to return to the old Union with honor and rights? In any case, reconstruction would involve the humiliation of defeat, along with the likely loss of all slaves, who might suddenly be enfranchised. The vast majority of Southerners had been saying openly that if it were merely a question between slavery and independence, slavery must go. Some planters, sensing the wind's direction, began selling slaves who had once been worth $1,000 for $50 in gold. Others still hoped for recognition by France, if not England. Since Napoleon III had placed the Austrian prince, Maximilian, on the throne of Mexico in 1864, it seemed natural to expect recognition by France.

But in early January Davis received a revealing letter from Dud- ley Mann, the Confederate commissioner in Brussels, which had been written on December 17.

From the Emperor of the French, we never had nor have now, any- thing favorable to expect. His Imperial Majesty is deaf to international justice and blind to its usages when he conceives that Mexico may possibly be involved in danger. It is quite certain, as I had long ago supposed, that there is a cordial understanding between the Cabinets of the Tuileries and Washington in relation to Maximilian. I now understand, upon good authority, that the latter is to consider the Monroe Doctrine as utterly obsolete, and that for this concession the former will decline for an indefinite period to establish diplomatic relations with us.

Our friends everywhere enjoy your recent speeches and your message. They like your confident and earnest language. Our enemies, too, know that you speak the truth, the whole truth, and nothing but the truth.

For some time Davis had expected little from Napoleon III, though he knew that the Emperor was not opposed to slavery. And it was altogether likely that the astute Seward had made a secret deal with the Emperor, who was now too deeply involved to let anything ruffle his Mexican adventure. But the President agreed to a last-hope plan of Benjamin's to send a commissioner abroad to ascertain conclusively if general emancipation could win recognition from France and England. So the President secretly sent Duncan F. Kenner of Louisiana with power to cooperate with Slidell and Mason, and even to supersede them if necessary. He was confident that if recognition depended upon emancipation the Confederate States would yield.

Kenner, along with Mason, was received courteously by Prime Minister Palmerston. Kenner read aloud to him the end of his instructions from the President, which stated the Confederacy's willingness to emancipate the slaves if slavery was the cause of Britain's nonrecognition. Lord Palmerston, who had always been pro-Southern, said that slavery had little or no bearing on England's refusal to recognize the Confederacy. The obstacles were the same: failure of the South to achieve some decisive military success and fear of Seward's threat to take Canada.

But Kenner's report was not to reach Richmond until March. In the meantime Congress wrangled.

Congress had assembled in sullen mood in November and the coming of the New Year had not made the situation more agreeable for the Chief Executive. His old brother, Joseph Davis, a refugee in Tuscaloosa, Alabama, wrote him:

I feel much anxiety and sympathy for you. I hope the badgering of Congress does not worry you. . . . Much of it is from personal resentment. I saw that would be the case when in Richmond in '61.

Since the fall of Vicksburg in July, 1863, Jefferson Davis had had little time to write his numerous relatives. He had often hesitated to write at all because of the difficulties of transportation and the possibility of his letters being intercepted by the enemy. But on Sunday, January 8, with the departure of his nephew-in-law, Colonel Keary, for Mississippi, he took the occasion to write a long letter from the heart to his nephew, Hugh P. Davis, who lived in Konnochetto.* The President had been quite anxious, he wrote, about the exchange of Hugh's son, a prisoner of war, and had done all in his power to facilitate it. But the enemy Government made it very difficult to secure the release of a Confederate. "We want all of our own soldiers," Davis wrote, "and we do not want to guard and feed Yankee prisoners."

Then he unburdened himself in a frank résumé of some of his disappointments and troubles. The letter, which was intended only for private eyes, is clarifying in regard to Davis's attitude towards certain controversial subjects.

The movement of the contending armies in Ga. has resulted very disadvantageously to us. I had hoped Genl Hood would have compelled Sherman to go North from Atlanta and perhaps to beat him by selecting a strong position in the mountains between Atlanta and Chattanooga, and such were the expectations of Genl Hood when I parted from him on the Chattahoochee. . . .

After Sherman started to the South East Genl Beauregard thought it impossible to overtake him but that his plans might be frustrated by a rapid advance into Tenn. The latter part of the opinion proved erroneous, the first part may have been right. Left with only cavalry, reserves, and militia to oppose Sherman's march, I directed the roads to be obstructed, bridges destroyed and all supplies near to his line of march to be removed or burned. His horses were poor and not sufficiently numerous to draw provisions and ammunition for his march. The faithful execution of those orders would have defeated his project.

If cattle and hogs had been driven off and foodstuffs that could not be carried away had been burned, as the President directed, Sherman, cut off from his communications, would have been ruined, as the Washington Government feared he was. "When," deplored Davis, "will our people learn to expect nothing from Yankee forbearance?"

* This holograph letter to Hugh Davis, which has never been published before, was shown the author by Jefferson Davis's great-niece, Mrs. Mary Lucy O'Kelley of Pass Christian.

Now Sherman is on the Atlantic Coast, can be readily supplied and reinforced for future operations. The malcontents seizing on the restlessness consequent upon long and severe pressure have created a feeling hostile to the execution of the rigorous laws which were necessary to raise and feed our armies, then magnifying every reverse and prophesying ruin, they had produced public depression and sown the seeds of disintegration.

He touched on his trials with Congress.

Now when we require the brains and the heart of the country in the legislative halls of the Confederacy and of the States, all must have realized how much it is otherwise. Our people have fought so as to command the admiration of mankind, they have nobly met the sacrifices of their position, never before was there so little despotism under such severe pressure. If there be a growing spirit of opposition to continued effort it is, I think, to be attributed to the bad conduct of those whose official position made it their duty to cultivate confidence and animate patriotism.

Even as the President was writing to Hugh, unexpected trouble was brewing in Congress.

In the first month of 1865 more fighting broke out among Confederate Congressmen than on the battlefields, where foul weather hampered activities. And certain Senators, such as Wigfall, automatically fought with their mouths and their pens anything the President advocated. Friends in the army tried to influence the pugnacious Texan to be reasonable. "I wish, my dear Wigfall," wrote General Wade Hampton, "that you would forget the differences of the past and try to re-establish the intimate relations that once existed between Mr. Davis and yourself. You can aid him greatly and you can serve the country by giving him counsel."

But Wigfall was staunchly in league with certain pro-Johnston Virginians who hoped to oust Davis from power.

In mid-January matters came to a little crisis between Davis and Congress. Virginia's Thomas S. Bocock, Speaker of the House, wrote the President that his State desired a complete change in the Cabinet, and he boldly added that if Davis did not make the change Bocock feared the House would pass a vote of no confidence in his Administration. After weeks in session, the Confederate Congress could apparently think up nothing better towards winning the war than for the President to change his Cabinet. It recommended that all but Trenholm, the new Secretary of the Treasury, should be dismissed. Secretary of War Seddon, stung by the insult from fellow Virginians, promptly handed in his resignation.

Davis begged him to withdraw it. He said he would not be dictated to by Congress; he would not abrogate his constitutional preroga- tives. And he was determined not to reinstate Joseph Johnston, which the Virginia delegation insisted on. "The clamor for General Johnston," Jones wrote, "seems to be the result of a *political* com- bination."

But Davis could not persuade the offended Seddon to keep his Cabinet post. So after a fortnight he chose General John C. Breck- inridge, one-time Vice-President of the United States, to succeed him. The selection, when announced, proved to be extremely popu- lar.

If the President would not oust his experienced Cabinet, his congressional critics had another scheme to embarrass him. Vir- ginia's William C. Rives, Chairman of the Committee on Foreign Affairs, was sent to General Lee to ascertain if he would assume sole authority in the Confederacy, proclaim martial law, and "guide the country through its present crisis." The astounded Lee categorically declined such a dangerous commission, which seemed to amount to a counterrevolution. He said he agreed with Davis's loyal friends in Congress that "if the President could not save the country, no one could." However, for the sake of the military's morale, Lee was willing, with Davis's approval, to take on the added burden of General-in-Chief of all the Armies.

The drastic *Examiner* on January 17 went so far as to suggest a convention to abolish the Constitution and remove the President. That same day Davis received a resolution from the General As- sembly of Virginia respectfully requesting him to put Lee in com- mand of all the Armies of the Confederate States. Such a move, it claimed, would promote the efficiency, operate to reanimate the spirit of the soldiers, and "inspire increased confidence in the final success of our cause."

The document was most tactfully worded, and expressed mani- fest confidence in Davis's "patriotic devotion to the welfare of the country." It also "dedicated the entire resources of the Common- wealth to the common cause" to strengthen Davis's hand and "to give success to the struggle of liberty and independence."

Despite the courteous tone and cordial expressions of faith, the intention of curtailing the Presidential powers was patent. At first Davis may have felt hurt. His wife was indignant. Davis, who could not possibly have any strained relations with his foremost General, handled the matter adroitly. To Lee he wrote:

It has been reported to me that you had changed your opinion in regard to the extension of your command, while retaining command of the Army of N. Virginia.

I therefore renew to you the proposition that you should exercise command over the Southern Atlantic States, together with Virginia and North Carolina, and now offer the larger sphere of all the forces east of the Mississippi River, or, if you think it practicable, that you should resume your former position of Commander of all the Armies of the Confederacy, with the addition of the immediate command of the Army of Northern Virginia.

He then carefully prepared a joint letter addressed to the President of the Virginia Senate and the Speaker of the House of Delegates. After thanking the General Assembly for its generous appreciation of faith in him, he spoke of the "uncalculating, unhesitating spirit" with which Virginia had consecrated the blood of her sons and natural resources to "the sacred cause of independence."

The opinion expressed by the General Assembly in regard to General R. E. Lee has my full concurrence. Virginia cannot have a higher regard for him or greater confidence in his character and ability than is entertained by me. When General Lee took command of the Army of Northern Virginia, he was in command of all the armies of the Confederate States by my order of assignment. He continued in this general command as well as in the immediate command of the Army of Northern Virginia, as long as I could resist his opinion that it was necessary for him to be relieved from one of these two duties. . . .

In conclusion, I assure the General Assembly that whenever it shall be found practicable by General Lee to assume command of all the Armies of the Confederate States, without withdrawing from the direct command of the Army of Northern Virginia, I will deem it promotive of the public interests to place him in such command, and will be happy to know that by so doing, I am responding to their expressed desire.

The next day, January 19, Congress passed a bill creating a Commander-in-Chief apart from the President. Davis signed it on January 26 and named Lee to the position. Lee wrote the President:

I know I am indebted entirely to your indulgence and kind consideration for this honorable position. . . . If I can relieve you from a portion of the constant labor and anxiety which presses upon you . . . I shall be more than compensated for any present burdens. . . .

Then, in what amounted to an implied rebuke to the Davis enemies, Lee wrote the Confederate Congress, "I am indebted alone to the kindness of His Excellency, the President, for my nomination to this high and arduous office." Davis's opponents, who had desired to deprive him of military power, were nonplused. They realized that Lee was not going to do anything without the President's sanction.

On February 6, the day that Breckinridge was sworn in as Secretary of War, Lee officially became Commander-in-Chief. On Lee's formal acceptance, Davis wrote him:

I have not failed to appreciate the burden already imposed on you as too heavy to enable an ordinary man to bear an additional weight. Your patriotic devotion I knew would prompt you to attempt anything which was possible, if it promised to be beneficial to the country.

The honor designed to be bestowed has been so fully won, that the fact of conferring it can add nothing to your fame.

Joseph Johnston's friends in the Senate immediately pushed through a request to Lee to assign Johnston to command the Army of Tennessee. Lee replied to their communication from "hd. Qrs. Armies C. States." In it he made clear his attitude towards President Davis's ultimate authority.

I entertain a high opinion of Gen Johnston's capacity but think a continued change of commanders is very injurious to any troops, and tends greatly to their disorganization. At this time as far as I understand the condition of affairs, an engagement with the enemy may be expected any day, and a change now would be particularly hazardous. Genl Beauregard is well known to the citizens of S. Ca., as well as to the troops of the Army of Tennessee, and I would recommend that it be certainly ascertained that a change was necessary, before it was made.

I do not consider that my appt. as Gen in chief of the Armies of the C. States, confers the right which you assume belongs to it, nor is it proper that it should.

On the authority of the President, General Lee, on February 11, proclaimed an amnesty for all soldiers absent without leave who would report for duty within twenty days. He appealed to their patriotism and set before them the choice between war and abject submission.

To such a proposal, brave men, with arms in their hands, can have but one answer. They cannot barter manhood for peace, nor the right of self-government for life or property.

On the same day Lee declared in a general order: "Our resources, fitly and vigorously employed, are ample." A Richmond paper carried a follow-up editorial that pleased Davis immeasurably.

Material exhaustion is not yet felt by the mass of the nation. . . . The extent of their territory is so great that its real occupation by the armed forces of two or three such nations as that we are fighting is inconceivable. The enemy is perfectly aware of this fact, and does not base his hope of subjugation on the practical application of main strength, but upon submission of the will, and consequent inability to contend to the last extremity, which he expects to see at some time spread over the land. . . . The Southern States are in no danger so long as the spirit of the people is what it has hitherto been.

CHAPTER XVI

FRUITLESS PEACE CONFERENCE

WITH STRONG MISGIVINGS, but in a state of composure, President Davis agreed early in January, 1865, to receive Francis C. Blair, Sr., for an interview on the subject of peace. The Davises and the Blair family had once been friends; the Blairs had been extremely kind to them in Maine in 1858, and Mrs. Davis had rented their Maryland house for a summer. Undoubtedly Davis did not know that Blair had been one of the chief begetters of the fratricidal war because he had admonished Lincoln to launch the "relief" ships for Sumter as the only way out of an insoluble political dilemma. But Davis was fully aware that the newspaper magnate was a wily politician, perhaps as devious as his one-time admiring friend Seward. The President, as eager for an honorable peace as anyone in the Confederacy, knew that if he did not receive Blair he would be accused by Judge Campbell and others of not wishing to make peace. And Varina urged him to let Blair come.

Blair arrived in Richmond on January 12, 1865. Colonel Ould conducted him to the Spotswood Hotel, where he stayed unregistered. Davis received him at his home that night. It was rumored that Mrs. Davis embraced him warmly. Blair confessed he had arrived without credentials or instructions; he emphasized that his visit, while made with President Lincoln's permission, was entirely unofficial. "My views are therefore to be regarded as merely my own," he said, "and perhaps merely the dreams of an old man."

With Davis's indulgence he read aloud a letter he had drafted. His main proposition was the cessation of hostilities and the union of the military forces of the North and the South for the common purpose of driving the French out of Mexico. Blair affirmed that Mr. Lincoln did not sympathize with the Northern Radicals who sought the devastation of the Southern States. He expressed his own earnest desire of stopping the further effusion of blood, and reminded Davis that every drop of his own blood was Southern. The Marylander also reiterated his belief in the doctrine of State sovereignty. ,

The chief difficulty of making a secret treaty with the United States to terminate the war, he said, was that of existing arrangements between the Confederate States and European powers. Unwisely, perhaps, the forthright Davis told him that now there was no such complication, and that he desired to keep State policy and all institutions free from foreign control. Later others wondered if that particular information was what Blair had come to ascertain: that the Confederacy had no secret treaty with France or any other foreign power.

The conference ended with Davis agreeing to enter upon negotiations with Lincoln to end the war, if the latter would receive Confederate commissioners. He drafted a letter for Blair to show to the President of the United States.

I have no disposition to find obstacles in forms, and am willing now, as heretofore, to enter into negotiations for the restoration of peace; and am ready to send a commission whenever I have reason to suppose it will be received, or to receive a commission, if the United States government shall choose to send one. Notwithstanding the rejection of our former offers, I would, if you could promise that a commission, minister, or other agent would be received, appoint one immediately, and renew the effort to enter into a conference with a view to secure the peace to the two Countries.

The news of Blair's visit with the President leaked out and aroused disfavor. Davis's friend Judge Lyons regarded Blair as nothing more than a clever spy. The *Examiner* was highly suspicious and asked in an editorial: "What right had Mr. Davis to allow the whispering old humbug to come here, spreading rumors and insinuating false suggestions."

Some days later, however, Blair returned to Richmond with a letter from President Lincoln dated January 18.

You have shown me Mr. Davis's letter to you of the 12th inst. You may say to him that I have constantly been, am now, and shall continue ready to receive any agent whom he or any other influential person now resisting the national authority may informally send to me with the view of securing peace to the people of our common country.

Davis read Lincoln's letter twice over in Blair's presence. He questioned him on the meaning of the words "our common country." Blair merely replied that it related to Davis's phrase about "the two countries." Davis saw that Lincoln was determined not to recognize the independence of the Confederate States. He knew that he himself as Chief Executive elected by the people had no authority to agree to reunion as long as there were Southern men under arms. The phraseology suggested that nothing but submission or a decisive victory would bring peace.

But he decided to give those opponents of his, such as his Vice-President, who so loudly clamored for negotiations, an opportunity to test their mettle with President Lincoln. He would have no peace himself unless an effort to treat was made. So, in the words of Professor Dodd, "Davis took advantage of this state of things to bring the machinations of Stephens and his friends to an end."

He summoned the Vice-President to ask his opinion. He told him all the facts of Blair's conversations. When he had finished, Stephens said he thought the program suggested by Blair should be acceded to, "at least so far as to obtain if possible a conference upon the subject." Davis then appointed Stephens to head a commission of three. The surprised little man wriggled to get out of the position; he suggested several other persons. But Davis overruled all his objections. He was determined that the chief agitator urging negotiations should head the commission.

As his fellow commissioners, Davis shrewdly chose two other prominent advocates of peace negotiations, R. M. T. Hunter, head of the Senate, and Assistant Secretary of War John A. Campbell, who had felt since November that the Confederacy was doomed.

The three commissioners were summoned by the President on January 25. The following document was read to them:

In conformity with the letter of Mr. Lincoln, of which the foregoing is a copy, you are requested to proceed to Washington City for an informal conference with him upon the issues involved in the existing war, and for the purpose of securing peace to the two countries.

On Sunday morning, January 29, the commissioners left, presumably for Washington.

Although an attempt had been made to observe the greatest secrecy, rumors had spread beyond Richmond and into the camps that peace was to be made. The news was received with distaste.

One soldier, C. C. Baugham, wrote from Camp Walker: "We have no idea of submitting after having endured all these hardships. . . . If we are true to ourselves, we will gain our independence despite present gloomy prospects." General Gorgas noted in his diary: "Old Blair has returned to this city from Washington and is again gone. Are we really to make terms with the enemy before we are half beaten? . . . Would that these birds of ill omen could be kept outside our limits. They do us no good."

Four days later Davis learned that his commissioners were still held up at City Point within the Union lines. Was Lincoln going to cancel the conference? Did he believe that the Confederacy was about to go under?

On both visits Blair had used well his shrewd old eyes and ears. He had noted the general shabbiness and the flagrant scarcities. He had seen citizens walking the streets with their heads down. Davis was informed that on the night of Blair's second visit to Richmond several public men whom he had known in Washington gathered about him. Among them was Judge Campbell, who, although a most able Assistant Secretary of War, had always been regarded by some Southern patriots as a spy in high position. Several of Blair's callers were inveterate Davis enemies. Blair learned that the Confederate Congress was infected by a Joseph Johnston cabal bent on undermining Davis's influence and that both houses of Congress were dangerously divided within themselves. On finding these gentlemen sunk in gloom, Blair had dilated on the fearful ruination that might be inflicted on the South if peace were not made soon. Doubtless Blair reported to Lincoln all the dark signs of depletion he had discovered. And between the two visits of Blair, the Confederacy had received a strategically damaging blow: Fort Fisher, which protected the all-important port of Wilmington, had fallen on January 17. President Lincoln would most likely stiffen his terms.

Notes passed back and forth between Washington and the Confederate commissioners over the phrases "two countries" and "one common country." Finally, on Thursday, Davis learned that the commissioners had been taken down the river to Hampton Roads, where in early July of 1863 on a previous peace mission Stephens had sweltered on shipboard for some days, and then, after the Confederate defeats at Gettysburg and Vicksburg, had been handed an insulting note and sent packing.

On Friday morning, February 3, the commissioners were finally conducted aboard the steamer *River Queen,* where President Lincoln and Secretary of State Seward awaited them. The meeting began agreeably. As the ninety-pound Stephens, who suffered keenly from cold, divested himself of a voluminous woolly greatcoat and began unwinding shawls, Lincoln looked on with quizzical amazement. Finally he declared pleasantly that he had never seen "so small a nubbin come out of so much shucks," and greeted the Confederate Vice-President with outstretched hand. The two had not met since 1848, during Lincoln's one term in Congress. When Stephens plunged into a lengthy discussion of the Monroe Doctrine and the desirability of the two countries joining forces to drive the French from Mexico, Lincoln impatiently declared that Blair had no authority from him to broach the topic of Mexico. He said that it must be understood that no terms short of laying down arms and reconstruction were to be considered. Through repetition Lincoln emphasized that nothing but submission would be tolerated, though both he and Seward carefully used the term "restoration of the national authority."

Urging an armistice, Campbell brought up the fact that Charles I had treated with revolutionaries when they were still armed against the crown. Unimpressed, Lincoln said he did not profess to be posted on history, but he did recollect that in the end Charles lost his head. Questioned about possible punishment for the leaders, Lincoln declared that they must accept "the consequences of the application of the law," but that he himself "was disposed to treat them liberally." The former Supreme Court Justice drew himself up and remarked that he had never regarded his neck as in danger. Lincoln replied sharply that there were many oak trees where the Judge lived and that the limbs afforded many convenient points from which a body might dangle.

In regard to slavery, Lincoln said that question would be decided by the courts. He himself would not have interfered with the institution except for the preservation of the Union. The House of Representatives had that week voted to outlaw slavery completely by a thirteenth amendment to the Constitution. Perhaps, as a sop to Hunter, Lincoln did say that, for himself, he would be willing to consider compensation to slaveholders. Seward interjected that the North had already spent too much to abrogate slavery. Lincoln countered that if it was wrong in the South to hold slaves, it was wrong in the North to carry on the slave trade and sell Negroes to the South and hold on to the money thus procured. But Lincoln admitted that he was not authorized to make a proposition for compensation, and he made no claim that his Congress would accept such a proposition.

In the end President Lincoln conclusively brushed aside all talk of an armistice, which the commissioners still urged. He could not be diverted from his insistence that Union was a *sine qua non* and that the disbandment of Southern armies was indispensable to peace. The conference, which lasted for three hours, broke up without any agreement.

Late Saturday night, February 4, Davis, who had not been sanguine of results, learned that his peace commissioners had reached Richmond at eight o'clock that evening. They were depressed and chagrined at the total failure of their mission. The next day Robert Kean, Campbell's admiring assistant and Head of the Bureau of War, wrote perceptively in his secret diary: "This ends this peace *fiasco* which must satisfy the most skeptical that we have nothing whatever to hope or expect short of the exaction of all the rights of conquest, whether we are overrun by force, or submit."

President Davis requested a full report in writing to present to Congress and the people. Stephens tried hard to worm out of making a formal report; he wanted the whole proceeding to be forgotten as quickly as possible. But Davis sternly demanded a statement. The commissioners conferred. Because Seward had craftily proposed that the conference should be confidential, they claimed they felt bound not to include in a written document the varied subjects discussed. So they prepared a brief report couched in roundabout, obscure language stating that "the message of President Lincoln to the Congress of the United States in December last, explains clearly and distinctly his sentiments as to the terms, conditions, and methods by which peace can be secured to the people."

When Davis received this unsatisfactory letter on Sunday, the fifth, he promptly sent for Judge Campbell, who told him everything that had occurred. As Campbell recalled Lincoln's asperity in his allusion to oak-tree limbs, Davis saw that the Judge had been somewhat shaken as well as surprised. But when he asked Campbell to add to the report the simple statement that Lincoln and Seward demanded submission, to Davis's amazement, Campbell refused. Was he being heedful of his neck? In his memorandum he had written frankly: "In conclusion, Mr. Hunter summed up what seemed to be the result of the interview: there could be no arrangement by treaty between the Confederate States and the United

States, or any agreements between them; there was left nothing for them but unconditional surrender."

That night Davis summoned Stephens and Hunter. They, too, refused to change the fuzzy wording of their document. So Davis appended a concise note for Congress, under his own name:

The enemy refused to enter into negotiations with the Confederate States or to give our people any other terms than unconditional submission to their rule.

It had all turned out much as the President had expected, only more conclusively. The finality was yet disappointing and disturbing. But Stephens's mouth was stopped. Hunter had no longer any hope of becoming President of the Confederacy. Judge Campbell might ruminate in silence on Lincoln's macabre remark about oak trees. Davis had been completely justified in his opinion of Lincoln's unyielding attitude. In later years he was to be surprised and saddened when, to curry favor for themselves, each of the three commissioners, separately, was to blame Davis for blocking the peace negotiations by his obstinacy.

The Hampton Roads Conference with its ultimatum of unconditional submission stirred the South to fierce resentment and fresh resolution. The President could take advantage of the failure of Stephens's mission to urge the Confederates to a final desperate effort to save the South from the vindictive plans of the Radical Republicans, which included the confiscation of the whites' property and the enfranchisement of illiterate blacks.

On Monday War Clerk Jones remarked "a more cheerful aspect on the people's countenances in the streets." He wrote:

All hope of peace with independence is extinct and valor alone is relied upon now for our salvation. Everyone thinks the Confederacy will at once gather up its material strength and strike such blows as will astonish the world.

Having sent his unequivocal note to Congress, that night Davis was inspired to make a direct appeal to the people of Richmond. At Metropolitan Hall on Franklin Street a public meeting was under way, which Governor Smith had called so that Virginia could adopt resolutions concerning the result of the conference. Without stopping to put on his best clothes, the President left his house. Unannounced, he appeared at the door of the hall. The surprised audience stirred with excitement as the thin, erect figure of their President in a worn gray suit walked down the aisle to the platform, where he was enthusiastically greeted by the Governor and led to the speaker's lectern.

As Jefferson Davis looked out over the assembly that jammed the hall, tumultuous cheers rang out. "A smile of strange sweetness came to his lips as if the welcome assured him that, decried as he was by the newspapers and pursued by the clamor of politicians, he still had a place in the hearts of his countrymen."

His pale, poetic, and definitely haggard face was illuminated as if by a lightning flash. At that moment he stood as the very symbol of the South, of all that was brave, noble, and good in the Confederacy. When the rapturous applause finally died down, he began to speak in his low voice with its peculiar sweetness of tone, which carried to the farthest corners of the auditorium. From his first utterance he had "an entrancing mastery of his audience," even of his personal enemies scattered here and there. Among those in the audience was one of the President's most persistent antagonists, Edward A. Pollard, assistant editor of the Richmond *Examiner*. Pollard had recently been released from a Federal prison; he had been captured some months earlier while attempting to go to England after the conscript law was changed so as to call up young *assistant* editors for military service. A brilliant writer, but notorious for his unscrupulous fabrications, Pollard was to do Davis more harm historically in postwar publications than any other single civilian.* Yet on this night Pollard was profoundly stirred by the man he had been hounding for three years. He wrote:

We have heretofore spoken of the power of Mr. Davis as an orator. On this occasion . . . the author does not recollect ever to have been so much moved by the power of words spoken for the same space of time.

Pollard recalled in wonder the "shifting lights on the feeble, stricken face," of "the beautiful and choice words that dropped so easily from his lips."

For more than an hour he held the audience by an appeal of surpassing eloquence. The speech was extempore, for he was frequently interrupted, and always spoke appropriately and at length to the subject suggested by the exclamations of the audience. . . . Mr. Davis frequently paused in his delivery; his broken health admonished him that he was attempting too much; but frequent cries of "go on" impelled him to speak at a length

* The direct quotations in this section are from Edward A. Pollard. Though in 1869 Pollard wrote a disparaging so-called *Life of Jefferson Davis,* Davis stated in Memphis in 1870 that he had "never met the creature" and knew of him only as "a malignant who managed to escape conscription."

which he had not at first proposed. . . . He spoke with an even, tuneful flow of words, spare of gestures, his dilated form and a voice the lowest notes of which were distinctly audible, and which anon rose as a sound of a trumpet, were yet sufficient to convey the strongest emotions, and to lift the hearts of his hearers to the level of his grand discourse.

The newspaperman could only summarize the tenor of Davis's speech as "imperious, unconquerable defiance to the enemy."

In commemorating the heroism and devotion of the private soldier, Davis drew a picture of their sufferings, and "in withering tones he cursed the speculators who had traded and profited in their distress." At the close he emphasized his own attitude with a vivid illustration drawn from history. He spoke with scorn of Louis Kossuth, the Hungarian revolutionary patriot, who had been highly honored in Washington. For Kossuth, Davis said, had been so weak as to abandon the cause of liberty when he still had "thirty thousand men in the field."

Davis spoke pointedly of the "disgrace of surrender." "What shall we say," the Southern leader demanded, "of the disgrace beneath which *we* should be buried if we surrender with an army in the field more numerous than that with which Napoleon achieved the glory of France, an army standing among its homesteads?"

Despite the increasingly crushing odds against the South in February of 1865, Davis's resolution was stronger than ever. Adversities had not made a nick in his iron will. He refused to admit that the terrible four years of privation, blood, and death had diminished the spirit of the South. Upborne by their leader's eloquence, his hearers felt themselves grow taller, and believed—for an hour at least—that the South would never bend a corrigible neck to its mighty foe.

The President left the hall with the elation of his hearers throbbing in his consciousness. But his unscheduled speech had been heard only by a few hundred. Pollard himself deplored the fact that the regular reporters were not present "to preserve a speech which should have been historical." If Pollard, Davis's malevolent detractor, could be so moved by his eloquence, faint-hearted friends in distant states would have been tremendously stimulated. Skulkers and deserters might have returned to service to drive the invaders back to their boundaries.

A few days after the President's triumphant address, many demonstrations with parades and speech-making were planned. Rallies were scheduled in the theater, in various halls, and in the African

Church, which white politicians were accustomed to request for meetings because of its vast seating capacity. Secretary of State Benjamin and R. M. T. Hunter were designated to speak at the African Church. Davis had invited his Vice-President to participate in the demonstration, but the chastened Stephens was too disheartened now to raise his voice, and he did not want to put on record anything Federal authorities might ultimately use against him. But he attended the meeting in the colored church. And so did the President. They both heard the shifting Hunter frankly tell the excited audience that President Lincoln had "turned from propositions of peace with cold insolence." "I will not attempt," the Senate's head declared with a shudder, "to draw a picture of subjugation. It would require a pencil dipped in blood to paint its doom."

Davis saw his Secretary of State turn on his most radiant manner. "Hope beams in every countenance," Benjamin declared, smiling encouragingly on the audience. "We know in our hearts that this people must conquer its freedom or die."

Then, undoubtedly with the President's approval, Benjamin plunged into the controversial subject of arming slaves. He averred that the white fighting men were exhausted and that the black men must recruit the army, and *at once*. He said that General Lee had told him he must abandon Richmond if not soon reinforced, and that the Negroes would answer. Since Congress had no authority to command them, the *States* must send them. He called on Virginia to set the example and prepare 20,000 Negroes for the trenches in twenty days.

At the last moment, when called upon, the President himself spoke briefly and impromptu. In stirring tones he predicted Confederate triumph within twelve months. Against his will Alexander Stephens was impressed. He wrote that he found Davis's speech "bold, undaunted, confident." Though he could "not concur in Davis's general view of policy," he admired "the heroism of the sentiments expressed."

After the demonstrations, when the President and Vice-President met, Davis asked Stephens what he intended to do now. "To go home," he answered wearily, "and stay home." Then after a pause he added, "And say nothing." He turned away, in the words of Von Abele, "looking like a walking dead man." The two would not meet again until they were bound for Federal prisons.

After all, the Hampton Roads meeting had not been entirely futile. It had strengthened Davis's hand by silencing Stephens and certain other malcontents, and by dispelling illusions of an easy negotiated peace. It aroused the nation to a high pitch of patriotism, if only for a few brief weeks. Even the contentious Congress was stirred to joint resolution, and released a patriotic address to the people. "Thanks be to God," it declared, "the haughty insolence of our enemies which they hoped would intimidate and break the spirit of our people is having the very contrary effect."

The Conference had in no sense altered the President's own attitude. His thought had ever been to fight to the finish, for he did not believe terms could be obtained. He would feel guilty of betrayal if, with armies in the field, he submitted to the enemy's demands. But now, as Grant made ready for his spring campaign, Davis more than ever was desperately in need of fighting men.

CHAPTER XVII

SHERMAN BURNS AGAIN AND CONGRESS EATS PEANUTS

————◄◦►————

AFTER SHERMAN'S FLAMING raid through Georgia, his for-bearance in the seaport of Savannah surprised almost everyone. Davis learned that he even permitted the Episcopal ministers to continue to pray for the Confederate President. "Jeff Davis," he said, "needs the prayers." Sherman's moderation at Savannah was looked upon by the Richmond *Examiner* (January 7, 1865) as "a dangerous bait to deaden the spirit of resistance in other places." And the Richmond *Dispatch* likened his restraint to "the repose of a tiger." "Let him taste blood once more, and he will be as brutal as ever."

As it was to turn out, the papers judged rightly. After halting in Savannah for more than three weeks, Sherman prepared for a puni-tive invasion of South Carolina, the state that had set off seces-sion. Colonel H. J. Kilpatrick saw that his men's saddlebags were well supplied with matches, if nothing else.

Sherman had begun moving from Savannah on January 19, with some 6,000 prisoners in the vanguard, almost half of them Negroes, ready with sharpened axes to lay corduroy roads through swamps where it seemed impossible that a road could be made. Davis had learned that Sherman, who before the war had been employed in the South, used blacks only for menial jobs, and that he had con-sistently refused to add Negro regiments to his forces.

To the astonishment of Davis, General Hardee, the Confederate engineers, and the Lincoln Government, Sherman had boldly plunged into the treacherous swamps just northwest of Savannah. No one but Sherman himself knew his destination. Charleston seemed the most likely objective.

In a fortnight Sherman had emerged triumphant from the bogs.

His "bummers" began marauding through lower South Carolina committing every sort of outrage, leaving utter desolation and misery in their wake. They even set fire to the resinous sap in the cavities of turpentine pines and created vast square miles of holocaust.

On February 5 the President received a telegram from Beauregard, who feared he would be impelled to give up Charleston. In considerable perturbation, Davis replied calmly:

You can better judge of the necessity of evacuating Charleston than I can. Such full preparations had been made that I had hoped for other and better results; and the disappointment is to me extremely bitter. The reinforcements calculated on from Reserves and Militia of Georgia and So. Car., together with the troops ordered from Mississippi must have fallen short of estimate. What can be done with the Naval Squadron, the Torpedo boats and the very valuable heavy guns at Charleston? Do not allow cotton stored there to become prize of the enemy as was the case at Savannah.

Then, as was generally his custom in a distressing situation, he added a note of cheer. "From reverses however sad, if you are sustained by unity and determination among the people we can look hopefully forward."

But it was soon apparent to Davis that Sherman was not headed for Charleston, but for Columbia, the state capital.

After being annoyingly contentious for two years, North Carolina's Governor, Zebulon Vance, suddenly became Davis's ally. Thoroughly alarmed at Sherman's demoralizing march northward, Vance made a patriotic appeal to the South. He railed against the thousands upon thousands of Confederate soldiers absent without leave, "lurking in the woods and swamps." He pointed out how relatively little Confederate territory was actually in the hands of the Federals—in Georgia, for instance, there was now only Savannah. "Thank God," he proclaimed, "the Confederacy does not consist in brick and mortar or particular spots of ground, however valuable they may be in a military point of view. Our nationality consists in our people. Liberty dwells in the hearts of her votaries. . . ."

As Davis read Vance's eloquent appeal with some surprise, he wished the Governor had expressed these high sentiments earlier instead of haggling and obstructing his Administration. Only now, at a dangerously late hour, Davis noted regretfully, was the South waking up to the possibility of utter ruin.

The day after Vance's patriotic proclamation, Hardee, on Beauregard's orders, prepared to abandon Charleston and march his troops to a rendezvous north of Columbia. Since Sherman had severed the railroad communications between the two cities, Charleston was completely cut off.

On February 18, the fourth anniversary of his inauguration in Montgomery, Davis got the news that Sherman had taken Columbia the day before without a fight. Though the Mayor had surrendered the capital to preserve it from destruction, most of the city had been burned, with tremendous loss of public property, including all the State buildings, factories, 1,300 dwellings, and even the Ursuline Convent, the latter deliberately set afire by Union soldiers, though Sherman had appointed guards for its protection. And on this same anniversary proud Charleston, which had withstood continual bombardments and attacks, was occupied by the enemy.

Smitten as Davis was by the loss of strategic Charleston and the wanton burning of Columbia, he steeled himself against depression. On Sunday afternoon, February 19, he went for a horseback ride with three of his aides. As he passed the house of the diarist Jones, he was "seemingly as cheerful as if each day did not have its calamity!" Jones wrote:

No one who beheld him would have seen anything to suppose that the capital itself was in almost immediate danger of falling into the hands of the enemy; much less that the President himself meditated its abandonment at any early day, and the concentration of all the armies in the Cotton States.

"And yet Congress has done nothing and does nothing, but waste time," Jones bewailed the next day. "It is too late to raise recruits for service in the campaign now in active operation."

The President was using all his influence behind the scenes to get some action out of Congress. On February 21 he wrote to John Forsyth, the prominent Mobile editor, who had sent him a clipping from his paper.

The article enclosed from the *Register and Advertiser* is a substantial expression of my own views on the subject of employing for the defence of our country all the able-bodied men we have without distinction of color. It is now becoming daily more evident to all reflecting persons that we are reduced to choosing whether the negroes shall fight for us or against us, and that all arguments as to the positive advantages or disadvantages of employing them are beside the question, which is, simply one of relative advantage between having their fighting element in our ranks or in those of our enemy.

The disconsolate General John B. Hood came to Richmond the second week in February to report to the War Department. At his own request, in mid-January, President Davis had relieved him of his command. Hood had turned the remainder of his battle-torn troops—some 20,000—over to General Richard Taylor at Tupelo. After a visit to his sweetheart and friends in South Carolina he had come to the capital. Davis was touched by the misery of the valiant Hood, who, on his own initiative, and abetted by Beauregard, had changed the strategy he and the President had agreed on to wreck Sherman's aggressive campaign in Georgia.

Hood's report was submitted to Breckinridge on February 15. When Congress demanded copies of the report and got them, Joseph Johnston's cohorts and admirers quivered with rage, though they made little effort to prove Hood's facts in error.

Hood declared Johnston's proclivity to retreat was evidenced from the first and "soon became a routine of the army, and was substituted for the hope and confidence with which the campaign opened." Dilating on the long withdrawal from Dalton, Hood added bitterly:

Thus for seventy-four days and nights that noble army, which if ordered to resist, no force that the enemy could assemble could dislodge from a battlefield, continued to abandon their country, to see their strength departing, and their flag waving only in retreat or partial engagements.

Yet Wigfall and others continued to clamor for Johnston's reinstatement, as if it were the sole important objective of Congress. Finally the President felt impelled to prepare a paper of some 4,000 words, stating his reasons for lack of confidence in Johnston. He reviewed the General's whole career from his first unnecessary retreat from Harpers Ferry in 1861, only to find in it consistent evidence of his failure.

My opinion of Genl. Johnston's unfitness for command has ripened slowly and against my inclination into a conviction so settled, that it would be impossible for me again to feel confidence in him as the commander of an army in the field.

The President had hardly signed the document when General Lee came to ask his sanction on the restoration of Johnston to command the Army of Tennessee. Johnston's appointment would do much to appease Congress, he thought. Lee had ascertained that Beauregard, whose health was indifferent, was quite willing to take a subordinate place. It was as apparent to Davis as to Lee that Beauregard had accomplished nothing these last five months, and now he had lost the people's confidence.

Davis found himself in a most difficult position. He realized that the politicians were almost too strong for him. They had forced Lee into his new place to bring about Johnston's restoration and were exerting strenuous pressure upon his best general. If Lee really thought Johnston's appointment might bolster morale, to make things easier for him, Davis was willing to give in. But he had little reason to expect any good to come of Johnston's reinstatement.

The Chief Executive did not present his own written document on Johnston to Congress; but he sent it to a Mississippi friend, James Phelan.* In an accompanying letter he explained that he had complied with Lee's request "in the hope that Genl. Johnston's soldierly qualities might be made serviceable to his country when acting under General Lee's orders." And to make his personal opinion quite clear, he said he hoped that in Johnston's new position "his defects would be remedied by the control of the General-in-Chief."

"The Great Retreater," as Mrs. Chesnut called Johnston in her diary, stayed on at Lincolnton, North Carolina, for a few days after Lee ordered him to the front. Under date of February 22 she noted:

> We [Isabella Martin and Mrs. Chesnut] were taking a walk and General Joseph E. Johnston joined us. He explained to us all of Lee's and Stonewall Jackson's mistakes. He was radiant and joyful, but we had nothing to say. How could we? He always impresses me with the feeling that all of his sympathies are on the other side. Still he was neither gruff nor rude today, as he can be when he chooses.

February 22, 1865, marked the third anniversary of Jefferson Davis's inauguration in Richmond "under the permanent Constitution of the Confederate States." Varina could only shudder when she recalled that dismal day of downpour when her husband took the oath of office in Capitol Square. She had been so overcome by the foreboding that her husband was entering a martyrdom, that she had suddenly left the scene. In reality, the three years that

---

* The whole illuminating paper may be read in *Official Records*, 99, pp. 1304–1311, or more conveniently in Rowland, Vol. VI.

followed had been more grueling for him than in her dire imaginings. With all her worldly knowledge and political experience in Washington she had not conceived how abominably some of his Southern compatriots would treat him. For it was the Southern malcontents, not the great Northern armies, who had drained his best energies. It was the self-seeking politicians, malicious editors, and egotistical generals who had caused him sleepless nights and strengthened the enemy's hands. Varina, who possessed a sharp tongue, short patience, and a quick temper, had marveled at the remarkable equanimity with which her husband had borne unjust criticism and calumny. And she wondered at his unshakable imperturbability at one crushing military disappointment after another. Now on this sad anniversary came another particularly heavy blow. Braxton Bragg with only 6,500 men against Major General John M. Schofield's 20,000 was forced to evacuate Wilmington. The last Confederate seaport on the Atlantic was now lost.

One of the principal debates among Congressmen for some weeks had been the recruitment of Negroes for army service. In the late fall, General Lee had concluded it would be advisable to enlist slaves as fighting soldiers with a definite promise of emancipation of those who joined in the battle for Southern Independence. On January 11, 1865, Lee had publicly declared that he was in favor of a well-digested plan of gradual emancipation. For, he said, "if the war continued, emancipation would certainly come. Whatever measures are to be adopted should be adopted at once. Every day's delay increases the difficulty. Much time will be required to organize and discipline the men, and action may be deferred until it is too late."

While Davis thoroughly agreed with Lee, he thought that the General did not understand how much such an innovation depended upon public opinion. He doubted if the "sovereign states" were yet prepared to support such a measure. By the Confederate Constitution, as well as the United States Constitution, the right of emancipation resided in the individual states.

Through private channels the President had been doing what he could to promulgate the radical idea. For the benefit of public thinking, at Davis's suggestion, Benjamin estimated that there were almost 700,000 Negroes of military age in those parts of the Confederacy not in possession of Federal troops. The North, declared the Secretary of State, had already put 20,000 Negroes in uniform to fight the Southerners, and they had proved serviceable soldiers. Lee had pointed out that the enemy would certainly use more Negroes against the Confederates if the Federals could get possession of them. "As the enemy's present numerical superiority will enable him to penetrate many parts of the country," he argued cogently, "I cannot see the wisdom of the policy of holding them to await his arrival, when we may, by timely action and judicious movement, use them to arrest his progress."

Lee now advocated that slaves be freed on entering service, and that those who volunteered for their freedom and had the consent of their masters should be enrolled immediately. The President was glad to have the popular Lee speak out, while he kept moderately silent so as not to stir up antagonism among his enemies in Congress.

In various quarters Davis found violent opposition to Negro recruitment. The Charleston *Mercury* went so far as to declare that "if the slaves were armed, South Carolina could no longer have any interest in prosecuting the war." Colonel Robert Ould wrote the Secretary of War that a strong reconstruction party would spring up in Virginia rather than adopt the President's idea about enlisting slaves. R. M. T. Hunter, who seemed obsessed by fear of losing his slave property, led a mighty opposition in the Senate. Some Congressmen argued that the Negro soldiers might desert to the North; others avowed that the Southern white privates would never endure close association with black men in uniform.

Despite the acrimonious debates in Congress, Davis was convinced that the South could bear the loss of its slave property far better than the failure of the cause of independence. Many of the Generals owned no slaves, and the vast majority of soldiers were not slaveholders. Davis had always maintained that slavery was merely "an inferior object of the conflict." If slaves were freed, the magic propaganda rug would be pulled from under Mr. Lincoln's feet. Thousands were echoing Mrs. Chesnut's cry of "Let slavery go, and glory be with it." Numerous rich young men were already planning to free their slaves after the war; they were tired of the heavy responsibility of caring for the Negroes from "the cradle to the grave."

Davis could understand, however, why many Southerners, aside from losing property and labor, were reluctant to put arms into the hands of the Negroes. They believed the North would try to stir them to mutiny. With the women and children unprotected at home while their menfolks were in camp, pictures of ghastly massacres such as the Haiti horror rose in countless minds. On the other hand, the

North had expected bloody uprisings after Lincoln's Emancipation Proclamation and had been surprised that not one had broken out. Davis himself did not fear bad behavior on the Negroes' part, and he was prepared to take the risk and free the slaves who would fight the invaders. But even Lee with his enormous prestige could not yet quite overcome the prejudice against arming Negroes.

On February 23, as a torrential rain fell on Richmond, the Senate voted on a bill to put 200,000 Negroes in the Confederate Army. Lee had already sent a letter to the papers declaring the measure necessary. But Hunter's influence largely defeated the bill. Where was the President now to get men to fill Lee's depleted ranks?

The next day in the cold rain Davis rode out to Camp Lee with the new Secretary of War, Breckinridge. There he mingled with some thousands of returned soldiers who had not yet been officially exchanged. He hoped to get them back into the ranks as quickly as possible. But they were in such an emaciated and rundown condition from the experience in freezing Northern prison camps that Davis could hardly speak for pity. Yet both he and Breckinridge did address the men briefly. As they attempted to rouse the fighting spirit, now and again a spectral figure of a man would shout "Furlough! Furlough!" to which they were, of course, entitled. In the wet and the wind the President became chilled to the bone. Someone insisted he go into a hut where there was warmth. He finally consented, and sat before the fire "looking ill and wan."

The next morning the President stayed in bed much later than usual. But when he walked to his office an observer noted that his head was "very erect."

Hunter appeared that day at the Capitol with "blood-shotten" eyes. To his surprise he had been reproached by many Virginia slave owners for his negative vote. "Now," they said ominously, "for lack of Negro soldiers Lee will have to leave Virginia and move South, and Virginia will become a slave-free state."

In his desperate need for troops, General Lee rode out with the President to Camp Lee on Monday, the twenty-seventh, to urge the soldiers returned from prison camps to forego the customary furlough and enter his army now as the spring campaign was about to begin. But the prisoners were too beaten down and spiritless to promise much to Lee. As the month of February ended, the President had no reason to be sanguine. And, as Lee said to his son Custis in disgust, "the Confederate Congress seems to do nothing but chew tobacco and eat peanuts." The hero General had not been more able than the President to stir Congress to action. His new high position had changed nothing except the status of Joseph Johnston, a matter of dubious value in Davis's eyes. But it had relieved the President of some responsibility and some blame.

In the meantime, Davis received sickening reports of Phil Sheridan's burning devastation of the Shenandoah Valley. On March 2 the remnants of Jubal Early's command at Waynesboro disputed his progress. The Confederates were widely dispersed or captured. The Valley was lost beyond redemption. Sheridan, with his well-fed cavalry divisions, was now free to join Grant. According to Dr. Freeman, "the news shook Lee to the depths."

CHAPTER XVIII

THE END APPROACHES

———◆◇◆———

AFTER THE DISASTER in the Shenandoah, General Lee came to Richmond and held "a long and free conference" with the President the first week in March. Grant had just declined a conference with Lee on a probable negotiated peace. The Union Commander had written:

I would state that I have no authority to accede to your proposition for a conference on the subject proposed. Such authority is vested in the President of the United States alone.

Lee told Davis frankly that the evacuation of Petersburg was but a question of time. He said he fully appreciated the embarrassment which would result from losing the workshops and foundry at Richmond, which had once been the Confederacy's main reliance for the manufacture and repair of arms, as well as the preparation of ammunition. But now excellent facilities had been created at Augusta, Selma, and Fayetteville, and a large armory was progressing well at Macon. Perhaps Lee thought it would be difficult to persuade the President to give up Richmond with its prestige. But under the necessities of war Davis had no sentimentality about the capital being the symbol of the Confederacy. He promptly asked: "Would it not be better to anticipate the necessity by withdrawing *at once?*"

Surprised at the President's readiness to leave Richmond, Lee said that his artillery and draft horses were too weak for the roads in their present condition, and that he would have to wait until they became firmer.

In Davis's words, "there naturally followed the consideration of the line of retreat." They agreed that Lee would retire to Danville, where supplies should be collected and a junction made with the troops under General Johnston. Then the combined force would be

155

hurled upon Sherman in North Carolina, with the hope of defeating him before Grant could come to his relief.

Davis and Lee both felt that those more southern states, freed from pressure and encouraged by this expected success, would send reinforcements to the army. Grant, drawn farther and farther from his base of supplies into the midst of a hostile population, might yet be defeated, and Virginia delivered from the invader. So Davis and Lee then believed, as Davis was to write in his *Rise and Fall.*

Now Davis promised that under the energetic new Commissary General I. M. St. John that every effort would be made to collect supplies in depots to be made easily available. And to improve the condition of the horses he instructed the Quartermaster General to send immediately large quantities of corn to Petersburg so that Lee could move soon.

Of this interview and the likely exigency of evacuating Richmond, Dr. Freeman later wrote: "The Chief Executive faced this dread event with unshaken courage, and . . . asked why Lee delayed: If the move had to be made, why should not it be undertaken forthwith?"

As Commissary General St. John briskly began building up the reserve supplies that Lee needed for his withdrawal, Davis yielded to the repeated entreaties of his eight-year-old son and namesake to visit the trenches. The President's nephew, Brigadier General Joseph R. Davis, took the excited boy with him on March 10 to live in a tent like a real soldier for a few days. Before he left little Jeff had a row with his ten-year-old sister Maggie, who told him she was glad to get rid of him. In contrition the next day she wrote a letter of amends and brought it to her father for his approval.

My Dear little Brother—

I miss you very much and wish you would come home. I am so very lonesome. I am very sorry that I told you that I would be glad if you would go. And what do you think Tippy did? Why he killed the biggest rat I ever saw and we made such a great fuss about him that you would have thought he never killed one before. Jimlimber sends his love to you and so does Mrs. Omelia send her love to you and sends you two kisses to you My Dear little Brother. I wish I could see your sweet little face, Darling, I am now tired, but I am your most affectionate Sister

Maggie Howell Davis*

* Tippy was a dog. Mrs. Omelia was the housekeeper, and Jim Limber was a little Negro boy whom Mrs. Davis had rescued from a savagely cruel father, healed his cuts and bruises, and virtually adopted him.

The author is indebted to Carl Haverlin of Broadcast Music for this letter.

A few days later the President received a letter written by little Jeff himself enclosed in a letter from General Joe. He replied on March 16.

My dear Son,

Your very gratifying letter came duly to hand, and I was happy that my dear boy was able to write to me about himself and to give me news from the trenches.

We all miss you very much and are only willing to spare you so long because you seem to be so happy with your Cousin Joe.

Your Mother and the children are well and are anxious to have you back.

It made me very glad to hear from your Cousin Joe that you were a good boy. With much love

Your father
Jeff'n Davis

While the President was writing his son, several of the Congressmen were already getting out their luggage to pack for the home trip. After four months of windy talk they had done little. Lee told Major General John B. Gordon, his youngest corps commander, that Congress simply did not appreciate the present critical situation. The President was informed that Congressmen had spent days arguing how many copies of daily newspapers should be placed each morning on the Congressional desks. Not until early March of 1865 could Congress even agree on a measure of taxation aimed to relieve the Treasury. The tax bill as passed called for twenty-five per cent on all profits from each business which exceeded twenty-five per cent of the capital invested in it!

Finally, after prolonged controversy and under General Lee's direct influence, the Confederate Congress grudgingly had passed a bill permitting Negro enlistments. But the imperfect law merely authorized the President to accept for military service "such able-bodied slaves as might be patriotically rendered by their masters." No inducement of freedom was offered. Weak as the bill was, Davis had signed it on March 13 as a token of right direction. In referring to it, the disappointed President merely said: "Much benefit is anticipated from this measure, though far less than would have resulted from its adoption at earlier date, so as to afford time for their organization and instruction during the winter months." *

After this supreme effort at legislation, exhausted by its own wrangling and do-nothingness and having "debated the recom-

* No Southern Negro in Confederate uniform was ever to reach the firing line.

mendations of the President's annual message for four months without result," the Confederate Congress moved to adjourn.

Davis, troubled and amazed, promptly sent a brief message to Congress "pointing out the necessitous condition of the country" and urging more legislation before adjournment. He reproved the members for designing to leave important matters unattended to as the enemy pressed nearer to Richmond. His style, as he was to write a fortnight later, "was not intended to provoke controversy," nor did it seem to him "to have been wanting in decorum and deference." But the Senate took offense and in secret session appointed a committee to reply sharply to the message.

Nettled by the President's criticism, however, Congress reluctantly stayed in session a few more days and passed some bills he desired. Then, despite a few protesting conscientious voices, it summarily adjourned on March 18, still apparently unable to sense the critical situation. A contemporary newspaper wrote in utter disgust: "Thus meanly expired a legislative body, remarkable in the annals of the world for its weakness and ignorance, whose record was a constant degradation of the Confederate name."

After the legislators had departed, the Senate's reply to the President's last admonitory message was published during the last week of March. It proved to be a spiteful attack on the Chief Executive. In that time of high tension and fear, hardly anything more damaging to the Confederate cause could have been perpetrated by the foe.

When Mrs. Howell Cobb down in Georgia read a newspaper account of the malicious charges, the distressed lady sent the President a clipping and urged him to reply publicly. In the midst of almost unbearable pressures, Davis answered Mrs. Cobb's letter. He told her that Congress had departed without giving him an opportunity to correct the many misstatements in the reply before it was published. He touched upon something from which he was to suffer the rest of his life: personal assaults, replete with misstatements, misinterpretations, and outrageous fabrications.

Faction has done much to cloud our prospects and impair my power to serve the country. . . .

If not *intended* to destroy the confidence of the people in me, it is certainly calculated to have that effect. Whether truth can overtake falsehood has always been doubtful, and in this case the race is most unequal. . . . The demand of the public taste for spicy articles will render it more to the interest of publisher to copy the assault than the defence.

The day after Congress adjourned, the President received an encouraging dispatch from North Carolina. Joe Johnston had at last won an engagement at Bentonville. As Lee had directed him, he had concentrated all his forces and waited to attack Sherman's left wing as it marched northeast, widely separated from the right wing. A few days previously Sherman had destroyed the valuable Confederate arsenals at Fayetteville and then had started to make juncture with the triumphant Schofield trooping inland from Wilmington. At Bentonville the surprised Sherman was seriously halted for the first time since he had left Atlanta in November. The day's fight ended in moderate Confederate success; Johnston captured four guns and nine hundred prisoners.

Johnston had only 20,000 men with him, but, in the words of Robert Henry, an extraordinary "rank" to command so little "file." Besides the three full Generals, Johnston, Beauregard, and Bragg, there were the Lieutenant Generals, Hardee, Stewart, and D. H. Hill. Heading the cavalry were Lieutenant General Wade Hampton and Major General Joseph Wheeler. There was a galaxy of other Major Generals, among them: McLaws, Hoke, Talliaferro, Loring, Stevenson, Walthall, Butler, Brown, Bates, Cheatham, and Patton Anderson.

When Davis received the cheering news of the small victory, "I hope," he commented in a letter to Lee, "that this is only the first of good tidings we may receive from that quarter."

It is a plain case for the application of the maxim with regard to the employment of a small army against a large one. Sherman's forces, worn by long marches, and necessarily completely ignorant of the country in which he is operating, must offer other opportunities for surprises and attacks in detail. . . . I hope General Johnston will find the opportunity to destroy at least to a great extent Sherman's army before it makes a junction with the other.

Davis's flare of hope did not last long. On the second day Sherman rallied his forces and beat back the outnumbered Confederates. On March 21 Johnston retreated to Raleigh. Two days later Lee relayed to the President a discouraging dispatch from Johnston: "Sherman's course cannot be hindered by the small force I have. I can do no more than annoy him."

In the meantime Lee was becoming deeply enmeshed in Grant's closing-in tactics. But he had one more daring move he wanted to try. With the mettlesome young General Gordon he planned a sortie against Grant near Fort Stedman, which, if successful, would threaten Grant's line of communications with his City Point base. Lee came to Richmond to consult with the President. Davis saw that it was a hazardous move. Now that the roads had hardened somewhat and the horses were stronger from their extra rations of corn, Davis wondered why Lee did not pull out for Danville. He had given Lee his sanction on the withdrawal in early March, but Lee seemed reluctant to abandon his position. As Davis wrote in the *Rise and Fall:*

Though of unusually calm and well-balanced judgment, General Lee was instinctively averse to retiring from his enemy, and had so often beaten superior numbers that his thoughts were no doubt directed to every possible expedient which might enable him to avoid retreat.

When Lee returned to headquarters he told Gordon of his conversation with the President, and Gordon reported in his memoirs:

Of Davis, Lee spoke in terms of strong eulogy; of the strength of his convictions, of his devotion, of his remarkable faith in the possibility of still winning our independence, and of his unconquerable will power.

At four in the morning of March 25 Gordon led his men in the surprise attack near Fort Stedman. At first the Federals were thrown back in confusion. But the enemy's tremendous odds in manpower finally turned the tide against the Confederates. The next day Lee reported to the Secretary of War the failure at Fort Stedman.

Gordon, according to his own words, now advised Lee "to abandon Richmond and Petersburg, unite by rapid marches with General Johnston in North Carolina and strike Sherman before Grant can join him."

Letters from the deep South had been pouring in to the President advocating the abandonment of Richmond and a movement of Lee's army into North Georgia and even down to Montgomery.

After March 25 the Petersburg siege, which had simmered down to quiescence, was about to burst forth. Grant planned a mighty attack to cut Lee off from the south.

Davis was in great perplexity. Lee was now Commander-in-Chief. The decision of when to give up Petersburg must be Lee's.

After his latest conference with Lee, Davis told his wife gently but with decision that she must prepare to leave the city. "My headquarters for the future," he said, "may be in the field, and your presence would embarrass and grieve me instead of giving comfort." Varina pleaded to be permitted to remain with him. "I understand your desire to assist and comfort me," he said. "But you can do this in but one way: by going yourself and taking our children to a place of safety." She saw he was deeply affected. "If I live," he told her, "you can come to me when the struggle is ended." Then he added, "But I do not expect to survive the destruction of Constitutional liberty."

Taking out the gold coins he had, he gave them to his wife, reserving only one piece for himself. He asked her not to request any of their friends to take care of the family silver, because it might get them into trouble if the Federals occupied Richmond. So she sent the silver plate to a dealer for sale, along with some of the furniture. Pieces of bric-a-brac which had a sentimental value she entrusted to some convent nuns. Then sorrowfully she began to pack the children's clothes.

On March 29 Davis sent a hasty note to General Gorgas.

Will you do me the favor to have some cartridges prepared for a small Colt pistol, of which I send the moulds, and the form which contained a set of the cartridges furnished with the piece. The ammunition is desired as promptly as it can be supplied.*

The next day the President brought his wife the pistol with the cartridges and showed her how to load, aim, and fire it. He was fearful that on this journey into the unknown she might be assaulted by marauders roving the countryside. "You can at least," he said, "if reduced to last extremity force your assailants to kill you." Because of the unsettled condition of the country, with Federal cavalry penetrating deeper into the South, no final destination could be certain. But her husband solemnly charged her to leave any place if she heard the enemy were approaching. "If you cannot remain undisturbed in your own country," he said, "make for the Florida coast and then take a ship for a foreign land."

Then Varina "made the mistake of telling Jeff," as she later said, that she had secretly bought several barrels of flour to withstand a siege and now purposed to take them south to feed her family. He forbade her. "You can't take anything in the shape of food from here," he said firmly, "for the people need it."

The two young daughters of Secretary of the Treasury Trenholm were to accompany Mrs. Davis and her children on this refugeeing journey. Her sister Margaret Howell, the Negro maid Ellen, James

---

* The original unpublished letter was given to the author by Jessie Palfrey Leake, granddaughter of General Josiah Gorgas.

Jones, the free colored coachman, and Jim Limber, the rescued black boy, made up the rest of the party, along with a twenty-year-old midshipman named James Morris Morgan, who was to be the party's escort.

At the last minute Davis decided to send Burton Harrison as protector to see that the President's wife and children were settled in the house rented for them in Charlotte, North Carolina. Burton just had time to dash off a note to his fiancée, Constance Cary, explaining his sudden departure. He hoped to be back in Richmond quite soon to find her "well and happy and light of heart." The next time Connie would see him he was behind Federal prison bars, emaciated and suffering from scurvy.

On Thursday afternoon, March 30, Midshipman Morgan presented himself at the Executive Mansion. Mrs. Davis knew well the pink-cheeked New Orleans-born young man. He had often been a guest in her home and was a close friend of her youngest brother, Jeffy D. Howell, also a midshipman. "There was not the slightest appearance of excitement or preparation," Morgan wrote later; "no one would ever have dreamed that a flight from a doomed city was about to take place."

The next evening at eight o'clock Morgan drove with the Misses Trenholm to the station. He saw Mrs. Davis's overloaded carriage driven by James Jones arrive with Mrs. Davis, her sister, the four children and Burton Harrison.

A dilapidated old passenger coach "long a stranger to paint" was the best that could be provided for the First Lady of the Confederacy. Varina took note of the lumpy seats covered with threadbare brownish plush. They looked anything but comfortable for a night's journey; she did not suspect they were infested with vermin. Winnie, the nine-month-old baby girl, and little William were stretched out on seats and were already asleep when the President came in. He spoke "pleasantly and cheerfully" to everybody. Then with Maggie and Jeff half-clinging to him he sat down by his wife and entered into earnest conversation. The engine blew a signal of departure. He kissed the children goodbye, embraced Varina, shook hands with the Trenholm girls and Midshipman Morgan and wished them *bon voyage*. When little Jeff begged to remain with his father and Maggie held convulsively to him, he almost gave way to his emotion. According to Mrs. Davis, "he thought he was looking his last upon us."

Burton Harrison followed him out of the coach. But the train did not start. The President and his secretary walked up and down the platform conversing. Finally, at ten o'clock, the locomotive gave another screech and a sudden lurch. Burton jumped onto the moving train. The President waved goodbye and returned to the empty White House.

He was at least relieved that if there should now be a sudden evacuation of the capital his loved ones were already gone. He did not know that just beyond Richmond the engine could not make the grade, and there the first family would sit in discomfort the rest of the night while it began to rain and the car roof leaked. Without remaining in Danville as she was invited to do, Mrs. Davis proceeded to Charlotte with a better engine. When she arrived at the leased house in a state of utter exhaustion, she found no conveniences for cooking. The owner, a Jew named Abraham Weil, kindly sent the family their meals from his own house for several days and would not hear of accepting payment.

The night of his family's departure, after his return home, the President learned that John Daniel, famous editor of the Richmond *Examiner*, was dead of pneumonia. The man who had attacked him with a virulent pen for years was not quite forty. Much of the Confederacy's discontent could be traced to this talented misanthrope, who, while believing wholeheartedly in the Southern cause, yet devoted his major energies to denigrating its Administration. In the beginning he had maliciously ridiculed Lee, and among the military he seemed to have personal admiration only for Joseph Johnston and ex-Governor Floyd. As the *Examiner* was perhaps the most popular paper in the South, almost every week soldiers in the camps had read some belittlement of their President.

Through his paper with its witty diatribes, which had served to shake the confidence of the Southern people, Daniel had amassed a fortune. A few evenings before his death the bachelor Daniel had talked of the elegant house he purposed to build on the old family estate in Stafford County. "With my possessions walled in," he declared with contemptuous pride, "I shall teach these people what they never knew—how to live like a gentleman."

It seemed strange, Davis thought, that Daniel could not have seen, if only for selfish reasons, that his fight against the Administration might in the end help to destroy the personal fortune that he loved so fiercely.

The next day, April 1, business in the Richmond offices went on as usual. The President wrote General Lee of the difficulty of finding iron to keep the Tredegar works employed.

The question is often asked, will we hold Richmond, to which my only answer is, if we can; it is purely a question of military power. The distrust is increasing and embarrasses in many ways.

That afternoon Phil Sheridan, who was dashing to cut off any attempted Confederate retreat west and south of Petersburg, attacked George Pickett's forces at Five Forks. Pickett had been fighting boldly and well and had pushed some six miles forward, almost to Dinwiddie Court House, on March 31. Then he had retired to a position covering Five Forks, where five dirt roads met just a few miles from Lee's line. On the morning of April 1 Pickett wired Lee that he must fall back under increased pressure from Sheridan. Lee sent an order that Five Forks must be held at all cost. The Confederates fought with such spirit that the Federal attacks slowed to almost nothing about noon. When it seemed that the day's action was over, Pickett and several other weary senior officers, including Fitzhugh Lee, went to a nearby shad-bake given by General Thomas L. Rosser to enjoy a little relaxation and the tasty river fish. Around three o'clock Sheridan and his horsemen swooped down on Five Forks, cut the Confederates to pieces, and took some 3,000 confused prisoners. Lee was furious with Pickett and ordered his removal. Grant, on learning of the Federal victory at Five Forks, commanded an immediate all-out assault on Petersburg. Davis went to bed ignorant of the calamity by which the mobile force that protected Lee's right flank had been swept away.

CHAPTER XIX

"A GOVERNMENT ON WHEELS"

————◈————

WHEN JEFFERSON DAVIS had his breakfast on the morning of Sunday, April 2, 1865, the day was bright and beautiful, the best of the year so far. Daffodils bloomed in the garden; apricot trees were bright with blossoms; the atmosphere was fragrant as well as fresh. No rumble of guns broke the peace. The muted call of church bells emphasized the quiet. Without the lively activities of his healthy brood, the mansion was silent. He was alone in the great house except for Mrs. Omelia, the housekeeper, and Robert Brown, the colored man who served him. Davis thought of his family settling in their rented house in Charlotte on this perfect day of burgeoning spring. He did not dream that they were still in the uncomfortable train coach, beset by delays, vermin, and a leaking roof.

When the President left the house at a quarter to eleven for a leisurely walk to Saint Paul's, he purposed to take Holy Communion, as he had the previous Sunday, with General Lee and Secretary of the Treasury Trenholm kneeling at the altar rail beside him. Now Trenholm was sick in bed and Lee was hard-pressed about Petersburg. But the aspect of Richmond was as serene as that of an English village in the first rapture of spring. No citizens were in evidence except churchgoers in their shabby Sunday best. Here and there, however, attached to residences, occasional little red flags stirred faintly, indicating that a house was for rent or that furniture was up for sale. People were selling possessions to buy food, or preparing to leave Richmond if the city was to be rendered.

Partly because of the diminishing civilian food supply, Davis had already advocated sending the women and children and aged to the south or west, as far as was practicable. If the exigency of direct assault on the city should come he hoped that only those who

165

could assist in its defense would be left. He had set the example by sending his own family to North Carolina. But he did not really expect any sudden evacuation. Only the day before he had had a conference with Lewis H. Harvie, President of the Richmond and Danville Railroad, in the presence of Secretary of War Breckinridge and Quartermaster General A. R. Lawton. So assured were they all of adequate foodstuffs collected on the railroads that could be got to Lee's army either on the Petersburg line or on a potential line of withdrawal to Danville that Harvie decided he might safely go to his country place for a fortnight's vacation.

On the peaceful street, as he neared the church, the President was suddenly accosted by Postmaster General Reagan, who informed him that a startling, though unofficial, dispatch had just been received at the War Office: Lee's thin line southeast of Petersburg had been broken. Much perturbed, but somewhat dubious—if the news were correct General Lee would surely have telegraphed him directly—the President proceeded with his accustomed dignity to St. Paul's and took his seat in his pew just in front of Constance Cary, his secretary's fiancée.

Those near his pew "scrutinized his face anxiously for some sign of good or bad news." But whatever anxiety was in his heart, he revealed nothing. In the words of Secretary of the Navy Mallory, his expression in repose "varied not from that cold, stern face which four years of harassing mental labor stamped upon it."

The service had begun when some slight disturbance occurred in the back of the church. A soldier had entered and demanded to see the President. The sexton walked rapidly down the aisle, whispered in the President's ear, and handed him a telegram. The eyes of most of the congregation turned from the altar to the President. He glanced at the scrap of paper and saw it was from General Lee. Lee announced his intended speedy withdrawal from Petersburg and the necessity of evacuating Richmond. Mrs. Gorgas, across the aisle, saw Mr. Davis turn pale. Constance Cary, directly behind him, plainly noted a "gray sort of pallor creep over his face." "With stern set lips and his usual quick military tread," she wrote, "he left the church, a number of other people rising in their seats and hastening after him, those who were left swept by a universal tremor of alarm." The Rector came down to the altar rail and tenderly begged his flock to remain and finish the service. "The occurrence probably attracted attention," Davis later wrote, "but the congregation of St. Paul's was too refined to make a scene at anticipated danger."

The possible evacuation had been foreseen for weeks and some preparations made, but the actual event was here much sooner than Davis or anyone in Richmond had expected. Davis went straight to the War Office to confer with Breckinridge. As many of the heads of departments as could be found on a Sunday were quickly assembled and given instructions.

The President hastily summoned his Cabinet. Benjamin took the mile stroll from his house at No. 3 North Main to the Capitol with his usual jaunty air: "His pleasant smile, his mild Havana, and the very twirl of his slender, gold-headed cane contributing to give to the casual observers an expression of casual confidence."

When all the Cabinet was gathered, the members sought to control their agitation, as the President "in a few words, calmly, solemnly" told the latest news from Lee and ordered the immediate withdrawal of the Government from Richmond.

Then the President summoned Harvie, the railroad president, who had hardly reached his country house, to confer with him and Breckinridge, particularly about the route the wagon supply train should take. Harvie rushed back to Richmond and prepared to travel with the Government to Danville.

Davis sent a dispatch asking if Lee could not hold off abandoning his Petersburg line one more day. If the Government moved from Richmond that night he feared it would involve "the loss of many valuables, both for want of time to pack and of transportation."

At three o'clock that afternoon Lee wrote a long, leisurely dispatch to the President, discussing details of plans for raising Negro troops. But he set eight o'clock that evening as the hour of the Government's evacuation, unless by that time he had managed to re-establish his broken lines.

The President was occupied until late in the afternoon arranging his own personal papers for convenient reference in the transaction of current affairs. He sorely missed his private secretary, Burton Harrison, whom he had sacrificed for his family's convenience. But his mind was very clear and orderly. Two of his aides, Colonel William Preston Johnston and former Governor F. R. Lubbock of Texas, worked zealously packing the executive papers. Wagons were backed up to the doors of various Departments and filled with boxes of documents and sent down to the Danville Railroad station.

All that remained of the treasure of the Confederacy, together with the private funds of the Richmond banks—some $500,000 in double-eagle gold pieces, silver bricks, gold ingots, and silver coin

—was packed in bags and boxes to go on a special train under the supervision of the Senior Teller of the Treasury Department, Walter Philbrook. It was guarded by sixty young midshipmen, who had been rushed to the capital from their training ship, the *Patrick Henry,* on the upper James. Among these was the President's youngest brother-in-law, Jefferson Davis Howell. The treasure train was ordered to proceed to Danville as soon as it was ready, independent of the movement of the Presidential train.

In the late afternoon General Breckinridge came to tell Davis there was no hope of remaining another day. Members of the Cabinet were ordered to join the President at the depot around ten o'clock.

Davis conferred with his Secretary of the Navy, who sent a momentous order to Admiral Raphael Semmes commanding the Confederate squadron in the James.

General Lee advises the Government to withdraw from this city, and the officers will leave this evening accordingly. General Lee withdraws his lines towards Danville this night . . . upon you is devolved the duty of destroying your ships this night and with all the forces under your command joining General Lee. Let your people be rationed as far as possible for the march and armed and equipped for the field.

After directing last necessary arrangements at his office, Davis started walking to his home to make what dispositions he could in the few hours that remained before the special train would leave. He saw women clad in black—almost everyone in Richmond mourned the loss of some kindred in the war—weeping in the street. Several persons accosted him to ask if Richmond was to be evacuated. He admitted the painful fact, qualified by the expression of hope that the Government would return under better auspices. With "generous sympathy and patriotic impulse," one lady, speaking for a group, declared, "If the success of the cause requires you to give up Richmond, we are content." Davis was deeply touched. "The affection and confidence of these noble people in the hour of disaster," he wrote later, "was more distressing to me than complaint and unjust censure would have been."

At home the President and Robert Brown got his luggage ready. Then he entrusted the bust of himself, which Varina treasured, to a friend who offered to put it where "it would never be found by a Yankee." Davis also gave him charge of a painting called "The Heroes of the Valley." An auctioneer arrived with an account of sales for $28,400 from silver plate and furniture Varina had given a firm to sell. Davis sent word to Mr. Grant, his friend across the street, who owned a farm, to come and get the milk cow he had so kindly lent the family. At the last moment, Davis thoughtfully had his favorite easy chair carried to Mrs. Lee, who suffered severely from arthritis.

Finally he entrusted the housekeeper, Mrs. Omelia, with charge of the house and its possessions. His saddle horse Kentucky was brought to the front door. Then he sat down quietly in his office to await notification that it was time to go to the train. What lay beyond he had no way of knowing. The message came; the President and Robert Brown started for the station.

As Davis looked up he saw the heavens were studded with bright stars. But the idyllic quiet of that Sunday morning seemed ages past. Richmond was now a frenzy of riotous activity. The outlying bridges became choked with refugees fleeing the expected Yankees. The streets to the railway depot were jammed. Marauders, white and black, ranged the business district, burst into shops and carried off spoils of every description. Convicts, deserted by fleeing guards, broke out of prison and created their own turmoil. Men with pails scooped up from gutters liquor that had been emptied from casks to prevent drunken disorder. Confusion and hysteria made a mockery of the years of restraint Richmond had known.

When Davis reached the station he had to force his way through the distracted, milling crowd. All the Cabinet members had already assembled except the Secretary of War, who was to attend to final duties concerning the evacuation and the destruction of armaments and the tobacco warehouse. Mrs. Trenholm, wife of the ailing Secretary of the Treasury, was the only lady in the Presidential party.

At eleven o'clock the train pulled creakily out of the station on its 140-mile journey southwest to Danville. As Davis looked about the dimly lit old coach the atmosphere was dismal in the extreme. Mrs. Trenholm was tending her stretched-out husband who was suffering torment from neuralgia. No one could sympathize more feelingly with that agony than Davis himself. John Reagan, the big-hearted Texan, known as a "Grand Old Roman," sat "silent and sombre," his black eyes glistening; but apparently he saw nothing but the stick he was whittling "to the little end of nothing." Mallory nursed his special grief: his James River squadron, which had so resolutely guarded Richmond from the ascent of enemy warships, would be blown up at dawn. The explosions would mark the last operations of the Confederate Navy east of the Mississippi.

Whatever melancholy thoughts coursed through Davis's tired brain, he had one bright expectancy to hearten him: the early arrival of Lee and his army at Danville, as they had planned.

Benjamin was the only one who kept his cheerful humor. As he relished a midnight snack, he tried to rally his colleagues with a buoyant "never-give-up-the-ship" air. He spoke reassuringly of other great national causes which had been redeemed from more dismal reverses than those the Confederacy had just suffered.

Sleep for the President and most of his companions was well-nigh impossible; the train was continually halting because of the road-bed's ragged condition. In the morning the party was refreshed by good things from the hampers of food the well-to-do Trenholms had brought along, including "inexhaustible supplies of 'Old Peach.' "

At Clover Station Lieutenant John S. Wise, eighteen-year-old son of the ex-Governor, General Henry Wise, had watched refugee train after train go past loaded to capacity with men clinging to the cars. He had seen the treasure train go by. And now came the Presidential train.

Mr. Davis sat at a car window. The crowd at the station cheered. He smiled and acknowledged their compliment, but his expression showed physical and mental exhaustion. . . .

While the train took on water, young Wise slipped aboard and had a chat with his brother-in-law, Dr. Garnett, the Davises' family physician.

After the cars got under way Wise stayed at the station and watched other trains that followed the President's. One bore the archives and employees of the Post Office Department; another, those of the War Department; still another, General Gorgas and his employees in Ordnance. "I saw," wrote the youthful officer, "a government go by on wheels."

The exhausting journey, which should have been completed by dawn, stretched out interminably to noon and to the middle of the afternoon. At the Danville station, city officials, committees of foremost citizens, and a host of simple townsfolk waited to welcome the President and his associates. The large Benedict House was prepared for the offices of the Confederacy. Davis was escorted to the mansion of Major W. T. Sutherlin on Main Street, set conspicuously on a little rise of ground, and he was made to feel that this was his home. "Nothing," he wrote later, "could have exceeded the kindness and hospitality of the patriotic citizens. They cordially gave us an 'Old Virginia Welcome,' and with one heart contributed in every practicable manner to cheer and aid us."

In his uncertainty as to the situation, Davis immediately asked for news from Lee. There was none. He wired his wife in Charlotte, merely informing her that he was in Danville. She had heard nothing of the evacuation until his telegram reached her.

Following his military instinct, Davis asked to be shown the fortifications. He found the entrenchments surrounding the town "as faulty in location as in construction." He ordered the matter remedied immediately, and urged energetic efforts to collect supplies of various kinds for Lee's expected army.

Though there was still no word from Lee on the fifth, the President issued a public proclamation.

The General-in-Chief found it necessary to make such movements of his troops as to uncover the capital. It would be unwise to conceal the moral and material injury to our cause resulting from its occupation by the enemy. It is equally unwise and unworthy of us to allow our energies to falter and our efforts to become relaxed under reverses, however calamitous they may be. . . .

It is for us, my countrymen, to show by our bearing under reverses, how wretched has been the self-deception of those who have believed us less able to endure misfortune with fortitude than to encounter danger with courage. . . .

Animated by that confidence in your spirit and fortitude which never yet failed me, I announce to you, fellow-countrymen, that it is my purpose to maintain your cause with my whole heart and soul. . . .

I will never consent to abandon to the enemy one foot of soil of any of the States of the Confederacy. . . . Let us not despond, my countrymen, but meet the foe with fresh defiance, with unconquered and unconquerable hearts.

Some persons may have regarded the bold words as stemming from desperation. As Davis later wrote wryly, "viewed by the light of subsequent events, the proclamation was oversanguine." But he made it very clear that he himself had no purpose to relinquish the struggle for independence, and at that time he was confident of Lee's continuing the war, with a probability of ultimate success.

Harper's Weekly made note of Jefferson Davis's firm resolve. In an editorial, in which it speculated on "what the rebels will do next," it said:

Their leaders are not men who will relinquish the struggle until the defeat and disappearance of their soldiers assure them that there is no alternative.

On the day of his proclamation, Davis wrote his wife briefly:

I have in vain sought to get into communication with Genl Lee and have postponed writing in the hope that I would soon be able to speak to you with some confidence of the future. . . .
The people here have been very kind, and the Mayor & Council have offered assistance in the matter of quarters, and have very handsomely declared their unabated confidence. I do not wish to leave Va. but cannot decide on my movements until those of the army are better developed.

Davis was relieved to hear from Varina that she and their "unruly" children were well. Mr. Weil, who owned the house she had leased, had treated them very kindly, "with the delicacy and hospitality of a gentleman."

Since your telegram upon your arrival at Danville we have nothing except the wildest rumors, all, however, discouraging.
I, who know that your strength when stirred up is great, and that you can do with a few what others have failed to do with many, am awaiting prayerfully the advent of the time when it is God's will to deliver us through his own appointed agent, I trust it may be you as I believe it is. . . .
Numberless surmises are hazarded here, as to your future destination and occupation, but I know that wherever you are, and in whatever engaged, it is in an efficient manner for the country. The way things look now the trans-Miss seems our ultimate destination—
Though I know you do not like my interference, let me entreat you not to send B.B. to command there, I am satisfied that the country will be ruined by its intestine feuds if you do so. . . . If I am intrusive forgive me for the sake of the love which impels me, but pray long and fervently before you decide to do it. . . .
Write to me my own precious only love, and believe me as ever your devoted wife—

In this letter Varina revealed not only her great confidence in her husband, but the fact that he had sometimes resented her "interference," and her advice was given with consummate tact. But Davis had no thought of giving Braxton Bragg the top command in Texas or anywhere else. Able and useful as Bragg was to him, Davis fully realized the man's inveterate unpopularity.

Various reports reached Davis in Danville that Richmond had suffered a disastrous fire caused accidentally when the storehouse of ammunition was blown up to save it from falling to the invaders. Block after block of buildings went up in flames. While the ruins still smoked Lincoln himself had appeared in Richmond. He had gone by gunboat up the James from City Point to a spot where the river was obstructed. Sailors then rowed him and his son Tad up to Rockett's Wharf. The President of the United States, holding his little boy by the hand, had walked almost a mile to the Confederacy's deserted Executive Mansion. Wearing a high silk hat and a long black overcoat, he had made quite an appearance, topping his guard and followed by a crowd of curious Negroes. In the mansion Lincoln went straight to Davis's office and sat down in his desk chair. He had a talk with Judge Campbell, Assistant Secretary of War, and the only man of high position left in the smoking city. Campbell took it upon himself under the circumstances to act as the head of state and he asumed that the Virginia Legislature would be allowed to carry on as usual. After reviewing the troops and taking a carriage drive to see the blackened ruins, Lincoln departed for City Point, where he was to stay until the fateful ninth. Davis had little thought to give to Richmond's fire or Lincoln's visit; he was too anxious about Lee.

The suspense of waiting for some word, any word, from Lee now became almost intolerable. Davis sent telegram after telegram to numerous stations trying to communicate with him, or to ascertain if anyone else had heard from him or knew his whereabouts.

CHAPTER XX

STUPENDOUS DISASTER

ALL AROUND THE edges of Lee's withdrawing army the ever-increasing Federals closed in and painfully harassed it. Sheridan was doing his vigorous best to cut off the retreat to the west and south of Petersburg. On April 6 at Saylor's Creek the Federals made an all-out attack on Ewell's corps, tearing it to bits and capturing a large part of it. Among the prisoners taken was General Custis Lee, whom the President had reluctantly released as his aide because he begged to get into combat. The engagement took, in killed, wounded, and captured, some 7,000 of the shrinking Confederate forces. It was the most calamitous blow the Army of Northern Virginia had received. The next day was moderately quiet on the battlefields, while the Confederates reckoned their losses and the Federals totted up their gains. That night Grant wrote to Lee urging surrender. The anxious President, in Danville, knew nothing of the catastrophes.

Finally, on April 8, Davis received a telegram from the Secretary of War, who, after completing the evacuation of Richmond, had proceeded to seek out Lee's headquarters.

I left General Lee at Farmville yesterday morning where he was passing the river for temporary relief. He will still try to move around towards North Carolina. There was very little firing yesterday and I hear none today. . . . The straggling has been great and the situation is not favorable. . . . We will join you as soon as possible.

Breckinridge's dispatch merely increased the nerve-searing suspense. But the President noted particularly that Lee would "still try to move around towards North Carolina." After dinner that evening he called a Cabinet meeting in the Sutherlins' dining room.

As they were seated about the table an imperative knocking at the front door broke the night's quiet. Robert Brown, the President's body servant, acting as an extra butler, opened the door cautiously to a wide-eyed, disheveled young man. Burton Harrison, who had returned that day from Charlotte and was taking notes, went quickly out to the hall and at once recognized him. Without ceremony he ushered into the room Lieutenant John S. Wise, who four days before had volunteered to seek out Lee and try to get word to the President about his situation. This gallant youth had ridden all that day and all the past night, making several hairbreadth escapes through enemy lines. He had risked his life to bring the President incredible news: Lee was about to surrender. He had seen the General twice. Lee had written on a piece of paper a few words to the effect that the Lieutenant would make a verbal report; he did not want to risk a detailed message being captured; if occasion arose he would give further notice. Wise handed the note to the President. Then he went to the other end of the table, stood facing Davis, and told his deplorable story. His hearers listened as men paralyzed by shock.

The President questioned the youth directly. "Do you think that General Lee will be able to reach a point of safety with his army?" Wise replied frankly: "I regret to say, no. From what I saw and heard I am satisfied that General Lee must surrender. It may be that he has done so today." Wise was conscious of a shudder around the table. After a pause he added hopelessly, "It is only a question of a few days at most." Then he swayed slightly with exhaustion.

For Jefferson Davis it was an agonizing moment, though outwardly he remained calm. Solicitously he asked the youth to talk with him privately after he had eaten the good dinner being prepared for him in the Sutherlins' butler's pantry.

Later, somewhat refreshed, Wise joined the President in the drawing room. He gave more details of the army's condition. He quoted General Lee from memory:

The enemy's cavalry is already flanking us from the south and east. You may say to Mr. Davis that as he knows, my original purpose was to adhere to the line of the Danville Road. I have been unable to do so, and am now endeavoring to hold the Southside Road as I retire in the direction of Lynchburg.

Wise said he had ventured to inquire if General Lee had any place where he contemplated making a stand. "No," Lee had replied, slowly and sadly, "no; I shall have to be governed by each day's developments." Then, with a touch of resentment and raising his voice slightly, he had added, "A few more Saylor's Creeks and it will all be over—ended—just as I have expected it would end from the first."

Davis sat silent for some time, "peering into the gloom outside." At the very beginning, he, too, had secretly doubted the probability of success if the North determined on full-scale war. It was ironic that it was Lee himself who had inspired in him an unflagging optimism after he began to win victories in the summer of 1862. Finally, the President asked Wise if he felt equal to another trip the next day after a good night's sleep. Davis would give him a brief letter of credentials and let him explain verbally his wishes to General Lee. The President then retired to his featherbed. But his mind was too perturbed to sleep.

After breakfast the next morning, Palm Sunday, April 9, the President handed Lieutenant Wise the letter and wished him Godspeed as he dashed off to rejoin General Lee. Then he sent Lee a telegram.

You will realize the reluctance to leave the soil of Virginia and appreciate my anxiety to win success north of the Roanoke. . . . I hope soon to hear from you at this point, where offices have been opened to keep up the current business, until more definite knowledge would enable us to form more definite plans. May God sustain and guide you.

Despite Wise's reiterated warning, Davis could not bring himself to believe that Lee would have to surrender the Army of Northern Virginia. No other army in American history, he thought, had ever possessed such a love of and faith in its commander, whose brilliant fighting had earned him a legend of invincibility against stupendous odds.

But even now as Davis dressed for church, General Lee, wearing a resplendent new uniform, beige gauntlets, and his yellow sash, was riding forth to make personal contact with General Grant. He would not receive the President's telegram until after his return from the confrontation.

With his Cabinet and the heads of agencies the President attended a union prayer service which the municipal officials had arranged. On the streets he remarked fagged stragglers from Lee's army arriving in the town. Some of them claimed they had fled to keep from being surrendered, so that they could continue the fight in North Carolina. In any case, the signs were ominous. But Davis still felt that his great General would find a way out.

Back at Lee's camp early on that Sunday morning, April 9, the commanding General and almost every other officer were in a dread state of perturbation. On April 7, Grant had written Lee respectfully urging him to surrender. When Lee had shown Longstreet the note, Old Pete had said, "Not yet." Grant had written again on Saturday, April 8. This letter, received after dark, had been read by lantern light. Lee had asked Colonel Charles Venable how he would answer it. "I would answer no such letter," he said firmly. But Lee said he thought it must be answered. So he wrote:

Though I could not meet you with a view to surrender the Army of N. Va. . . . I shall be pleased to meet you at 10 A.M. tomorrow on the old stage road to Richmond between the picket lines of the two armies.

That day the Southern troops had moved toward Appomattox Court House; the advance regiments had arrived by midafternoon. "There had been no sight of the enemy all day." That night of April 8, around a campfire, Lee called Generals Longstreet, Gordon, Pendleton, Fitzhugh Lee, and a few others to him. They discussed among other things the fate of the Southern people if Lee surrendered. There was talk of forcing a passage through enemy lines, saving some portion of the army and continuing a desultory warfare until the Government at Washington should grow weary. Hope was expressed that "they might reach the mountains of Virginia and Tennessee with a remnant of the army and ultimately join Johnston."

Late in the night a decision was reached to make one more fighting try. Fitz Lee's cavalry and Gordon's infantry, supported by General Armistead Long's artillery, would strike the Federal line near Appomattox at sunrise in an effort to break through. Longstreet would bring up the rear.

Before dawn Gordon commenced his battle with fierce energy, but by six o'clock he sent Lee word that he had fought his corps to a frazzle and that he could do nothing more unless heavily supported by Longstreet.

"Then," said Lee, who was already dressed in a new uniform, "there is nothing left for me to do, but go and see General Grant, and I would rather die a thousand deaths."

A colonel standing near-by impulsively cried out, "Oh, General, what will history say of the surrender of this army in the field?" "Yes," Lee replied, "yes, I know they will say hard things of us. They will not understand how we are overwhelmed by numbers. But if it is right to surrender this army then I will take all the responsibilities."

General E. P. Alexander, the famed artillerist, who could not bear the thought of surrender, came up and suggested that the army should be disbanded "to scatter like rabbits and partridges in the bushes," and reassemble either with Johnston or the Governors of their separate States and keep up the struggle.

Lee frowned on the idea of his army becoming something like guerrillas. "And, as for myself," he said, "you young fellows might go bushwhacking, but the only dignified course for me would be to go to General Grant and surrender myself and take the consequences of my acts." Alexander was to write later that he felt Lee had answered his suggestion from a plane so far above it, that he was ashamed of having made it. Yet he persisted and, carried away by his welling emotion, spoke in a rush:

If there is a chance to cut our way through, I'll answer for the artillery making a good fight. If there is any hope for the Confederacy it is *delay*. If this army surrenders, every other army will give up as fast as the news reaches it. . . . *You* don't care for military fame or glory, but *we* are proud of your name and the record of this army. We want to leave it to our children. . . . A little more blood or less now makes no difference. Spare the men who have fought under you for four years the mortification of having to ask Grant for terms and have him say Unconditional Surrender. . . . General, spare us the mortification of having you get that reply.

Lee patiently listened to his artillerist's pleading outburst. Then he said quietly:

I expect to meet General Grant this morning and surrender this army to him. But he will not demand unconditional surrender; he will give us as honorable terms as we have a right to ask or expect.

Half-blinded with tears, Alexander turned away and went to join Gordon, who was still fighting as hard as he could with his inadequate force.

When Lee's aide, Colonel Walter Taylor, came up just then, the Commander-in-Chief told him he was going to Grant to surrender and desired his company. For a moment Taylor stood speechless. Then he replied frankly: "Speaking for myself, any other fate is preferable."

. . .

By the time the President had returned to the Sutherlin home from church, General Lee and General Grant had come together just after noon at Appomattox Court House in the house of Wilmer McLean, whose former home had coincidentally stood on the field of Manassas.

Grant had noticed in the distance the western foothills to which Lee's army might possibly escape. He did not know that the Army of Northern Virginia had shrunk to some 28,000, that about half of Lee's troops had already dispersed, that Lee had perhaps no more than 9,000 infantry with muskets, and that the men were again virtually destitute of rations—Sheridan had captured the trains sent from Lynchburg the night before. Grant was sure that Lee would never submit to unconditional surrender, which Pemberton had refused to do at Vicksburg. So his terms were generous: officers and men were to be paroled, under strict obligation not to take up arms against the United States until properly exchanged; all artillery and portable arms were to be relinquished; but the sidearms, personal baggage, and horses of the officers were to be retained. All the parolees would be permitted to go to their homes immediately. When Lee suggested that many of the private cavalrymen and artillerists also owned their own horses, Grant considerately made the concession that the men too could keep the horses personally owned. Then he called for rations to be furnished immediately for Lee's hungry soldiers.

When Lee sorrowfully rode back to his headquarters, two solid walls of men rushed to the roadside to greet their General and broke into wild cheering. Colonel W. W. Blackford, who rode just behind the General, wrote:

Tears filled his eyes and trickled down his cheeks. . . . The men's cheers changed to choking sobs as with streaming eyes and many cries of affection they waved their hats. . . . Each group began in the same way with cheers and ended in the same way with sobs all the way to his quarters.

Grim-hearted men threw themselves on the ground, covered their faces with their hands and wept like children. Officers of all ranks made no attempt to hide their feelings, but sat on their horses and cried aloud. . . .

One man held his arms wide over the crowd and shouted, "I love you just as well as ever, General Lee."

Some who were near enough passed their hands gently along Traveller's flanks. Lee had sufficient control to fix his eyes on a line between the horse's ears.

Finally at a large white oak tree the General dismounted. As soldiers crowded upon him, Lee said, "Men, we have fought the war together, I have done my best for you. My heart is too full to say more."

When Colonel Blackford reached a fighting South Carolina unit commanded by General John Geary and told him the army was surrendered, he was never to forget the stunned expression on Geary's face.

He quivered as if he had been shot and sat still in the saddle a moment and then, returning his sabre, which he held still drawn in his hand, he said, "Then I'll be damned if I'll surrender." And that night he passed out of the lines to join Johnston's army.

Jefferson Davis, unaware of the climactic event at Appomattox, continued to believe that his foremost commander would manage a way out. He took consolation in recalling a recent statement of Lee to him: "With my army in the mountains of Virginia I could carry on this war for twenty years more."

So, on Monday morning, the President, though anxious, imperturbably went on conducting affairs of state. That afternoon he was seated in his improvised office with several of his Cabinet when a panting courier burst into the room with a dispatch: General Lee *had* surrendered at Appomattox Court House. Davis, who had the extraordinary faculty of seeming never to be surprised at anything, no matter how calamitous, sat very still. Though his features hardly changed expression, pallor spread over his face. He handed the message to the man nearest him. The piece of paper passed from hand to hand. The men "looked at each other gravely and mutely." For some moments a silence ensued, more eloquent of stupendous disaster than words.

Almost immediately, scouts arrived, announcing that an enemy cavalry force was approaching Danville from the west. There was no time to lose; the Government might be captured. The President gave orders for an immediate withdrawal to North Carolina. He sent a dispatch to Joseph Johnston saying it was reported that Lee had surrendered and asking him conditionally to meet him at Greensboro. Efficient Burton Harrison directed preparations: the repacking and reloading of documents for the journey south. Fortunately the treasure train had been sent on to Greensboro several days before.

It was raining hard when the President returned to the Sutherlin house to prepare again for travel. His hostess met him at the door. He told her "almost in a whisper" that Lee had surrendered and that he must leave at once.* The faithful Robert began packing his luggage. General Gorgas came to the President for orders. He found Davis "evidently overwhelmed by this astounding misfortune." The Secretary of War, Davis said, was expected the following day and would instruct him.

When the President said goodbye to Mrs. Sutherlin, she offered him a bag containing a thousand dollars in gold. Tears of gratitude welled in his eyes. "I cannot take your money," he said. "You and your husband are young and will need it, while I am an old man, and—I doubt if I shall need anything much very long." He reached into his pocket and brought out a little gold pencil for her to keep for his sake. Then he remembered to write a note of appreciation to the Mayor of Danville, thanking him and the City Council for the courtesies extended him and his associates.

When the President arrived at the station the greatest confusion prevailed. The night was dark and the mud more than ankle deep. Trenholm was now so ill that he had been brought in an ambulance. The drivers of quartermaster wagons yelled contentiously. Getting the horses into the freight cars was proving dangerous business. Mutual shouts of inquiry and response as to missing individuals or baggage rose above the curses of soldiers and civilians determined to board the train in defiance of the guards. Burton Harrison had stationed armed men to exclude all persons and material not specially authorized by him to go aboard. The guards were kept busy in repelling the multitude eager to embark. Frantic people sought transportation at any hazard, even though rumors now ran that the Yankees had already cut the railroad to Greensboro. One General R—— from the "torpedo bureau" was very insistent that he and his several daughters be given places. Harrison had refused him, but the man got access to the President. In kindness to an old friend, Davis finally said that Harrison should make room somehow for the General and his daughters.

Through the muddy maelstrom at the station the President entered the coach with dignity. Harrison had assigned him a whole seat to himself for his better comfort. But when there was apparently no seat for one of General R——'s daughters, Davis courteously permitted her to share his seat. In the words of Harrison she

* Mrs. Sutherlin wrote that though the President was naturally "in a most anxious frame of mind" during his week's stay, he was "always pleasant and agreeable."

proved to be a young lady "of a loquacity irrepressible." For two hours she plied the tired President diligently with a thousand trivial questions while the train was delayed because the fires in the locomotive fed with damp wood could not get up enough steam to move. "There we all were," wrote Harrison, "in our seats, crowded together, waiting to be off, full of gloom at the situation, wondering what would happen next, and all as silent as mourners at a funeral; all except indeed the General's daughter." She was quite oblivious of the President's obvious impatience with her chatter. But annoying as she was, she probably distracted his mind from thoughts that would have hurt him more.

At last the train started and proceeded cautiously over the bridge of the River Dan into North Carolina. Only a few hours later Stoneman's seasoned raiders arrived and destroyed the bridge. The President and the Confederate Government had barely escaped capture. When Davis was told of his narrow escape he merely commented colloquially, "A miss is as good as a mile."

Back in Richmond War Clerk J. B. Jones, who had indefatigably kept a diary since the summer of 1861, was about to bring his record to a close. On this black April 10 he wrote in despair:

It is true! Yesterday Gen. Lee surrendered the "Army of Northern Virginia." . . . There *were* 290 pieces of artillery belonging to this army a few weeks ago. This army was the pride, the hope, the prop of the Confederate cause. . . . All is lost. No head can be made by any other general or army—if indeed any other army remains. If Mr. Davis had been present, he never would have consented to it; and I doubt if he will ever forgive Gen. Lee.

Not one breath of criticism of Lee escaped Davis's lips then or at any time during his remaining quarter of a century of life. In Davis's later written words, "General Lee had succumbed to the inevitable. He surrendered to overwhelming force and insurmountable difficulties." Davis could understand, as perhaps no one else could, the heartbreak it had caused Lee to act as his duty prompted him. But he himself had been as surprised as he was grieved. For Lee had been his mainstay as well as the South's most illustrious soldier, and never until two days before had Davis conceived of even the possibility of his surrender. His thinking on Lee's unconquerable spirit was much the same as that of Bob, the youngest of the General's three sons.

Captain Robert E. Lee, Jr., riding toward Appomattox in the late afternoon of April 9, met a body of cavalry with General T. L. Rosser at its head. They had cut their way out and were going to Lynchburg and thence to join Joseph Johnston. Rosser informed Bob that General Lee had surrendered. Young Lee was astounded; he absolutely refused to believe that his father had capitulated. Finally several of his personal friends in Rosser's outfit came up and insisted that it was a fact. "I had never heard the word 'surrender' mentioned," he wrote in *Recollections and Letters of General Lee,* "nor even suggested in conversation with our General or our army." Stunned, he turned sadly and went along with Rosser's men to Lynchburg. There he found some wagons from Lee's headquarters which had been sent back together with some horses and servants of the staff. Not believing for an instant that the struggle was over, despite his father's surrender, Bob took charge of the wagons and with several officers started for Greensboro.

Judith Brockenbrough McGuire had called on Mrs. Lee two days after the evacuation of Richmond. She had found her "busily engaged in her invalid's chair, and very cheerful and hopeful." "The end is not yet," she had said brightly, as if to lift the hearts of those about her. "Richmond is not the Confederacy." Like Bob, Mrs. Lee was incredulous when she was told that her husband had capitulated to Grant. But even after the surrender was a certainty, Mrs. Lee, "ardent advocate of the noble cause," would rally her despairing callers by insisting, "General Lee is not the Confederacy." *

* Mrs. McGuire's diary was published shortly after the war anonymously as *By a Lady of Virginia.*

CHAPTER XXI

HOPEFUL PRESIDENT ON HORSEBACK

AS THE TRAIN bearing the Confederate Government crept into Greensboro on the morning of April 11, Davis turned his thoughts away from the calamitous, if unofficial, report of Lee's surrender. Even if Virginia were irretrievably lost to the Confederacy there were still Johnston's 36,000 men in North Carolina. Forrest and Dabney Maury had their seasoned troops in Alabama; Dick Taylor still commanded an army in Mississippi, and Kirby Smith was strong in Texas. In Davis's mind the South was far from the physical necessity of surrender. But he feared the Southern people might be deluded into trusting in the generosity of the enemy. Some persons, he knew, were fatuously doubting that slavery would be actually lost in a peace; others believed it would be a case of gradual emancipation. Would the news of Lee's surrender increase the delusion of a painless reconstruction already at work undermining the people's resistance? Davis was quite willing that the slaves should be emancipated, but constitutional liberty as Thomas Jefferson had envisioned it was all in all to him, and he preferred anything to submission.

The chill reception at the Greensboro station increased the President's anxiety. No welcoming group was on hand to greet him and his party. The atmosphere was one of sullen indifference. This hilly region of North Carolina had at no time been enthusiastic about the Confederacy. Greensboro had been a nucleus of pro-Union sentiment and now the townsfolk feared reprisals from Federal troops if hospitality was shown to the Administration. Stoneman and his 6,000 destructive raiders were not far away, and Sherman's dread soldiers were pushing Joseph Johnston out of Raleigh.

Only one Cabinet member was offered lodging: Secretary of the

Treasury Trenholm and his wife were welcomed effusively and borne off to a commodious mansion by a rich citizen, John Motley Moorehead, who, it was maliciously said, hoped to cajole the Secretary into swapping some gold in the treasure train for his Confederate bonds. Colonel John Taylor Wood, who had rented half of a modest house for his refugee family, had prepared a small second-story bedroom for his uncle-in-law, the President—despite the protestations of the frightened landlord. As no other Cabinet or staff member received an invitation, the men prepared to make themselves as comfortable as possible in the dilapidated cars in which they had arrived.

General Beauregard came to the station to greet the President. The meeting was cordial, and they had a private talk in the coach. Beauregard said he expected General Johnston to arrive the next day. Davis was relieved to hear that Captain William H. Parker, former Superintendent of the Confederate States Naval Academy, had taken the treasure train on to Charlotte. His guard of sixty young midshipmen and the precious load had passed through Salisbury down the line not many hours before Stoneman had cut the railroad and raided that town. Parker had left in Charlotte some $39,000 in gold for Johnston's troops.

When the President reached Colonel Wood's lodgings, several Confederate officers called almost immediately to consult with him. At noon Davis telegraphed Johnston at his headquarters near Raleigh.

I have no official report from General Lee. . . . The important question first to be solved is at what point concentration should be made. . . . Your more intimate knowledge of the data for the solution of the problem deters me from making a specific suggestion on that point.

When he spoke of "concentration" he made it plain that he had no thought of giving up the struggle. He wanted Johnston to be thinking of his next move before they met.

The next morning General Johnston arrived and set up temporary headquarters in one of Beauregard's boxcars. Soon word was received that the President desired to see them. Davis had come from Wood's house to the "official" coach on the siding and was waiting there with his Cabinet. His resolution had been strengthened by some rest and sleep. He was not unmindful of the irony of the situation, that the two Generals who liked him least and who had opposed him most were the men he would now have to inspirit to keep fighting. After greetings had been exchanged, Davis began the session by saying that he hoped to recruit a sizable army by bringing in the deserters and conscripting the men on the draft lists.

Surprised, Johnston's first significant expression was a desire to open correspondence with Sherman in regard to a truce that might lead to termination of the war. Davis, however, was confident that the United States Government would not accept such a proposition, and a failure of such negotiations, he said, would have a demoralizing effect both on the troops and the people. "Neither soldiers nor citizens had shown any disposition to surrender," he declared, "or had reason to suppose that their Government contemplated abandoning its trust—the maintenance of the Constitution, freedom, and independence of the Confederate States." No true Confederate, he believed, was prepared to accept peace on the terms of surrender at discretion.

Reading the cold, tight-lipped expression on Johnston's face, the President proposed to adjourn the conference until Secretary of War Breckinridge arrived with more definite news about Lee's army. Some of Lee's men were already coming into Greensboro with the avowed purpose of continuing the fight.

That afternoon Robert E. Lee, Jr., who had just arrived from Lynchburg, came to pay his respects. He found Mr. Davis "calm and dignified," and in conversation with "several officers of rank." He heard the President say that "the cause was not lost, though sorely stricken," and that "we could rally our forces west of the Mississippi and make good our fight."

"While I was in the room," Bob Lee wrote, "Mr. Davis received the official communication from General Lee of his surrender." Bob happened to be standing with John Wood at the President's side when the dispatch was brought in. Davis read it slowly, and then, without comment, handed it to young Lee. Turning away, the President "silently wept bitter tears." "He seemed quite broken at the moment by this tangible evidence of the loss of his army and the misfortunes of its General. All of us, respecting his great grief, withdrew, leaving him alone with Colonel Wood."

Jefferson Davis was fortunate in having his first wife's nephew with him at this crushing moment. He had loved Sarah Knox Taylor profoundly and her death three months after their marriage had transformed the gay young man into something of a stoic. Now, with Lee's official notification of surrender clutched in his hand, Davis again had an acute intimation of heartbreak.

General Breckinridge, after numerous delays, reached Greensboro in the night, confirmed Lee's surrender, and gave out figures. Johnston and Beauregard sought him out, said that they were agreed that the cause was lost, and the war should be ended.

At ten o'clock the next morning,* the thirteenth of April, the Cabinet gathered in the President's small upstairs room in John Wood's house. According to Reagan, the meeting was "most solemnly funereal," "for it was apparent that they had to consider the loss of the Cause." The "hero of Sumter," Beauregard, his hair quite white now, entered the crowded room with General Johnston. When all were seated, the President, as was his custom at Cabinet meetings, began with pleasantries. Then for some minutes a general conversation was indulged in. Remarking the grim expression of Johnston's mouth, Davis was not disposed to take up immediately the business for which they were assembled.

Finally he began by admitting fully the gravity of recent disasters. But he said he did not consider Lee's surrender fatal to the Confederacy's hopes. He believed that the struggle might be continued until the North was so wearied of war that she would be willing to make a negotiated peace. With Southern armies still in the field, he said, the South had some hope of getting reasonable terms. He expressed his conviction that the Confederacy's fall would involve ruin, both material and moral. He believed that confidence in the righteousness of the cause, if equally felt by his compatriots, would make the Southerners "do and dare to the last extremity." Pointing out that the main part of Lee's infantry had been composed of men from farther south who had absented themselves before the surrender "to go homeward," he had had reports of their avowal to continue the struggle. "I think," he said, "we can whip the enemy yet, if our people will turn out. We must look at matters calmly, however, and see what is left to do. We have not a day to lose."

Turning to his most bitter enemy, North or South, the President said politely, "We should like to hear your views, General Johnston."

Without hesitation and in a tone and manner that Mallory called "almost spiteful," Johnston jerked out concise, decisive sentences.

* Reagan says "morning," which is correct. Mallory mistakenly puts the meeting at night.

"My views are, sir, that our people are tired of the war, feel them-selves whipped, and will not fight. Our country is overrun, its mili-tary resources greatly diminished. . . . My men are daily desert-ing in large numbers. . . . Since Lee's defeat they regard the war as at an end. If I march out of North Carolina her people will all leave my ranks. . . . My small force is melting away like snow be-fore the sun and I am hopeless of recruiting it. We may, perhaps, obtain terms which we ought to accept."

As Johnston spoke, Davis listened "without a change of position or expression," his eyes fixed on a small piece of paper which he folded and unfolded. A tense silence followed Johnston's rush of words. Then Davis asked in a low, even tone, "What do you say, General Beauregard?"

"I concur in all General Johnston has said," Beauregard replied quietly.

Another silence. Then, without varying his tone or expression, and keeping his eyes fixed on the scrap of paper in his hand, the President asked Johnston what he proposed. "You speak of obtain-ing terms."

Davis recalled the several attempts to open negotiations with the Federal Government; the only terms offered at Hampton Roads were "a surrender at discretion." He had not called this interview with the senior Generals to learn their opinion about negotiations with the Lincoln Administration, but what it was advisable and feasible to do with their army as a military problem. Yet he realized that he must express willingness to treat with the enemy.

Johnston said he believed that Sherman would be ready to offer terms. With the President's permission he would propose an inter-view, embracing a cessation of hostilities during the negotiations. Davis yielded to the judgment of four members of his Cabinet and of the two Generals—only Benjamin holding his own views.

"Well, sir," Davis said, "you can adopt this course, though I am not sanguine as to ultimate results."

Mallory sat down at the desk and offered to be Johnston's aman-uensis. But the General insisted that the President dictate the note. Johnston signed it.

Then, believing that the enemy Government would decline to make terms, the President asked Johnston what line of retreat he would follow to the southwest. When Johnston expressed his choice, the President promised to order Commissary General St. John im-mediately to begin to place supplies at depots along Johnston's chosen route. He expected Johnston to make a stand at Charlotte, and if forced to yield, to retreat southwest "with Texas as a final goal." He felt that Johnston's superiority in cavalry would protect him from harassing pursuit.

The meeting, which had been extremely trying to the proud, unbending spirit of Davis, broke up. In the Cabinet's opinion, the President did not fully comprehend the widespread demoralization of the South in these last days. Or rather, his advisers believed that his own indomitable courage and singleness of purpose blinded him to what he could not accept.

The Cabinet members earnestly appealed to the President to provide for his own safety in the likely failure to obtain acceptable terms from Sherman. They discussed his possible escape to Mexico or to the West Indies from the Florida coast. Johnston told the President that Sherman had intimated that on the authority of President Lincoln Davis might leave the country on a United States vessel and "take with him whoever and whatever he pleased." To this Davis replied coolly that he would do no act which would put him under obligations to the Federal Government. Besides, if necessary, he purposed to go to Texas and there continue the struggle for liberty. He had "no idea whatever," he affirmed, "of leaving Confederate soil as long as there were men in uniform to fight for the cause."

Though apparently indifferent to his personal safety, Davis was beset by anxiety for his wife and children. Federal raiders had already cut the railroad between Greensboro and Charlotte. That same April 14, as General Bonham was leaving on horseback for Charlotte, some seventy miles south, Davis dashed off a note for him to take to Varina. It revealed that he was less hopeful than his Cabinet believed.

I will come to you if I can— Everything is dark—you should prepare for the worst by dividing your baggage so as to move in wagons. If you can go to Abbeyville it seems best as I am now advised— If you can send everything there, do so— I have lingered on the road and labored to little purpose— My love to the children and Maggie— God bless, guide, and preserve you, ever prays

Your most affectionate
Banny

But Mrs. Davis had already left Charlotte and reached Chester, where she was "joyously received" by General and Mrs. Chesnut.

However, hearing of another threatened raid, she was "not making an hour's stay which is unnecessary." She had previously written her husband on the thirteenth that she was leaving with "the specie train," for "they had a strong guard and two responsible men." "I am wordless, helpless" she confessed. "Would to God I could know . . . horrible rumors I hear of you. . . . May God preserve your life for your dear wife."

The Presidential party left for Charlotte with a protective escort of Tennessee cavalry commanded by Brigadier General George G. Dribell. Davis, Breckinridge, Mallory, Reagan, and the President's staff were mounted. The sick Trenholm rode in an ambulance along with old General Cooper, Attorney General George Davis, Benjamin, and Benjamin's brother-in-law, the diminutive and exquisite Jules St. Martin, who had been Chief Clerk in the Department of Justice.

In Greensboro, the ebullient Frank Vizetelly, artist and correspondent of the London *Illustrated News*, had joined the party and was now the only journalist in the Confederate caravan. He prepared to make pen-and-ink sketches for his publication along the way.

Heavy rains had fallen, and the roads were sticky with red mud. When the ambulance came to hills so steep the horses could not make the grade, the distinguished passengers had to get out and push. Benjamin beguiled the dismal time with his recitations of English poetry, for which he had made a reputation for himself in Richmond drawing rooms. In his silvery, resonant voice he would intone the stanzas of Tennyson's *Ode on the Death of Wellington*. Then from a seemingly inexhaustible supply he would light a fine Havana and fill the air with its pungent incense. As he wafted the cigar in the darkness, its glowing end seemed like a signal proclaiming all was well.

But the going was so rough and exhausting that after ten miles camp was made. This night the President and some others were entertained at "a house on the top of the hill," and served "the first good meal since leaving Virginia." The fear of visitation from Yankee raiders held this rugged part of North Carolina in a general chill like that of Greensboro. Hospitality was so scant that thereafter the President himself often stayed the night in roadside camps. But he carried it off with grace, as one inured to hardship. "Throughout his journey," Mallory was to write in *McClure's Maga-*

zine, "Mr. Davis greatly enjoyed the exercise of riding and the open air, and decidedly preferred the bivouac to the bedroom; and at such times, reclining against a tree, or stretched upon a blanket, with his head pillowed upon his saddle, and under the inspiration of a good cigar, he talked very pleasantly of other days, and forgot, for a time, the engrossing anxieties of the situation."

To some of his intimates, the traveling President seemed to relax for the first time in months, to feel temporarily relieved of responsibilities. His companions found him "singularly equable and cheerful," and his conversation bright and agreeable. He talked of horses and dogs, of woods and field, of roads and how to make them, of Byron and Walter Scott, of the habits of wild birds. His customary close observation and his remarkable memory made him a most charming companion when he was disposed to talk. When the party came to rivers he taught the uninitiated something about fording, and to the escorting soldiers he was "like a father, offering advice."

CHAPTER XXII

BITTER NEWS AT CHARLOTTE

———◆———

AT SALISBURY ON Easter Sunday, April 16, the President and several of his party were house guests of the Reverend Mr. Thomas A. Houghton, Rector of St. Luke's Episcopal Church. At tea the President appeared cheerful, and talked with a group of friends until late in the evening. Because Federal cavalry had raided the town only the week before, Burton Harrison, to better insure the President's safety, slept on the rectory veranda with some of the guards.

When the travelers reached Charlotte three days later, Harrison was informed that accommodations had been secured for every official except Mr. Davis himself. Because Stoneman had threatened to burn any place in which he was received, even Mr. Weil, who had let his house to Mrs. Davis, feared to domicile the President, though he happily was host to Benjamin, St. Martin, and Harrison. Only one lodging was offered the President: a house on the town's main street at the corner of Tryon and Fourth. It was owned by L. F. Bates, a man from Massachusetts, local agent of the South Express Company, and later believed to have been a spy. Bates was a convivial bachelor, who kept a "sort of open house with a well-stocked sideboard." Though Harrison knew that it was no seemly place for the President, he had to accept it. There Davis was to stay with his three aides, William Preston Johnston, John Taylor Wood, and ex-Governor F. R. Lubbock.

Bates, called a "graceless scamp" by some of the citizens, was not at home to receive his distinguished tenant; he had gone to the railway station to meet him. The front door was locked, but one of the party went to the back door and came through the house to let Mr. Davis in.

While the President was standing on the second step, the telegraph agent, Major John Courtney, rushed up and handed him a dispatch from General Breckinridge, who was at Sherman's headquarters near Raleigh. Davis read the missive in stunned silence.

April 19, 1865

His Excellency President Davis

President Lincoln was assassinated in the theatre in Washington on the night of the 11th inst.

Seward's house was entered on the same night and he was repeatedly stabbed and is probably mortally wounded.

John C. Breckinridge

After a second reading, he passed it on to a prominent businessman named William Johnston, who stood nearest among "the large concourse" that had come to greet him. "Here is a very extraordinary communication," Davis said. "It is sad news."

At that moment the street was suddenly filled by a column of Kentucky cavalry riding up in a cloud of dust. "The men waved their flags and hurrahed for Jefferson Davis." Some of them halted before the door and called for a speech. Standing on the steps, the President thanked the soldiers for their cordial greeting and paid a high compliment to the gallantry and efficiency of Kentucky's horsemen. He expressed his own determination not to despair of the Confederacy and urged the men to remain with the last organized band upholding the flag. Pleading fatigue from travel, he excused himself. Mr. Johnston then read aloud the dispatch from Breckinridge. Someone shouted. The President raised a hand to check cheers. Then he passed into the house. The crowd dispersed in a kind of awe.

Davis was deeply troubled. To Burton Harrison he said, "I am sorry. We have lost our best friend in the court of the enemy." He realized at once how much more harmful to the Southern States Andrew Johnson, the Tennessean, would be. He later wrote to Crafts Wright, an old friend in Chicago: "The fact was that without any personal regard for Mr. Lincoln, I considered him a kind hearted man and very much to be preferred by us to his successor." Of Lincoln's death Davis was to state frankly in the *Rise and Fall:*

For an enemy so relentless in the war for our subjugation we could not be expected to mourn; yet, in view of its political consequences, it could not be regarded otherwise than as a great misfortune to the South. He had power over the Northern people, and was without personal malignity towards the people of the South; his successor was without power in the North, and the embodiment of malignity towards the Southern people.

It was more than a full day before Davis got particulars of Lincoln's murder. The date on the Breckinridge dispatch was an error. On Good Friday, April 14, the President had attended a performance of *Our American Cousin* at Ford's Theater in Washington, and in his box he had been shot in the back of the head by the actor John Wilkes Booth. The assassin, a younger brother of the country's foremost tragedian, Edwin Booth, was known as an ardent Confederate sympathizer. In his fanatical zeal to help the South he had committed an infamous crime, which was to do Jefferson Davis and the Southern people incalculable harm. Brooding over what he regarded as the terrible and unjust wrong being done to the South, Booth had joined with a small band of conspirators to wipe out the top Federal officials. Davis's one-time admiring friend, Secretary of State William H. Seward, confined to his bed because of injuries in a carriage accident, had been stabbed in the throat, gashed across the cheek, and left for dead. Seward had not died, however; but the next day Mr. Lincoln had passed away.

No brief period in United States history ever held such dramatic events as the seven days preceding Easter of 1865. Each signified catastrophe to the South, beginning with Lee's surrender at Appomattox on Palm Sunday and ending with Lincoln's death on Holy Saturday. Davis belatedly got the dismal news that on Wednesday, April 12, the city of Mobile, the last major Confederate center, had fallen. And on April 14, the day Lincoln was shot, Robert Anderson had raised the American flag over fallen Fort Sumter exactly four years after he had surrendered it to the Confederates.

Charlotte would ever be a town of bitter memories and tragic news to Jefferson Davis. Here he now received General Lee's explanation of his surrender on Palm Sunday. It seemed as if the fate of the Confederacy had turned upon an unsent order. In Lee's report, dated April 12, Davis read with more than considerable surprise:

Upon arriving at Amelia Court-House on the morning of the 4th with the advance of the army on the retreat from the lines in front of Richmond and Petersburg, and not finding the supplies ordered to be placed there, nearly twenty-four hours were lost in endeavoring to collect in the Country subsistence for men and horses. This delay was fatal and could not be retrieved.

Davis felt certain that no orders for supplies at Amelia Court House had been received; and so it was to be proved conclusively. No one in the Confederate Commissariat had received any word about sending supplies to Amelia Court House. And no one in the commissary department of the Army of Northern Virginia had knowledge of such a request. The fatal delay was due to Lee's not having given that order himself or not making sure that such an order had been given and received.*

When Lee's army had arrived at Amelia Court House on April 4 and found no supplies, he had to appeal to the neighboring farmers to furnish food for his army. The one day's delay in collecting foodstuffs made it almost impossible for him to reach Danville or Lynchburg with his army. Lee later wrote that he had expected to find "plenty of provisions, which had been ordered to be placed here by the railroad several days since." But he did not say in his final report that he himself had ever given such an order, nor did he name any man who had given such an order.

Davis always believed that the harassed Lee thought he had made such a request, or that perhaps in the excitement of the speedy withdrawal from Petersburg he had not made himself clear. The great man's one fault was that sometimes his orders were not sufficiently specific.

Whatever the facts, fate had dealt the South another mocking blow, for if rations had been at Amelia, Lee's army could have reached the hills of Lynchburg. The "fatal one day's delay" was like Sidney Johnston's unnecessary bleeding to death in the hour of his victory at Shiloh, like the dramatic appearance of Ericsson's *Monitor* at Hampton Roads, like the lost orders at Antietam when England was preparing to recognize the Confederacy, like the shooting of Stonewall Jackson by his own men, like the untimely demise of President Lincoln.

North Carolina's Governor, Zebulon Vance, who had missed Davis in Greensboro, now caught up with him at Charlotte. When

---

* Douglas Freeman in *R. E. Lee,* Vol. IV, pp. 509-10, refers to an article in "Southern Society Papers," (3, p. 7ff.), which quotes a series of letters from General St. John and numerous other officers denying that Lee had requested supplies to be sent to Amelia Court House. "These letters," writes Freeman, "are convincing proof that no specific directions naming the village had ever been received." Freeman goes on to ask, "Was Lee mistaken or were his orders misunderstood?" Colonel W. H. Taylor, who as his aide was very close to Lee, is authority for declaring that no such orders were sent from General Headquarters.

General Johnston had notified the Governor of his intention to uncover Raleigh, the State capital, Vance had begun immediately to transfer the records and the tremendous accumulation of military stores to Salisbury and other western points in North Carolina. Listed among these supplies were: "40,000 blankets, enough stout English cloth for 100,000 uniforms, shoes or leather equivalent to 10,000 pairs, 150,000 pounds of bacon, 40,000 bushels of corn, vast quantities of cotton cloth and yarn, 6,000 scythe blades, and a stock of precious imported medicines." The President must have reflected somewhat bitterly what a difference these hoarded commodities would have made to Lee's men during the grueling siege of Petersburg. But he had been unable to persuade the Governor to relinquish his stores.

Davis was in consultation with his Cabinet when the chubby and now disheveled Vance presented himself and said respectfully: "Mr. President, I have come to see what you wish me to do." Davis welcomed him cordially and explained the military situation at some length. "We must double our efforts to meet the present disaster," he said encouragingly. "Moral influence is wanting, and I am sure you can do much now to revive the spirit and hope of the people." To Vance, Davis appeared "full of hope" as he spoke of the probability of all the Confederate armies retreating beyond the Mississippi. He intimated a desire that the Governor should accompany him with those loyal North Carolina troops who were willing to follow. "He was very earnest," Vance later wrote, "and displayed a remarkable knowledge of the opinions and resources of the people of the Confederacy, as well as a most dauntless spirit."

At length Secretary of War Breckinridge, who had just returned from Johnston's headquarters, interposed: he did not think the President had sufficiently answered Vance's question. "What would you tell him to do?" Davis inquired. Breckinridge suggested that since the hopes of accomplishing what the President desired were so uncertain, the Governor should remain in North Carolina to help his people.

"Well," said Davis with a sigh, "perhaps, General, you are right." When Vance agreed that he did feel a sense of duty to remain, Davis rose, pressed his hand in farewell, and said: "God bless you, sir, and the noble old State of North Carolina."

During the several days' halt at Charlotte while awaiting information from Johnston, despite grim news of every kind, the

President's cheerfulness continued. One morning he declared brightly to Burton Harrison, "I *cannot* feel like a beaten man!"

Davis was somewhat heartened by the spirit expressed in a letter from General Wade Hampton dated April 19. This valiant South Carolinian strongly opposed Johnston's surrender.

The military situation is very gloomy, I admit, but it is by no means desperate & endurance & determination will produce a change— There are large numbers of the A.N.V. who have escaped and of these many will return to our standard if they are allowed to enter the Cavalry service. . . .

The main reason urged for negotiation is to spare the infliction of any further suffering on the people— Nothing can be more fallacious than this reasoning. *No* suffering which can be inflicted by the passage over our country of the Yankee armies can equal what would fall on us if we return to the Union. . . .

Give me a good force of Cavalry and I will take them safely across the Mississippi—and if you desire to go in that direction it will give me great pleasure to escort you.

I write you, my dear Sir, that you may know the feelings which actuated many of the officers of my command— They are not subdued, nor do they despair. . . . If you will allow me to do so, I can bring to your support many strong arms and brave hearts.

Hampton was apparently one of the few who foresaw what Davis had prescience of. The great delusion was at work, undermining the resistance of the Southern people. Against all the counsels of Davis, war-wearied Southerners, who had sacrificed so much, were prone to believe that the pictured harsh realities of subjugation were largely imaginary.

A follow-up letter from Hampton, who had missed Davis at Greensboro, expressed his own resolution in even stronger terms.

My only object in seeing you was to assure you that many of my officers and men agree with me in thinking that nothing can be as disastrous to us as a peace founded on a restoration of the Union— A return to the Union will bring all the horrors of war coupled with all the degradation that can be inflicted on a conquered people.

As rumors spread through the Confederate camps that Johnston was contemplating capitulation, his men began to desert in alarming numbers.

A letter from Varina at Abbeville, S.C., dated April 19, reached the President. Only recently had she learned of Appomattox.

The fearful news I hear fills me with horror—That Genl Lee's army are in effect disbanded. . . . I do not believe all, yet enough is thrust upon my unwilling credence to weigh me to the earth. Where are you, how are you—what ought I to do with these helpless little unconscious charges of mine, are questions which I am always asking myself.

Painful as the last question was to him, since he had no answer, at least he was relieved to know that his family was safe. The children were well, Varina wrote, and played happily all day; their Billy and little Jim Limber, the adopted Negro boy, were "fast friends." "No such heartfelt welcome," she said, "had been extended as the one received in Abbeville." They were being entertained in the beautiful home of their old friend Armistead Burt, whose wife was a niece of John C. Calhoun.

On April 22 the President called a Cabinet meeting in the directors' room of the Bank of North Carolina on South Tryon Street, to discuss the terms of the Sherman-Johnston agreement, which Breckinridge and Reagan had brought.

Davis learned that Sherman had first met Johnston on the eighteenth at a place between the rival picket lines and offered the same terms Grant had given Lee. Johnston had replied that his position relative to Lee's did not justify such a capitulation, but suggested an endeavor to arrange terms of a permanent peace. Sherman was sympathetic to the idea. He, too, was eager for the war to be finished. And he had a predominant fear that if negotiations should fail, "pursuit and capture or destruction of Johnston's army would be extremely difficult." As Federal General J. M. Schofield, Sherman's second in command, was to write in his *Forty-six Years,* "Johnston's army was not surrounded and its surrender could not have been compelled."

Sherman had been willing to receive Secretary of War Breckinridge as a military man, but not as a Cabinet officer. Though Postmaster General Reagan, who had been sent by Davis, had not been permitted to sit in at the conference, at Johnston's request he drew up tentative terms of peace. When Sherman scanned Reagan's text he declared it verbose, and wrote out his own shorter basis of agreement, while substantially following Reagan.

As President Davis now read the convention it provided: First, the continuance of the armistice, terminable on forty-eight hours' notice. Second, the disbanding under parole of all the Confederate armies "now in existence and the depositing of their arms in their several State capitals." Third, the recognition by the Executives of the United States of the several State Governments. Fourth, the re-establishment of the Federal Courts. Fifth, the people and inhabit-ants of all the States to be guaranteed, "as far as the Executive can," their political rights and franchises. Sixth, freedom for the people from disturbances by the Executive on account of the pact. There was no mention of slavery.

When the agreements had been drawn up in duplicate and sent to the rival Governments for ratification, Sherman was very pleased. He told his troops that soon "there would be peace to the Gulf of Mexico." In a private letter he wrote to a friend in the North:

The South, broken and ruined, appeals to our sympathy. To ride the people down with persecutions and military exactions would be like slash-ing away at the crew of a sinking ship.

But what Sherman hoped to avoid was exactly what the vin-dictive Stanton and other Radical Republicans like Charles Sumner and Thaddeus Stevens purposed.

As Davis read the peace terms, he saw they were generous. But he knew that Sherman had exceeded his authority, and he felt that the Federal Government would not ratify the agreement. The pro-posals were so broadly phrased as to cover political reconstruction. Though in accord with Lincoln's ideas of leniency, which he had recently expressed to Sherman at City Point, they were the antith-esis of the Radical pattern for treatment of the South as intended by the powerful Republican vindictives. Davis did not believe that the Washington Government would have agreed to the concessions, even if Mr. Lincoln had still been living.

Of Andrew Johnson he expected malevolence, without even knowing how delighted the Republican Radicals were with him at first. After a delegation had talked with the new President follow-ing Lincoln's death, Ohio's Ben Chandler exclaimed gleefully, "By the gods, there will be no trouble *now* in running the Government." For Johnson had said, "Treason is a crime, and crime must be pun-ished. Traitors must be impoverished." According to G. W. Julian of Indiana in his *Political Recollections:*

While everybody was shocked and grieved at Lincoln's murder, the feeling was nearly universal that the accession of Johnson to the Presi-dency would prove a godsend to the country. Aside from Mr. Lincoln's known policy of tenderness to the rebels . . . his well-known view on the subject of reconstruction was as distasteful as possible to the radical Re-publicans.

Notwithstanding his belief in the futility of his own sanction of the Sherman-Johnston proposals, Davis withheld official approval until the members of his Cabinet submitted individual written opinions. He could not now disregard history. In effect, his signature as President would mean that he agreed to reunion and to the end of the Confederate States as a nation.

On the morning of April 23 the Cabinet carefully prepared separate reports; some members wrote at considerable length. While his advisers were engaged in setting down their opinions, Davis took the opportunity to write to Varina—the first real letter since he had left Richmond three weeks past.

Davis wrote from the fullness of an overburdened heart, revealing a melancholy he concealed from those about him. He had to prepare his wife for the possible end of the Confederacy and to hint at his own intolerable dilemma. His heart and his mind had hitherto been fixed on his duty to his country as its official chief and symbol. Now he was harrowed by his concern for the welfare of his loved ones. Where could they reach a haven from harassment and want? Home to Brierfield they could not go, for the United States Government had seized the house and with insulting intent had made it a domicile for stray Negroes. He was in dire perplexity.

"Your own feelings," he wrote, "will convey to you an idea of my solicitude for you and our family, and I will not distress you by describing it." In understatement he made her know the shock he had sustained in the sad ending of the noble Lee's forces.

The dispersion of Lee's army and the surrender of the remnant which remained with him, destroyed the hopes I entertained when we parted. Had that army held together, I am now confident we could have successfully executed the plan which I sketched to you and would have been today on the high road to independence. Even after that disaster, if the men who "straggled," say thirty or forty thousand in number, had come back with their arms and with a disposition to fight we might have repaired the damage; but panic has seized the country. . . .

At this very hour, when in other rooms the several Cabinet members were debating with themselves reunion or a prolongation of war, the President wrote of the undesirable alternatives confronting him.

Genl. Johnston had several interviews with Sherman and agreed on a suspension of hostilities, and the reference of terms of pacification. . . . To us, they are hard enough, though freed from wanton humiliation and expressly recognizing the State Government.

The issue is one which it is very painful for me to meet. On one hand is the long night of oppression which will follow the return of our people to the "Union"; on the other, the suffering of the women and children, and carnage among the few brave patriots who would still oppose the invader, and who, unless the people would rise en-masse to sustain them, would struggle but to die in vain.

Then he spoke *de profundis:*

I think my judgment is undisturbed by any pride of opinion. I have prayed to our Heavenly Father to give me wisdom and fortitude equal to the demands of the position in which Providence has placed me. I have sacrificed so much for the cause of the Confederacy that I can measure my ability to make any further sacrifice required, and am assured there is but one to which I am not equal— My wife and my Children— How are they to be saved from degradation or want is now my care.

Finally, he made suggestions which Varina might act upon as circumstances prescribed.

During the suspension of hostilities you may have the best opportunity to go to Mississippi, and there either to sail from Mobile for a foreign port or to cross the river and proceed to Texas, as the one or the other may be more practicable. The little sterling you have will be a very scanty store and under other circumstances would not be coveted, but if our land can be sold, that will secure you from absolute want. . . .

For himself, he intended to force his way to Texas. "If nothing can be done there which it will be proper to do, then I can go to Mexico, and have the world from which to choose a location."

As he closed the letter, emotion almost overcame him:

Dear Wife, this is not the fate to which I invited you when the future was rose colored to us both; but I know you will bear it even better than myself. . . .

Dear children, I can say nothing to them, but for you and them my heart is full, my prayers constant, and my hopes are the trust I feel in the mercy of God.

Farewell, my dear, there may be better things in store for us than are now in view, but my love is all I have to offer, and that has the value of a thing long possessed, and sure not to be lost. . . .

He gave the missive to Burton Harrison to take in person to Varina in Abbeville. His efficient, comforting secretary was to remain with his wife and assist her in her flight to safety.

As Harrison prepared for immediate departure, the Cabinet presented their written opinions. Although some were quite long and expressed in language apparently calculated for posterity, Davis read each statement carefully. He seemed to be postponing for some painful minutes the sealing of the document. When sifted, the opinions were in substantial agreement with that of Attorney General George Davis, who, in one particular sentence, summed up the matter succinctly:

Taken as a whole the convention amounts to this: that the States of the Confederacy shall re-enter the old Union upon the same footing on which they stood before seceding from it.

The President's counselors urged him to sign. Even Benjamin had now changed his opinion: the South, he said sadly, could expect no better terms from the foe. Davis noted with special interest one qualifying provision in Reagan's statement, which he read aloud.

But if the terms of this agreement should be rejected, or so modified by the government of the United States as to refuse a recognition of self-government, and our political rights of person or property, or to refuse amnesty for past participation in this war; then it will be our duty to continue the struggle as best we can, however unequal it may be; as it would be better and more honorable to waste our lives and substance in such a contest than to yield to the mercy of a remorseless conqueror.

Looking about the table, as if in query, the President saw that this qualification was evidently the sentiment of the Cabinet. He took up the pen, and in a steady hand affixed his signature to the agreement.

But barely an hour after the document reached Johnston's headquarters on the twenty-fourth, that General learned from a disappointed Sherman that the new United States Government had categorically rejected the peace proposal.

The reaction in Andrew Johnson's Cabinet had been violent against Sherman's terms. Stanton expressed vehement rage, "lost his head completely," and in the public press openly accused the Union's second General of disloyalty, implying that "he had been bribed by Jeff Davis gold."

Sherman now declared that he must resume the war and that he would start firing at eleven on the morning of the twenty-sixth, unless Johnston surrendered on the same terms as Grant gave Lee, "purely and simply."

The outcome did not surprise Davis. As he wrote later, the opinion he entertained in regard to President Johnson and "his venomous Secretary of War, Stanton" did not permit him to expect "that they would be less vindictive after a surrender of the army had been proposed than when it was regarded as a formidable body defiantly holding its position in the field."

General Johnston wired the President for instructions. After the briefest consultation with his Cabinet, Davis ordered him to retire at once with his cavalry, some light artillery, and as many infantry as could be mounted on draft horses. The rest of the infantry were to be disbanded and a place of rendezvous appointed. The route of retreat had previously been agreed upon and supplies placed along it. Davis believed that Johnston would be strong enough to encounter anything between North Carolina and the Southwest.

The President was now urged to leave Charlotte without delay. As hurried preparations were being made, George Davis, the courtly Attorney General, came to him with a personal problem. His home in Wilmington was in the hands of the enemy. His motherless children were staying with family friends, but without means of support. Jefferson Davis, anxious about the safety of his own little ones, sympathetically said at once that the North Carolinian should remain and look after his children. The two Davises parted with many expressions of affectionate regard.

The President had entered Charlotte escorted by cavalry brigades under General J. P. Dibrell of Tennessee and Colonel William C. P. Breckinridge of Kentucky. Now he left the city with the increase of three more brigades. One was composed of the remnants of those famous raiders who had created terror in Ohio under the late John Hunt Morgan, and was now commanded by his brother-in-law, Brigadier General Basil Duke. The other commanders were Brigadier General S. W. Ferguson and Colonel J. C. Vaughn. The Secretary of War, General Breckinridge, was in command of all— between two and three thousand cavalrymen. With the wagons of baggage and supplies, the Davis cavalcade would stir up a lot of dust on dry roads and some excitement every day.

When the Presidential party passed into South Carolina it began to move through territory that had scarcely been touched by the war. Shortly the retreat began to resemble a triumphal tour. Citizens lined the streets of towns and villages. Schools were dismissed so that the pupils could glimpse the President of the Confederacy. Along the way Davis was stopped by tearful women, bereaved of husbands, sons, or brothers, eager to greet him and looking to him for the country's salvation. When Preston Johnston, riding at his side, said that it must be gratifying to see people still with so much confidence in him, he looked pained. "It is that which makes me most miserable of all."

According to Colonel Lubbock, as the party neared a commodious mansion at Fort Mills, some seventeen miles below Charlotte, ladies stood at the gate, strewed flowers before the President, and insisted that he and his friends spend the night, which they did. Next day George Trenholm, who was now too ill to continue the journey, resigned his office as Secretary of the Treasury. In the letter of regretful resignation, he said:

I cannot retire without expressing the profound impression made upon me by your public and private virtues, and the grateful sense I entertain of the kindness and courtesy that I have received at your hands, in our official intercourse.

The President appointed John Reagan to assume Trenholm's duties. And he thanked Trenholm for his "lofty patriotism and personal sacrifices" and for the zeal and ability with which he had managed the Confederacy's finances and for the confidence he had inspired at home and abroad.

Davis shortly learned that, contrary to Presidential orders, Johnston had surrendered his army on April 26, before the President himself was out of North Carolina. Sherman had proffered ten days' rations for some 25,000 Confederates. In his last General Order, Johnston blamed "recent events in Virginia for breaking every hope of success by war."

Johnston's surrender caused Davis bitter indignation. The surrender of Lee on similar terms he accepted as justified, because Lee's army was virtually surrounded. He had never expected a Confederate Army to surrender while it was still able either to fight or retreat. In his opinion, Lee had capitulated only when it was impossible for him to do either one or the other. But Johnston was free to move his army westward out of Sherman's way. By paroles, Johnston had now rendered some 36,000 Confederates under arms impotent. His unauthorized action in surrendering had made almost impossible the continued resistance by which Davis had hoped to secure better terms.

Even now, however, Davis did not abandon all hope. And as Professor William Dodd was to write: "The success of Sherman and a victory over Lee would not have meant final disaster to Davis, who expected to maintain his ground with small forces after the manner of Washington in the Revolution, and wring recognition from the North even after defeat in the open field."

CHAPTER XXIII

THEY WITNESSED THE FALL
OF A GREAT CHIEF

———◄◉►———

ON THE MORNING of April 29, before leaving the home of Colonel A. B. Springs near Yorksville, Davis called together on the lawn his four remaining Cabinet members and the senior officers of his military escort. They discussed the most practicable route for the retreat to Texas, where the President purposed to re-establish the Confederacy.

As they proceeded, making one-night stops, Davis and the high officials were entertained in mansions along the route. This section of South Carolina, where John C. Calhoun had lived, had been untouched by the war, and the hospitality was like ante-bellum days.

At Unionville, in the home of Brigadier General William H. Wallace, Davis was served fresh strawberries—the first of the season. And there he received a letter from Varina in answer to his brought her by Burton Harrison. She urged him not to risk capture by going out of his path to join her.

Your very sweet letter reached me safely and was a great relief— I leave here in the morning at 6 o'clock for the wagon train going to Georgia— Washington will be the first point I shall "unload" at—and wait a little until we hear something of you—

Let me beseech you not to calculate upon seeing me unless I happen to cross your shortest path toward your bourne.

Then, referring to the lines in his letter censuring himself for bringing the present calamities upon her, she rose to absolve him.

It is surely not the fate to which you invited me in brighter days, but you must remember that you did not invite me to a great Hero's home, but to that of a plain farmer. I have shared all your triumphs, been the *only* beneficiary of them, now I am but claiming the privilege for the first time of being all to you now that these pleasures have passed for me.

206

Varina hoped to put the two oldest children in the best school she could find, "either in England or elsewhere," and then join him with the two youngest in Texas. She spoke of the uncommon kindness of the people of Abbeville.

Here they *are all your friends,* have the most unbounded confidence in you. Mr. Burt and his wife have urged me to live with them—offered to take the chances of the Yankees with us—begged to have little Maggie— done everything in fact that relatives could do— I shall never forget all their generous devotion to you.

But she made emphatically clear her opinion that nothing further in the way of resistance could be made *this* side of the Mississippi.

I have seen a great many men who have gone through—not one has talked fight. A stand cannot be made in this country; do not be induced to try it— As to the trans-Mississippi, I doubt if at first things will be straight, but the spirit is there, and the daily accretions will be great when the deluded of this side are crushed out between the upper and nether millstone.

Davis knew that she was right about further battling east of the river. But with Kirby Smith's army and such troops as could be got across the Mississippi, he felt that the Confederates could move out on the Texas plains "where they would not be flanked by rivers and railroads." In a region of unlimited supplies, he believed he could hold out for more acceptable terms and avoid the military rule and the humiliations of such a reconstruction as the Radical Republicans promised to instigate. His important consideration now was to conduct a war reduced to such narrow proportions that the South might obtain a quasi-treaty of peace which would at least secure political rights to the States and "immunity from plunder of the people's private property." Some Radicals, like Sumner in the *Atlantic Monthly,* had openly advocated confiscating the whites' estates and giving them to Negroes. But neither Jefferson Davis nor anyone else perhaps pictured the full shame of Carpetbag and Negro rule, which actually was to ensue, along with the disfranchisement of most politically mature white men in the South.

Davis had been encouraged in his hopes of continued resistance by troops who had escaped Johnston's surrender and were coming into Charlotte. According to Mallory, "they seemed determined to get across the river and fight it out; and, wherever they encountered Mr. Davis, they cheered, and sought to encourage him."

During the journey through South Carolina the President and

his four remaining Cabinet members mingled with the soldier guards and talked freely with them. The men speculated among themselves on who would escape capture. They felt sure that the President, General Breckinridge, and Reagan, the old Texas Ranger, could escape if they really wanted to. But they thought that plump Benjamin, who could not ride a horse comfortably, would surely be caught. This they regretted, for the jovial Jew with his vivacity, his anecdotes, and his unfaltering cheer had delighted them. He was so completely different from the "evil genius of the Confederacy" that he had been pictured as in Joe Johnston's camp.

As the party rode toward Abbeville, the President and Reagan took the lead well in advance of the others. On the roadside, passing a cabin with a well in the front yard, Davis stopped and asked a woman on the doorstep for a drink of water. As he was drinking from the dipper, a boy baby crawled out of the door and down the steps. The woman, who had been eyeing the distinguished-looking rider, asked hesitantly if he were not the President. When he admitted he was, she pointed to the child and said, "He is named for you." Davis reached in his pocket and took out a small gold piece and asked her to keep it for his namesake and tell him about the incident when he was old enough to understand. Riding on, he told Reagan it was the last coin he possessed.

When they reached Abbeville on May 2, the President was escorted straight to the Burts' home, now embowered in climbing roses in the height of bloom. He was warmly welcomed into the same room which Mrs. Davis had so recently vacated when she had started for Washington, Georgia. The Burts had pressed her to stay, but she had expressed her unwillingness to subject them to the danger of having their house burned. Colonel Burt had declared chivalrously that there was no better use to which his house could be put than to have it burned for sheltering his friend's family. Burton Harrison, too, had urged her to remain, but Mrs. Davis and her sister were fearful that they might be treated by Yankee soldiers in the manner that some Georgia ladies had suffered at the hands of Sherman's men.

A courier from Washington brought the President a hurried note from his wife, who had just heard of Johnston's capitulation.

I cannot refrain from expressing my intense grief at the treacherous surrender of this Department. May God grant you a safe conduct out of this maze of enemies— I look at the precious little charges I have and wonder if I shall be with you soon again. . . . Pie was vaccinated on the roadside, as I heard there was smallpox on the road. . . .*

Oh, my dearest precious husband, the one absorbing love of my whole life, may God keep you free from harm.

Davis was torn with desire to protect his family, but he had immediate government business to attend to.

The President's three aides now destroyed quantities of official papers. Some of the more valuable ones Preston Johnston gave to the secret keeping of his hostess, Mrs. Henry J. Leovy of New Orleans, temporarily taking refuge in Abbeville with her husband, Colonel Leovy.

At four o'clock on the afternoon of May 2, Davis called for the five commanders of brigades comprising his escort to confer with him at the Burt home. Dashing Basil Duke, homespun George C. Dibrell, and the three other brigade commanders were shown into a room where the President was seated beside Secretary of War Breckinridge. The informal meeting had the aspects of a council of war. As Duke later wrote, "I have never seen Mr. Davis look better or show to better advantage. He seemed in excellent spirits and humor; and the union of dignity, graceful affability, and decision, which made his manner usually so striking, was very marked in his reception of us." †

After a little conversation of a general nature, the President said: "It is time that we adopt some definite plan upon which the further prosecution of our struggle shall be conducted. I have summoned you for consultation. I feel that I ought to do nothing now without the advice of my military chiefs." He smiled as he used this expression, and Basil Duke could not help thinking that "such a term addressed to a handful of brigadiers, commanding altogether barely three thousand men, by one who so recently had been the master of legions, was a pleasantry, yet he said it in a way that made it a compliment."

After the President had accepted statements as to the equipment and condition of the five respective commands, he proceeded to declare his conviction that the cause was not lost any more than hope of American liberty was gone amid the sorest trials and most dis-

---

* They had halted briefly at a plantation, where the owner had taken a scab from an infected Negro child and performed the vaccination on the Davis baby.

† Basil Duke's article, which appeared in the *Southern Bivouac*, August, 1886, and is reprinted in its entirety in fine print in *Battles and Leaders*, Vol. IV, pp. 762-766, is one of the most vivid eyewitness pieces on the last hours of the Confederacy.

heartening reverses of the Revolutionary struggle. Energy, courage, and constancy might yet save all. "Even if the troops now with me," he added with quiet emphasis, "be all that I can for the present rely on." "Three thousand brave men," he said, "are enough for a nucleus around which the whole people will rally when the panic which now afflicts them has passed away." He asked for specific suggestions as to future war operations.

A strained silence ensued. Davis saw the officers glance at each other in frank amazement and distress. They hardly knew how to reply, since their views were so opposed to those he had uttered. Duke wrote:

Our respect for Mr. Davis approached veneration, and notwithstanding the total dissent we felt, and were obliged to announce, to the programme he had indicated, that respect was rather increased than diminished by what he had said.

The brigade commanders finally admitted that the events of the last few days had removed from their minds all idea or hope that a prolongation of the contest was possible. The people, they said, were broken down and worn out. An attempt to continue the war, after the means of supporting warfare were gone, would be an injustice to the South.

The President coolly asked why then they were still in the field. They answered that they were desirous of affording him an opportunity of escaping the degradation of capture. They would ask their men to follow them until his safety was assured, and would risk them in battle for that purpose, but would not fire another shot in an effort to continue hostilities.

Davis reacted as if he had been struck an unkind blow by a trusted friend. For a moment he sat speechless. Then he declared abruptly that he would not listen to any suggestion which regarded only his safety. After another moment of silence he recovered himself. In the face of unanimous opposition, Davis roused himself to make a last eloquent plea. He spoke of his deep faith in the righteousness of the Confederate cause. He appealed to "every sentiment and reminiscence that might move a Southern soldier." He begged the officers to accept his views and agree to continue the struggle for liberty. When he had finished, they merely gazed at him in sorrow.

Jefferson Davis realized that his leadership of a people and a cause was ended. He became deathly pale. "All is lost indeed," he murmured bitterly. He rose with difficulty. As he turned to leave the room, he swayed unsteadily and his military shoulders sagged. As his footsteps faltered, General Breckinridge stepped up hastily and offered his arm.

When Breckinridge returned the men were still sitting in solemn quiet. They had just witnessed the fall of a great chief.

Breckinridge, who had taken no part in the discussion, said he would urge upon Mr. Davis "the necessity and propriety of endeavoring without further delay to get out of the country." It was determined that the march be resumed for Washington, Georgia, at midnight.

Everyone, except the guards on duty, was ordered to get what sleep he could. But at ten o'clock Basil Duke was roused by General Breckinridge, who told him the Confederate treasure was at the Abbeville railway station. It had been moved hither and yon, by wagon train and by railway, from place to place, to escape threatened capture. Since there was no available railroad to Washington, Duke was instructed to provide a sufficient number of wagons to move it by dirt road. He did not like the job of handling money, but he picked fifty men as guards and obtained the wagons. He found the treasure in open boxcars, packed in small iron chests, money belts, shot bags, and various boxes, "some of them of the frailest description." By the flickering light of tallow candles, Duke and his trusted helpers rummaged through the dirty boxcars and gathered up the treasure, vastly overestimated by Federal General Halleck to be worth five million dollars.

Competent, courageous naval Captain William H. Parker, who had been in charge of the Confederate treasure ever since it had been packed in Richmond, now officially turned over the gold and silver specie and the bullion to Acting Secretary of the Treasury Reagan, and made his final report. The teen-aged midshipmen, who had proved such vigilant and uncomplaining sentinels in their fatiguing marches and long hours on guard duty, were disbanded, to make their way to their homes as best they could.

The President, who had agreed to the urgency of getting on further south, mounted his horse at midnight. But he refused to be hurried. After the party crossed the Savannah River on pontoon bridges near the village of Vienna early in the next morning, he and some others got breakfast and fed their horses at a nearby farmhouse.

Here Davis had a private conference with his loyal Secretary of

State, Judah Benjamin. He sent him on a secret mission to attend to Confederate business in Havana and Nassau; afterwards he was to join the President in Texas.* Pretending to be a Frenchman who was known to be traveling in the South and who had the same initials as Benjamin, the Secretary of State set off cavalierly for Florida behind a jogging nag, accompanied by Colonel Leovy, who would guide him for a fortnight.

Before Benjamin departed, he was given gold for travel expenses. And now the President ordered that the silver coin, amounting to one hundred and eight thousand dollars, be paid to the troops in partial discharge of the arrears of pay due them. Each brigade received about thirty-two dollars per capita, officers and men sharing alike.

When Basil Duke expressed impatience at the slow progress, Captain Morgan replied, "At least Mr. Davis is traveling like a President and not like a fugitive."

The cavalcade finally reached Washington. Davis had been in the saddle almost twelve hours in stormy weather. He had stood the trip remarkably well, and outwardly he was not despondent. As one of his escort said, "He manifested none of the airs of a would-be political martyr."

The quaint old town of Washington, Georgia, which dated from Colonial days, was the center of a region of rich planters, among them Robert Toombs, Davis's first Secretary of State, who had later sought to ruin him. The town had escaped Sherman's fiery march, and when the Presidential party arrived it looked as peaceful and assured as in 1860. Davis noted that the buildings on the public square had graceful galleries running the length of the second stories. Hospitality was offered the President and his staff in the home of Dr. and Mrs. J. J. Robertson, who scorned the consequences that might befall them from the oncoming Federal troops. The Robertsons lived in spacious apartments above the bank on the north side of the plaza. As M. C. Clark wrote, "At Washington, where the bitter end was known to be reached, the welcome, though fearful, was full of love, warmth, and tenderness."

* An original, unpublished letter from Benjamin in the Jefferson Hayes-Davis Collection now at Transylvania University, Lexington, Kentucky, states this categorically. The letter is dated London, September 1, 1865; and some of it is quoted later in this volume.

The President was handed an undated note left by his wife urging him not to try to meet her.

I dread the Yankees getting news of you so much. You are the country's only hope, and the very best-intentioned do not calculate a stand this side of the river. Why not cut loose from your escort? Go swiftly and alone with the exception of two or three. . . . May God keep you, my old and only love.

Though he was far more concerned about the fate of his loved ones than he was about his own personal safety, Davis knew that Varina's advice was sound. Calling for Captain Given Campbell, a Kentuckian commanding his escort, he explained conditions. His company was not strong enough to fight a large detachment of Union cavalry, and too large to pass without observation. So he inquired if there were ten men who would volunteer to go with him without question wherever he chose to go. Campbell returned with the answer that the whole company volunteered on the proposed terms. Davis was touched at this brave manifestation, but told the Captain to form a party of ten men only of his own choosing.

Secretary of the Navy Mallory now told the President that his own family responsibilities would prevent his going to the Trans-Mississippi. He therefore resigned his position. But he offered to guide Davis to the southern part of Florida, from which he might escape by ship to Texas. To prevent the President's capture, Colonel Charles E. Thornburn, who had been a purchasing agent for the Confederate Navy and who had joined the President's staff at Greensboro, arranged for a boat to be in readiness on the Indian River to take him to Cuba, the Bahamas, or Texas. Davis, however, reasserted his determination not to leave Confederate soil while a Confederate regiment was on it. So Mallory bade him an affectionate farewell and departed by train to join his refugee family in La Grange, Georgia.

Davis's host, Dr. Robertson, who was cashier of the bank, made the building available for a last official meeting. Here Davis "spoke with his accustomed calm," and still maintained his hope of uniting the scattered Southern forces in the Trans-Mississippi. He was keenly aware of his historical responsibility as the elected head of a Government. As President he had no constitutional authority to dissolve the Confederacy. As the Commander-in-Chief of the remaining armed forces, he would not surrender himself unless overpowered. And capture could not really reflect on his honor or prestige.*

President Davis's last authoritative act was to commission as Acting Treasurer of the Confederacy young Captain Micajah C. Clark of Richmond, who had been a confidential clerk of the Executive Office. When the meeting was over, Mr. Davis took a little rest before continuing his journey, while Reagan delivered that part of the treasure belonging to Richmond banks—some $230,000— to proper agents, who temporarily deposited it in the local Washington bank. The silver bullion, worth about $30,000, was stored in a warehouse. James A. Semple, a bonded naval officer, was given $86,000 in gold to take to Savannah or Charleston, concealed in the false bottom of a carriage. The gold was to be shipped to a Confederate agent in Nassau, Bermuda, or Liverpool for the Confederate Government's account.

To Clark was turned over the remaining gold specie, amounting to about $35,000, and Davis's personal luggage, consisting of a trunk and two chests. Some distance beyond Washington, Clark was to give each of the Presidential aides and Colonel Thornburn $1,500 in gold for expenses en route to Texas, plus some $10 in silver. Reagan asked for and would get $3,500 for himself and for the President, who carried no money at all. Clark was to take the remaining $25,000 straight on to Madison, Florida. The sum was to be used eventually by the Confederate Government in Texas.

Among Clark's selected eight guards was young Tench F. Tilghman of the distinguished Maryland family and a great-grandson of George Washington's noted aide-de-camp. Others included three of Mrs. Joseph Davis's nephews, the Philadelphia-born Van Benthuysen brothers, the youngest being named for Jefferson Davis.

Clark secretly sewed the President's Letter Books and certain other valuable papers in a quilt and hid them in Washington, to await a more propitious time.

When Davis emerged from the residential part of the bank building ready for travel, scores of admirers crowded to greet him and pay their respects. Ladies in summer dresses carried offerings of

---

* General Basil Duke, who was with Davis in his last hours in Washington, wrote: "I have never believed that Mr. Davis really meant or desired to escape after he was convinced all was lost. . . . He and his party were admirably mounted, and could easily have outridden the pursuit of any party. . . . I can only believe that he had resolved not to escape." Duke's supposition is reasonable, in that Davis would have welcomed a public trial. But it was Davis's solicitude for his family that brought about his capture.

spring flowers. While his aides were visibly impatient to be gone, Davis, with his innate courtesy, let each woman godspeed him in her own good time.

Davis then thanked the soldier guards for their services and bade them an affectionate farewell. For the first time, his servant Robert saw tears in his master's eyes. Young Tench Tilghman, who kept a diary, was so moved that he knew not the words to express himself at "witnessing the head and representative of a great and mighty people fleeing for his life." To Tilghman, Davis at the very end gave the impression "of being yet hopeful," though his gray eyes had lost "some of their lustrous power." Finally the President mounted his horse and made his last bows to the crowd. Then, with head erect, sitting his horse superbly, and looking nothing at all like a fugitive, he rode from the town.

The last drawing Frank Vizetelly made during the war for the London *Illustrated News* was of Jefferson Davis, hat in hand in the public square of Washington, saying goodbye to officers of his guard. "It was there," he wrote, "that President Davis determined to continue his flight almost alone. With tears in his eyes he begged the men to seek their own safety and leave him to his fate. With Postmaster General Reagan, his three aides, and a small cavalry detachment he headed southward for Florida." Vizetelly, who had come to admire Davis greatly, quietly contributed a note for £50 sterling to aid in the President's escape.* Shortly he began his circuitous route back to England, bearing his sketches and notes, which when published attracted world-wide attention.

Years later M. C. Clark, who had been with the President ever since the exodus from Richmond, wrote in summation of the prolonged journey:

I saw an organized government disintegrate and fall to pieces little by little, until there was left only a single member of his Cabinet, his private secretary, a few members of his staff, a few guides and servants, to represent what had been a powerful government. . . . Under these unfortunate circumstances, Mr. Davis's great resources of mind and heart shone out most brilliantly. He was calm, self-poised; giving way to no petulance of temper at discomfort; advising, consoling, laying aside all thought of self for our unhappy and despairing people, and uttering words of consolation and wise advice to every family where he entered as guest.

* Vizetelly's fifty-pound note, captured by Federal Colonel B. D. Pritchard, was finally turned over to the War Department on October 21, 1865.

CHAPTER XXIV

THE CAPTURE

————◄◎►————

WHEN THE PRESIDENT was some miles from Washington, the troops who desired release were given their formal discharges. At the request of General Breckinridge, Basil Duke and Colonel William Breckinridge each took 350 of their respective brigades and marched westward on different roads to confuse the Federals reported to be on the Davis trail.*

John Reagan stayed on through the afternoon and half the night winding up the Post Office business. He took occasion to call on Robert Toombs. After some conversation his host inquired if he needed money or horses. Reagan said he had enough to get him across the Mississippi. Then solicitously Toombs wanted to know if the President had money. Reagan replied that he had none, but that he himself would have enough for both. Toombs wanted assurance that the President was well-mounted. Reagan said that he had his tireless bay "Kentucky" and another first-class gray,† which Robert E. Lee, Jr., had presented to him at Greensboro.

"Mr. Davis and I have had a quarrel," Toombs said regretfully; "but we have none now. If he desires I will call all my men around here to see him safely across the Chattahoochee at the risk of my life."

Reagan, who knew the precise cause of Toombs' animosity, al-

---

* For some days General Breckinridge remained in camp just north of Washington with a small force as a nucleus to attract any units desiring to fight on. Upon the news of Davis's capture, he escaped to Florida, met John Taylor Wood, and after harrowing adventures together, they reached Havana on June 16. Eventually they went to England.

† Reagan mistakenly wrote in his *Memoirs*, p. 214, that General Lee had sent to Mr. Davis "his gray war horse Traveler as a present."

ways regretted that he did not reveal to him the truth. In 1862 Toombs had sought promotion to the rank of Major General, and twice Reagan had approached Davis on the subject. "The President, while speaking kindly of General Toombs," Reagan wrote, "said that he had in no case made a promotion against the objection of superior officers; and both General Lee and General Magruder objected to his advancement." Davis preferred to take the animus of Toombs rather than cause dissension in the army by revealing Lee's objection. Reagan had begged the President to let him tell Toombs the facts, but Davis felt that he would be betraying Lee and had refused to allow Toombs' quarrel to be transferred from him to Lee. This tendency of Jefferson Davis to accept blame which rightfully belonged to others was akin to that "pride in humility," which often cropped up in members of the Davis family. It was undoubtedly something of a flaw, even if partly on the side of virtue. In Toombs' case, his relentless enmity to the President caused calamitous trouble in Georgia and helped to wreck the Confederacy.

When Reagan finally caught up with the President and delivered Toombs' message, he said, "That is like Bob Toombs. He always was a whole-souled man. If it were necessary I should not hesitate to accept his offer."

After two nights of riding and camping out together the Davis party and the Clark treasure party separated at Sandersonville. The expense money was distributed as planned. Clark, with the remaining $25,000 and the President's baggage, took the direct road south to Madison, Florida. Davis turned southwest towards the Chattahoochee. Now shed of almost all impedimenta, his escort expected to move with rapidity. Cheer prevailed, even as they coursed a desolate, uninhabited region. The President's escape seemed certain.

But during the evening, while encampment was being made on the east bank of Oconee River, Preston Johnston walked down to the ferry. He heard that Mrs. Davis's wagon train had passed and that a group of disbanded soldiers planned to rob it that night. At this intelligence the President, who had barely dismounted, got back in the saddle. "This move will probably cause me to be captured or killed," he said to his companions. "I do not feel that you are bound to go with me, but I must protect my family."

When he rode off, the entire company followed. After some hours of hard going Captain Campbell declared that his men's horses were too exhausted to proceed without a rest. But Davis was too disturbed to tarry. He rode on; his aides and his body servant, Robert, behind him.

It was near morning when the President caught up with his wife's party in camp. He had taken several wrong roads in trying to locate her trail. According to one, he had ridden an estimated "sixty miles without drawing rein."

Davis remained with his amazed wife the rest of the night. He and his small staff and the escort, who had rejoined him, rode with her the next day. They all camped together the following night. His solicitude for his family, his escort muttered among themselves, will yet bring about his capture.

In truth, though he was loath to admit it, Davis, within a few weeks of his fifty-seventh birthday, was now excessively tired. Except for John Reagan, ten years his junior, most of the men of both parties were young enough to be the President's sons. Excellent horseman that he was, at his age a ride from Greensboro, North Carolina, to south Georgia was not exactly recreation. Despite his outward composure, the tragic and exciting happenings beginning with the Richmond evacuation had seared his innermost being. And now his agitation over his family's safety had brought on a racking attack of facial neuralgia. He was grateful to be able to lie prone in the ambulance for some hours while the march proceeded.

At last Mrs. Davis persuaded him to leave her, with her wagons, ambulances, and encumbrances. So with his little band the President rode southwest towards Abbeville, Georgia. That night, after his men had lost their way in a torrential downpour, he finally crossed the Ocmulgee River and occupied a deserted house on the outskirts of the village.

Hearing that 3,000 enemy cavalry were at Hawkinsville, only twenty-five miles to the north, Davis sent a courier posthaste to advise Burton Harrison to move on at once. In the dead of night Mrs. Davis and the children were roused from their tents, and in a storm of thunder, lightning, and rain her party pushed on to Abbeville.

Burton Harrison, who for four days had been suffering from dysentery and a low fever, found the President wrapped in a blanket on the bare floor of the abandoned house. Davis was so tired that he did not get up to speak to his family outside in the ambulance. He urged Harrison to proceed at once; he would overtake them, he said, "as soon as his horses had had more rest." Mrs. Davis's party continued in pouring rain, over roads so poorly marked and so obstructed by fallen trees that the soaked drivers often "had to wait for lightning flashes to see their way."

Some hours later the President and his company overtook Mrs. Davis, and they traveled with her more than twenty miles. John Wood noted in his diary that both Mr. and Mrs. Davis accommodated themselves well to gypsy life in the woods. "This morning," he wrote, "I saw them at the branch washing *al fresco.*"

About five o'clock on the afternoon of May 9 Harrison ordered camp to be made just south of a little creek to the north of Irwinsville, Georgia, some fifty miles from the Florida line. While the fires for supper were being started, Preston Johnston rode into town to buy eggs. Davis purposed to leave after he had eaten. He would follow his original plan, which, though he had lost two days in seeking to protect his wife, was cogent enough. As expressed to his aides and later stated in his handwriting upon the proof of Burton Harrison's article "The Capture of Jefferson Davis" for *Century Magazine* of November, 1883:

My purpose was to cross the Chattahoochee below the point where the enemy had garrisons, and as Taylor and Forrest were still maintaining themselves in the field, to join them and await reinforcements, or otherwise to cross the Mississippi immediately.

But on this fateful evening Davis did not know that five days before, on May 4, General Richard Taylor had surrendered all the land and naval forces in Alabama and Mississippi at Citronelle, Alabama, thus making his escape through those states virtually impossible. Nor was he aware that a proclamation, signed by President Andrew Johnson, accused Jefferson Davis of masterminding the assassination of Abraham Lincoln. This tack put Federal pursuit on a very different basis. Various Union contingents in Georgia were now furiously seeking him. From Macon, Georgia, on May 6, Federal General J. H. Wilson had announced in scattered handbills:

One hundred thousand dollars Reward in Gold will be paid to any person or persons who apprehend and deliver Jefferson Davis to any of the military authorities of the United States.
Several millions of specie reported to be with him will become the property of the captors.

On May 8, only the day before, a harsher directive had been sent to the Federal commanders to guard well "every port and ferry on the Ocmulgee and Altamaha rivers" and "to make every effort to capture or kill Jefferson Davis, the rebel ex-President, who is supposed to be endeavoring to cross."

A traitor had reported to the military at Hawkinsville that Mrs. Davis's party had passed through Abbeville, Georgia, and now Lieutenant Colonel B. D. Pritchard, commanding the Fourth Michigan Cavalry, was rushing to Irwinsville by a parallel road in the hope of capturing the "treasure train."

Though no one in the Davis camp suspected the imminent danger, everyone agreed that if the President was to attempt to reach the Trans-Mississippi by whatever route, he should move at once "independent of the ladies and wagons." Harrison secured his "positive promise" that as soon as something to eat could be cooked he would say goodbye and ride at least ten more miles that night before stopping. After arranging the tents and wagons, Harrison, worse for his dysentery and fever, lay down on the ground without any supper and fell into a profound sleep.

When Johnston returned from the village with eggs, he told of a rumor that a marauding party intended to attack the camp that night. Davis decided to wait for a couple of hours or so to see whether there was any truth in the report. His horse remained saddled, hitched close to the road, with his pistols in their holsters. Being desperately tired he stretched out fully clothed in his wife's tent to rest and went sound asleep.

Reagan and others, expecting the President to call them any minute, sat up quite late, and then they themselves dropped off to sleep. Under cover of darkness Colonel Pritchard had moved up from Irwinsville and posted one battalion in front of the Davis camp and another across the creek in their rear. In the gray dawn an independent unit, the First Wisconsin Cavalry, under Colonel Harnden, came in sight of the Federals in the rear, and each taking the other for Confederates opened up a fusillade with repeating rifles.

Burton Harrison was still in a deep sleep when James Jones, the colored coachman, who was up at dawn boiling water to wash Winnie's diapers, ran up to announce that the Yankees had come. Then the coachman rushed excitedly to call the President. Harrison was amazed to learn that Mr. Davis was still in camp.

Davis had already been awakened by the firing, which he supposed to be the work of the marauders. He jumped up, fully dressed in the gray suit in which he had slept, and said to his wife, "Those men have attacked us at last. I will go out and see if I can't stop the firing. Surely I will have some authority with Confederates."

On opening the tent flap to answer Jones's cries of alarm, he saw deployed troopers in blue coats. Turning to his wife, he said, "The Federal cavalry are upon us." Terrified, she implored him to fly. Reluctant to leave his family, he hesitated, and, as he wrote later, "lost a few precious moments before yielding to her importunities." In the semidarkness he grabbed a waterproof sleeveless raglan which was similar to his, though it happened to be his wife's. As he strode off, Varina impulsively took off her dark shawl and threw it about him.

The unarmed Davis had gone about fifty feet when a trooper on horseback ordered him to halt and surrender. Giving the man a defiant answer, Davis dropped the shawl and waterproof and advanced towards him. The man leveled his carbine. But Davis came forward, intending "to put his hand under the man's foot, tumble him off on the other side, leap into his saddle and attempt to escape." It was a trick he had learned from the Indians in Wisconsin in his youthful soldiering. His terrified wife, knowing his reckless bravery, rushed forward with a cry, and threw her arms about his neck. She may have saved his life, but, since success depended on instantaneous action, his opportunity to escape was lost. Other troopers dashed up. The President was captive. "God's will be done," he said in a low voice and turned away slowly. Because the morning was damp and chilly, he walked on past the tent and sat down on a fallen tree by a campfire.

During the wild confusion of the next few minutes, Colonel Lubbock struggled stoutly with soldiers who were trying to rob him of his horse and saddlebags. Preston Johnston lost his $1,500 in gold and his most treasured possession, the pistols his father, Albert Sidney Johnston, wore when he was killed at Shiloh.

John Taylor Wood escaped, after inducing the soldier who halted him to step aside into the bushes with him, where he bribed him with two twenty-dollar gold pieces to let him get away altogether. If Wood were captured, he knew it might go exceedingly hard with him, for he was not only an officer of the army and the President's aide, but as a naval officer he had taken and sunk several Northern vessels and was condemned in the metropolitan papers as a "pirate." Later, recording in his diary the dawn commotion, Wood noted that "the President was calm, his wife greatly excited." "She," he wrote somewhat ambiguously, "by her appeals, the children by crying, the servants by fear howling, destroyed all."

While the troopers were disputing over booty, Harrison emptied the contents of his haversack into the fire. Along with some official letters and telegrams he burned love letters and the photograph of his fiancée, Constance Cary, to save it from desecration.

In the midst of the plundering, Davis heard a piercing shriek of agony that rose above the hubbub. In his haste to pry open a locked trunk with a loaded musket, an unfortunate Yankee soldier had shot off his own hand. Out of this trunk later was procured a new hooped skirt which Mrs. Davis had never worn, and which indeed could hardly have been worn during the inconveniences of travel by ambulance. Yet a week or so later this skirt was to figure in an absurd accusation that Jefferson Davis was wearing it as a disguise when captured.* The North, sensitive to the fact that its own papers had ridiculed Abraham Lincoln for entering Washington for his first inauguration disguised, wished to attach a worse humiliation to Davis. It was sometime after the capture that the fiction was concocted and used to hold the ex-President of the Confederacy up to national ridicule. The story of Davis attempting to escape in woman's dress, carrying bags of gold, was intended as propaganda to inflame the credulous mob, not the intelligent Northerners. He was to be pictured in cartoons running through bush and briar in cumbrous hoop skirt. One would draw him cavorting in hoops, while melodramatically brandishing a dagger. The great Barnum would present him to the public in mocking tableaux.

It was almost an hour after the capture before Colonel Pritchard came up to Mr. Davis. He had been investigating the encounter between the two Federal detachments and the casualties that had

---

* In his first dispatch of May 11, Colonel Pritchard made no mention of any such circumstance as Davis being disguised when captured. In General Wilson's two dispatches to Stanton on May 12, which announced the capture to the War Department, there was no hint. Lieutenant Colonel Harnden of the First Wisconsin Cavalry, who arrived just after the Michigan troops, wrote a full report and made no allusion to Davis in female clothes.

Andrew Bee, a Norwegian tanner, and Captain James H. Parker, who contested for the glory of capturing the Confederate President, both denied that he was disguised. Bee wrote that he saw Davis emerge from his tent: "He had on a military suit, cavalry boots and all, and a gray flannel blouse. . . . He was pulling on an ulster without sleeves. Mrs. Davis followed him and threw his traveling shawl over his shoulders." Parker flatly denied the fabrication in the Portland (Maine) *Argus:* "I am no admirer of Jefferson Davis. I am a Yankee, full of Yankee prejudices, but I think it wicked to lie about him. . . . I saw the whole transaction from the beginning. . . . Jefferson Davis did not have on any garments such as are worn by women. . . . I defy any person to find a single officer or soldier who will say upon honour that he was disguised in woman's clothes."

resulted. He was amazed to find that he had captured the President
of the late Confederacy. He had been seeking the treasure supposed
to be with Mrs. Davis's train.

Davis protested the pillaging that was proceeding apace. But
Pritchard straightway claimed for himself Mrs. Davis's splendid
carriage horses, which had been repurchased for her by the citizens
of Richmond. Soldiers robbed her not only of gold pieces, but even
of some of "the baby's tiny garments," as she was to write Francis
P. Blair, Sr., on June 9, 1865. All about the dewy grass Davis beheld family articles scattered as unwanted: among them Varina's
and Margaret Howell's Bibles and Prayer Books. "You are an expert
set of thieves," he remarked contemptuously to one man, who coolly
replied "Think so?" When, though only partly cooked, his children's
breakfast was snatched from the fire and gobbled up by enemy
troopers, Davis rose in a fury of indignant protest and spoke harsh
words to Pritchard.

The ex-President finally asked that his family be allowed to proceed on their journey; surely the Colonel did not need to interfere
with women and children. But Pritchard said he must take everyone to headquarters in Macon.

The march to Macon took four days. The captured men rode in
columns of two, being lent their own horses temporarily. The
Davises traveled in the ambulance. As the ex-President sat silent on
his way to a highly uncertain fate, Margaret Howell could not control her emotions. She sobbed hysterically, and greatly upset the
children.

When on the third day the guarded captives came upon a cavalry
camp, a brass band on the roadside struck up a spirited rendition
of "Yankee Doodle." Here, during a halt, Pritchard and the rest of
the company learned of the proclamation offering a reward of $100,-
000 for the capture of Jefferson Davis. The charge, presumably in-
vented by Secretary of War Stanton and Judge Advocate Joseph
Holt of the Bureau of Military Investigation, was that he had participated in the plot to murder President Lincoln. Colonel Pritchard,
gleeful at his own good fortune, gloatingly brought a handbill
announcing the proclamation to Mr. Davis. Burton Harrison saw him
read it "with a composure unruffled by any feeling other than
scorn." Noting the name of his implacable enemy Andrew Johnson
as the signer, Davis said to his wife and Harrison: "The miserable

scoundrel who issued that proclamation knows it is false. Of course, such an accusation must fail at once; but now it may render these people willing to assassinate me."

The attitude of the Federal troops did change into menacing hostility. Jibes and expressions of detestation were heaped upon the Davises. Captain Charles T. Hudson, the Davises' special guard, became particularly crude and offensive. In 1890 Mrs. Davis was to write: "Colonel Pritchard, though evidently laboring under an invincible prejudice, even an active sense of hate, tried to give us as little unnecessary pain as he could, but of the horrors and sufferings on that journey it is difficult to speak."

Just outside Macon the Davis ambulance was halted and the soldier guards lined up on either side of the road. Fearfully the children crept up close to their father. Little Maggie put her arms tightly about him. He calmed and comforted her by softly repeating lines from the Psalms. During the hour's halt, as the soldiers stood at ease, they shouted their malice in words which Mrs. Davis considered "unfit for women's ears." When Colonel Pritchard returned with a brigade to conduct the prisoners into Macon, these men also testified to their belief in Davis's guilt "in rudest manner."

In Macon the Davises were conducted to the Lanier Hotel, which General Wilson had made his headquarters. Stout guards at the entrance opened ranks, faced inward, and presented arms as the ex-President passed. He received the salute as "an expression of the feeling brave men show to a fallen foe." Wilson had provided a commodious room for the Davis family. Dinner was brought on a covered tray. When the cloth was removed Davis was touched to see a bunch of short-stemmed roses among the dishes. With tears in his eyes the Negro waiter said, "I could not bear for you to eat without something pretty from the Confederates." *

After dinner Mr. Davis had an interview with the Union General. The one-time Secretary of War inquired about old West Point friends and Wilson answered pleasantly enough. In reply to a direct question about Lee, Davis declared him "the ablest, most courageous, most aggressive, and most beloved of all the Confederate Generals." At length Wilson brought up President Johnson's proclamation. Davis said carefully that there was one man who knew the accusation to be false: "the man who signed it. Johnson knew that I preferred Lincoln to himself."

* Mrs. Davis declared in her *Memoir*, Vol. II, p. 643, she kept one of the roses, pressed.

Wilson, "manifesting a courteous, obliging temper," * asked how Davis would prefer to travel to Washington City. Because of the small children, Davis expressed preference for the easier route by water. Wilson accorded him his choice.

Davis reminded Wilson that some of the captured men were already on parole, that they had merely volunteered to assist his wife to a place of safety. He requested that they be allowed to keep their own horses and go to their homes. Wilson seemed to agree that this should be done. But their horses were confiscated and they were sent to prison in complete disregard of the protection promised when they surrendered. Among them was Mrs. Davis's youngest brother, Midshipman Jefferson Davis Howell.

From the hotel the next day Mr. and Mrs. Davis, flanked by guards, were driven to the station in what Mrs. Clement Clay called "a jimber-jawed, wobble-sided barouche, drawn by two raw-boned horses." Margaret Howell, with the children and their colored nurses, followed in a "carry-all." It was a beautiful May day with garden flowers in profuse bloom and early Georgia peaches swelling on the trees. As the procession passed "the alien crowd hooted in derision." At the station a gaping throng had congregated to see the fallen President. More insulting shouts penetrated the air. One of the Northern soldiers yelled with mordant good humor to a sorrowful Southern onlooker, "Hey, Johnny Reb, we've got your President!"

"And the Devil's got yours!" the Rebel shot back with a sardonic grin.

For more comfort in the train, Mr. and Mrs. Davis seated themselves on opposite sides of the aisle. Senator Clement C. Clay from Alabama entered under guard. He had given himself up at La Grange on learning that he, too, was accused in Johnson's proclamation of plotting the murder of Lincoln and that a reward of $25,000 was offered for his capture. His wife, Virginia, one-time scintillating belle of Washington society, came in behind him. She had persuaded General Wilson to let her accompany her husband, whatever his destination might be.

Clay sat down beside Mrs. Davis, and they began a deep conversation. Mr. Davis rose and embraced Virginia. "This is a sad meeting, Jennie," he said, offering her a seat beside him. She remarked his pallor. She bowed to Burton Harrison and the aides. The

* Years later Davis was greatly surprised to read in The Philadelphia *Press* a malicious criticism of himself by Wilson, full of absurd fabrications.

coach filled up with soldiers. The car door slammed. A command "Order arms!" was barked. The floor reverberated with the thud of musket butts. The prison train got under way.

Reaching Augusta at dusk after a fatiguing journey, the prisoners were driven to the river landing and put on a tug without cabins. Fiery young General Joseph Wheeler, who had opposed Johnston's surrender, now joined the prison party, and so did Alexander H. Stephens. Ill and trembly, the ex-Vice-President looked peculiarly miserable in his greatcoat and shawl in the balmy mid-May weather. Davis bowed to him remotely but courteously.

In the saloon there was not a chair or a couch. For Mr. Davis, who was suffering intense pain in his eye, two valises were stacked one on top of the other, as a seat. Mrs. Clay insisted on bathing his temples with eau de Cologne.

At Port Royal, outside Savannah, the prisoners were transferred to an ocean-going side-wheeler named the *William P. Clyde*, which was to sail up the coast protected by the guns of the warship *Tuscarora*. A tug of jeering soldiers and their painted female companions came alongside and began firing coarse questions at Mr. Davis, who retired to his cabin.

The Davis children now had to part with their little Negro playmate Jim Limber. The ex-President sent a note to his old friend Federal General Saxton requesting him to look after the boy's education. Mrs. Davis later wrote that Jim "fought like a tiger," when he realized he was to be separated from his friends.

CHAPTER XXV

THAT LIVING TOMB

IT WAS a rough voyage and the Davis servants were incapacitated by seasickness. Neuralgic pain made Mr. Davis extremely restless, and when the waves were not too turbulent he would pace the deck with his delighted baby, Winnie, in his arms.

Sometimes he would converse with Reagan or Clay or Wheeler, careful to keep the talk away from sadness. Although several persons feared that he might be on his way to execution, according to General Wheeler: "President Davis showed not the slightest trepidation, but reviewed the situation as calmly as if he had no personal interest in it. He discussed the war, its men and its incidents, in the same dispassionate way that a traveler might speak of scenes and incidents in some foreign land."

And now that they were linked in common misery, he would exchange polite pleasantries with his one-time Vice-President, Alexander Stephens. It was oddly ironic that on his way to his grim but still unknown fate Davis should be companioned by this impractical, contentious man who had been a continual thorn in his flesh.

Davis fought down the bitterness that rose in his breast as he thought of those willful men who had, in one way or another, helped wreck the South's hopes for independence. Alexander Stephens by comforting deserters and stirring disloyalty had perhaps done more than any single public figure in the South to weaken the coherence of the Confederacy. Now that they were both encompassed in ruin, Davis could have more than a dash of pity for this frail, dejected little man. Whether contrite or not, or ever realizing the wrongness of his behavior, Stephens was to live to write in his old age: "I was not very friendly and in no way chummy with Mr.

Davis, but I wish to say that he was the bravest and most courageous man I ever knew."

On May 19 the *Clyde* anchored off Fort Monroe to await orders. Davis learned he was not to be taken to Washington after all. For three days the ship lay at anchor and Davis was not told what the Federal Authorities intended to do with him, but he was correct in his supposition that he would be imprisoned in Fort Monroe. Brick masons and blacksmiths were turning gun rooms into prison cells for Clement Clay and himself. Secretary of War Stanton had been casting about for a properly tough jailer. The current commander of the fortress was considered too soft. Stanton would not trust a West Pointer or even a regular army man. As Secretary of War, West Pointer Davis had become extremely popular with the military men because of his generous army reforms. Stanton finally found his man in young Nelson A. Miles of Massachusetts, a former clerk in a crockery shop, who, because of his energy, ambition, and toughness, had risen rapidly to become a Brevet Major General in the Volunteers. Ulysses S. Grant himself had recommended Miles. He telegraphed Halleck that Miles was being sent: "the object being to put an officer at Fort Monroe who will by no possibility permit the escape of the prisoners to be confined there."

The first Confederate to be taken off the *Clyde* was young Jefferson Davis Howell, paroled midshipman, who, nevertheless, was to be sent to prison because he was the President's brother-in-law. With a cheerful smile he said to his weeping sister, "They have come for me; goodbye, do not be uneasy."

At ten o'clock on the twentieth, guards called for Stephens and Reagan. The two were to be put aboard the *Tuscarora* and sent to chill Fort Warren in Boston Harbor. Stephens, who half-expected execution, came up and placed his frail little hand in Davis's, who merely pressed it sympathetically before turning away.

Reagan was depressed more for his Chief than for himself. Davis urged him to read the Sixteenth Psalm, in which, he said, he had often found consolation. The Texan opened his Bible and read the words of David:

> Preserve me, O God: for in thee do I put my trust. . . .
> The Lord is the portion of mine inheritance and of my cup: Thou maintainest my lot. . . .
> Therefore my heart is glad, and my glory rejoiceth: my flesh shall rest. . . .

Later, in writing of his parting from Davis to the Reverend Mr. J. W. Jones of Richmond, Reagan added, "I loved him as I never loved any other man."

General Wheeler, Preston Johnston, and Lubbock were sent to Fort Delaware. The only one destined for Washington City was young Burton Harrison, from whom the authorities hoped by rigorous treatment to extract some incriminating evidence against the ex-President. For Davis the parting with Harrison was the saddest of all. They had become deeply attached to each other. Harrison had not fought on the battlefields, because his Chief had found him too valuable in Richmond; but nevertheless he was an outstanding hero of the Confederacy. He had often risked his life for the President, and had served him with an efficiency, devotion, and indefatigable cheerfulness that perhaps no other private secretary in history ever surpassed.

As Harrison, debonair to the end, went over the ship's side to the tug, Jefferson Davis saw the absolutely final dissolution of the Government and the Cause he had been chosen to head. Though he had himself been a most reluctant secessionist, he knew that he would most likely be made the scapegoat for all the woes of the South. On his single head would eventually fall the responsibility for the so-called "sin" of secession, while the unfair propaganda press of the North would keep the people inflamed with hatred.

Finally it was learned for a certainty that Davis and Clay would be imprisoned in Fort Monroe. One-time Secretary of War Davis well knew that the fortress was the most formidable of all Federal strongholds. Its granite walls rose thirty feet and some of the solid portions were ninety-five feet thick. The solidity had earned Monroe the soubriquet of the Gibraltar of the Chesapeake. A moat surrounded the fort, a mile and a quarter around, the width varying from sixty to one hundred and fifty feet; the depth of water averaged eight feet. No one could possibly escape from such a prison. But escape was the last thing Jefferson Davis wanted. He longed for a speedy trial in which he might clear his name and that of the Confederate States.

As the Davises and the Clays waited uncertainly at anchor in the sea-reflected heat, Davis's neuralgic pain did not abate. However, Mrs. Clay wrote, "Always an intellectual cosmopolitan, he made observations on the natural phenomena about us, commenting from time to time on the beauty of sea or sky."

On the morning of May 22 a sultry, drizzling rain fell, like an obbligato to the gloomy speculations on shipboard. After lunch, when the rain ceased, a stir of activity was noticed on the wharf and in the water. Little Jeff, his eight-year-old face drawn with fright, rushed to his mother, who was lying down. "They say they have come for Father!" he cried. "Beg them, oh, beg them to let me go with him!"

Escorted by an officer, Mr. Davis shortly came up to his wife on deck. "It is true," he said, "I must go at once." Her face clouded; she was stricken with terror. She remarked that the guards who had come to fetch him were German mercenaries in blue coats. Her husband leaned close and said in her ear, "Try not to cry. They will gloat over your grief." Varina, who was by nature a highly emotional woman, struggled valiantly to restrain her grief. "The desire to lessen his anguish," she later wrote, "enabled me to bid farewell quietly." Davis braced himself, kissed his wife and children quickly, and went down the gangplank into the small boat. His wife recalled in her *Memoir:*

As the tug bore him away from the ship, he stood with bared head between the file of undersized German and other foreign soldiers . . . and as we looked, as we thought, our last upon his stately form and knightly bearing, he seemed a man of another and higher race.

When he was out of sight, Varina rushed to her cabin, threw herself on the bunk, and gave way to uncontrolled weeping.

Assistant Secretary of War Charles W. Dana, officially reporting to Stanton, noted, "In leaving his wife and children, Davis exhibited no great emotion, though he was violently affected." On his landing, it seemed to Dana that Davis "bore himself with a haughty attitude. His face was somewhat flushed, but his features were composed and his step firm." Dana did not know that the flush came from a fever.

When the tug landed at the Engineer's Wharf, gloaters were on hand to jeer. Brash General Miles rudely seized the august prisoner by the right arm. Preceded by a cavalry detail and followed by half a dozen soldiers with rifles at ready, the ex-President was marched off the long way around as in a spectacular. Behind came Clay, his arm grasped by Pritchard, and followed by more soldiers. The procession passed between files of uniformed men, then over a bridge, and through the Water Battery Postern.

Jefferson Davis was escorted to casemate No. 2; Clement Clay to casemate No. 4. Upon each side and between, in casemates 1, 3, and 5, off-duty guards were housed.

The ex-President was taken through the courtyard room into what had been the gun room. The low, deep embrasure looking onto the gray moat had been fitted with heavy iron bars. Openings had been walled up, and the place smelled suffocatingly of fresh plaster. Two heavy wooden doors leading from the outer room had been temporarily installed and secured by horizontal iron bars. At both doors stood sentinels with loaded muskets. Within the cell itself two armed guards had been commanded to pace incessantly. Four sentinels walked the parapet overhead. Four others were stationed on the glacis beyond the moat facing Davis's barred window. Six men stood outside in front of the casemate's entrance. Every two hours the guard was relieved. Every fifteen minutes the officer of the day was required to take a peek into the cell to see that the prisoner was still there. If the ex-President had been so minded, he might have taken a little pride that one man was deemed so dangerous.

Though some seventy-odd soldiers were detailed to guard Davis, locked within an inner cell with only one stoutly barred window that gave onto a moat and with a lamp ordered to be kept burning night and day at his cot's head, Stanton had still further "security" measures in mind. In his name Dana gave the following order to the jailer:

Brevet Major-General Miles is hereby authorized and directed to place manacles and fetters upon the hands and feet of Jefferson Davis and Clement C. Clay whenever he may think it advisable in order to render their imprisonment more secure. By order of the Secretary of War.

Ambitious young Miles decided to please his superiors by executing at least part of the humiliating and totally unnecessary measure on his chief prisoner. The next morning he would order heavy leg-irons to be prepared for the helpless ex-President.

The New York *Herald* of May 23 gave out to the world its editorial version of the imprisonment, calculated to satisfy the most vengeful.

At about three o'clock yesterday, "all that is mortal" of Jeff'n Davis, late so-called "President of the alleged Confederate States," was duly, but quietly and effectively, committed to that living tomb prepared within the impregnable walls of Fortress Monroe. The 22nd of May, 1865, may be said to be the day when all the earthly aspirations of Jeff'n Davis ceased. . . . No more will Jeff'n Davis be known among the masses of men. . . . He is buried alive.

But one Northern editor was not to be placated with any mere "living tomb" treatment. "We hope soon," he announced, "to see the bodies of these two arch traitors, Davis and Clay, dangling and blackening in the wind and the rain."

CHAPTER XXVI

THE TORMENT BEGINS

———◆———

SURVEYING HIS WHITEWASHED cell, State Prisoner Davis stooped to look through the iron bars of the low opening. He could see nothing except grayish moat water and the masonry wall of the parapet beyond. "Which way does this embrasure face?" he asked one of the pacing guards. No answer. Raising his voice slightly, Davis repeated the question. Stony silence. Supposing the first soldier to be deaf, he turned to the other. By the twitching of an eye, the second revealed that he understood but was not allowed to speak. Davis realized that his confinement was to be solitary, though two human beings were ceaselessly with him.

That night he was brought an unpalatable ration of boiled beef and bread, covered with a grayish hospital towel. The only utensil provided was a wooden spoon. According to reports, neither knife nor fork was provided because the authorities, who were looking forward to his execution, pretended that the prisoner might slit his throat or puncture an artery, due to some feeling of guilt.

Mr. Davis left the prison fare untouched. He was too gravely concerned about the fate of his wife and children to eat. To calm his mind, he sat on his hard iron cot and opened his Bible at the Sixteenth Psalm. The Bible was the only personal possession left him besides the clothes he wore. General Miles had taken all of his other belongings to headquarters.

On the second day of the ex-President's imprisonment, Miles called for Captain Jerome B. Titlow of the Third Pennsylvania Artillery. He had an order, he said, from Secretary of War Stanton that he might put Davis in irons if he thought his safety required it. When Titlow expressed incredulity, Miles showed him the order signed by Assistant Secretary of War Charles A. Dana.

233

While the General admitted that it was entirely optional, he had definitely decided to iron "Jeff," as he contemptuously called his prisoner. Titlow remarked on the mighty guard constantly on duty, the iron bars, the moat, the total impossibility of his escape. Miles agreed to forgo wrist-irons, but ordered Captain Titlow to have the company blacksmith prepare heavy leg-irons, and put them on that very afternoon.

Just before the sundown relief, Captain Titlow entered Davis's cell with the blacksmith, H. C. Arnold, and a helper. The prisoner was sitting on his cot reading his Bible by the light of the lamp that had been kept burning bright all night. He had had no sleep at all. The ex-President looked up in astonishment at the stout smith, who carried dangling leg-irons connected by a ponderous chain.

"I have an unpleasant duty to perform, sir," the Captain said.

"My God," Davis exclaimed in unbelief, "you don't intend to iron me!"

"Those are my orders, sir." Titlow's reluctance was palpably sincere.

Davis rose, his face livid. "But the war is over; the South is conquered. For the honor of America you cannot commit this degradation. No such outrage as you threaten me with is on record in the history of nations. The world will ring with this disgrace."

Captain Titlow, much embarrassed, repeated, "Those are my orders, sir."

"I shall never submit to such an indignity," Davis said with some heat. "It is too monstrous. I demand that you let me see the Commanding General."

Titlow told him that Miles had left the fort. "Then postpone the execution of the order," Davis requested, "until someone telegraphs to President Johnson. There is some terrible mistake."

"The orders are from Washington, sir," Titlow said. "And my orders are peremptory."

No one moved.

"Mr. Davis," the Captain said persuasively, "you are an old soldier and know what orders are; it is needless to say that an officer is bound to execute an order given him."

Gesturing towards the solid masonry, the iron bars, the guards within a few feet of him, Davis declared, "It is obvious there could be no necessity for such an order to make my imprisonment secure."

"My duty," Titlow replied, "is to execute this order. It is folly for you to resist."

Davis answered that he was a soldier and knew how to die. Pointing to a sentinel, he said, "Let your men shoot me at once."

Titlow was silent. Davis had his right hand resting on the back of his chair and one foot on it. His manner led Titlow to suppose that no further resistance would be made. "Smith, do your work," the Captain ordered. Then he turned to the embrasure to avoid witnessing the deed.

As the blacksmith stooped to place the clasp of the shackle round the ex-President's ankle, Davis seized him with frenzied strength and threw the brawny fellow across the room. Recovering himself, the furious blacksmith made for the prisoner with lifted hammer. He would have struck him down if Titlow had not caught his arm. Simultaneously, one of the sentinels lowered and cocked his musket and advanced on Davis. Titlow quickly interposed, and in a loud voice ordered the men not to fire. The next moment Titlow saw Davis and a sentinel struggling, both having hold of the musket. Titlow called to the officer in the outer room to bring four of his best men at once, unarmed. As the sentinel finally wrenched the musket from the prisoner's grasp, four stalwart soldiers made their appearance. "Men," Titlow said, "I wish you to take Mr. Davis, with as little force as possible."

All four instantly closed on him. The contest was brief. The prisoner was thrown on his cot and held down by the four men. Though he could not see the blacksmith approach with the irons, as he felt him grasp for a leg, with a last supreme effort, Davis kicked him off.

"The prisoner," Titlow noted in a written report, "showed unnatural strength." It was all the four men could do to hold him while the blacksmith riveted the clasp round one ankle, his helper holding the sledge hammer. The other clasp was locked on with a heavy brass lock, "the same as is in use on freight cars," Titlow wrote.

After Titlow sent the men to their quarters, Mr. Davis lay perfectly motionless. Just as the Captain was leaving, the prisoner raised up on his cot and with considerable effort put his feet to the floor. With the harsh clanking of the chains, he gave way. "It was anything but a pleasant sight," Titlow wrote, "to see a man like Jefferson Davis shedding tears, but not one word did he say."

Later Mr. Davis regretted his resistance. He said he had been taken by surprise and was appalled to realize his shackling might be symbolic of the treatment intended for the prostrate South. In the margin of his personal copy of *The Prison Life of Jefferson Davis,* he wrote, "My resistance resulted from a sense of right and duty; though desperately, it was calmly and quietly made."

The day after the shackling, General Miles notified Assistant Secretary of War Dana:

Yesterday I directed that irons be put on Davis's ankles, which he violently resisted, but he became more quiet afterwards. His hands are unencumbered. . . . The females were sent to Savannah today.

Miles may have felt magnanimous in refraining from manacling Mr. Davis's wrists. His want of sensibility is shown in the *Official Records* by his reference to the anguished wives, Mrs. Davis and Mrs. Clay, as "the females." The General's expression of contempt accorded with his treatment of the ladies while their ship was still at anchor. He refused to tell Mrs. Davis where she was to be sent or to permit a physician to call on Margaret Howell, who was ill with fever. All during their stay in the harbor "little tugs full of mockers, male and female, steamed around the ship offering insults."

At Fort Monroe, on the morning of May 24, Dr. John J. Craven, chief surgeon, was put in charge of the distinguished prisoner's health. Craven, a kindly man in his early forties, with sandy hair and beard and light blue eyes, had practiced medicine in Newark, New Jersey, before the war. He had two hobbies: natural history and his diary. The latter was to prove fortunate for the prisoner, as its publication in book form in 1866 helped secure his release. Craven was alarmed at the ex-President's appearance. After his first visit he wrote: "Mr. Davis presented a very miserable and affecting aspect, his eyes restless and fevered, his head shifting from side to side for a cool spot on the pillow. His pulse was full and at ninety, tongue thickly coated, his extremities cold and his head troubled with a long-established neuralgic disorder." He was "so emaciated that his skin chafed easily against the slats" of the iron cot, which was covered with only a thin mattress. His hard pillow was stuffed with hair. Craven ordered an additional hospital mattress and a softer pillow, for which Davis thanked him courteously.

For days the prisoner had not been able to get any sleep. All night a lamp flamed by his bedside. Two guards incessantly paced the hard floor of his cell, and every two hours there was clatter and barked orders when the guard was changed in the outer room.

During the first interview with Craven, Mr. Davis mentioned tobacco, "though not complainingly, nor with a request that it be given." But the good doctor wrote to Major Church, the Assistant

Adjutant General, advising that the prisoner be allowed tobacco. Soon he brought Davis the meerschaum pipe and the tobacco Miles had taken from him. "I hardly expected it," the prisoner said, very pleased. "And I did not ask for it, though the deprivation has been severe. During my confinement here I shall ask for nothing."

On a subsequent visit, the physician found Davis calmer, the feverish symptoms steadily decreasing. But he said that the footfalls of the two sentries within his chamber made it difficult for him to collect his thoughts. "However, with this," he said, touching his pipe, "I hope to become tranquil."

When Dr. Craven urged him to walk up and down the room as much as possible to aid his digestion, the ex-President showed him the broad abrasions on his thin ankles. "I can hardly stand erect," he said. "These shackles are very heavy. If I move, the chains trip me." The doctor thought of devising some means to pad or cushion the irons so they would not chafe the prisoner so intolerably. But then he decided to urge General Miles to remove the shackles entirely so that the prisoner could get some essential exercise—"at least until he could begin to digest his food."

Davis was desperately worried about his wife and children on the sea. He had futilely requested that his family be permitted to go to Richmond or Washington or Charleston, where Mrs. Davis had many friends. He had then asked that they might be allowed to go abroad on one of the foreign vessels lying at the Roads. Finally, he had been informed that they must return to Savannah on the old transport ship on which they had come. Until he heard of the family's arrival on land, he told Craven, he could know no peace. He was concerned about the weather, for the ancient *William Clyde* was hardly a seaworthy vessel. How are the winds? he asked. In his casemate, being unable without much pain to creep to the embrasure, he could not tell how the wind was blowing.

Mrs. Davis had much to contend with, he said. Ellen, the children's faithful colored nurse, had been forced by her husband to abandon the ship at Hampton Roads. All the other servants, too, had debarked, except Robert Brown, Davis's devoted valet, who went with the family to Savannah and was to be their greatest comfort in this time of distress. "My only consolation," Davis said, "is that some of my paroled people are on board, and soldiers make excellent nurses. Perhaps the roughness of their camp life makes the contrasted playfulness of infancy so pleasant. Charles XII of Sweden, Frederick the Great, and Napoleon were illustrations of this peculiarity. The Duke of Wellington is the only eminent commander of whom no trait of the sort is recorded."

Davis did not know that after the prison door had clanged shut on him on May 22, while Mrs. Davis lay prostrate in her cabin bunk, two highly rouged women detectives came aboard the *William Clyde* to search the ladies, who were stripped to their shifts. Then Colonel Pritchard demanded Mrs. Davis's waterproof raglan, which the ex-President had had on when captured. She was happy to give it to him, for she thought it would disprove the assertion that it was essentially a woman's garment. A few hours later a tougher raiding party came aboard, led by the detested Captain Charles Hudson. He demanded the shawl she had thrown about her husband, and brought her a cheap one to replace it. His men then went through her trunks, appropriating whatever took their fancy, and carried off, she later wrote, "most of the children's clothes."

Arriving in Savannah, battered in body from the rough voyage and bruised in heart, Mrs. Davis could find no carriage to convey the party to the hotel. So they trudged "immigrant fashion" to the Pulaski House. Robert took all the luggage he could manage. Margaret Howell, who had now almost recovered from her illness, carried the baby girl. And Mrs. Davis, who had lost her voice from a cold caught when water came through her cabin roof, walked stumbling up the street, shepherding the children, who bore parcels.

At the hotel she did find rooms. Immediately detectives were placed to watch her and to note all her visitors. She was told by the Federal General in charge that she would be permitted to pay her expenses, but that she would not be allowed to go outside the limits of Savannah. She was thus virtually a prisoner.

In Fort Monroe, for a man of Davis's refinement, the conditions of his imprisonment were almost unbearable. Not for a moment was he without a hostile gaze upon his slightest movement: when he stripped to take a sponge bath, or when nature's call made it necessary for him to use the portable commode, which was wheeled into the cell. General Miles decided when Davis should change his underwear. His tough beef, cut into hunks, he had to eat with his fingers, if he ate at all.

Until some soldiers talked to reporters, Miles, Stanton, and particularly Judge Advocate General Holt, were all gratified at the ignominy of Mr. Davis's imprisonment. But the sensational news of the shackling was leaked out to correspondents of the Philadelphia *Inquirer* and the Philadelphia *Telegraph*, which published the first accounts with all the ugly details. The New York *Daily Tribune* had the news on May 27. Putting a captive Chief of State in irons aroused clamorous disapproval throughout the North. Though instructed by the press to hate Jefferson Davis, the Northern public in general found it abhorrent to insult and torment him.

Some newspapers noted that the infamy was perpetrated by the order of the very War Department over which the victim had once presided with honor and conspicuous success. A few persons blushed to recall that Davis as Secretary of War had accomplished so much good that even his political enemies conceded that he had not been surpassed in that particular Cabinet post.

By the end of May the entire United States knew that chains had been put upon the helpless ex-President of the Confederacy. In the South nothing could have been calculated to increase to greater intensity the bitter sectional hatred that already flamed. Clear-sighted Northern politicians were distressed because of the bad odor such a deed would attach to the United States Government. Among those who took Stanton to task was the powerful New York Republican, Thurlow Weed, a close friend of Seward and once an admiring political enemy of Davis. On May 29 the shocked Weed wrote somewhat commandingly to Stanton from Albany:

I could not believe the accounts of Ironing Davis, but they *seem* authentic. If true, it is a great error and a great calamity. . . . I hope that this dreadful cloud may not obscure the glory of other Achievements.

The fact—if fact it be—is even less revolting than the details. . . . The world is with us. But this wholly unnecessary severity with a *State* Prisoner will lose us a great advantage.

The London *Times*, fearing that the American Government might go even further, said editorially:

It is purely in the cause of the American Union that we urge the impolicy of shedding the blood of a man whom a little success would have transformed from a traitor to a monarch. The stake has been played fairly, and lost entirely, and the victor should be content with success.

When public feeling against Stanton rose to a crescendo, he sent a peremptory order to General Miles to unshackle the State Prisoner. On a Sunday morning the blacksmith came back and broke the leg-irons which had chained him for five days. That afternoon, when Dr. Craven called at the casemate, Mr. Davis rose, both hands extended in gratitude.

Mrs. Davis, under police surveillance in Savannah, had read the grim details of the shackling, with thoughts, as she wrote Dr. Craven, "that stopped her heart's vibrations." On June 7, the physician received a piteous letter from her:

Shocked by the most terrible newspaper extras issued every afternoon, which represent my husband to be in a dying condition, I have taken the liberty of writing you. . . . Would it trouble you too much to tell me how he sleeps—how his eyes look—are they inflamed?—does he eat anything? —It seems to me that no possible harm could accrue to your government from my knowing my sorrow. . . .

If you are only permitted to say he is well, or he is better, it will be a great comfort to me, who has no other left.

Dr. Craven was forbidden by General Miles to answer this letter or any of Mrs. Davis's communications. But he was touched, particularly by a prayer which Mrs. Davis said nine-year-old Maggie had composed and taught her little brothers to repeat in concert for their "grace" at each meal.

Dear Lord, give our father something he can eat, and keep him strong, and bring him to us with eyes that can see and in his good senses to his little children, for Jesus' sake, Amen.

Craven would often find the coarse food on the prisoner's plate untouched. Knowing that his patient required light and nutritious food for his very life's sake, the doctor sent over one evening from his own quarters some tea and toast. When he called later, he found the prisoner-patient cheered by this show of kindness.

But on June 9 the physician recorded in his diary:

Found Mr. Davis relapsing and very despondent. Complained again of intolerable pains in his head. Was distracted night and day by the unceasing tread of the two sentinels in his room and the gabble of the guards in the outside cell. The arched roof of the casemate made it a perfect whispering gallery, in which all sounds were jumbled and repeated. . . . It was well formed for a torture room of the Inquisition.

Even after the shackles had been removed, Davis was to be subjected for months to the kind of confinement that would have driven many men mad.

In the darkest days of his confinement, one ray of hope penetrated the prison cell. It was a surprise letter from the eminent New York attorney Charles O'Conor, then the acknowledged head of his profession in the United States. Dated May 31, 1865, it had been sent "open" through the War Department and addressed to "The Honorable Jefferson Davis." After some official delay, it reached the prisoner on June 7, four days after his fifty-seventh birthday.

Gentlemen who have no personal acquaintance with yourself, and who never had a connection by birth, residence or otherwise with any of the Southern States, have requested me to volunteer as counsel for the defense, in case you should be arraigned upon an indictment which has been announced in the newspapers. . . . I beg leave to tender my services accordingly. I will be happy to attend, at any time and place that you may indicate, in order to confer with yourself or others in relation to the defense. . . .

The attorney said he inferred that the Department of War, if it permitted the transmission of this letter, would give Mr. Davis full permission to confer with his counsel in writing or in personal interview, if he accepted O'Conor's professional aid.

Davis was deeply gratified. But he had no stationery on which to reply. General Miles was in a quandary; he sent a dispatch to the Assistant Adjutant General in Washington to ask if he should furnish writing material for the state prisoner to answer O'Conor's letter. He was instructed to furnish paper for this "specific purpose."

On the single sheet allowed him, the ex-President gratefully accepted the attorney's generous offer. But, since his arrival at Fort Monroe, he said, all knowledge of passing events had been so rigorously excluded that he was quite ignorant as to any proceedings instituted against him, as well as the character of the evidence on which they were to be founded. Consequently he could not judge what kind of testimony would be required for his vindication.

Though reluctant to tax you with the labor of coming here, I must request you to obtain the requisite authority to visit me for the purpose of a full conference.

The answer, inspected by the Secretary of War, the Secretary of State, and the Attorney General, was finally deemed "an improper communication" and returned for emendation. Davis, deleting his expression of gratitude, patiently framed a new acceptance. But his answer never got beyond Washington.

After ten days had passed without a reply, O'Conor complained to Stanton and requested permission to have "a personal interview

with the accused." The Secretary of War coolly refused, stating that
Davis was "not in civil custody." Nevertheless, O'Conor prepared
to act as leading counsel in whatever trial was held.

Other outstanding Northern lawyers, among them George Shea,
also proffered their services. The Governor of Mississippi wrote
O'Conor that his State would pay him a fee of $20,000 for defending
the ex-President. But O'Conor declared he desired "to serve America by furthering prompt justice" and would accept no financial re-
muneration whatever.

When Dr. Craven called on June 11, he found the prisoner's febrile symptoms somewhat abated. Davis thanked him warmly for
some fruit sent with his breakfast. He was very fond of fruit, and
he spoke of the various fruits of the tropics and their excellent
adaptation to the wants of the inhabitants. Craven had a little
daughter named Annie, who felt sorry for the lonely prisoner and
who began preparing special dishes for him to be smuggled in
with his tray of prison fare.

Dr. Craven had come to believe that the dampness of the cell
was really dangerous for the prisoner's health and caused the stric-
ture in his chest. The fresh plaster had not dried; the walls sweated.
The sun could not penetrate the cell, and the water of the moat
"stirred up noxious vapors." Finally, the doctor insisted to General
Miles that the prisoner was in imperative need of "different pabulum both for his eyes and his mind." The Medical Inspector of the
Department agreed. With no one to speak to except the physician,
nothing to read but the fine-print Bible, nothing to look at but the
whitewashed walls or the dull moat water, the solitude was having
a most deleterious effect. Besides, the prisoner's nights were extremely tedious, being almost without sleep. The officers' sabers still
clanged on the brick floor when the guard was changed every two
hours. The guards' shoes squeaked maddeningly. The lamp still
shone constantly on the prisoner's pillow.

Ill, with his nerves kept on raw edge, the ex-President had also
to submit to innumerable petty indignities, as well as the intolerably distracting noises that tried him to the limit of his endurance.
However, there is only one record of his losing control with a Federal private and it may either be an exaggeration or a fabrication.
After his release from service, Elisha Kisner of the Third Pennsylvania Artillery told how "old Jeff," as he called him, once seized
him by the throat.

Davis was lying on his bed, apparently trying to get a nap, and our orders were to pace his room constantly, but under no consideration to speak or enter into any conversation with him. My shoes, which were then new, screeched as I passed his bed and this seemed to annoy him. Once as I passed him, he turned to me and growled, "I wish you'd make less noise." I replied, "I wish you'd keep quiet." Then he turned over with his face to the wall, and I kept walking back and forward past his bed. In a minute or two he growled again, "Can't you keep quiet?" To this I replied, "Can't you hold your jaw?" Then he got up and commenced to walk the floor, mad as a caged lion. I passed him and turned to go back, when I met him about the middle of the room. Just as I was about to re-pass him he suddenly sprang at me, and with his left hand caught me by the throat. I struggled to get loose, but he held me as though I had been in a vise. I could not use my gun, as he held me close to him. I struggled for breath, but he had shut off my wind. The scuffle drew the attention of the other guard and also the officer outside, when he rattled his sword against the iron-grated door, and then old Jeff let loose of me and went back to his bed. I tell you I was weak in the knees when he did not let go, and though he only held me a moment or so, it seemed like an hour. . . . He was a spunky old cuss, I tell you.*

Soon after the collaring episode, while Davis was napping, one of the guards drew his picture on the wall with a piece of crayon, representing him dangling from a rope. An uncomplimentary inscription beneath the picture completed the insult. When Davis saw it on awakening he called it to the attention of the officer of the guard, who had the drawing washed out.

For the most part Jefferson Davis earned the respect of his guards, as he endured the endless nerve-racking tramping on his floor with extraordinary self-control. The men knew as well as he that the constant pacing up and down had been instituted, not for security measures, but purely to torment him. Some went out of their way to tread lightly. Kisner was one of the exceptions.

Because of Dr. Craven's report that the continuous pacing of guards within a few feet of the prisoner's bed was counteracting all his efforts to quiet his patient's nerves, on June 23 General Miles moved them temporarily into the outer room. Here they could keep up their relentless watch through the two iron-grilled doors.

When the physician called next day he found that Davis had had his first good night since his incarceration. But his eyes troubled

---

* The statement of Elisha Kisner, an employee of the Waterson Planing Mill Company, appeared in the Watsonville (Pa.) *Record* and was widely quoted.

him, and there was that persistent throbbing pain in the back of the neck. He spoke of the deleterious effect upon the eyes of reflected light from whitewash, and diverged to the phenomenon of the mirage. Davis remarked that mirages in the Egyptian and African deserts were chiefly observed in the afternoons after the sands had been thoroughly heated by the blazing sun. "Science," he said, "is fast explaining all the mysteries of the earth on which ignorance in preceding ages founded its superstitions and the magicians built up a belief in their reputed power."

Davis dreaded photophobia; he had seen a few cases of it, and had heard that it was the keenest agony to which nerves were susceptible. Injured as his sight was already, with one eye completely blind, he sometimes had the fear that he might end in total blindness. "Not that I may expect many pleasant things to look upon, Doctor," he said with an ironic smile; "but I need sight for my defense, which must also be the defense of the cause which I represented, and which my sufferings have been aimed to degrade."

Davis believed that continually reading the fine print of the Bible severely taxed his sight. Might he not have something else to read and in larger print? "Utter inaction for a mind so busy as mine has been is impossible," he remarked. "I must either furnish it with external employment or allow it to prey upon itself. Nature has provided all varieties of pabulum to the vision, resting it on one color when weary with another, changing the forms on which it had been employed with every object of nature. To employ the vision continually on one size of type must be injurious."

Craven agreed that Davis did need other pabulum, and asked for books from the fort library. He had mentioned to General Miles the necessity of the prisoner's getting some exercise and fresh air, which was usually allowed even for condemned criminals in penitentiaries.

On June 23 the physician received a second distressful letter from Mrs. Davis. She was pursued, she said, by dreadful pictures thrown before her every day in excerpts from Northern correspondents and published in Southern papers "in which the agony inseparable from defeat and imprisonment is represented to have been heightened for my husband by chains and starvation."

Can it be that these tales are even in part true? That such atrocities could render him frantic? I know it is not so. I have so often tended him through months of nervous agony without even hearing a groan or an expression of impatience, that I know these tales of childish ravings are not true.

But there was something about the rumors that convinced her that they were not altogether false.

Will you not, my dear sir, tell me the worst? Is he dying? Taken from me with only ten minutes warning, I could see that he was quite ill; indeed suffering from fever at the hour of our separation. . . .

With a blaze of light pouring upon the dilated pupils of eyes always sensitive to it, chains fettering his emaciated limbs, coarse food served, as the newspapers describe it, in the most repulsive manner—hope seems denied to me. . . .

Please try to cheer him about us, for we are kindly cared for by Southern friends who love him here. Will you not trouble to write me, only this once?

Again Dr. Craven was strictly forbidden to reply to Mrs. Davis. But he gave the prisoner the comfort of knowing that his family was being cared for by kind people in Savannah.

CHAPTER XXVII

THE PERSECUTION CONTINUES

———————⫷◉⫸———————

AS THE DAYS passed, Dr. Craven looked forward with keen anticipation to his visits with the former President. He confessed in his journal that he was enchanted by Mr. Davis's conversation and amazed at his prodigious memory. He marveled at the remarkable range of his knowledge, "from warfare to optics and acoustics, to the culture of oysters, to Hogarth, to engineering, the works of Isaak Walton, tropical fruits, the habits of the loggerhead turtles, statuary, Edmund Burke, and scores of diverse subjects."

In the beginning no reading matter had been allowed Davis except his Bible. Then after some hesitation Secretary of War Stanton, who himself professed to be an Episcopalian, had permitted him to have his Prayer Book. By July first the prisoner was allowed not only devotional books, but histories from the fort's library and some magazines. He also received occasional newspapers, principally the New York *Herald*, which in 1861 had vehemently opposed Lincoln's coercion of the seceded States, but now spoke of Davis in most uncomplimentary terms. Periodicals were carefully selected "with a view to their loyal principles, lest his mind be corrupted by any hint of rebellious doctrines." Through the *Herald*, Davis got news of the miserable political and economic condition of the Southern States.

Craven admired Mr. Davis's composure in bearing excruciating neuralgic pains and his efforts to endure his humiliations without complaint. But on Sunday morning, July 11, after a nerve-racking, wakeful night, for the first time Davis sent for the doctor. Craven found the ex-President "very desponding, the failure of his sight troubling him, and his nights almost without sleep."

His present treatment was killing him by inches, and he wished shorter work could be made of his torment. He had hoped long since for a trial, which should be public and therefore with some semblance of fairness. The odious, malignant and absurd insinuation that he was connected in some manner with the great crime of Mr. Lincoln's assassination was his chief personal motive for so earnestly desiring an early opportunity of vindication.

But apart from personal considerations, Davis said, he was evidently made the representative through whom the action of the seceding States was to be argued and decided. For this reason he strongly desired to be heard in behalf of the defeated, and, to him, still honorable cause of State Rights. He accepted defeat, he said, as a man has to accept all consequences of an accomplished fact. But the last remaining labor which life could impose on him as a public duty was to vindicate the theory and justice of his cause, by showing on the authority of the Constitution that in seceding his people had committed no crime but had merely asserted a right.

He spoke to Craven of his New Hampshire friend, ex-President Franklin Pierce, as a fair public man who had studied Constitutional law thoroughly. If he were given choice of counsel, he would desire Pierce as one of those whose advice he would think most reliable. Davis had recently read in the New York *Herald* that Senator Reverdy Johnson, a Maryland Unionist, as well as Charles O'Conor, had professed readiness to assume his defense. For this, he felt grateful personally and for the South. "My own fate," he declared, "is of no importance in this matter, save to the Government on which history will devolve the responsibility for my treatment."

"My people," Davis explained, "attempted what your people denounced as a revolution. My people failed; but your people have suffered a revolution which must prove disastrous to *their* liberties unless promptly remedied by legal decision. State sovereignty, the cornerstone of the Constitution, has become a name." Then he added somewhat bitterly: "There is no longer power or will in any State that would dare refuse compliance with any tinkle of Mr. Seward's little bell."

In answer to some professional medical questions, Davis asked with strange intensity, "Doctor, have you ever had the consciousness of being watched? Of having an eye fixed on you every moment, intently scrutinizing your most minute actions, and the variations of your countenance and posture?"

To have a human eye riveted on you in every moment of waking or sleeping, sitting, walking, or lying down, is a refinement of torture on anything the Comanches or Spanish Inquisition ever dreamed. They, in their ignorance of cruel art, struck only at the body; and the nerves have a very limited capacity of pain. This is a maddening, incessant torture of the mind, increasing with every moment it is endured.

He paused, and then went on:

Letting a single drop of water fall on the head every sixty seconds does not hurt at first, but its victim dies of raving agony, it is alleged, if the infliction be continued. The torture of being incessantly watched is, to the mind, what the water-dropping is to the body, but more afflictive, as the mind is more susceptible of pain. . . .
The human eye forever fixed upon you is the eye of a spy, or enemy, gloating in the pain and humiliation which it itself creates.
I have lived too long in the woods to be frightened by an owl, and have seen death too often to dread any form of pain. But I confess, Doctor, this torture of being watched begins to prey on my reason. The lamp burning in my room all night would seem a torment devised by someone who had intimate knowledge of my habits, my custom having been through life never to sleep except in total darkness.

The medical aspects of this conversation with the prisoner Dr. Craven duly reported to Miles. He then prescribed weak brandy and water with meals to aid digestion. But he knew that this simple remedy would not relieve the prisoner's real trouble.

Shortly after the Sunday visit to the cell, on July 11, Dr. Craven received another letter from Mrs. Davis begging news of her husband. No answer, she said, had been returned to her first three letters. All the harrowing newspaper accounts of her husband's treatment had been in accord in representing the physician as kind to the prisoner, and the last one had reported that the physician's "wife and little daughter were also kind enough to attend to his wants." She thanked God for him, and for his "manly disregard of everything but the suffering man before you."

Davis, who longed to be allowed to communicate with his wife, said ruefully to Craven: "Even criminals condemned to death for heinous crimes are allowed not only correspondence with their wives, but interviews at which no jailer stands within earshot."

Aroused by an incendiary press, a host of Northerners had been willing at first to assume that Jefferson Davis was implicated in Lincoln's assassination, as President Johnson had openly proclaimed.

But virtually no one in high authority believed the absurd accusation, not even the vindictive Thaddeus Stevens. Judge Advocate General Joseph Holt, however, pretended to credit it. This most hateful of all defecting Southerners apparently conceived it to be his "special duty to accomplish the ruin of Mr. Davis." Knowingly or unwittingly, Holt became the dupe of a shady character who called himself Sanford Conover. (The real name of this accomplished perjurer was Charles A. Dunham.)

Conover, for a handsome consideration, offered to produce witnesses who would swear that Jefferson Davis had plotted with them the murder of Lincoln and his Cabinet. Now and again, he would bring these fakers from the underworld of Manhattan, one by one, to Washington, where in an obscure hotel he would rehearse them for days in their bogus accent and testimony, and then bring them before the Bureau of Military Investigation to make their false depositions. Holt gloated with gratification over the suborned witnesses. However, Colonel L. C. Turner of the Bureau of Military Investigation, an honorable man, became suspicious. He aided a congressional committee in an investigation and secured the confession of one of the frauds, named Campbell. Conover fled. He was eventually captured and jailed. He confessed fully. In the words of Colonel Turner, the depositions were "cunningly devised, diabolical fabrications of Conover's, verified by his suborned and perjured accomplices."

When, on July 7, the innocent boardinghouse keeper, Mrs. Surratt, was executed by decision of a military commission for complicity in Booth's crime, many Northern papers expressed indignation. A few, however, renewed the clamor for the blood of "the Great Criminal"—Jefferson Davis. Speaker Colfax, later proved a grafter and an official plunderer, declared in the House of Representatives that justice should see Jefferson Davis "hanging between heaven and earth as not fit for either." But ex-President Pierce comforted Mrs. Davis with the assurance that her husband would never be brought to trial, "as the evidence on which the Government relies is a tissue of wicked fabrications from the perjured lips of the lowest upon the earth."

On June 17, Davis's personal trunk, which was taken by M. C. Clark to Florida and hidden by the wife of Senator Yulee, had been discovered, seized, and brought to Washington. Agents of the War Department examined it zestfully. But not one scrap of incrimi-

nating evidence could be found in the hundreds of family letters
and confidential notes from members of his staff and political associates.

Secretary of War Stanton was now in a real quandary: on what
grounds should Davis be tried? In the middle of July the Cabinet was
still discussing what should be done. Chief Justice Chase held firmly
to his conviction that the ex-President should not be tried for treason. "If you bring these leaders to trial," Chase said, "it will condemn the North, for by the Constitution secession is not rebellion."
To endeavor to prove in a court of law that Jefferson Davis had
been the Chief Executive of belligerents was ridiculous, for the fact
had been common and universal knowledge for four years. "Lincoln wanted Jefferson Davis to escape," Chase declared; "and he
was right. His capture was a mistake. His trial will be a greater
one. We cannot convict him of treason. Secession is settled. Let it stay
settled."

From Georgia, Varina Davis, who knew that before the war Horace Greeley had written in most flattering terms of her husband's
statesmanship, made an impassioned appeal to him for help. She
enclosed a cutting from the Savannah *Republican,* assailing her
husband in libelous terms, and wrote with passion:

> How can the honest men and gentlemen of your country stand idly by
> to see a gentleman maligned, insulted, tortured and denied the right of
> trial by the usual forms of law? Is his cause so strong that he must be done
> to death by starvation, confined air, and manacles?
>
> With all the archives of our government in the hands of your govern-
> ment, do they despair of proving him a rogue, falsifier, assassin and
> traitor—then they must in addition guard him like a wild beast, and chain
> him for fear his unarmed hands will in a casemated cell subvert the gov-
> ernment? Shame, shame. . . . Is no one among you bold enough to de-
> fend him? . . .

Greeley, intrepid Abolitionist editor of the New York *Tribune,*
was moved by the frantic plea of a distracted wife, and sent
Mrs. Davis a letter of sympathy and encouragement. He took care
that none should accuse him of clandestine correspondence by
boldly addressing the envelope to "Mrs. Varina Davis, wife of Jefferson Davis, from Horace Greeley," and sending it open through the
Secretary of War and thence down to Georgia.

Greeley, who had once insisted that the Southern States had a
constitutional right to secede, urged Judge George Shea of New
York to press for an early trial for the prisoner. But to satisfy him-

self that Davis was completely innocent of any charge of cruelty to Northern prisoners at Andersonville, Shea journeyed to Montreal to examine those Confederate archives that had been stored there for safekeeping. Reading hundreds of documents and letters, he was convinced of Davis's innocence. He and Greeley now joined with Charles O'Conor in pushing for a speedy trial. But Stanton continued evasive.

When Mrs. Davis read a dispatch from a Boston paper, headed "Glimpses into Jeff Davis's Desk. Interesting Correspondence," she seethed with resentment. In heated protest she wrote to her husband's one-time friend, Secretary of State Seward. "The only legacy the Government has left my children," she declared, "is the record contained in these letters of their father's love, and the constant unpremeditated exhibition of his moral rectitude." She begged to have these private letters back "when the Government was done with them." Seward did not reply.

Still trembling with outrage, Mrs. Davis wrote to Judge Shea on July 14 complaining of her plight in being detained in Savannah and forced to spend far more than she could afford. And she had even been denied, she said, the comfort of telling her husband how his "baby prisoners" were or of sending him a single word of love. It was understandably a bitter outcry from a bruised heart.

When his life was apparently hanging by a thread the Government had not the humanity to send me a notice of it, but every agony of his was published, accompanied with jeers of valiant editors, and hawked about the streets in extras. . . .

I am accused of no wrong, yet I am confined here without redress. . . .

For our downtrodden people I crave "amnesty"—whatever that may be—permission to breathe God's air, and gain their bread by the sweat of their brows. But for me and mine, we crave no amnesty. We have been robbed of everything except our memories— God has kept them green. . . .

There is no bond uniting us to the Northerners. A great gulf of blood rolls between us. My spirit shrinks appalled from attempting to cross it.

In referring to her husband's only "offence" in believing in Constitutional law, she shrewdly called it "an inexpedient assertion of an undeniable right."

In his desperate effort to find a shred of evidence to support absurd accusations, she said contemptuously, Stanton had set investigators "mousing among the archives." Again she complained of agents "polluting with their unhallowed gaze the precious records of my few happy hours, and selling garbled extracts to those papers whose readers need a gentle excitement."

Mrs. Davis thus bared her resentment and grief to one of the compassionate Northern attorneys who had volunteered to champion her husband's case.

I am unhinged by sorrow, and forget that you have not lived in an invaded country and that your ire has not been lighted at the funeral pyre of friends and homes forever lost.

Judge Shea was sympathetic, and immediately made renewed efforts to secure Mrs. Davis's complete freedom from military surveillance.

On July 20 Dr. Craven was requested by General Miles himself to make an emergency call on State Prisoner Davis. The doctor found him "in a very critical state; his nervous debility extreme; his mind more despondent than ever heretofore; his appetite gone, complexion livid and pulse denoting deep prostration of all the physical energies." Realizing the responsibilities of his position, he was duly alarmed. "If Mr. Davis were to die in prison without trial, subject to such severities as had been inflicted on his attenuated frame," Craven wrote, he was convinced that "the world would form unjust conclusions, but conclusions with enough color to pass them into history."

Davis asked his doctor if nothing could be done to secure him the justice of a trial before death. "If death without trial is the object of the Washington people," he said, "I wish they would take quicker means of dispatching me." He was led to suspect that the authorities might even intend for him to die in prison, because, he said, "a trial must surely develop many things unpleasant to those in power." And it would indubitably place much of the responsibility for the suffering of prisoners at Andersonville on Grant's refusal to make exchanges. Again he emphasized that he was most eager to vindicate at law the theory and justice of the Confederate cause, showing by the authority of the Constitution that the Southern States had only asserted a right in withdrawing from the compact of States. "This," he repeated, "is the last remaining labor which life can impose on me as a public duty."

Davis was troubled about the slow progress of "reconstruction." "Every man's experience," he said, "must teach him that quarrels between friends are best healed when they are healed most promptly."

When Craven left the cell he set down these spontaneous rumi-
nations of Davis, and wrote: "This conversation impressed me
much, and has been recorded with peculiar care."

As to the absurd notion that the ex-President would attempt to
escape, which General Miles still pretended to fancy, Craven declared:

If all the doors and gates of the fort were thrown open he would not
leave. The only duty left to him—his only remaining object—was to vindicate the action of his people, and his own action as their representative,
by a fair and public trial.

On the morning of July 24, as Jefferson Davis was reading his
Bible he looked up to see the husky young Commanding General
at his door. Miles announced that the prisoner would be allowed
an hour's exercise on the ramparts daily, the privilege to begin
that afternoon.

Davis brightened considerably; he looked forward to the exercise and a sight of something besides white walls and moat water.
He had not breathed fresh air since his incarceration two months
earlier. He could stretch his legs, gaze on the ocean, and breathe
freely again. He awaited the hour with eager anticipation.

But when Miles himself appeared at his cell door that afternoon
and announced that he would always accompany the prisoner,
Davis's spirits sank. With this hostile young upstart, whom he had
every reason to detest, he could not hope to benefit fully by the
exercise. As Miles grasped one arm and the Officer of the Day the
other, Jefferson Davis started on his first stroll under the blue sky
since he was marched to his cell on May 22. Four guards with
bayoneted rifles walked close behind as the party climbed the
stairs to the parapet.

From the grassy ramparts Davis beheld the gently heaving sea
and moving ships. He had an affinity for the ocean; he had ever
found it soothing and healing. He paused and took a deep breath.
Suddenly he was aware of a crowd watching him with curiosity.
Apparently by some foreknowledge, people had come to gaze upon
the famous captive as he took his first unsteady steps.

The Confederate ex-President thought of the Indian Black Hawk,
who had also been imprisoned once in Fort Monroe. It was the
young Lieutenant Jefferson Davis who had been put in charge of

the old captive warrior in Wisconsin to take him by steamer down to St. Louis. Black Hawk had spoken of Lieutenant Davis with gratitude in his autobiography:

We started . . . in a steamboat under the charge of a young war chief who treated us all with much kindness. He is a good and brave young chief with whose conduct I was very much pleased. . . . People crowded to the boat to see us, but the war chief would not permit them . . . knowing, from what his feelings would have been if he had been placed in a similar situation, that we did not wish a gaping crowd around us.

Dr. Craven, observing Davis's walk from a distance, wrote in his diary, "While his carriage was as proud and erect as ever, not losing a hair's breadth of his height from any stoop, his step had lost its elasticity, and he had frequently to press his chest, panting in the pauses of exertion. . . . He was so weak that the hour allowed proved twice too much for him, and he had to be led back with only half his liberty enjoyed."

When the good doctor inquired that night how he had enjoyed his exercise, Davis merely replied that "the sense of breathing air not drawn through iron bars was a glorious blessing, only to be fully appreciated by prisoners." He did not refer to his revulsion at the gapers or the arm-in-arm proximity of his hateful jailer.

A few days later Craven was pleased to find that the hot application he had ordered for the back of the prisoner's neck had relieved his pain and that he no longer saw "a cloud of black and amber motes rising and falling before his sight." He noted, too, that the nervous twitching of Davis's eyelids had almost ceased. Davis had begun to read with interest Macaulay's *History of England*, which he had always intended to do, but had never found the time.

Craven soon learned that the varieties of view and the animation of the scenes observed from the parapet had invigorated Davis's eyesight. His continued debility the physician judged to be partly caused by the miserable plight of the South. Davis said:

In the better days of the Roman Empire, it was the policy of conciliation, following that of military conquest, which achieved the desired results. . . . Their leaders were justly treated, and no efforts were spared to make the new order of things sit lightly at first, and even pleasantly in a few years on the necks of the subjugated provinces. Generosity is the true policy, both of individuals and nations.

Once, in response to Dr. Craven's questions, Davis discussed naval gunnery at length. On his first walk he had noted the fifteen-inch Rodman guns which stood *en barbette* on each bastion of the fort. They had been adopted before 1861, and as Secretary of War Davis had used his influence to have them accepted. He commented on the extraordinary recent improvements of ordnance. He remarked that Swedish iron was the best, but he thought that experiment would prove that the iron in Eastern Tennessee was especially good for the American climate.

Then Davis casually "discussed the atomic theory or relationship of particles." He spoke of "the effects on iron fibre of different temperatures and treatments, or by hammering, rolling, cooling" to such a minuteness of detail that the doctor declared he could not hope to follow him.

One day Craven found the prisoner lying on his cot near the window, watching through the bars of the embrasure the flight of fish hawks, which told fishermen of the shoals of varied fish near the coast. Davis said that he had been reading unhappy accounts in newspapers about the plight of ex-slaves who no longer had masters to support or guide them. The Government seemed to have trouble with the officers appointed to take care of the Negroes. It would be a far better plan to remit their care and future to the several States and to those Southern men who had been reared with them and knew their peculiarities. Judging from the reports, he said, the Northern civilians who rushed South with carpetbags at the end of the war, professing sympathy for the Negro as their motive, were "most unsafe to arrange the destinies of ignorant and helpless people." According to reports, these so-called "philanthropists," suddenly given control of wealth for distribution among the Negroes at loose ends, had quickly gravitated into corruption.

In the agricultural districts Davis feared it would be difficult to make a start because most of the draft animals, horses, mules, and oxen, had been slaughtered during the war. But with industry and the influx of capital from the North and Europe, Davis saw no reason why prosperity could not be re-established in half a dozen years. "But," he said, "this restoration depends on the Administration's pursuing a wise and generous course and allaying the irritations and fears of the conquered South."

Some days later Davis had a shock when he met Clement Clay on the ramparts walking like himself under guard with "four bayonets pacing behind him to prevent his escape." Clay was looking so wretched that Davis realized more acutely his own humiliating condition. As they passed, the two old friends paused and exchanged greetings in French. The officers, not understanding the language, became suspicious, and Clay was swiftly marched off to another section of the ramparts and not permitted to encounter the ex-President again.

Davis asked the doctor solicitously about Clay's state of health and about his food. At first, Craven said, he had received soldier's rations, but lately, because his condition demanded it, he had been sent trays from the hospital. Davis begged the doctor to do whatever he could for Clay's relief, and "to hold up his hands."

In 1866 Craven was to write in his book:

Let me here remark that, despite a certain exterior cynicism of manner, no patient had ever crossed my path, who, suffering so much himself, appeared to feel so warmly and tenderly for others.

One day, when Craven commented on the Bible and the Prayer Book* lying on the prisoner's bed, Davis admitted that their fine print pained his eyes, but he declared there was compensation for the sacrifice in what he read.

Davis, who as Secretary of War had assisted and stimulated the work of the chaplains and religious organizations in the army, was forbidden to join in any chapel service at Fort Monroe. So in his isolated cell he read the lessons in the Prayer Book and silently conducted his private devotions.

It was undoubtedly Davis's religious faith and meditations that helped save him from losing his reason. He still had faith that Divine Grace would not let him crack under his torments. During frequent periods of the day and night he drew within himself to commune. While he made petitionary prayers for the welfare of his family and for the relief of the South's misery, he asked nothing for himself but the ability to endure.

In his harsh incarceration Davis had come to realize deeply that "without humility the spirit of the Lord cannot dwell within one." He knew that there could be no harmony if one held to hate and a desire for revenge. Though tried to the limit of his endurance by Miles's petty tortures and diurnal digs on the walks, Davis struggled not to hate the man, though he could never rid himself of contempt.

"There was then living no more devout exemplar of Christian faith and its value as a consolation than Jefferson Davis," Craven was to write.

* The books may be seen in the Confederate Museum in Richmond.

There was no affectation of devoutness or asceticism in my patient; but every opportunity I had of seeing him convinced me more deeply of his sincere religious convictions. . . . There was a vital earnestness in his discourse, a clear, almost passionate grasp in his faith; and the thought would frequently recur that a belief capable of consoling such sorrows as his evidenced a reality which no sophistry of the infidel could discredit.

Through the sweltering midsummer Davis continued to worry about his children. He read disturbing reports from Savannah. Four-year-old Billie had been bribed by Federal soldiers to sing in public "We'll Hang Jeff Davis to a Sour Apple Tree." Many unhappy instances had occurred. A Negro sentinel had aimed his rifle at little Jeff and threatened to shoot him for addressing him as "uncle," a form considered polite usage in the South when greeting an older colored man. Two women from Maine who found Jeff in the hotel parlor one day had threatened to thrash him because "his father was such a villain."

Towards the end of July Mrs. Davis decided to send the three elder children to Canada for better safety and to schools where they would not be annoyed. Robert Brown, the colored servant, had been urging her to get the children out of the country. Finally, Mrs. Howell and the three older children, with the faithful Robert and a newly acquired Negro nursemaid, sailed for New York. On the voyage, when a "Yankee" made insulting remarks about his father to Jeff, Robert interposed and asked if the white man considered him, a Negro, his equal. The man replied, "Certainly." "Then take this from your equal," Robert said, and knocked the fellow flat on the deck. The ship's captain exonerated Robert.

Before they left Savannah, little Maggie was told by her mother that she might probably get a letter through to her father if she said nothing that the Federal authorities would find objectionable. The child thought long and hard, and then after careful labor, for she was only ten, she produced a paraphrase of the whole Twenty-third Psalm. The letter began: "My Darling Father, the Lord is Your Shepherd, you shall not want." With tear-filled eyes, she brought the sheets to her mother and said appealingly, "This letter will not make the Yankees mad, will it? They won't object to the Bible, will they?" Maggie's missive was mailed, but it was never delivered to the prisoner.

CHAPTER XXVIII

"THE WORLD'S
MOST FAMOUS PRISONER"

———◄◉►———

AS THE MONTHS passed, the weakness of any "case" against Jefferson Davis became more apparent. Andrew Johnson realized the wisdom of Lincoln's desire that Davis escape to some foreign land. But methods dishonest as well as honest were still rigorously employed to discover evidence against the Confederacy's President. Even the private letters of his attorney were tampered with in the United States Post Office. Charles O'Conor wrote James Murray Mason on August 6, 1865, that he had "met with much delay and some loss of letters entrusted to the mails" since his announcement in the press as a counsel of Mr. Davis. He said he had become very cautious in his correspondence and had even taken the precaution of having letters sent "under cover of some inconspicuous person with instructions to make delivery to him in person." O'Conor predicted:

No trial for treason or any like offense will be had in the civil courts. Notwithstanding the Surratt murder and its flagitious concomitants, the managers at Washington are not agreed as to the safety of employing military commissions to color a like outrage upon any eminent person.

While O'Conor continued to use every available means of securing justice, George Shea traveled extensively, searching for documents that might throw light on the main issues. William B. Reed of Philadelphia, distinguished attorney and one-time minister to China, had recently tendered Davis his professional services in a handsome letter. Davis requested permission to acknowledge his kindness by letter; it was not granted.

Early in August Judge Shea thought he had won for Mrs. Davis the privilege of leaving Georgia. She might come North if she

258

pleased. "Welcome to New York!" Shea wrote her on August 3. "While here are your husband's chief political enemies, you will find your chief personal friends." Horace Greeley had told him to say that he had received assurances that "all was right at last in Washington." "He [Greeley] is a good and firm friend of those who need a friend, and unswerving in the day of defeat and danger."

Mrs. Davis had no desire to go to New York. She longed to visit her husband. But she was grateful to be able to leave Savannah. She accepted an invitation from Mr. and Mrs. George Schley of Mill View, Georgia, five miles in the country from Augusta. The Schleys refused to take her as a paying guest. She moved to their guesthouse with her baby Winnie and the new nurse, Mary Ahern, "a sweet-tempered, kind creature," who had been born in Ireland and brought to Georgia when three years old. Her father had cultivated a little place near Savannah, which had been devastated by Sherman. Mary was a Catholic, and she had been recommended by convent nuns. The baby and Mary Ahern adored each other at sight, and Mary was to remain with the Davises for more than a dozen years.

On returning from Baltimore, Dr. Craven called on the prisoner on August 14 and was disturbed by his condition. "A pustule, somewhat malignant in character, was forming on his face, which was much inflamed and swollen." That evening when he called again he found the prisoner "in a high fever, the swelling of the face spreading to his back and neck with indications of erysipelas." In his discomfort, Mr. Davis expressed a longing for his colored servant, Robert. Though born a slave, he said, Robert had "a moral nobility deserving honor." And no one could know better than he the incomparable comfort of having a devoted Negro to minister to one's needs.

The next day the physician found Davis suffering more acutely, "a cloud of erysipelas covering his whole face and throat," and "a painful carbuncle greatly inflamed on his left thigh." Davis had just read about the so-called "elections" in Richmond in which unscrupulous men had been given all the important positions. Sadly he had come to realize that the policy of "woe to the conquered," which he had feared, would prevail. "It is a cruel farce," he said, "to permit an exercise of the elective franchise, with a proviso that the electors must cast their ballots for men they despised or hated! To ask men who have fought, sacrificed and lost their all for a cause to wheel suddenly and vote into power men they despise as renegades and cowards is the sin of attempting to seethe the kid in its mother's milk."

"Mr. Lincoln," Davis went on ruminating, "naturally longed for the glory and repose of a second term to be spent in peace. At the time it occurred, his death, even by natural causes, would have been a serious injury to the prospects of the South. But the manner of his death, frenzying the Northern mind, was the last crowning calamity of a despairing and defeated, though righteous, cause."

The prisoner's spirits, Craven noted, were "exceedingly dejected." Davis hoped that no sensational reports of his illness would get into the public press. But reporters swarming about the fort told all with highly colored exaggerations.

Down in Georgia Mrs. Davis was agonized over the lurid accounts of her husband's condition. She implored Dr. Craven to give her correct news. Though he was not allowed to reply, the physician persuaded Miles to permit Davis to write to his wife. On August 21 Davis composed his first letter to his wife with extreme care, because it was to be scrutinized by censors.

I am now permitted to write you under two conditions, viz., that I confine myself to family matters, and that my letter shall be examined by the United States Attorney General before it is sent to you.

This will sufficiently explain to you the omission of subjects on which you desire me to write. On the subject of future action towards me . . . of the purpose of the authorities I know nothing.

He did not speak specifically of his present acute illness, but merely wrote, "Be not alarmed by speculative reports. You can rely on my fortitude, and God has given me much of resignation." In this and in future letters from prison, Davis's chief thought was to comfort Varina. Being eighteen years her senior, he had ever had a protective attitude, and knowing her impulsive, headstrong nature, he did his utmost to protect her now, even from his prison cell.

The confidence in the shield of innocence with which I tried to quiet your apprehensions and to dry your tears at our parting, sustains me still. . . . If your fears have proved more prophetic than my hopes, yet do not despond. "Tarry thou the Lord's leisure, be strong, and He will comfort thy heart." Every day, twice and oftener, I repeat the prayer of St. Chrysostom.

Two days after Davis wrote to his wife, Dr. Craven found him "a little improved, the febrile symptoms subsiding." Though he could not eat any ordinary food, he found "the coolness and moisture of fruits agreeable."

Smiling, he asked to be allowed to keep the spoon which had come that morning with his breakfast. Five spoons recently sent with his tray from the doctor's quarters had been kept by guards as trophies. His briarwood pipe had also been taken; and soldiers had sent home as souvenirs napkins the ex-President had used, and locks of his hair left by the barber.

Observing the doctor brush away with his foot some crumbs scattered near his bedside, Davis restrained him. The crumbs were for a mouse he was "domesticating." It was the only living thing he now had power to benefit.

A momentous event came on August 25 when General Miles permitted Davis to have a knife and fork. He could now cut his own food, and he would no longer have to peel peaches with a spoon. Miles had given up the pretense that Davis might attempt suicide out of remorse.

At daylight on September 1, Captain Titlow, who looked in on the prisoner, feared he was dying and rushed to rouse Dr. Craven. To the physician "Mr. Davis seemed to be sinking rapidly." His pulse indicated "extreme prostration of the vital forces." Craven prescribed both constitutional and topical remedies. And he wrote in his journal that "in docility and a strict adherence to whatever regime was prescribed, Mr. Davis was the model patient of my practice."

Craven noted the mold that had gathered on the prisoner's shoes and on crumbs which the pet mouse had not consumed. No life could prosper in such a damp atmosphere, he believed. Though men in robust health might defy these miasmatic influences, with a man so physically reduced as the prisoner an atmosphere that generated mold was very deleterious. Craven reported the danger to General Miles, and strongly recommended a change to more healthful quarters.

During his acute illness, Davis mentioned the parallel of his imprisonment to that of the Marquis de Lafayette in the dungeons of both Magdeburg and Olmütz, the most powerful fortresses in Prussia and Austria respectively. Lafayette, too, had been denied fresh air and knife and fork. One of the worst torments the Frenchman endured, Davis said, was human eyes fixed upon his every movement day and night. When Lafayette's kind doctor at Olmütz declared the prisoner could not live unless allowed to breathe better air, his jailer replied that the Frenchman "was not sick enough yet." General Miles apparently did not think Davis yet quite sick enough.

Even when the prisoner was too ill to sit up, Craven remarked that his memory remained "clear and precise." "The power of his memory appeared almost miraculous," he later wrote. "A single perusal of any passage that interested either his assent or denial he could repeat almost verbatim."

Various Officers of the Day who had begun to have brief conversations with the State Prisoner were amazed at the range of his knowledge. One morning a captain entered Davis's cell followed by his bull terrier. The Mississippian instinctively began judging the dog's "points," commenting "with all the minuteness of a master." As the officer questioned him further, Davis reviewed the qualities of bird dogs, which he knew best: setters, pointers, and retrievers. He then proceeded to comment on bulldogs, German poodles, and greyhounds. Later the dog-fancying captain said to Dr. Craven, "I thought I knew something about dogs, but hang me, I need to go to school to Jeff Davis."

From Mill View, Mrs. Davis, who had read sensational accounts of her husband's failing health, wrote him in despair on September 14.

I wake and weep, watch and pray to be granted strength to wait, to possess my soul in patience. . . . It was mistaken kindness in you to refrain from telling me how unwell you were. Do you not know I could take my death warrant from your lips better than joyful tidings from another?

She was happy to be able to say that she had been followed with constant solicitude and affectionate letters from Mrs. Robert E. Lee; Elizabeth Blair, daughter of Montgomery; Mrs. Grant, their generous Richmond neighbor; the Harrisons, Mr. Burt, and a host of others. "Everybody is so kind," she wrote. "May God bless you and keep you, dearest honored husband. The all absorbing love of my whole life seems so poor a tribute to your worth."

At Dr. Craven's insistent urging General Miles finally agreed that Davis might be moved to more salutary quarters. An upper room was selected in Carroll Hall, originally used for officers' quarters, and plans were under way to put in grated doors and iron-barred windows.

On September 24 Davis was well enough to take his walk again. He was greatly cheered to learn from the doctor that within about a week he would be moved to new quarters. And he was happy to hear that General Lee had accepted the presidency of Washington College at Lexington, Virginia. He spoke of the rare good fortune of those students who would be under Lee's tutelage "with his Christian faith, his stainless integrity, and his numerous accomplishments."

Another week passed and Davis was still in the dank cell.

"My days drag heavily on," he wrote his wife early in the morning of October 2. "To what, I have no means to direct, or to foresee. Having no communication with the outer world except with you, and in that restricted by the *judgement of the Commanding Officer as to what should be sent.*" He explained that he could not write daily as she wished, for he was not permitted to keep stationery; each sheet handed him had to be accounted for and returned written or blank.

Later that very morning the ex-President was moved to a second-story room in the northwest bastion of the fort. Davis's good-sized corner room in Carroll Hall had a fireplace in the center of the end wall. The opposite wall opened into the room occupied by the officer of the guard and was divided by an iron-grating door. The two doors on the side walls opened into a corridor and a veranda respectively. They, too, had iron bars, and one had in addition a panel shutter in which were inserted two panes of glass. Sentinels paced just outside the prisoner's room; one along the gallery; one along the passageway; and still another in the guardroom. Davis might be watched from three directions.

The furnishings were Spartan. A basin and pitcher stood on a chair with a broken-off back that served as a washstand. In a chimney recess were an empty bookshelf and pegs on which to hang clothes, but the prisoner was not allowed to have any garments except those he wore. He still changed his linen according to General Miles's whims. A pleasing refinement, however, was a folding screen which enabled him to wash unobserved. For four and a half months heretofore he had had the eyes of sentries on him not only when he bathed, but when he used the portable commode.

On October 11 Davis wrote his wife a cheerful letter about his new room.

The dry air, good water and a fire when requisite have already improved my physical condition. . . . I am deeply indebted to my attendant physician, who has been to me much more than the terms usually convey.

Despite the agreeable change of habitation, Davis had been enduring some painful physical experiences. He had not been able to exercise for nine days because "a carbuncle with a succession of points," which rose in his right armpit, prevented him from putting on his coat.

He had recently read a religious book by the Reverend Mr. Krumacher and had been impressed "by the dignity, the sublime patience of the model of Christianity, as contrasted with the brutal vindictiveness of unregenerated man." Davis commented:

Misfortune should not depress us, as it is only crime which can degrade. Beyond this world there is a sure retreat for the oppressed; and *posterity justifies the memory of those who fall unjustly.*

For the first three months in prison, he confessed, he had had hardly two hours of consecutive sleep. Now it was better: sentinels did not pace *in* his room. But even so he got only broken sleep because of the changing of the guard and the perpetual footsteps of the sentinels outside.

I have not sunk under my trials, am better than a fortnight ago, and trust I shall be sustained under any affliction it may be required me to bear. My sight is affected, but less than I would have supposed if it had been foretold that a light was to be kept where I was to sleep, and that I was at short intervals to be aroused, and the extended pupil thus frequently subjected to the glare of the lamp.

In her most recent letter Varina said she had been dreadfully upset by a malicious article in the September *Harper's Monthly*. It was written by Beauregard's former Chief of Staff, Colonel Thomas Jordan, and seemed calculated to inflame Northern minds against the ex-President, and at the same time make him appear to the South as a meddling incompetent. Beauregard himself had appended a note to the article, which Varina deemed "hostile and offensive."

Davis responded calmly in an effort to moderate his wife's righteous indignation.

I have not seen Jordan's critique, and am at a loss to know where that game was played and lost by my interference. If the records are preserved they dispose summarily of his romances, past, passing, and to come.

History is ever repeating itself. . . . The unfortunate have always been deserted and betrayed; but did ever man have less to complain of when he had lost power to serve? The critics are noisy—perhaps they hope to enhance their wares by loud crying.

From Mill View on October 3, 1865, Varina wrote to William Preston Johnston, who had recently been released from Fort Delaware and was now in Montreal, where he had shown most kind attentions to the Davis children. She was very grateful to him, but she had been hurt, she said, because he had been so long in writing her. In her "aching heart," she had been "accusing" him.

All through her life Varina was touchy, and often deeply offended when people did not write as promptly as she expected. She suffered for slights never intended or never given. She was aware of this flaw in her nature, and in her letter to Johnston she deplored it, begging his forgiveness for a fuss she had picked with him in the last days of the flight.

Have you thought of our quarrel on the road? I have, and it had made a painful impression, a longing to be forgiven. I was unjust, but so goaded I could not tell the difference—a touch seemed to stab. When I am ill at heart I am wild, and vagaries possess me.

Varina said that her husband wondered "why no one answered the 'fictions' published against him." But Jefferson Davis had not complained of his friends' neglect. He understood that most of them were struggling to survive and he realized that only time could mollify the Northern animosity that had been built up against him.

One old friend who did speak out in strong terms in defense of Jefferson Davis was Judah P. Benjamin. Immediately on arrival in London on August 30, 1865, he gave an interview to the *Times*, in which he extolled the Confederacy's President and absolved him of all blame. On September 1 he wrote Mrs. Davis, after consulting with C. J. McRae, the Confederate business agent abroad, and learning that he had placed £2,000 to her credit in London. Benjamin explained that this equivalent of $12,500 represented the President's salary due him up to June 30.

He had learned of the President's capture in late May when he himself was in Florida endeavoring to get to Cuba.

God knows what I have suffered since my first reception of the horrible news that my beloved and honored friend was in the hands of the enemy.

After every imaginable contretemps and danger, I reached London nearly four months after I parted from the President, charged by him to perform certain public duties in Nassau and Havana, and then to rejoin him in Texas.

He described in detail the vicissitudes he had endured in Floridian swamps and several near-brushes with death. Then he ended:

Knowing your devoted love for your husband, I cannot imagine how you have survived the terrible distress which must have overwhelmed you when the extent of the calamity became apparent as revealed by his barbarous treatment—

Goodbye, my dear Mrs. Davis— God bless you and your little ones— I dare not trust myself with the expression of my feelings for your noble husband, for my unhappy friend—

In mid-October Dr. Craven received another pitiful plea from Mrs. Davis.

I dread paralysis for him, his nerves have been so highly strung for years without relief. If you can, prevail upon the authorities to let him sleep without a light. He is too feeble to escape, and could not bear a light in his room when in strong health. The sequel of these attacks has always been an attack of amaurosis, and in one of them he lost an eye.

By interdiction Dr. Craven could not reply. But he did persuade General Miles to let the lamp wick be turned lower.

Davis shortly learned that Margaret Howell had arrived safely in Montreal on October 17, accompanied by his nephew General Joe R. Davis. Varina did not dare write him that Margaret had taken the valuable Confederate Letter Books concealed in the false bottom of her trunk and that they were now safely stored in the Bank of Montreal.

One morning in late October John Mitchel, the third political prisoner incarcerated at Fort Monroe, secured his release and was permitted to take leave of Davis "through the grates." He found the ex-President "in morning dishabille and looking haggard." "But I assure you," he wrote Mrs. Davis, "when he dresses to go out he looks well, steps as firmly and holds his head as high as he ever did on Capitol Square."

"I am sustained by a Power I know not of," Davis wrote consolingly to Varina on November 3. Daily he read from a small worn copy of Thomas à Kempis's *Imitation of Christ*. One day, after he was permitted to keep a pencil, he wrote at the top of Chapter 48, entitled: "Of the Day of Eternity and the Miseries of this Life,"

"Great comfort in this." And in the text he underlined the following passage:

When shall I enjoy a solid peace, a peace never to be disturbed and
always secure, a peace both within and without, a peace everywhere
firm?

Davis took some consolation from newspaper reports of various
committees in America and abroad bestirring themselves in his
behalf. A delegation of Baltimore ladies had called on President
Johnson bearing a petition with thousands of signatures urging him
to free the Confederate ex-President. In the issue of October 29
the Philadelphia *Inquirer* reported that an Italian committee from
New York had had an audience with Johnson and presented a
petition from Milan pleading for Jefferson Davis. At least the eyes
of the world were on the Washington Administration.

As November 10, the day set for Henry Wirz's execution, approached, certain authorities in the capital again prepared to take
desperate measures to incriminate the Confederate ex-President.
Shortly before the hanging, a proposition was made to Wirz in his
cell, and also to his attorney in the presence of his confessor,
Father Boyle, that "a high Cabinet officer" would see that his
sentence would be commuted if Wirz would implicate Jefferson
Davis with Andersonville. "I would not," he declared valiantly in
his last hours, "become a traitor to him or anyone else to save my
life."

General R. B. Winder, who was also in the prison, later wrote to
Mrs. Davis:

The door of the room which I occupied while in confinement at the
Old Capitol Prison was immediately opposite Wirz's door, both of which
were occasionally open. About two days before his execution I saw three
or four men pass into the room, and upon their coming out, Wirz told
me that they had given him assurances that his life would be spared and
his liberty given him if he could give any testimony that would reflect
upon Mr. Davis, or implicate him directly or indirectly, with the treatment
of prisoners of war, *as charged* by the United States authorities—that
he indignantly spurned these propositions and assured them that he had
never been connected with Mr. Davis, either officially, personally, or
socially . . . that the offer of his life could not purchase him to treason
and treachery to the South.

From the beginning of Wirz's trial Davis had been convinced
that the evidence of the officer's cruelty was deliberately fabricated.
In later years he was to write of Henry Wirz:

Arrested while under protection of a parole, tried in time of peace by a military commission of officers, in a service to which he did not belong, denied the favorable testimony of those who came, and subpoenas for other witnesses of like character—without these ordinary means, granted to the accused in all civilized countries, he died a martyr to conscientious adherence to truth.

If such a mockery of justice had fallen to the lot of Wirz,* Davis could not but wonder, in spite of the best defense counsel in America, what certain corrupt officials like Joseph Holt might try to perpetrate against himself.

When Dr. Craven had called on the State Prisoner one autumn day, he confessed that his light suit of gray tweed was too thin for the increasing chill on the windy ramparts. The good doctor promptly requested that a friend of his in Washington see S. W. Owen, Davis's old tailor, who had his measurements on file, and order an overcoat of "heavy black pilot cloth."

The news of the overcoat got into the papers. On November 8 the New York *Herald* informed the world:

Jeff. Davis' new overcoat was sent down to Fortress Monroe today. The garment is an expensive one in accordance with Davis' fine taste in matters of dress and is paid for.

When young Miles read the item in the paper he was in a blazing fury. It was the first he had heard of the transaction. He had been growing increasingly resentful of the cordiality between the fort's chief surgeon and State Prisoner Davis. He sent for Craven, who faced the General unruffled. The doctor maintained that his patient's frail health necessitated a warm overcoat for his winter walks, for the winds of the coast were cold and piercing. He was surprised that any objection should be made.

A series of letters of specific inquiries from Miles ensued about the price of the coat and who paid for it. The tailor replied that the price of the coat was $125, and that "parties" in Washington had called at his shop and left the money to pay for a much more expensive coat than the doctor had ordered. This payment, Craven said, had been made "without his approval, knowledge or consent."

Miles seethed for a week. Then on November 18 he sent Craven

* According to Professor Randall of the University of Illinois, the frustrations of justice in the case of Wirz were "even more shocking" than "the ghastly miscarriage of justice" in the execution of Mrs. Surratt. (*The Civil War and Reconstruction*, p. 803.)

a peremptory and spiteful command: "In future, your conversation with the prisoner will be confined strictly to professional matters."

This silencing order was a hard blow to the ex-President. To be able to talk freely with the sympathetic physician amid the daily irritations had helped to preserve Davis's sanity. And Craven had felt himself most fortunate to enjoy the talk of "a superbly informed and fascinating conversationalist." He regarded Miles's tyrannical order as "cruel and unnecessary." But, as an army officer, Dr. Craven felt bound to carry out the order. So, perforce, on November 19, 1865, his diary concerning "the world's most famous prisoner" came to an end.

Mrs. Davis read varied accounts of the "overcoat incident." Sometimes, sinking with despair, she would write her husband unrestrainedly in melancholy mood. "The dreary, dreary days, and weeks, and months—" she began a letter on November 13. "I grow hard and sullen with sorrow."

She was troubled about the "awful responsibility" she felt for their children scattered about in Canada—"without your counsel, your decision."

I always knew where the glory and pride of my house lay, but never until now have I realized how entirely the strength was in your possession. Twenty-one years of happy dependence upon the wisdom and love of another so much better and wiser does not fit one to stand alone.

Late in November Davis was pleased to receive from his wife a dressing gown and some nightshirts and handkerchiefs. In thanking her, he took occasion to comment on her exquisite needlework: "the mark on the handkerchiefs no fingers save yours could make."

Then he spoke ironically of something he had just read in a newspaper:

My incarceration followed four years of terrible war. The North put forth its whole capacity on land and sea, by ball and bayonet, striving to retain the South in one Government with it; the South strained every nerve to maintain a separate existence. By the newspaper, to-day, I see that the North, as represented in Congress, stands quite united to keep the South *out* of the legislative halls of the Union, and the South, wistfully looking at the closed entrance, stands outside—and then she is told she has all the time been inside.

Still he tried to be philosophic about the deplorable situation and to steel Varina to bear worse things that might come.

Truth and the common sense of justice will generally protect the innocent, where the trial is according to the due course of law, and is sure to vindicate the memory of a victim.

When we shall pass into the future state of *pure intelligence*, so as to judge not by external signs but by inner motives, how different men will appear to each other from the estimates of their carnal life! . . . I live and hope.

While he was writing, one of the sentinels began to stamp so heavily on his back-and-forth tramping that he seemed determined to distract the prisoner from his task. "Until another and more quiet walker comes on, and I recover from the effect produced by the attempt to write under such difficulty, I will desist."

In early December the prisoner received from his wife a most encouraging report of his children in Canada. Jeff's schoolmistress in Lennoxville, Mrs. Morris, had written to say that he was "very truthful and loveable." The Archbishop of Halifax urged Mrs. Davis to let him educate Jeff at any college of her choice in Canada or England. Little Billie, staying with his grandmother in a village halfway between Maggie in Montreal and Jeff in Lennoxville, was fat and flourishing.

The most heartening news of all came in a surprise letter from ten-year-old Maggie. Though many previous notes from her had been intercepted and returned, the Washington authorities had at last decided that no great harm could come from the prisoner's receipt of an occasional note from his children. Maggie's letter from the Sacred Heart Convent, Sault au Recollet, was dated November 30, 1865.

My precious Father
It gave me great pleasure when I found out that I could write to you. . . .
Darling Father, all I want in this convent is you and sweet Mother and sweet little Pie Cake, for I am treated so kind. Precious Father, the Arch Bishop of Halifax came to the convent and was very kind to me and in remembrance of you gave me some beautiful presents, which consisted of a prayer book which was butifuly bound with Ivory and the clasp is pure Silver and he also gave me a pretty little gold Cross—it is set with rubies and in the centre is an emerald. Precious Father I send you these little pictures with more affection than I can express.

Six more sentences about her school progress and the family members in Canada followed, each beginning "Precious Father."

Though touched and inspirited by his first letter from his affectionate little daughter, Davis now knew some bleak days because of Miles's order that forbade conversation with his physician. But on December 11 occurred a simple event, which greatly lifted his heart. After repeated efforts, Charles Minnegerode, Rector of St. Paul's in Richmond, had secured permission from the Washington authorities to visit the prisoner. Miles reluctantly conducted the clergyman to the ex-President's prison room.

In these six wearing months Davis had not been allowed a visitor. At his rector's unexpected appearance before the grated door it was difficult for him to control his emotion. Minnegerode had considerable difficulty in controlling his own.

"The noble man showed the effect of the confinement," he later wrote, "but his spirit could not be subdued, and no indignity—angry as it made him at the time—could humiliate him."

I was his pastor, and of course our conversation was influenced by that and there could be no holding back between us. I could come to sympathize and comfort and pray for him. At last the question of Holy Communion came up. He was very anxious to take it. He was a purely pious man, and felt the need and value of the means of grace. But there was one difficulty. Could he take it in the proper spirit—in the frame of a forgiving mind, after all the ill treatment he had been subjected to? He was too upright and conscientious a Christian man "to eat and drink unworthily"—i.e., not in the proper spirit, and, as far as lay in him in peace with God and man.

The clergyman left the prisoner alone to meditate on the matter, while he inspected the fort. He had spoken about the Communion service to Miles, who had agreed to make preparations. A couple of hours later, he was again escorted by the General to the prison door. Minnegerode was gratified to find Davis ready to commune, "to pray 'Father, forgive them.' "

It was a most solemn hour. A goods box covered with a white cloth served as an altar. Night had fallen, and the fortress was shrouded in silence. General Miles ordered the three sentinels to stop their pacing. They stood like statues. It was the first utter quiet Davis's frayed nerves had known in more than half a year. Though Miles himself declined to leave, he had the grace to turn his back on the scene and lean against the mantelpiece in the anteroom as Jefferson Davis knelt and the minister spoke softly: "Take, eat, this is my body which is given for you."

After his rector's visit Davis was better prepared to endure the dark December days in which prison rigors continued unabated.

On Christmas Day, as a bitter present to Jefferson Davis, General Miles removed Dr. Craven completely from attendance. When the physician came to say goodbye, the prisoner, out of inexpressible gratitude, gave him his last valuable possession: his meerschaum pipe.

Craven also carried away some fascinating memories and sheaves of notes on conversations with the prisoner, which he was to put into book form and publish the following summer as *The Prison Life of Jefferson Davis.*

CHAPTER XXIX

THE WIFE JOINS HER HUSBAND
IN PRISON

DR. CRAVEN HAD been replaced by a physician General Miles thought more suitable to State Prisoner Davis: one whose political opinions were "sounder." Craven himself was disturbed about the appointment of Dr. George Cooper, whom he believed to be "the blackest of Black Republicans." Neither Craven nor Miles was aware that, for all his gruff and forbidding manner, Cooper was a man of good heart and no politician where the health of a patient was concerned, and perhaps they did not then know that his wife was a Virginian. Though at first assuming a stern professional demeanor—any sentry might be a spy—Dr. Cooper was to turn out to be a sore disappointment to Miles. For, like his predecessor, in spite of himself, he was soon to become impressed by Mr. Davis's qualities and the charm of his conversation.

When Dr. Minnegerode came to Monroe in February, 1866, and administered Communion for the second time, he talked with various officers, who had come increasingly to admire the prisoner for his fortitude. Encouraged, Minnegerode determined to face Stanton.

In Washington the Secretary of War received the Rector of St. Paul's coldly and spoke not a word in reply to anything he said. Finally, the clergyman suggested that "without the least danger of any kind as to Mr. Davis's safe imprisonment, he might enjoy some privilege, especially the liberty of the fort, or there would be danger of his health's failing completely." Stanton burst out: "It makes no difference what the state of the health of Jeff Davis is. His trial will soon come on, no doubt. Time enough till that settles it."

Meanwhile Davis's chief attorneys, O'Conor and Reed, mixed contempt with bitterness in their correspondence about the regime which stalled at bringing their client to trial. O'Conor avowed on

273

February 12 that the Government was remediless in the premises, "unless it dares to slay without form or ceremony."

As Davis's close confinement and the constant jar of three pairs of tramping feet told dreadfully on him, Dr. Cooper grew increasingly anxious. Above everything else, he reported to Miles, Davis's nervous system cried out for a respite of stillness and he felt that the prisoner should have "the liberty of the fort." Such liberty could hardly facilitate escape.

In anxious fear that her husband might lose the sight in his good eye, in January Mrs. Davis had devised a black silk mask with no eyeholes, but only slits for the nostrils, with strings to be crossed behind and tied lightly on his forehead.*

After nine months of suffering the lamp's flare, the prisoner was permitted by Miles to use the shade both at night and when he rested by day. When Davis wrote his wife of the tremendous relief it gave him, Varina replied joyously: "I am so triumphant about my shade for your eyes."

This month brings to my heart many delightful though sad memories— the long walks in the Hurricane gardens with their rose borders and mocking birds and your sweet voice in my ear as we walked and talked of our future when we should be married, and at home— And how I used to see you dash by the carriage so free and strong, and think you the strongest of men.

Now I know you are the dearest, the purest, and best of men, and love you so much better than *then* that it seems wonderful to me to compare that feverish childish passion with this waking certainty.

Soon Dr. Cooper managed to have the lamp's flame dimmed further. But despite her eloquent pleas to the authorities Mrs. Davis was still denied permission to visit her husband. However, on Federal General Stedman's recommendation, she was permitted to leave Georgia and go anywhere she pleased except to Fort Monroe. Burton Harrison, who had been released from a miserable incarceration in Washington on January 25, joined her in March and accompanied her to Mississippi. Burton's mother lived in Oxford, and he had not seen her for almost four years.

The party consisted of five, including the baby, Winnie, her white nurse, Mary Ahern, and the colored man, Frederick Maginnis, who had offered himself to Mrs. Davis for employment in Savannah. Ma-

* The mask may be seen today in the Confederate Museum at Richmond.

ginnis, a striking-looking mulatto with long mustachios, had been a former servant of General Beauregard. He had taken a fancy to the President when he served him at Manassas just after the battle in 1861. Davis remembered the man well.

From General Joe Davis's place in Canton, Mississippi, Varina wrote her husband on March 8 about her journey across the South. Davis, who usually had no taste for gossip, was now interested in his wife's accounts of people, places, and conditions, and he was pleased to read that her trip had been "marked at every step by kindness and consideration from those who met me with the knowledge of who I was." All the railroads had given her free passes. She had been "profusely entertained" in Macon, Georgia, where she had spent several days with the Howell Cobbs. She mentioned scores of his old friends and admirers by name and gave him their specific messages. She had felt rather shabby in her old gray poplin at the dinner parties and an evening reception, but she had "borne up." In Atlanta she had been warmly met at the station and well entertained. At Holley Springs, Mississippi, Burton Harrison had left her at her request, so as not to lose any time in seeing his mother at Oxford thirty miles away.

Some Union officers stationed in the war-ruined town of Holly Springs treated Mrs. Davis "with most marked courtesy"; one of them carried some of her luggage from one train to the other. The friendly Winnie, she wrote, had taken "an immense fancy to the Yankees." On the way to Canton, she discovered that the amiable Federals had cut all the buttons off the baby's little dress to send to their children as mementos.

The first day in Canton, after greeting numerous relatives and beholding the new poverty, Varina had "a sinking feeling." Though spring had come, she wrote, and the lark sang high in the air, she felt "weak and chilly and thirsty, like chills," as she claimed she often did in the Mississippi climate.

Davis answered on March 13 in a long letter.

Your reception at Macon was such as I anticipated from my own experience. The kind manifestations made by the negro servants are not less touching than those of more cultivated people. I liked them, and am gratified by their friendly remembrance.

All his life, everywhere he went, Davis was liked by the colored people with whom he came in contact, and loved by those who served him. "Like you, I feel sorry for the negroes," he wrote. He believed that "the ordinary laws governing the relation of labor to capital" would gradually solve the new problems, "if they were *let alone.*" But, between the races, he predicted, hostility would inevitably come about if Northern "interference" continued.

In his prison room, Davis read Varina's next letter—dated New Orleans, March 18—with more gratification. It seemed, she wrote, that she had never before seen so many old friends in one place. Nearly all the Confederate Generals were there: Dick Taylor, Hampton, Wheeler, Preston, Longstreet, Humphrey Marshall, Dabney Maury, and numerous others. All of them sent messages of love and respect —except, of course, Beauregard, who did not call. The warmest words of all, she said, came from the Virginian General Maury. "He spoke of you in manner alike honorable to him and precious to me —as did everyone in the different degrees of graceful power and expression which each possessed."

It is impossible to tell you the love which has been expressed here for you—the tenderness of feeling for you. People sit and cry until I am almost choked with effort to be quiet. But it is a great consolation to know that a nation is mourning your suffering with me—and to be told hourly how far above reproach you are—how fair your fame. I am overwhelmed by the love which everything of your name attracts.

Varina could hardly persuade the New Orleans merchants to accept payment for the articles she bought to replenish her four-year-old wardrobe. But she refrained from telling her husband that with certain Louisiana families the Davises were as unpopular as before the war; for they were still regarded as "nigger-lovers," who had spoiled their people and tried to raise them up too high.

Though Varina had complained despairingly of the effect of the Mississippi climate only ten days before, now she wrote:

My health is very good—iron and treatment have quite set me up again, and I am better than I have been for many months, indeed very well again.

Davis knew that this buoyant sense of well-being was due not merely to iron or medication but to the favorable attention Varina was receiving.

Though she remained fifteen days in New Orleans, she wrote her husband only one letter from the city. Her later apology was that she had not had a half-hour to herself during the whole day "from nine in the morning until eleven at night."

I could not then write because the baby is your child and everything must be pitch dark and quiet as silence and sleep can make, or she wakes and cries piteously.

Varina went up the river to Vicksburg on the *Stonewall* and she was not permitted to pay for her passage. On board she remarked a large number of discharged Negro soldiers "going to Davis Bend with pistols, trinkets, and calico to sell there."

In the early morning at Vicksburg she walked up to see Joseph Davis at his boardinghouse. Birds were singing in the garden, "where lilacs, yellow jasmine, hyacinths and violets were in full blossom." Brother, she wrote, was changed in that his hair had grown whiter, but he was "as well as any old gentleman of his age and as bright." He had a rockaway and two mules in which one of the Negroes drove him about. He seemed to like "the excitement of being in a little town."

Joseph would have long since received back his property, she said, but "he refused to pay the blackmail which a Genl. Thomas of the Freedman's Bureau offered to levy against him." So he could not get it "until a court is assembled upon his charges against the Genl, which he hopes will be soon." Since he was "quite out of money" Varina gave him $400 from her meager supply.

The Negroes have almost taken Vicksburg—they swarm—but they toil not, neither do they spin.

Some of the family servants from Brierfield came to pay their respects. They were getting along well enough, they said, but "twasn't like old times." A few talked "like proprietors of the land," but they were all "respectful and friendly." They sent affectionate remembrances to their former master.

Varina gave Ben Montgomery twenty dollars to provide some comforts for Uncle Bob, who had been robbed by the Yankees and was now a hundred years old. Her letter ended with the further assurance that everyone she had met was "full of love" for Jefferson Davis. "But," she added, "who of our people is not, excepting only Joe Johnston, Beauregard and Jordan, the meanest and basest of mankind."

Varina had not gone to Brierfield, for the Freedman Bureau had placed strange Negro tenants in her house. And her stay in Vicksburg made her think that there was nothing of their possessions in Mississippi to recover. It was even worse than Davis himself had believed. Where was he to take his large family after he was free?

While Mrs. Davis was in Vicksburg, the New York attorneys intimated that she would receive permission from President Johnson to
visit her husband. So Burton Harrison immediately rejoined her and
accompanied her north.

Varina wrote cheerfully from the New York Hotel, where she was
"kept in the parlor until twelve at night from ten in the morning."
She had talked with Mr. O'Conor and was "well satisfied with his
course." Dick Taylor was in the city and had been as "affectionate
as a brother and a son." Any day she expected a permit from President Johnson to go to her husband.

After ten days of impatient waiting for the President's permit,
Mrs. Davis decided to join her mother and children in Canada and
the indispensable Harrison went along to look after her. The first
letter Davis received from Montreal, dated April 14, started off with
lamentations about Howell family troubles. Her mother was ill in
bed with bronchitis in a wretched boardinghouse. Margaret was in
a state of nerves, had no appetite, and cried out if she heard a loud
noise. Her sister Jenny Waller, married to a grandson of President
Tyler, was looking wretched and going to have another baby in
June. Three of her four Howell brothers were jobless in Canada. But
of his own children she could give glowing reports. Little Maggie
was extremely happy at the convent.

Our beautiful Billie—immensely grown—fat as a little possum—and
so sweet and loving to his "Mudder." . . .

Jeff is morally unchanged, which is very much to us. The only change
I see is that he has learned to fight. He fought a boy sixteen for pretending to believe that you were in petticoats at your capture. I understand
the boy did not intend to hurt him, but only to make him show spirit.

I told Jeff your last message, and he seated himself in a chair, covered
his face, and sobbed out, "the dear, dear fellow, will I ever see him
again?"

Jeff, she explained, had picked up many British expressions from
the schoolmasters and students at Lennoxville, "dear fellow" being
among them.

On April 20 Davis's walk was extended to two hours. To get out-
of-doors for two hours away from the maddening tramp of army
boots was a boon of no small significance. "You cannot imagine," he
wrote, "how one shut out from all direct communication with his
friends dwells upon every shadow and longs for light."

After Clement Clay was set at liberty on April 17, 1866, Jefferson Davis alone of all the Confederate State Prisoners remained behind bars. The press noted significantly that Clay had been jailed on exactly the same charge as Davis. But no hint was given as to when the ex-President would be brought to trial or released.

At last Congress appointed a committee to report on the facts on Davis's case and recommended his trial by a Commission of the Court. The War Department had turned over all its "evidence" to the jurist Francis Lieber. After he had examined thousands of letters, he declared: "Davis will not be found guilty and we shall stand there completely beaten." In the meantime Jefferson Davis languished in prison.

But late in April the State Prisoner was permitted an interview with his counsel. The allegation of complicity in the murder of Lincoln having so egregiously failed, and also the attempt to blame the Confederate President for conditions at Andersonville, the Administration had finally been driven to the charge of treason. O'Conor confidently expected to win the case.

In early May of 1866 Jefferson Davis was indicted in the Circuit Court of the United States in the District of Virginia, Judge John C. Underwood presiding. In his "charge" to the jury of Davis's peers, which included black and white illiterates, Underwood infuriated the South by beginning: "Jefferson Davis, yeoman, not having fear of God before his eyes, nor weighing the duty of his said allegiance, but being moved and seduced by the institution of the devil, and wickedly devising against the peace and tranquillity of the United States to subvert, and to stir, move, and incite insurrection, rebellion and war . . ."

Mrs. R. E. Lee expressed her disgust at Underwood's language in a letter to Mrs. R. H. Chilton on May 6:

Have you read Underwood's charge to his grand jury, 5 of whom are negroes? It is the most remarkable piece of composition I ever read, the most *false* and *vindictive*—that such a creature should be allowed to dispense justice is a perfect *farce*. I think his meanness and wickedness have affected his brain.

A fortnight after Mrs. Davis's arrival in Canada a rumor ran through Montreal that the Confederate ex-President was dying. Frantic, she rushed to a telegraph office and wired President Johnson: "Is it possible that you will keep me from my dying husband?" He responded with permission for her to go to Monroe, "subject to conditions to be stated at the fort."

At four o'clock of a raw morning—May 3—Mrs. Davis arrived by ship with her baby, who was still nursing, and Frederick Maginnis. For some hours she sat in an open-shed waiting room, expecting to be conducted to the fort. Then she went to a little hotel not far away and had breakfast. Finally, after a six-hour wait, a pleasant young lieutenant named Fessenden made his appearance. He took her parole that she concealed no deadly weapons, charmed the baby, and eventually brought her into the presence of her husband's jailer. Mrs. Davis made a brave effort to treat General Miles courteously, though she considered him as "utterly lacking in taste or gentlemanly instincts," and, as she wrote a friend: "a tiger and a beast, and, think, only twenty-six years old!"

Followed by the dramatic-looking Frederick, who carried the baby, Mrs. Davis was taken through three lines of sentries, each requiring a password. Ascending a stairway at Carroll Hall, she was admitted into the guardroom, where three young officers were sitting. After a year of anguished separation, Varina was trembling with emotion as she approached the bars of the prisoner's room. Then she beheld in horror what they had done to her husband. She almost cried out at his "shrunken form and glassy eyes." "His cheek bones," she later wrote, "stood out like those of a skeleton. Merely crossing the room made his breath come in short gasps, and his voice was scarcely audible."

Mrs. Davis was not prepared for the crude conditions of his surroundings. She was revolted to find "the bed so infested with insects as to give a perceptible odor to the room." Her husband "knew so little of such things that he could not imagine what annoyed him so at night, and insisted it was some cutaneous affection." Within a half-hour, the constant passing of the sentinels by the door and the windows made her so jumpy that she could scarcely keep her eyes still.

While Varina was with the prisoner, his dinner was brought in. She examined it closely. Though it was "quite good enough," it had been slopped from one dish to another and was covered with a gray hospital towel. To a man of refined taste, rendered weak by illness, she thought it was anything but appetizing. But Dr. Cooper's wife had kindly added oysters to the menu that day. A card read "By order of Dr. C." Mr. Davis ate one oyster and then could not take anything else. Varina was alarmed to remark that because of his low vitality even that morsel gave him stomach pains.

To the wife, who had a far less forgiving nature than her hus-

band, it was remarkable to find that he "was bitter at no earthly
creature," though he did express "supreme contempt for the petty
insults inflicted hourly upon him by General Miles." "My memory,"
Mrs. Davis was to write in her *Memoir*, "does not furnish a record
of the thousand little stabs he gave his emaciated, gray-haired prisoner."

Suffice it to say that he used his power to insult and annoy to the utmost, and in ways previously unknown and not to be anticipated by gen-
tlefolk. . . . We excused much to General Miles, whose opportunities to
learn the habits of refined people were said to have been few; and his
sectional feeling was very bitter. But that he should not have been moved
at the age of twenty-six by the evident physical and mental anguish of
his prisoner, and should have devised ingenious tortures for him, we
could not understand.

Although Miles wanted to put Mrs. Davis on the side of the
fort with the camp women because he thought it would be an im-
propriety for the wife of "Davis" to associate with Federal officers'
wives, Brigadier General Burton, second in command, persuaded
him to let her have a casemate. Varina quickly set up housekeeping.
Miles fixed short periods for Mrs. Davis's visits with her husband.
After several appeals on her part, however, he allowed her to spend
evening hours with him. But, as she wrote, "If the General came
over to the guardroom and found us cheerfully talking together,
whether at seven, at eight, or at ten o'clock, he left the room and
sent an order for me to go home. Once or twice he personally called
at the bars and said 'shutting up time.' "

Though permitted to visit her husband daily, Mrs. Davis was not
allowed to walk on the ramparts with him. Miles reserved that privilege for himself; it afforded him a daily opportunity to needle the
ex-President with mocking remarks about the South or make offensive
attacks on his admired friends. One day, as Davis and Miles rested
briefly on a bench along the ramparts, the young General sneeringly
accused John C. Calhoun of financial dishonesty. Davis rose in indignation and started walking rapidly towards the fort's entrance
gate. No remonstrance of Miles or the flustered guards could stop
him until he reached the sanctuary of his prison room. On another
day, while Mrs. Davis was with her husband, Miles came up to
the prison room and said something so insulting that Davis forgot his
usual forbearance and sprang at the bars. "But for these," he cried,
"you should answer to me now!" Miles recoiled.

In a letter to President Johnson, Dr. Cooper recommended a change of regimen and better treatment "unless the Government desires the captive to die under his sufferings." The President took it under advisement, and finally an order came for the guards to desist from their ceaseless tramping.

Gifts from friends and from unmet admirers, like the Bishop of Montreal, began to arrive. The Catholic prelate sent the ex-President a case of green Chartreuse from his own cellar. Dr. Cooper immediately "prescribed" the liqueur as a stimulant to aid digestion.

Miles resented all the sympathetic attention his captive was receiving, even the occasional oysters from the surgeon's wife. When he learned that some ladies from St. Louis had sent a dressing gown to the prisoner in a package addressed to Mrs. Davis, he took her sharply to task. "This fort," he shouted, "shall not be made a depot for luxuries and such delicacies as oysters for Jeff Davis. I shall have to open your packages and see that this is not done."

Mrs. Davis's dark eyes blazed, and she lost her "hard-earned patience." Drawing herself up to her imposing height, she looked him in the eye and said, "I am not your prisoner. You would not find yourself justified by the laws in infringing on my private right." Miles stared at her in astonishment. Then he backed away and muttered, "I guess I couldn't." He made no further threat to inspect her parcels.

To satisfy himself as to Davis's condition, President Johnson sent his Secretary of the Treasury, Hugh McCulloch, to Fort Monroe to call on him. Mrs. Davis, who was not allowed at the meeting, requested a private interview. General Miles refused to let her talk with the cabinet minister except in his presence. Emboldened by McCulloch's sympathetic manner, Mrs. Davis laid the whole matter before him in Miles's hearing and spoke of the countless indignities and little torments the Commanding General had devised. When she mentioned oysters as something her husband could digest and which Miles objected to his having, the Secretary regarded the young commander with a quizzical smile. "General," he said, "oysters on the seacoast are hardly to be classed as luxuries, are they?"

On May 23 Dr. Cooper sent a letter to Mrs. Davis in answer to a pressing inquiry from her.

I have done all in my power to keep his health up, but I must own I see him becoming more and more weak day by day. He has been well cared for in the matter of food; the tramp of the sentinels he no longer hears. . . .

Notwithstanding, he fails and the only thing left is to give him mental and bodily rest and exercise at will.

This can be only by having the Parole of the Fort with permission to remain with his family now residing there.

Whether or not Varina sent this letter to some friend who passed it on to the New York *World*, Cooper's report on Davis's depressed health became public. Almost immediately a strong editorial appeared in the *World*.

It [the report] cannot be read by any honorable and right-minded American, no matter what his sectional feelings or his political opinions may be, without a sickening sensation of shame for his country and burning flush of indignation against the persons who have prostituted their official position to inflict upon the American name an ineffaceable brand of disgrace by the wanton torture of an invalid, lying a prisoner in the strongest fortress of the Union. . . .

The American people will have a serious account to settle with the functionaries who could thus misrepresent them in the eyes of Christendom and of history.

Articles of a similar tone began to appear in other Northern papers. Miles was outraged. On May 26 he complained bitterly to Adjutant General Townsend, declaring that he had only obeyed orders from the War Department and that the press was doing him great injustice. Two days later he wrote again to Townsend attacking Dr. Cooper in a communication marked "confidential."

I regret to say that I think Surgeon Cooper is entirely under the influence of Mr. and Mrs. Davis, the former of whom has the happy faculty that a strong mind has over a weaker to mould it to agree with its views and opinions. Surgeon Cooper's wife is a secessionist. . . . Yesterday he had a private interview with Davis and Messers. O'Conor and Shea.*

Towards the end of May Mrs. Davis went to Washington to plead her husband's case before President Johnson. It took some courage because of the malice he had harbored against Jefferson Davis for almost two decades. She arrived on a Saturday, and many old Washington friends called to pay their respects, with what the New York *Tribune* of May 28 designated "unseemly haste." Among

---

* The full letter of Miles in *Official Records*, 121, p. 919, makes interesting reading as do his communications in the pages following.

noted callers were Senator Willard Saulsbury of Delaware and Senator Reverdy Johnson of Maryland.

Under the caption "A Sensation" the astounded correspondent of the *Tribune* wrote:

The great sensation of the Capital today has been the appearance of Senator Saulsbury at the Church of the Ascension "clothed and in his right mind" as an escort for Mrs. Jeff Davis. After church a noted Rebel procured an open buggy, and took a Sunday evening drive with Mrs. Davis about the principal streets of the city.

Senators Johnson and Saulsbury persuaded the President to appoint an hour to receive Mrs. Davis.

Somewhat to her surprise, Andrew Johnson greeted her most civilly; he even seemed friendly. "But we must wait," he told her. "Our hope is to mollify the public to Mr. Davis." She told him the public would not need to be mollified but for his own proclamation that Davis was an accessory to Lincoln's assassination. "I am sure you did not believe it," she said. The President admitted he did not, but that others in authority claimed they did, and he himself had been in the hands of wildly excited people. He intimated that he had been compelled by Stanton and Joseph Holt to issue the proclamation, and that Holt insisted he had proof of Davis's complicity.

Mrs. Davis said quietly, "If Booth had left a card for Mr. Davis as he did for you, Mr. President, just before the assassination, I fear my husband's life would have paid the forfeit."

Johnson merely bowed assent, and then after a moment's silence, he said that now time was the only element lacking to Mr. Davis's release. He confessed that he, a Democrat, was laboring under the enmity of Radical Republicans in both Houses of Congress, and that if they could find anything upon which to base an impeachment they would attempt to degrade him.

At that moment Thaddeus Stevens, "a lopsided man" in Mrs. Davis's words, burst into the room and threatened the Chief Executive in "such a manner as would have been thought inadmissible to one of the servants." When the intruder had left, Johnson said, "You see a little of the difficulty under which I labor." Then he suggested that Mr. Davis ask for a pardon in writing. But Mrs. Davis told him that he would never do such a thing.

When Varina returned to Fort Monroe and related her Washington experiences, she said that the President had affirmed he made it an inflexible rule never to grant a pardon unless the individual seeking clemency asked for it himself.

Jefferson Davis adamantly declined, as Varina had expected. To ask for pardon, he said, was a confession of guilt. Not only did he have a clear conscience, but the record of such an application would prejudice the case of the South as well as his own.

While Mrs. Davis was in Washington, pleading for her husband's release, O'Conor and Shea had been closeted with the prisoner at Fort Monroe. They discussed matters of procedure to be followed in the Richmond court trial during the first week in June. They left Davis hopeful of early freedom.

When the court in Richmond opened on June 5, two days after Davis's fifty-eighth birthday, four of his attorneys were on hand. Philadelphia's William B. Reed demanded to know what was to be done with the Davis indictment. He declared that he desired a speedy trial on any charge that might be brought against Mr. Davis in any civil tribunal in the land.

We may be now here representing, may it please the Court, a dying man. For thirteen months he has been in prison. The Constitution of the United States guarantees to him not only an impartial trial, but a speedy trial.

After two days of talk, the Assistant United States District Attorney affirmed that the prisoner had never been in the custody of that court but was held as a State Prisoner "under order of the President, signed by the Secretary of War." Reed then made a formal move for Jefferson Davis's release on bail. But his gesture came to naught.

O'Conor sent Burton Harrison to Fort Monroe to break the sad news that he had not been able to effect the anticipated release. Davis was painfully disappointed, but, as Harrison wrote his mother, "he bore it in good part."

Varina, however, blew up in a fury of frustration. In her impatience, she began to annoy the attorneys with importunate letters. Harrison cautioned her to be more discreet and temperate in her remarks, reminding her that she sometimes had difficulty in controlling her feelings. From having lived in the house with the family in Richmond he knew well that Mrs. Davis's headstrong nature often made matters difficult for her husband. Finally, he wrote her firmly:

Mr. O'Conor has received a letter from you within a few days, and asks me to say that he thinks it better that he should not write to you again for the present.

Varina accepted the rebuke humbly. Burton was one person with whom she never quarreled, no matter how overwrought she might be. When calm, Varina quite understood her own tempestuous tendencies. She freely confessed in a letter to Mrs. Howell Cobb:

As for me, I am like a wild animal about trouble—I can better afford to lick the lance which rankles in my heart, than bear the surgical examination which may teach the mode for its extraction. I take refuge in mocking.

In July Mrs. Davis piteously appealed to Reverdy Johnson to intercede again with the President to secure more liberties for her husband. "Now his fevers return daily," she wrote, "and he is so patient, so uncomplaining, so entirely quiescent in this death in life. It breaks my heart."

When it was announced that State Prisoner Davis was permitted to receive letters from friends, one of the first to arrive was from Mrs. Robert E. Lee. It was boldly addressed to "Ex-President Jefferson Davis." Though posted in June of 1866, the body of the letter had been written in late May, 1865. Mary Lee now said that on learning that the prisoner was not permitted correspondence even from his wife, she had kept her letter until the ban was lifted. "I do not know," she wrote, "that I can write anything more expressive of my feelings towards you than this letter penned a few days after I heard of your imprisonment, so send it now with the love and prayers of all my family."

The letter was accompanied by Mrs. Lee's "favorite hymn"; she had copied all six verses in the hope that it might bring consolation.

My heart has prompted me, my dear friend, ever since I knew of the failure of our glorious cause, to write to you and express my deep sympathy, how much more since I learned of your captivity, your separation from your beloved family and your incarceration in a solitary dungeon. If you knew how many prayers and tears had been sent to Heaven for you and yours, you could realize that you were not forgotten. We did so long to hear that you could reach in safety some foreign clime where you could enjoy the repose and consideration which seems to be denied you in your own country. . . . The only consolation I can now offer you besides our deep attachment and remembrance of you, is contained in the words of my favorite hymn which I have transcribed for you. . . . As I know not if this letter will be allowed to reach you I will not say more. You can imagine all we would say and feel and know that one sentiment animates the hearts of your true friends and, among them, believe, there is no one truer than

Mary C. Lee

A postscript was appended: "You don't know how I value the chair you sent me."

Davis was signally touched by Mrs. Lee's solicitude. They had been fond of each other, and she had given repeated evidences of her admiration for her husband's Commander-in-Chief. He noted with gratification her phrase "our glorious cause."

Among other early letters that affected him was a manly, tender one from the unlucky General John C. Pemberton, the Philadelphian who had cast his lot with the Confederacy. After his valiant defense of Vicksburg, when starvation finally caused capitulation, the friends of Joseph Johnston had turned the South so unjustly against the Northerner that President Davis was unable to secure another command for him, though he had done his best to alleviate the man's wounded feelings. Pemberton, who had been brought up luxuriously, was now trying to eke out a frugal living from a small farm near Warrenton and "striving against inexperience and many adverse circumstances." But he assured the ex-President that he did not regret the course he conscientiously took, and only lamented the results as they affected the South and Davis himself.

I hope and believe it is unnecessary for me to say how frequently my thoughts have been with you, and how deeply I have felt the wrongs which have been done you. I can never forget the uniform kindness and consideration with which you honored me even to your own prejudice and which manifested itself most, when I was most under the ban— neither need I tell you how sincerely I have deplored the effect upon your health of the long and cruel incarceration you have suffered for our common cause.

In midsummer Dr. Craven's book *The Prison Life of Jefferson Davis,* based largely on his conversations with the State Prisoner, was published. Craven wrote that he had not intended to release the book until after the trial so that it might not interfere with the public opinion or the due course of justice. But friends of his thought that the North should know something of the prisoner's true character, as well as the conditions of his imprisonment. In the introduction, which had been written before the New York *World* editorial had appeared in May, Craven said:

It must be remembered that during the past year Mr. Davis has lain a silent prisoner in our strongest fort, unable to reply by so much as a word to the myriad assaults which have been made both on his private character and public course. This is absolutely the first statement in his favor . . . and the case against that prisoner must indeed be weak which cannot bear allowance of a single voice to be raised in his defense, while seven-eighths of the Northern journals have been industriously engaged in manufacturing public sentiment to his injury. . . .

His self-control was the feature of his character, knowing that his temper had been high and proud, which most struck me during my attendance. . . .

As for the rest, the character of Mr. Davis, we believe, will receive justice in history. . . .

The book created a stir and immediately became a best seller. A few Northern reviews were scornful. *Harper's Weekly* remarked with sarcasm that Davis had "a physician who apparently sat at his feet to catch the drops of wisdom which fell from his mouth; a physician who has prepared a book about the prisoner whom he calls 'ex-President' and 'distinguished captive.'"

Though Davis winced to read some expressions Craven had put into his mouth that were inconceivable to his nature or his breeding, he recognized the work as obviously that of an admiring friend. The revelations created much Northern sympathy for the prisoner, as well as indignation at Miles's sadistic treatment. Jefferson Davis could now expect a fairer trial and perhaps an early release.

CHAPTER XXX

"IT IS THE PART OF FIDELITY
TO WAIT FOR MORNING"

WHILE JEFFERSON DAVIS was eagerly anticipating his trial, the Federal authorities decided to postpone the case until the first Tuesday in October when Chief Justice Chase could preside. Charles O'Conor again sent Burton Harrison to Fort Monroe to report the unhappy turn of events. It grieved Burton to bring such ill tidings. But at least he could tell the prisoner that O'Conor was already working on a new plan. Perhaps the postponement was not altogether bad; for many persons, including General Lee, seriously doubted that the Confederate ex-President could get a fair trial in a United States court.

In view of the new turn of events, Harrison decided to go to Europe to see his fiancée, Constance Cary, who was staying in Paris with her mother. Davis encouraged him. Harrison insisted that he would return before the trial; he said he was determined not to marry until his Chief had gained freedom.

Varina was again in black despair, because, as she told Burton, the best lawyers in New York seemed at a loss "to see Mr. Davis's way out of this living tomb."

Throughout August Davis received letters from sympathizing friends and many little tributes of affection. From an ex-private of the Army of Tennessee, now living in Charleston, came a gift of cognac and a note couched in such formal phrases as one might suppose fitting for a deposed ruler.

B. G. Wilkins, paroled prisoner of war . . . presents his respectful compliments to Mr. Davis and begs His Excellency's acceptance of 3 Bottles Cognac and 1 Bottle of Vinegar, each excellent of its kind, having been sent Mr. Wilkins direct from Bordeaux by his venerable friend Monsieur Nartigue, a proprietor of high consideration in that vicinage.

Mr. Wilkins regrets that circumstances have prevented his making a more worthy offering. But he avails of the occasion to assure His Excellency of the profound sympathy of his countrymen in this his dark hour of trial and sorrow. . . .

Thus writing, he prays God to have you in His Holy Keeping.

One letter that especially warmed Davis's heart was from the loyal General Wade Hampton, who had opposed Johnston's surrender.

If there is any mode in the world by which I can serve you, it will give me the greatest happiness to do so for I need not tell you that my esteem & affection for you are unchanged, or changed only by becoming greater than they were. . . . Every true heart at the South feels that you are vicariously bearing the griefs of our people, & from every corner of our unhappy & desolate land constant prayers go up to Heaven for your deliverance.

But the unhappy economic situation in South Carolina, at which Hampton hinted, distressed Davis.

In this state the condition of the people is deplorable, & I look for a famine next year. The corn crops are a total failure, & there will not be cotton enough made to buy bread. And the prospect for the future is quite as gloomy. . . .

The fate of the Negro I regard as sealed. . . . Thank God, we are no longer responsible for him. My own negroes have given most gratifying evidence of their "loyalty" by remaining with me & behaving quite as well as they ever did, & of course I am trying to make them contented & happy. . . .

Davis deplored the fact that so many Southerners were emigrating to Brazil and other foreign lands to avoid living under Yankee domination. He thought the Southerners should stick it out for the good of the nation, he wrote his wife, who had gone again to Mississippi.

I hope the reports of growing despondence, because of political action leading to organizations for expatriatism, have been exaggerated. All cannot go, and those who must stay will need the help of all who can go away. *The night may seem long, but it is the part of fidelity to watch and wait for morning.*

Being silenced in prison, Davis could not speak to the South, but Varina would undoubtedly pass on his thought here and there, and small ripples of influence might result.

. . .

Davis shortly learned that several outstanding Northerners were interceding with the President in his behalf. Gerrit Smith, the noted Abolitionist leader and philanthropist, was among those who signed a petition begging the release of Jefferson Davis. In a letter to Andrew Johnson of August 24 Smith reinforced his signature in strong language:

I deem very long confinement in prison without a trial an insult to the South . . . and a no less deep dishonor to the Government and the country.

A little later Smith put himself on public record:

We have neither moral nor legal right to put on trial under the Constitution, those whom we have recognized as belligerents and under the protection of the law of war. . . . The South, in her vast uprising, reached the dignity and rights of a party to a civil war.

As the sympathy of powerful Northerners became more manifest and pressure from all sections increased, at the end of August President Johnson ordered Brevet Major General Miles to be mustered out of the Volunteer service. Miles protested bitterly, blaming his dismissal on "the base slanders and foulest accusation which the disloyal press has heaped upon me." Since he had been Davis's jailer for fifteen months, he begged to remain one month longer, until the prisoner was removed from Fort Monroe for his trial.

The President rejected his request, and on September 1 General Miles was relieved of duty.* His departure marked the happiest day the Davises had known since the capture in May, 1865. The petty cruelties inflicted by the callous young man had finally redounded against himself and added to the fame of the ex-President. Davis reflected that it was sad that Miles had not known the Chinese dictum which puts a high price on vindictiveness: "The fires you kindle for your enemy will eventually burn you more than him." For the rest of his long life Nelson Miles would be explaining, apologizing for, or blaming on others his base treatment of his distinguished captive.

Brigadier General Henry S. Burton, the new commander at Fort

---

* Shortly Miles entered the regular army with the rank of Colonel and was sent to the West to fight Indians, whom he slaughtered with remarkable dexterity. He married a niece of General Sherman and ultimately became the Commanding General of the United States Army.

Monroe, proved a humane and civil jailer. Within the bounds of his directives he was most considerate of the feelings of the prisoner and Mrs. Davis. Davis was shortly allowed "the freedom of the fort," and his wife accompanied him on his walks on the ramparts.

Dick Taylor had two interviews with President Johnson in Washington and begged permission to visit his brother-in-law in prison. He had expected Johnson to be difficult. As he wrote in *Destruction and Reconstruction,* Johnson had succeeded Lincoln, "breathing fire and hemp against the South." "He had loudly proclaimed that he would make treason odious by hanging traitors" and had promptly ordered the arrest of General Lee, which General Grant had had the power to resist.

Johnson received the son of President Zachary Taylor courteously but would give him no answer to his special requests about Jefferson Davis. Taylor found him to be of "an obstinate, suspicious temper. . . . Like a badger, one had to dig him out of his hole." Johnson confessed that between him and the Republican leaders such seeds of discord were already sown that he would be saved embarrassment if Thaddeus Stevens and Charles Sumner could be induced to recommend Taylor's permission to visit Davis.

Stevens, the Republican leader in the House, frankly told Taylor that he wanted "no restoration of the Union under the Constitution," which he called "a worthless bit of old parchment." The white people of the South, he said, should never again be trusted with power, for they would eventually unite with Northern "Copperheads" and control the Government. He declared that the only sound policy was to confiscate the property of the Southern whites and divide it among the Negroes.

In regard to Jefferson Davis, however, he was convinced that nothing would be done with him, "since Johnson had only pluck enough to hang those two poor devils, Wirz and Mrs. Surratt." If the leading traitors had been promptly strung up, well and good: now the time for hanging was past. But he thought it was silly to refuse permission to visit Davis, though he himself did not intend to relieve Johnson of that responsibility.

Senator Sumner, in high-flown language, put Taylor off with quotations from the classics, modern poets, and Mrs. Stowe. Seward, who entertained him at dinner with "fatted calf" for the prodigal, seemed to favor the object of his mission. At least as far as Taylor could "gather his meaning under the cloud of words with which he is accustomed to cover his slightest thought."*

Taylor finally worried Johnson into giving him permission to visit Jefferson Davis. He took a boat at Baltimore and arrived at Fort Monroe early in the morning. General Burton did the son of President Taylor the honor of receiving him at the dock and escorting him to his quarters for breakfast.

It was with considerable emotion that Dick Taylor reached the barred room in which the ex-President was confined. The two men had been devoted friends since 1831 in the wilds of Wisconsin when Taylor was just a boy and young Lieutenant Davis was courting his sister, Sarah Knox. Now they met in silence and merely clasped hands. Taylor could not speak. Finally Mr. Davis said, "This is kind, but no more than I expected."

"Pallid, worn, gray, bent, feeble, suffering from inflammation of the eyes," Taylor wrote, "he was a painful sight for a friend."

When they sat down, Davis "uttered no plaint," but confessed the light kept burning all night in his room had "hurt his eyes a little" and that the noise made every two hours by relieving the sentry "prevented much sleep." "However," he said, "everything has changed for the better since General Burton, who strains his orders from Washington to the utmost in my behalf."

Taylor related details of his visit to Washington, of his reception by Johnson and half a dozen other strategic persons. Optimistically he declared that if he could not secure his brother-in-law's immediate release on bail, he felt certain that he could obtain permission for Mrs. Davis to live with him.

"You may solicit favors for me," Davis said. "But I decline to solicit any for myself." At the hope of having his wife with him, however, his countenance brightened. He asked numerous questions about the condition and prospects of the South which Taylor answered in as favorable a light as he could, without absolutely lying.

But he told his former Chief that during the visit to Washington he had witnessed "the martial tread of hundreds of volunteer Generals, just disbanded." "Gorged with loot," he said, "they spent it as lavishly as Morgan's buccaneers after the sack of Panama. Their women sat at meat, resplendent in jewels, the spoil of Southern matrons. The camp followers of the army were there in high

---

* In the opinion of Gideon Welles, Seward's attitude to Davis at this time was extremely vindictive.

carnival and in character and numbers they rivaled those attendants of Xerxes." In fact, he declared, courtesans swarmed everywhere, around the Capitol, "in the very ante-chambers of the White
House." Of a tolerant disposition, Taylor confessed that he did not
feel called upon to cry aloud against these enormities, but he certainly had "some doubts concerning Divine justice."

At last, through the efforts of Taylor and others, executive permission was given for Mrs. Davis and the baby to live with the prisoner. A four-room apartment in Carroll Hall was assigned to them.
Friends in Baltimore and Norfolk sent furniture. With her talent for
making those about her comfortable, Mrs. Davis soon gave their
prison quarters the semblance of a home. Ellen, the colored nurse,
who had been forced to leave the ship in Hampton Roads in May,
1865, returned as housemaid. Frederick Maginnis became the ex-
President's body servant, helping to nurse him back to health, as his
beloved James Pemberton had done in the terrible Wisconsin winter
of 1832. Davis found Beauregard's former man just as Varina described him: "a courteous, refined gentleman in his instincts."

Once, when an impertinent woman rang the Davis doorbell and
told Frederick that she wanted to see "Jeff," the Negro replied that
he knew no such person.

"Aren't you his servant?"

"You are entirely mistaken, madam," he answered with cool for-
mality. "I happen to serve the ex-President of the Confederacy."

Though Davis was now immeasurably better off in creature comforts and could take his wife and his baby girl in his arms without
being watched, his health was too shattered to be easily restored.
Dr. Cooper "exhausted his skill" in trying to build up the prisoner's
strength. Mrs. Davis herself was a tireless and dedicated nurse. For
a time her husband could sleep only when read to, and Varina, so
she wrote, sometimes "read aloud until day broke." She kept a finger
on his feeble pulse, for the physician warned her that the walls
of his heart were so weak that a very sound sleep, if too prolonged,
might cause it to stop forever. When the pulse became barely perceptible, she would rouse him, give him a sip of Chartreuse or make
him eat a bite of something.

Many Northerners still held the image of the fiendish Jefferson
Davis which the press had sedulously created. Among those thoroughly deceived was Mary Day, a young woman from Bowling
Green, Ohio, who came to visit her brother, Captain Selden Day,
one of the prisoner's guards. She had been horrified to find that her

brother now lived in Carroll Hall directly under "the archtraitor." But one day the Captain took her to meet Jefferson Davis and to thank his wife for reviving him with cordials when he had been stricken with a malady erroneously thought to be cholera. Mary Day had a pleasant shock, as she later wrote.

I was speechless with amazement as I gazed at the thin, strong features framed with grey locks; one eye faded a little more than the other, but both lightened by a smile that was almost angelic! And the most arresting of all was a quality in his voice that seemed to go directly to one's heart. Back in Ohio, we had been singing with great enthusiasm, "Hang Jeff Davis on a sour apple tree." I had expected to see Mr. Davis a most unlovable creature, almost with hoofs and horns, so strong had been the feeling against him in the Middle West. . . . Now I understood why the doctor of the fort who attended Mr. Davis when he was first imprisoned had lost his position on account of friendship and deep interest in his patient, and why another physician who succeeded him very soon developed the same friendly feeling towards his prisoner.*

Later, when Margaret Howell came to Fort Monroe, she nursed Mary Day through an illness, and in her Southern way would add rose geranium leaves to the tempting trays she brought. The Ohio girl learned that Rebels were different from what the papers had pictured. She often called on the Davises and noted that though the husband and wife were of different caliber, "they were equally charming and seemed to complement each other." Never once in Mary's hearing did Mr. Davis ever mention the war or his own imprisonment.

Almost from the beginning, Mrs. Davis, with her tact and charm, had won the favorable regard of the Northern officers' wives. Of course, Mrs. Cooper, born in Old Point Comfort, was "a secessionist at heart." But Varina's favorite was General Burton's wife, "a warm-hearted, sympathetic, talented Mexican"—really a Spaniard from old California. Since Mrs. Burton was resentful of the Government's interference in Mexico's affairs, she and Varina would often sit together and secretly "abuse the Yankees."

In late September, under the new regime, some of Davis's friends were permitted to call. Ex-President Franklin Pierce, who had never swerved in his personal devotion, came from New Hampshire to reassure him. Wade Hampton made a long visit. Among others, General John C. Preston and General John B. Gordon paid their respects.

* Mary Day Burchenal wrote an interesting piece about the Davises as she knew them at Fort Monroe in *Holland's Magazine*, October, 1931.

As Davis was looking eagerly to his trial in early October, with resultant vindication and freedom, a happy message reached Fort Monroe: Burton Harrison was returned from Europe and would soon see him.

The day after Harrison's ship docked in New York Charles O'Conor sent for him. Washington authorities had decided to postpone the Davis trial until the spring of 1867. Harrison was charged to bear the melancholy tidings. It was a grievous task, but no one was better fitted to temper the bitterness of bad news than the engaging Burton.

Davis found him looking splendid and entirely recovered now from scurvy and other ill effects of his harsh imprisonment. He stayed for two days beguiling the Davises' crushing disappointment by bright recountals of his European travels, telling them about his Connie and her mother and various friends abroad. He delivered affectionate messages from Dudley Mann, the Slidells, and others in Paris. Robert Toombs was living richly in Paris, but thoroughly detesting his self-imposed exile. In fact, he complained that he was eating an acre of his Texas land every day he lived abroad. The first time Harrison had seen Toombs since their stop in his Georgia hometown during "the flight" was at the Théâtre du Châtelet. "The spectacle," Harrison said, "was one of the most splendid ever put upon the stage there and the French people were in raptures over the dazzling beauty of the scene. Toombs, fashionably dressed, sat in an orchestra chair, regarding it all with the stolid composure of an Indian—with an expression of countenance suggesting that he had a thousand times seen spectacles more brilliant at Washington, Georgia." That, too, was so like Toombs! Davis thought, thoroughly enjoying the story.

When Burton returned to New York, a miasma of gloom settled on the Davis household. Hope had been deferred too often. It was hard to face another bleak winter in prison. Varina wrote sadly to her mother in Canada on October 18:

Jeff grows hourly weaker, more exhausted. He has now to cling to the banister, and to use his stick in descending the steps, and staggers much in walking. This decision of Mr. Johnson that he must be left to the Republicans, that he can do nothing for him, seems to promise that his life will be spent in prison. It is in the power of the judge to postpone his trial from one time to another and this they have done— I am too grieved, too agonized to talk of this. God knows what we shall do—what we can do.

Malie [Brodhead] is kind in staying here, for it is a wretchedly dull place.

In late October John R. Thompson, the poet-editor, just returned from England and his excellent but fruitless propaganda work on *The Index,* came to see the prisoner. He brought him an English overcoat and a verbal message from Thomas Carlyle, which pleased him very much. Carlyle had said that he thought Jefferson Davis had "more of the heroic in him than any other actor in the drama and that he was one of the great and good men now on this planet."

That same day Varina wrote Horace Greeley pleading that he make some impressive gesture towards securing her husband's release. Greeley replied with a sympathetic and hopeful letter. On November 9 a telling editorial appeared in the *Tribune.* Greeley reviewed the case of Jefferson Davis and pointed out that his counsel had made repeated efforts to bring his case to trial. But "one legal tangle had followed another," until now "Congress, President and Chief Justice were in a complete muddle on the subject." Greeley urged the prisoner's immediate release and took President Johnson to task for not publicly retracting his charge that Jefferson Davis was involved in Lincoln's assassination. Davis was particularly pleased with this passage:

It is neither just nor wise to send forth a prisoner of state with the brand of murder on his brow; and a naked failure to prosecute is but equivalent to the Scotch verdict, "Not proved." . . . A great government may deal sternly with the offenders, but not meanly; it cannot afford to seem unwilling to repair an obvious wrong.

The day after Greeley's editorial appeared, Richard Taylor wrote that he was putting more pressure on President Johnson. He had just had a three hours' talk at the White House. He felt certain that Mr. Davis would be paroled, to appear in court when the Government called him to trial. He also confidently expected a general amnesty to be announced shortly. With Greeley's editorial and Taylor's optimistic letter Davis's health seemed to improve.

In late November, Mary Stamps, the widow of Davis's nephew Isaac Stamps and daughter-in-law of his sister Lucinda, came to see him. There was no one outside his immediate family whose presence could have given him more joy. A sort of spiritual affinity existed between this young woman in her early thirties and the fifty-eight-year-old man. During the dread uncertainty of Gettysburg,

Mary had been staying with the Davises in Richmond and, when almost distracted by strange forebodings of her captain husband's agonized dying, she had been comforted by her uncle.

In appearance Mary had changed little since that July of 1863 except that with the responsibility of two fatherless little girls to rear she had matured. Her cool, classic beauty was enhanced by the touch of personal tragedy. Her rich brown hair held the same copper lights, but her sea-blue eyes had new depths.*

Mary had brought a perplexing problem for Uncle Jeff. At the home of her father, Governor Humphreys, in Jackson, Mississippi, Joseph Davis, the octogenarian brother, had come to see her on important business. He had told her to tell Jefferson that as the duration of his imprisonment was so uncertain, he hoped to act for him in the sale of the Brierfield place. In what he considered his brother's best interests, he had arranged to sell Brierfield along with his own Hurricane property to Ben Montgomery, his former slave. The sale price for both properties together was $300,000. The sale of Brierfield was, of course, subject to Jefferson's approval. Montgomery had little or no cash, but he and his able sons, Thornton and Isaiah, were to pay six per cent annual interest on notes through the crops they would raise.

In one sense it was fortunate that Joseph, who had given his young brother the Brierfield land in 1835 when it was virgin wilderness, had never had it properly deeded to him. If it had stood in Jefferson's name on the court records, it might have been confiscated by the Federal Government as traitor property. Varina had repeatedly insisted and even created scenes to effect the legal transfer. But she had only angered Joseph; and in case of Jefferson's death he did not want the property to go to her and the Howells.

Davis was surprised that Joseph wanted to sell the plantations to the Montgomery Negroes. He had expected to farm his land himself when he was released, and he looked upon Brierfield's extensive acres as his children's heritage. He liked Ben Montgomery and his sons, whom he had helped to educate. Ben had often acted as his overseer during his years in Washington and Richmond and he had found him quite as satisfactory as the white overseers who came and went. Joseph thought that Ben, being a Negro himself, could better control the labor. And he had great faith in his drive; for, as he said, Ben was ambitious to be a rich man.

* See Strode's *Jefferson Davis: Confederate President*, pp. 417-18, 432, 440, 450-451, 468-69.

For some days Jefferson Davis thought over all that Mary Stamps related. He "expressed himself as not being hopeful of a good result from the sale."* Mary assured him that Joseph Davis had not claimed any right to dispose of Brierfield, but on the contrary he had emphasized that he had acted for his brother subject to his consent. The fact that he desired his approval showed clearly that Joseph considered Brierfield Jefferson's property.

Since his release from prison seemed uncertain and since property in his own name might be confiscated, Jefferson Davis reluctantly agreed to let Joseph sell Brierfield.† But it was a painful wrench.

With her family in Canada clamoring for a visit, Varina took advantage of Mary Stamps's presence at Fort Monroe to get her to manage the household and be company for her husband while she went to Montreal. Shortly, Davis received a letter from his wife, written December 8.

I ought to go away from home to know how rich I am— You seem a thousand feet high compared with the rest of the world. I seem to feel sanctified by the one last long kiss as we parted and the memory of your love gives me confidence to do anything but risk your displeasure.

How do you and Mary get on I wonder—I think I can see you strolling around the Ramparts and sitting around the best lamp shade ("mine own contrive") to read. Do give my best love to Mary.

Four days later Varina wrote details about each member of the family. Davis was peculiarly touched at the part about his youngest son, William.

Billy got in bed this morning and said, "Mother, do you know lots of stories?" So I told him of your childhood and manhood and at last told him who you were. He was charmed and said, "Oh take me to see him, do please. I want to see how he looks!" So I will bring him with me, and Ellen will take care of him. Now this is very near my heart, but if you are *set against it and fixed,* say so, and of course I shall give up the project.

Davis could not bring himself to accede to his wife's desire to have five-year-old Billy at Fort Monroe. As poignantly as he longed to see both his boys and Pollie, he could not bear for them to have

---

* The words in quotation marks are taken from the original handwritten court proceedings in the trial for the reclamation of the Brierfield property of Jefferson Davis (1874-1878). The court record in manuscript, a thick volume of more than 500 pages, is in the Mississippi Department of Archives in Jackson. Mary Stamps's main testimony appears on pp. 148-154.

† "I have closed the contract with Ben," Joseph Davis wrote his brother on March 26, 1867.

the unhappy memory of seeing their father in prison. So he telegraphed a negative answer.

After Varina's departure the Carroll Hall apartment had been rather quiet. Mary and Mr. Davis were not given to talk when they had nothing significant to say, while Varina was by nature uncommonly garrulous. Silence depressed her and she liked bustling activity around her. Her dynamic personality could put the atmosphere of any room into vibrations.

To Davis, Mary was more like a soothing balm. They were extremely harmonious together. In the evenings she would read aloud to save his eyes. In the afternoons they would stroll together along the ramparts, observing the moving ships and the dark December sea.

Mary had one personal problem to discuss: she did not like living dependent at her father's. Though she was decidedly feminine, Mary had a man's logical mind. As a young married woman she had studied law to encourage her husband's interest and found it stimulating. All through her teens she had delighted in teaching the Negroes on her father's plantation. She wanted to be independent, to teach school or have a school of her own. Her father insisted that she stay at home with him and his young second wife, of whom Mary was quite fond. To force her to remain, he refused to release her share of her dead mother's estate.

Jefferson Davis himself had somewhat old-fashioned ideas about woman's place being in the home. But when he ascertained that Mary was determined to make her own way to support her little girls and that she had no intention of marrying again, he agreed that she might respectably teach in a young ladies' seminary. He promised to try to influence her father, who had been a cadet with him at West Point.

Varina wrote long full letters from Canada and complained that no one at the Fort would write her. She had received "only one brief letter and that most unsatisfactory"; not a line about Pie from Mary Ahern, who had been "instructed to write every single day." But Pie flourished during her mother's absence and was the pet of Fort Monroe.

As Mary Stamps prepared to return home by ship from Norfolk to New Orleans, Davis could hardly bear to part with her. Despite the perturbing business about the sale of Brierfield, her visit and presence had brought him a certain peace.

Varina's imminent return was heralded in a letter of December

16 with a score of instructions concerning household matters. Among other things, Frederick was to buy five pounds of raisins and five pounds of currants.

Chop raisins very fine to put in a stone jar . . . engage some suet against I come. Tell Jullet to make a pound and a sponge cake and ice them—to make a batch of potato pies—and tell Frederick to lay by some eggs.

If Mary has not left you, which I fear she has, give her my best love, and thanks to her.

Varina said she was bringing back to Fort Monroe Margaret Howell, who was "highly nervous and very discontented." She had also invited Malie Brodhead for Christmas with all her Pennsylvania children, including his namesake, Jefferson Davis Brodhead. Frederick was to see about procurement of extra beds at once.

In his own state of nervous debility, which had just been relieved by a quiet fortnight, Davis read of his wife's vigorous return with mingled emotions.

CHAPTER XXXI

OUT OF PRISON

———◆———

ANOTHER CHRISTMAS AWAY from his three eldest children came to Jefferson Davis in Fort Monroe. But it was consoling to have his wife and baby under the same roof with him and devoted servants to minister to him. On this Christmas of 1866 when he looked out of door or window it was not through iron bars. No lamp burned at night. He was not waked every two hours by the changing of the guards. But he was still a prisoner whom his accusers would not bring to trial.

Christmas Day was centered about the little girl's pleasure. Pie received a magnificent doll from a Richmond Sunday School class and a score of other dolls. Illustrated story books came in such profusion that they made a little library.

Outstanding among the gifts to the ex-President from strangers was a large inscribed photograph of Pius IX. At the bottom was written in Latin: "Come unto me all ye that labor and are cast down; and I will refresh you." About a carved decoration at the top of the wooden frame hung a chaplet of thorns woven by the Pope's own fingers. The signature of Pius was attested under the seal of Cardinal Barnado. Sympathetic attention from as far away as Rome and from such an illustrious source was gratifying indeed. Knowing that the presentation of the Pope's signed photograph was an honor generally accorded only to royalty or top prelates, Davis was deeply touched.* And he had special need of cheer at this time, "when," as he said, "the invention of malignants was taxed to the utmost to fabricate defamations to degrade me in the estimation of mankind."

* The framed photograph with the crown of thorns hangs on the walls of the Confederate Memorial Hall in New Orleans.

With the New Year of 1867, Davis's future was no clearer than it had been in the fall. "Indeed," as Varina wrote a friend, "it seems to grow darker in the little distance I am permitted to look."

In February conditions in the South and for the South were worsening, as Jefferson Davis read in the papers. A letter of February 10 from his niece, Mrs. Brodhead, in Bethlehem, Pennsylvania, was the opposite of reassuring. Everything in Washington, she said, was "in dire confusion." Thaddeus Stevens was trying to get through Congress "a monstrous bill to bring more disaster on the South." On her uncle's behalf she had sought the help of many influential men in her state, including Governor Bigler and Simon Cameron, Lincoln's first Secretary of War, who had stoutly opposed his sending the "relief" ships to Sumter.

Every one I met of our friends seem very desponding, fear every kind of trouble—business of all kinds seem prostrate and then this mad Congress, no one can tell what will be the result. Gen. Grant, they say, was undoubtedly consulted about Stevens' bill. . . . I dare not hope anything from the Northern Democrats. It grieves me not to have something cheering to write, it has kept me for so long a time silent.

"The newspapers turn me sick with terror," Varina wrote Mary Stamps on Sunday, February 17, 1867.

We suppose from all we can gather that the Southern States were last night, Saturday, under martial law, restored to the condition of territories and civil law abrogated. . . . The night will be long and dark for this generation, and for how many others? Plunder will destroy the land, and life sighed out in military prisons by more suffering, for by the provisions of this new bill the military commanders over the districts have the power to condemn and execute by court martials.

In mid-March Mrs. Davis went to Baltimore to confer with more lawyers and to have some imperative dental work done. She was the guest of John S. Gittings, an old friend of her husband's. In her first letter on the eighteenth she wrote that Hettie Cary, the reigning belle of Richmond during the Confederacy, had come to see her at once.

Hettie is sadly changed, though still beautiful. She cried all the time nearly that she sat with me. She said if I only could kiss Mr. Davis's hand and look at him, it would comfort me.

"At last I am on my way to the Dentist," Varina continued, "pale with fright, but plucky to all outside appearance." She was to have five teeth extracted. Maryland's Governor Pratt had called to see her about "the" case. Dick Taylor was in New York, but hourly expected in Baltimore.

Varina was inspired to seek the assistance of John W. Garrett, President of the Baltimore and Ohio Railroad. She was told that he was the only man who might soften the adamant Secretary of War Stanton, who was under special obligation to him for facilitating troop movements during the war. And before the war Stanton had been counsel for Garrett's railroad. Garrett was reputed to be one of Stanton's very few friends. In secrecy, wearing a thick black veil, Varina was taken to Garrett's Baltimore home by an attorney friend. Would he not use his influence with Stanton to effect her husband's release? she begged; for he was "slowly dying in prison." She assured him that Secretary of the Treasury McCulloch, the only Cabinet minister who had seen her husband, would support his aid. She presented her husband's case so well that she made a profound impression on Garrett. He decided to go to Washington the following Saturday.

Garrett first called on the sympathetic McCulloch, who was somewhat astounded at "the fool's errand," and then on the Attorney General, Henry Stanbery. The latter told him Stanton was sick and would see absolutely no one. But Garrett drove straight to his house, and was ushered into the sickroom, where Stanton lay inert on a lounge.

As Garrett informed Mrs. Davis next day, he immediately and frankly stated the purpose of his surprise visit. Stanton became very angry and "exhibited much displeasure." But Garrett was one man Stanton could not back down. He told him that Davis's death in confinement at Fort Monroe would be most inconvenient to the authorities of the United States. He said that at least two Cabinet ministers favored his release, and that President Johnson was only waiting for Stanton's approval. Finally, after a heated discussion, Garret's logic and humanity won. In his weakened condition, Stanton said he would not object to the Attorney General's arranging for the prisoner's release. Garrett thanked him and drove back to the amazed Stanbery's office, where preliminary papers were drawn up. On his return to Baltimore, Garrett dispatched a man to New York to invite Horace Greeley to come to see him at once to discuss bondsmen, of whom Greeley had offered to be one.

When Garrett told Mrs. Davis all that had happened so quickly, she was overcome with tears of gratitude and relief. While Stanbery could give no specific promise as to time, he thought Davis might be released in a fortnight. Charles O'Conor went to Washington to arrange the terms of the release. Among Northerners who were willing to put up $25,000 each for bail, besides Horace Greeley, were Gerrit Smith and Cornelius Vanderbilt.

Suffering agony from her teeth, but buoyed up by Garrett's optimism, Varina wrote her husband in repressed excitement. She was in such pain, she said, with "the killing of nerves, and punches and plugging," that she could hardly think at all. Davis noted her unwonted cautious style and her odd metaphor:

At last I can see some little way into the millstone which weighs us down. Mr. Garrett seems to think that the Secretary of War is now favorably inclined to your release, and to hope much.

Davis looked eagerly for Varina's return and her full story. But she stayed on in Baltimore having more teeeth extracted. Davis received a letter from her dated Friday, April 5, in which she said that she was up for the first time since Monday. The dentist did not want her to risk exposure yet by traveling.

Though he now missed his wife very much, the broken man took great pleasure in playing with his baby daughter. He told her stories and charmed her with recitations of Scott's and Burns's poems. He would sit on the floor and help her build elaborate houses with blocks. The officers' wives were most kind and solicitous. They seemed delighted when Winnie paid them a visit. Davis remarked that his youngest child had that rare faculty of making people love her. And she was remarkably bright; already at two and a half she could repeat lines of poetry.

On April 25 Varina was still in Baltimore, but just ready to leave. Mr. Reed was on his way from Philadelphia to see her. Everyone assured her, she wrote, that her husband's release was near at hand. "I have had so many disappointments," she said somewhat confusedly, "that I am greatly stirred up, but not hopeful, where others seem so certain."

Feeling wretched physically, she pathetically demanded protestations of love.

Little Winnie must make much of her old toothless mother when she gets her, and Maggie must make believe I am indispensable to her. As to you, I must demand a great deal of petting in return for the thinking I have done about you.

Before the end of April Varina returned, still aching, but triumphant. Her persistence and courage had seemingly proved effective.
By winning the support of Garrett she had accomplished more than
her husband's coterie of able attorneys had been able to do. But
Davis could not give himself over to unrestrained joy. He had fed
on promises too long. Varina, however, prepared to pack.

Franklin Pierce now paid another visit to his friend, whom he
always called "General" Davis. He was still more convinced, he said,
that the Government would never dare bring him to trial, to risk
having its charge of treason turned into a legal vindication of secession. Pierce's visit and his unswerving devotion were extremely
heartening to the prisoner. Davis told him that when and if he was
released on bail he would go straight to Canada to be with his
older children, whom he had not seen for two years. Beyond that,
he had no plans; he would have to await the pleasure of the court.

On the first Monday in May, 1867, Charles O'Conor summoned
Burton Harrison to New York and told him he must undertake a
momentous journey. He handed him a writ of *habeas corpus* for
Jefferson Davis, which had to be signed by the Clerk of the Court
in Richmond.

After the signature was secured, Harrison went down the James
River with a Federal marshal to Fort Monroe, on Friday, May 10,
which chanced to mark the second anniversary of Davis's capture.
The prized document was delivered to General Burton, who was
officially ordered to prepare "to present the body of Jefferson
Davis" in the United States District Court on May 13. Harrison
spent Friday evening with the Davises in their quarters amid
packed luggage; he prayed that it would be the last night his Chief
would ever sleep in prison.

On Saturday, Mr. and Mrs. Davis, accompanied by General
Burton, Dr. Cooper, and Harrison, took the boat *John Sylvester* for
Richmond. General Burton, who had always been as kind as regulations permitted, now dispensed with guards altogether. Though
still the jailer, he asked for no parole, and on the river acted like a
member of a pleasant party on an outing. At the little landings on
the James clusters of people gathered to pay their respects to their
former President. At the estate called Brandon, the ladies of the
house, relatives of Burton Harrison, came aboard bearing bouquets.
They embraced Mr. Davis, wept over the ravages prison life had
made in his appearance, and shed tears of joy at his expected release.

At Richmond, among the concourse on the wharf were many

Negroes whom "Yankee emissaries" had instructed to show insolence. But the presence of soldiers kept them in order—"or perhaps
it was the dignity of the ex-President," who descended to the wharf
on Burton Harrison's arm. At the sight of Mr. Davis, the men in the
crowd silently took off their hats. Mrs. Davis was seated in the carriage of James Lyons, her husband's old friend and now one of his
attorneys. General Burton, Dr. Cooper, and Harrison entered an
open carriage with Mr. Davis. All along the streets men stood with
hats in hands, while women waved handkerchiefs from the windows.

A reporter on the Richmond *Enquirer* carefully noted Mr. Davis's
appearance after his two years in prison.

He wears a full beard and mustache, which in a measure conceals the
ravages made by sorrow and suffering upon his face, but his countenance,
although haggard and care-worn, still preserves the proud expression and
the mingled look of sweetness and dignity for which it was ever remarkable. His hair is considerably silvered, but his eye still beams with all the
fire that characterized it in the old time, and he seems every inch a king.

When his carriage reached the entrance of the Spotswood Hotel,
Davis saw that the sidewalks were banked thick with bareheaded
men with grave faces. In the hotel he was given the very rooms he
had occupied six years before when he had arrived from Montgomery as President of a new nation, which the Southerners expected
to be everlasting. In his private parlor scores of old friends called,
bringing flowers. The ordeal proved trying, and it was a great relief when at last the family was left to rest.

The next morning, Sunday, the Davises remained in their rooms
except for a secret trip to the cemetery to lay flowers on the grave
of their boy Joseph, who had been killed in a fall in 1864. After
church and during the afternoon Mr. Davis received friends and
kissed all the pretty girls. Harrison noted that "he kissed the prettiest again on their departure." He wrote to Connie in Europe: "No
stranger would suppose for an instant that the quiet gentleman who
receives his visitors with such graceful elegance & dignity is the
State prisoner . . . whose trial for treason against a mighty Government today attracts the interest of all mankind."

After the respite of Sunday, tension again gripped the city on
Monday, the day set for the trial. Few citizens felt really assured.
There was no telling what tricks the abominable Judge Underwood
had up his sleeve. Some feared that as soon as the military relin-

quished Davis, Underwood would throw him into the local jail. During the morning hours, in all parts of town, women knelt in prayer, while the men on the streets "wore the most anxious faces." The citizens' nervous excitement was kept under control, however, because they were warned that any public outburst might prove compromising for the "accused."

Varina was not going to the courtroom; she would stay in her room and pray in private. When her husband left her, she thought he looked very well in his black suit with the flecks of gray. To avoid the crowd in front of the hotel Burton Harrison slipped his Chief out the back door to a carriage waiting in the courtyard with a small military escort.

Before the legal proceedings began, privileged persons, including some ladies and the press, had been allowed into the courtroom, which was in the old Customs House. Eager crowds packed the stairways and passages. A few minutes before eleven Mr. Davis's counsel of six entered and took their seats. All were men of distinction. Charles O'Conor and Judge George Shea were the New Yorkers. Philadelphia's William B. Reed, a prominent Democrat of Pennsylvania, was the third Northerner. Virginia was represented by her best legal minds: Robert Ould, John Randolph Tucker, and James Lyons.

Just before the clock struck eleven, the double doors were opened and the public rushed in to take every available seat. While the clock was still striking, the famous Horace Greeley entered, and was greeted with warm handshakes by gentlemen on both sides behind the bar. The crowd buzzed with pleasure because the papers said definitely that Greeley had come to sign Mr. Davis's bail bond.

At last Jefferson Davis, somewhat flushed with nervous excitement, appeared, following General Burton in full uniform, and trailed by the court marshal. He was conducted to a comfortable chair, used as the prisoner's dock, by General Burton with "more of the manner of a sympathizing friend than of his keeper." Though the ex-President showed marks of extreme weakness, he seemed cheerful and bowed to several friends. As George Davis, last Attorney General of the Confederacy, wrote his son:

Mr. Davis is only the shadow of his former self, but with all his dignity and high, unquenchable manhood. As he entered the densely crowded courtroom, with his proud step and lofty look, every head reverently bowed to him and a stranger would have sworn that he was the judge and Underwood the culprit.

After a few moments, the marshal crossed the room and asked Burton Harrison to take a chair beside the prisoner. Harrison wrote that in taking his seat next to "the accused" he felt "as exalted as if he were enthroned beside a king." Shortly, to everyone's surprise, further courtesy was offered: Mr. Davis was invited to leave the prisoner's dock and sit within the bar, close to his counsel. Throughout the proceedings Harrison was beside his Chief.

Everything went smoothly, as the Attorney General had assured the defense counsel, though Underwood in his preliminary remarks managed to get in some unnecessary jabs at Mr. Davis's sensibilities. Then the Judge declared that the prisoner had now passed from the control of martial law and was "under the protection of American Republican law and was in the custody of the marshal." People held their breaths in apprehension. Davis wondered what species of law "American Republican law" could be. But O'Conor announced the readiness of the defense and said he desired immediate trial. William M. Evarts, counsel for the United States, replied that the case could not be heard at the present term. Again the crowd was breathless, until, as by prearrangement, Judge Underwood declared the case bailable. Motion for bail was then made; the prosecution consented. After a stump speech by Underwood praising the magnanimity of the United States Government, the bail was fixed at $100,000. O'Conor announced there were at least ten gentlemen in court who were willing to go surety.

The several Northern gentlemen went up to sign the bond, beginning with Horace Greeley, followed by Gerrit Smith and Augustus Shell, who signed for Cornelius Vanderbilt. Seven others signed. Then the marshal was directed to release the prisoner.

The crowd in the courtroom burst into unrestrained shouts of joy. The first to congratulate Mr. Davis was General Burton, followed by Dr. Cooper. Someone rushed to a Maine Street window of the Customs House and yelled at the top of his lungs, "The President is bailed!" A mighty roar rose from the people below. The cry of delight was taken up from street to street and re-echoed from hill to hill.

As people surged around Davis, he whispered to Burton Harrison to get him out as quickly as possible. With O'Conor on one side and Ould on the other, the ex-President came out of the Bank Square door. He was greeted not with hurrahs, but with the Rebel Yell, ear-splitting, triumphant.

Dr. Minnegerode and Burton Harrison rode in the open vehicle with Jefferson Davis. "Our carriage passed with difficulty through the crowd," the clergyman wrote. "The rejoicing Negroes, with their tender affection, climbed upon the carriage, shaking and kissing his hand, and calling out, 'God bless Marse Davis.'"

All along the way to the Spotswood Hotel, the ex-President was saluted by that Rebel Yell. But when his carriage reached the hotel entrance, a grave silence fell upon the throng. The men seemed too moved to shout. As Jefferson Davis rose to step down, one deep voice commanded, "Hats off, Virginians!" "Five thousand uncovered men," wrote Harrison, "did homage to him who had suffered for them." In a tribute of emotional silence, Mr. Davis descended and entered the hotel.

The people on the stairs and in the upper hall pressed back in respect. Mrs. Davis received her husband in their suite. After embracing his wife, Davis turned to Dr. Minnegerode and said: "In my sufferings you have comforted and strengthened me with your prayers. Should we not now kneel together and return thanks?" Mrs. Davis led the way into the adjoining room. Harrison locked the door. Around a center table the three persons who had meant most to Jefferson Davis in his tribulations dropped to their knees with him. Each silently in his own way expressed his gratitude. And then, overcome by emotion, each of them realized that the others were crying. In the words of Minnegerode, "There, in deep-felt prayer and thanksgiving, closed the story of Jefferson Davis's prison life."

When Burton Harrison at last opened the door, joyful friends rushed in and enfolded the ex-President in loving embraces.

Because the excitement was so wearing to him, Mrs. Davis and Harrison thought it best to get Mr. Davis out of Richmond as quickly as possible. Harrison got the family aboard a steamer for New York that night.

At the dock Davis bade an affectionate farewell to his jailer, General Burton, and sailed away while Richmond celebrated. The animosities of war were at least momentarily forgotten. Burton and Dr. Cooper were invited to a series of feasts. For the first time since war's end, the best houses of Richmond entertained "Yankees."

Throughout the South there was jubilant rejoicing at the announcement that "the caged eagle" was once more free. But the rejoicing was mingled with regret that Jefferson Davis had not been allowed his coveted opportunity to vindicate the cause of the Confederacy "in the courts of the country and in the hearing of the world."

Because of his long imprisonment, the scandal of his shackling, and the nobility with which he bore indignity and suffering, the popularity of Jefferson Davis in the South was marvelously revived. During the last agonizing year of the war, when the South's resources wore to shreds, he had known a sharp diminution in popular acclaim. But now he found himself hailed with all the pride and devotion that were first accorded him as President of the Confederate States of America.

CHAPTER XXXII

REFUGE IN CANADA

———⫸◉⫷———

JEFFERSON DAVIS, though outwardly calm, was in a highly nervous state when his party, piloted by Burton Harrison, arrived at the New York Hotel in New York. Sympathetic visitors poured in to see him, but other persons with scowls and mutters of hostility collected outside in the street. To get the Chief away from this new strain, Burton took "possession of him bodily" and drove him to the seclusion of Charles O'Conor's home at Fort Washington on the Hudson. "He is looking very thin and haggard," Burton wrote his mother, "and has very little muscular strength. But his spirits are good."

Even Burton did not fully realize what a terrible toll prison and the Miles regime had taken of his Chief's vital forces. And though reprieved, Davis was not free. He had no means of employment, no salary on which to support his wife and children; and now not even a home to take them to.

After a few days of the O'Conors' attentive care, however, Davis considered himself strong enough to go on to Montreal. He did not want to delay seeing his children. To avoid attention it was thought best for him to precede his family by a day. Even so, some of the railroad people must have sent word in advance, for he was hooted in the New York stations along the route.

The evening of his departure Mrs. Davis and Margaret Howell were taken to the theater by friends to see the Italian tragedian Ristori in her farewell performance. The next day Mrs. Davis followed, with her sister, the baby, Mary Ahern, and, according to a Montreal paper, "two servants of color." * In the meantime Mr.

* Frederick Maginnis and Ellen had been married at Fort Monroe just before Jefferson Davis was released.

312

Davis had a touching reunion with his children, his mother-in-law, and three of his wife's brothers.

At first the family was domiciled in a cheap boardinghouse, and Mr. Davis was described as shunning crowds, "keeping indoors or going out incognito." One reporter recognized him walking with a stick and looking "dreadfully worn and thin."

Letters of congratulations on his release, which had been sent to Richmond, finally caught up with him in Montreal. Four had special import for him: those from Franklin Pierce, James Murray Mason, John Reagan, and Robert E. Lee. The last three were addressed directly to him; the first to Mrs. Davis. Pierce had written on May 14 from Concord, New Hampshire, immediately on receiving a telegraphic announcement that his friend had been released. Pierce hoped that "General Davis for his health's sake" would not return to the South during the summer months now at hand.

My cottage at Little Boon's Head will be ready to receive all your family by the middle of August. The latter part of that month and the whole of September is usually delightful there. The place will be as quiet as could be desired—and I need not express how much pleasure I should find in trying to make everything agreeable to you.

Pierce had sent a package of books by express and some photographs of his dead wife, Jane. Davis, deeply grateful for Pierce's generous offer, feared that acceptance would subject the New Englander to harsh criticism and perhaps worse, for during the war some rabid anti-Southerners had threatened to burn his Concord home.

Mason, who, since his return from Europe, was living near Toronto, urged Davis to come to Canada.

Of all things I should desire once more to be with you. . . . But above all, I have thought it might be to you a matter of some moment to be and remain in a country freed from the tyranny and brutality now dominant at our once happy homes.

You will, I know, be harassed with letters, and therefore trespass on you no farther than to express my sincere and unqualified appreciation of all that marked your career in our late noble struggle.

General Lee had been painfully distressed over Davis's tormented and prolonged imprisonment. As long as Davis suffered in prison, Lee could not fully enjoy the shade of Washington College's trees and the privilege of educating Southern youth. Against all Davis's warnings, he had believed that the North would be appeased by the South's surrender and that Virginia would promptly take its former place in governmental affairs. Now he had the most melancholy evidence of the Radicals' vindictiveness. Neither Lee nor his sons, nor virtually any Southerner under forty known to him was permitted to vote. It had troubled him sorely that he, still a paroled prisoner of war, had been in no position to make a public move in Davis's behalf.

You can conceive better than I can express the misery which your friends have suffered from your long imprisonment and the other afflictions incident thereto. To none has this been more painful than to me, and the impossibility of affording relief has added to my distress. Your release has lifted a load from my heart which I have not words to tell, and my daily prayer to the great Ruler of the World is that he may shield you from all future harm, guard you from all evil and give you that peace which the world cannot take away.

That the rest of your days may be triumphantly happy, is the sincere and earnest wish of your most obedient faithful friend and servant.

In Montreal, Davis was still so weakened from his prison ordeal that ordinary noises of the city tormented him. According to his wife, the voices of people "sounded like trumpets in his ears." It distressed him that he was disturbed by the activities of his own boisterous, happy children. Varina would try to keep them with her, while he sat in a room with Mrs. Howell and the two talked softly of happier days.

In an effort to rouse him from an appalling lassitude and to get him away from the city sounds, Varina persuaded him to accept an urgent invitation of James Murray Mason to visit him in the village of Niagara near Toronto. Mason and Colonel Charles Helm, the former Confederate agent in Havana, came to Montreal to fetch him. In *Soldiering in Canada* Lieutenant Colonel George T. Denison tells of the ex-President's arrival on the river boat at Toronto.

I heard a couple of hours before the steamer arrived that Mr. Davis was coming on her. I went around and started a number of friends to pass the word through the city for as many as possible to come down to the wharf and give him a reception. By the time the vessel arrived a crowd of several thousand people filled the landing place. I got on a pile of coal with a number of friends to give the signal and start the crowd to cheer. As Mr. Davis appeared on the gangway with Messrs. Mason and Helm, I was so astonished at the emaciation and weakness of Mr. Davis, who looked like a dying man, that I said to a friend near me, "They have killed him." Then I called for cheers, and nothing could have been more cordial and kingly than the welcome he got.

Davis, utterly unprepared for the rousing demonstration in Toronto, could only bow his thanks. He inquired about the Canadian officer who led the cheering. So, while waiting for the afternoon boat to cross Lake Ontario to Niagara, Mason sent for Denison and invited him to go with them for dinner and to spend the night. Delightedly he accepted the invitation. Somewhere along the way, in answer to a question, Davis told Denison that he thought it was arranged for Howell Cobb to be President, but when the convention met in Montgomery, he himself in his absence had been chosen, though he had desired to command an army of defense. Denison remarked that perhaps the Southern people wanted a man who would fight it out obstinately to the very last. "Well, Colonel," Davis said with a wan smile, "if that was what they wanted, that was what they got."

With the enthusiastic reception at Toronto still ringing in his ears, Davis sniffed the lake breeze with zest. "I feel," he told his companions, "that I am once more breathing free air."

At the Niagara wharf Davis was met by his old friends General Jubal Early and Beverly Tucker, and other Confederates who had taken refuge from Federal wrath just across the border from Buffalo.

Suppressed excitement ran through the Mason household at the approaching visit of the Confederacy's leader. Mason's ten-year-old granddaughter, Eliza Ambler, later wrote her recollections of the visit to add to her husband's memoirs.[*] She had last seen Mr. Davis that memorable Sunday in St. Paul's when he received the message from General Lee to evacuate Richmond. "Now," she wrote, "I was so moved at his coming that I rushed upstairs to my room, where I hoped to see him in his approach to the house."

At last he appeared walking with my Grandfather, and looking so old, so careworn, emaciated and depressed that after one glance I turned from the window sobbing so violently that I could not control myself to go and greet him with the rest of the family. . . .

That evening several of our friends dined with us, and we had the best dinner party we could arrange in honor of our guest. My Grandfather was

[*] Eliza Ambler married L. M. Blackford, for three decades principal of the famed Episcopal High School of Alexandria, Virginia. The hitherto unused material in this section was furnished the author by their son, the Reverend Mr. Randolph F. Blackford of St. Petersburg, Florida.

not then a religious man, and we used no form of prayer or grace. At dinner, surrounded by a large and joyous crowd of gentlemen, the President clasped his hands and bent his head in reverent devotion. I was awestruck. It was the first silent grace I had ever witnessed, and his expression seemed to me the beauty of holiness.

After dinner townspeople gathered before the house and the village band serenaded the ex-President. Davis made the crowd a little speech.

Gentlemen, I thank you sincerely for the honor you have this evening shown to me. It shows that true British manhood to which misfortune is always attractive. May peace and prosperity be forever the blessing of Canada, for she has been the asylum for many of my friends, as she is now an asylum to myself. I hope that Canada may forever remain a part of the British Empire, and may God bless you all, and may the British flag never cease to wave over you.

The crowd cheered. Mr. Davis excused himself and retired. Beverly Tucker and some others said the impromptu speech should be printed in the local paper and began trying to recall it. Having noted that little Eliza Ambler had listened with peculiar intensity, Tucker asked her if she could repeat the speech. Because the eloquent words were simple enough to fix the attention of a ten-year-old girl, she was able to give it verbatim.

As Mr. Davis sat on the veranda alone the next morning, her small brother John and she approached him shyly. He called them to him, petted them, and took John on his knee, speaking affectionately of their father and telling them about his own four little ones. "He encouraged us to talk to him, and I think we felt more utterly at home with him than any older man I ever remember meeting."

John had a small gamecock named "Bayard," and he would take Mr. Davis to his grandfather's chicken yard to watch Bayard sparring with a great Shanghai rooster called "Sir John Falstaff." Mason was glad to note that the cocks, as well as the children, diverted his friend's mind. The chickens were Mason's pet hobby and care, and he got Davis to help him gather the eggs.

After four or five days Davis was so much improved that he attended an agricultural fair with Mason and the grandchildren. Eliza Ambler wrote:

We were very much pleased by the attention universally bestowed on our illustrious guest, and charmed by the affability with which he spoke to all the good country folk, questioning them and talking to them with interest, and showing a familiarity with their life which delighted them.

Though pressed to remain for a long visit, Davis, greatly refreshed in spirit, felt he must return to his family. Mason accompanied him as far as Toronto to put him on the Montreal boat. This time Davis was spontaneously cheered. He could say later that he felt the loving hospitality in Niagara among devoted Southern friends may have saved his life.

On his return to Montreal Jefferson Davis was to know real Canadian hospitality. For John A. Lovell, the wealthy and cultivated publisher, rescued him from his miserable boardinghouse. Lovell insisted that all the Davises be his guests while a suitable furnished house was being found for the family. Lovell lived in a great mansion facing the square of Christ Church Cathedral. Though his was a large family, the house held numerous empty guest rooms. Because of Lovell's charming insistence, the Davises moved with the entire family, including Mrs. Howell, already an intimate friend of the Lovells, and Margaret and the servants. At Lovell's home Jefferson Davis met many of the prominent people of Montreal. While he himself always retired early, Mrs. Davis would remain in the drawing room entertaining the Lovells' dinner guests "sometimes until past one in the morning."*

Davis had hardly got back to Montreal when Mason wrote him, inviting him for a return visit.

I brought back with me from Toronto a supply of fishing tackle, and yesterday and today, in an hour or two, caught herrings enough to supply my table for a week— Ah! what you have lost by the perverse habit of having your own way. Do write me of anything in which I can serve you.

Again Mason wrote on June 17: "Aren't you coming this way? The weather is now delightful, and the fields green and inviting."

The repeated invitations were tempting to a man who had never cared for cities. But Davis felt he had to put out feelers in Montreal for some respectable employment. It was not a little frightening to him that he yet seemingly had scant strength to face the enormous responsibility of supporting in decent style a wife, four children, a young sister-in-law, and to a large extent his wife's mother. For nearly twenty years the Howells had had little money. Davis's two

---

* The above material comes from reminiscences by Mrs. Lovell and a daughter, Jane Lovell Foster (Mrs. W. B.), furnished the author by Edgar Andrew Collard, Editor of the Montreal *Gazette*.

younger brothers-in-law, Beckett and Jeffy D., were now jobless in Montreal. William, who had fled to Canada right after Johnston's surrender, had secured only an insignificant position.

On June 12 Davis wrote to C. J. McRae, the former Confederate business agent still abroad, in answer to a letter sent him in care of Mason. Davis had hoped that an arrangement could be made which would enable him to go to England.

Deprived of means of support of my family I had it in contemplation to form a business connection at Liverpool by which a subsistence might be earned. Here there is nothing for me to do, and until the pending prosecution of me is settled, it would be impossible for me to engage in any regular pursuit in our country.

A furnished house for the Davises had at length been found at 1181 Mountain Street between St. Catherine and Dorchester; the rent was paid by anonymous Confederate donors until September. It was a narrow, three-story house, with steep front stairs leading up to the drawing-room level. The façade was marked by high, stone-arched windows, and a black iron fence surrounded the green patch of garden. Though severe and unattractive, it was not at all a bad house; and it was later to be occupied by William Henry Drummond, the Canadian poet.

As soon as the family was settled, to rouse her husband from his lassitude Mrs. Davis suggested that he begin writing *his* history of the war. So he sent for the Confederate letter-and-message books that Margaret Howell had brought in a false bottom of her trunk and deposited in the Bank of Montreal. Mrs. Davis was prepared to copy all the passages he would mark as significant and to arrange them by dates. For the first days Davis merely read desultorily. Before long he came upon the telegram he had sent General Lee from Danville on April 9, 1865, the day of Appomattox. It began: "You will realize the reluctance I feel to leave the soil of Virginia and appreciate my anxiety to win success north of the Roanoke."

With a stricken expression on his face he pushed the book away from him. Recalling the shock of surrender and all the anguish of the terrible struggle, Davis rose and began pacing the room. Then he said to his wife in a low, strained voice, "Let us put them by for a while. I cannot speak of my dead so soon." It was to be a full decade before he could bring himself to face the task again.

. . .

Though in his first months in Montreal Davis declined invitations to dinners and "to go on fishing trips in the Canadian woods," he attended a gala performance of *The Rivals* at the Theatre Royal on Côté Street on the evening of July 18. Friends insisted that the ex-President put in an appearance, for the play was given as a benefit for the Southern Relief Association, a charitable organization which raised funds to help destitute Southerners. According to the papers, the theater that night was crowded with "the elite of the city."

Because he feared he could not sit through the whole comedy, Jefferson Davis did not arrive until the first act was over. Some of the audience then saw "a tall, very thin man in a black suit enter, carrying a broad-brimmed white hat and a slender yellow cane." He quietly took his place in the dress circle, along with three ladies of his family and his son Jeff. Murmurs ran through the house, and within moments the entire crowd from "pit to private box" was on its feet cheering lustily. One of the overenthusiastic Britishers shouted, "We shall live to see the South a nation yet!" Wild calls for "Dixie" rang out, and the orchestra spiritedly struck up the Confederate tune. Finally Davis rose and gravely bowed his acknowledgments. His gesture was followed by another outburst of prolonged applause.

One who had a seat only a few feet from the ex-President wrote his impressions of the "haggard and broken man." "Not even the wild cheering of the crowd moved him to smiles, and it was not until the play drew towards a close that his face showed pleasurable emotion."

After the performance, when Jefferson Davis and his party prepared to enter their carriage, tremendous cheers rang out on the street. As he drove away an unknown man dashed up and thrust a note into his hand. When he reached his house and a light he opened the sheet with curiosity. It bore one word: "Andersonville." The pleasure of the evening was spoiled by the implied unjust accusation.*

When news of the Davis ovation reached the United States, some Northern papers expressed indignation that a man on bail, "a war criminal," should be received in Montreal as a hero. The New York *Tribune* went so far as to declare:

* The material about the benefit performance of *The Rivals* is taken from the Montreal *Gazette* of August 18, 1962. It appears on the editorial page in the widely known column "All Our Yesterdays" by the paper's distinguished editor, Edgar Andrew Collard.

The fuss made over the arch rebel on this occasion proves that the Canadians are in a very bad condition of mind. They won't recover their equanimity until they are formally annexed to us.

Davis had sought to avoid attention in Montreal and declined to talk to newspaper correspondents. But when J. G. Ryan, an agent for the Southern Hospital Association of New Orleans, seeking charitable contributions in Canada, came to Jefferson Davis for an open letter of endorsement, the Southern leader was happy to oblige, as it was a cause near to his heart. "A free, brave Christian people," he wrote of the Canadians, "may not be slow to hear and respond to the call you make."

In his plea for funds Ryan had intended to deliver an address "fully exposing the terrible wrongs that the carpetbaggers were inflicting upon the South." Davis counseled him against such a course and induced him to change the tone of his speech. "The enemies of the South," he said, "the venal politicians and ignorant fanatics would make great capital of your strong language." Later Ryan wrote: "I was so overpowered by his Christian patriotism that I curbed my own desires to hold up Radical devilism to public scorn."

But Davis was in no sense blind to the South's misery. To General Chilton he wrote on July 20, 1867, that he had learned that "his fellow Confederates were being brought under the systematic persecution of the conquerors."

The worst fears which I entertained as to the consequences of a surrender of the armies without terms have been realized. Each concession has been the means of securing further progress in the Destruction of the South. My trust in earthly powers is gone.

Two days later, however, he had a spark of hope; for he wrote his brother Joseph about a possible business connection.

I will leave in a few hours to visit a copper mine in which I have been offered an interest, and hope to make something out of it; of course not much, as I have no capital to put in, but in mining there is a profitable employment to be found.

Yet in the same missive, he confessed it tired him both mentally and physically even to write a letter.

The problem of his children's schooling was a serious concern for Davis, and running a house in Montreal was proving too expensive for his dwindling means. So the Davises determined to go in September to board at a hotel in Lennoxville, a village in the eastern part of Quebec Province, where young Jeff had already spent a happy year in school. Both sons would get excellent instruction in the grammar school connected with the estimable Bishop's College, where many Confederate boys were enrolled. Mrs. Howell went to pay a prolonged visit with an old Southern friend living in Bennington, Vermont. Agreeable employment for the colored servants, Frederick Maginnis and Ellen, was found in Montreal. Winnie's white nurse, Mary Ahern, and Margaret Howell went on to Lennoxville with the family.

Jefferson Davis now took up a new kind of life in a humble hostelry right on the main village street. It was called Clark's Hotel* and catered mostly to traveling salesmen and itinerant show folk. The food was substantial, but hardly appetizing to a semi-invalid; each day, it seemed, there was "a choice of beef or beans, puddin' or pie." But Varina wrote Mrs. Howell Cobb that they were "tolerably comfortable."

Davis found Lennoxville a pretty little place, with the Massawippi River winding between the village and the shaded grounds of Bishop's College on heights less than a mile away. Diagonally across from the hotel, a block away, the small but pleasing St. James's Episcopal Church was set in a small garden. Surrounding the town were green hills with sleek cattle, wheatfields, and appealing bucolic vistas, which Philip Henry Gosse, the famed English writer, had described so vividly in *The Canadian Naturalist,* published in 1840.

Fortunately there were several interesting English families living in Lennoxville temporarily for business reasons. A favorite couple were the Rawsons, who lived in a large red and white house on a hill about a quarter of a mile from the hotel. Cultivated and charming, they became the Davises' most intimate friends and frequently invited them for dinner. Closer by, only three blocks from the hotel, up a graduated slope stood the Cummins's many-gabled house, "Rock Grove," also painted red with white trimming.†

Because of the noise of the business street, Davis would often seek refuge in the Cummins's pleasant shaded garden or commodious drawing room. There were four Cummins children in the

* On the site of Clark's Hotel now stands the Lennoxville Post Office.
† The Cummins house has been divided into two apartments; the Rawson house has been converted into a "cocktail lounge," connected with a motel.

house, wards of Lord Mountcastle. Stephen, the only boy, has left a memoir of Davis evenings at Rock Grove.

The Davises would sit in the big drawing room where a group of young people gathered about the piano and sang old Southern songs. Sometimes the children would sing sitting in a circle on the floor, and Mr. Davis, with his eyes closed and a smile on his face, would lightly beat time with his fingers on Cissy Stotesbury's shoulder as she sat beside him.

In Lennoxville Davis began to find relaxation of mind and body. He liked the stroll across the picturesque stone bridge over the Massawippi and along the shady lanes to the College Hill. He found pleasure in playing chess with the Reverend Mr. William Richmond, one of the instructors at Bishop's. He could be amused and pleased when he visited the boys' school, and the lads would gather on the lawn and sing lustily:

> *Oh, the muskets they may rattle*
> *And the cannon they may roar,*
> *But we'll fight for you, Jeff Davis,*
> *Along the Southern shore.*

But the mail brought news to disturb his convalescence. An aggressive Christian missionary to Japan and China, named Paul Bagley, had taken an ardent interest in trying to secure Davis's release. Apparently he had President Johnson's ear and several times while Davis was at Fort Monroe he had written to induce him to apply for pardon. He had begged the President to withdraw the infamous Proclamation against him since the "witnesses" had proved to be false. Now, in a much-forwarded letter, Bagley said that the President had been visibly disturbed by his recountal of an interview with Judge Underwood, who was to try the Davis case in Richmond.

I told him that Judge Underwood had proposed to me that I had done enough for Davis and now to give him up . . . that he could get negroes enough on a jury with a few white men to convict him, that he, U., would only take his Mississippi property away from him by fine and would try to have it bid in at half a dollar per acre by his, D's, old slaves, and that I could then go down there and preach to them.

Johnson said it "used to be fashionable to try a man before they hanged him." . . . My information from Judge U. moved Johnson very much.

Underwood apparently did not know that his plantation had already been sold to Negroes.

In early October Davis received the first warning of a plot to kill him. The writer was a Thomas Worthington of Ottawa, a stranger who said he had strongly sympathized with Mr. Davis and "the gallant South" in the struggle for liberty. On sailing from Prescott to Ottawa on the St. Lawrence on September 26, Worthington had made the casual acquaintance of "a seemingly respectable Yankee from New Hampshire," who told him of "a settled determination" on the part of Davis's enemies "to take the law into their own hands." While he was no alarmist, he said that his conscience would not have been at ease if he had not told Mr. Davis of this murder threat.

Shortly afterwards Father John H. Finnegan, a Jesuit priest and teacher in Montreal, learned of a more "definite" conspiracy. When Finnegan had gone to Cape Vincent, New York, to apprehend a runaway student, he heard of a plot to assassinate the ex-President, "the deed to be done by two negro barbers." It was a complicated affair, but the priest thought the conspiracy would not be put into effect until Mr. Davis went to Richmond for his trial. William Howell in Montreal also wrote him about the purported plot. On November 6, 1867, Davis answered his brother-in-law, enclosing a copy of the letter from Father Finnegan.

That there exists a conspiracy in the States to murder me, and that many persons are engaged in it, I have been assured by letters of various dates and from various places. . . . There is a proverb that threatened men live long. I hope to be an example of it.

We are about as when I last wrote to you. I hope your information as to Varina's prompt return will prove correct, as her presence here is more than desirable.

Varina had been called to the sickbed of her mother in Bennington, Vermont, and she had already been gone almost a fortnight. The household at Lennoxville had been much upset, for just after Mrs. Davis left, Mary Ahern, the baby's nurse, had been laid low with some malady.

Dr. Robertson, the family physician in Lennoxville, now told Mr. Davis that it would be most unwise for him to face the rigors of a Canadian winter; when he went South to his trial he should stay there until spring.

CHAPTER XXXIII

"PERTINACITY IN MALICE"

———◈———

AS THE TIME drew nearer for the late November trial in Richmond, Jefferson Davis received numerous invitations: notably, from his Rector, the Reverend Dr. Minnegerode; from the proprietor of the Spotswood Hotel, who had his old apartment ready for him; and from Judge Robert Ould, one of his Virginia attorneys. Ould was insistent that Mr. Davis stay at his home, where people "could not get at him."

Before deciding on his host, Davis looked forward daily to his wife's return to Lennoxville. But at this critical juncture Varina was racked with indecision and anxiety. The outcome of the trial might change the course of their lives, and her husband would need her in Richmond; but her mother in Bennington had taken an alarming turn for the worse. When Davis's mind should have been as unclouded as possible, he was greatly troubled by a family crisis. In the end he started for New York alone. After a few days with his New York counsel, he proceeded to Richmond and stayed with Judge Ould. Word reached him there that Varina had taken her mother in a desperate condition to the home of the Lovells in Montreal.

On November 24 Davis conferred with his three Virginia lawyers: James Lyons, Beverly Tucker, and Judge Ould. That night he received a telegram that gave him a shock: Mrs. Howell was dead. Her funeral was set for November 27 at Christ Church Cathedral in Montreal. But he could not attend; his trial was to begin on the twenty-sixth. He had not believed his mother-in-law to be so dangerously ill. Only a year and half older than himself, she would not be sixty-two until January, 1868. Davis had been extremely fond of her, and he was truly grieved.

On the afternoon of the twenty-fifth General Lee, accompanied by Custis, arrived in Richmond for the trial and registered at the Exchange Hotel. His second son, William H. Fitzhugh, called Rooney, was awaiting him. Widower Rooney was to be married to Mary Tabb Bolling of Petersburg on the twenty-eighth. Lee had been in Richmond only once in the two and a half years since June of 1865; and that day's brief visit had been on college business. He was not entirely sure how some Richmonders felt towards him. But when he came out into the lobby after supper he was greeted enthusiastically and praised for his work in Lexington. According to the Richmond *Whig* of November 26, "Strangers and Northerners joined with Southerners in seeking to shake his hand." "It was the first time since the war," wrote Freeman, "that a promiscuous crowd in any Southern city had the opportunity of showing its affection for him. He may have been surprised and moved by this sponta-neous warmth of welcome."

Leaving the hotel, Lee paid a few brief visits and then went to the house of Judge Ould to meet Jefferson Davis, who had not seen Lee since the end of March, 1865. No specific record of their meet-ing exists, but doubtless it was charged with suppressed emotion, for the men had been close. Though Davis had never uttered one breath of criticism, Lee somehow felt that the President had not approved of his surrender. And now both men were under indict-ment, and Richmond, the once proud capital of the Confederacy, was a part of Military District No. 1 and garrisoned by Federal troops. Lee wrote his wife the next day: "Mr. Davis looks astonish-ingly well and is quite cheerful. He enquired particularly after you all."

The next morning, when Davis presented himself at the Federal building, ready and eager to be tried, he was informed that Chief Justice Chase would not put in an appearance. In an anteroom he met General Lee, and, according to Freeman, they had "a long and pleasant chat while they waited."

Lee was finally taken to the jury room and questioned by a mixed jury of Negroes and whites. For two hours he was made to tell of military movements about which the entire world knew. This testimony was considered "proof of armed insurrection against the authority of the United States." Finally William Evarts of New York, on behalf of the Government, proposed that the third Wednesday of March, 1868, be assigned for a new trial.

Davis, who was not even called to the stand, was keenly disappointed. His nerves had been keyed up to his defense. Now again he was reprieved but not free.

Custis Lee and his brother, William H. Fitzhugh Lee, came to press Mr. Davis to attend the latter's wedding the next night in Petersburg. It would be an easy trip, only twenty-two miles, in a special coach attached to the regular two o'clock train. The wedding festivities might relieve his mind of the strain of the last three days. Davis appreciated the attention. He liked the huge, strapping Rooney and he was devoted to Custis. He might have accepted the invitation had not his mother-in-law been buried this very day.

Finally Varina arranged matters in Canada for her absence of several months and joined her husband in Baltimore. Instead of going direct to New Orleans by train they sailed via Havana. As Judah P. Benjamin had written Mrs. Davis two years before, while the ex-President was in prison, some funds for the children's education had been deposited in a Cuban bank. The Davises had desperate need of money; among other things there were school fees to pay in Canada.

The Davises reached Havana the week before Christmas of 1867. The city was in fiesta, decked with flowered arches in honor of the new Captain General just arrived from Spain. As Davis remarked the colorful façades, rose, lemon, pale blue, he had poignant memories of the subtropical city in December, 1835, whither he had gone to recuperate from fever and grief at his first bride's tragic death. The Davises were guests of a Southern woman, Mrs. Sarah Brewer, who kept a successful hotel, at which she had liberally entertained Confederates during the war and after. In her parlors they received many Spanish gentlemen and their ladies, who came to pay their respects and to express sympathy with the Confederate cause. Davis found that he was free to draw on the moderate sum in the Cuban bank.

When he reached New Orleans, the warmth of his welcome surprised him. The lobby of the St. Charles Hotel was jammed with well-wishers, and some men strove to embrace him with unabashed tears pouring down their cheeks.

At Vicksburg Davis saw with his own eyes the destruction wrought by the Union army. But he rejoiced that his aged brother, despite his crushing reverses in fortune, was in good spirits. Joseph Davis seemed relieved that he no longer need feel responsible for the health and happiness of the plantation Negroes. Ben Montgomery and his sons now had the worry and the challenge. Jefferson Davis took a sad journey to Davis Bend and beheld the damage the enemy had made there, including the complete destruction of Hurricane. He stayed only a few hours, greeting the friendly Negroes, who had once been his "people." Again he felt like "a returning ghost," as he had when he re-entered Richmond from Fort Monroe in May, 1867.

Davis had expected to receive some interest on the sale of his property to the Montgomerys. But they had had hard luck because of river floods and both army and boll worms. So the interest was forgiven them for the first year. Instead of receiving any cash from cotton, Davis took greenbacks from his own slim funds to contribute to the care of the superannuated Negroes, who no longer belonged to him. The ironies of his return became as palpable as painful. The place which he had spent the best years of his life developing into a model plantation was now possessed by former slaves. And Negroes were living in his brother's Greek temple library, where he had studied constitutional law and read world literature. Though the bluecoats had burned all the books, they had left the building itself intact. While Davis had only the most kindly feeling for the Negroes themselves, who for the most part still addressed him as "Marse Jeff," he returned to Vicksburg darkly depressed.

Shortly he left for family visits to his two eldest sisters, Anna, Mrs. Luther Smith, at "Locust Grove," St. Francisville, Louisiana, and Lucinda Stamps at "Rosemont," Woodville, Mississippi. Then he went to Canton to see Susannah, his brother Isaac's widow and the mother of General Joseph R. Davis. As he left Canton for Jackson a score of the town's girls came into the coach to bid him a last goodbye. The conductor held up the train's departure until he had kissed them all. Varina noted that he had not lost his interest in pretty young women.

At Jackson, Governor Benjamin Humphreys, who so far had managed to keep his office despite the carpetbaggers, gave a "quiet" reception for the ex-President. Because the capital was garrisoned with Northern soldiers, Davis wanted no ostentatious welcome.

Here and there he remarked instances of drastic changes in the old way of living that hurt his heart. One of the proud Virginia Dabneys, who had moved to Mississippi before the war and prospered, was not only completely ruined, but left without a single servant to help in the home or the fields. The head of the house refused to permit his four young lady daughters to do certain menial tasks like washing clothes. He himself would boil their garments and the bed linen in an iron pot in the backyard and scrub them with homemade soap.

Varina had expected her husband's visit among devoted relatives to recruit his health before the trial set for March. But he saw too much misery, and in private he was more dispirited than he had been in Canada.

In answering an invitation of Colonel George H. Young of Waverly plantation near Columbus, Davis, on February 25, expressed some degree of his melancholy.

The desolation of our country had made my visit sad, but the heroic fortitude with which our people bear privation, injustice and persistent oppression fills my heart with pride. It cannot be that so noble a race and so fine a country can be left permanently subject and a desert. . . .

The belief that I might embarrass my friends by visiting them, has caused me to restrict my trip to the amount of travel necessary to reach the home of my nearest relatives. . . .

I start this morning for Richmond, but it is probable the trial will be again postponed. Having robbed me of everything I had, my enemies do not now allow me the poor privilege of going to work.

While Davis was on his way to Richmond he learned that the House of Representatives had voted to impeach President Andrew Johnson. A fierce political struggle in Washington was approaching a climax. The preceding August, Johnson had suspended Stanton from the office of Secretary of War. Stanton had become insufferable and Johnson would no longer take his insults or stand for his backbiting accusations. In February, against his vigorous protest, Stanton was finally dismissed from the Cabinet. The Radicals were furious, and decided they had sufficient cause to prefer impeachment charges against the President for "high crimes and misdemeanors." Johnson had, they said, been too free in granting pardons. He had disregarded the repeal of the clement section of the Confiscation Act, and had even pardoned about two hundred Union deserters. Senator Charles Sumner wrote John Bright in England: "A. J. is now a full-blown rebel . . . in spirit he is as bad as J. D."

In Richmond Davis found his doubts confirmed. The Government's counsel fought shy of trying such a dangerous case while a hate-charged fight between the President and the Radical Republicans raged. Charles Dana wrote William Evarts, the counsel for the

United States, that the Johnson administration would be disgraced by the failure of its case against Davis.

But Evarts was now to be withdrawn from prosecution of the Davis case to defend President Johnson. The best that the Government's counsel could do to save face was to claim that the former indictments against Davis were defective and to substitute a new bill against him. On March 26 he was charged with many acts of treason, among which was a conspiracy with Robert E. Lee, J. P. Benjamin, John C. Breckinridge, and seventeen other named persons. This indictment was "found on the testimony of Robert E. Lee" and seven others.

To the court's inquiries as to whether Lee had not been acting under Davis's instructions, the General answered that he "always consulted with the President when it was practicable to do so," and "they always finally reached the same conclusions." But he insisted he must bear the responsibility for his own acts.

Immediately after leaving the jury room Lee came to Davis to tell him what had occurred; he had virtually been offered a chance to escape blame by transferring to the ex-President the responsibility for his own overt deeds. Naturally, he had repelled the suggested offer.

With a sense of humor, Lee also told him that as he presented the truth as distinctly as possible, he looked up to see what effect he was producing upon the Grand Jury. Immediately before him "sat a big black Negro, whose head had fallen back on the rail he sat on; his mouth was wide open and he was fast asleep." Lee said that if he had had any vanity as an orator it would have received a rude shock.

In the end, Davis's case was again postponed until May. It was a cruelly wearing situation. When the Davises left Richmond, General Lee was deeply distressed over his friend's plight. He wrote his son Rooney on March 30:

Mr. Davis said that he did not know what he should do or what he could turn to for a support. As long as his trial is hanging over him, of course, he can do nothing. He can apply his mind to nothing, nor could he acquire the confidence of the business community in anything he might undertake, from the apprehension of his being interrupted in the midst of it.

On this same day, the trustees of Randolph-Macon College at Ashland, Virginia, decided to offer Jefferson Davis the Presidency of the institution. They sent a committee to meet him in Baltimore, where he broke his journey to Canada. Mr. Davis was very pleased with their interest and the offer. But he said regretfully: "Gentlemen, I am a prisoner of State, released on bail. I feel that I cannot risk the fortunes of any institution by becoming connected with it until the odium cast upon me is removed. If I were free I would cheerfully consider your proposition."

It was in a sadly frustrated state of mind that Davis reached Lennoxville. Immediately, on April 16, he wrote James Murray Mason and enclosed a long newspaper account of the court proceedings. He assured him that despite the outcome Charles O'Conor remained "attentive and diligent" in his behalf. He mentioned new obstacles to securing justice and asked Mason's opinion on several matters.

In Virginia they now have negro jurors, and nearly all the intelligence and respectability of the community have been excluded from the jury lists by acts bearing on their political opinions. The prospect of a fair trial is certainly bad. . . .

If A. J. is removed by the pending impeachment, it cannot be worse for me. May God grant that it be not worse for the country.

Mason replied promptly, expressing indignation at the inconclusive turn of events, but assuring Davis that Chase had a certain honor in regard to the law.

Those ignorant brutes who now govern affairs act so strangely to delude the mob at their heels, that it is impossible to know the object of their movements. In one thing they are consistent—pertinacity in malice.

The Chief Justice stands committed to hold the Court before his country. . . . With the world looking on, he cannot rule that to be law which he knows is *not* law.

Bad as it all is, I am yet encouraged in the double aspect, first that there will be no trial—or if there be, that the Chief Justice dare not pronounce it treason.

But how long was this protracted game of the Federal authorities going to bedevil Jefferson Davis? He desperately needed remunerative employment, and he still hoped to get to England to sell shares in the Canadian copper mine he had inspected the preceding summer.

The May of 1868 was a month of peculiar tension for Jefferson Davis. His friends everywhere were fearful of his fate if Johnson was impeached. Since there was no Vice-President, the President Pro-tem of the Senate, Benjamin Wade, would become the nation's Chief Executive. Wade was one of the South's most malicious foes; his son had led a Negro regiment in Tennessee. With the Radicals in complete control, Davis's very life would be in jeopardy. The cool-headed Charles O'Conor advised his client to flee to Europe if Johnson was convicted.

Varina was frantic with apprehension. The situation was highly ironical: the implacable man who bore Davis an ancient grudge and who had signed the proclamation accusing him of Lincoln's assassination now stood between him and possible death.

Davis knew through the papers that the Radicals were doing their utmost to whip up animosity to Johnson. On May 12, General Robert C. Schenck, Chairman of the Committee on Impeachment, sent identical telegrams to scores of party leaders in doubtful states.

Great danger to the peace of the country and the Republican cause if impeachment fails. Send to your Senators public opinion by resolution, letters, and delegations.

The Radical organs raged against "the four Republican apostates" who were going to vote "not guilty": Senators Fessenden, Trumbull, Grimes, and Fowler. Maine's Fessenden, a man of high principles, was abused as if he had been a Benedict Arnold. Under the strain of attacks Grimes of Iowa was stricken with paralysis.

Senator Edmund G. Ross, a quiet little man from Kansas, found himself in a most difficult position. Poor and mildly ambitious, he saw yawning before him his own political grave if he voted for Johnson. In that corrupt time, when the unprincipled Ben Butler was engineering the impeachment and offering to pay Ross well for his vote, moral scandals were fabricated against the Kansan. He was threatened with investigation on the charge of bribery. Telegrams from his state demanding a vote for conviction poured into his office. But Ross was quietly determined to do right, as he saw it, "even if the Heavens fell."

Wade, however, felt so sure that Johnson would be convicted that he submitted his list of new Cabinet members for General Grant's approval. Though Ben Butler would be Secretary of State, Grant said he had no objection to anyone on the list.

On May 26, 1868, the atmosphere in the Senate chamber was as charged as that day in January of 1861 when Jefferson Davis made his farewell address. A final vote would decide whether or not

Andrew Johnson would be thrown out of the Presidency. In Canada most of the papers predicted conviction.

The Radicals had an assured thirty-five votes for impeachment. They needed only one more for a two-thirds majority. Eighteen Senators stood determinedly for Johnson. Edmund Ross was the only doubtful man, and the Radicals thought he would hardly dare vote against them. The voting went precisely as expected, until Chief Justice Chase came to the name of Ross, who sat idly tearing foolscap into slim strips, as was often his custom. "Mr. Senator Ross," asked Chase, "how say you, is the respondent, Andrew Johnson, President of the United States, guilty or not guilty of a high crime and misdemeanor?"

The personal life of Jefferson Davis as well as the political fate of Andrew Johnson hung on Ross's answer. The people in the gallery held their breaths. Senators on the floor sat stiffly at their desks like "petrified men." The little Kansan rose slowly to his feet. Then, clear as a bell, came his answer: "Not guilty." Johnson had the bare nineteen votes necessary to save him.

Before adjournment the Chief Justice announced that he was ordering an entry in the journal that the President had been acquitted. In Lennoxville, Jefferson Davis could take a freer breath. A man named Ross* whom he had never met had made a mighty difference in his life.

Two days after Johnson's acquittal William Evarts returned to the Davis case as counsel for the United States. On May 28 Evarts and O'Conor agreed that the case would not be called on June 3 as rescheduled, or before some day in October "agreeable to the court." Davis was packing to make another tiresome journey to Richmond when a telegram from O'Conor stopped him. He was now assured of free movement at least until October. But this cat-and-mouse torture was so trying to his nerves that his steps again became unsteady.

---

* In Kansas, Ross was burned in effigy, and when his term in the Senate expired, he retired poverty-stricken from political life. Though warned never to return to his home state, he opened a little printing shop in Coffeyville. Shortly after he was established, a prominent Radical named D. R. Anthony from Leavenworth, a gigantic bully, attacked him in his shop and beat him with a stick so unmercifully that he never regained his health. Ross lived in penury until Grover Cleveland became President and appointed him Governor of the Territory of New Mexico. Just before his death Congress granted him a pension as a Union Veteran of the Civil War. In 1956 John F. Kennedy made Ross one of the heroes of his *Profiles in Courage*.

Towards the end of June Davis suffered a serious accident. One morning, as he started down the hotel stairs carrying Winnie in his arms, he missed his step at the top and plunged headlong to the bottom. He had the presence of mind as he went down to drop the little girl on a landing. In the lobby he lay unconscious until Dr. Robertson came. The physician found Davis in a state of shock; he had injured his head and broken two ribs. His first words, when he came to, were about the baby's safety. Then he asked the physician not to let his wife see him die. When his patient did not rally after several days in bed, Dr. Robertson became gravely worried. But Davis seemed wholly indifferent to his situation.

His English friends, the Rawsons, came to propose that he go abroad with them. They were sailing "home" for a vacation on the *Austria* from Quebec on July 25. The doctor prescribed a sea voyage as the best hope of preserving what meant more than life itself, "his splendid intellect." The idea of an ocean voyage pleased Mr. Davis. And he had received intimation of a worth-while position awaiting him abroad. He would go to England and take his entire family. On July 6 he dictated an inquiring, hopeful letter to Howell Cobb.

I have decided to go to Liverpool to see what may be done in establishing a commission house, especially for cotton and tobacco. An Englishman of very high character and social position who has been extensively engaged in the India trade as a commission merchant has proposed to me a partnership. . . . I write to you to inquire what may be expected in regard to shipments by your friends and neighbors.

Mrs. Davis, who had written the letter for him because the broken ribs pained him continuously, added a postscript.

I trust that at least we see our way clear to be raised above the wretched sense of idle dependence which has so galled us. . . . I beg that you will write us plainly what has been your success in trying to get promises of cotton. I am sorry to say that Mr. Davis looks wretchedly. I think much of his indisposition is induced by his despair of getting some employment.

In another week Davis was up and about and began saying his goodbyes to numerous Lennoxville friends. The night of the seventeenth Mr. and Mrs. Davis dined with the Cummins family at Rock Grove. Since he had no thank-you gifts to present for months of hospitality, Davis inscribed to Jennie Cummins his Bible, the one that had consoled him in prison and was full of marked passages.

Years later Jennie's brother, Stevie, was to present it to the Confederate Museum in Richmond, "as a precious relic of the good and great man whom I was fortunate to know in my youth."

In the two days' wait in Quebec, Davis, though still suffering from his fractured ribs, found beauty in that jewel of an old French town set on a hill. He visited the Cathedral of the Holy Trinity, the oldest Episcopal Cathedral in the hemisphere, a gift of King George III to Canada in 1804. He noted particularly the unique basketwork design of the beautiful ceiling and the slab over the remains of the Duke of Richmond, at whose Brussels house was held the ball that Byron described when the Battle of Waterloo began. Davis was interested in the story of the Duke's strange death. Richmond had been inspecting the new British settlements in Ontario when he was bitten by his host's tame fox. On the return trip overland he became oddly ill: at the sight of a river he was terrified and tried to flee. Little was known about hydrophobia in those days in the Canadian wilderness, and the nobleman's end was one of unrelieved agony.

On July 26, 1868, Jefferson Davis, together with his family and the Rawsons, boarded the *Austria* for Liverpool. But he still felt exhausted, and the roughness of the voyage pained his mending ribs. The Rawsons, old sailors, were most attentive, and ministered to the seasick children. Eleven-year-old Jeff, by far the sickest, thought his end had come. Rawson gave him ginger beer to drink, which brought him round. When all next met on deck one day after the sea had calmed, Jeff came up to Rawson's chair, doffed his cap, made him a manly bow, and said, "I have to thank you, sir, for saving my life with ginger beer." Even his father could not help laughing. It was perhaps the first time the ex-President had actually laughed in three years.

Halfway across the Atlantic, Davis began perceptibly to recover. As he got farther away from the sad plight of the South his melancholy began to dissolve. He walked the deck without his stick. When the ship reached Liverpool, resounding cheers of welcome rang out along the docks. A hundred friends were there to receive him. Davis's spirits lifted. He came down the gangplank as if he were a completely free man and still the head of a great people.

CHAPTER XXXIV

FLOATING UPROOTED

———◆———

FOREMOST AMONG THE well-wishers at Liverpool to receive the Davises on August 4, 1868, were their intimate Virginia friends, the Norman Walkers. In late 1862 Davis had appointed Walker "Resident Distributing Agent" in Bermuda, where many blockade runners were based. After the collapse of the Confederacy Walker had sailed with his family for England on May 13, 1865, to make a home there. Eventually he had opened a shipping and a cotton-buying business, which flourished richly for a decade. It was a special joy to Varina Davis to embrace on foreign soil Georgiana Walker, whom she had liked perhaps the best of the Virginia ladies. The two had not seen each other for five years now, and Mrs. Walker declared in her journal that they "talked for twelve hours almost without stopping," adding that she had heard few tongues as clever as Varina's.

More surprisingly, she wrote that on this day she had "never seen the ex-President so attractive and charming." "Before," she noted perceptively, "he had always had the weight of a nation upon his Soul"; but now he appeared "so placid and calm and gentle, like the soft waves of the sea after a mighty storm."

James Smith, a prominent business leader of Glasgow, was also at the dock to greet the ex-President. Davis had not seen Smith since 1855, when he had gone back from Mississippi to his native Scotland after the death of his wife. He had turned his acquired capital from cotton planting into a sizable fortune in Glasgow. An ardent pro-Southerner, he had given a battery to the Confederacy; and his brother Robert had been killed fighting in gray. Smith had come in person to press the Davises to stay with him in his great house near Glasgow. He offered to show the family Scotland's historical scenery, the journey to cost the President absolutely nothing.

Other cordial invitations from Britishers Davis had never met awaited him at the Adelphi Hotel, where a reception was given him that night. One of the warmest notes was from Alexander James Beresford-Hope of Sedgebury Park, Kent, urging an immediate visit. Mason had talked most affectionately of this cultivated Cambridge man, who had entered Parliament at the age of twenty-two as a Conservative and who had made several stirring speeches in behalf of the Confederacy. He was married to Lady Mildred, daughter of the Marquis of Salisbury and sister of the South's ardent champion Lord Robert Cecil, who had suffered a nervous collapse when the Confederacy's cause was lost. Davis did not feel strong enough yet to stay with even the most cordial of strangers, and the first thing he had to do was to find a school for his boys.

Because of a case in a London court involving him, Judah Benjamin had not been able to meet the boat. But he came as soon as he could and made himself charming and ready to serve.

When the Davis boys were placed in a good school at Waterloo just outside Liverpool, the rest of the family went to stay with the Norman Walkers at Llandudno, their summer place in North Wales. The ex-President did not feel quite up to the travels through Scotland yet. Above everything else he wanted quiet, and he found peace in Llandudno, which lay between the sea and the Welsh mountains. Davis, who was Welsh on his father's side, found the simple, provincial people congenial. Having a special interest in mining, he enjoyed going down into coal mines and noting the processes used. It seemed that about half of the miners were named Davis. He met numerous other Davises; and one well-to-do old lady named Davis was so taken with him that she wanted to make him her heir if he could trace the slightest relationship. He thanked her, but did not try to prove a connection.

Davis gradually grew stronger at Llandudno. Soon he received an invitation from the Earl of Shrewsbury to stay with him at Alton Towers at the time of the annual flower show. Since he shortly had a business engagement in London, Davis accepted. On September 3 he took a train to Buxton. As there was no public conveyance at Alton, he hired a "fly" and drove over the highlands to Derbyshire. He found it an excellent way to enjoy the appealing English countryside.

"The gardens and grounds are very extensive," he wrote his wife from Alton Towers, "and more beautiful than anything I could have imagined."

Everything is on a scale of great magnificence, but these people do not seem to feel their grandeur so I am quite at ease. They are very cordial and earnest in the wish that I stay and write you to join me.

After luxuriating in English county hospitality for a few days, Davis went on to London for his first business appointment, but there was no tangible result.

In October the Davises went to stay at Leamington in Warwickshire, not far from Warwick Castle and Stratford-on-Avon. It was the hunting season, and many civilities were accorded them by the gentry. Among those who entertained them as house guests were Lord and Lady Leigh at Stoneleigh Manor. According to Varina in her *Memoir*, "Mr. Davis attracted all who saw him."

Late in October Davis received sad news from America: Howell Cobb had dropped dead in a New York hotel. Not only was he grieved at the loss of his loyal friend, but he had looked to Cobb to supply the cotton and tobacco for the commission house in Britain he hoped to establish. Though Davis had discovered that the first English firm he had thought to join was not really sound, he had leads to other connections. He had also learned that certain Northerners in Britain were throwing out ominous hints that it would be unwise to form any business tie-up with Jefferson Davis, who was, they pointed out, "only a prisoner on bail."

Just before sailing from Canada in July, Varina had written Mrs. Cobb that her "husband's soul was wearing out his body," that inactivity was killing him, and that he would recuperate only if he could get something tangible to do. "It is fearful to hold your earthly hopes upon an 'if!'" she exclaimed. She was thankful that others she loved were not in their sad plight, "floating uprooted."

In November, 1868, Jefferson Davis was still "floating uprooted." He had to adjust himself to several disappointments—to develop still more of a "frustration tolerance."

Happily, however, scores of persons in London were most kindly attentive to Davis. Colonel Arthur Lyon Fremantle, who had toured the South as an observer for the British Army in 1863, and had spent an evening with the President in Richmond, was eager to guide him about historic London. Now "Sir" Arthur, he conducted Davis through the Tower of London and also took him to

the House of Commons, "where the appearance of the ex-President
of the Confederacy created great interest." He put Davis up at his
club, as Benjamin did at his.

On a damp, darkish tenth of November, Davis dined with Judah
Benjamin at the Junior Athenaeum. He went half an hour early and
wrote Varina on the club stationery about another business disappointment.

I found the head of the House from which favorable results were expected was out of town and would not return until Thursday. The prospect of a direct sale is not encouraging, but there is reason to expect some
important papers from Canada.

It is very sad to be separated from you, but as I cannot cheer you I will
not give you a reflection of this dismal London day.

Even the buoyant Benjamin could not greatly cheer Davis,
though he entertained him well and often. Benjamin had one long
final talk about Confederacy matters with his former chief, and
thereafter he was reluctant ever to touch on the subject again. He
spoke feelingly of his grief over the South's defeat, but said that his
life-long ability to dismiss any painful memory had served well.
The past was behind; the future now seemed incredibly promising
for him in his newly adopted country. Benjamin's star was rising
rapidly, he was gaining remarkable prestige in his law practice. In
the last years of the war he had sent cotton to England and had
made good investments. Though his frivolous gentile wife still refused to leave Paris, his devotion never abated, and he contented
himself with periodic crossings to France to see her and their
daughter.

The political news from America was anything but comforting
to Davis. General Grant, the new President, was reported to have
come completely under the influence of the Radical Republicans,
who advocated a harsh policy of reconstruction. In the November
Presidential election results, Davis discerned a dark factor that to
him bode ill for the future of Anglo-Saxon culture in the United
States. Though Grant had won by a large electoral majority over
the Democrats' weak candidate, Horatio Seymour of New York,
the popular majority had been surprisingly small: only 306,000
out of 5,715,000 votes cast. Six Southern states were under the
Radicals' domination, with most of the educated white men disfranchised; and three other Southern states did not participate in
the election at all. The newspapers declared that the Negro vote

exceeding 500,000 had decided the election. Whereas before 1868 the Negro vote in America had been almost nonexistent, now it swayed the decision. Davis foresaw how politicians of both parties, scrupulous and unscrupulous, might traffic for the favor of the Negro electorate in the years to come.

In December the Davises took a furnished flat at 18 Upper Gloucester Place, Dorset Square, London. It was a simple apartment, but in a good neighborhood near Regent's Park, where Mary Ahern could take Winnanne to play on clement days.

Davis had one special thing to be thankful for: his attorneys had managed to get him released from the necessity of crossing the Atlantic for his trial set for the end of November. This time Chief Justice Chase presided at the court in Richmond. On November 30, 1868, Robert Ould of the defense asked that the indictment against Jefferson Davis be quashed. On Thursday, December 3, the defense took a new tack. O'Conor affirmed that since the Fourteenth Amendment had been passed and Davis could no longer hold public office, that disqualification was punishment enough for any charge against him. He maintained that the Constitution itself afforded positive proof that disqualification of citizen rights was considered punitive.

On Saturday morning, December 5, the Chief Justice announced that the court had failed to agree upon a decision. Judge Underwood had opposed dismissing the case. But Chase instructed the reporter to record himself as saying that the indictment should be quashed and all further proceedings barred by the effect of the Fourteenth Amendment.

Jefferson Davis soon received word that he might consider himself free. Though the case was left dangling, O'Conor assured him that he would not be troubled. And by a general amnesty proclamation issued by President Johnson on Christmas Day, 1868, Davis was no longer a prisoner on bail. Varina was mightily relieved that her husband was at last free from "the clutches of the Yankees." But Davis himself always regretted that his case was not tried, for he thought it would prove to the world that the Southern States had the constitutional right to secede and the North would stand convicted of making an unjustifiable war.

Just after Christmas, responding to repeated urgings, Davis, with his wife, went to Paris, for he had the hope that some business connection might turn up there. It gave him particular joy to be with his devoted friend A. Dudley Mann, who had been the third

Confederate commissioner abroad, along with James Murray Mason and John Slidell. The widowed Mann was living comfortably at 17 Boulevard de la Madeleine, and he also had a modest retreat in the country near Chantilly. He intended to remain in Europe, he said, for he could not endure the idea of living in an America controlled by Radical Republicans. The rich Slidells also purposed to live permanently in France. Their daughter, Mathilde, now the Baroness Erlanger, had married into great wealth. On New Year's Day the Slidells gave a dinner for the Davises and invited numerous Southern friends.

The William McKendree Gwins entertained the Davises royally at Neuilly, where they resided in grand style. Davis recalled the elaborate parties the Senator from California had given in Washington in the 1850's. He was glad that Gwin still retained his fortune. Varina made note that most of their friends in Paris were living on their incomes and had no active connections with business. The only one among them who seemed to earn her own bread was the esteemed Emily Mason, sister of James Murray. She had given her patrimony to more needy relatives and was now teaching in a fashionable school. Varina could not help remarking on the fact that while their Southern friends abroad were retired and financially secure, her weary sixty-year-old husband, with four young children to educate, looked to start a brand-new career.

Having never been in Paris before, the Davises were taken on numerous excursions by their friends. Napoleon III courteously sent a member of his staff to offer an audience to the ex-President. And Empress Eugénie expressed her willingness to receive Mrs. Davis. But Davis had no admiration for the Emperor, for he felt he had been hypocritical in his dealings with the Confederate commissioners. So, because he could not meet him with sincere cordiality, he did not avail himself of the offer. However, a military review was held in his honor, at which Slidell accompanied him.

Dudley Mann, for his part, urged the Davises so ardently to settle in Paris that they looked at several houses. But already there was in the air a scent of revolt that was to end the Bonaparte dynasty. And somehow Davis could never feel quite comfortable with the French people. However, they inspected a convent school with the thought of sending thirteen-year-old Maggie there for a season to acquire a good French accent. Mann eagerly offered to act as her guardian, and the Slidells, Emily Mason, and others promised that they would endeavor to keep her happy.

When Mrs. Davis returned to London, her husband stayed on and moved in with Mann on the Boulevard de la Madeleine.

Except for a persistent cough, which he blamed on the dampness of London, Davis was now extremely comfortable. The two friends, congenial from their first meeting in Washington, never tired of talking. As Mrs. Davis testified in her *Memoir:* "They gravitated towards each other at once, and loved like David and Jonathan until extreme old age." Mann had been known as one of the best conversationalists in Virginia. He had had the advantages of travel, served the United States Foreign Office in Germany and Hungary and had been the American Minister to Switzerland in the 1850's. Now his memory was stocked with his recent years in Belgium and France and such outstanding events as his inspiriting audience with Pope Pius IX in 1863. Sitting before Mann's fire, enjoying his pipe, Davis could relax as he had not relaxed in seven long years. Although the two often dined out, Davis was more pleased when they stayed quietly at home. Toinette, Mann's Belgian cook, took overt joy in preparing favorite dishes for "The President."

Everything was serene with Davis's immediate living except for the remembrance that he had young hostages who had to be provided for, whereas Mann's only son was grown, married, and prosperous in the States. And now a forwarded letter from his brother Joseph reached him with depressing news. The crops at Hurricane and Brierfield had been a failure, and there would be no check for his share in the mortgage interest. "I am becoming more feeble," his brother wrote, "and hear and see more imperfectly." Little but sadness seemed to be expected from Mississippi.

However, another letter, which his wife forwarded to him in Paris, brought him a modicum of pleasure. It was from an Episcopal minister, The Reverend Mr. W. F. Brand, Varina's favorite pastor, who was having untold difficulties in trying to run a boys' school near Baltimore with an empty treasury.

I saw here [on Cobbs Island] a goodly company of hearty Yankeehaters. Hate is a hateful thing, of course, even if its object be a Yankee, and a preacher of Godliness ought to preach forgiveness of wrong & a spirit of charity— So I did on Sundays— But, as I was sick, I did not feel in me much strength to resist the tendencies of the sons of wrath— Ah me! . . .

Does it hurt you to hear that all the world did not approve Mr. Davis policy—or what they supposed his policy? Where thro all time will you find the man who escaped censure? Of how many in all time, who have

held exalted stations, will you find such things said as are confessed of
Mr. Davis by his opponents? With one voice are assigned to him perfect
honesty, & purity of motive, truest patriotism, & entire submission to
the guidance of a sense of right. These qualities I heard attributed to
him last week in Va. by the most decided condemner of the Prest. whom
I have seen. And on my asking who in the South would have better filled
the chair, the answer was—"I am obliged to say that there was not one
single better man for the place." So I think we may be satisfied. . . .

Because Davis's cough did not yield to treatment, a French
physician prescribed a fortnight in Italy. However, since he had no
citizenship and could not apply to the United States minister for a
passport for Italy, Davis decided on the dry mountain air of Switzerland, where travel regulations were less strict. He had the vague
idea of discovering a suitable place for his family to settle while
the children were being educated. He wrote his wife:

My opinion of Paris as a place for education has not changed for the
better, but rather for the worse. . . . The shops have been unusually
brilliant in their windows of late, as Lent approaches; and crowds of men
and women are gathered in places where prints and toys are exhibited;
and occasional observation has taught me that whereon the number of
gazers is great one may expect the presence of prints of nude women
and toys expressive of amorous passion.

When Davis returned from his Swiss sojourn to Boulevard de la
Madeleine, his cough was completely gone. After another fortnight of Mann's devoted attention and courtesies from other obliging friends, old and new, Davis left for London. In his letter of
thanks to his host he said feelingly: "The quiet days passed with
you remain to me the one happy appreciation of recent years."

But back at Upper Gloucester Place, Davis was feeling more
uprooted than before, for little Maggie was being outfitted for a
brief season at the Convent of the Assumption in Paris.

When in May the family funds in London became perilously
low, Davis thought of going to Mississippi straightway to see if he
could raise some money. But his London physician said the walls
of his heart were not yet strong enough, and Varina begged him to
wait until the South's hot weather was over and he could go in more
safety.

All through the spring and early summer invitations from the
distinguished and important poured into the Davis mailbox or were

delivered by servants in livery. But Davis accepted only a few of them, and Varina often felt that she did not have the proper clothes.

Lady Eardley offered them her London house at 4 Lancaster Street for a season. When they first dined with her, Davis was surprised to see his own portrait hanging on her wall. Her father, who had been British Consul at Mobile, was recalled because of his Southern sympathies. Now Jefferson Davis stood godfather to her baby niece.

In Essex, a county adjoining London, the Davises were several times the guests of Mrs. C. E. Barrett-Leonard at her Tudor mansion. Among titled persons who sent them invitations were the Marquess of Westminster and the Duke of Sutherland, Lord Lovell, Lord Bulwer-Lytton, the well-known author of *The Last Days of Pompeii,* and Lord Lothian, who had published in 1863 a strong pro-Southern book intended to influence the British Parliament to recognize the Confederacy.*

Lord Campbell, one of the ex-President's most eloquent admirers, called one day, accompanied by Charles Mackay, the Scottish poet and one-time editor of the London *Illustrated News.* Mackay had met Davis in Richmond, when he was briefly a correspondent for the London *Times.* He suggested an alluring month's vacation in Scotland with himself as guide.

In July Mrs. Davis received a formal note of invitation in the handwriting of a younger brother of the Duke of Northumberland.

Lord Henry Percy presents his compliments to Mrs. Jefferson Davis & begs to inform her that his brother the Duke of Northumberland has requested him to write to her & say that he will be at Lyon until Tuesday the 20th & that he & the Duchess will be very glad if Mrs. Davis & Mr. Davis would come down any day to luncheon at half past 1 or in the afternoon later as agreeable to them. If Mrs. Jefferson Davis will let Lord Henry Percy know the day they would like to go he will let his brother know.

Varina sent a note of regret saying that her husband was ill and she feared they could not come before the twentieth. Lord Percy wrote again, but more informally.

Dear Mrs. Davis,

I am sorry to hear Mr. Davis is so unwell. My brother returns to Lyon

---

* Lothian gave Davis a handsomely bound, inscribed copy of his book, which is in the possession of Jefferson Hayes-Davis of Colorado Springs.

about the 26th 27th & remains there for a spell & they will be very glad indeed if Mr. Davis is well enough to come. I shall do myself the honor of accompanying you.

> With my compliments,
> I am yours very truly
> Henry Percy

But by the time the second invitation arrived, Davis had succumbed to Charles Mackay's enticing suggestion to take a month's journey through Scotland.

CHAPTER XXXV

THE TRIP OF HIS LIFE

———◆◉◆———

ON THE LAST Saturday of July, 1869, Jefferson Davis sailed with
Charles Mackay for Edinburgh. It was to prove a memorable and
salubrious trip. Endeavoring to leave troublesome thoughts behind,
Davis enjoyed the invigoration of a water voyage along England's
east coast. The North Sea was smooth, the weather was propitious,
and Mackay proved the perfect traveling companion. From the
Tweed northward the ship was rarely out of sight of some place of
historical association, as Davis was to write Varina from the Royal
Hotel in Edinburgh. The ship passed "close to the Towers of San-
tallan and the rock where Rosenwood came down to the water."
The captain obligingly brought the vessel so close to the Bass rock
that the passengers could see the remaining portion of the old
prison and myriads of gulls sticking to the sides of the rock, "so
little acquainted with the destructive tendencies of 'civilized' man
that they remained sedentary, though the boat whistle screamed in
passing."

In his first day at Edinburgh Davis saw the Castle, Holyrood
Palace, the old Parliament, and the house of John Knox. He wrote:

The fog hangs over King Arthur's seat and we have postponed the ascent for a brighter day. We are pressed to go hence to visit a gentleman
who lives near to Melrose Abbey and to Abbotsford.

Davis reveled in a visit to the ruins of Melrose Abbey and Dry-
burg Monastery, where Sir Walter Scott, one of his favorite au-
thors, was buried. At Abbotsford, the current owner, Mr. Hope
Scott, showed him relics seen only by very special visitors. Davis
examined with keen interest the original manuscripts of several of
the novels, Scott's diary, and some portions of the autobiography.

The travelers changed plans according to mood and circumstance. They had turned aside from a direct journey to Glasgow and, as Davis wrote his wife from Selkirk, were now at "a pretty country house on the bank of the Ettrick."

The country about the Tweed, the Ettrick and the Yarrow is the best combination of the beautiful, the useful, and the grand that I have beheld. There is in the people the warmest hospitality and cheerful greetings—Many ask for you and regret your absence.

I send you a few sprigs only of interest because of the localities where they were gathered. The little daisy was plucked from the ground near the depository of the Heart of Bruce. The harebell grew near to the Tomb of Scott. Another, the smallest, from Arthur's seat. The little white flower is from the plain where Lord Marmion is described as pausing enraptured with the beauties of the Firth of Forth and the plains of Down Edin.

But, he said, he would not force her to read more of "this talk so like a guide book." They were leaving the next day to visit Mr. John Blackwood, the noted editor and publisher.

From "Strathtyrum," Blackwood's estate, Davis wrote Varina on August 2. "I am in this old Cathedral and sea-bathing town, now St. Andrews', formerly St. Rule's, and am the guest of Mr. Blackwood, the proprietor of your favorite magazine." Blackwood's daughter, who became Mrs. Gerald Porter and in 1898 published her memoirs of her father, set down her recollections of Jefferson Davis as their guest.

Perhaps one of the incidents of the Strathtyrum life most clearly impressed upon my childish recollections was the visit in 1869 of Jefferson Davis, the ex-President, the gallant leader of the Confederacy, who for two years previously had been languishing in prison awaiting his trial. . . .

The day he was to arrive we were all assembled on the doorsteps, and as the carriage swept round to the door we saw the ex-President slowly and very courteously raising his hat as he caught sight of his host and hostess, in the way peculiar to those accustomed to bow to large crowds. We felt that it was quite like entertaining royalty, and we ought to have had a band playing, and a guard of honour. He wore a dark-blue military cloak, and his appearance was in every way dignified and commanding. His tall slight figure was remarkably upright; only the pale drawn face told the tale of disappointed hopes and physical suffering. . . .

He was delighted with Scotland. The bracing climate seemed to invigorate his health, and the universal courtesy and friendliness shown to him could not have been otherwise than very gratifying. . . .

Mrs. Porter described a special instance of the spontaneous friendliness of the Scots to Mr. Davis. On Sunday, after attending the Episcopal church, Davis drove with the Blackwoods to see the ruins of the cathedral which had been built seven centuries before and were enclosed by a wall that had been a part of the ancient monastery. Davis lamented the demolitions by John Knox's misguided followers, excited to rage by one of Knox's sermons. He remarked that the church had been built of such good material that it might well have lasted another seven centuries. While the party was exploring the ruins, "a little crowd of fishermen and seafaring folk gathered quietly outside the wall to have a glimpse of Mr. Davis." The Blackwood carriage was waiting at a door in the wall, through which Davis could see the bright blue water of the bay and the group in the foreground framed as in a picture. As he advanced to the open door, the men began to press forward. One huge, bronzed fellow in blue jersey stepped up and murmured: "I'd like fine to ha'e a grip o' yer haund." The ex-President grasped the man's hand, and then raised his hat courteously to the rest of them. As the carriage drove off the crowd broke into loud cheers. "My father," wrote Mrs. Porter, "considered their enthusiasm did them credit." And Blackwood hastened to explain to Davis "the great personal compliment it was intended to convey."

In her memoir Mrs. Porter summed up her impressions of the Southern statesman.

Any one who had the privilege of knowing Mr. Davis personally could not fail to be attracted by the straightforward, manly uprightness of his character, which was apparent in everything, and withal the charm of his manner, a mixture of dignity and simplicity, that compelled a certain respect which his kindly courtesy only made more impressive. His fine figure was seen to great advantage on horseback, and he looked like a cavalry officer all over.

Though Davis enjoyed some pleasant horseback rides in the country around St. Andrews, he did not try to play golf in the town where the sport originated. But "on the ground dedicated to the 'Royal game of golf,'" he picked three harebells and enclosed them in a letter to his wife. In that mid-Victorian age when ladies wore lockets containing the hair of loved ones, it was considered a pleasing attention to send wild flowers from one's travels.

Davis relished his literary conversations with Blackwood, who was then publishing George Eliot and other current English luminaries. His firm had just brought out Queen Victoria's *Journal*. Anthony Trollope had been the most recent house guest at Strathtyrum. The ex-President found the Blackwoods as charming as they were accomplished. They seemed delighted with him, for they pressed him to return for a longer visit. Mrs. Blackwood had him write to his wife requesting one of his photographs.

The day that Davis and Mackay left for a tour to Loch Lomond John Blackwood wrote Colonel L. W. M. Lockhart:

Jefferson Davis has been with me for the last four days, and I have just seen him off by the train. He is a grand old man. I could mount and draw sword for him at a moment's notice.

While in St. Andrews Davis realized that at last his sleep was sound. He had enjoyed every hour and every mile of the trip. He had only one small concern: he had had to leave London just before his daughter Maggie, now fourteen, was to return from the convent school in Paris. From Callander he took time to write her about the circumstances of his absence. Then he plunged into a reminder of the beautiful scenery and the places connected with characters in Scott's poetry and fiction, which he had read to her when she was a little girl.

I am now at what is often called the Gate of the Highlands of Scotland. The mountain of Ben Ledi is in full view from the window of my room, you will recollect it in connection with the description in the "Lady of the Lake" of the scene when Roderick Dhu showed his men to Fitz James.

This is the scenery described in the first canto of the Poem, and it is with special pride that the course taken by the stag is pointed out to visitors.

It is wonderful to remark how thoroughly Scott's descriptions have entered into the minds of the people hereabouts as History. At Stirling Castle I saw the room in which King James stabbed Earl Douglass and the window is pointed out from which the body of the murdered Earl is said to have been thrown. Beneath that window I picked the two white flowers enclosed. . . .

The leaves of Box and the Harebell were gathered at the little garden shown as that of Queen Mary when she was a child and placed for safety on the Island of Luchmahorne in Loch Ard.

The chapel and palace are in ruin, the Island has no other occupant than a small flock of sheep, but the grand chestnuts and the humble box remain as mementoes of the unhappy Queen of Scotland.

Davis was pleased that the descriptions of the lochs made familiar by Scott's *Lady of the Lake* were "wonderfully true to nature." But, he wrote Varina, "the beauty and grandeur of the scenery could only be realized by visiting it." He picked some wild flowers for her on "Ellen's Isle," as even the boatman on Loch Katrine called it. They grew at a spot where the hut assumed to be the home of Roderick Dhu had stood. At the head of Loch Earn he and Mackay saw the grave of Rob Roy. Since boyhood an admirer of the proud and sturdy Scots, Davis delighted in this sentimental journey to the land of legendary heroes. By book-post he sent Varina a handsome copy of *The Lady of the Lake* with illustrations that would give her "a fair idea of the terrain."

"The good people of the Highlands," he wrote, "have given me much genuine hospitality and have often complained that you and the children had not come with me." Did he realize in his heart that one reason he had improved so much in health was because he did not have the encumbrance of a family? He had only his own convenience to think about, and not children's little ailments and mishaps or Varina's uxorial worries or Margaret Howell's aptitude for antagonizing people by her clever sarcasm. He was traveling with a hearty male companion, a poet of Perth, highly respected locally, to whom all doors opened wide. And wherever his identity became known, the ex-President was treated with high honor.

When Davis made a pilgrimage to the thatched birthhouse of Robert Burns, his favorite poet after Shakespeare, at Alloway just outside Ayr, a surprise awaited him. On his arrival he noticed that the two lady custodians, great-nieces of the poet, regarded him with a strange, fluttering interest, though Mackay gave no indication of his companion's identity. When they led him into an inner room where stood the curtained bedstance in which the poet had been born, to his amazement he saw, beside a portrait of Burns, a framed likeness of himself. Bemused, he turned a questioning glance from the photograph to the smiling pair. "We read in the papers," one of them said, "that Mr. Jefferson Davis was in Scotland, and we felt sure that he would be coming to pay his respects to Robert Burns some day, so we prepared a little welcome." They had put fresh summer flowers in vases ornamenting the "auld clay briggin," which the poet's father had built for his bride, Agnes Broun, in 1757.

Because of his life-long love of Burns, the sight of the River Doon carried special overtones for Davis, as did the town of Kilmarnock, where the first edition of his verse was printed. In a day of half-mist and half-August-sunshine, all Ayrshire suggested an idyll to Jefferson Davis.

At the Glasgow railway station he was met by his local host and old friend James Smith, and James Smith, Jr., and several prominent Scottish gentlemen who had been sympathetic to the Confederate cause. In the parlor of the Imperial Hotel, contiguous to the station, an informal reception was held. On this August 9, the air was quite cool, and at the Smith home, "Benvue," Dowanhill Gardens, Davis welcomed the fire that blazed cheerily in his bedroom.

Davis gave no interviews, but in its account of his arrival the Glasgow *Herald* of August 10 spoke of him as "a spare, tall man, considerably bronzed by the weather" and noted that he seemed "to be the better for his tour in this country." Davis realized that now his "prison pallor" was indeed gone.

In the next day's *Herald* the reporter followed his movements with interest, but at a respectful distance.

Modesty seems to be the characteristic of the ex-President of the Southern States. Yesterday, quite unobtrusively, he visited many of the "lions" of the city. About 11:00 o'clock, accompanied by Dr. Mackay, he visited the Cathedral. Mr. Davis afterwards paid a visit to the celebrated Parkhead Forge, where he evinced an unmistakable interest in the process for the manufacture of armour plates, a process now so much used for our ships of war.

About two o'clock, Mr. Davis entered the Exchange, where, in expectation of a visit, there was a crowded attendance. The assemblage opened a passage in the centre of the hall, up which Mr. Davis walked and at the end of the room entered his name in the Visitor's Book. Leaving the building Mr. Davis was loudly cheered.

Davis, who had a lively interest in scientific discoveries and processes, visited the "Cooking Depot" at Trongate, where the manager minutely and satisfactorily explained the system which had "gained a name all over the Kingdom for economy and efficiency." Then he inspected the shipbuilding yard of Messrs. Napier and Govan. At Dumbarton he amazed the shipbuilders with his technical understanding of their jobs.

On the eleventh Davis took a day of rest at Benvue and met for the first time Mackay's fourteen-year-old adopted daughter, half-Italian, half-English, later to become a famous best-selling novelist known as Marie Corelli. Pictures of Mr. Davis and his Scottish friends were taken on the veranda of the Smith mansion.* That evening his host gave a dinner at which thirty gentlemen were present.

It was hard for Davis to tear himself away from Smith's hospitality. But the next morning he sailed on the *Iona* for Oban. Instead of the quicker way by train, he elected to proceed from the Glasgow bridge wharf to glimpse the scenery on both sides of the Clyde and to see the newly established industries.

The Glasgow *Herald* reported that Mr. James Smith and a number of other friends accompanied Mr. Davis for some distance down the Clyde.

On leaving the Broomielaw quay, there were a large concourse of persons. Mr. Davis was followed by large cheers, which he acknowledged by raising his hat and bowing repeatedly.

A similar demonstration was accorded him at Greenock, Dunoon, Innelian, Rothesay and Tignabrusich; the crowds who were assembled at the different piers exhibiting an eager desire to have a sight of the famous President of the Southern States. While passing down the river, the view Mr. Davis obtained of the numerous vessels of the shipbuilding yards seemed to interest him considerably. The weather was delightful.

At Greenock Lord and Lady Abinger boarded the ship and sailed with Mr. Davis as far as Oban. He and Mackay were to be their guests at Inverlochy Castle in Kingussie. Lady Abinger was the niece of General John Bankhead Magruder, who had been a cadet with Davis at West Point. The Abingers proceeded straight home, but Davis and Mackay stopped for a day at Oban, toured the Island of Mull, and visited Fingal's Cave and the ruins of Iona where, as Davis wrote his wife, "in the dark ages Christianity found a nursing mother."

At Inverlochy Davis again basked in luxury and loving attention. He thought the scenery about the castle "the grandest of all the sublime spectacles I have met in Scotland." He liked the mists and changing lights and shades which characterized the Scottish mountains. The August air he found bracing and tonic, and he enjoyed salmon fishing one day and grouse shooting another.

After the exhilarating days with the Abingers, the travelers went by the Caledonia canals and lochs to reach the railway between Inverness and Edinburgh. Davis's last letter to his wife from Scotland was written from Dochfour House, Inverness, the old capital city, where Macbeth had reigned with a bloody conscience.

* One of these group photographs hangs in Davis's pavilion study at Beauvoir.

When Davis parted with Mackay in Edinburgh, for sentiment's sake they exchanged walking sticks. Today the stick that Jefferson Davis used on his Scottish tour reposes under glass at the John Harvard House, Stratford-on-Avon, which Marie Corelli bought, restored, and gave to England as a memorial to her foster-father and to the original benefactor of Harvard University.

In London again, Davis faced the problem of a business connection. He wrote Varina, who had taken the children to Yarmouth, the seaside resort:

The heat and smoke and dust of London seem all the worse as compared to the pure and cool air of the Scottish highlands.

I went to the city this morning, but found the matter still hanging and was disposed to consider it a matter for somebody else who had more years to work, but was requested to wait until evening when I should see what I should see.

Davis, who had recently passed his sixty-first birthday, realized that commercial firms were looking for vigorous young men. Though the weight of years had seemed to melt away from him in Scotland, now he suddenly felt old. Yet, when he reached Yarmouth, Varina had not seen her husband in such good health in many a year. He had liked the land of Burns and Scott so well that he wrote Mackay: "I would fain spend the balance of my days in Scotland."

By mid-September Davis was constrained to consider seriously an offer of the presidency of a life insurance company in Memphis, Tennessee. He decided to go back to America to examine the situation and temporarily leave his family abroad. Varina was immeasurably depressed. An insurance business hardly seemed fitting for an ex-Secretary of War of the United States and the ex-President of the Confederacy, and she abhorred the thought of their returning to the South, which was now under harsh military rule.

As Davis prepared to depart he received a letter from Dudley Mann in Paris, dated September 18, 1869.

I have a vast number of *last words* to say to you. . . . But I cannot refrain from the utterance of my ardent wish that you will at your earliest convenience prepare your *Book*. This is a requisition which the world of enlightened man makes upon you. And, if you will permit me, I will add that it is due to the truthful history of our times, and to a more enlarged understanding of your own honest, virtuous fame.

I wish, indeed, that there was something worthy of you to go to in America; but in my belief there is nothing, absolutely nothing. . . . May your noble soul, which has borne so much, be equal to the wrathful tormentings of the merciless North.

To make it less painful for Varina and himself, Davis insisted on saying goodbye at the London railway station rather than at the ship's pier. The next day, September 25, just before the steamer sailed from Southampton, he wrote her a note of farewell, using the portfolio of writing materials she had provided as a *bon voyage* gift.

Long after we were under way your sad face as last seen was before me. I wished as you walked off to run after you and see you in the cab, for in your failure to look back I had the evidence of the struggle you had made to suppress the manifestation of your emotion. . . .

Give my tenderest love to all our children. When I awoke this morning the sorrowful realization that I could not have their morning kiss came upon me with a force which belongs so specially to the waking hour.

After parting with her husband, Varina had been seized by a foreboding and had wept bitterly. Shortly she wrote:

I dread the return to America as a country in which we are to live and die, more for you and for our children than for myself. And I turn sick with the thoughts of what you will undergo while you see the ideal people of your life's long love change into a mere temporising people of expedients—

This death in life is the most harrowing of all sorrows. May God give you strength to bear it. I have loved the people of our country through sympathy with you, but have not partaken thoroughly of all your expectations.

When Dudley Mann learned that the best position the ex-President could yet find was with an insurance company, he lamented:

I had fondly indulged in the hope of a different pursuit for you. I wished to see you so situated that you would benefit humankind by your rare wisdom and your general knowledge. Strange, strange indeed are the ways of earth when such "a Light" as yours is concealed under a "bushel."

On September 28, 1869, when Davis was three days out on a very rough sea, Robert E. Lee was writing a revealing letter to Colonel R. S. McCullough of his Washington College faculty, who was trying to raise money in New York to improve the curriculum. Lee expressed himself frankly as to his attitude concerning secession, hoping his opinion might win those Northerners hesitating to make contributions.

Every brave people who considered their right attacked & their Constitutional liberties invaded, would have done as we did. Our conduct was not caused by any insurrectionary spirit nor can it be termed rebellion, for our construction of the Constitution under which we lived & acted was the same from its adoption, & for 80 years we had been taught & educated by the founders of the Republic & their written declarations which controlled our consciences & actions. The epithets that have been heaped upon us of "rebels" & "traitors" have no just meaning, nor are they believed in by those who understand the subject, even by the North.

Jefferson Davis could have approved wholeheartedly of everything Lee said. But something in the last paragraph of Lee's letter marked a great contrast to his own present circumstance.

I think I shall be obliged to get relief in some way & long for quiet & such retirement as my condition requires. I have continued in my present position and in public life longer than I intended, & believe that it is time for me to seek repose now so congenial to my feelings.

Davis, who at the time was being tossed about physically on tempestuous waters, was greatly in need of repose of mind. While Lee longed to retire even from a somewhat sheltered academic world, Davis was sailing to begin a new life in an unsuitable field of business in a broken South.

CHAPTER XXXVI

BUSINESS IN MEMPHIS

———◆◉◆———

AFTER AN UNCOMMONLY rough Atlantic crossing, Jefferson Davis's ship reached Baltimore on October 10, 1869. His brother Joe and his great-niece Lise were at Barnum's Hotel to greet him. The agent of the Carolina Insurance Company also met him, with full powers to negotiate for Davis's connection with the company, but he said he had lost the satchel with the papers showing the condition of the institution and its mode of transacting business. Davis "did not feel quite satisfied with the signs," as he wrote his wife, but he hoped he might regard the matter more favorably when he got to Memphis. He was also disappointed not to find a reply about a position he was seeking with the Southern Pacific Railroad. Davis would have found quite congenial an administrative position with a railway company. He had always been fascinated by railroads; he believed they would have tremendous influence in bringing progress and prosperity to the country, and one of his far-sighted acts as Secretary of War had been to have three routes to the Pacific surveyed.

Friends "by the battalion" called on him. They seemed eager to do something for him, and none of them approved of his going into the insurance business. But what was he to do? Farming was out of the question; he no longer owned Brierfield.

After four days in Baltimore, to save his octogenarian brother the fatigue of a journey by land, Davis sailed with him and Lise on the *Cuba* for New Orleans, October 15.

In New Orleans friends urged Davis to settle there and "spoke of good things in the future for him," but everything was "contingent." In general they deprecated his connection with the life insurance business. One who showed acute distress that the ex-President seemed

355

destined to hide his light under the traffic of insurance was Mary
Stamps. She felt the waste of her uncle's special talents even more
poignantly than Dudley Mann. Regardless of his necessity to support his family she urged him to wait just a little longer until a
better position offered itself.

Following some soul-searching arguments with himself, Davis
wrote Varina from Vicksburg on November 9.

If I had fewer necessities or more means I would in deference to the
sentiments of friends decline the offer of the Co. But soberly, indeed
sadly, looking at my needs and those of others near and dear to me, I am
inclined to "gather grass by every mile that's justified by honor." . . .

I have compounded with my pride for the material interest of my family, and am ready to go on to the end as may best promote their happiness.

He told his wife that she might remain abroad and give the
children the advantages of the English schools for some time to
come, or cross the ocean at a favorable season and put the boys
and Maggie at school in Baltimore, "where you will find a pleasant
residence." As a third choice Varina might come with the girls to
stay with him "for all except the summer months." His one thought
was to please his wife.

While I live, there is reason to believe the money necessary for an eco-
nomical mode of living will be at my command and subject to your order.
So choose freely.

In Vicksburg, recent Governor Benjamin Humphreys, the father
of Mary Stamps, called on Mr. Davis and related some of the
shocking conditions under carpetbag and Negro rule. An ex-Federal
General named Adelbert Ames had rushed down from the North
as one of "the scavengers seeking profit from the prostrate South"
and had assumed the position of Military Governor of Mississippi.
Ames's wife was Blanche Butler, the only daughter of "Beast" Ben
Butler, whom some Southerners ranked foremost "among the thiev-
ing Yankees."

When Humphreys had refused to vacate his office, Ames had
forcibly taken possession of the Executive Mansion in Jackson. The
legally elected Governor had called witnesses to behold his second
wife and his three beautiful young daughters descend the great
staircase at high noon and march under guard to a waiting carriage.
Out in the front garden "a crowd of grinning negroes had assembled

to see the fun" * and a file of soldiers was lined up outside the gate. Mrs. Humphreys had her box of silver put into the carriage *with her* and then drove off to Mrs. Barr's boardinghouse.

Davis was even more distressed to hear of certain prominent Southerners turning into "scalawags" for the equivalent of a handful of silver. It particularly pained him that General Longstreet had now gone over to the Republicans lock, stock, and barrel; his reward: a customs house job in New Orleans. Lee's "War Horse" had published a letter in scalawag newspapers expounding his idea that the Southerners as "a conquered people" could not escape "the terms of the conqueror." Proud Southerners hastily denounced Longstreet's attitude.

The day after Davis conversed with Humphreys, he wrote in understatement to Mary Stamps:

Your father called on me yesterday; he was well, but not pleased with the political condition of the state, of which I will only say it could hardly be worse.

To me there is something very sad in this time to which I see a proud, honorable people reduced. I have lived for the fame of our people and looked in the darkest hour to posterity to right the wrongs to which we were forced to yield; if we consent, thus becoming parties to our own degradation, I shall die hoping that our posterity spurn the example and pass over our memory to that of a more worthy era.

In Memphis Davis registered at the Peabody House. When he conferred with the Directors of the Carolina Insurance Company, he liked them well enough, and to a degree he was satisfied as to the institution's solidity. One of the men stepped down from the Presidency to a lower office, and the board elected Jefferson Davis President, with a salary of twelve thousand dollars a year and traveling expenses.

By November 23 he had entered on the duties of his new post. He purposed to try to extend operations eastward as soon as possible, so as to increase both income and security. He had the secret hope that it might become desirable to transfer the parent company to Baltimore as a larger monetary and commercial center, depend-

---

* Mrs. Humphreys' account of the expulsion in letters to friends, later reproduced in Publications of the Mississippi Historical Society, Volume III, is interesting in details. Ames was snubbed by the gentlemen of Jackson, and in the first week of his occupancy the only callers were "several delegations of colored ladies, who were met by the sentinel and ushered in."

ing, of course, on the prospects of business in the Atlantic States.

Though reasonably comfortable at the Peabody, Davis found it difficult to get the proper rest because of the hotel noises and a continual stream of callers. Some persons came to offer services; some to commiserate with him; some to try to stir up bitter memories; and, now and again, one to borrow money. A few long-time friends, however, offered him real companionship and agreeable hospitality. Benedict Semmes and his attractive family had settled in Memphis after the war. William R. Hunt had a well-chosen library from which Davis could get all the reading matter he wanted, as well as peace and quiet in Hunt's house. Colonel and Mrs. Minor Meriwether showed him continual courtesies. The day when he paid the Meriwethers his first call the Colonel brought in his handsome seven-year-old son named Lee, who had been rushed in from play, scrubbed, and dressed in his best suit to meet "the President." Lee was presented as the boy who had been born in a stranger's house at Columbus, Mississippi, on Christmas night, 1862, a fortnight after Sherman had banished the pregnant mother from Memphis.* Davis put his hand on the boy's head, looked at him intently as he ran fingers through the blond hair, then said: "He is a fine boy, Colonel. He will be a true son to the South."

But when Davis discovered that Elizabeth Meriwether was one of the leading spirits in seeking contributions to build the Davises a house worthy of them, he promptly stopped the movement and asked that the money already collected be given to destitute Confederate veterans.

Davis kept himself absorbed with his business so that he would not ruminate on the ignoble political situation. "I do try to do what is before me," he said in a letter to his wife. "I find it more pleasant to look into the future than to the past." Yet relatives and old friends would write him of their hardships and their inability to pay the ruinous taxes levied by the carpetbag authorities against their properties. He had a special worry about his niece Helen Keary, the widowed daughter of his long-dead brother, Samuel, who had lived as one of the family at the Executive Mansion in Richmond and who was now struggling to make ends meet on an Arkansas farm. Her mules had been taken from her because of tax debts, and no one could run a farm without mules.

---

* See Strode's *Jefferson Davis: Confederate President*, p. 354, for an account of the incident that had made Davis so indignant. Lee Meriwether was still enjoying life on his hundred-and-first birthday, December 25, 1963, his mind bright and nimble.

Conditions, however, were not as bad in Tennessee as they had been in 1866. For some time now white women had been able to walk on the sidewalks of Memphis, though there had been a year when they had to walk in the streets because Negroes sauntering deliberately four abreast might brush them into the gutters. Even now in his Oxford, Mississippi, home the idealistic L. Q. C. Lamar was disconsolate to stand at twilight at his cottage and remark friends walking in the middle of the road for safety's sake.

Davis learned that things were no worse than they were because on Christmas Eve, 1865, in the small town of Pulaski, Tennessee, some young men, to cheer the monotony of their penniless positions, had started a social club. First they called it "Kuklio" from the Greek word meaning "band." Then, with the Scottish word "clan" added, the name evolved into Ku Klux Klan. The band went serenading their sweethearts, and to add a dash of romance and mystery shrouded themselves in sheets and sometimes draped their horses, too, with white. On beholding the ghostly troop, superstitious freedmen who had been behaving badly underwent a change. Triflers returned to work in the fields and rogues stopped their petty stealing. After the night riders paraded the farm roads and colored districts of towns, the Negroes hesitated to be impudent to their white employers, as carpetbagger agitators had been inciting them to do. When it was discovered that the young men's masquerade, which had begun as a lark, had helped intimidate the Negroes, the movement spread to other communities. At length, in the Maxwell House at Nashville, the first national gathering had been held in secrecy in the spring of 1867, just about the time Jefferson Davis was released from prison on bail. General Nathan Bedford Forrest was its first chief, and the aim of the Ku Klux was set down as "the protection of women and property and civilization itself."

For a long time it was not known who commanded the Klans in other states, but gradually the identity of the leaders became rumored. They turned out to be superior men of moral force: General James H. Clanton in Alabama, a distinguished lawyer who had opposed secession; in Mississippi, General James Z. George, one-time Senator and jurist; in Georgia, General John B. Gordon, war hero and statesman; in Arkansas, General Albert Pike, soldier, scholar, and poet.

Even in Tennessee, which was better off than most Southern states, Davis found certain situations had been extraordinary, indeed. At an afternoon party at Colonel Meriwether's, largely attended by ex-Confederates, the hostess pointed out the ironic fact that the only man in the gathering who was permitted to vote was the black servant passing the lemonade. She said that a North Carolina friend had written her of a similar situation in Governor Vance's state. At a banquet attended by "three ex-Governors, two ex-members of Congress, besides a number of lawyers, doctors and prominent business men," the only persons in the banquet hall who could either vote or hold public office were the colored waiters.

Davis learned that though the Klan had proved effective in checking numerous domestic outrages, it had virtually no control over voting abuses in any Southern state. Strange things had happened earlier in 1869. Judge Louis Dent, President Grant's brother-in-law, who had come to Mississippi after making Washington his residence, was persuaded by some of the state's Democrats, together with conservative Republicans, to accept the nomination for Governor on the National Republican ticket. Dent had expected his wife's brother to support his candidacy. But to his surprise the President repudiated his cause in an historic letter in July, 1869; he had little respect for the moderate kind of Republican party Dent advocated. Instead, Grant threw his support to the "scalawag" J. L. Alcorn, a native planter and a one-time leader of the state's Whig party, who detested Jefferson Davis and all other Democrats. Alcorn, with several Negroes on his ticket, won almost the entire black vote. In the Mississippi Legislature now sat forty former slaves, many of whom could not sign their names. By mid-August of 1869, as Claude Bowers was to write decades later: "Grant's feet had already been set in the path he was to follow for eight years as the militant champion of Republican Radicalism at its worst."

Davis had been established in his Memphis office hardly three months when, on February 25, 1870, a Negro named Hiram R. Revels took the seat in the United States Senate which Davis had vacated after Mississippi seceded in January, 1861. Revels was a man of some education, but he was not a Mississippian. He had moved from St. Louis into the state along with the first white carpetbaggers. According to the current newspapers, in Washington a great to-do was made of the incident of the colored man's seating. Senator Charles Sumner of Massachusetts gave a "mixed" dinner party in his honor, and later in the Senate chamber he spoke of "an historic event marking the triumph of a great cause." Some pointed out the event also marked the climax of Sumner's revenge on the South for the public caning he had once received at the hands of a young South Carolinian for insults to his Senator uncle. In any case, when the Negro Revels assumed Jefferson Davis's seat and desk in the Senate, in the view of Bowers, "the dramatic event illustrated the full flowering of the policy imposed upon the South."

Jefferson Davis, ever a strict constitutionalist and a believer in Jefferson's ideology of State Rights, abided in silence at the situation in Mississippi. Nor did he speak of worse conditions in Arkansas, just across the river from Memphis. A former Union soldier named Powell Clayton had stayed on in that state after the surrender to amass a fortune. Daring, dominating, shrewd, and unscrupulous, he got the Negroes and incoming carpetbaggers to back him for Governor, and then despotically began plundering everything he could lay hands on. Soon his supporters filled all the important offices. With Washington's approval he armed Negroes to enforce his extortion policies. He created his own punitive militia to carry out his will. And according to T. S. Staples in *Reconstruction in Arkansas* his militia cost the taxpayers over $300,000. Clayton passed out lists of men opposing his will with the reputed remark that many of them might well be executed. The Federal Government was said to ignore his depredations; for was he not helping to insure Grant's re-election? The Republican Congressional Executive Committee assured him that Federal troops would be at his service if he proclaimed martial law, and the editor of *The Daily Republican,* Clayton's official organ, frankly stated: "We'll make Arkansas Republican or a waste-howling wilderness."

Davis heard other blood-chilling stories from Arkansas that could hardly be credited. And yet Claude Bowers, after scrupulous researches, was to write six decades later that with the proclamation of martial law under Clayton, "soon two thousand undisciplined Negroes were preying on the people of ten counties, stealing, arresting, imprisoning, executing, looting houses, and occasionally violating women."

Disfranchised like most of his friends, Davis could only stand aghast on contemplating what American civilization had come to. Not only in Arkansas, but in many other parts of the South, men, women, and children were living in a nightmare. Davis reflected that during the war, while most of the able-bodied white men were absent from their homes fighting the invaders, the Negroes had behaved commendably. Though many Northerners had eagerly expected a servile insurrection, cases of outrage committed by any of the four million Southern blacks were rare indeed. But now, with hate, rudeness, and vengeance instilled in them by agents of the Northern Loyal League, who advocated social equality for the South, the bemused Negroes had undergone a drastic change. High-up carpetbaggers would order state bond issues, pocket most of the proceeds, and leave the South saddled with staggering debts for years to come.

Jefferson Davis looked upon these Reconstruction "measures" not only in dismay but as something inconceivable in the United States, and yet such lawless acts were continually occurring. His private judgment on them in 1870 was no more severe than that of historians decades later. Professor W. M. West of the University of Minnesota was to write in 1922:

The atrocious Reconstruction Acts had been followed by anarchy and misgovernment in the South. . . . Thousands of Northern adventurers, drawn by the scent of plunder, had thronged thither to exploit the ignorant negro vote and to organize it as the Republican party.

Woodrow Wilson was to sum up Reconstruction neatly as "A carnival of public crime under the forms of law."

From his wife's letters Davis could sense between the lines her reluctance to join him just yet, even though she wrote, "I shall do precisely as you wish," and declared that she was prepared to face life in a new town "where so much would be expected" of her. But now she was having pain with her eyes and annoyances "to be expected by women in the forties."

I try very hard to overcome nervous excitability, but last winter racked me sorely, and I have been so tried for the last seven years that I think now a heavy sorrow would drive me mad—ten years hence I will be more able to resist nervousness than I am now—but at middle age a woman loses much of her power for a few years—this may account for much of the nervous depression under which I labor.

Davis was sympathetically understanding and, since he was getting adjusted to the insurance business and traveling on business in other states, he did not insist that his wife join him. Later, Varina enclosed a letter from Mrs. Howell Cobb in Georgia urging her not to return to the States *yet*.

As long as you can bear the separation—remain in England. You know not what may be in store for you and yr children in the present state of political affairs. . . . Looking only to yr safety and peace, I would stay away as long as possible. There will be no peace to the country during Radical rule, and there is much cause of apprehension that things will grow worse.

In March came the news that Margaret Howell was to be married in England. Varina wanted to know just how much he could afford to spend on the trousseau. Margaret and she would go to Paris to get the clothes, and she would try to "keep within five hundred dollars." Varina made no pretense of being pleased with the match. The husband-to-be, Carl de Stöess, a native of Alsace-Lorraine, was in the importing business in Liverpool. He was a widower twenty years Margaret's senior, with a seventeen-year-old son. But his "morals are irreproachable," Varina wrote, "and his manners good." He had "an agreeable social position" and owned "a pleasant, small house." But Davis realized his wife's disappointment that her sister was not making a more advantageous marriage.

A letter from Margaret followed, asking his consent.

I am sure, my dearest brother, you will believe that your eldest child desires to show you all the love and affection that a life of love and kindness to her would imagine her to show.

The wedding was set for April 28, and both Margaret and Varina rather foolishly expected the ex-President to cross the ocean to give the bride away. Davis was fond of Margaret, whom he had supported and educated since she was a little girl, but this request was almost too much.

Because of the Jefferson Davis name as President on the Carolina Insurance Company stationery, its business increased, and so did demands on Davis's time. Old friends wanted jobs and favors. Braxton Bragg, who did not have an attractive personality, but was able, had the agency of the company in New Orleans. Wade Hampton, who was most personable, was made a Vice-President to head a branch office in Baltimore. "Constitution" Browne, the Britisher, who had been one of President Davis's aides, was given a job selling insurance and shortly made Secretary of the firm. Clement C. Clay, Jr., did not want employment, but sought to borrow money from the company.

Davis now traveled about the South stimulating new business for the company. His health was definitely better. He had gained weight, as he wrote on April 3, 1870, and he expected to leave Memphis on business before "the sickly season" began.

Davis's friends in Memphis often congratulated him on his good physical condition. As Mrs. Meriwether observed him in 1870:

He had endured that which might well bow any man's shoulders, but not even a dungeon and chains had been able to subdue that great man's lofty spirit. He still held himself as erect as an Indian, his head set well and firmly on his shoulders, his eyes still held their native fire and force. He was tall and slender, his step was firm and steady. Mr. Davis' features were finely chiseled; his face, his glance, his general aspect denoted benevolence and impulses that were pure and good.

If anyone in his presence denounced his jailer, General Miles, Mr. Davis invariably remained silent and at the first opportunity changed the subject. He never complained of his treatment or of his fallen fortunes.

In several letters during the spring Varina complained of eye trouble—some sort of inflammation. Since Davis himself had long ago lost the sight of one eye and had almost lost the sight of the other in prison, he was peculiarly apprehensive about his wife's eyes. Yet, as he wrote her encouragingly on May 31, "no atmosphere could be more favorable than London for weak eyes."

Varina would write despairingly about her eyesight in one letter, and in another she would proudly declare that she had "saved a fortune" by sitting at her sewing machine before seven in the morning and, except for meals, staying there "until evening dark." Yet in this very letter, she closed with the announcement: "I am blind for sure!"

Davis continually begged her to spare her eyes, and reminded her that since the children could scarcely be old enough to take care of themselves when he "should go hence forever," she would be more necessary to them than she was in their infancy.

Then he touched upon her confession that she held too much bitterness in her heart to take Holy Communion.

I am sorry you do not commune in the Church. It is a help to the Peace which passeth understanding, and the heart when most bruised is most ready to receive the messenger.

In thanking his little girl for her first "letter," he enjoined Winnanne to try to make her mother happy. "Keep her amused at night so that she may have no need for a light which will hurt her eyes."

Varina's letters indicated such fluctuating moods that her husband could not divine her true state of health or mind. In a letter of June 22 that bespoke her despondency—"If I see again, I will make you another comb case, one that tears will not drop upon and spoil the

leather and cause me to work new ones before one is done"—
Varina told of gay parties during the London "season."

I shall dine at Mrs. Dallas' *again* on Thursday—and dined a few days
ago with Lord Lytton and many other people. Lytton is handsome—and
has eyes like yours were when your miniature was painted—and more
than agreeable, though much spoiled. He is very anxious for me to go to
Knebworth, but I do not think I shall.

The children, she said, required her more than Robert Browning
or Owen Meredith or any of the great people that she would meet
there. She closed her letter rather oddly: "With the most anxious
and affectionate hopes that could agitate the heart of one so alone
as I am in the world, Believe me yours, Varina."

Davis was gratified that London was not neglecting his wife. But
"alone" in London society, and with her four children about her!
Though Davis had a keen understanding of his mercurial, complicated wife—"you know my very heartstrings," she once wrote
him—sometimes her moods baffled him. He could never be sure how
serious were the ailments she claimed for herself or for the children.
He was deeply appreciative of her brilliant mind and her charm,
and remarkably patient with her tempers and vagaries. She fascinated him and held for him a strong sexual attraction, but at
times she fatigued him greatly. Now he wondered how Varina, who
was being entertained by Bulwer-Lytton, Lord Campbell, and a
string of sophisticated notables in London, would content herself in
Memphis, Tennessee.

CHAPTER XXXVII

UNDER ONE ROOF AGAIN

———◆———

THE STOCKHOLDERS OF the Carolina held their annual meeting on June 28, 1870. Davis was re-elected President and shortly left for Virginia and Maryland on business. In Richmond the heat was as oppressive as in Memphis. So before going to Baltimore he sought cooler air at The Greenbrier, White Sulphur Springs, where he found many old friends, among them the devoted James Murray Mason and scintillating Mrs. Chesnut, whose frank admiration always delighted him. The guests numbered about five hundred persons, all more or less of the same background and tastes.

Mason pressed Davis for a visit to "Clarens" in Fairfax County, a commodious house he had purchased when he left Canada. It was only eight miles from Washington. "I never go *there*, of course," he said, "nor have I seen any man from north of Mason and Dixon since I returned to Virginia—except once the rascally Yankee tax-gatherers." Mason was disgusted with the "truckling of certain persons the South was wont to rely on." "But you remember," he said, "that even among the Apostles, tho' but twelve, one renounced the Master and another backslided." Hopefully, he added, "The Yankee Government must fall to pieces of its own rottenness."

In his fashion, Davis, savoring "the delicious air, shade and greensward," enjoyed his few days at the resort. When confronted by a friend with Joe Johnston's accusation that he had lost a mighty opportunity and perhaps victory by not sending all the South's cotton to Europe at the beginning of the conflict, Davis replied with sharp clarity.

General Johnston is not the only ignoramus who does not know that the crop of 1860-61 had mostly gone forward before the birth of the Confederacy. It all belonged to individuals. The Confederate Government had not the money to buy it, nor the ships to transport it. The next crop was imprisoned by the blockade, and much of it in the interior, closed by lack of transportation facilities by land or river.

Then he dismissed the argument with a wry smile. "Every vain-glorious empiric," he remarked, "can announce something as proposed or possible, however empty it may be, and find people who will accept it."

Davis was gratified to hear repeated the story of General Lee's cordial meeting with the Northern General Rosecrans at The Green-brier in late August of 1868. Habitués reported that Lee had said to Rosecrans, who detested the Radical Republicans, that if he had dreamed what the Federal Administration would do to the South with their Reconstruction, he would not have surrendered at Appomattox but cut his way through to the hills.

After Davis's departure one of the fellow guests wrote, "I never heard Mr. Davis laugh, but I never heard him utter a complaint, or even allude to the cruel treatment he had received." He was averse to speaking of politics in the South, but when pushed, he did "express contempt and disgust for three or four prominent Southerners, who, when he was a prisoner, turned their poisoned pens against him."

Refreshed in mind and body, with business attended to, Davis sailed on the *Russia* for Liverpool on August 10, 1870, to fetch his family home. He always derived some benefit from an ocean voyage, even in rough seas, and this passage was pleasantly smooth. He read a great deal and occasionally talked with new acquaintances. Everyone on board was discussing the Franco-Prussian War then in progress. Davis found that the men of "Yankee proclivities" were for the Prussians, and those of the South for the French.

As the long days at sea passed, his thoughts turned reflectively to Mary Stamps, whom he had come to admire more and more in her gallant perseverance to support herself and her two fatherless girls. He had seen her on business trips to New Orleans and she had once been in Memphis to get his advice. "As distance is magnified between us my thoughts draw closer to you," he wrote Mary.

It is well for us in these days of sorrow and disappointment that we have too many demands on our time for much of retrospect. On shipboard one has an enforced leisure and my memory has summoned the past. It is however the happy quality of my memory to preserve the pleasant more readily than the painful; and among the stores it has brought none were sweeter than those to which you have so largely contributed. Conferring happiness amid the horrors of a prison you excelled nature's busy little chemist which extracts honey from the bitter leaf. My dear little Molly, I hope we may see happier days and that it may be my good fortune to return to you a fractional part of the joys you have bestowed upon me. . . .

Think of me always as your own property and whenever I can serve you be assured of the pleasure it will give me to show how devotedly and lovingly I am your uncle.

That something which might be called "spiritual compatibility" between these two idealistic beings had even increased since the prison visit of 1866.

In England Davis found his four children flourishing. The little girl talked like a child twice her age. Independent-minded, but winning, she knew how to please when she wanted to. Maggie was quite lovely at fifteen, almost a young lady. The boys had grown enormously. Their mother said she could find no ready-made English suits to fit them and had to have their newest jackets made by a tailor. Thirteen-year-old Jeff took a man's size in the chest, and Billie at nine required a thirteen-year-old's clothes.

With little heart for the task, Varina began to make preparations for the voyage to America. She dreaded to return to the deplorable condition of the South, and she had a disturbing foreboding about Memphis. Davis attended to small matters of business and endeavored to make contacts for the future. He saw numerous British friends, including Lord Campbell and the Beresford-Hopes, but he could not accept all the invitations that came. Benjamin, who was on vacation in France with his wife and daughter, wrote him on September 6:

I shall be in London early next month when I hope to have the pleasure of once more pressing your hand and having a talk over old times, as well as of the future prospect of our loved common land.

Benjamin was becoming still more renowned as a barrister, and Davis knew that he was cut off forever from any real association with the States. He doubted if he would see his one-time Secretary of State, because he was trying to get passage for his family at the end of September. But Varina complained of her health and did not think she could be prepared to leave even on October first. So the voyage was postponed until the sixth.

In London Davis received the news that his aged brother Joseph had died on September 18. He felt as if he had lost a father. To his great-niece Lise he wrote:

You who, better than any other, can sympathize with me in this sad bereavement, will appreciate how bitter are the waters in which I am overwhelmed.

Finally, on October 6, Davis sailed for Baltimore—alone. He enjoined his wife to get George Campbell to assist her in securing rooms "on a vessel of some days' later departure."

While Davis was at sea, on the twelfth, Robert E. Lee died. When the ship docked he learned of the saddening event. A reception committee waited upon the ex-President to ask him to deliver the address at a memorial service for Lee scheduled in Richmond on November 3. The Lee family begged his acceptance, which he heartily gave.

In a moving ceremony of Confederate Soldiers and Sailors held at the First Presbyterian Church for the purpose of organizing the Lee Monument Association, Jefferson Davis made his first public address since the war. According to the Richmond *Dispatch* of November 4:

As Mr. Davis rose to walk to the stand every person in the house rose to his feet, and there followed such a storm of applause as seemed to shake the very foundations of the building, while cheer upon cheer was echoed from the throats of veterans saluting one whom they delighted to honor.

The *Dispatch* quoted some 1,600 words of the speech. Among the paragraphs reproduced were those which revealed Davis's close friendship with Lee.

Robert E. Lee was my associate and friend in the Military Academy, and we were friends until the hour of his death. We were associates and friends when he was a soldier and I a congressman; and associates and friends when he led the armies of the Confederacy and I presided in its Cabinet. We passed through many sad scenes together, but I cannot remember that there was aught but perfect harmony between us. If ever there was a difference of opinion it was dissipated by discussion, and harmony was the result. I repeat, *we never disagreed*.

In praising Lee, Davis declared—undoubtedly with Joseph Johnston in mind—"I never in my life saw in him the slightest tendency to self-seeking. . . . He has been charged with 'want of dash.' . . . I never knew Lee to falter to attempt anything ever man could dare."

"Of the man, how shall I speak?" he asked, and paused. Then he estimated Lee in a one-line epitaph: "His moral qualities rose to the height of genius."

Davis touched briefly on the final overwhelming days of the war.

When in the last campaign he was beleaguered at Petersburg, and painfully aware of the straits to which we were reduced, he said "With my army in the mountains of Virginia I could carry on this war for twenty years longer." . . . In surrender he anticipated conditions that have not been fulfilled.

In closing, Davis's voice was low and soft, but carried distinctly to those standing in the back of the church.

Here he now sleeps in the land he loved so well, and that land is not Virginia only, for they do injustice to Lee who believed he fought for Virginia alone. He was ready to go anywhere on any service for the good of his country. . . . Here the living are assembled to honor his memory and there the skeleton sentinels watch over his grave.

This day we write our words of sorrow with those of the good and great throughout Christendom, for his fame is gone over the water.

According to the *Dispatch* Mr. Davis spoke "with his accustomed thrilling, moving eloquence." The drive for the fund to erect a monument to Lee was started auspiciously.

When Mrs. Davis finally arrived in Baltimore she established the two boys in Mr. Brand's church school, as her husband had prearranged. Maggie had been left in England under the guardianship of her Aunt Margaret. Davis expected his wife, with Winnie and Mary Ahern, the white nurse, to join him in Richmond and accompany him to Memphis. He had written that he was anxiously looking for her arrival and that it was "very desirable" for him to go on to Memphis as soon as possible because of business obligations. But Varina was detained in Baltimore by this and that. So he returned to Memphis alone.

Arriving at his hotel on a bleak November 8, the place seemed peculiarly drab and cheerless. In his piled-up stacks of mail he sought for some cheering word from Mary Stamps. Disappointed to find none, he wrote to her that night.

As you are constantly in my thoughts, it is not tolerable for me to suppose you have not been thinking of me—though you have said nothing.

In your last letter long, long ago, you spoke of changing your residence.

Where are you, and how are you situated? Beloved, all which concerns you interests me and you should not leave me in darkness.

Do not, my own sweet Mollie, take up the burden of life so gravely as not to write sometimes to one who loves you so well that he is not willing to see you cover the light within you with that awful bushel: the routine of business.

In his brother Joseph's will Jefferson Davis had been named the first of four executors. But he was not mentioned as the owner of Brierfield plantation, which Joseph had given him in 1835, though it had never been actually deeded to him. However, $20,000 was bequeathed to each of the four Davis children. Of course, this was only a paper bequest, for Joseph Davis had no cash, and only when and if the Montgomery Negroes paid their $300,000 indebtedness—due in 1876—on the combined areas of Davis property, could the money be realized.

Davis's position as one of the executors was complicated and embarrassing. He felt it his duty to his family to claim Brierfield as his possession; yet on accepting the obligations as a trustee of the will, he was presumably estopped from laying claim to part of the estate. Joseph had seemingly not declared his brother's ownership of Brierfield in order to protect it from the probability of Federal confiscation. But Lise Mitchell Hamer maintained that her grandfather did not want the property to fall to the possession of Varina, whom he thoroughly disliked.

Davis was in a dilemma. Either he would lose his property or face the publicity of a lawsuit which would provide his enemies with a fresh opportunity to misrepresent him. And the notoriety of a suit might be deleterious to the insurance company. Davis had been through so much strife that he could not bear to be involved in a new controversy. He attempted to convince Lise and Joe Mitchell, the principal heirs, of the justice of his claim, but failed to do so. Since he now seemed financially secure with a good salary, and because he loved Lise, he was inclined to give her his cloak as well as his coat.

Plantation affairs, however, had not gone well. The Montgomerys had been put to considerable expense for levees to control the Mississippi at flood times. Their white neighbors, who were resentful to Joseph for selling the estates to Negroes, did not cooperate in the water control. Though the Montgomerys were able agronomists, the black laborers did not seem to like Negroes for employers. The ambitious Montgomerys worked the hands harder than the Davises had ever done. Itinerant Negro preachers appeared and stirred up discontent. Tenants moved away and then moved back again, restless and disappointed, finding, like other former slaves, that freedom did not mean being rewarded for doing nothing. Davis could see little hope in a situation which was not of his making.

When Mrs. Davis finally arrived in Memphis it took resolution for her to adjust to hotel living in a small provincial city. But she always put her best foot forward in company, and Memphians, according to Mrs. Meriwether, found her "jolly and full of humor." She was much entertained. She assumed an interest in charities and in the St. Lazarus Church; she acquired a new prayer book, and again "communed." In the meantime her husband and she sought a dwelling house. Though hotel life "did not agree" with either the little girl or herself, Varina postponed a decision in the hope that her husband might be yet offered a more suitable position in some larger city.

Since Davis's return to the States in the fall of 1869, friends had been sending him newspaper cuttings of "slander and mendacities" and urging him to answer. Edward A. Pollard had published a so-called *Life of Jefferson Davis*, with the catch subtitle: *A Secret History of the Southern Confederacy Gathered Behind the Scenes in Richmond.* The book was an attack on the Confederate President and his Administration, craftily mixed with half-truths, and occasionally larded with sincere praise. In his preface Pollard, who had been an assistant editor of the *Examiner*, claimed to be "peculiarly fitted to be the biographer of Jefferson Davis" and said he "was near him during the whole war." But Davis had not to his knowledge ever met his detractor.

In the North Pollard's book was gleefully seized upon by certain historians, as well as by a press hostile to Davis. Between Northern journalists and Davis's Southern enemies there seemed to be some sort of collusion to deface any favorable image of the Confederate President. Davis was indignant at Pollard's malicious twisting of facts and incensed by his insulting remarks about Mrs. Davis. But he tried to ignore the defamations, and he kept silent.

Although his insurance business consumed his energies, friends and strangers continually urged him to write "his book." From Lexington, on December 11, 1870, William Preston Johnston, recalling his accolade at the Lee Memorial service, was pressing:

When I see how steady is the trust and affection reposed in you by the great mass of the Southern people, I feel that you owe it to yourself not to die without vindicating the truth of history. It has rarely been the lot of a man who has acted great deeds to be able by education and circumstances to tell the story of them.

I do not believe any man ever lived who could dare to tell in the light more fully what was done in the dark, than you can.

It seems to be a friendly duty to warn you not to forget your design.

Davis had no intention of forgetting his design, but a livelihood for his family was the immediate prime necessity.

In early March of 1871 Davis was delighted to receive an affectionate letter from General Fitzhugh Lee announcing his approaching marriage at Alexandria on April 19. "There was a time," he began characteristically, "when I cared for but little outside of a good horse and cavalry sabre." He now craved Davis's presence at his wedding: "it would be inestimably dear to me," he wrote.

Therefore please make one of your Cavalry men happy by letting him say to his great-*grand*children that you were present at their great-grandfather's wedding.

The virile Fitz obviously had lost none of his charm, and he added the inducement that the ex-President "would be able to delight with a visit" his good friends James Mason and General Samuel Cooper, both of whom lived near Alexandria and would be at the celebration.

Mrs. Davis's continued ill-health and discontent troubled her husband. General practitioners could find nothing wrong with her except "nerves," so she was put under the care of a homeopathic physician. At the first hot blast in May, 1871, Davis sent his wife and baby to the supposed cooler clime of Maryland, where she had numerous friends and where the three eldest children were in school. (Maggie had returned from England and was living at Mrs. Cary's select boarding school in Baltimore.) But when Varina wrote him a birthday letter on June 3, she was anything but cool. "It has been the most intense heat that I have ever felt—a boiling suffocating heat that leaves one no energy to look out, or even to brush off the flies."

She enclosed a note from "poor little Mary Stamps." "The crack," she wrote, "has I fear come before I thought it would." Mary had bought a large house and was trying to run a girls' school. Varina believed that nothing under three thousand dollars would help her. "Poor child, I do not think that she or I would ever succeed in business."

In replying, Davis seemed to sense a guarded resentment of his nephew's widow, for he wrote:

I am truly grieved at the unfair assessment of Mary Stamps, if you seem to conclude the sale of the house means the failure of her enterprise. Do you think we could relieve her? I can wish, but what can I venture in the face of our wants and uncertainties?

He was directly appealed to by other relatives for help. His niece, Lucy Boyle, who had inherited Locust Grove from his sister Anna, was in straitened circumstances. She was about to lose the plantation where his bride Sarah Knox had died and was buried. Because of mortgages and high taxes, she could be relieved "by not less than twelve thousand dollars." "Poor thing," he wrote Varina. "I am sad and perplexed about her. . . . I can work and fast and wear shabby clothes and walk everywhere I have to go, but this doesn't furnish a fund sufficient for half it would please me to do for others."

To make up for her criticism of Mary Stamps, whom she really admired, Varina responded with a very loving letter on June 16, 1871.

I am more than gratified that you knew I would write on the third. . . . I not only wrote to you, but dreamed that I walked with you and that we talked of love and I felt old and you seemed young and so you are to me—ever young and beautiful and beloved.

Then she penned an apology.

I am ashamed of a letter I wrote you a few days ago—a seeming mad letter full of highstrikes. However I erred on the side of love and you will the more readily excuse me. I know when I think of it that I should not have been inconsiderate about poor Mary Stamps.* . . . Of course I knew that three thousand dollars you could not give. I have less sympathy with Lucy's course, because she ought to have refrained from many expenses she has incurred, and yet I am so poor an economist, so unequal to many of the really grand acts of self-denial that she had practiced that I am the last person to throw a stone. My idea is that the

---

* In 1877 Mary Stamps became the first woman principal of the Girls' High School in New Orleans. At her death in May, 1900, the *Picayune* declared she was the foremost woman educator in Louisiana.

more you do in her case the more you may do, for I think a fortune could be swamped on their affairs and then they would be involved.

We have not had helpful families on either side, have we? And you, dear old love, how faithfully you helped my people in every way. The Lord has a blessing for all that you have done for others.

It had seemed only natural and right to Jefferson Davis to help his own or his wife's relatives whenever they called on him or when he sensed their need. Though he had done ten times as much for the Howells as for his Davis kin, he had never complained or even hinted that it was not his pleasure to help Varina's parents and brothers and sisters. Now he felt only depressed and self-reproachful that he was unable to meet the necessities of the two widows on his side of the family, Mary Stamps and Lucy Boyle. But Varina with her practical sense had been right to warn him not to involve himself deeply in others' misfortunes. So he sent Mary a check for $300, which she accepted as a loan.

In the last week of June, 1871, at the Board meeting of the Carolina, Davis was again re-elected President. He thanked the directors, the more, because his annual report had frankly pointed out what he regarded as defective policies and practices of the company and he had suggested changes which might have offended their *amour-propre*.

In response to an urgent request of Bishop William Green, a founder and present Chancellor of the University of the South, Davis attended the Commencement at Sewanee, Tennessee, on July 12. He made an address, and was sorely tempted to accept the Vice-Chancellorship, or Presidency, of the college, which was offered to him. He liked the mountain atmosphere, as well as the academic milieu, and he was particularly devoted to the Bishop, who, because of his spirituality, was sometimes called "the St. John of the Church." The one drawback, besides the isolation which he knew would go hard with Varina, was the salary. Davis could not support his wife and educate four children on $2,000 a year. So he regretfully declined.

On his return from a week in Sewanee, Davis found a letter from Mary Stamps. In answering he came closer than ever to expressing his devotion.

I had counted on a sight of you as you went to the Springs and not even the many disappointments I have borne enable me to bear the new

one with proper resignation. Thank you, darling, for thinking of me so
often and so affectionately; be ye sure it is returned with interest, even
more than would be charged by a street broker of these dull times. I will
not tire your loving heart with a recital of my Iliad, and like yourself hope
to be in better spirits when we meet again. Often my memory recalls the
events of our last meeting and again it delights to live over the hours we
passed in quiet communion with each other. How happy it is for care-
worn mortals that they can sometimes wrap the past and the future in
the present, and not less happy is it that memory preserves the sweet so
much more tenaciously than the bitter.

After sending "immeasurable love," he signed his letter conven-
tionally "Cordially and faithfully, Your Uncle Jeff."

Mary Stamps was in a way Jefferson Davis's ideal of womanhood:
high-minded, selfless, unworldly. And he was to her the near-
perfect man, whom, with her cool appraisal, she admired to the
edge of adoration. Though he was older than she by twenty-seven
years, in their brief meetings each found a peace that was consen-
tient and imponderable.

At Christmas, 1871, all of the Jefferson Davis family were finally
settled "under one roof" at 129 Court Street. Except for a few brief
months in Montreal in 1867, it was the first time in six years that
they had had a house since the flight from Richmond in the spring
of 1865. Although he paid $100 a month rent, Davis himself did
not care much for the place, because "the rooms were small and the
plan cranky." But they had the best possible neighbors in the Benedict Semmeses, who had moved next door in October. The whole
neighborhood was good, if the drainage in the back garden was not.
Varina, who had spent all the "sickly season" in Maryland, had gone
to Richmond in September and recovered a large part of the furniture she had sold, and also quantities of ornaments, books, and
pictures that had been kept for her by friendly convent nuns. She
had also bought several new good pieces at reasonable prices. With
her inborn talent for homemaking, and with three servants, the
family lived comfortably.

After their year in Brand's school in Maryland, Davis had wanted
his sons at home with him in Memphis, and Mrs. Davis thought that
they should be under their father's influence. Yet mindful of fourteen-year-old Jeff's eventual college education, he had taken him to
Lexington, where Mrs. Lee and Custis, now President of Washington College, had been most hospitable. But Jeff had been so en-

chanted by the drilling cadets of the Virginia Military Institute on the other side of town that he straightway set his heart on V.M.I.

Now in public school at Memphis the boys seemed completely happy. They both had engaging ways and were immediately popular with their schoolfellows. Billie had a much more alert mind than Jeff, who did not get good marks. Billie became tremendously attached to his father, of whom he had seen so little in his ten years of life. Though buoyant with animal spirits, he would often go to his father's office and sit there absolutely quiet, merely watching him at work, just as Maggie had enjoyed doing when she was a little girl. Mrs. Davis, fearing the youngster would annoy him, tried to restrain Billie, but her husband said: "You will not grudge me our little gentleman's company, when you know how I enjoy his presence."

Billie, a complete democrat, liked riffraff quite as much as the sons of his parents' friends. One day when General Ransom came to one-o'clock dinner, Billie proudly ushered in six urchins he had impulsively invited to dine. He had corralled them in the street to help him finish some ambitious gardening project in the back yard. They had done their work, and he would reward them with a filling dinner. Mrs. Davis, who was remarkably adjustable in sudden household emergencies, had the table extended and the hands washed. The ex-President, who instinctively understood boys, put them at their ease and entertained them at his end of the table, while his wife took care of the amused General at the other.

During most of the summer of 1872, although she sent the children to cool resorts, Mrs. Davis persisted in her purpose to remain with her husband in Memphis. He worked steadily through the heat and traveled much, trying to shore up his company. On August 6 he wrote his lifelong friend James Phelan, who was seeking health in the East and who felt that the ex-President should not work so hard:

The silkworm spins her cocoon before she dies, and Man should provide for his family before he is borne from his house. Life has not been to me of the dramatic kind, but would call it a long tour of fatigue, marked by a succession of unjust reports. . . .
Were I your physician my dictum would be a sea voyage. To mate with the inconstancy of his mind, man's body requires change; when diseased the more extreme the change the better.

Doubtless few persons who knew Jefferson Davis's story would have agreed with him that his life had been undramatic. Though there had been no scandal in his career, it had been marked by uncommon adventures from the age of seven, when he went pony-back from lower Mississippi to the Dominican school in Kentucky, down to the shackling at Fort Monroe. Now the insurance business was faltering, and in the next year's panic would provide its own disruptive drama.

CHAPTER XXXVIII

CRASH

————◄◆►————

THOUGH JEFFERSON DAVIS was constantly being urged to use his influence in public affairs, he had kept silent about political matters. However, in 1872, he did let his preference for Greeley over Grant as the next President be known. Davis was well aware that Greeley, who had at first considered secession legal and argued for peace, had later fought the Confederacy with his pen almost as relentlessly as Grant had hammered it with his guns. He did not favor Greeley because he had helped to rescue him from prison; for he believed that Greeley had acted merely "out of devotion to the cause of justice."

Davis thought that under Greeley conditions in the South would be less appalling than under the current administration. Grant's reassuring tenders of leniency, implied in the peace parley with Lee at Appomattox, had long since been discounted; he was completely under the influence of the Radical Republicans. The remembrance of Lee's faith in the North's generosity recalled to Davis his own dark prophecy of April 23, 1865, that if Joseph Johnston did not continue the fight a "long night of oppression will follow the return of our people to the Union." But postwar Northern oppression had proved even more dreadful than his most dismal imaginings.

To still disquieting thoughts, Davis worked harder at the insurance company's business. In September, 1872, he was in Baltimore conferring with Wade Hampton, president of the Maryland branch office. On the eighteenth he wrote Varina: "We have many troubles here for the Carolina and I am ill at ease." In a letter eleven days later he explained further:

379

Though I have been here longer than anticipated, my work is not done. Whatever had been done or commenced by others was much worse than nothing. There is a fatal weakness in most men—that of conceding too much for the sake of avoiding controversy or offense. Thence come my present difficulties.

Davis had barely got home on October 10 when tragedy struck almost without warning. Billie came down with diphtheria, and in a few days he was dead. Jefferson Davis had now lost three of his four sons. Only fifteen-year-old Jeff remained. Billie had been the handsomest of the Davis children and obviously much brighter than Jeff. The father endured his inexpressible grief stoically, as the city and the South grieved with the parents. Among the letters of condolence that poured in from all about the country one that gave him special comfort was from Mrs. Lee to Varina. Mary Lee, who had recently lost a beloved grandchild, said she could really appreciate "your great sorrow in the loss of your noble boy."

I write to express my deep sympathy tho' I feel that Mr. Davis and yourself know of the interest we take in all that concerns you, both of joy and grief.

You must give our love to all the children and to Mr. Davis, in which Custis begs especially to participate. He is just the same, quiet and grave, and I have almost relinquished the hope of ever seeing him married.

With the death of Billie all affairs seemed to turn worse for the family in Memphis. Mrs. Davis complained that her limbs were numb, and she suffered spells of mental depression. Doctors still could find nothing wrong with her organically, and recommended "cheerfulness." The insurance company business was going badly. Yellow fever, malaria, typhoid, effects of old wounds, and various diseases had taken the Southern men off at far earlier ages than actuarial calculations anticipated. Many citizens were too poor to pay their premiums, and some solicitors were anything but aggressive. On the whole Davis had put good men in charge of various agencies: men popular, well-bred, honest. As John S. Preston, his general state agent for Virginia, wrote, he himself was "running down—remorselessly—the impoverished Virginians," but it was hard to get his subordinates to *work* at selling policies. Some were too proud to seek and ask.

Davis not only had the cares of his company, but a tremendous personal correspondence to attend. Numerous strangers sent unsolicited "material" for his book, often relating their personal exploits in the hope he would mention them. Scores wrote begging *his* help with books *they* were writing. Much essential material, however, came in from important Confederate Generals like Dabney Maury, Stephen D. Lee, and I. M. St. John, the last Commissary General of the Confederacy. Not only from the South but from the North came letters urging Davis to write his book, many pointing out that Lee had intended to write his story, and *now he was gone*. William B. Reed, the Philadelphia lawyer who had been one of Davis's defense counsel and had recently moved to New York City, volunteered his personal services gratis.

Let me ask you as I have done perhaps impatiently in every letter I have written. Is your record and the record of the Confederacy never to be written? . . . I cannot tell you how much pleasure it would give me to assist in such a work.

In general, Davis considerately answered this enormous inflow of mail; writing letters helped to relieve his grief over the loss of Billie, on whom he told a friend he had "pinned his highest earthly hopes." With tender care he wrote, December 6, 1872, to ten-year-old Jefferson Davis Smith in Stewartsville, Missouri, a lad just about Billie's age.

The interest I feel in you, not merely as my own namesake, but because of your bold avowal of your name on all occasions during the war when you were questioned by our enemies induces me to write to you and request that you will reply to this letter and tell me about your studies and what branches are most attractive to you. It is rarely given to any one to acquire with equal facility in the different departments of knowledge, but zealous labor will overcome special difficulties and bring ever increasing capacity to learn.

In the partially developed condition of our country, the apothegm that "knowledge is power" has more than the physical application, but it is not alone for material use that I would have you gather knowledge. To be wise is not merely to be great, but also to be good. Glory properly belongs to duty well performed and happiness only dwells with him whose conscience is at peace with itself. It may not be your fortune to fill high stations, but if it should be, value them as the means of greater usefulness, and thus deserve, though you should not receive, the thanks of those you have served.

This letter to a boy would have been lost like hundreds of others except for Ella Smith, a niece-in-law, who sent it to Mrs. Davis in 1890, because she thought "it contained too much good advice for all American boys to be kept in private circles."

Ever since his return from abroad Davis had continued to correspond with certain prominent Britishers, notably A. J. Beresford-Hope. In a letter of February 28, 1873, thanking him for kind attentions and some books, he took occasion to remind the conservative Britisher of his good fortune at being free, despite the encroachments of radicalism.

The contrast between your government and that of this country, may at least give you the consolation of knowing how much worse off you might be than you are. The liberty of the law, administered by learned and respectable men, is a blessing best appreciated by those who have it not.

Jefferson Davis was alone in the Memphis house most of the summer of 1873. At the end of May, Varina had taken Winnie with her nurse to the cooler clime of Canada, where there was a pleasant gathering of Southerners at Drummondsville near Niagara. Maggie and Jeff, Jr., were paying guests of the Preston Johnstons in Lexington, Virginia. Davis struggled with insurance problems; the Carolina business was at a crisis. The board asked him to go to New York to try to borrow $150,000.

The time could hardly have been more inauspicious for securing a sizable loan. The year of 1873 was marked in the United States by financial panic, which had begun the year before. Commercial failures followed one upon another with enormous liabilities. As industries closed down, hundreds of thousands of laborers were thrown out of work, and bread lines formed in Northern cities. When shaky banks collapsed, sound ones were ruined by "runs" of frightened depositors. Stock quotations dropped alarmingly. The strained and unnatural situation between the Federal Administration and the Southern people served as a discouragement to normal enterprise. Investigations of private frauds and official corruption shook the public confidence.

Davis reached New York just two months before the New York office of Jay Cooke and Company, powerful and respected firm of financiers, closed its doors, and the New York Stock Exchange stopped operations. But he laid frankly before bankers and insurance men the figures of his company. From the New York Hotel on July 12, he wrote his wife:

I have had a vexatious time and all to no purpose. The great number of deaths at the South during the last year has alarmed the Insurance men.

They fear the rate will continue, and rightly conclude that if it does, the business there must be ruinous in the end. I have done everything except ask for money as a personal favor. That I have been urged to do, and have, as you will anticipate, refused to consider. It is a sad hour and, however unjustly, must be seriously damaging to my future prospect for business.

In Baltimore a few days later Davis ascertained that the only prospect seemed an arrangement with the Piedmont and Arlington Company. The whole matter was very disagreeable and mortifying to him, and he felt that he would indeed be glad to be out of the business, even at the sacrifice of his own investment in the Carolina. His distress was revealed in his next letter to Varina.

To go back empty-handed and encounter the gloomy looks of the despondent and the malignant grins of the evil prophets is not a cheering prospect, and I have done much and will do whatever may be done consistently to avoid a total failure.

But just before he left Baltimore he made an arrangement by which he hoped "to get rid of his company's troubles." Stopping overnight in Louisville, on his return to Memphis, he received a telegram from Wade Hampton stating that something odd had happened after his departure and that the deal had fallen through.

The day after arriving in the Memphis house, empty except for the two colored servants, he wrote his wife that he was now making another attempt to wind up the insurance affairs.

To save those for whom we acted and to get out creditably is my object. Loss of my investment as well as past labor is probable. To feel secure of exemption from blame is something to one who values his self-respect above popular praise. That something is likely to be all we retain.

On Sunday, July 27, after attending service at the St. Lazarus Church, of which he had become a vestryman, Davis wrote his wife a long letter about business affairs.

Those who organized the Carolina and involved it in all the difficulties which now oppress it, are so insensible of their responsibility and so happy in shifting the burden to my shoulders, that so far from having their aid to effect such a loan as you suggest, they cannot be induced promptly to pay their own notes. It was that which drove me East to seek relief. Perhaps it would have been justifiable to quit a crew that was scuttling the ship, but I thought only of my obligation to the owners, and felt like the seaman who last leaves the wreck.

I hope to save the policy holders, and then my conscience will be easy though my pockets be empty.

At the close of a day's hard and painful work on August 4, Davis found himself obliged to go on to Richmond the next morning to meet with Wade Hampton. But Hampton was delayed because of his wife's illness. So, while waiting in Richmond, Davis was persuaded by General Jubal Early to come to the Montgomery White Sulphur Springs and speak to the Virginia Historical Society at its annual conference. Except for his eulogy of Lee at the memorial service in November, 1870, Davis had hitherto declined all invitations to speak at scheduled meetings; for he had almost invariably been misquoted whenever out of courtesy he responded with a few remarks at dinners given for him on business trips. But now he was moved to go to the conclave.

In the course of his brief speech he made two statements which aroused the "loyal" journals in the North and upset the serenity of some "excessively discreet" newspapers in Virginia, owned by Northern capital. Davis declared that the South had been "cheated rather than conquered." "Could we have foreseen the results of surrender," he said, "we would have been free today." He explained that if the humiliating Reconstruction had been envisaged, the South would not have surrendered. He referred to the earlier resolutions of Congress and the proclamations of President Lincoln which maintained that the war was conducted solely for the preservation of the Union and that the State governments would remain intact with their constitutions, laws, customs, and institutions the same as before.

If it had been anticipated that it was the purpose of Washington to destroy the regular State governments, enfranchise the negroes, and subject the white people to their rule, did any sane man doubt that the Confederate Government and its armies in the field would have been more thoroughly *sustained* than they were?

Davis also declared that if the objects of the War of Northern Aggression had been avowed in the beginning, many thousands in the North who took sides against their Southern brothers would have withheld their support. And as Carl Sandburg was to write in *A Lincoln Preface*, "at least one-fourth of the Northern people always believed in the Southern cause."

One statement of Davis to which some Virginia editors particularly objected was that he had never yet seen a Southern *woman* who was reconstructed. Davis had strongly in mind, among others, Mrs. Lee, who, though now in her last illness, had never lost her devotion to what she called "our glorious cause."

Because Davis urged the children of the South to cherish the principles of freedom and State Rights, for which their fathers and forefathers had fought, his words were interpreted by Northern foes as an attempt to incite fresh rebellion, which was, of course, anything but his intention. Yet he made it impressively patent that no disfranchisement, hardship, persecution, or malignant report could diminish one jot his love of liberty.

Without anticipating the little furor his speech was to kick up, Davis returned to Richmond to meet Wade Hampton. While they were in conference, Davis received a telegram announcing that the Carolina had been sold to the Southern Life of Memphis. Davis was astounded; from what he knew, this company was in a near-bankrupt condition. Hampton thought the Memphis action was "a trick." Davis more charitably chose to consider it "a blunder." Yet he wrote his wife in Canada, "The evil genius of the Carolina took possession and destroyed all for which my trip was made."

A few days later he wrote more fully of his frustration:

The seed sown when I was in New York had germinated and there was assurance that I could soon get $150,000 of new stock taken on the condition of taking a charter in Md. and removing the parent office from Memphis to Balto. Thus the debts of the Carolina would have been paid at once. . . .

Back in Memphis, Davis found that the matter had indeed been most loosely and unwisely conducted, that the managers of the Southern Life had got every advantage and that the debts of the Carolina were only to be paid "as its means should furnish the money."

"It was," he declared, "hard to avoid being offended at so serious an injury." The bad deal had taken place behind his back while he was absent from Memphis. Robert Boyle alone had protested vigorously against the Board's drastic action. Yet Davis tried to make excuses for the directors: "The only thing which is perceptible of indirection is the evident desire to keep the business in Memphis, for local advantage. The rest, I believe, was due to panic, ignorance and want of caution." He was personally embarrassed by the necessity of paying notes of $5,650, which still stood against his $15,000 worth of stock. Now he would have to raise the cash by selling some fire insurance and mining stocks he owned.

Here I am alone in this big house, with furniture too fine and too valuable to sacrifice. No definite object is in view from which to derive the income we require and the little we have will be little indeed if it all be saved for you and the children. But a truce to gloomy forebodings, and let us hope in this little family world of ours as in the great world of which we are a part, the darkest hour is that which precedes the dawn.

In solitary meditation on Sunday, he calmly reviewed the action taken by the Board of the Carolina during his absence. "To avoid the necessity of going before the public in the language of censure," he sent in his resignation as President.

The resignation was accepted and his salary stopped immediately. Now four years older than when he had sailed back from England in 1869 to take the insurance position, Jefferson Davis would have to make a fresh start in the business world.

In the midst of the business calamity, Davis was hearing repercussions of his address at Montgomery White Sulphur Springs earlier in the month. He had been attacked by a few Southern newspapers for what some timid editors called his "bold indiscretions." General Jubal Early, President of the Virginia Historical Association, was among the stoutest of Davis's defenders. He sent Davis a sheaf of cuttings—of attack and defense.

One article by Early that particularly pleased Davis appeared in the Petersburg *Index and Appeal* of August 26, 1873.

If we did fight for the principles of civil and constitutional liberties, then where is the Virginian who will dare to say that he does not desire that those who are to come after us shall cherish and maintain those principles?

But it is said that it was imprudent for Mr. Davis to say anything because his words were likely to be seized hold of and distorted from their true meaning. Really this is a strange doctrine for a country claiming to be Republican in its institutions, and where liberty of speech has been regarded as one of the great bulwarks of freedom. . . .

Are not all our acts, sayings, customs, the constant theme of misrepresentation, perversion and abuse in the daily papers, pictorial journals and books in the North. If we cannot have political independence, let us have independence of thought at least.

In another article published in the Chester *Reporter* on September 5, 1873, he lashed out at those Southern papers that unjustly criticized Mr. Davis. "The howl raised in the North," the General declared contemptuously, "found response in the weak-kneed and time-serving among the presses of the South that were saying unbecoming things about the ex-President."

In our judgment such stuff as this has done the South ten thousand times more damage than all the speeches Jeff Davis ever made. It shows to our conquerors that we don't respect ourselves. . . . They would crush out of our souls the love we feel for the causes for which we fought, because in that sentiment they recognize an unrelenting enemy to the warfare they are waging on civil liberty itself.

Jefferson Davis spoke no word in his own defense. He had nothing to retract, and Early's strong articles said all that was needed.

"The tide of my fortune is at the lowest ebb," Davis wrote his wife from Memphis on September 7. He had that morning received a letter from Judge Clayton of Alabama advising him that the iron company stocks, which he had bought on the Judge's advice, were "under a cloud" and that Clayton himself had sold his shares at a heavy loss.

On receiving the news of the business catastrophe and her husband's unqualified resignation, Mrs. Davis collapsed. Her health had greatly improved during her summer sojourn in Canada. But now she was naturally undone at the thought of again "floating uprooted."

To get away from his depression in Memphis, Davis went to Louisville to think matters through. He telegraphed Varina to join him there at the Galt House as soon as she was able to travel.

When she finally reached Louisville, Mrs. Davis begged her husband to go at once to England for his health's sake because of the terrible strain he had been under the last two years. She grasped at the faint hope that though he was now sixty-five—retirement age—he might secure some worthy business connection abroad.

Having lost heavily in the Carolina and being desperate in his need to support his family, Davis, as a last resort, felt it his duty to repossess his Brierfield plantation. Goaded by Varina, he decided that he should go through with a painful lawsuit for his children's sake. And now that he was no longer the President of Carolina Life, his involvement in the courts could not hurt the company.

Judge Thomas Farrar of Vicksburg, a kinsman of Varina, advised him that he might recover Brierfield "if prompt measures were taken," but that in 1875 "the action would be barred by limitation." When Joe and Lise Mitchell (now Mrs. M. E. Hamer) definitely refused to recognize their great-uncle's ownership of Brierfield, Davis agreed, in some agony of spirit, to file suit for the recovery of his property.

In early November, the death of Mrs. Lee in Lexington grieved Mr. Davis, for Mary Lee and he had had a most sympathetic bond. He wrote Custis:

> The grief you feel is intensely shared by me, for your mother was to me the object of highest admiration and most respectful regard. A bitter experience has taught me how vain are the words of consolation in such sorrow as yours, but you have the comfort of knowing that the loss is ours, the gain is hers.

While Varina settled again uncertainly in Memphis, Davis went to Vicksburg to consult with his lawyer, W. B. Pittman. In December he met with Ben and Isaiah Montgomery, and the other executors of Joseph's will. It was agreed to relieve the Montgomerys by reducing their interest payment for the year 1873 from $18,000 to $15,000 and postponing that settlement until October, 1874. So there would be no cash for Davis this year.

Ben Montgomery gave Mr. Davis a written statement of the understanding between himself and Joseph Davis to the effect that Brierfield was to be returned to his brother whenever he chose to demand it. Pittman examined the facts of the case and felt convinced that he could recover the property.

On the last day of 1873 Davis was still in Vicksburg attending to business before proceeding to New Orleans. He would take the next river boat, for since his favorite sister, Lucinda Stamps, had died earlier in the year, it seemed vain for him to detour by carriage to Woodville. "The last link," he wrote Varina, "that bound me to happy childhood is broken."

> Though wearied and worried, I am no worse than when we parted. . . .
> With kindest wishes to your considerate neighbors who have there endeared themselves to me, and kisses innumerable for my precious, grand old Waafe, I send again the greeting of a happy New Year.

CHAPTER XXXIX

DIM CASTLES IN SPAIN

———————◆◎◆———————

WHEN JEFFERSON DAVIS arrived in New Orleans in the fore-noon on January 5, 1874, he found a letter from Dr. Blackburn, his Memphis physician, urging him to take the prescribed sea voyage, and another from his wife pleading the same thing. Both Varina and the doctor were now concerned about a swelling of his feet that had started in Vicksburg.

In replying Davis minimized his physical trouble and said that since there was no letter from Liverpool awaiting him he did not want to go abroad unless money was to be definitely gained by it. "I am now at Mary Stamps'!" he wrote. At this distressful time, away from his wife, he felt the need more than ever of Mary's sympathetic understanding.

Varina had sent his trunk to New Orleans for the European voyage she insisted he should make. In answering her latest letter Davis said: "You write as though my voyage was begun, and I feel as if I should not leave you." He then touched on a sour matter:

J. E. Johnston's book is in the press. The advance sheets exhibit his usual malignity and suppression of the truth when it would affect his side of the cause unfavorably. Hood is quite excited and anxious for *others* to fight Johnston. *Says* he will make a reply to the part specially affecting himself.

Varina wrote on January 12:

Your sweet and precious letter written in pencil is before me. How sweet it is to an old broken-hearted woman to be addressed by the love of her youth it is not granted to me to tell you. . . .

But your letter grieved and shocked me, as well as gave pleasure. I

389

thought you had finally determined to go abroad. I will come down to wish you a pleasant voyage and fold you in my arms; but do not, oh do not, come back, dear love. Do not. You know that a little more enfeeblement may take the water now settled in other parts to your heart. *Now* you are easily curable—*then*— Then what would become of me? Only and dear love, think of this and go—go at once.

She reminded him that he could do nothing in the Carolina but shudder under the rule of "brass and iron" and see shears made of those metals fleece his friends. He could not help in the Brierfield suit just now. Above all, he could not answer General Johnston's "miserable, paltry attacks" until he had recovered his strength and elasticity. "Let the public fight him for a time, and 'you go a-fishing.'"

Then, with touching wifely concern, she urged him to get Mary Stamps to procure burr artichoke leaves, chop them fine enough to fill a whisky bottle lightly pressed full and pour in the best whisky. He should take the tonic three times a day. "It is intensely bitter, but is a specific for dropsy. . . . Will you take it for me, will you do it, because I love you to distraction?"

The S. S. *Alabama,* the finest ship sailing from New Orleans to Liverpool, was in port and scheduled to leave the next Saturday. Reluctantly he booked passage. But he wrote Varina that if it were not for her anxiety he would stay until their affairs had been more satisfactorily arranged.

On the seventeenth Dr. Choppin performed a minor operation on his foot and drew off about seven ounces of water. Because the injection of iodine caused considerable irritation, Davis was forced for a day to stay "undressed," which he did not like at all.

Mary Stamps had written Varina inviting her to be her guest, but Davis was unwilling for his wife to travel alone, as she would have to pass through Vicksburg, where there was seething tension between Negroes and whites. Varina, however, fearing her husband might at the last minute balk at sailing, unexpectedly arrived in New Orleans the day before he was to leave. She brought him a pair of warm woolen slippers she had knitted for the voyage. The next day she went with him in a carriage to the dock, saw him aboard, and then drove quickly away.

On January 25, 1874, Jefferson Davis sailed down the Mississippi, a prelude to his third eastbound crossing of the Atlantic. Though the ocean voyage was peculiarly rough even for February, it was beneficial to him, as an increase in strength and appetite clearly indicated. He had never failed to find some curative balm in the trackless sea. When the *Alabama* entered the Irish channel he was loath to debark.

In Liverpool both the Norman Walkers and the de Stöesses claimed him as a house guest, so he stayed first with the former in elegant luxury, and then in moderate comfort with the latter. His old friends and acquaintances pronounced his appearance more robust than when he had left England four years earlier.

Varina had been right to urge a sea voyage, to put out of his consciousness for a time both the Memphis business debacle and the South's humiliation. She hoped for some miracle that would make it possible for them all to live respectably in Europe during these dreadful years under Radical rule. But after one week in Liverpool a touch of homesickness revealed itself in a letter to his daughter Maggie. Davis was still the American patriot.

The weather is chilly and damp, and my thoughts ever turning to the land which holds my heart's treasure, brings often to remembrance the sunny days of our own land. Though you all cried out with one voice in denunciation of Tom Payne's love for America, it is not possible for me to find elsewhere "so fair a land."

He did not lack attention abroad; he was pressed for visits from James Smith in Glasgow, Dr. Blandy and others in London; Dudley Mann in Paris. Dinner parties were given for him. Callers were numerous.

He made contact with British insurance companies, which in correspondence had seemed to look favorably on his association with them. Introduced by Major Walker, Davis called on the manager of the Royal Insurance Company in Liverpool. He was told that their head in New York doubted the wisdom of establishing a separate agency for the South. The British directors had just learned from their New York agent, an Englishman, that the animosity against Jefferson Davis individually was so great that his appointment "would imperiously affect" their business in the North. Davis wrote his wife:

How far dread of the Yankee may render it impossible for me to get anything in this country is doubtful. . . . I could hunt or fish or chop or hoe, but could not in that way make enough to support our wants. God guards the sparrow, and will, I pray, keep watch over my dear Wife and children. The world keeps pace with fiction and so the liars rule.

In a state less than sanguine he went on to London to see what could be done there. While Davis was the guest of the Campbells at 47 Princes Square, Bayswater, a former London acquaintance, J. B. Jennings, kindly undertook the task of intermediary to learn whether any of the strong companies desired to engage in American business. Thus Davis was spared the embarrassment of seeking employment. He had already had pleasant relations with Jennings during previous visits to London. And he had written the Londoner at the end of September, 1870, a line that stuck in his mind: "When we get those castles in Spain reduced to possession, my powers to show my appreciation will be great." But the castles instead of being possessed by 1874 had receded to dimmer distances. Yet there was one business possibility that might unfold in the near future: the sale of Southern land to emigrants.

While waiting for developments, Davis went to Paris to stay with Dudley Mann, who was now living at 51 Rue de Luxembourg. Ex-Governor Frank Lubbock of Texas, who had never deviated in his loyal devotion to Davis, accompanied him and got a room near Mann's place. The reunion with his two friends did much to assuage Davis's anxiety.

A long letter from Varina reached him in Paris. She was moving to 98 Court Street, a much larger house down the street, which she had rented for $60 a month, instead of the $100 they were paying. It was in need of repair, but they would live in only a part of the house. She and the children were busy packing for the move. Varina had been suffering from "numbness" and insomnia, and she had had her heart examined "critically." The doctor could find no disease connected with that organ and believed that her "nervous system had sustained so many severe shocks that it had temporarily succumbed." "It would be a real grief to me," she wrote, "if you were to come home before your health is established, which I have not a doubt it can be by plenty of sunlight, fresh air, generous food and exercise."

Though neither Paris nor London was noted for sunlight in March, Davis did have excellent food, agreeable exercise, and cheering companionship. In Paris he enjoyed seeing his friends. Emily Mason, Baroness Erlanger, Rossine St. Roman, and the younger Mary Lee, who was spending the winter abroad, called on him and sent affectionate messages to Varina. A friend arranged for him to visit the Chamber of Deputies at Versailles during a critical session to decide the form of government for France, monarchy or republic. Never in his life had he witnessed a more stormy meeting. "I thought the French especially logical," he wrote, "but their present condition does not justify the belief."

On a Sunday, after Mann and Lubbock had read aloud the Episcopal morning service, the three friends went to the Chapel of the Invalides. It was a colorful ceremony, with the French veterans "in many stages of decay and disability, each bearing a smart tricolor, and with military orders on their breasts." From time to time in different parts of the service an old officer gave commands, and the *invalides* would raise their flags or rest the butts of the staffs on the floor. A number of boys, orphans of gallant soldiers, constituted the band. Davis reflected on the signal respect France paid its veterans.

It was a spectacle which could but painfully remind me of our neglected braves and their unprovided orphans. It is well that virtue is its own reward, for sometimes it would otherwise be without compensation.

Davis saw few traces of the recent siege in Paris, except that the Tuileries Palace had been burned by the Communards. The Orleans princes had gone to reside near Chantilly, and Mann thought Mrs. Davis would find his little house there a pleasant residence. Mann was full of projects to keep Davis a resident in France. One was to turn his country place into a farm to breed horses. Davis smiled to himself at Mann's impracticality and wrote Varina, "What a wild herd we could have on that domain of barely seven acres." It seemed impossible for Davis's friends in Paris to comprehend the measure of his family's requirements.

He stayed in Paris much longer than he had expected, because of tentative propositions there "to organize a land company to aid our people and to secure emigration to the South." At length, in mid-April, he returned to London, and for almost a fortnight he met with various committees. He found the English ignorance of the South astonishing—they seemed to think the carpetbag rule to be that of true Southerners and they could not understand that the tremendous bond indebtedness was created by alien adventurers and Negroes.

At every step Davis found in London businessmen "a dread of displeasing the Yankees," which presented a formidable obstacle to his success. On April 26, 1874, he wrote his wife:

From each overthrow of a hope, I rise proud in the consciousness that my sin is the love of my country. . . .

Perhaps I may effect something for our people if not for myself. There is a difficulty in my case growing out of what I owe to our people if not to myself, which is that the dignity conferred upon me does not permit me as another might to ask employment by personal application.

Dear old wife, I hear you say—we can fast, we can toil in secret, but we cannot *crawl* in public.

In the end, the tentative propositions in London were so inconclusive that Jefferson Davis returned to America in late May, improved in health, but still "floating uprooted" with castles in Spain even more dim.

Varina had wanted to get her husband away from the ugly situation created by Radical rule. But on his return to the States in early summer of 1874, conditions, instead of improving, seemed more intolerable. Some said the Northerners were leaving no stone unturned to make the South a "Negro heaven," so that the Negroes would not be tempted to move North. Little was left undone by the carpetbaggers and certain misguided New England schoolmarms to encourage "cupidity and animosity" in the Negroes. Now, in mid-1874, nine years after the South had surrendered, Davis found that the black night of Reconstruction was far from ending. In his home State of Mississippi, Maine-born carpetbagger Adelbert Ames, former Military Governor and United States Senator, had recently defeated James Alcorn, the planter-turned-Republican, for Governor. Davis read of the Mississippi Legislature of 1874 as "the culmination of negro representation." The Lieutenant Governor, who presided over the Senate, was a Negro named Alexander K. Davis. Another Negro, J. D. Shadd, was elected speaker of the House. Of the seventy-seven Republicans, twelve Democrats, and few scattered Independents in the House, fifty-five were Negroes. The three counties of Warren, Hinds, and Adams, with which Jefferson Davis had been most closely associated, were represented in both Senate and House almost entirely by colored members.

Not only were the positions of Secretary of State and Superintendent of Education held by colored men, but a newly created Department of Immigration and Agriculture, "palpably useless and injurious" was headed by a Negro. The opposition declared that this so-called department "served for the expenditure of many thousands of dollars merely to keep two or three almost unlettered colored men in a room of Jackson's Capitol under the false pretense

that they were engaged in immigration and agricultural enter-
prises."

When Davis went to Vicksburg in July on legal business connected with Brierfield the racial tension was approaching a crisis.
The blacks in Madison Parish, Louisiana, just across the river from
Vicksburg, were being organized by carpetbag adventurers into
companies to "march on Vicksburg" and attack the whites. The
action hinted at a kind of delayed servile insurrection after the
slaves were freed. A climax was reached on July 9, 1874, when an
offensive and belligerent Negro named Davenport, Clerk of Chancery, made a speech, which was reprinted in the city papers. He
declared that the time was not far distant when miscegenated mar-
riages would occur daily. Barriers could be broken down, he report-
edly said, for "the white women might now see that the Negro was
the coming man." Did not Negroes have control of both city and
state governments? He claimed that if he himself were not married,
he could get the daughter of one of the best Vicksburg families.
And he further boasted that if he were in the matrimonial market,
he "would buckle on a brace of pistols and meet the woman's
father or brothers who would dare interfere with his affairs."

In the face of such threats a "white man's ticket" was nominated
in Warren County. Many Negroes, including those on the Mont-
gomery-Davis plantations, supported it, and it was elected in August. Though a race riot had been predicted, this time President
Grant had refused Federal arms "to keep the peace" and thus assure a Radical victory. Despite the "cyclonic intensity" of the day,
no overt act of violence occurred. This election in Vicksburg with a
split Negro vote marked a turning point in the political affairs of
Mississippi, though not the end of trouble.

When the Carolina Insurance Company was finally liquidated,
Davis's investment of $15,000 was totally lost. The Davises now
lived in such strict economy in Memphis that their condition bordered on penury. Their niece Helen Keary, on hearing exaggerated reports of their destitution, offered them a home on her humble
Arkansas farm.

Evenings passed quietly in the Memphis home. Mrs. Davis
would generally read aloud from some classic. One night, in the
family circle about the lamp, she read from *The Tempest*. When
she paused after a scene between Miranda and Ferdinand, the ten-

year-old Winnie sighed deeply and exclaimed, "Oh me! I hardly think that a woman takes as naturally to men as she did."

Having time on his hands now, Davis consistently began gathering material for "his book" and exchanging numerous letters with prominent Confederates about controversial matters. He sought the aid of Philip Phillips, the Jewish ex-Congressman from Alabama, whose wife had been a victim of Ben Butler's brutality, and who was now practicing law in Washington. Davis asked him to secure from the War Department a box taken by Sherman's men in Mississippi containing numerous private papers which were important to him in regard to the Brierfield suit. "There are others," he wrote, "valuable only to myself, such as family letters running back to the time when I was a school boy; some commissions and diplomas which were also a part of the capture." He would be much obliged if Phillips would get "at least so much of them as the officers of the Government shall not consider of any possible use to them." There was also his trunk containing personal belongings and letters, which had been in charge of Senator Yulee's wife in Florida and which had been seized by General Isaac Vogdes. Phillips promised his good offices and set to work.

To his friend General George W. Jones of Iowa, Davis wrote asking that he secure a family album containing pictures of his dead children and other relatives. It had been advertised for sale by an ex-Federal soldier named D. C. Moore, who had stolen it from Mrs. Davis's trunk.

In September Davis made a brief business trip to New Orleans and just missed a sanguinary battle between whites and blacks on Canal Street. General Longstreet participated in the fight and ordered his Negro police to fire on white citizens arrayed against them. Davis had heard that the animosity against the ex-Confederate General was extremely bitter, that none of Longstreet's old Confederate comrades would deign to speak to him, and that he suffered such complete social ostracism that his wife had gone to Michigan to stay.

The year before, in 1873, when a carpetbagger named W. P. Kellogg had been declared by Washington to be the elected Governor of Louisiana, Longstreet had been given charge of the New Orleans police, a force composed mostly of Negroes. Pent-up resentment against Washington tyranny and the corrupt excesses of carpetbag rule—the state debt rose from $10,000,000 to $50,000,000 in five years and taxes increased about 500 per cent—had brought about the establishment of a White League purposed to gain political control. On September 14, 1874, the colored police, reinforced by militia, attempted to capture the White League's store of rifles and ammunition. Citizens prepared for battle. Longstreet rode out in front of his Negro forces and called on the whites to disperse. A mighty Rebel Yell rose, tinctured with more hate and contempt than had ever been vented against impersonal Yankee troops. Though emotionally affected, Longstreet ordered his men to fire. In the first blasts over thirty were killed. Longstreet himself was one of the more than 100 wounded. Federal troops arrived and put an end to the street fight.

Davis read in the New Orleans *Republican* of September 27 that a reporter had heard several men say that they would shoot Longstreet on sight. Another paper blasted him as "the betrayer of the dearest interests of the South." Davis was more grieved than he was indignant. Longstreet's behavior seemed another case of "such things don't happen."

Just before the end of September, Davis's trunk which had been seized in Florida arrived in Memphis. It had been opened in the presence of Philip Phillips and officers of the War Department. Adjutant General E. D. Townsend had made a list of the contents and sent Davis a memorandum. Everything the trunk had contained was returned, except some antiquated pistols and some woolen clothing, which was so badly moth-eaten that it was destroyed in Washington. Davis noted the items of the inventory. There were ledgers and portfolios, bank passbooks and canceled checks, scores of telegrams, and carefully marked packets of family letters. One envelope contained locks of hair, photographs, and a letter of Andrew Jackson, dated May 2, 1831. One package contained letters of condolence on the death of their little boy Joe. There were letters from Ben Montgomery before and during the war about plantation affairs. Among Davis's personal effects were a cotton dressing gown; six linen shirts; a satin embroidered dressing case containing two razors, a comb, and a corkscrew; a pair of gold tweezers; and a Rogers and Son razor strop. Phillips had thoughtfully divided the five boxes of cigars found in the trunk among War Department officials.

In thanking Phillips for his trouble Davis lamented the fact that the Government had chosen to keep his double-barreled pistol, which he had used in Indian campaigns when he was a young Lieutenant in the U. S. Army, fresh out of West Point.

The special papers he had hoped to recover in connection with the Brierfield lawsuit, however, were in the box seized in Hinds County and sent by General Sherman to Washington. Davis hoped that "under the kind offices of Genl. Vincent" the box might yet be found and sent to him. But in 1964 the box and its contents had still not been unearthed in the Archives of the War Department.

The family album, which General George W. Jones had secured in Iowa, arrived in Memphis by express. By a ruse Jones had got it without paying the forty-five dollars the ex-soldier demanded. Jones had taken his attorney as constable with a writ to Moore's house in the country and simply repossessed it.

In late October Lise Hamer and her brother Joe Mitchell had filed an answer to Davis's bill, denying his claims to Brierfield and pleading an estoppel. Davis now asked his wife to put in writing recollections of a letter from Joseph proposing to buy Brierfield and of subsequent conversations with Joseph in Vicksburg. From her memorandum Pittman would know what to include in interrogatories for her deposition. He had hoped to keep Mrs. Davis entirely out of the controversy. "Had the other party been fair and truthful," he wrote, "it would not have been necessary to introduce you as a witness. If you still prefer not to testify, you are free to decline."

During Davis's December visit to Vicksburg the enormity of the political and financial corruption in Warren County came to light as the newly elected men took office. In this river town of less than 12,500 population the bonded debt had increased from $13,000 in 1869 to $1,400,000 in 1874, a large part of which had been pocketed by colored officials. Such graft was discovered that the Grand Jury, on which there was a Negro majority, made forty indictments against officials, including the chancery clerk, circuit clerk, and the ex-circuit clerk, T. W. Cardoza, now State Superintendent of Education—all Negroes. This Cardoza was already under indictment for larceny in New York. On December 2, 1874, the county taxpayers met and sent a delegation, headed by an ex-Union white officer, to demand the immediate resignation of the culpable county officers. Some five hundred citizens, including many ex-Union white soldiers, marched in a body on the courthouse to see that the resignations were carried out. The deposed Negroes rushed to Jackson to complain to Governor Ames, who ordered the ousted Sheriff Crosby to return to Vicksburg and resume his office and to summon a posse to enforce it. If necessary, Ames promised to call out the state militia.

Davis read in the Vicksburg *Herald* that couriers were dashing about the county notifying the rural Negroes to rendezvous at appointed places for the march on Vicksburg to reinstate Crosby in the sheriff's office. The taxpayers' Mayor, Richard O'Leary, issued a proclamation about the reported attack on the city. Alarms were first sounded at three o'clock in the morning and the citizen soldiery began to stir. At about nine o'clock fire bells rang a general alarm. A hundred men on horseback rode out to meet the approaching Negroes just inside the city limits. The officer in charge proceeded forward alone and urged them to disperse. Though the colored sheriff, under guard in the courthouse, also sent word to the Negroes to return to their homes, they became defiant and announced that they had come for a fight and were determined to have it. Firing commenced on both sides. After sixteen Negroes had been killed, many wounded, and their leader captured, the rest took flight. Sheriff Crosby resigned.

On December 21 President Grant, though wearied with Ames's continual demands for Federal troops to support his corrupt rule, issued a riot order, and Congress appointed a committee to investigate the Vicksburg violence.

Because the Warren County taxpayers had finally taken a bold stand against misrule, a State convention of taxpayers assembled in Jackson on January 5, 1875, to take some united action on the turpitude of Reconstruction. Jefferson Davis noted that members included such leading citizens as ex-Governors B. G. Humphreys and Charles Clark, ex-Senator A. G. Brown, ex-Representative Reuben Davis, a couple of Generals, and the brilliant L. Q. C. Lamar, who was later to become a Justice of the United States Supreme Court.

A memorial of grievances was prepared and copies sent both to Governor Ames and to the President of the United States. It portrayed the desperate situation in Mississippi and expressed indignation at the exorbitant taxation—an unbearable burden laid upon a people of agriculturists, "whose crops were in all degrees of failure." Oftentimes after the crops were ready to harvest, some Northern agitator or colored preacher would appear, stir the laborers to discontent and cause them to move away, leaving the crops to spoil in the fields. The memorial emphasized the needless and corrupt waste of county and state funds by an alien government.

Despite all the protests, Governor Ames still had power to enforce his will. On January 15, 1875, he reinstated Crosby as sheriff, and in February the notorious Davenport resumed his old office as clerk of chancery. Warren County was again "the focus of observation of the abomination of carpetbag rule."

In the early months of 1875 Davis had only to look at his home county to behold a microcosm of the South's misery and humiliation. Davis's young friend L. Q. C. Lamar said he had fallen into a daze of melancholy. From Oxford, Lamar wrote a friend:

Spies and secret detectives swarm through the country, dogging the footsteps of our best citizens, following up with arrests, arbitrary searches, indefinite and unexplained imprisonments, trials before vindictive and partisan juries for the purpose of insuring convictions.

Lamar felt that the Southerners had laid down their arms in good faith, had indeed submitted to the Northern interpretation of the Constitution. "Yet the administration of President Grant," he wrote, "had never ceased to treat the Southern people with contemptuous distrust, severity, and vengeance."

One thing that gave Jefferson Davis peculiar distress was the bitterness that Northerners had stirred up between the races. He himself had done much to create and maintain a cordial feeling between them; he and his brother Joseph had always been known throughout Mississippi as "friends to the Negroes." He considered a race riot incited by outsiders a shocking disgrace. He had said in prison that if not interfered with by the North, race relationships in the South would regulate themselves. But recently they had been so drastically interfered with that Davis feared it might take a very long time before harmony was restored.

CHAPTER XL

AS DAVIS SEEKS A LIVELIHOOD,
BLOODY SHIRTS ARE WAVED

———————◆———————

JEFFERSON DAVIS HAD always had two special economic interests besides agriculture: the development of mines and railroads.
In 1875 his attention was turned towards both with a hope of
achieving a livelihood. In late February he went on a rough pros-
pecting tour into Arkansas. Reaching Little Rock at half past two
in the morning of February 22, after an early breakfast, he set out
in a buggy for the Kellog Mines. There he found the deposits of
mixed metals, but more lead than silver, zinc, or copper. The next
morning, provided with a "rubber overcoat," he started off on horseback in the rain, accompanied by an engineer who was an ex-
Confederate soldier. In a miserably poor region he was the guest
of the engineer in his log cabin set in desolate backwoods. He
learned that potential mining land might be purchased for perhaps
five dollars an acre, but not being a practical miner he was at a
loss to decide on the value of the dug-up specimens of earth.
Though matters were inconclusive, Davis somewhat enjoyed his
uncomfortable outing, for it diverted his mind from his unhappiness
over the Brierfield lawsuit.

In May, while he was in Jackson, Mississippi, on legal business,
telegrams of invitation poured in from Texas. The press announced
his coming to appear at the Agricultural Fair at Houston, before he
had actually consented. So he felt obligated not to disappoint his
friends. At Houston, when Davis stepped out of the train at 7:45 in
the evening of May 10, he received an overwhelming greeting. His
old friend ex-Governor Lubbock was on hand, along with Mayor
J. C. Lord, various distinguished citizens, and the Houston Light
Guards drawn up in military formation. After the Mayor's speech
of welcome and Davis's response, a voice in the crowd yelled "Give

him a Texas cheer, boys," which was rendered with a rousing will.
The party then entered carriages, the Light Guards taking escort
positions in front and rear. The procession proceeded to the residence of his host, Major T. R. Franklin, a well-to-do naturalized
Englishman.

After a day of public appearances an editorial appeared in the
Houston *Chronicle:*

The enthusiasm which the presence of Mr. Davis has inspired among
those in attendance upon our Fair must be very grateful to him, and
doubly so when it is considered that he is now only a private citizen,
wrecked in fortune and stripped of power. . . .

If this man who has been a target for criticism, who was the head and
front of a stupendous failure, *made so by us,* who has been imprisoned
and maligned . . . we say if Jefferson Davis had come among us a President, a Ruler . . . he would not perhaps have been taken so warmly to
the hearts of our people. But as a plain, unostentatious citizen, verging
on his three score years and ten, with his form erect in the pride of his
integrity, and his head unbowed by the recollection of any betrayal of
trust, he has received the warmest tokens of admiration from our people.

Davis wrote his wife on May 15 that he had been "so strongly
urged to go to Austin and Dallas" that he had consented to do so.

The people here in Houston have been more than kind and in general
wish to make it my interest to remain with them. Some propose the Presidency of the Agricultural Mechanical College, which is immediate; others
the Presidency of a Railroad to the Pacific, which is prospective. But I
have declined the first, and nobody has power to offer the second. The
route from Austin to Dallas passes by Bryan, the site of the College, and
gives an opportunity to see it.

As the proposed new railway line would be financed largely by
Northern capital, there was doubt about his being offered the railroad position. But now a special train was put at his command for
his travel in Texas, and the Mayor and City Council of Houston
gave him a gala dinner on Saturday night, before his departure for
Dallas. He wrote Varina:

The weather here is hot, in the sun. The country is beautiful, abounding
in flowers. There is a refined society, a goodly number of old Mississippians and their descendants. The people have a robust, healthy look, and
are cheerful and confident of their future.

Varina feared that her husband's enthusiasm for Texas and the
Texans for him would take the family there to live, and she was

anything but joyous with anticipation. On his sixty-seventh birthday, June 3, she wrote him a letter, in which she said:

When I find myself looking forward with dread to our Texas hegira I feel that our times are short and that I need not care when the evening of mine closes, just so it is calm and finds my day's work done. But I only meant to ask God's blessing upon another year on which you have entered.

Though Davis could sympathize with Varina's tone of melancholy, it saddened him, particularly when he recalled that she was not yet fifty.

A fortnight after her birthday letter, Varina suggested that he might like to go to California for a summer trip—an excursion was coming up which guaranteed the round trip for $180. Jeffy D. Howell, his wife's youngest brother, whom he had reared and loved as a son, now made his headquarters in San Francisco and was the Captain of S. S. *Pacific*. He was eager for a visit from his brother-in-law, and he wrote that he often saw Senator and Mrs. Gwin and many Southerners in California "still devoted to the lost cause," who looked upon Jefferson Davis "as the Representative man of our people." The summer before, when he was commanding the Sandwich Islands steamer in the central Pacific, Jeffy D. said, he could have shown his brother a glorious time, for the present King, Luna-lilo the First, was a great chum of his and had frequently taken him hunting. But Davis had too much on his mind and too little in the bank to think of going to California.*

Though while in Houston Davis had verbally been offered the Presidency of the Texas Agricultural and Mechanical College, he now received a formal offer from Governor Richard Coke, dated June 14, 1875. His salary would be $4,000 a year "with a residence, properly furnished, and as much land as he desired for gardens." The Governor declared that the Texas people "would never cease to love and honor" him, and that he knew of no living man whose

---

* In the autumn of 1875, while commanding the old passenger ship *Pacific* on the run between Seattle and San Francisco, Jeffy D. Howell lost his life. On Thursday, November 4, shortly after clearing the harbor of Seattle in a fog, the *Pacific* was run into by a sailing vessel and both ships were wrecked. Captain Howell got his three hundred passengers and the crew into lifeboats and rafts. Then he stripped to his underwear for swimming and stayed with his ship until she sank. He managed to reach a small raft, with an old lady who had insisted on clinging to him. Finally, after four nights and three days of exposure, cold, sleeplessness, and hunger, his strength gave out and he was swept into the sea. When his body was washed ashore, a gold ring was taken from his finger and sent to the grief-stricken Varina.

name and efforts could do so much towards accomplishing the
building up of the college.

Gratified by the warm tone of Coke's letter, for a month Davis
considered accepting the position. In the meantime his family protested stoutly that the burden would be too great a strain. And
Davis did doubt that his wife could ever become adjusted to the
searing heat of Texas and the isolation of Bryan.

When it became generally known in Mississippi that the Presidency of Texas A and M had been offered him, Davis received
many letters and many callers insisting that he decline and spend
the balance of his life in Mississippi. An alluring new prospect was
presented. Some men in Vicksburg and New Orleans, who had been
fortunate in salvaging part of their capital from the general wreck-
age, were interested in a newly formed British company, called the
Mississippi Valley Association. Its purposes were to induce European immigration into Mississippi by grants of virgin lands and
to collect from British capitalists £1,500,000 to build merchant
ships to develop direct trade connections between the Mississippi
River region and both England and South America. The scheme
was as yet somewhat nebulous, but Davis was asked to head the
movement on this side of the ocean. A dream of empire still
underlay the surface of Davis's thoughts, and he envisioned the re-
establishment of New Orleans as a queen among seaports and foresaw a bright future for the whole Mississippi Delta.

On July 14 Davis finally declined the Texas offer. It had been a
hard decision, for he felt that Texas was perhaps destined one day
to be "the most useful, most necessary and most important" State
in the Union. In the first week of August Davis wrote the London
members of the Mississippi Valley Association a conditional acceptance if they would make "the needful arrangements for compensation."

Though involved with personal concerns, Davis was keenly interested in the doings of the Mississippi Democratic State Convention, which had met in Jackson on August 3, 1875. L. Q. C. Lamar,
a delegate from Lafayette County, was an eloquent leader in every
movement. Davis read of his great speeches on the convention floor,
which served as "a bugle call to action" for the white people to
throw off the oppressive yoke that was destroying them. On August
15, 1875, the Executive Committee issued a printed address to the
people of the State. It was a bitter arraignment of the current situation and in no uncertain terms it spoke of "a Governor who is an

alien and an adventurer." It frankly wrote down the Negro Lieutenant Governor as "patently incompetent and under suspicions of bribery," and explicitly charged that the Negro Superintendent of Education already stood indicted by a Northern grand jury for numerous felonies.

Our legislative halls are controlled by a combination of ignorance and corruption which baffles all hope of reformation. The men who impose our taxes are entirely dissevered in sympathy and interest from those by whom they are paid.

The memorial pointed out that the rate of taxation had been increased more than 1,500 per cent in six years and ended:

The overthrow of such government and the defeat of such a party is the supreme necessity of the hour and has become the duty of every honest man.

Jefferson Davis had silently wondered how his compatriots could have borne so long such oppression without protest. A decade had passed since Lee's surrender at Appomattox and Washington was still protecting corrupt administrations with Federal troops.

Because of the pending lawsuit, Davis spent a large part of the oppressive summer shuttling between Vicksburg and New Orleans hunting up witnesses and overseers' mislaid account books decades old. An even greater bitterness had arisen between the defendants and himself than he had anticipated. Lise, his great-niece, whom he had loved as a daughter, was now under the influence of her new husband as well as her brother; she had written him some letters that hurt him deeply.

Finally, by agreement of counsel, the case was postponed until the October term in chancery. In the meantime Davis was continually being pushed by friends to write his book. Major W. T. Walthall was particularly insistent in wanting to help him. But in his present financial condition Davis could not afford to pay him a salary. However, he wrote, if the courts would only view his law case *without prejudice*, he would have the leisure for work on the history.

Like yourself I have argued against the idea of leaving history to posterity. While admitting that the future historian may alone be able to write without bias and therefore to make a history in the higher sense of the word, surely unless contemporaries furnish the material posterity cannot judge of events and describe their causes.

After the publicity about the crowd-drawing appeal of the ex-President at the Houston Fair, invitations began coming in from Northern states to speak at fall fairs. From Columbus, Indiana, a pressing invitation arrived, professing "a very general sentiment of the highest regard for yourself pervading our community." Davis decided to go as a gesture of conciliation between the two sections. But when it was announced that the Confederacy's leader had been invited to speak at the Bartholomew County Fair, a violent storm of opposition was raised. According to the Columbus *Ledger* the protests came mainly from "the warriors who hired substitutes, or had to go out as hundred days' men. Not many of them ever saw a rebel. Perhaps none of the loyal howlers ever killed one. So they announced that they would set themselves right on that charge by killing Jeff. Davis."

The Fair Committee, however, unanimously stood by their invitation in spite of the threats, but Davis courteously declined. It had been his hope to help draw the two sections together, he said, not separate them further.

From the Winnebago County Agriculture Society of Rockford, Illinois, came an invitation to speak at their exposition on September 14. For an hour's address the honorarium would be $400. When Davis did not reply promptly, a second invitation arrived, guaranteeing him "a grand ovation of 40,000 hearers, and a compensation of $500."

Davis accepted in good faith. But the announcement that the former Confederate President was to appear at the fair aroused such unexpected opposition from some Grand Army veterans that the Committee felt it wise to cancel the engagement, lest "a single word might be spoken to offend Mr. Davis."

So Davis sent a tactful telegram revoking his acceptance; and in a letter he expressed his eagerness "as in former years to promote the interest of our great Valley of the Mississippi and believing that with mutual confidence and intelligence much could be done for their advancement." "My only regret," he added, "is the loss of opportunity to promote public interest."

Letters from Northern strangers arrived, deploring the fact that Davis would not appear at the Winnebago Fair and condemning the manifestation of ill will. One, dated August 20, 1875, from an ex-Union soldier, J. V. Admire, the Postmaster of North Topeka, Kansas, declared that the sentiments that dictated Davis's acceptance were "noble and generous."

Those who were seriously displeased, forty-nine times in fifty, are political prostitutes, who thrive upon a popular frenzy towards which they contribute as much zeal as they manifested in keeping out of all danger during the war. . . .

We hope the day is not distant when all attempts to foster this bitterness will be frowned down.

In early September, just as Davis was preparing to leave on a speaking tour in Missouri to work up interest in the Mississippi Valley Association, James Redpath, the well-known lecture manager, came to Memphis to try to engage him for a speaking tour in the East. Unfortunately, Davis was too occupied to receive Redpath at his house or call at his hotel. He sent a courteous note of explanation and said he was leaving on the "Memphis and Ohio" for St. Louis at noon and wondered if they might be fellow passengers.

In the talk on the train the men took a liking to each other. Redpath, who had been born in England and emigrated to America when he was eighteen, had been an ardent Abolitionist. After serving as war correspondent for the New York *Tribune,* he had become Superintendent of Education in South Carolina, where he had established colored schools and orphanages. But with the recent show of hostility to him in the Midwest, Davis did not feel the time was propitious for him to lecture in the East. He could not have suspected that a man of such different background as Redpath would become his admiring friend and within a few years would be staying with him and assisting him in preparing commissioned articles.

On this western journey Davis was accompanied by a reporter from the Memphis *Appeal* and also by his own handsome eighteen-year-old son Jeff, whom he had asked the authorities at V.M.I. to excuse for a late arrival in the fall term. Now, as Davis wrote his wife from the Southern Hotel in St. Louis on September 9, "Jeff seemed to enjoy himself everywhere and behaved generally in a quiet, decorous manner."

On September 8 Davis had spoken at an agricultural fair in De Soto, and that evening he had traveled to St. Louis intending to stay only the night. But according to both the St. Louis *Dispatch* and the *Republican,* he was prevailed upon to remain an extra day. The papers stated that he spent the day receiving visitors and being taken on a tour of the town and to the theater in the evening.

On page two of its September 11, 1875, edition, the New York *Times* carried seven columns of liberal extracts of Davis's speech at De Soto. The piece was headlined "Jefferson Davis—His Address

in Missouri—A Tribute to Early Settlers—The Mississippi Valley and
Its Resources." While there was nothing political in any of the Missouri speeches, New York was concerned because Davis was advocating direct trade between the Mississippi River towns and Europe and South America, thus by-passing New York and avoiding
transshipment. Freight rates by boat, Davis said, were only one-third
as expensive as by railroad. He urged a bond of union of all the
Northern and Southern peoples of the Mississippi Valley. He hoped
that sturdy Europeans would be invited to settle among them. And
he strongly "urged the necessity of education for everybody, from
the highest to the lowest, and advocated the establishment in the
Mississippi Valley of at least one great University."

In conclusion Davis said to his enthusiastic hearers:

Let me express the heartfelt wish that all your days may be days of
happiness, that all your paths may be those of peace, that your future may
be equal to that grand development of which I believe your country capable. And though I, with many years upon my head and trials which
have multiplied the drain upon my life, cannot hope to see consummated,
I shall die praying for you, men, women and children, every good of
which you are worthy.

After speaking to ten thousand persons in Fulton, Missouri, the
ex-President, with Jeff, went to visit the Governor of Missouri at
Jefferson City. He had no rest en route, for passengers continually
came up to greet him. By the time he reached the capital he was
hoarse from talking on the train and speaking in the open air. But
in Kansas City on the fourteenth he spoke before fifteen thousand
at another fair. And he was feeling "much improved in health,"
though he had only time to send Varina eight brief lines after midnight, when husky Jeff was sound asleep.

On the morning of the eighteenth father and son left for Denver.
Later, by stagecoach in a severe snowstorm, Davis drove to inspect
a mine situated 10,500 feet above the sea. At Clear Creek Canyon
the mountains towering above were already thick with new snow
and the air so cold that even Jeff was glad to hover around the
stove. Davis could write Varina sincerely, "I am quite well, much
better than when we parted." Did it ever occur to him that he was
almost invariably in better condition when he got away from his
wife's constant concern about his health and her own? When he left
Memphis she had been suffering from "spells of suffocation" that

would last fifteen or twenty minutes and put the entire family into a fright.

At Manitou Springs, the fashionable health resort for asthmatic and consumptive patients, Davis visited some old friends. While there, invitations from Kentucky arrived, urging him to visit his birthplace at Fairview during the October fair. On October 9 there was a mighty demonstration at the fairgrounds when Jefferson Davis appeared and made a brief speech. Kentuckians gave him an ovation even beyond that of the Texans. He wrote Varina:

The reception here has surpassed anything I could have expected . . . a wild burst of affection exceeding anything I ever had before.

Women who had lost and suffered and bearded men who have served in battle melt into tears and vainly try to express their love.

It was his first visit to his birthplace since he had left it at the age of two. When he went to see the log house of his babyhood, a very old woman, who had been a teen-age hired girl in the Davis family, showed him the very corner where stood the bed in which he was born, and she pointed out the exact location of his crib. It was a moving and exhilarating experience, and Davis returned to Memphis in good spirits, though nothing concerning his affairs was conclusive and he was still more or less floating uprooted.

On a business trip to Montgomery, Alabama, on November 16, Davis on impulse went down to the Gulf Coast to see the lots his wife had long ago selected for their future home when he would retire from the United States Senate. He arrived in the night and took a room at a little inn in the village called Mississippi City near Biloxi. He rose early and walked to the beach. "The moaning of the winds among the trees," he wrote Varina, "gave me a sense of rest and peace which made me wish to lay me down and be at home until this trial is past." After breakfast he hired a horse and buggy and inspected his undeveloped property. The fence was entirely gone and the bushes were so thick that he doubted whether the clearing work he had paid for had ever been done. He drove on towards Biloxi to call on Mrs. Sarah Dorsey at her small estate "Beauvoir." But the lady, whom he had known well as a girl in Natchez, had departed for her Louisiana plantation the previous Saturday. "It is a fine place," he wrote. It had a "large and beautiful house, and many orange trees yet full of fruit." Davis, standing alone on the cultivated space of land between the house and the beach in the shadow of spreading live oaks, fell in love with Beauvoir on that day, November 18, 1875, not dreaming that he would spend the last dozen years of his life there and die in legal possession.

Now he only felt that the pervading silence was sweet and good. With that stillness, made more perceptible by the gently heaving sea, Davis felt that silence was for prayer and in its very self was like a prayer. What a blessed place this might be in which to take refuge from the obtrusive world, from conversations that bored him, from recurrent poisoned attacks on the lips of Northern politicians. It was this sweetness of solitude, this peaceful oblivion that Davis craved above all else.

Just as Jefferson Davis could not divine that this sight of Beauvoir pointed to the greatest future blessing in his long and fateful life, so he had no conception that a domestic event of New Year's Day, 1876, was to prove an invaluable boon to his declining years. At the unorthodox hour of nine o'clock in the morning he gave his lovely daughter Margaret in marriage at St. Lazarus Episcopal Church in Memphis. The groom was a young bank cashier named J. Addison Hayes, whose future was unpredictable. But he was to turn out to be as perfect a son-in-law as a man could desire. Hayes, from a North Carolina family, was all that could be asked for in blood and breeding. He was also as selfless as he was able, and later he would become affluent. Davis had had a father's natural distrust in giving over his adored "Pollie" to any other man's authority. He had noted her scores of beaux and gentlemen callers and wondered who would win her. She had unerringly chosen the best.

The odd hour of 9:00 A.M. had been set because of train and honeymoon schedule. But Varina had insisted on a full-scale wedding with bridal veil and a dozen attendants. The elegant white silk Worth wedding gown made for Margaret Howell had needed only slight alterations. Though the invitations were so numerous that the packed church could not hold all the guests, those asked to the wedding breakfast at the Davis home after the ceremony were confined for economy's sake to the families and the wedding party. The marriage of the Confederate President's daughter was a news item of national interest and was carried in papers throughout the land.

A few days after his daughter's marriage Davis learned in Vicksburg that the presiding judge of the chancery court had decided the Brierfield case against him on the ground of estoppel, a bar preventing a party from asserting a claim inconsistent with a position previously taken. If he had been able to sue immediately upon knowing the contents of Joseph's will, estoppel could not have been introduced by the opposing lawyers. "As it was," Davis wrote his wife on January 11, 1876, "the Chancellor had argued the merits of the case in such a manner as to suggest either bribery or political consideration. He misstated testimony and omitted every fact in our favor." But Davis expected his lawyers to take the case to the Mississippi Supreme Court, "where," he said hopefully, "unless our *luck* runs as heretofore we may expect the decree of the Chancellor to be reversed."

Almost exactly contemporaneous with his defeat in chancery came a poisonous attack from a Radical Republican Senator that was more of a national press item than Maggie's wedding. With the approach of the eleventh anniversary of the war's end a universal amnesty bill, which would restore civil rights to all Confederates, was before Congress. The country expected its passage; Jefferson Davis's lost citizenship would be restored, rendering him once more eligible to Federal office. At the last hour, James G. Blaine, Senator from Maine, whose ambition was to be the next President of the United States, rose to attract publicity for himself. He offered an amendment to include the words: "With the exception of Jefferson Davis."

A storm of protest immediately raged in the Border and Southern States. John Preston of Kentucky presented to his State Legislature a resolution that Kentucky should not participate in the 1876 Centennial until there was *universal* amnesty. One Kentucky paper declared: "The idea of making Jefferson Davis a vicarious sufferer for acts for which he is no more answerable than thousands of his followers is one which every honorable Southern man will resent." Despite the protests, Blaine would not be moved from his position. He seized the chance to display his famed eloquence and further vent his vindictiveness.

While Senators listened in astonishment, on January 9, 1876, Blaine launched upon the bloodiest bloody-shirt waving since Appomattox. He charged that Davis was "the author, knowingly, deliberately, guiltily, and wilfully of the gigantic murders and crimes of Andersonville prison, in comparison with which I here before God measuring my words, knowing their full extent and import, declare that neither the deeds of the Duke of Alva in the Low Countries, nor the massacre of St. Bartholomew, nor the thumb screws and engines of torture of the Spanish Inquisition, begin to compare in atrocity." Davis, he claimed, had deliberately sent Winder to Andersonville "to construct that den of horrors." He avowed that Davis, "by a wink of his eye, by a wave of his hand, by a nod of his head," could have stopped that atrocity. He ended with a melodramatic protest "against crowning with the honors of full American citizenship the man who organized that murder."

Blaine, like Seward, keenly realized the power of printed words in the press to stir the public, and he expected his speech to win him the Republican nomination. He knew perfectly well that Davis was in no sense responsible for the unavoidable conditions of Andersonville. He knew by Federal statistics that proportionately more Southerners had died in Northern prisons than Northern prisoners in Southern camps. He was aware that Stanton and Grant were responsible for the suffering on both sides because of their refusal to exchange prisoners. He could easily recall that during the three months of Wirz's trial, even though 160 witnesses, most of them suborned, had testified, not one unrefuted sentence had been found to connect Davis with the suffering.

Listening in shocked amazement to Blaine's outrageous display of demagoguery, Senator Benjamin Hill of Georgia got control of his emotions sufficiently to rise on the floor to answer Blaine with withering contempt. He pointed out that when Wirz was offered life and liberty upon the one condition that he would implicate the Confederate President in the crime of which he stood accused, the prisoner had gallantly replied, "I would not become a traitor against Davis or anybody else, even to save my life." Hill quoted Wirz's confession to Father Boyle just before his hanging: "I do not know anything about Jefferson Davis." "What Wirz would not do *to save his life*," proclaimed Hill with devastating effect, "Mr. Blaine would do *to secure a political office.*"

Davis's defenders were by no means all Southerners. Senator Samuel S. Cox of New York prepared a derisive reply to Blaine and delivered it on the Senate floor, January 10, 1876. He seized the opportunity to blast the whole Reconstruction policy as manipulated by the Radicals. Indeed, his attack on the Federal Administration was perhaps stronger than anything a Southerner had ever made.

Ten years after the termination of war, the Radical Republicans still proposed the bad rule of force and the bravado of brigadiers to coerce

States and upturn established institutions. Though it often babbled of concord and made festive speeches about fraternal feeling it returned to the low instincts of party advantage and discordant legislation.

Poison, not oil, was poured into the South's unhealed wounds of war. . . . Undisciplined ravage and reprisals of fraud were followed by rancor and unrest. The friends of the Radicals actually talked extermination, but the better angels of our nature fled aghast from the spectacle.

When a great scholar wrote to the conquering Charlemagne how to treat the subjugated Huns, his advice was: First, send gentle-mannered men among them. Second, do not require the tithe. Better lose the tithe than prejudice the people. Treat mortals with kindness. One sacred stream flows for us all.

But when the Federal Congress sent its decrees to the South and the emissaries of discord to execute them, it was a question which was the worse curse, the agents of the Government or the fraudulent taxes! . . . No forgiveness to the enemy, no measures of moderation.

Then came the juggling pretenses of amnesty; now and then, for treachery and party service, individual disabilities were removed. During this decade of wrong, outraging every lesson of history and every tenet of political philosophy, every code of humane law and every attribute of divine justice, most of the leading men of the stricken South remained disabled.

Then Senator Cox directly accused Blaine of "partisan services and base treachery to recruit his failing ranks." He declared that Blaine in his attack on Davis "had made the invidious exception that marred the general harmony which was about to pervade the land." He charged Blaine with killing the general amnesty bill which included Jefferson Davis "to keep alive the very embers of despair." He ended with an expression of contempt. "The gentleman from Maine is known to be a candidate for the Presidency, but that is no reason why he should be a mean man."

Almost any literate American might understand that the purpose of Blaine's melodramatic tirade was, as James Lyons wrote to Davis, "to mislead the white men of the North and the negroes of the South into voting for him." "Goaded by rage," the Richmonder pointed out that Blaine had a second purpose:

to stain and stir the history of the South and the War, and thus to draw off the attention, if he can, of posterity, as well as the present voter, from the truth; and from the aggressions and vices of his own party.

As letters of indignation poured into his house, Davis took Blaine's outrageous personal attack calmly enough, though he was profoundly gratified by Senator Cox's blasting exposé of the evil intent of Reconstruction. His anxiety now was for the South and the quick removal of its civil disabilities. He wrote to J. Proctor Knott, Chairman of the Committee on Amnesty, urging that the passage of the Amnesty Bill should not be endangered on account of an objection to the inclusion of himself in its provisions. "I express my regret," he said, "that any of my compatriots should suffer by identification with me." Then with a characteristic Davis touch, he wrote:

Further, it may be proper to state that I have no claim to pardon, not having in any way repented, or changed the convictions on which my political course was founded, as well before, as during, and since the war between the States.

Congressman Knott found Davis's letter "perfectly consistent with the genuine dignity and manliness, illustrated by your whole career, public and private." "If," he wrote him, "you knew me personally, it would perhaps be unnecessary for me to assure you that such an exhibition of a chivalrous self-abnegation on your part has increased if possible my admiration of your character."

Of course every intelligent mind in the country understands perfectly well that the objection to embracing you in the provisions of the bill was merely to pander to the meanest passions of the rabble and to furnish materials for the miserable scoundrelly demagogues in ensuing campaigns for the Presidency.

Though the Universal Amnesty Bill was finally passed with Blaine's exclusion of Jefferson Davis, his pernicious tactics had lost him the Republican nomination. However, Blaine was later to hold other high offices, through which his involvement in railroad scandals would make taller headlines than his sensational attack on Jefferson Davis.

CHAPTER XLI

THE DARKEST HOUR—AND
THEN A HAVEN

———⟨◉⟩———

IN FEBRUARY, 1876, Jefferson Davis was in New Orleans conferring with members of the Mississippi Valley Association. He was elected President of the American branch to be established in that city. The work would devolve on him much travel, including an early trip to England. His salary was to be $6,000 with liberal traveling expenses. The Vicksburg members had already sent him $1,000 for initial expenses. On March 2, 1876, he wrote Varina on the new stationery headed:

INTERNATIONAL CHAMBER OF COMMERCE AND
MISSISSIPPI VALLEY SOCIETY

EUROPEAN DEPARTMENT	OFFICE AMERICAN DEPARTMENT
OFFICE, LONDON, ENGLAND	33 CAMP ST., NEW ORLEANS
HON. JOHN CROSSLEY, PRESIDENT	HON. JEFFERSON DAVIS, PRESIDENT

Finally it was arranged for Davis to sail in May to consult with the English directors of the Association. In the meantime he prepared suggestions for the new company and attended to many unpleasant details in regard to the Brierfield lawsuit that had gone to the Supreme Court. To economize he took a ground-floor parlor-and-bedroom suite in a house on Bourbon Street, two blocks from Canal. In better days it had been the home of a friend, but now it was owned by a respectable mulatto woman. J. U. Payne, his factor and close friend, unreconciled to the ex-President's new living conditions, begged him to take his guest room. But he gently declined, saying that he worked at his office all day and really only slept at his apartment.

On the evening of March 21, Mr. Davis took Mary Stamps to see the new American stage star, Mary Anderson, who was only sixteen

415

and who had become famous overnight in the preceding year when she had made her debut in Louisville as Juliet. Davis found her "tall and beautiful, with a fine, deep voice," but "somewhat untrained," though she "showed great power under excitement." In writing Varina of his only "lark," he said, "My mind ran back, when looking at her in high passion, to what Fanny Kemble was in her youth." He did not say that Mary Anderson in her classic beauty bore a striking resemblance to Mary Stamps.

Thornton Montgomery, the elder of Ben's sons, came down from Davis Bend to see him, because his father and he had again failed to pay the drafts that had been taken in settlement the year before. The low price of cotton was the excuse, and partially accounted for the failure. Philosophically, Davis wrote his agitated wife:

When what would be satisfactory cannot be had, it only remains to take the best which is attainable. My dear, dear Winnie, be patient. You have heard there is luck in leisure; perhaps by taking the latter we may gain the former.

Davis was obliged to make one last trip to Vicksburg before going abroad. After conferring with his attorney, he wrote encouragingly:

Pittman is sanguine of the decision by the Supreme Court. We have Chalmers in the place of the "Yankee" Tarbell, and Campbell in place of the Radical Payton, and may hope for *justice,* if there be such a thing in this world to those who have only the right for their might.

In the last week before sailing, Varina finally made up her mind to accompany her husband to Europe. He was glad, because he feared she might not recover her health unless she got entirely away from the South and its bitter memories. On May 24, Davis, with his wife and eleven-year-old daughter Winnie, sailed for Liverpool on the S. S. *Memphis.*

England was inexpressibly lovely at the June climax of bloom when Davis went to stay with the George Campbells at their country place in Surrey not far from London. He needed counsel before he met with the British officers of the Mississippi Valley Association. Mrs. Davis and Winnie would remain with Margaret de Stöess in Liverpool for a while, and then he would seek lodgings for them all in London. Davis's talks with Campbell hinted at probable disappointments to come. And when he did meet with the Executive Committee, he was anything but assured.

The splendid scheme for developing trade between the Mississippi Valley and England and South America had proved too visionary to attract much British capital. And Northern interests had frowned on the undertaking. The promise of merchant ships, which the Southerners expected the English to provide, was not met. Though Davis was to stay on for four months trying to right affairs, he began to realize, after delays and failures of committee-men to attend meetings, that his dream of bringing prosperity to the Mississippi Valley might come to naught.

While this dark situation was unfolding, the Davises settled in a furnished apartment at 78 Upper Gloucester Place, Dorset Square. With the accumulation of disappointments, Varina collapsed in July and became so painfully ill that for weeks she could not bear to have her husband leave her side. The doctors said this and that. But she was suffering from that most corroding of diseases: despair.

Her husband, relying on those spiritual sources that had sustained him in prison, remained erect. And now the problem of Winnie's education also confronted the parents. An unusual decision was reached: Winnie would enter the Misses Friedlander's School for Girls in Carlsruhe, Germany. The establishment had impeccable recommendations; it was under the patronage of Her Highness, Luise, Grand Duchess of Baden, and daughter of Kaiser Wilhelm I of Prussia. The royal palace was only a few blocks from the school. Emily Mason in Paris approved. It was often the custom of well-to-do Americans in the last half of the nineteenth century to give their teen-age daughters a season or two of European education. Several Southern girls of prominent families attended the Carlsruhe school, among them a playmate of Winnie's from Memphis, Pinnie Meredith, who was at this time their guest in London. And Mrs. Davis hoped that some special blessing would come from Winnie's education in an exclusive continental school.

Davis was certain that Winnie had the capabilities of profiting by the regime of the German establishment. She was remarkably bright and imaginative, and, except for her inability to spell cor-rectly or punctuate, quite advanced for her years. Although shy, she was somewhat full of herself and desirous of attention. Davis thought it well for his little girl to get away from her mother, who was inclined to smother her with constant solicitude for her health. But he felt a pang at the thought of a long separation. Because he could not leave his wife prostrate in bed in London, he sent Winnie to Carlsruhe with a friend and had to say goodbye at the London station. He would never forget her "sad little face, as she sat crouch-

ing in the corner of the railway carriage, too absorbed in her grief
to notice his last salutation."

In one of her early letters to her mother from Carlsruhe, signed
"your loving Baby," Davis noted Winnie's acute homesickness, as
well as her description of new wonders. He feared that she might
find the transition from childhood to adolescence peculiarly difficult.

We went to see the Emperor today as a school and all stood in a row,
the little children had reaths on their heads but we went in black dresses
and our uniform hats (which are dark bleu with cock feathers) we had
flowers and we had to throw them but we all missed them so we picked
them up and threw them to the Crown Prince and we missed him, so I
got a rose for you which I send. It is very cold heare and you remember
how I used to put my feet on you at night, well I cant do it now so I must
take my bibel to bed with me and when it gets warm I put my hand on it
and try to think it is you. I have done some thing that gives me great
hope I prayed very hard that you and father would be hear in a month
and so I asked the Lord to let me know by the Bible, if I saw yes it would
be yes if no—no, and it came yes 3 or 4 times, and I was so glad.

The "season" in London with all its delightful entertainments
had passed and Davis had accepted virtually no invitations, for he
was more or less immobilized at his wife's bedside for weeks. He
could not afford a nurse, and Varina was miserable if he left her.

During this distressful period Davis gradually admitted to himself the defeat of all his brave plans for enriching the region of the
Mississippi River and helping to make New Orleans one of the
world's outstanding ports. He had done all he could for his family
in the way of business. None of his efforts had prospered. Circumstances had played against him at every point. Though he
sought valiantly to cheer his desponding wife, his own heart was
like lead.

Now there was nothing left for him but to write his book explaining to the world the Cause of the Confederacy. He determined
to return to America and begin the work. If he could not provide
properly for his family or boost the economic state of the South,
he might at least do something for the morale of the Southern people.

In October Davis was finally able to leave Varina and go to
Carlsruhe to visit Winnanne, while his wife recuperated at the de
Stöess home in Liverpool. Miss Rosalie Friedlander, the headmistress, insisted on his being a guest in her house. He spent the
evening of October 30 in the midst of the pupils, whom he found

"very genteel and showing affectionate regard for each other." The girls were charmed by the Confederate President. Winnie had gained in weight, was quite well, and seemed content. The next morning before breakfast she came into his bedroom to give him a morning kiss, just like old times.

Davis was pleased with everything about the school and impressed by the beauty and elegance of Carlsruhe's park, which stretched up to the Duke of Baden's palace, and where the girls often walked. As he prepared for his return journey to England, he could honestly write Varina—as he did in scores of extant letters—"I am better than when we parted." He was glad to discover that Winnie, who was sometimes recalcitrant, was really a favorite with the Friedlanders, who knew how to handle her. He felt convinced that his child was in the right school.

When the business arrangements in London seemed to end in total failure and profound apologies from the Britishers, Davis sailed home on the *Adriatic* in mid-November, leaving his wife boarding with the de Stöesses in Liverpool. On the ship he reread Thackeray's *The Newcomes* and wrote an encouraging letter to Varina, begging her to relax and to leave the cares of the family to him. As usual, the sea voyage lifted his spirits.

When he arrived in Memphis, Margaret Hayes and young Jeff found their father looking better than they had seen him since the war, and far more cheerful than they could have thought possible under the existing circumstances.

In Vicksburg he learned that plantation affairs had again gone badly and that there would be no cash. On December 9 he reported to the Board of the Mississippi Valley Society in New Orleans on the strange tergiversation of the London members. His news was received with more disappointment than indignation and it was decided to wait for the plan of some Trust and Loan Company the Britishers now wanted to substitute.

Boyle, in Memphis, to whom Davis had turned over money to lend at safe interest, was now being hounded by some "Yankee" lawyers, who seemed bent on ruining Davis as well as Boyle. The latter was shortly forced into bankruptcy. Davis had really reached the end of his row. He would start work on his book. Major Walthall was ready and eagerly waiting. Appletons, the New York publishers, were prepared to pay advances for Walthall's assistance. But where was Davis to find the quiet place in which to write?

. . .

Everywhere he went he heard excited chatter about the November election and fresh disclosures of corruption among officials of the Grant Administration. The shaking of heads and the wagging of tongues were manifest across the continent. Though Grant was deemed innocent of rascality himself, he had apparently chosen a goodly number of rogues for his friends. Energetic Northern papers rehashed uncomplimentary stories like that of the President's driving about Washington behind horses caparisoned in magnificent harness with breastplates of gold engraved with Grant's name. This harness was a gift from his friend General John McDonald, supervisor of internal revenue at St. Louis and chief manipulator of the scandalous "Whisky Ring" conspiracy, formed by distillers to defraud the Treasury of internal revenue and to line their own pockets. Charges of guilt had pointed a relentless finger at Grant's Private Secretary, General O. E. Babcock; only the President's intervention had saved him from disgrace and prison.

A House investigation had disclosed that Grant's Secretary of War, William W. Belknap, had taken bribes for selling trading posts in the Indian Territory. He had been impeached but had resigned immediately to avoid trial. Grant's Minister to the Court of St. James, R. C. Schenck, was so involved in the Emma Mine Scandal that when the President attempted to save his appointee's skin, the New York *Tribune* acidly remarked that "General Grant always stands by a friend in trouble, though it involves the Government in disgrace." And railroad scandals, in which James G. Blaine was implicated, were pointed up as perhaps the worst of all. The flamboyant Blaine, who had expected to be the next President, was now pilloried in cartoons.

These exposés of roguery among Grant appointees had seriously damaged the Radical Republicans. A large contingent of the North's voters, revolted by the prolonged vindictive treatment of the South, was eager to vote Democratic. Conditions in the Southern States during the last year, as Davis noted, had, however, already improved considerably. As Professor J. G. Randall eventually wrote: "In spite of the Grant administration, self rule by conservative whites in the South had gradually been obtaining control of State governments." At the time of the 1876 election only three Southern States remained completely under Radical and military rule: South Carolina, Florida, and Louisiana.

Davis, who had been in England on the last election day, learned immediately on his return that the Democratic candidate, Samuel

J. Tilden of New York, had received a quarter of a million more votes than Republican Rutherford B. Hayes of Ohio, as well as a significant electoral percentage. The morning after the election the New York *Tribune* had displayed a banner headline "Tilden Elected." But the *Times,* which had become fanatically Republican, urged the party leaders not to concede yet.

Emboldened by the powerful *Times,* the Republicans claimed election irregularities in Florida, Louisiana, and South Carolina. But even without the electoral votes of these normally Democratic States, Tilden lacked just one vote of having the necessary 185 for a majority. The decision was held in abeyance until the Republican election boards of the three Southern States could throw out enough Democratic votes to give all three States to Hayes. Davis wrote his wife from the St. Charles Hotel in New Orleans on the night of December 9:

The excitement over the fraud in counting the vote of Louisiana is intense here, but they have become accustomed to injustice and will suffer long.

The next day Davis left to visit some relatives near Biloxi and to try to find a quiet place in which to write undisturbed. Again he inspected his lots near Mississippi City and hired a man to clear out the underbrush. He considered putting up a small cottage, although the last thing that Varina had said to him when he left England was "do not get a house on the Gulf Coast." While he was in a perplexing quandary, fortune smiled in a most unexpected way. Mrs. Sarah Dorsey, hearing that Mr. Davis was in the vicinity, invited him for a visit at Beauvoir. Her husband had died earlier that year and her cousin, Mrs. Cochran, also an old friend of the Davises, was living with her.

Davis had known Sarah Dorsey since she was a child. She was the daughter of a rich Louisiana planter, who also had properties in Mississippi and Arkansas and maintained a home in Natchez. Not only had she been a girlhood friend of Varina, but she had often visited the Joseph Davises at Hurricane. On one side her ancestry went back to the Northumberland Percys. Her education had been completed in England, where she had made many friends among the British nobility. In 1853 she had married one of her father's overseers, Samuel Worthington Dorsey, a Marylander of good family. After the death of her parents, Dorsey had managed her properties well. Sarah Dorsey was as ardent a Confederate as Mrs. R. E. Lee, and even after the war, in 1871, she had stoutly upheld the Confederate cause in London drawing rooms. In that year she had known Thomas Carlyle and Christina Rossetti well, and had met Judah P. Benjamin for the first time. She corresponded with pundits in India. Four books of hers had been published under the pen name of Filia. After her husband's death, a few months before Jefferson Davis returned to the States, Mrs. Dorsey had rented her Louisiana plantations and decided to make Beauvoir her permanent home.

When Davis arrived at Beauvoir as a guest in mid-December he was again struck by its pervading peace. The immediate grounds were extensive, shaded by magnolias, cedars, and live oaks draped in pale gray moss. The sea stretched before the house and a large orange grove lay behind it. Beyond were pine woods traversed by a clear brook, its banks a tangle of bay, wild azalea, sweet olive, and yellow jasmine. Then came six acres of scuppernong vineyards and beyond those the Louisville and Nashville Railroad cut through the property. Across the tracks stretched a virgin forest of long-leaf pine, which belonged to the 600 acre estate.

When Mrs. Dorsey learned that Mr. Davis was looking for a retreat in which to write his long-postponed book, she took him to see her east pavilion-cottage. It was a square building of one large room, the roof composed of four triangles meeting in the center. A pillared gallery ran completely around. The back gallery might be enclosed to make a small bedroom and a dressing room. Carpenters could line the walls of the study-sitting-room with bookshelves. Mrs. Dorsey had plenty of good servants, and could provide meals. Davis might work in uninterrupted peace. Would he like to write his book at Beauvoir? his hostess asked.

By offering Mr. Davis a refuge without encumbrances, Mrs. Dorsey relieved him of the embarrassing delay in his program of writing. Here he had at last found the ideal place for his work. He was inexpressibly grateful. But he absolutely insisted on paying for his board. Mrs. Dorsey said that fifty dollars a month would include board for Robert Brown, his faithful one-time body servant, who had taken the Davis children to Canada in 1865 and who was now in Memphis eager to return to his former employer.

Sarah Dorsey looked upon the arrangement as a peculiar blessing to herself. She offered to be Mr. Davis's amanuensis for stated daily hours. A bluestocking with a passion for literature, she did not have the talent to write something she could be really proud of herself, but she could help the ex-President of the Confederacy. With her active intellect she longed for something to anchor her days to. She considered that Jefferson Davis had not been properly appreciated by the Southern people, and she, who had met scores of famous persons, regarded him as "the noblest of all the men she had known." She understood that during the last sixteen years he had been under the most grueling strain, and she felt privileged to provide for his comfort.

While carpenters were renovating the cottage, Mrs. Dorsey found a suitable place in the neighborhood for Major Walthall to live. Walthall had recovered the official letters and documents which in May, 1865, had been left with Mrs. Leovy in South Carolina for hiding. The work would soon be actually under way.

When Davis returned to New Orleans on business just before Christmas, he found that the Congressional committees inquiring into the election in Louisiana filled all the hotels, so he went to stay at Mary Stamps's, where it always seemed restful. On Christmas Eve he wrote Varina all his news and sent the letter to Carlsruhe, where she was spending the holidays with Winnie and expected to remain for an extended stay. It was sad for him to realize, he said, how his loved ones were "scattered far and wide" at this season when families should be together. Though he rarely mentioned politics to her, he wrote:

I will not weary you with details of our political muddle, as it is commonly called, but will give you my hopeful opinion that Tilden will be our next President. The scenes through which we are passing would be ridiculous if less tragical, and may well induce those who doubt the capacity of man for self-government to say I told you so.

By February, 1877, Davis was comfortably settled in the cottage at Beauvoir, and he and Walthall and Sarah Dorsey were working assiduously on the book. The routine at Beauvoir was both peaceful and stimulating.

At long last Jefferson Davis had found a haven. Often, after the revival of sad memories by the writing, he could lie awake at night and find balm in the murmur of the sea rolling up the beach. And in the afternoons, tired from the concentration on composition, he would stroll in the forest, where he found the sighing of the wind in the pines soothing. Sometimes he would take a detour down a path to a fern-bordered spring and sit in meditation.

But Davis was still not free from legal or personal worries. Young

Jeff had done so poorly in his studies at V.M.I. that the authorities had tactfully suggested he be withdrawn. Jeff had gone to Maggie Hayes in Memphis and vainly sought a job there. His father now brought him to Beauvoir to salve his pride in giving him the pretense of helping on the book by taking down occasional dictation. The youth was good-looking, witty, and happy-hearted, but, like his Howell uncles, he seemed to have little aptitude for gainful employment. In commenting on Varina's disappointment in their son, Davis wrote: "My dear, we do not understand the boy, and I fear I never shall."

As had been his custom whenever absent from Varina on their wedding anniversary, he wrote her on February 26, 1877. Though he could be tenderly loving, he could not pretend to be joyous. He spoke of "the goblet of sorrows they had together drained to the dregs."

The world goes wrong with me; men prove false, business affairs turn in other courses than would subserve my interest. The South, our loved country, is misrepresented, cheated, and the fetters of oppression riveted upon her.

And Jefferson Davis shortly found that he had erred in predicting that the Democrat Tilden would be the next President. A new law had been passed in Congress, January 29, 1877, creating an Electoral Commission—five members from the Senate, five from the House, and five from the Supreme Court. It consisted of eight Republicans and seven Democrats. On February 9 the Commission began debating the matter. South Carolina's electoral vote, though Democratic, was given to Hayes. In Louisiana, in one parish alone, some 1,500 Democratic votes were thrown out as illegal, and that state was eventually declared for Hayes. Finally, on March 2, just before inauguration day, Florida was given to Hayes, and by one electoral vote he was declared to be "elected by the will of the people." Though the Democrats had been cheated out of the election, the protests were not as vehement as they might have been, for Hayes had promised the South the absolute end of military rule.

Some Republican commentators assured the public that the action of the Commission rested on "sound constitutional law." But Jefferson Davis groaned to think what injustice could be perpetrated under a twisted interpretation of constitutional law.

On Monday, March 5, 1877, Hayes was duly inaugurated. He named a Cabinet that was free of the now generally detested

Radicals and that included a Tennessean as Postmaster General. He did not delay long in making good his promise to withdraw Federal troops from the South. On April 10, when they decamped from Columbia, South Carolina, the carpetbag Governor also left, after bitterly denouncing Hayes. The State's foremost citizen, Wade Hampton, Davis's close friend, became Governor.

A fortnight later the end of Grant's Radical program came in Louisiana, too, when the last Federal soldier was withdrawn. After twelve years of suffering a humiliating tyranny, the South was finally free for "peaceful self-government," which the new President proclaimed was indeed an "imperative necessity." In his inaugural address Hayes had spoken of the "question of government or no government," of "social order or a return to barbarism." After the twelve years of abuse since the death of Lincoln, it seemed to Davis something like a new language to hear the Northern President say, "it is a question of fellow-citizens and fellow-men."

CHAPTER XLII

"BITTER, BITTER WORK"

IN THE ROUTINE of his quiet work at Beauvoir, Mr. Davis was disturbed by his wife's discontent in Carlsruhe. At first she had stayed in the Misses Friedlanders' guest room and had charmed everybody. But she had gradually come to expect so much service that she began to feel unwelcome, and after two months she moved to a pension. She was not pleased with it. And a letter Davis wrote to Winnie on March 17, 1877, made her the more restless. He spoke of looking hopefully forward to his daughter becoming a well-educated young lady, and "last and greatest, to the formation of a vigorous, healthy constitution."

Knowledge and high aims are to human character what cultivation is to fertile land, the necessary means to keep down noxious weeds. You have an example in Miss Friedlander; who would expect her to be troubled about a ribbon or to engage in gossip and back-biting?

Your Brother Jeff is with me, he reads some French, and some medicine, occasionally writes for me, and seems quite contented here.

I dictate daily for 3 or 4 hours, for a book of reminiscences of my public career. Mrs. Dorsey acts as my amanuensis and Major Walthall assists in compiling and hunting up authorities.

The mention of another woman as his assistant infuriated Varina. She liked to think, and particularly to have the world think, that her husband was entirely dependent upon her. Later, when an interview Mrs. Dorsey had given a reporter appeared, it revealed to the public that she was helping the ex-President with his book. Varina was in a rage. It had not occurred to Sarah Dorsey that she was doing anything offensive to Varina. She had believed that a friendly article in a newspaper would be good publicity both for

426

Mr. Davis and the book in progress. But Varina could not accept it in that light. She thought that Mrs. Dorsey was vaunting herself.

Mrs. Davis had been writing of her continued wretched health—she now was convinced that the trouble was in her spine—and announced her intention to make "a speedy departure from Carlsruhe." So Davis sent his letter of May 1, 1877, to Liverpool. He may have been more tenderly tactful than sincere when he wrote: "You cannot be more anxious to be with us than I am to have you here, but my love bids me to ask you not to embark until you feel able to bear the journey by sea and by land." He suggested that she might find it pleasant to take Winnie to Scotland for the summer. But he reassured her about the Gulf Coast:

You dread the heat and insects here. I am writing by a fire, and sleep without a bar. But, darling, I am not a fixture and you shall live where you will and I can.

The Brierfield law case, he said, had been argued before the Supreme Court of Mississippi and Pittman expected a favorable judgment. But the sudden death of Ben Montgomery had further complicated the tangled affairs of Montgomery and Sons as purchasers of the Hurricane and Brierfield.

Because his mother was so displeased about Mrs. Dorsey's assistance, twenty-year-old Jeff, Jr., wrote her a very loving and appeasing letter on May 7. Jeff, a true Howell, reveled in the easy routine of Beauvoir and found pretty girls aplenty in the neighborhood to keep him entertained, and a niece of Mrs. Dorsey living in the big house was quite taken with him. Jeff knew how well things were going with his father and himself, but he was deeply devoted to his mother.

Father is well—interested in the task of writing. He is looking better than I ever saw him, although very anxious about our darling Mother.

I am reading law and expect to study hard & be a pleasure to my darling Mother, who becomes more and more dear to me everyday— Indeed, Mother, my heart does become so full that I can't express half that I feel or that I know you already know so well.

The other day I longed for you to be behind the door when my Father was talking about you! He told me that you were a woman worthy the worship of any son—I felt just like picking him up and kissing him. . . .

Good night, my all in all, and believe me that I am more affectionate and devoted than any other son was before, Your boy,

Jefferson Davis, Jr.

Mrs. Dorsey remarked that Mr. Davis was deeply concerned about his wife. He worried about what he could do with her if she returned immediately to America in ill-health. So she invited Varina to come and stay at Beauvoir. But Varina did not deign to reply. In a note to Walthall Mrs. Dorsey mentioned that Mr. Davis was in a "very troubled condition of mind."

His movement must be governed by his wife's health and its requisitions. He hates to make the effort to travel—but I shall not be surprised *if he finds himself compelled to cross over to England at any time.*

In the end, however, Varina spent the summer with Winnie and Margaret de Stöess and her two children at Buxton, the English watering resort.

In early June Davis went to Memphis to become acquainted with his first grandchild, who had been named for him. While there, he learned that he had won his Brierfield suit in the Mississippi Supreme Court "in every particular." Then followed the upsetting news that the defendants would not accept the decree, but insisted on having the case "reviewed." This meant more expense and delay, and, in the meantime, there was no income from crops.

Davis had hardly got back to work on the book when his infant grandson died. The young mother was in despair. She needed a change from the sad scene in Memphis and she wanted to be near her father. Mrs. Dorsey lovingly invited Maggie and her husband to spend Addison's July vacation at Beauvoir. They came and stayed in the west *garçonnière*. Davis insisted on paying board for them.

Maggie, who had thought she did not like Mrs. Dorsey and had felt a certain resentment against her "because she preferred the conversation of men to that of women," now became quite fond of her. She wrote her mother of Mrs. Dorsey's solicitous attentions, and said that she believed she would now like the Gulf Coast.

But Varina had no intention of even trying to like this region that her husband found delectable and good for his writing. In a letter of August 2, 1877, she wrote with ill-concealed resentment:

I see by an allusion that you have called your book "Our Cause." I have so often hoped, though so far away, that you would find it necessary as a matter of sympathy to tell me of its plan and scope, and of its progress—but I know I am very far off—and—"other things."

In almost every letter from his absent wife Davis found something to cause him pain and time-absorbing explanations.

Davis wanted Winnie back in America. But Varina was averse to bringing their daughter home with her. In a letter reporting her delight in having Winnie with her at Buxton, Varina declared the child was "in much better health and very much improved in temper and manners too, so biddable, and so cheerful, and so considerate." Then she added:

The place where you desire to live seems to render an education of the higher sort impossible there, and the humid climate of New Orleans is poison for one of her rheumatic tendencies.

The child's "rheumatic tendencies" were something utterly new to the father.

One paragraph really hurt:

Winnie yearns so over her family it is quite touching. She says "Now let us imagine ourselves a little home." She has already bought a little piece of work for "our home" and is busy over it.

After Buxton, Mrs. Davis took rooms in London in September and prepared Winnie for her return to Carlsruhe. She herself, she said, might embark on the *Spain* for New York early in October. About Mrs. Dorsey and Beauvoir she made her feelings acidly clear.

I am sorry not to have written Mrs. Dorsey—but I do not think I could satisfy you and her if I did and therefore am silent. I do not desire ever to see her house—and cannot say so, and therefore have been silent. Nothing on earth would pain me like living in that kind of community in her house. . . . When people here ask me what part of your book she is writing, and such like things, I feel aggravated nearly to death. I have avoided mentioning her in my letters for I felt too angry at the last squib in an illustrated paper to be reasonable. Please thank her for me for her kindness to you all, and excuse my silence as you will.

Varina would not grant her husband's request to cable him when she actually left England. She did not want him to meet her in New York and try to persuade her to come to Beauvoir. In his uncertainty as to her movements he telegraphed Burton Harrison, who was now an established lawyer in New York, to meet the *Spain* when it docked, in case his wife was aboard. Harrison and Constance met the boat, and put Mrs. Davis on the train for Memphis.

Though Davis and Mrs. Dorsey were expecting to receive her at Beauvoir, Varina settled down in Memphis with the Hayeses. As soon as her husband learned of her arrival there, he, with Jeff, Jr., went to see her, hoping to bring her to Beauvoir. But the reunion of husband and wife was not exactly harmonious. Varina refused to be placated, nursed her hurt, and was extremely cool in private. She declared that she would never go to board at Sarah Dorsey's. Davis stayed on about ten days trying to mollify his wife and get her to join him at Beauvoir.

On October 28, 1877, while Davis was in Memphis, Nathan Bedford Forrest was brought to the city in a dying condition from his cotton plantation of President's Island in the Mississippi River. General Dabney Maury told Davis that Forrest had said: "I am completely broke up. I am broke up in fortune, broke in health, broke in spirit." The ex-President went to see his great cavalryman. He was shocked and grieved at his emaciated appearance. Apparently suffering from diabetes, Forrest, who had been a powerful six-footer, had shrunk to one hundred pounds. Davis sat by his bedside and held his hand. Besides their love of the Confederacy, Davis and Forrest had in common the belief that railroads might be the key to the South's prosperity. Though Davis had never got to be head of a railroad as he had hoped, Forrest had been President of the Selma, Marion and Memphis line, which his fierce energy and shrewdness had created and promoted; but in the end he had met with failure. On the evening of the twenty-ninth, Forrest died. He was buried from the Court Street Cumberland Presbyterian Church, which he had joined less than two years before. Jefferson Davis was one of his pallbearers.

Depressed by his wife's attitude and Forrest's sad end, Davis returned to Beauvoir to resume work on his book. Jeff remained in Memphis, where Addison Hayes shortly got him a small position in the bank.

To Mrs. Dorsey's further invitations to stay at Beauvoir, Varina replied not a word. Major Walthall also wrote to her, dilating on how pleasant the routine there was. In a restrained letter she thanked him for telling her how her husband was looking. "He does not often speak of himself," she said, "and I am always more or less anxious about him." She explained that she felt her daughter's health was so precarious that she could not leave her yet: "so I cannot say at what time."

To Connie Harrison in New York Varina wrote with quivering sarcasm on November 7:

In the course of human events I shall go down to Mr. Davis's earthly paradise temporarily. . . . The beauties of nature are for those who either have a hope of reaping the fruits of many seasons, or can make them immortal in verse or color—or else for man haters.

She declared that she herself dearly loved *people;* they acted on her dullness "like steel on flint." "Mr. Davis inclines to the 'gentle hermit of the dale' style of old age—so behold we are a tie—and neither achieves the desired end."

Varina thus revealed the temperamental differences between her husband and herself. She was out of sympathy with his un-worldliness. Being almost eighteen years her senior, he was per-haps too old for her now; and, somewhat shattered in health and broken in heart, he had but one great passion left: to vindicate the South. In the full vigor of her middle age—she was only fifty-one —Varina had little taste to share the scholarly life of a recluse. With a talent for the world, she was conscious of her gifts and aching to use them. Davis was fully aware of her side in the problem of personalities. He well understood that Varina came from hot-blooded, choleric, high-tempered Cavalier stock. And though by temperament she was a jealous and possessive woman, Davis looked upon his wife as an enchanting companion, gay, humorous, and fascinating—when she was in the mood. Conversely, he merely suf-fered in silence when she lost her self-control or was deliberately rude and quarrelsome.

Though Davis had given in to Varina's preferences countless times before, now he refused to tear himself away from the near-ideal conditions for writing. Besides, he knew they did not have enough money to live respectably in a city like Baltimore, where she wanted to reside. But Varina was determined to hold out as long as she could against the inevitable. It was a blow to her pride that she could not pry her husband loose from the Gulf Coast.

During the Christmas holidays of 1877, when General Jubal Early paid a visit to his old Commander at Beauvoir, Mrs. Dorsey ap-proached him on the subject of Mr. Davis's financial condition. During his first year's residence with her, Mrs. Dorsey had become aware of his near-destitution. She had discovered that he had been living on the principal of a small sum he had managed to invest through his nephew-in-law, Congressman Charles Brodhead of Penn-sylvania. She began the conversation with Early on the veranda, and then she asked him to walk with her on the beach, where they could not possibly be overheard. She told him that she felt that she would not live long and that it was her intention to leave her estate to Mr. Davis, but that it must be kept absolutely secret, for he would not permit anything of the kind if it came to his knowledge. From experience, she had learned that any income from plantations, especially those subject to floods, was uncertain at best. She realized that her "tragic hero" craved above everything independence. And she had determined to contribute all she could to save him from that most dreaded of all conditions: financial dependence.

Despite his legal worries and Varina's hold-off attitude, Davis was feeling unusually fit in early 1878. In a birthday letter to Maggie Hayes on February 25, he reported, "Minnie Howell says she never saw me 'so fat'; and I send you *that* as bulletin of my condition."

As an effort to win Varina, Davis sent her a frascata and an orange flower in a letter of March 30, 1878, and wrote: "The air is now perfumed by the blooming orange trees." A few days later Robert brought him a plate of dew-fresh strawberries. They were the first ripe ones of the season; and, following an old Southern superstition, Mr. Davis made a wish on the first bite. He then wrote Varina that he had wished that she would join him.

Robert, who now slept in the narrow dressing room Jeff had occupied, was a great comfort to his master. He wrote to Winnie in Germany that his man was "one of the few of the pattern of old fidelity yet remaining." Robert had so earnestly begged for a likeness of her that he had given him the photograph of her as a flower girl at Maggie's wedding.

After Mrs. Davis had ignored two of her warm invitations, Mrs. Dorsey offered to go in person to Memphis to persuade her to come to Beauvoir. But, on April 18, Varina warned:

There is only one thing, my dear Husband, that I beg of you. Do not—please do not let Mrs. Dorsey come to see me. I cannot see her and do not desire ever to do so again. Besides I do not wish to be uncivil and embarrass you, and I would certainly do so against my will. Let us agree to disagree about her, and I will bear my separation from you as I have the last six months and hope for better times the history being once over.

Though Davis was sorely disturbed by Varina's attitude to his benefactress, his work progressed. And now that he was deep in what his friends continually reminded him was his "duty to posterity," he would not be put off by Varina's displeasure. But he tried to draw her into the writing by appealing to her for help. He really needed her assistance on numerous points. Like himself, she was blessed with an extraordinary memory, and she would always answer clearly to the best of her ability. She even confessed to a "grateful sense of being permitted to help." She rightly warned him against any unnecessary "bandying words" with his critics. She pointed out that it was "the cue of Yankees" to call him and his friends out into innumerable contests; "it confuses and disturbs your mind and their end is answered."

Though Varina had once been convinced that he could never be happy until he had written his defense of the Confederacy and explained his part in it, she now appeared to look upon the book itself with resentful eyes.

I know you must be greatly harassed by painful things and I am mean enough to care nothing for posterity and a great deal for the peace of your declining years. So I heartily regret that you have attempted the history, since it has been, and must ever be, such bitter, *bitter work*.

Varina knew well that there was no romantic attachment between her husband and Mrs. Dorsey, for she was too certain of her hold on him, as well as of his personal probity. But her ostentatious aloofness caused considerable wonderment and whispers of gossip.

Mrs. Dorsey's almost reverential attitude to Jefferson Davis was revealed in a letter to Dudley Mann, April 25, 1878. Mann had hinted to her that he would like to return to America to spend his last years in the neighborhood of his "ever dear" friend. She replied by inviting him to Beauvoir.

I have had the great joy and honor of Mr. Davis' society in my house during the past year. You who appreciate him so truly can comprehend what a privilege this is to me. Mr. Davis feels a sort of responsibility towards me from having been so closely connected in the bonds of dearest amity with my father and his family. He has always kept a kind of oversight of me and now I am left entirely alone and desolate in the world, he is kinder and more considerate than ever. I hope and think that my house will be, at least, *one* of his homes as long as he lives; I am anxious that he should make use of it exactly as if it was his own and should esteem it a great consolation if I could add in any way to his comfort and happiness. So, dear Sir, if you should really choose to come to America in order to be near him you can come to me, *sans ceremonie*. The first desire of both of us will be to make this noblest of men as happy as we can.

Mrs. Dorsey had already entertained a string of prominent Confederates, who had come at Mr. Davis's bidding to clear up certain controversial points for his book. She would put them up for the night or for days, and she enjoyed being hostess at these historical conferences.

Good news came to Davis in a Western Union telegram from Jackson on May 20, 1878. His lawyer, W. B. Pittman, wired: "Your case again decided in your favor. Former decree of Supreme Court stands."

The court held that Jefferson Davis's bill was good and not inequitable, that he was entitled to Brierfield, and that at the same time his children were entitled to the $80,000 in notes that Joseph had bequeathed to them.

It was Mary Stamps's testimony that had swayed the judges; particularly the fact that Joseph Davis had asked her to see his brother in prison to secure his permision to let him sell Brierfield to the Montgomerys. Almost everyone in Mississippi believed the decision just. And even the anti-Davis Chicago *Tribune* declared: "The courts were compelled to decide in favor of Jefferson Davis, because the law was plainly on his side."

Davis could not be overelated at his victory, however, so much bitterness had been stirred up. His once beloved Lise had turned caustic against him. Four years of worry and expense had led up to the final verdict. The Montgomerys had been able to pay only a few interest installments and nothing on the principal. But Brierfield was now again his possession, and he would at least have land to hand down to his son. Because of the bequest to his children the Hurricane property would have to be resurveyed and acreage added to Brierfield.

In a daring effort to bring about a reconciliation with Mrs. Davis, Sarah Dorsey issued invitations to the Gulf Coast gentry to a party in honor of the absent lady. Without knowing whether or not Varina would appear she prepared and garnished her best guest room in the big house.

Varina had long before come to realize that the Hayeses were tired of her, though with customary Southern family politeness they had tried to conceal the fact. Addison Hayes had done all in his power to make her feel at home, and she had written her husband that she "thanked God every day for Addison." But when Maggie invited a young friend to be her house guest, Varina in a huff had moved to Mrs. Allen's boardinghouse. Discontented there, she packed a trunk and arrived at Beauvoir the very morning of the party.

With the guests she put on her most gracious manner, and "reigned with queenly dignity," the phrase used by the New Orleans *Times Democrat,* which sent a reporter to cover the event. None of the company dreamed that just before the guests arrived Varina had lashed out at Sarah Dorsey in an uncontrolled fit of temper and rushed off into the woods, where the agitated hostess sought her out and appeased her. Such storms were generally as quickly over with Varina as a summer squall on the Gulf. Though she had left the whole household shattered by her outburst, she appeared in the drawing room serene and scintillating.

While Varina did not exactly eat humble pie, by August she was settled at Beauvoir as a paying guest. For Mr. Davis's peace of mind and his writing, Mrs. Dorsey made every possible concession. On August 4, 1878, she answered Dudley Mann's queries about his friend's condition.

His health is quite good, and I hope he is started on a peaceful and vigorous old age. He rides horseback occasionally—walks about freely and is interested in everything surrounding him. Mrs. Davis, I regret to say, does not find that the heat of this semi-tropical climate agrees with her health. She suffers from the warm weather, which renews the life of Mr. Davis and which is an absolute necessity for my well-being. We see many people who come and go at will. So that Mr. Davis does not suffer from ennui.

Varina's ruffled feathers were gradually smoothed down. She took over Mrs. Dorsey's job as amanuensis and began to find that the Gulf Coast had attractions. After a few weeks at Beauvoir, she could write Emily Mason in Paris:

We may be, I suppose, considered settled here for a long time to come, as Mr. Davis has his material here for his work. We board with Mrs. Dorsey and there is no one else in the house. She has a charming temper and makes us very comfortable, and thus she secures companionship when otherwise she would be alone. I am very fond of her, but do not like the climate. . . . We have won back Brierfeld, but no money with it.

In a letter from young Jeff on September 19 to his father, he said: "I am delighted to know that my darling mother has at last found something that she likes about the Sea Coast. I felt sure she would like it after a while." Jeff was now doing satisfactory work in the Memphis bank, and he was in love with a girl named Bessie Martin.

This letter was the last Jefferson Davis ever received from his son. A virulent form of yellow fever swept up the Delta from New Orleans beyond Memphis, which was put under strict quarantine. During the early days of October the Davises were painfully anxious about their children. In answer to a query of concern, Davis wrote his friend Bishop William M. Green at Sewanee:

We are surrounded here by the dread scourge, which has this season desolated our land. Our children near Memphis are in like condition; but a merciful Providence has thus far spared them. We ask your prayers for further safety.

One afternoon an ominous telegram was delivered to Mr. Davis's study. It was from Addison Hayes. Young Jeff was stricken with the fever. The next day Davis sent an emphatic refusal to the proposition that his "dear little Pollie" should attempt to nurse her brother. Professional nurses should assume the case, he said, "under Addison's watchfulness."

Powerless to aid and fretting under the restraints which keep us from you all, our misery may be imagined.

Give my heart's tenderest love to my dear daughter and son, if he can safely receive a message from his father, who would willingly die to save him.

Because of quarantine regulations, Davis, who was not well at the time, could not go to his son's bedside. Major Walthall, who had had experience with the disease, valiantly volunteered to try to reach him, and did slip through the quarantine. Maggie telegraphed almost every day. On October 15 Jeff took a turn for the better, and Maggie wired confidently that the crisis had passed. But on the sixteenth Jeff suffered a violent relapse, though retaining his full faculties. While regarding some bud chrysanthemums a friend had sent him, and holding four of the blossoms in his fevered fingers—two red, one white, one yellow—he suddenly died. Walthall telegraphed the father: "He died quietly and peacefully at five this afternoon. Burial tomorrow at ten."

Jefferson Davis, anguished by the loss of his fourth son, wandered hither and thither about the mansion grounds and through the forest all the next day in search of ease for his grief. On October 18 he penned a note to Addison Hayes, thanking him for all his kind offices. "The last of my sons has left me," he lamented. "I am crushed under such heavy and repeated blows. The many and humble prayers offered before my boy was taken from me are hushed in the despair of my bereavement."

The death of his last son just on the threshold of manhood was the climax of a prolonged series of bitter blows with which Jefferson Davis had been struck. They had begun in 1835 with the loss of his first bride. Then at intervals came the deaths of three young sons. And now when he looked to have a supporting strong arm in his old age—that consolation was snatched from him. The conquest of the Confederacy and his tortured imprisonment he could accept as the machinations of man. But the loss of all of his four sons was something else. This time he could not say, "Thy will be done." Not only had his own prayers gone unheeded, but also those of Bishop Green, the most spiritual of the Episcopal hierarchy, who had been praying that Jeff's life be spared. In a second letter to his son-in-law, at the culmination of questioning grief, Davis seemed to balance precariously on the precipice of doubt.

In her own inconsolable sorrow, the mother became ill with brain fever. For long days and nights Mrs. Davis lay upon what she feared would be her deathbed. Sarah Dorsey gave herself over to constant and tender nursing. For almost a fortnight she did not leave the sickroom except for short intervals. And gradually Varina recovered.

On the evening of November 10, a Mrs. Weed, who had managed to leave Memphis now that frost had come, came to see Mr. Davis. She brought him the four flowers Jeff had been holding in his hand when he died. He sent them as something precious in a letter to Varina, who had gone to help nurse a child relative in another coast town.*

Davis confessed in his letter that he was suffering from an attack of neuralgia, the first in a long, long time. But he found the pain rather welcome for the "distraction it created from less endurable ills." He closed: "With love of many years undimmed by shadows dark as ever fell on man."

It was not until November 27 that Davis could bring himself to write to his little girl in Germany about her brother's death.

I write in the cottage where he and I worked together before he went to take a place in the bank at Memphis. Around me are many objects as-

---

* The four flowers, dried but intact, were found by the author in the letter in Colorado Springs. They may be seen today in a transparent plastic box at Beauvoir, their colors clearly distinguishable, though faded.

sociated with him and dear, very dear, for his sake. I have bowed to the
blows, but in vain have sought for consolation. So many considerations,
not selfish, plead for his longer stay on earth that I only shut my eyes to
what it is not permitted me to see, and stifling the outward flow, let my
wounds bleed inwardly.

Then to cheer her he told her that Robert had just been in and
was pleased to see some recent photographs of her. "He says he
cannot tell you how much he loves you, but hopes you know it."

My dear child, I long for your bright, loving face. In my bereavement
it seems doubly hard to be separated from you. Yet I remember your
stoical heroism when you started from London, and try to feel, as you
spoke, that the necessity for education had to be met.

My darling, my sweet Winanne, may God have you in His Holy keeping prays

Your Father

CHAPTER XLIII

INHERITANCE

———◆◇◆———

DURING THE WEEK of Jeff's fatal illness and those that followed immediately after his death a huge quantity of unopened correspondence had piled up on Mr. Davis's desk. Finally, he began to read his mail, much of which contained material for his book. Senator Hill of Georgia had sent him in October his recollections of three important events: the removal of Joseph Johnston before Atlanta, of Blair's visit to Richmond, and the appointment of the Hampton Roads commissioners. Concerning this last incident Hill had written some years before in a heated controversy with Alexander Stephens. And in his accompanying letter Hill now stated clearly what reliable historians have later pointed up:

It is painful, I confess, to review our Confederate struggle. I am so fully convinced that our failure was the result of unwise cabals against you by some of our leading men, and notably from Georgia, that it is exceedingly unpleasant to me to think of them.

Hill did not need to mention by name Governor Brown, Robert Toombs, and the Stephens brothers. And Davis had abundant evidence that Alexander Stephens even now rarely lost an opportunity to snipe at him, continually misrepresenting facts. In his incredible lack of reality he still blamed Davis for the loss of the war. At the end of his letter, Hill remarked hopefully: "I do not despair of seeing you once more in the Senate of our nation." But Davis had no desire whatever to re-enter the political arena.

Throughout December and January, Davis relieved his grief over his son by plunging even deeper into his literary labors. In February, 1879, while Varina was in Memphis paying her first visit to the Hayeses since she had left, Mrs. Dorsey offered to sell Beauvoir

439

to him. She felt that he had found his right home and she wanted
him to be comfortable in his old age. The property deed was signed
on February 19, 1879. The sale price was $5,500, to be met in three
installments, of which the first was paid immediately.

Though Varina admitted that Mrs. Dorsey had nursed her
through brain fever with "unwearied care," and said that "no one
had ever so nearly approached the skill of her mother," she still
could not completely stifle her resentment. In a letter to Maggie,
Davis commented: "The sick man knows the physician's step, but
when he is well cannot remember his face." Sarah Dorsey realized
that Varina's attitude towards her would always be a problem. She
was selfless enough to be willing to bow herself out of the picture
and out of her home. She would live perhaps on one of her Louisiana plantations. Feeling the need of medical attention, she consulted a physician in New Orleans. She learned that she was suffering from cancer; but she told no one.

Now Davis took note that the political and economic situation in
Mississippi had vastly improved in the two years since Grant. His
friend, L. Q. C. Lamar, who had been seated in the United States
Senate in 1877, had proved both stalwart and diplomatic in pleading the cause of the shattered South and pushing through bills for
public improvements. He had won golden opinions of the North
by his reasonableness and his brilliant eloquence. In March, 1879,
Davis was heartened to read of Lamar's bold defense of him on the
Senate floor. To prevent Davis from getting a Mexican War pension,
Senator George F. Hoar of Massachusetts had waved the bloody
shirt and compared the hero of Buena Vista with the traitor Benedict Arnold. Lamar rose swiftly, and in telling, extemporaneous sentences he nobly fixed Davis forever in his proper place.

Jefferson Davis stands in precisely the position that I stand in, that
every Southern man who believed in the right of a State to secede stands
in. The only difference between myself and Jefferson Davis is that his
exalted character, his preeminent talents, his reputation as a statesman, as
a patriot, and as a soldier, enabled him to take the lead in a cause to
which I consecrated myself.

When Mrs. Davis returned from Memphis and found that her
husband had bought Beauvoir and that Mrs. Dorsey had departed,
she settled down to the inevitable and took an absorbed interest in
his book. Her husband had particular need of her, for Walthall's as-

sistance was interrupted now and then by bouts with ill-health. It was difficult for the three of them to keep down rancor, as they delved into misstatements, alibis, and fabrications of Generals like Joseph Johnston and politicians like Stephens and Hunter. At her husband's dictation, Varina carried on a tremendous correspondence in the search for facts and corroborations of this and that.

Stacks of new material arrived every day: from W. L. Trenholm, Confederate Secretary of the Treasury, General Early, General St. John, Secretary of War Seddon, and scores of others. General Josiah Gorgas sent Davis voluminous pages about the operations of the Ordnance Department, with painstakingly exact numbers of siege guns, rockets, infantry arms, and even to "1,456,190 friction primers and 146,901,250 percussion caps and 56,893 curry combs." *

Seddon, in a detailed letter on various controversial points, admitted that his recommendation of Joseph Johnston for the command of the Army of Tennessee had been a mistake, and that "the President was right in his original misgiving." The entire Cabinet had later urged Johnston's removal, he reiterated, when it realized that Johnston had no intention of holding Atlanta, and Davis had been the last to agree.

From London came a long letter from Judah P. Benjamin, dated February 15, 1879, which strongly strengthened the mass of testimony about the failure of Johnston as a fighting General. One sentence conclusively summed up his peculiar deficiency:

From a close observance of his career I became persuaded that his nervous dread of *losing a battle* would prevent at all times his ability to cope with an enemy of nearly equal strength, and that opportunities would thus constantly be lost which under other commanders would open a plain path to victory.

Prominent persons throughout the South in the late seventies continued to beg Davis to sign whatever amnesty paper was necessary so that he could again represent Mississippi in the United States Senate. In March, 1879, James Lyons pleaded:

Now, my dear beloved friend and leader, let not these Republican villains oppress you and humiliate the South any longer, but come forward as soon as the new Congress meets and ask to be released from the iniqui-

---

* Gorgas prepared this long detailed brochure for Davis's use in his *Rise and Fall* as a labor of love for his Chief. The manuscript remained in the Gorgas family for decades and now is among the Gorgas papers, a gift to the University of Alabama Library.

tous oppression which has been put upon You, but under which we all suffer. If a sacrifice, recollect that it will be another sacrifice for the country for which you have suffered and sacrificed so much.

Later Lyons became somewhat annoyed because Davis refused to ask for pardon, and wrote Walthall of his impatience.

Mr. Davis is in every great quality vastly above the great mass of mankind, and yet he is too self-reliant and has too much contempt for the opinions of those who differ from him. . . . Shakespeare has well described him in his description of Henry the Fifth by his father,

> "He is gracious if he be observed,
> He hath a tear for pity, and a hand
> Open as day for melting charity,
> Yet notwithstanding, being incensed, he is flint."

Please tell Mr. Davis, with my love, that he *must* make the sacrifice, no matter how great—for the South.

When Davis read this comment on himself by his friend Lyons he smiled and agreed with some of it, but strongly denied that he had contempt for opinions that differed with his.

Mrs. Dorsey's cancer proved to be of the fast-killing type, and though she had successfully survived an operation, at the end of June the doctors realized there was no hope. Davis went to her bedside in New Orleans.

Early in the evening of July 3, he was told that she would not last the night. She had been expecting the end for days, and was "resigned, calm and hopeful, and at peace with the world." Davis sat by her side when she received Holy Communion. Then with a pencil and a pad, at her request, he noted down certain deathbed bequests to nieces, cousins, friends, servants: a silver pitcher and a special set of china here, a glass bowl and a painting there, a sum of money to this servant and that. She assured him—as she stated in her will—that she owed absolutely nothing to her brothers. She had given them money and property in the past, and, in her opinion, they had proved ungrateful and had squandered her gifts. Even after she was unable to converse, her mind remained clear and composed. She asked Davis to repeat the Beatitudes to her, and at the end of each verse she would gently nod her head. At four o'clock in the morning of the fourth of July, she ceased to breathe.

Later that day Davis wrote Walthall asking him to compose an obituary notice for the *Sea Shore Gazette* and "any other papers you may choose."

You know more than most others how self-sacrificing she was, how noble in sentiment, how grand in intellect, but you cannot know how deeply grateful I am for her years of unvarying kindness and service. And therefore cannot realize how sorrowfully I feel her loss.

Jefferson Davis accompanied the body on the river boat to Natchez, where Sarah Dorsey was buried beside her husband in the family plot.

When Mrs. Dorsey's New Orleans lawyer read the will, Davis learned that she had left Beauvoir to him. And more, she had left him everything she possessed, including three plantations in Louisiana. Her will stated with extreme clarity:

I owe no obligation of any sort whatever to any relative of my own. I have done all I could for them. . . .

I therefore give and bequeath all my property, real, personal, and mixed, wherever located and situated, wholly and entirely, without hindrance or qualification, to my most honored and esteemed friend, Jefferson Davis, ex-President of the Confederate States, for his own sole use and benefit, in fee simple forever; and I hereby constitute him my sole heir, executive, and administrator. If Jefferson Davis should not survive me, I give all that I have bequeathed him to his youngest daughter, Varina. I do not intend to share in the ingratitude of my country towards the man who is in my eyes the highest and noblest in existence.

Naturally Mr. Davis was deeply grieved by his friend's passing. He was more touched by her devoted admiration than her beneficence. Sarah Dorsey had been his salvation at the time of his greatest need. And now from beyond the grave she would be blessing him to his last breath. In providing Jefferson Davis with a proper home for his old age, Mrs. Dorsey also unwittingly furnished America with a shrine worthy of a statesman's memory.

Eventually Mrs. Davis would realize how unjust she had been to Mrs. Dorsey; in her *Memoir,* published in 1890, she remarked that "her uniform kindness to him and her deference to his wishes had endeared her to him, and he felt her death very much."

Two of Mrs. Dorsey's relatives, a brother, Stephen Percy Ellis, and a half-brother, Mortimer Dahlgren, contested the will and had some uncomplimentary things to say about their sister and Mr. Davis. But the inheritor was not much concerned. And on March 10, 1880, the court in New Orleans decided everything in Davis's favor. However, the "fortune" was nothing like as much as many persons imagined. Davis had to assume all of Mrs. Dorsey's debts, and the best of the Louisiana plantations rented for no more than $2,500 a year.

Though blessedly settled in an agreeable home of his own, sometimes the tragic past would press upon him. In a winter letter to the ailing L. B. Northrop, inviting him for a visit to the warmer climate of Beauvoir, Davis wrote:

Our home was given its name by its former possessor to express a beautiful prospect. The air is soft. In winter especially the sea breeze is invigorating. The oranges are shining golden on the trees, and our pine knot fires soar in the chimneys; in their light I try to bury my unhappiness.

However, as the first volume of his book neared completion in April, 1880, Mrs. Davis could write to Winnie cheerfully: "Your father is as well, though of course not so vigorous, as any man of thirty."

In speaking of his work, though, she hinted at the emotional toll on them both.

The weary recital of the weary war, to be compiled into a splendid but heartbreaking record of cherished hopes now blasted, brave warriors bleeding and dying, and noble men living, yet dead, in that they are hopeless—this tremendous record he is giving to the world, and all the while, as he writes, the graves give their dead and they stalk before us all gory and downcast—but all that gallant proud army, ready if they could again put on their fleshly shield to do battle for their rights.

The first volume was to be sent to the publishers within a few days. Mrs. Davis ended her letter joyously: "Our garden is ablaze with gladioli and perfumed with reseda and mignonette."

On June 27, 1880, Winnie became sixteen. On her birthday her father wrote that he was coming the next year to fetch her home.

CHAPTER XLIV

ESTO PERPETUA
AND MONSTROUS CALUMNY

IN EARLY NOVEMBER, 1880, while Jefferson Davis was pushing himself hard to complete his work, Father Alvan J. Ryan, priest of St. Mary's Church in Mobile, made a spontaneous offer of assistance. The priest, who had been a fervent advocate of Independence, had served as a Confederate chaplain in the field and was a popular poet. Father Ryan wrote:

Since I saw you last I have been thinking and thinking day and night about *your* work and *our* defense. It ought to be the "Sacred scripture" of our Confederacy. And you ought to be almost *inspired* to give to the world of false policies the doctrines of deathless Principles.

On his own initiative the priest had asked Bishop Lynch at Charleston for certain data, and he had sent inquiries to priests who had been stationed at Andersonville, and to numerous other Catholics for material which he would be forwarding shortly.

Now, my dear Sir, if I can (and I can) be of aid in any way, in such a work, my services (for it would be a service of love for the cause and reverence for yourself) are at your wish (of course gratis). . . . Day and night I would be willing to work for you, because you, in dark days, worked for all—and among the all, there is no one living that gives you a heart-loyalty and love more sincere than mine.

It was generous letters like this one from a pastor of a different religion that kept Davis's heart warmed while he proceeded with his monumental task. But he did not accept the services of Father Ryan, because Appleton's had just sent Judge W. T. Tenney down from New York to help speed the work. Tenney, with his objectivity and literary perception, was to prove efficient in the finishing stages of the bulky manuscript. He was, as well, a pleasant house guest.

445

During the last half-year of the writing, however, Davis did not have complete peace for reflection and composition, for visitors were continually descending upon him. Margaret Howell de Stöess with her two children came from England in the fall of 1880 and stayed through the next spring.

In February, 1881, for a night and a day, came twenty-six-year-old Poultney Bigelow to pay his respects. His father, John Bigelow, when Consul General in Paris, had effectively corralled poverty-stricken Germans and shipped them to New York to fight against the Confederates. The cosmopolitan Poultney, a school friend of the German prince who would become Kaiser Wilhelm II, had already gone around the world in a sailing ship. Davis found him a bright raconteur, and they sat talking through most of a Sunday under the great trees that shaded the lawn.

Maggie and Addison Hayes were also at Beauvoir on a visit, and Bigelow noted the "closeness of the family." He remarked that Mrs. Davis was "handsome, as well as strong-minded," and "like her husband, ever dignified, gracious and tactful." When the time came for the late-afternoon train, the entire family walked with the Northern guest to the place a quarter mile behind the house which the L & N had designated a flag-stop.

As they sat conversing on a log, awaiting the New Orleans-bound train, a strange large dog came along and attacked the Davises' Newfoundland. The animals were shortly engaged in a terrific fight, with jaws interlocked. While the women were agitating in fright and neither Hayes nor the young guest dared to interfere, Mr. Davis "leaped up into the Catherine wheel, flung the combined jaws across his knee, and with bare knuckles hammered into the foaming mouths with such swiftness and force that he achieved a parting of the astonished animals." Then the old gentleman reseated himself on the log and calmly resumed the conversation that the dog-fight had interrupted.*

A few weeks after Bigelow's visit, Mrs. Davis wrote Maggie at Memphis: "The labor is very heavy now as the book draws to a close." But her father, on the whole, was well, she reported; "his face pink and fresh looking."

Charles O'Conor, the New Yorker who had been the ex-President's chief counsel in 1865-67, wrote Mrs. Davis on April 7, 1881,

---

* Poultney Bigelow tells the story of his visit to Beauvoir in *Seventy Summers*, Vol. II, pp. 221–225. Long after Davis's death he continued to correspond with Mrs. Davis and sent her cards at Christmas.

telling her of his "new abode" on Nantucket Island and inviting the Davises to stay with him as they returned from fetching Winnie from Europe. Although he realized they were impatient to get away, he hoped very much that Mr. Davis would "finish his book leisurely and deliberately."

I wish it to come forth full armed and capable of resisting all just criticism. On its great subject the whole of literature is *bribed* or *intimidated*. His ability and knowledge are ample and he should take all the time needful to give results fair play.

When O'Conor's letter reached Beauvoir the book was on the verge of completion—after three years of labor. On an afternoon some days later Davis took a prolonged siesta, and at eight in the evening he began dictating to his wife. His mind, she noted, was extremely lucid. The statements emanating from life-long political convictions flowed cogently. He dictated slowly but assuredly to midnight and beyond. On what when cast in type became the next to last page of the original edition (page 763), Davis made clear not only his own stand, but his grave concern for the future of the United States. It was his firm opinion that the Federal Administration had revolted from its established way of Constitutional Government.

This overthrow of the rights of free men and the establishment of such new relations required a complete revolution in the principle of the Government of the United States, the subversion of the State governments, the subjugation of the people and the destruction of the fraternal Union. The work has been done. Will it stand? Have the eternal principles of the Declaration of Independence been hid from our sight forever?

When the cause was lost, what cause was it? Not that of the South only, but the cause of Constitutional Government, of the supremacy of law, of the natural rights of man.

Mrs. Davis did not complain of fatigue; she felt the spell of her husband's inspiration and wrote on steadily. Finally, as the hour hand of the clock was approaching four in the morning, Jefferson Davis carefully dictated his "Conclusion," consisting of four paragraphs. Outside there was intense stillness; the night creatures were now silent, the birds were not yet astir. Only the gentle heaving of the Gulf onto the passive sand made a muted liquid music.

In his brief recapitulation, Davis stated that his first object in the work had been to prove by historical authority that each State, as sovereign parties to the compact of Union, had reserved the power to secede whenever "the ends for which it was established did not answer." And so it followed that on the part of the United States Government "the war was an act of usurpation, and on the part of the South, merely the defense of an inherent, inalienable right."

His next purpose, he said, had been to show by the gallantry and devotion of the Southern people in their unequal struggle how thorough was their conviction in the justice of their cause.

In asserting the right of secession, it has not been my wish to incite to its exercise. I recognize the fact that the result showed it to be impracticable. But this did not prove it wrong. And now that it may not be again attempted, and that the Union may promote the general welfare, it is needful that the truth, the whole truth should be known, so that the crimination and recrimination may forever cease, and then, on the basis of fraternity and faithful regard for the rights of States, there may be written on the arch of the Union, *Esto perpetua.*

Davis leaned his white head back against the chair and momentarily closed his eyes. His wife held her pen poised for a moment and then looked up to signify that she was ready for the next sentence. With a tired smile he said, "I think I am done."

"And so," Mrs. Davis was to write in her *Memoir,* "was finished his life's work for his countrymen."

The final chapters were sent to New York before April ended. In the last week of May, 1881, Davis journeyed to Montreal to arrange for the publication of his book in Canada by Longmans. On arriving he was grieved to find that his old friend and benefactor John Lovell had lost his entire fortune. The great house in which the Davises had been guests had been converted by Mrs. Lovell into a school for twenty-one girls, and she was its cheerful headmistress. "I have had numerous calls," Davis wrote his wife, "and when I wanted to lie down and rest the rap rappings came at my door."

It is now early spring, the apple and cherry trees covered with bloom, and the fields and lawns look very charming in their full suit of fresh grass.

He got his contract and returned home by way of Toronto to New Orleans.

Finally, in June of 1881, *The Rise and Fall of the Confederate Government* was published in two thick volumes. The book was sold largely by subscription in various bindings with a wide differential in price. Southerners, although still pinched for cash in 1881, scrimped to purchase the work, and today the two volumes may be found in many libraries of descendants of "old families."

Naturally the history was welcomed and praised in the South, but the North was extremely chary and still disinclined to listen to the Southern view of the Confederate cause and the conduct of the war. The Northern newspapers on the whole ignored *The Rise and Fall*. Only brief mentions were made in even professedly Democratic organs. A few magazines reviewed the work grudgingly. The *Nation* resented Davis's emphasis that slavery had been injected into the contest as a political rather than a moral question, that the emancipation proclamation had been a war measure, as President Lincoln freely admitted. And it disliked Davis's holding to the fact that the issue had been between centralization and State Rights. An adverse criticism of Davis and his book by General Longstreet appeared in the New York *Herald*. *Appleton's Review*, however, reprinted some high commendations from English periodicals.

The cool reception of his work in the North was but another of the countless disappointments that had come to Jefferson Davis in the last twenty years. He struggled to accept the situation philosophically, and trusted to the judgment of posterity.

The Davises had planned to meet Winnie in Paris the middle of July, but they had to postpone the voyage several weeks. Against their arrival, Winnie, after leaving Carlsruhe, was to spend some weeks in Paris with Emily Mason and take, in Mrs. Davis's phrase, "some singing and painting lessons from a master." "Emily Mason will take your heart at once by her elegance and tenderness," the mother wrote. "Enjoy every hour you can, my precious, as to lay up a store of jewelled memories with which to decorate your old age."

On August 17, 1881, the Davises finally sailed from New York on the *Bernard Hall*. It had been almost five years since Jefferson Davis had kissed his daughter goodbye in Carlsruhe on November 1, 1876. Winnie had been very much of a little girl then, and a darling, if somewhat spoiled. Now at seventeen she had become a young lady, tall and willowy. She did not possess Maggie's beauty, but she was good-looking and had an obvious distinction. Shy and pensive in repose, she had a kind of radiance about her when she spoke. In her large clear gray eyes there was an expression of pleasant expectancy. Like the Davis side of the family, she was not only fair-haired, but reserved and warm at the same time.

Her father noted that she spoke English with a slight German accent, which she was indeed never to lose completely.

Davis wondered if his wife had not made a mistake in keeping their daughter in Europe during five years of the formative stage of her life. A look now and again would come over her as if she had lost something that could not be recaptured, that she had endured a kind of exile, however beneficial. But what was done was done, and Winnie's continental education had enhanced her qualities. Years later, however, after her father's death, she was to write an article for the *Ladies Home Journal* protesting the fashion of Americans educating pre-college-age daughters abroad.

Emily Mason was to recall quiet September evenings in Paris when they all played a "game of quotations." She was amazed at Mr. Davis's alert and sure memory at seventy-three. However unusual or obscure the couplet or epigram, he seemed to have the answer on the tip of his tongue. And if given a first line of Burns, he could often recite the poem to the end.

While Mrs. Davis and Winnie shopped and enjoyed the social life of Paris, Davis went out to Chantilly to spend his last weeks abroad with Dudley Mann. Davis cared little enough for the bright capital, but he reveled in the beautiful French countryside, and he and Mann enjoyed long walks about the Chantilly racecourse.

One letter from his wife made a special impression on him. Mrs. Davis and Winnie had been taken by a friend to Sèvres to see "the glowing china." She wrote:

The world seemed to me to be the throne of ceramics. As I looked upon the angel forms depicted there, the longing of my life to create something that would live after me was greater than ever. A vague kind of awe came over me in looking at a vase of men running footraces, which had been baked 350 years before Christ's coming.

Perhaps that unfulfilled artistic urge in Varina was what made her so restless, so impulsive, so quick to fly off the handle, so possessive, and so eager for admiration. She had the desire to create some work of art, but neither the genius nor the determination to produce it. This frustrated yearning may have motivated to an extent her obsession with health and doctors.

Now she wrote that she was dreadfully worried over the health of Winnie, who had been a very healthy girl those five years in Carlsruhe. She had taken her to a Paris doctor, and he had ventured to suggest that Winnie was suffering from "overwork." This absurd diagnosis astounded her father. "I am at a loss to understand what the Doctor means by overwork," Davis replied promptly. "My baby may have been fatigued by going about, but her mind has not been oppressed."

When Mrs. Davis came to Chantilly to pay him a brief visit shortly afterwards, she became concerned over *his* health. So to please her he put on "the thick socks he had purchased in Canada," and after her departure he wrote that his feet did feel warmer for the change. Varina urged him to come to Paris at once for a medical examination. She wanted him "rejuvenated," she said. He replied dubiously:

If you were in America it would be easy to find patent medicines promising more than a Parisien medicine, and I have not "the face to be shaved" by either. It is not for me to renew my youth or by the equally silly fiction to find restoration in some spring. Let us "accept the situation" in this, the natural and inevitable decay of all earthly things, and by cheerfully yielding to the law, mitigate its device.

It is not that I am obstinate . . . and so I will come to town if the day is bright and will hear your Doctor; but whether I will take his prescription is more than doubtful. Plainly I have not force enough to resist much treatment and prefer to die a natural rather than an experimental death.

In late November, Jefferson Davis bade a last goodbye to his friends in France and England and sailed for New York with his wife and daughter. He had had three months of relaxing vacation and now he could look forward to twelve days at sea. He expected no more crises in his eventful life. He purposed never again to hold any kind of political office. Even though the North had largely given his book the silent treatment, he had done his duty for the South's cause and history, and there was some encouragement in the news that its sales had recently picked up. The Brierfield property was in his possession. Beauvoir, a home of dignity for his old age and for his family after him, had been provided in a peaceful spot of earth, in sight and sound of the sea with which he had such affinity. He felt that nothing serious could touch him further, except dying, and he had not the faintest fear of death.

When the *Necker* docked at Hoboken at one P.M. on December 7, Davis was happy indeed to set foot again on American soil, which he loved so well, though he was still denied American citizenship. He told a correspondent of the Cincinnati *Enquirer* that the voyage had turned out to be stormy, with water twice in the saloon, but that he had never in his life suffered seasickness. He smilingly declined to express an opinion on the political situation, and merely said that he was looking forward to retirement in the peace of Beauvoir. Eager to get home as quickly as possible, the Davises, conducted by Mr. Derby from Appleton's, went straight from the ship to the Pennsylvania Railroad station.

Eleven days later, Davis's sense of happiness was shattered by a highly unlikely event: Joseph Johnston accused him of stealing the Confederate treasure.

On December 18, 1881, there had appeared in the Philadelphia *Press* an extraordinary story with a blazing headline: *Confederate Gold Missing*—General Johnston Calls Jefferson Davis To Account For Over $2,000,000 In Specie. The writer of the interview with Johnston was a highly reputable reporter named Frank A. Burr. The long, detailed article declared that only $179,000 was accounted for of the Confederate treasure, which Johnston estimated "on good authority" at $2,500,000.

When the reporter had asked, "What became of the money?" Johnston had replied with a peculiar smile, "That I am unable to say. Mr. Davis has never given any satisfactory account of it, and what is a strange thing to me, the Southern people here never held him to an account of it." The insinuation was obvious. Though Davis had been falsely accused of many things, not even his worst enemies had charged him with dishonesty.

Johnston's attack on Davis's integrity created indignation in the North as well as the South. The General's friends tried to believe that he had not uttered the monstrous libel. Some persisted in hoping that the reporter had fabricated the interview. General Dabney Maury published a clear defense of Davis in the Richmond *Dispatch*, and gave his version of the disposal of the treasure. He sent Davis a cutting, and wrote:

> The pestilent interviewer F.A.B. has unintentionally done you a kindness by showing you how warmly you are treasured by true Confederates. If our enemies really desire to split the "solid south" they have adopted the wrong means—for this vile slander has rallied us to you very warmly.
>
> You will be received with an ovation in Richmond, where we, now especially, honor what is staunch and true.

After the mighty commotion the piece raised, Johnston, according to the Washington correspondent of the New York *World*, claimed he did not know Burr and "was beguiled into the conversation he had reported."

But Burr soon made it absolutely clear in print that he had quoted Johnston correctly. The reporter himself wrote Mr. Davis a frank letter describing his meeting with Johnston on a train going to Richmond, and riding with him in the omnibus to the Exchange Hotel. He had met Johnston before; *"before our accidental meeting on the cars my character and occupation were thoroughly fixed upon his mind."* After dinner that evening he had gone to the General's room. When their conversation was interrupted by a business engagement, Burr said they had parted to meet again to finish the interview. He had immediately dictated the first conversation to his stenographer. The next day the conversation was "continued for some time." Burr had offered to submit a copy of the conversations to the General for revision. "Johnston said, no, that that was not necessary . . . and he added jocularly that *'no man ought to make a statement to a journalist that he was not willing to stand by.'* "

Burr enclosed letters he had received from their mutual friend Senator Benjamin Hill of Georgia, who had telegraphed the reporter to ascertain the truth. In his reply to Hill, Burr maintained that his article "was a very temperate review of what passed between Gen. Johnston and myself."

The drift is decidedly against Gen. Johnston. I am, of course, more than pleased that the effort to impeach the accuracy of the work and to charge a breach of faith on my part has utterly failed.

The controversy seems to have done Mr. Davis a great deal of good rather than harm.

Hill wrote Burr again on December 27, 1881:

I am sorry for Genl Johnston. He has always had a respectable party of admirers in the South. He will have none now. His reputation and his character are both ruined. . . . I knew he was suspicious, spiteful, jealous, but I assumed he was sincere and truthful. Now I have a conscious knowledge that he is sadly untruthful. His absurd insinuations against Mr. Davis are as disgraceful in spirit as they are unfounded in fact. . . . Poor fellow. He has fallen sadly and I can see no recovery for him.

The same day Hill wrote to Davis:

Poor Johnston has ruined himself at last unless he can save himself by a retreat. If he can do anything at all he can retreat, though I think even that oft practised habit will fail him this time. In truth, I am sorry for him though he does not deserve even pity.

The whole Southern people are your defenders and the calumny has only served to show once more how devotedly they love you.

Johnston made a feeble effort to calm the tempest by sending a "disclaimer" to the editor of the *Press*. He stated that the article was based on a conversation which he "did not take to be an interview." He added with malicious insinuation: "In that conversation, therefore a good deal was said which nothing could induce me to say for publication." He pretended to believe that his "disclaimer" would completely settle the matter as far as he himself was concerned. But he was wrong in his assumption. Johnston had lost the respect of even some intimate friends.

Day after day, in various newspapers, ex-Confederate officers and administrators picked holes in Johnston's accusation. All agreed there was only a fraction of the gold Johnston had suggested amounted to $2,500,000. Now John Reagan, who on the retreat had become acting-Treasurer, published an account of the disposal of the funds.* He gave out the exact figures of silver and gold coin divided among the soldiers along the way from Greensboro to Washington, Georgia. That part of the treasure belonging to the Richmond banks was shortly returned to their vaults. Virginia's Captain M. C. Clark, the very last acting-Treasurer of the Confederacy, to whom Reagan turned over his office at Washington, Georgia, wrote a detailed story of specie and paper at the end. "No gold was found on President Davis when captured," Clark declared, "for he had none. He could have received it only through me and I paid him none."

Aiming at his fellow-Virginian, Joe Johnston, Clark declared:

The old Confederates brought nothing out of the war, save honor; for God's sake and the precious memory of the dead, let us preserve that untarnished and defend it from slanderous insinuations.

Davis particularly deplored the fact that Johnston's attempt to besmirch him had appeared just as he and his family reached America. It had poisoned the homecoming for Winnie, who had been kept abroad five years partly to spare her sectional prejudices. He had hoped that now she would know only happiness "in our common country." But with the explosion set off by Johnston, a Southerner, Winnie was confused to say the least.

Shortly after the New Year of 1882, William Preston Johnston,

* See Chapter XXIII.

now President of Tulane University, made a long "statement" for the press.

For twenty years President Davis has breasted a storm of obloquy and calumny from every quarter. Yet, today, he stands unscathed, the representative man of the most glorious epoch of Southern history, so that in all our part of the Union it is hard to find a man who has done his duty by his country who would not prefer a word of approval from his lips to a crown of gold from the hand of his best detractors.

Having stood so near him for four years no veil of his character was possible even if he had wished it.

At Beauvoir Davis gradually began going through his enormous accumulation of mail. From all over the South men who were among the last in control of the small Confederate treasure wrote to offer data. A letter from F. C. Randolph, Colonel of the Seventh Alabama Cavalry, was typical of the general feeling of outrage.

I cannot refrain from expressing to you my own sentiments of abhorrence of the unjust, wanton, outrageous and cowardly charges and imputations made against you by Genl. Jos. E. Johnston. . . . If after the publication of his so-called memoirs, anything was wanting to stamp Johnston as a man of small brain, and still smaller soul, this unmanly assault upon you has supplied that want.

In late January Judah P. Benjamin of London published in the New Orleans *Picayune* "a full and conclusive exposure of Johnston's slander." But Davis kept absolutely silent, though dozens of newspapers invitingly urged him to use their columns "to reply." His silence proved golden; throughout the nation it was favorably commented upon. Johnston began to reap the bitter fruit of what one paper in remarkable understatement called "a mean transaction."

Among the letters that had accumulated during the four months' absence was one from Mary W. Rhodes, a woman of Northern birth, who was a friend of the Lees and the Davises and whose father had been a friend of Franklin Pierce. She wrote that the two volumes of the *Rise and Fall* were lying on her table under the portrait of General Lee. As she read his book, she said, "past scenes were recalled."

In one of my interviews with Genl. & Mrs. Lee they both spoke of you with deep feeling, and Mrs. Lee pointed to a large easy chair which she said you had sent to her when you were on the eve of departure from Richmond, remembering *even then* her invalid condition. She spoke with tears of your suffering in prison and the cruel separation from your family.

Mary Rhodes had spent another evening with the Lees at their home in Lexington in 1868. The General was not well, but he got his hat and cloak and walked her back to her hotel. "During the walk," she wrote, "the General again spoke so feelingly and kindly of you."

We parted at the Hotel door—an earnest and, on my part, tearful parting. I entered the hall and passed nearly thro it, when looking back I saw the General still standing by the door. Seeing me turn and stop, he came to me, took both my hands in his, pressed them to his heart, and oh his look! The *soul* that was there!

He died of a broken heart. Found every pledge broken, every promise falsified—and his noble heart pierced to the core, gave way.

Mrs. Rhodes's last glimpse of the General was so poignant that it started in Davis a train of unhappy memories.

At Mardi Gras Mr. Davis broke his country routine to go to New Orleans "to attend" Winnie, who was Lady-in-Waiting to Mary Lee, the reigning Queen of the Comus Court. At seventeen Winnie was thus launched auspiciously in what is called "society."

CHAPTER XLV

"KEEP THE MEMORY OF
OUR HEROES GREEN"

————◆————

IN MID-APRIL, 1882, after much persuasion, Jefferson Davis agreed to make an address in New Orleans. The Reverend Mr. J. William Jones of Richmond, Secretary of the Southern Historical Society, had begged him to speak at prominent Southern centers in the interest of the Society and declared that then all the money needed to keep it going might be raised.

Davis had no inclination to embark on any extended tour, but on April 25 he spoke at the French Opera House in New Orleans. In the brief course of his remarks he explained that his aim in compiling *The Rise and Fall of the Confederate Government* was "defense as well as history." He pointed out significantly that "the other side" had written and was continually writing its views of the recent war.

We wish to present ours also, that the future historian by considering both may deduce the unbiased statements which no contemporary can make. We want our side of the war so fully and exactly stated that the men who come after us may compare and do justice.

In speaking of the South's having no army at the beginning of the war and how men left their families and peaceful occupations, he said:

At first call of their country they rallied around their flag like a wall of fire to defend the rights their fathers had left them.

Could there be cause more sacred than this? If there be anything that justifies human war, it is defense of country, of family, of constitutional rights.

The unanimity of our people and the heroism of our soldiers have caused us to be the admiration of the world. It is our duty to keep the memory of our heroes green. Yet they do not belong to us alone; they belong to the whole country, they belong to America.

From New Orleans Davis went up to his plantation, though, as he wrote Addison Hayes, he feared from alarming newspaper reports "that little of our land was to be seen." Hayes, the "blessed son-in-law," had taken over the business management of Brierfield when Davis went to Europe in 1881, and he was to keep the accounts for the next three years and relieve his father-in-law of much responsibility. Continual trouble, however, arose from overseers, who often were also the storekeepers. But the inefficiency and petty dishonesty of overseers was a small matter compared to the danger of the rampaging Mississippi River that in April, 1882, seemed bent on washing Brierfield away. The immediate job in hand was to rescue the tenants, remove the cattle, and wait for the roiling waters to recede.

In mid-May, after the terrible spring overflow had begun to subside, Mrs. Davis went with her husband to Brierfield to help the people. They were greeted by a little brass band of which Burgess Montgomery, a first cousin of Thornton and Isaiah, was the leader. It was the musical Burgess who had written Mr. Davis asking his "kind assistance in procuring uniforms," which he had given as far as he was able. And Mrs. Davis had got the measurements of each band member and "selected suits to advantage." Years later, on January 7, 1895, Burgess Montgomery was to write Mrs. Davis from the office of the Secretary of the Treasury in Washington, where he was employed, reminding her of that 1882 visit, "looking after the interests and distresses of those with whom he and you were so long related." "Each time Mr. Davis came," he wrote, "it was always a great pleasure to call the Band out for a serenade in honor of his distinguished and welcome presence in our midst." He had never ceased to be grateful, he declared, to Mr. Davis for "contributing to the needs of the many that were rendered destitute by the floods, who would otherwise have undergone severe hardship and suffering were it not for the generous and immediate aid extended them by President Davis."

All through the 1880's recurrent help to tenants was to be a drain on the family resources. In the days before Red Cross or Government relief of disaster, it was the Southerner's burden to care for his "people," though they had long ceased to be slaves and he was under no lawful obligation to succor them when they were idle.

On the third Monday of May, 1882, Beckett Howell, Mrs. Davis's next youngest brother, came to Brierfield to act as overseer. Now forty-two, Beckett, who had once served as a smart, handsome naval officer with Admiral Semmes on the *Alabama,* was a tired, gentle-tempered fellow, who seemed utterly defeated. After the war he had failed at everything he had tried. He had finally been reduced to attempting to raise a crop on rented land with a lame arm and one mule. So Davis brought him to Brierfield. Beckett was overjoyed to be again riding a horse and directing "hands." And the Negroes seemed happy to have him as "boss," for they knew he understood them. But Beckett's joy was to be short-lived, for in October he became sick and died.

Through the winter and spring of 1882 Mrs. Davis had been reading accounts of the sensationally successful lecture tour of an eccentric young British poet named Oscar Wilde. When she learned that he was to deliver a lecture in Memphis on June 12, she regretted that it would be inconvenient for her to visit the Hayeses at that time.

But Maggie sent her a copy of a thin paper called *Meriwether's Weekly,* dated June 17, 1882, which further excited her interest. Lee Meriwether, who was now nineteen, had had an interview with Wilde in his suite at Gaston's Hotel in Memphis. His older brother had said to him, "Wilde wears knee breeches and keeps a sun-flower pinned to the lapel of his coat, but there's more to him than that. Go and interview him."

Young Lee had found Wilde's sitting room "in disorder, with magazines and photographs strewn on the floor, and on the table were the two volumes of Jefferson Davis's *Rise and Fall* published the year before." He was amazed that the long-haired Britisher should have purchased such an expensive book or was even interested in the subject. Lee told him that he had been Mr. Davis's neighbor in Memphis and during his childhood had known him well. "Jefferson Davis is the man I would like most to see in the United States," Wilde said, and declared that it was remarkable that it took "Northern armies numbering three million soldiers four years to whip him."

He asked where Davis lived now. Lee told him on the Gulf Coast about four hundred roundabout miles from Memphis. "That's a long way to go to meet anyone," said the poet-lecturer, "but not too far to go to see such a man as Jefferson Davis."

Wilde's manager, however, had already secured an engagement

in New Orleans and he arranged one in Mobile two days later. In time, Wilde wrote the ex-President a most winning letter, asking to be allowed to stop at Beauvoir and pay homage. Mrs. Davis urged her husband to invite him to stay the night. Davis was reluctant; he could not help but conclude that, despite his tremendous success on the lecture platform, Wilde with his knee breeches and sunflower was a bit silly. At best, Davis did not care much for worldly people, nor did he fancy people for their fame.

In the Mobile *Register* of June 23 Davis read an announcement which had undoubtedly been inspired by Wilde's manager.

We understand that ex-President Davis has invited Mr. Wilde to pay him a visit at Beauvoir, his Mississippi home; and that the aesthete has accepted. . . . It is scarcely conceivable that two persons can be more different than the ex-President of the Confederacy and the "Apostle of aestheticism," as known to report; and we confess to sufficient curiosity to desire to know the bent of their coming, protracted interview.

Wilde was reported by the New Orleans *Picayune* to have "very sensible views about the Southern Confederacy." In an interview he spoke of his great admiration for the ex-President. He had never seen the Chief, he said, but had followed his career with much attention. "His fall after such an able and gallant pleading in his own cause, must necessarily arouse sympathy." The case of the South in the late war Wilde compared to that of contemporary Ireland.

It was a struggle for autonomy, selfgovernment, for a people. I do not wish to see the Empire dismembered, but only to see the Irish people free. . . . People must have freedom and autonomy before they are capable of their greatest result in the cause of progress. . . . I look forward to much pleasure in visiting Mr. Jefferson Davis.

But it is doubtful if Wilde got as much pleasure as he expected in the meeting. Though Mrs. Davis and Winnie and a visiting cousin, Mary Davis, found Wilde enchanting as a conversationalist, Mr. Davis felt something indefinably objectionable in his personality. Even at twenty-six, Wilde's thick, sensual lips gave him a slightly gross look. At dinner Davis let his wife and Wilde carry on most of the conversation; he remained courteous, but aloof. Pleading doctor's orders for some temporary indisposition, he excused himself early. Wilde had felt restrained in the presence of this sincere man. By simply being himself, Davis had held up to Wilde a mirror which reflected an image that was not flattering.

But after his host had retired, Wilde brightened perceptibly and charmed the three ladies beyond words. Mrs. Davis made a very good pencil sketch of the poet while he chatted. And he presented her with a copy of a recently published English edition of his poems and inscribed it glowingly. The four talked until after midnight. When Mary Davis, who was to grow into a proper spinster, had undressed for bed, she went to the window and stared out enraptured. There on the beach in the moonlight she beheld the tall figure of Oscar Wilde sauntering up and down the sand with a handful of pebbles, which he moodily tossed, one by one, into the shallow waves.

Wilde had charmed most of America, but not his American hero. After the Britisher had departed next day, Mrs. Davis chided her husband for not being more cordial to their celebrated guest. He only said quietly, "I did not like the man," and would give no reason.

When he went out to his pavilion office, Davis found propped up on his desk a twelve by ten photograph of the lecturer-poet. It was inscribed "To Jefferson Davis in all loyal admiration from Oscar Wilde, June—'82 —Beauvoir."[*]

In mid-July, 1882, Davis received from General W. N. Pendleton, the Episcopal rector artillerist, an earnest request that he deliver the Memorial Address at the inauguration of the Lee Mausoleum in Lexington on June 28 of the next year.

For controlling reasons we judge and feel that Providence permitting, as we trust and pray, the just tribute to Genl Lee on the occasion, can be more fitly rendered by yourself than by any other mortal.

It was the particular wish of Custis Lee, who had succeeded his father as President of the college, he wrote. And while the bachelor Custis, "lonely as he is," would "press" for him, Pendleton's own plain household "would longingly open heart and arms and doors" to Mr. and Mrs. Davis and any others of his family.

The fighting preacher was taking no chances, for he added:

---

[*] The photograph may be seen at Beauvoir today. The book of verse and Mrs. Davis's sketch of Wilde are possessed by Davis's great-granddaughter, Mrs. John Wolcott Stewart of Santa Barbara, California.

Material about Wilde's visit was given the author by Lee Meriwether, Mrs. Stewart, and Anna Farrar Goldsborough, a blood relative of both Mr. and Mrs. Davis, who wrote the story as she had got it from Mary Davis who, though terribly shocked over Wilde's later years, "was never mentally free of the man's charm."

As an honoring friend, may I not ask you to set about at once preparing the Address desired? So as to have it ready, if granted life and vigor to deliver it. Or to let us have it for others' use, should the Lord remove or disable you.

Davis was amused by the parson's care for insurance against contingencies.

At the beginning of August Mr. Davis and Winnie were alone at Beauvoir; Mrs. Davis was with the Hayeses in Memphis. It was a relief to have a respite from visitors. But he still had a tremendous correspondence to wrestle with. To Maggie in Memphis he wrote:

As for me quiet is most desirable, and my correspondence is more occupation than agreeable. All sorts of people write to me about all supposable matters, and if I don't answer they generally write again. Those who fall in debt must think like Prince David I have a refuge for all such— rather they must think I have the Philosopher's stone with which to turn Yankee maledictions into gold, for they do not ask to join the refugees, but to have money sent to them. It would cost me very little to repeat my action with the so-called bread rioters, whose clamor I hushed by turning my pockets wrong side out, and telling them to take the contents.

Robert, who had been away on a long vacation, returned on August 7 and brought joy to the little household. Robert was a privileged servant, and he could turn his hand to almost anything, from pressing Mr. Davis's clothes and nursing the Davis granddaughters to building a chicken house. Robert straightway began making a new fence for the orange orchard. As Davis wrote his wife, "Robert does what he pleases, when he wants, and extra help is hired for him when he asks for it."

Before August had run its course the Beauvoir quiet was shattered, for Mrs. Davis returned with Maggie and the two little girls. Then again came the inflow and outflow of more visitors; some to pay devoted respects, some out of sheer curiosity. But everyone had to be given refreshment, if not a full meal and a bed. Stopovers had been rendered more convenient by the L & N Railroad officials, who had erected a small station pavilion a few hundred yards behind the house.

So Beauvoir became increasingly a place of pilgrimage—for veterans who had fought for the North as well as for the Confederacy. People of high estate and low turned up, as did Northern historians and editors. General Fitzhugh Lee and the Reverend Mr. J. William Jones, Secretary of the Southern Historical Society, visited Mr. Davis, as did Bishop Green, Chancellor of the University of the South, and General George W. Jones of Iowa.

Journalists commented on the attractive, high-ceilinged reception hall, big as a double drawing room, through which the Gulf breezes blew. The walls and ceiling were decorated with discreet frescoes in pastel shades, painted by a German artist named Meuhler when the house was first built. The room was comfortable with lounges and bright with flowered chintzes. Here, when there was distinguished company, Mrs. Davis served tea from a handsome silver service and her Sèvres cups. After-dinner coffee was served here too, often in little porcelain cups with filigree silver holders, a gift to the ex-President from the Sultan of Turkey.

A Northern-born woman reporter from the New Orleans *Picayune*, Catherine Cole, was delighted with "the mellowness" of Beauvoir, the "cool, sweet drawing room," the library filled with books, the old-fashioned back garden with its walks bordered with mignonette, and the roof of the detached kitchen "buried under a snow of white roses."

Varina Davis was a born chatelaine, and her activities extended beyond the household routine to the ducks and the geese and the packing of grapes for the New Orleans market, as well as to her rose garden. She boasted that she could pick five hundred roses a day, if she wished. But for an accessible celebrity, who also happened to be a gentleman with ingrained hospitality, fame was a drain on pocketbook as well as on strength.

Many of the visitors were unadulterated bores, but one whom Davis really enjoyed was a young newspaperman named Walter Hines Page. Davis was sitting alone on the veranda of Beauvoir when the future Ambassador to the Court of St. James came eagerly up the broad front steps. Page found Mr. Davis "elegant in manner, unbent by age, and his conversation of rare interest." He felt the spell of Davis's "beautiful speaking voice," which he rightly believed had much to do with his swift advancement in political life.

Davis refused to talk of the war, but he listened to Page's boyhood reminiscences. Having been born at Cary, North Carolina, in July, 1855, Page was almost ten when Sherman arrived just before the war's end. He related how the Sherman "bummers" in their search for hidden silver had opened all the flour sacks in the Page house and then in their anger at not finding any hidden loot had scattered the precious flour in the bedrooms and on the stairs. With their bayonets they had ripped open the feather mattresses and

had shaken them out, so that for days the household carpets were
covered with flour and feathers. When there was virtually nothing
to eat left in the place, a kindly Federal captain had invited the
hungry boy to dine at the officers' mess, but young Walter had
spurned his offer, declaring, "I'll starve before I'll eat with Yankees." Page recalled seeing the wounded and the starved Confederates struggling home from Northern prisons, "men with bodies so
thin and steps so uncertain that they might be expected to stagger
and fall in pieces."

Davis told Page that one particular purpose in his writing *The
Rise and Fall* had been to give young students of politics a chance
to get their history from original sources. But he admitted that in
the Southerners' desperate struggle to exist after the war, interest
in the secession question had waned sharply.

In March of 1883 Davis was greatly disquieted by a strange turn
of events affecting his promised speeech at the Lee Mausoleum in
Lexington. General Pendleton, chairman of the program, who had
been concerned that the ex-President might die before the event,
had himself died in mid-January of 1883. A man unknown to Davis,
Professor J. J. White of the Washington and Lee faculty, had then
become chairman. On March 13, in writing the ex-President details about the forthcoming event, White had casually mentioned
that General Joseph E. Johnston would preside. On hearing this
distasteful news, "not previously communicated or anticipated,"
Davis sent his regrets.

General Jubal Early had come to Beauvoir to persuade Mr. Davis
to change his decision. But he went away with the conviction that
Davis's position was correct, and he fully sympathized "with the
feelings and motives which prompted his withdrawal."

Though circumstances prevented Davis's much-heralded appearance at Lexington, he attended in New Orleans the laying of the
cornerstone of the Army of Tennessee monument, which was to be
surmounted by a statue of Albert Sidney Johnston. When the
orator of the day had delivered his address, continued calls from
the crowd urged Mr. Davis to speak impromptu. It was easy for
him to be eloquent about Sidney Johnston, who, he told his hearers,
had received him at West Point "as an elder brother might do."
They had served together side by side, he said, both on the Indian
frontier and in Mexico.

I have seen him in the most trying situations, and I never saw a man whose mind worked so quickly, whose voice was so calm, whose purpose was so fixed, and whose bearing was so great. Physically grand, intellectually great, morally sublime, his life was devoted to duty. Indeed in the conscientious discharge of that duty, he died upon the field of Shiloh in a moment of victory . . . had he lived but half an hour longer, Grant would have been a prisoner. I loved him so that I dare not trust myself to speak of him as my heart would prompt me. . . . When he came to us from California it appeared to me that a great pillar had been put under the Confederacy, and when he fell on the field of Shiloh, that ruin stared before us.

"Very few eras of history have been marked by great soldiers," Davis declared. "It is seldom that a generation produces one; but I think I may defy criticism when I say that the Confederacy had three great soldiers—three who would compare with the greatest soldiers of ancient or modern times." *

The glowing occasion was marred by the behavior of General Beauregard, who left ostentatiously in a towering rage, as the veterans and civilians cheered Davis and the memory of Albert Sidney Johnston. The next day Beauregard wrote an angry letter to a newspaper in an attempt to dim Sidney Johnston's glory and defend himself. Davis felt compelled to answer it. So controversy, which he had been trying to avoid, was revived.

More than ever now, Davis did not want to risk encountering a scene at Lexington, where the jealous Joseph Johnston would have to endure his eulogy of Lee. So Davis sent a letter to Custis Lee, fully explaining his position and expressing his deep disappointment at not being able to be present.

The persistent hostility of Genl J. E. Johnston to myself arose from the fact that I did not recognize him as superior in rank to Genl. Lee, culminating in gross misrepresentation in his book published after the war and crowned by his vile slander in regard to Confederate treasure. Confederates generally looked upon this last act as a disgraceful manifestation of a sometime concealed hostility, and I could not with due self-respect appear before a meeting over which he was to preside. But this was not all; he had been the envious detractor of Lee during the war and in print tried to rob Lee of the credit due him for his successes in the seven days' battle.

* The city of New Orleans had already erected handsome monuments to Lee and Jackson.

After giving several instances of Johnston's "insubordination" and Lee's "generosity, magnanimity and self-abnegation," Davis concluded:

Now, sir, I hope you will appreciate why it is so objectionable to me to see the envious detractor of Lee presiding where honors were to be paid to his memory.

Davis ordered floral offerings to be placed on the graves of Lee and Jackson on the dedication day in Lexington, as an expression of "how very near and dear their memories are to our household."

When the ceremony did take place, General Johnston made himself conspicuous by his absence. J. William Jones, ardent admirer of both Davis and Lee, presided and made the chief address.

For Jefferson Davis the hot months of July, August, and September, 1883, passed in comparative quiet. Few Northerners risked the Gulf Coast in the malarial season. Visiting relatives, however, came for a few days or a week, and Varina grew weary. She did not always restrain her temper before the family as she did before strangers. The kinfolk were sometimes astounded by her blazing blowups, while at the same time they marveled at "Uncle Jeff's self-control." But he himself sensed that his wife's outbursts were a release from the tension of having to live a retired life against her will, when it was the only kind he could now endure. He could recall how she had pictured herself in a letter from Augusta while he was in prison. Something derogatory in a newspaper had infuriated her. "I walked until I could walk no more," she wrote. "Then I cried. Then I walked again. But you have often seen me in trouble. I do not have to explain it to you."

One of Mrs. Davis's relatives said that Mary Stamps must have seemed "like a cool spring of water to Uncle Jeff after the heat of Aunt Varina's tempestuous outbursts." But Davis never allowed anyone to criticize Varina in his hearing. Only once was there evidence of his judging her, even indirectly. On one occasion when he went to New Orleans to see Mary Stamps at the home of her daughter Lucy, who had married Varina's kinsman Edgar Farrar,* he found that she had moved to temporary lodgings. She had left the Farrars because of some unpleasantness with a Howell relative who had

---

* Edgar Farrar was a grandson of Varina's Aunt Jane, noted in the family annals for throwing a loaded silver coffeepot in her husband's face and for being one of the first—if not the first—women in Mississippi to get a divorce.

come on a visit. When Mary began to tell him about the situation, Davis placed his hand over hers and said quietly, "You do not have to explain to me, Mary. I know. They are wild people."

With October, Northern visitors again began to appear at Beauvoir. Among them was one to whom Mr. Davis took a fancy: Hilton U. Brown, a twenty-four-year-old reporter for the Indianapolis *News*. He was spending his honeymoon traveling about the South. He had brought his bride to see Jefferson Davis. At Biloxi he had hired a buggy and had driven the five miles through the dense, sandy forest of virgin pine to Beauvoir, which he found partly surrounded by orange groves and vineyards. Ringing the bell, Brown wondered, as he later wrote, if the ex-President would see "this presumptuous young Yankee reporter."

When Mrs. Davis came in, after Robert had announced them, she assured him warmly: "Certainly Mr. Davis will see you. He is delighted to meet strangers from afar."

Mr. Davis approached us cordially with outstretched hand and the greeting could not have been more gracious. . . . His step was light, his bearing that of a gentleman of easy approach. In a moment we were made as welcome as if we were old acquaintances.

The personable young man explained that he was President of the national Phi Delta Theta Fraternity and that while in Montgomery some of his brothers had taken him to the spot on the Capitol terrace where Mr. Davis had been sworn in as President and that the incident had inspired his visit.

Davis was willing to talk of the future, but not of the past. In answer to direct questions he said:

To get here you have come through some of the pine forests which abound in the South. Now the country has been getting its lumber largely from the middle-west and the north. The deciduous forests, and the pine and the hemlock north of the Ohio, will one day not far off, be exhausted, and the country will then turn to the south where we have not only hard wood in Arkansas and all the mountain and hill country, but the best pine in vast quantities extending across the southern part of the Gulf States.

And lumber is only one of the factors of the future wealth of the South. You know that iron and coal have been discovered in several southern states and already these are being used industrially at Birmingham and elsewhere. We are learning how to rotate crops, and agriculturally there is a great future for the South. We shall give you tropical fruits in abundance, and your big cities will have fresh vegetables from the south after snow flies in your streets.

Our cities are building up—New Orleans, Atlanta, Birmingham, Memphis—while the vast state of Texas is just awakening. There is every reason to be hopeful for the future of the South with its resources undreamed of in the exclusive cotton days and we are already beginning to feel its new industrial impulse.

Mrs. Davis entertained the honeymooners when her husband excused himself and went into the orchard.

Presently he came back with an arm load of orange boughs heavy laden with golden fruit. Carrying these in one arm, he offered the other to Mrs. Brown and escorted her down the steps. At the buggy he helped her into the vehicle as gallantly as a bridegroom, and more gracefully than the amazed and blushing but grateful groom could have done, and placed them in her arms.

Perhaps Mr. Davis never knew that he had contributed to the young reporter's financial welfare. An article on the Confederate Chief caused his salary to be raised from $10 to $13 a week.

CHAPTER XLVI

EMBODIED HISTORY OF
THE SOUTH

———◄◦►———

THOUGH JEFFERSON DAVIS had persistently eschewed politics and disappointed his friends by not serving again in the United States Senate, the Mississippi Legislature at length persuaded him to let them honor him in a formal ceremony. The date set was March 10, 1884.

At the Capitol, where the two houses met in joint convention, every space was occupied. Galleries and windows were filled. Jefferson Davis entered the hall on the arm of Governor Robert Lowry, followed by the Supreme Court Judges and other officials. It was Davis's first appearance in a legislative assembly in almost two decades. "His entrance was greeted with the wildest enthusiasm," the papers said. Lowry wrote in his *History of Mississippi:* "Cheer after cheer went up, handkerchiefs waved, and the grand old man knew that he was appreciated by his own people."

When quiet was obtained, G. D. Shands, the Lieutenant Governor and presiding officer of the joint convention, presented Mr. Davis as "the embodied history of the South." Davis's speech exemplified the man; it was dignified, thoughtful, positive, winning. His voice still held its stirring quality. He spoke of Mississippi's bright future and of the present "transition state, which is always difficult, both in society and nature." Then he came to the crux of an old argument.

It has been said that I should apply to the United States for a pardon, but repentance must precede the right of pardon, and I have not repented. Remembering, as I must, all which has been suffered, all which has been lost, disappointed hopes and crushed aspirations, yet I deliberately say, if it were to do over again, I would again do just as I did in 1861.

469

Momentarily the audience held its breath, particularly those politicians who feared to give offense to the North. Then, after a burst of applause, Davis continued.

No one is a arbiter of his own fate. . . . Our people have accepted the decree. It therefore behooves them, as they may, to promote the general welfare of the Union, to show to the world that hereafter, as heretofore, the patriotism of our people is not measured by lines of latitude and longitude, but is as broad as the obligations they have assumed and embraces the whole of our ocean-bound domain.

An intense atmosphere of deep feeling pervaded the assemblage as Davis concluded:

I will now, Senators and Representatives, and ladies and gentlemen, bid you an affectionate, and, it may be, a last farewell.

The people sat utterly still for some moments. "The reverent and pained expressions on their faces" showed that they accepted the farewell in its literal impressiveness. Finally the thundering applause burst forth.

Davis's political philosophy was consistent to the end. He was still single-minded in his loyalty and devotion to the principle of State sovereignty. With all his heart he hoped that the States would never yield too much to the supremacy of a central government.

When he returned to Beauvoir Davis thought that he had made the last speech of his life, and he expected to settle down to enjoy as far as possible the privileges of old age. But as long as a man owned a plantation on the splendid, lawless river he could never know complete freedom from worry. Almost immediately after his arrival at home a telegram called him to Brierfield where a flood was again threatening to inundate his fields. Shortly Davis was supervising the day and night work of strengthening the levees, which just barely kept ahead of the rising waters.

Lise Hamer had sought her great-uncle's advice about levees. She now seemed contrite for having tried to keep his Brierfield property from him. The bitterness on both sides had begun to soften in 1882, when Davis wrote her: "I have not felt such alienation from you as your letter indicates you believed to exist." All his remaining years he would be helping Lise to control the flood waters and trying to persuade their neighbors to share in the expense.

The flood evil of the spring of 1884 was not averted. In April the Brierfield tenants again had to flee their houses. The fear of floods was one reason that it was difficult to attract proper labor.

Davis spent a June fortnight in New Orleans conferring with various owners of land on Palmyra. He hoped "to get a levee which would give full security to the island and attract all the labor wanted." But the other landlords expected him to put up most of the cash for the construction work. Davis had to go again into debt —an added $6,000—the one thing he dreaded to do.

The Davises, in these latter years, had an exceedingly small income. All the receipts seemed to be needed to keep Brierfield going. One well-meaning, prideful overseer named Cameron ran the plantation debt up to near $10,000 in one year. Davis wrote Lise Hamer that he was laboring "under much occupation and more tribulation."

To meet current living expenses Davis was forced to sell, parcel by parcel, most of the six hundred acres of timber to the north and behind Beauvoir. And now a severe blow indeed came when Addison Hayes, who handled the financial business of Brierfield, developed tuberculosis and prepared to move to the dry atmosphere of Colorado Springs. Davis felt that the last stout supporting prop had been taken from him.

Though living in relative privacy, occasional assaults from the North reached him. At a meeting of the Grand Army of the Republic in St. Louis in the autumn of 1884 General Sherman concocted a sensational new charge. Twenty years after the conflict he rose to state publicly that it was "not a war of secession from the United States, but a conspiracy." He claimed he had been "behind the curtain and seen letters and heard conversations that could not be repeated." He charged that Jefferson Davis was "a conspirator," that his object was "to get a fulcrum from which to operate against the Northern States and to make Northerners slaves." He avowed that he had seen a letter from Davis to a man whose name he could not mention because he was now a Senator, and that Davis had threatened to turn Lee's army against any State that might attempt to secede from the Confederacy.

This accusation appeared first in the St. Louis *Republican*, and was then quoted widely. On November 4, 1884, Davis wrote the editor of the *Republican*:

This public assault, under the covert plea that it is based upon information which regard for a United States Senator does not permit him to present, will, to honorable minds, suggest the idea of irresponsible slander.

It is thus devolved upon me to say that the allegation of my ever having written such a letter as is described is unqualifiedly false; and the assertion that I had any purpose or wish to destroy the liberty and equal rights of any State, either North or South, is a reckless falsehood, especially because it was generally known before, as well as during the War between the States, I was an earnest advocate of the strict construction of State-rights theory of Mr. Jefferson. What motive other than personal malignity can be conceived for so gross a libel?

If General Sherman has access to any letters purporting to have been written by me, which will sustain his accusations, let him produce them or wear the brand of a base slanderer.

When challenged to produce the letter, Sherman was unable to do so.

Senator Zebulon Vance, former Governor of North Carolina, to whom Sherman presumably referred, sent a statement to the St. Louis *Globe-Democrat,* denying he had ever seen or heard of such a letter. Every letter written to him on a political topic by President Davis, he said, was to be found faithfully copied in the official Letter Books of the Executive Department of North Carolina. Those letters were seized by General Sherman's troops and were now stored in the War Department in Washington.

Sherman claimed that yet a number were left at the State House and the Governor's mansion, which he had occupied in April, 1865. Among them, he said, was the particular Davis letter referred to in his St. Louis speech. Vance declared categorically that no documents or letters whatever were left at his residence. The reasons given by Sherman to corroborate his statement, he said, were such as "would scarcely recommend themselves to a respectable lawyer."

On the Senate floor Vance defended the South as well as the ex-President.

It may be that Northern gentlemen who were on the victorious side during the Civil War cannot properly appreciate the feelings of those who were on the side of misfortune and defeat. They seem to regard it as quite a sin and shame that we do not readily join in the denunciations that are heaped upon him who was our leader in that war, and hasten to condemn him on all occasions as the surest way of excusing our conduct and commending ourselves to the good opinion of our late opponents. Surely no man of even the lightest sense of honor in his composition would respect any Southern man who would thus debase himself. Surely the most flagrant and rampant trafficker in issues of sectional hatred would respect more an adversary who came to him walking upright on his feet than one crawling.

When Sherman made the new claim that the questionable letter had been burned with some of his other papers in the Chicago fire, the whole country scoffed. A Washington paper of January 13, 1885, boldly announced in a headline: "General Sherman's Mendacity Thoroughly Exposed."

Though the fabricated "conspiracy" of Davis was disproved, the talk of the slander did not die easily. Senator John Sherman later reiterated on the floor of the Senate his brother's charge against Davis so that it would be set down in the Congressional Record. But owing to the power of partisan hostility and the Ohio politician's influence, the Senate declined to write into the record the testimony showing the accusation to be false.

Concerning Senator Sherman's tactics Davis replied in a public letter:

The epithet of "traitor" which Senator Sherman in debate applied to myself is his mode of retaliation for my denunciation of his brother. I have been compelled to prove General Sherman to be a falsifier and a slanderer in order to protect my character against his wilful and unscrupulous mendacity.

As the Republican party renounced the issue of treason when it abandoned my trial in 1867, not at my instance, but in face of my defiance, its leaders of the present day but stultify themselves in the cry of traitor, which they raise at the mention of my name.

Davis finally dismissed General Sherman with contempt.

He stands pilloried before the public and all future history as an imbecile scold, or an infamous slanderer— As either he is harmless.

Jefferson Davis's chief attackers in his last decade, Joseph Johnston and Sherman, became closer friends. Their common hatred of Davis and their failure to stain his integrity proved a magnetic bond. As Johnston became more and more discredited in the South he sought consolation in the North and was pallbearer at numerous funerals of former Union Generals. Ironically, in February, 1891, he was to catch his death from standing uncovered in New York's icy damp, while serving as a pallbearer to the much younger General Sherman.

In the late spring of 1885, while the Sherman slander was still simmering, General Grant was nearing death from cancer of the throat and valiantly working to complete his memoirs to pay his debts and leave a competence for his wife. The Boston *Globe* called on Jefferson Davis for an expression on Grant's career. But Davis declined to respond. "General Grant is dying," he said. "Instead of seeking to disturb the quiet of his closing hours, I would, if it were in my power, contribute to the peace of his mind and the comfort of his body."

Within a week Davis received a cutting of an editorial from the Macon (Georgia) *Telegraph and Messenger.*

As these lines are written General Grant may be dead. Jefferson Davis must soon follow. It will not be forgotten that Jefferson Davis, as Secretary of War, saved Grant, a sub-lieutenant, from lasting disgrace by permitting him to resign in the face of a court martial. If the North expects the South to weep for Grant, may not the South expect the North to dismiss its malignity at the side of the open grave and treat Jefferson Davis, the United States officer, the United States Senator, and once Secretary of War, with becoming respect?

General Grant heroically finished his two-volume work on July 1 and lingered on until July 23. During his last weeks most of the Southern papers expressed sympathy and kindly feelings. As the foremost Union General, Grant was given a magnificent funeral. Northern papers printed eulogy upon eulogy, passing over his unfortunate years in the Presidency and dwelling almost wholly on his military activity.

Not long after General Grant's funeral the New York *World* sent a reporter to Beauvoir to check on Davis's physical condition. The man was impressed by his personality, as well as by his state of health.

His manner is genial and very kindly, with the charming courtesy characteristic of the high-bred Southern gentleman. Seventy-seven years of age, Mr. Davis has yet a fresh and vigorous look. His hair, moustache and whiskers are white in part, but his eye is bright and cheerful. His face in repose is almost severely intellectual, but the smile which lights up his mouth, and his quietly cheerful laugh, dispel the first impression of coldness. Few of our public men have the quiet fascination of manner, the old-fashioned grace and the charming conversational powers of Jefferson Davis. His memory is capacious and retentive. One might with a facile phonographic pen collect great stores of reminiscences from his lips.

Then the New York reporter revealed a facet of Davis that only intimate friends knew much about:

A patriotic regard for the public *safety* imposed silence upon Mr. Davis while the war continued, and a magnanimity which they have neither deserved nor appreciated, coupled with a proper sense of personal dignity, have impelled him since to refrain from the refutation of many misstatements by his enemies, utterly scandalous and inexcusable.

At Beauvoir Mr. Davis now enjoyed a pleasant routine, as the reporter remarked. Never a devotee of early rising, he customarily rose at nine, read his mail, and answered some of it. Often he rode about his small estate; though he was approaching eighty he still enjoyed being in the saddle. In the evenings he would read poetry or history or enjoy a lively game of euchre, at which he was expert. He liked the salt water bathing and never tired of the sound of the sea.

But housekeeping on the Gulf Coast was not easy for Varina, who had grown excessively stout and found the heat trying. The servant problem was ever difficult. Robert remained faithful, but cooks and gardeners came and went. As Varina would not cut down on her style of living, she was often dreadfully tired. Strangers in quantities continued to visit Beauvoir; and she did her best to entertain them, however simply, in a manner befitting an ex-President.

A visitor Mr. Davis enjoyed in 1885 was Alexander K. McClure, a noted Philadelphia editor and publisher, who came to Beauvoir to discuss writing commissions. Despite Davis's own financial difficulties, his optimism about the South's future surprised McClure; the publisher had found other Southern leaders glum over the rehabilitation problem, the low price of cotton, the discriminatory freight rates. Davis was pleased to hear from McClure that President Lincoln had often spoken in his hearing with great respect of both himself and Lee. The publisher was convinced that if Lincoln had lived Davis would never have suffered imprisonment. Davis himself had always so believed.

On October 29, 1885, when Davis read of General George B. McClellan's death, the news started a chain of recollections. As Secretary of War, Davis had discerned the young man's superior qualities when he was a mere lieutenant, and he regarded McClellan as "the most able and scientific" of the Northern commanders in the late war. He also reflected on how McClellan, a Democrat, had suffered from political associations. If Lincoln had left him in command after he had saved Washington and the Union at Antietam, Davis believed that he might have taken Richmond. And had McClellan been elected President in 1864, he felt sure that the South would have been treated with justice and decency. Davis also believed that eventually an impartial study of McClellan's career would lead to a more just appraisal. American history had so far been written largely by historians sympathetic to the Republican Party's traditions.

Foremost actors in the fratricidal war had been departing ever since Lee's death at sixty-three in 1870. Many Confederate Generals much younger than Davis were already dead. John Cabell Breckinridge had died in 1875. Braxton Bragg at sixty-five had dropped dead on a Texas street in 1876. Admiral Raphael Semmes had died in August, 1877, and Davis himself had been a pallbearer at Forrest's funeral in the fall of that year. His brother-in-law, Dick Taylor, had died in New Orleans in April, 1879, and four months later John Hood had succumbed to yellow fever on August 20. All of these high officers, Davis could reflect, had been loyal to him. Finally, in 1883 his most annoying political enemy, Alexander Stephens, had died.

Three of the foremost Confederate Generals, however, were still alive in 1885: Joe Johnston, Beauregard, and Longstreet; the first two actively hating Davis, and the third "playing odd games with the Yankees." (Longstreet, the most unpopular of them all in the South, was to live until 1904, the very last of the Confederate high command.) Also left alive now were six of Davis's warm admirers among the Generals: Jubal Early, Dabney Maury, Stephen D. Lee, the redoubtable cavalryman Fitzhugh Lee, South Carolina's Wade Hampton, and Georgia's John B. Gordon. These six were to keep in close touch with the ex-President until his death and to speak eulogies after his passing.

Davis had been growing old almost imperceptibly, with a kind of mellowed gentleness. He had, however, by no means lost his savor for living. Despite his plantation worries and the threats of poverty, he did not want quite yet to have the thread of life broken. Optimistically, he wrote an aging friend, who was eagerly looking to the end: "My downs have been so many, and the feeling of injustice so great that I wish to hold on and see whether the better days may not come."

One day in late March of 1886, after an extensive visitation of guests, a New York reporter came unexpectedly to Beauvoir to get Mr. Davis's opinion on certain current events. Davis was in bed and could not see the man. Mrs. Davis was exhausted. But Winnie received him graciously, and then went to speak with her father.

She returned bearing a penciled note. Mr. Davis said he was not in office, nor was he a candidate for office. So he felt that he had the right "to lead the life of retirement in which the will of others as well as my own has placed me." But shortly after this plea for privacy, Jefferson Davis was to be thrust again into a white-hot glare of national publicity.

CHAPTER XLVII

"ALL THE SOUTH IS AFLAME"

———◆———

IN LATE APRIL of 1886, the State of Alabama was preparing to lay the cornerstone of a monument to its Confederate dead at the Capitol in Montgomery, close to the spot where Jefferson Davis had been sworn in as the Provisional President of the Confederacy. Mr. Davis had been invited as the guest of honor at the ceremony. A committee headed by Montgomery's Mayor, Colonel W. S. Reese, had waited on him at Beauvoir; but Davis had declined. About a fortnight later Reese made a trip to New Orleans to get Davis's bosom friend and factor, Jacob Payne, to persuade him. But Payne said the ex-President could not endure "the worries and fatigue" of such a trip, and that it was useless to press him. Nevertheless, Reese, on returning to Montgomery, stopped off at Beauvoir to try once more. This time he found Mr. Davis in bed and was asked to sit beside him. Reese finally repeated his urgent invitation. Davis still demurred; he feared the consequences of such a trip. He did not want to risk stirring up sectional strife or be embarrassed by fresh manifestations of Northern animosity.

Reese had learned through Mrs. Davis that the President's "heart and life now seemed wrapped up with the happiness of his young daughter Winnie." So he said that if he passed away without giving Alabama and the South the opportunity of publicly showing their love for him, his daughter would never know how dear he was to the hearts of his people. Reese had struck the right chord. Davis reflected for a moment, and "then his countenance lit up, and with that calm, firm voice, he said: 'I'll go; I'll go.'"

When it was announced that the ex-President would make a public appearance in Montgomery, other cities, including Charleston and Richmond, clamored for a visit of honor. Atlanta wanted

478

him to attend the unveiling of a statue to the late Senator Benjamin H. Hill, who had been Davis's ever loyal friend and advocate. Henry W. Grady, golden-tongued orator and a leader of the New South, promised a special train to fetch him to Atlanta.

Savannah begged him to speak at the unveiling of a monument to Nathanael Greene, the Revolutionary hero from Rhode Island, who had spent the last years of his life in Georgia. Davis finally accepted the Atlanta and Savannah invitations. He regarded Hill as the best of the Georgians; and his father had fought under General Greene, who was somehow related to Davis's mother Jane Cook.

On April 27 Mr. Davis and Winnie left Beauvoir for Montgomery in the special railroad car, which had brought Mayor Reese and prominent citizens to accompany them. Maggie Hayes had come to Beauvoir for the celebration and brought her two little girls and the baby boy, Addison Jefferson, who had been born in Memphis shortly before the family moved to Colorado. But at the very last hour, she and Mrs. Davis had to forego the trip, because the boy was stricken with what turned out to be scarlet fever.

Leading Northern newspapers had sent reporters to cover "the progress" of Jefferson Davis. Among the group was Frank Burr, the Philadelphian, who had reported Joseph Johnston's accusation of theft and who now worked for the New York *World*. Wherever the train stopped en route crowds at the stations went wild with enthusiasm and tossed flowers. The *World*'s reporter wrote: "Half a carload of floral offerings were showered upon him during his trip and thousands of other tokens of love."

As Davis's train drew into Montgomery it was greeted by the boom of cannon and "the old familiar yell of the Southern multitude." The thousands of people crowding about the station made it difficult for the ex-President and Georgia's General John B. Gordon, who was his special escort, to reach their carriage drawn by four white horses. Despite a light rain, according to the *World*:

The boom of artillery grew louder and the crash of small arms and fireworks mingled strongly with the cheers of the half-wild populace as the procession moved. Added to the flash of colored fires from the curbstones was the constant discharge of Roman candles, rockets and bombs. The flames of the variously colored lights and lanterns which lined the streets and the lighted windows and brilliant electric sparks helped to make a perfect archway of fires more than half a mile long.

The crowd pressed upon the carriage at every step, trying to touch Jefferson Davis, making the journey to the Exchange Hotel slow. The Montgomery Grays in their Confederate gray, preceded by the band playing "Dixie," marched before the carriage, while the Montgomery Blues in regulation uniform followed.

When the Exchange Hotel was reached, the crowd had swelled in volume until the streets and squares were "a sea of faces." As the carriage drew up in front of the entrance a huge motto "Our Hero" caught Davis's glance. And just as he alighted a set piece of fireworks extending nearly across the square flashed in flame the words "Welcome, Our Hero!"

Mr. Davis seemed overwhelmed by the heartiness of his reception, and as he was led into the hotel he continually bowed right and left with an evident show of emotion. When he reached the top of the stairs on the second floor, a crowd of ladies awaited his coming. In the excitement of the moment some of them lost their self-possession and literally threw their arms about his neck. As he went down the hall to room number 101, which he had occupied in 1861, they scattered flowers in his path. "His apartment, floor, bed, furniture were so strewn with roses," said the *World*, "that it may truthfully be said that he walked on a bank of flowers."

It had been just a quarter of a century since Jefferson Davis had first slept in Room 101 on the night before his inauguration. His welcome had been even more wildly demonstrative now, in April, 1886, than in February, 1861, when William Yancey had introduced him in the memorable words, "The hour and the man have met." Tragic years had intervened since Davis had dreamed of a nation of freedom with the old State sovereignty.

What Davis thought this night as he lay under a silk quilt which had once covered Lafayette, no one knows, but the next morning he saw the town swathed in the national colors. Business houses and private residences alike were hung with the Stars and Stripes. Soldiers marched up and down the streets. Early-morning trains disgorged hordes of passengers along with several extra brass bands. As citizens crowded the main thoroughfare, "thousands of throats gave and echoed enthusiastic hurrahs." The morning's Montgomery *Daily Dispatch* announced in colloquial language: "We are fixing to paint the sky. Now let Dixie reign."

A faithful and stalwart policeman stood on guard outside the door of Mr. Davis's room to keep out all except those who had special credentials. But the ex-President was almost overwhelmed with visitors. Among them was the still pretty widow of Clement Clay, who had been incarcerated with him at Fort Monroe. And Dr. W. O. Baldwin, his physician of 1861, brought his four-year-old granddaughter, Jean Craik, to sit on the ex-President's knee. She was so enchanted with his silver hair and mellow voice that she did not squirm once during the long visit.

Towards noon the rain ceased and the sun shone. Various bands appeared from side streets. Militia in blue and in gray lined up ready for the procession to the Capitol. Mr. Davis entered the carriage with the four white horses. Ex-Governor Watts, who had been in his Cabinet in Richmond, sat beside him. Mayor Reese and Governor O'Neal faced him. General Gordon escorted Winnie Davis in the second carriage. All the way up Dexter Avenue the excited populace was yelling, and Mr. Davis continually bowed.

When the former President sat between two great Corinthian columns on the Capitol portico he looked out upon a crowd that was much larger than that at his 1861 inauguration. When the rain came again, the enthusiastic people did not disperse. Davis noted that Winnie's eyes now and then filled with tears at beholding how the people honored her father.

When Mr. Davis was introduced "as the highest type of Southern manhood," deafening shouts were so prolonged that Mayor Reese had difficulty in quieting the crowd.

Davis had been promised that on this occasion he would not have to make a speech; for his written address at the cornerstone ceremony was to be delivered the next day. So he merely thanked the people for their ardent demonstration, which, he said, surpassed that of twenty-five years before. But he took occasion to remind them that their war was "the only kind of which Christianity approved—a holy war of defense."

Well do I remember seeing your gentle boys so small, to use a farmer's phrase, that they might have been called seedcorn, moving on with eager step and fearless brow to the carnival of death. I looked upon them when their knapsacks and muskets seemed heavier than the boys, and my eyes filled with tears. Many of them found nameless graves. But they live in memory and their spirits stand out, the grand reserve of that column which is marching on with unfaltering steps toward the goal of constitutional liberty.

After General Gordon's eulogy of Jefferson Davis, the artillery resounded with thunderous salutes. Later in the afternoon Mr.

Davis attended a reception in his honor and that night he was taken to the Montgomery Theatre to a benefit dramatic performance for the Soldiers' Monument.

The next day Jefferson Davis spoke at the laying of the cornerstone. His resonant voice could be heard by most of the vast assemblage. His theme was reconciliation between the sections, but he declared the monument would commemorate "the deeds of Alabama's sons who died that you and your descendants should have the inheritance your fathers in the War for Independence left you." "The war between the states," he insisted, "was not revolution, as sovereigns never rebel."

Though yielding nothing of his love for the cause that was defeated, he emphasized that duty pointed to the present and the future, and he urged the citizens "to promote the welfare and happiness of their common country." He could not say "our common country"; for, being still excluded from the benefits of amnesty, he was a man without a country. He stuck rigidly to his written manuscript, in order that no hostile newspaper could twist his words. When he was done, guns roared a salute, and the people's throats became hoarse with cheering.

Mr. Davis attended another reception in the Governor's chambers, returned to his hotel, dined, and then drove to the cemetery to help decorate the graves of fallen soldiers.

Frank Burr marveled in his report to New York:

How this old man, who is fast nearing his eighty years, has stood the exactions of the past two days is a mystery to everyone. He has been moving about a great deal, and has met hundreds of people and shaken them by the hand. Yet he seems well and in the best of spirits. This welcome has evidently given him a new lease on life.

Burr continued:

The committee from Atlanta reached here tonight with three special cars, and Mr. Davis will leave for that place early in the morning. All along the route great preparations have been made to do him honor. All the South is aflame, and where this triumphant march is to stop I cannot predict.

On Friday morning, April 30, at 9:30, Mr. Davis left for Atlanta. A throng had gathered at the station "to get another look at the calm face and stately form of the venerable ex-President." Applause, band music, and the boom of guns once more greeted him. Davis was amazed to see the three special cars covered with flowers, flags, and bunting. Even the rods under the cars carried red, white, and blue streamers. An enlarged portrait of himself was secured on one side of his coach and on the other the name "Davis" was written high in immortelles. Within his coach flowers in silver baskets hung from the ceiling. A Pullman berth had been prepared for him so that he could recline in quiet between stations.

Many papers agreed that his progress was "one prolonged ovation." At the little junction for Tuskeegee five hundred colored and white people mingled to cheer him. At Auburn the cadets were drawn up in line and gave Mr. Davis a Presidential salute of twenty-one guns. Ladies in summer dresses stood on tables outside the station; some were even seated on the station roof. The Hon. Hoke Smith introduced him to the crowd of one thousand as "the most beloved of our countrymen."

It was the high noon of springtime in Alabama and Georgia. All the gardens were in bloom. Wherever the train stopped, according to one reporter, people had "brought their rarest blossoms and laid them at the feet of their old Chieftain." So Jefferson Davis made a number of two-minute speeches, "literally standing knee-deep in flowers."

In Atlanta, after wild confusion, the ex-President and his party finally entered the assigned carriages and started for the residence of Mrs. Benjamin Hill, his hostess, half a mile up Peachtree Street. Some 6,000 public school children in double column threw flowers upon the pavement before the Davis carriage and into the vehicle itself. With 40,000 cheering people lining the street, Davis had to keep his hat off almost all the way.

The news of the ex-President's coming had filled the trains approaching Atlanta from four directions. By Friday night the first 15,000 visitors had arrived. On Saturday the trains brought in 35,000 more. The Atlanta *Constitution* declared that "at no period in her previous history" had the city "had within her borders such a host." "From a score of states, including those of the far North, the people have come to do honor to the revered Davis."

Next day, in introducing Jefferson Davis to the crowd about the Hill monument, Henry W. Grady declared in the grandiloquent style of the time: "Never King inhabited more splendid palace than the millions of brave hearts in which your dear name and fame are forever enshrined."

Davis's address was brief, hardly more than five minutes. After his dignified eulogy of Benjamin Hill, the tenor of his remarks was "ours is a day of peace."

While the echoes of applause were still reverberating, Grady led Winnie before the crowd and presented her as the "Daughter of the Confederacy." "Hats flew into the air and the cheering was like thunder."

During the ceremonies, when the enormous crowd which included some 50,000 Confederate Veterans was in a tumult of enthusiasm over Jefferson Davis, a man on horseback in Confederate gray approached the speaker's platform. He held himself erect and wore a lieutenant general's insignia. Some recognized him as James Longstreet. He had not been invited, for since his behavior in Louisiana he had been spurned by the South. Now, apparently, he had come to make his peace; if not to beg forgiveness, to remind the crowd of his wartime services to the Confederacy.

When he was within some ten feet of the canopy under which Davis sat, someone whispered to him that it was General Longstreet. The crowd, which had been cheering Davis, became intensely still—what would the ex-President do? Longstreet dismounted and slowly approached. Davis rose and went forward. Then in an impulsive gesture he held out his arms. The men embraced. The eyes of Lee's Old War Horse were wet. Some men in the crowd thought of the return of the Prodigal Son as Longstreet was offered a seat on the stage.

The Atlanta *Constitution* commented on Davis's theme of reconciliation and the whole ceremonial celebration thus:

Ours is one country; all that has been done in it to the credit of the American character is the heritage of the whole country, not solely of one section.

But not all the North viewed it as such. Papers like the Cincinnati *Commercial*, which pretended to believe that the Union was in danger whenever an ex-Confederate opened his lips, now foresaw menace in Davis's triumphant tour. A portion of the "loyal" Republican press became excited over some Davis utterances. An indignation meeting was held at Albany, New York, because of the favorable attention he was receiving.

Yet the Atlanta *Constitution* quoted from some hopeful manifestations of understanding in a piece that had appeared in the Philadelphia *News* and in another from the Springfield (Mass.)

Republican. The latter spoke of the "unswerving purpose, bravery and resolution" of the Southerners.

And when the end came it was the defeat of men devoted to what was in their estimation a patriotic purpose. . . . Now they gather to commemorate the lost cause, with no desire to recall it, only to recognize it for what it was to them, to assert it to the world and go about their affairs again.

That is the way we read the honors to Jefferson Davis. . . . How could we respect the Southern people if they did not believe in the thing they undertook to do . . . if they did not honor their leaders and their soldiers, nor exalt their services and their sacrifices? They do well to cherish the sentiment that hallows their story.

To the special car which bore Jefferson Davis to Savannah had been added fresh festoons of flowers and the inscriptions "Buena Vista" and "He Was Manacled for Us." Representing his heroic military record and his martyrdom, the slogans "fired the Southern heart." The trip was another prolonged ovation. In Savannah Mr. Davis was the guest of the Comers on Taylor Street facing the Square, and during his four days there the house was often surrounded by a crowd hoping to see him. Several times he appeared on the iron balcony, bowed his appreciation, and spoke a few words. Each morning before he was out of bed his hostess would send up an eggnog to give him strength to meet the demands of the day. And as he descended the stairs for breakfast, seven-year-old Mary Comer would be at the foot waiting to present him with a boutonniere she had gathered dew-fresh in the garden.

On May 6, 1886, Jefferson Davis made two speeches: one honoring the centennial of the Chatham Artillery, and the other paying tribute to the memory of Nathanael Greene, who had helped win independence from Britain. In this second speech Davis, who had been quite cautious in his previous remarks, let himself go too far. He had sensed in some of the Savannah businessmen a dread of "offending the Yankees," even a desire to please Northern capitalists by pretending the South had done wrong. So in this speech he spontaneously inserted a tinge of defiance.

In 1776 the Colonies acquired State sovereignty. They revolted from the mother country in a desperate struggle that was the cause for which they fought. Is it a lost cause now? Never. . . . The independence of these States, the Constitution, liberty, State sovereignty, which they won in 1776, and which Nathanael Green, son of Rhode Island, helped to win for Georgia, can never die.

When he had finished, there was a mighty surge in the crowd, and the stage was filled with shouting veterans eager to grasp the ex-President's hand. The old statesman was in grave danger of being crushed, as the men, wild with enthusiasm, shoved and pushed to touch him. After some exciting confusion, a lane was at length cleared and Mr. Davis was escorted through the applauding crowd to his carriage.

As some Northern reporters telegraphed the "inflammatory" paragraph to their papers, friends advised Davis to correct the impression. Davis knew how the North hated to be confronted with the parallel of the two wars: one that made Washington a hero, and the other that tried to make Lee and himself traitors. So he determined to make amends that evening at Governor McDaniel's banquet in his honor. "There are some," he said, "who take it for granted that when I allude to State sovereignty I want to bring on another war. I am too old to fight again, and God knows I do not want you to have the necessity of fighting again." He paused as the reporters jotted down his statement. But then, looking into the faces before him, after a moment's reflection, he declared: "However, if that necessity *should* arise, I know you will meet it as you always have discharged every duty you felt called upon to perform."

His triumphal tour ended on a note of unvanquished belief in the right of the South's cause. But he had no doubt said too much. Now, hostile papers attacked him, as if he had blown the roof off the house. Some of them made up preposterous slanders. One went so far as to claim that he had said that now that Lincoln and Grant were dead and in hell, he himself was ready to die. A few Northern papers, however, expressed admiration for the consistency of Davis's stand and were impressed by the tremendous enthusiasm of the Southern people for their defeated leader. The Lowell (Mass.) *Sun* wrote:

Jefferson Davis suddenly emerges from his long retirement, journeys among his people and everywhere receives the most overwhelming manifestation of heartfelt affection, devotion, and reverence.

Such homage is significant, startling. And it is useless to attempt to deny, disguise, or evade the conclusion that there must be something great and noble and true in him and in the cause to evoke this homage.

When Davis returned to Beauvoir, dreadfully fatigued but happy and proud, he found, along with some Northern press cuttings condemning his ardent speeches and misquoting him, a stack of letters from Northerners expressing felicitations. One, written on New York Press Club stationery and dated May 10, 1886, was from Gideon J. Tucker, prominent New York-born lawyer and editor, who had once been Secretary of State of New York.

As one of those who through the long and dreadful Civil War, always opposed Coercion and deplored bloodshed, who believed that the cause of representative government was cruelly damnified by the people of my section, I cannot refrain from congratulating you at this moment upon the consistency and dignity of your course.

I trust your life may yet be prolonged sufficiently to see some returning reason come to the people of the North, and lead them to consider what a spectacle they presented to the world from 1861 to 1865, when, under the name of freedom, they fought for dominion.

Considering the enthusiasm of his triumphal journey, Davis was gratified to know, without any possibility of misconstruction, how dearly his Southland esteemed him. And, best of all, Winnie had been witness. As one paper, commenting on the tributes, said, "If they make the remaining years of his life happier, then they have not been in vain."

Without doubt the glowing trip did sweeten the memories of his last days. For months Mr. Davis received letters of pride about his public appearances. One that he particularly treasured came from Bishop William Green, Chancellor of the University of the South.

I was with you in spirit during your late "ovation" in Alabama and Georgia; and no heart among those vast crowds sent up warmer thanksgiving to God, at seeing such just and long-due honors paid to you, insufficient as they were to repay you for what you have suffered for them. It is good to see how truly you are loved by all our people.

After Davis's return to Beauvoir it took some days for him to recover from the nervous depletion. And then he was again handling a mass of correspondence, supervising his grape culture, and preparing requested articles for magazines.

Except for the increase in visitors following the nation-wide publicity of his triumphant trip to Alabama and Georgia, Jefferson Davis had a comparatively restful summer in 1886. But in October he was faced with a compelling sentimental journey. In 1885 admiring Kentuckians had subscribed money to purchase what had been the birthplace of Jefferson Davis in Fairview to erect a Baptist Church there as a memorial to him. A deed of gift had been made out to Mr. Davis in December, 1885, and he in turn had deeded the land to the Bethel Baptist Association. Now a brick church had been erected and was to be dedicated. His presence was called for.

Davis girded himself for the arduous trip to his native state. He went on the condition that his route of travel be not made known and that he would not be expected to make a speech at the ceremony.

In Fairview he was given an engraving of the log house in which he had been born and which had been torn down to make way for the church. He saw the tablet with an inscription which said that Jefferson Davis had been born on the site of the new edifice and that he had made a gift of the land to the Bethel Baptist Church as a thank offering to God.

Davis listened to eulogistic speeches and the ritual of dedication. When it was all over, the demand for him to speak was so insistent that he finally rose and spoke briefly of his faith in a God who favored no special sect. "I am not a Baptist," he said, "but my father, who was a better man than I, was a Baptist." He mentioned President Holley of Transylvania, a Northern Unitarian, who had taught him when he was a college lad a kind of universal love without prejudice. He spoke of the Kentucky pioneers, who, like his father, lived "in a day before the dawn of sectional strifes." In their beautiful, pristine surroundings, he said, it was no wonder that the early Kentuckians had learned that God was love.

After the eminent visitor had shaken hundreds of hands, he took a last look at his birthsite, which he would never see again, and returned to Beauvoir. Twenty years after his death, on his birthday in 1909, six thousand persons gathered to dedicate the Jefferson Davis Memorial Park. And today a white obelisk to his memory rises 351 feet above the green plain, on the same side of U. S. Highway 68 as the Bethel Church. At the time of its construction it was, next to that of George Washington, the second tallest monument in the Western Hemisphere.

CHAPTER XLVIII

HAPPY BIRTHDAY AND
A BOMBSHELL

———◦◈◦———

JEFFERSON DAVIS'S OPINION had often been sought by both sides of public controversies, but he had remained silent. On two occasions, however, he felt impelled to express himself for the nation's welfare. One concerned a court of arbitration to secure the confidence of both capital and labor, which H. W. Pope of Texas was advocating. Davis was willing to write a statement for publication, and it was reprinted widely.

The old war between capital and labor has called forth the best intellects of Europe. It has disturbed commerce, overthrown Governments, produced anarchy and crept from the wreck without solving the problem. With us the contest is in its incipient state, and happily it may be that something can be done to check its growth.

Davis, who believed stoutly in free enterprise, declared that we should not legislate to destroy the motive of self-interest, which "lies at the foundation of material progress." "The standard of comfort," he pointed out, "rises proportionately to the increase of wealth in a country." He believed that the organization of a court of arbitration would require both "liberality and discretion."

Decisions should be based on something like a cooperative principle of industrial partnership, in which the wages of the employee should be measured by the profits of the corporation. If in this manner a community of interest could be established, the welfare and contentment of both would seem to be a possible result.

In regard to new agitation over a proposed constitutional amendment in Texas prohibiting the manufacture and sale of intoxicating liquors, including beer and wine, Davis reluctantly consented

489

in 1887 to write a letter at the request of his friend ex-Governor
F. R. Lubbock.

Reared in the creed of Democracy, my faith in its tenets has grown
with its growth and I adhere to the maxim that "the world is governed
too much."

To destroy individual liberty and moral responsibility would be to erad-
icate one evil by the substitution of another. . . . The abuse, and not the
use, of stimulants, it must be confessed, is the evil to be remedied.

You have already provision for local prohibition. If it has proved the
wooden horse in which many a disguised enemy to State sovereignty as
the guardian of individual liberty was introduced, then let it be a warning that the progressive march would probably be from village to State,
and from State to United States.

Davis foresaw the trouble and the law-breaking that might
evolve from State or National prohibition. Though the latter did
not come until some thirty years later, it begot an era of bootleg-
ging and gangsterism far worse than he could have envisioned.

Now Davis found himself the center of bitter controversy. Some
of his words were "emblazoned on banners and transparencies at
anti-prohibition meetings." Liquor dealers widely quoted the Confederate ex-President. The prohibition measure failed in Texas.
The temperance people blamed Jefferson Davis and he was roundly
abused not only in Texas but in his own State and elsewhere. In
a public speech Dr. Charles B. Galloway, Bishop of the Methodist
Episcopal Church, South, declared scornfully: "How sad that the
last words of a soldier, sage, and Christian should become the shib-
boleth of the saloons!"

Though stung by the criticism, Davis merely repeated with
emphasis his belief that in the end prohibition would work more
evil than good. "There are better remedies for offenses against the
peace and good order of society," he maintained, "than such a
departure from our principles of constitutional government."

Why not trust to religion and science . . . to prevent the formation of
habits of intemperance, rather than at the sacrifice of personal liberty and
moral responsibility to undertake by coercive means the reformation of
the drunkards?

Early in 1887 Jefferson Davis suffered a personal loss that grieved
him far more than the harsh attacks of the Methodists. At dawn
on the second Sunday of February his devoted friend Bishop Green
died at Sewanee. A few days later he received a letter from Mrs.

Margaret Weber, who had been at the deathbed. She told of the churchman's last illness and peaceful passing, and how he often spoke of Mr. Davis. The very night before his death, she said, he called for Alfriend's *The Life of President Davis* to be brought to his bed and told his children gathered about him, "He is a noble man, and everyone should read this book that he may know how to live." Davis was deeply moved to hear this opinion of him by the good Bishop. He wondered if the time would be short before death came to himself.

In that summer of 1887 Davis lent a kindly ear to an experiment in living headed by Isaiah Montgomery, who as a teen-age lad had rowed him out to catch the Mississippi river boat on the first stage of his journey to his inauguration as President of the Confederacy. Certain colored citizens desired to organize a segregated community ruled entirely by themselves, "free from the restraints and prejudices of the civilization they had known." They seized the opportunity of the completion of the L N O & T Railroad line between Vicksburg and Memphis, when company officials let it be known that they were eager to populate a wilderness of deltaland along its right of way.

Jefferson Davis urged the railroad executives to let Montgomery and his friends have an initial 840 acres for the new colony at a nominal fee: seven dollars an acre, half payment down, the balance to be paid within five years. The tract chosen lay in Bolivar County, about halfway between Memphis and Vicksburg. As Montgomery wrote Mrs. Davis, his committee hoped "to train and educate the youth that they may be well qualified to take up farmwork and bring to it a higher development, instead of being drawn away by the peculiar attractions of town and city life." Montgomery was eventually to become the first mayor of the town called Mound Bayou. Though Mr. Davis was not to live long enough to know of the colony's fine progress, Isaiah Montgomery continued to let Mrs. Davis hear from time to time of its healthy and continuous growth.*

---

* On April 12, 1902, Montgomery wrote Mrs. Davis that the land holdings of the Mound Bayou Corporation had increased to 20,000 acres, "with many improvements in the way of business establishments and cottages, with schools and churches fairly represented." The first child born in Mound Bayou, B. A. Green, became a Harvard graduate and served seven consecutive years as mayor.

In 1960 the town's population was 1,354, all colored, and in the entire segregated community dwelt some 8,000 Negroes. The citizens are highly respected by the neigh-

In midsummer when committees in Georgia began arranging a grand reunion of Confederate Veterans in Macon to coincide with the State Fair to be held in the last week of October, 1887, they brought pressure upon the ex-President to meet with the surviving soldiers of the Confederacy "perhaps for the last time." Mrs. Davis and Margaret Hayes, who had missed his triumphal appearances in Montgomery and Atlanta, would now be able to go with him, as well as Winnie. So, with some misgivings, Davis accepted.

A delegation headed by the young Georgia writer, Harry Stillwell Edwards, arrived at Beauvoir in a special railroad car to escort the Davis party to Macon. Edwards was first received by Winnie, and was immediately struck by her grace of manner: "her face radiant and expectant, full of dignity, of elevated thought."

The long ride eastward to Georgia proved an ordeal. For at every stopping place, as Edwards wrote, "veterans and sons and daughters of veterans stormed the train and took him by assault."

The enthusiasm was indescribable: we seemed to be borne forward upon the crest of some mighty wave in a sea of voices. Flowers covered us, and the train ran under triumphal arches.

At Montgomery newspaper correspondents from the East and the North joined the train, some representing journals that were still bitter against Mr. Davis personally as well as politically. However, since the car the ex-President occupied with his family and a few privileged friends was under his personal control, none could be admitted without his sanction. Being a journalist, Edwards was appealed to by the other reporters to gain entrance and introductions. At length he submitted the question. "Admit them!" Davis said promptly and proudly.

Winnie, less shy than Margaret, immediately became the hostess; she greeted the reporters in the vestibule and laughingly pinned little Confederate emblems on their lapels. According to Edwards, she shortly had them "under the spell of her strong personality." Although some of the Northern correspondents got telegrams from their papers demanding sensations, Davis was to suffer nothing uncomplimentary at their hands.

When at certain stations crowds pushed into the private coach, Winnie, who sat beside her father, quietly but firmly drew his frail hand out of the way of the grasping fingers and offered hers in-

---

boring white people in the county and throughout the State as loyal Americans. The original jail was demolished years ago, "as there was no need for it."

stead. When she reached Macon her hand was sore to the touch and for days she could not put on gloves.

The train that bore Jefferson Davis to his last reunion reached Macon in the night of October 23. He was told that fifty thousand visitors had poured into the little town, where he had been brought as a prisoner in May, 1865, after his capture near Irwinsville. Now a torchlight parade greeted him, and a thousand flares accompanied him to the handsome hillside home of Captain and Mrs. Marshall Johnston, where he and Mrs. Davis were to be house guests.

A ball in Winnie's honor was given the next night at the elegant Coleman mansion next door. Davis did not attend, but he remarked the hundreds of Japanese lanterns stretched festively along the drive and across the veranda. Except for attending an eleven-course dinner for dignitaries, he stayed as quiet as possible and let his womenfolk do the round of social functions.

On what was called "Veteran's Day" five thousand old soldiers began a march from the center of town to the Johnston place where Mr. Davis was to receive them. They had been instructed to pursue in orderly procession the circuitous carriage route up to the Johnston front door. But as they approached the property and saw in the distance the white-haired ex-President waiting on the veranda with his wife and daughters, they broke ranks, and those who were able leaped the long iron picket fence. Shouting joyously the old soldiers rushed pell-mell to greet their Chief and in their enthusiasm almost overpowered him. Twenty men at a time would try to grasp his hand, their eyes brimming with tears. A few bore faded battle flags, saved from capture a quarter century past. As one veteran pushed up to Davis with his treasured flag and began to drape it about his body, the old commander pressed his face into its tattered folds to hide his own tears. Then he staggered slightly with a physical constriction in his chest. "The brave heart that had not quailed under imprisonment and vilification," Mrs. Davis wrote, "gave way under the weight of his people's love and almost stopped beating."

A physician ordered complete rest. There was to be no more exposure to fanfare. But Davis would not disappoint his people, and on Saturday, with his wife and the Johnstons, he drove to the Fair Grounds, where thousands awaited him with their children. The carriage stopped at the bandstand on the inside of the half-mile track, and as the Davises walked up the flight of steps to the stand, the band burst forth with "Dixie." It was Atlanta of 1886 over again, but with more excitement and emotion.

After the ex-President had been introduced, he rose and stood with his left hand resting on a table for support. Then the master of ceremonies asked for the orphans of the Appleton Church Home to come up first to greet him; then the babies and children under twelve. All these little ones shook hands with both Mr. and Mrs. Davis, and a few got kissed. Then came the older children and the adults. It was a fitting scene for a hail-and-farewell, but it was too exhausting. Drawing on an iron will he got through his brief address to the veterans. As they began to shout and rush forward, some officials managed to get Davis quickly into his carriage. He was put to bed as soon as they reached the Johnston house. His physician was now seriously alarmed, and some Northern newspapers reported the ex-President as near death.

On November 1, 1887, as Mr. Davis lay critically ill, Bishop J. N. Galleher of Louisiana, thinking that he "might be pleased to have an old soldier of the Confederacy" minister to him and his family "at a time of such import," offered by telegram to come at once to Macon. However, the patient rallied and insisted he was well enough to travel. So, on the third, his anxious family brought him back to Beauvoir.

Jefferson Davis had made his last appearance before a general reunion of Confederate Veterans. But his eventful, star-crossed life was not over yet, as many reporters assumed. He had another extraordinary crisis to face in 1888. Winnie, "The Daughter of the Confederacy," had fallen in love with a "Yankee."

On January 18, 1888, Joseph Pulitzer, the remarkable Hungarian immigrant Jew, editor of the already powerful New York *World*, stopped for a brief visit with the Davises. He was traveling in his private car with his wife on his way to California. Mrs. Pulitzer had been born Kate Davis in Virginia and though she was no real kin to Jefferson Davis, she liked to assume that she was. The Pulitzers had previously come to be quite fond of Winnie when she had stayed with them in New York the preceding year. Now they hoped to persuade her to go with them to the West Coast. To Mr. Davis, "the two-fold temptation of comfort and economy in seeing a new part of the country was attractive," but Winnie was unwilling to leave her frail father, and she had a secret that lay heavy on her heart. However, she promised to visit the Pulitzers in New York in late spring.

Davis found the forty-one-year-old editor as sound as he was dynamic; he esteemed him for his phenomenal success as journalist and publisher and gainer of honest wealth. Pulitzer, a State Rights Democrat, had come to admire Davis during his prison days. Later he was to be impressed by Mrs. Davis's letter writing, which he declared "should be placed in the highest rank"; and because of her original turn of phrase he was to offer her a correspondent's position on the *World* after her husband's death.

Though Jefferson Davis had thought he was through forever with public speeches after his collapse in Macon, a delegation of young men who were holding a convention at Mississippi City in March, 1888, persuaded him to speak one last time. The meeting hall was only a six-mile buggy ride from Beauvoir. Davis wanted to leave some admonitory words to Southern youth that might have both a harmonizing and stimulating effect.

But when he began in his accustomed evocative, "Friends and fellow citizens," he caught himself and said:

Ah, pardon me, the laws of the United States no longer permit me to designate you as fellow citizens, but I am thankful that I may address you as friends. I feel no regret that I stand before you a man without a country, for my ambition lies buried in the grave of the Confederacy.

Then, surveying his youthful audience intently and being pleased with what he beheld, he spoke words that were prophetic as well as memorable.

The faces I see before me are those of young men; had I not known this I would not have appeared before you. Men in whose hands the destinies of our Southland lie, for love of her I break my silence, to speak to you a few words of respectful admonition. The past is dead; let it bury its dead, its hopes and its aspirations. Before you lies the future—a future full of golden promise; a future of expanding national glory, before which all the world shall stand amazed. Let me beseech you to lay aside all rancor, all bitter sectional feeling, and to take your places in the ranks of those who will bring about a consummation devoutly to be wished—a reunited country.

In his address there was no talk of battlefield valor or moving sacrifice. It was a simple statement urging the South's young men to lay aside ill will and prepare to share in the expanding glory of the United States, for he foresaw the future amazement of the world at its rising power and achievements.

Davis reached his eightieth birthday on June 3, 1888. He had requested that no fuss be made. He desired only quiet. He was rather weary of the people who still came to Beauvoir singly or in battalions. On May 17 Mrs. Davis had written her eldest granddaughter in Colorado Springs that three hundred people were coming to see her grandfather the next day. She dreaded the crowd, she said, but was "filling the hearths with palmetto greens" and arranging flowers.

On June 3 people were kept at a distance, all except a single reporter from the New Orleans *Picayune,* who was granted a brief birthday interview. The reporter found no trace of melancholy in the one-time Secretary of War and President of the Confederacy. He was "immaculately dressed, straight and erect, with traces of his military service still showing in his carriage, and with the flush of health on his pale, refined face." And he revealed "a keen interest in current topics, political, social, religious."

The day was cheered by a deluge of letters and telegrams of felicitation. Presents came from friends and strangers. The State of Mississippi sent a silver crown. A box of lemons arrived from a former Negro servant, Milo Cooper, in Orlando, Florida, who often sent fresh fruit. Even Bettie, the little fifteen-year-old maid and adopted daughter, bought him a gift "with her last fifty cents." In 1879 Mr. Davis had found the five-year-old Elizabeth Tillman destitute and had taken her into the Beauvoir household as a sort of ward. He paid for her education at a Louisiana school and in the summers she stayed at Beauvoir and helped with the housework and ministered to the guests. She was a cheery and appealing child; every member of the family loved her and guests were captivated by her.*

In the midst of the quiet family celebration of June 3, Davis remembered to send a check to the Reverend Mr. Charles Hinsdale, Northern-born Rector of the Church of the Redeemer in Biloxi, of which he was himself a vestryman. A covering note was enclosed, marked and underscored *Private.* It bespoke Davis's depressed financial situation, which caused him considerable embarrassment.

Enclosed I send as a contribution a small sum, which you must regard not as the measure of my will, but of my ability.

To *you* is made the confession that circumstances have made me poorer than an average fisherman; but other demands are held subordinate to the cause of Him who died for the redemption of fallen man.

When the birthday was over, Mrs. Davis wrote Major William Morgan, an intimate Gulf Coast friend, that her husband "did not

* Bettie eventually married a handsome Indian named Henry Hooks, a noted rodeo rider and hunter who became a friend of Theodore Roosevelt.

altogether suffer from the sense of having no place 'among the men that be.'" However, she went on to comment sadly: "It is a frightful thing to drop out of one's place and never find it again."

After Jefferson Davis entered his eighty-first year, he was shortly plunged into an activity of writing. The *North American Review* and other periodicals asked for articles on various subjects.

James Redpath, now managing editor of the *North American Review*, came to Beauvoir in the summer of 1888 to persuade the ex-President to write an article on Andersonville to satisfy the Northern public concerning charges made long before by Senator Blaine. At first Davis declined. He was loath at his advanced age to be drawn into any further controversies. But the Scottish-born Redpath was charmingly persistent, and the proffered honorarium of $250 for each article was a consideration for one in constrained finances. The *Review* also wanted a piece on Robert E. Lee, and other subjects.

Redpath, lifelong political enemy, who had been captivated by Davis when they first met in 1875, now became quite attached to the old statesman, and he enjoyed the slow-paced life on the Gulf Coast, as well as the interesting visitors who came to Beauvoir. One day Davis confessed to his hope of having some first-rate student of American history write a Short History of the United States, which would do justice to the South and its people. And before Redpath returned to New York in late August, he had got Mr. Davis himself started on "A Short History of the Confederate States," as well as on three articles.

On September 6, Mrs. Davis, in acknowledging Redpath's affectionate bread-and-butter letter, wrote that they all missed him greatly. "Your love was reverently delivered to him and warmly welcomed." "Gen. Lee" is done, she said. Her husband had "popularized" his article, avoided military critique and controversy, such as Longstreet's lateness, and shown "the heart of the man through the eyes of one who knew and loved him."

Redpath shortly published an illuminating interview with the ex-President. And Mrs. Davis, in thanking him for his "tender way" of speaking, declared, "He deserves all you said, but 'apples of gold in pictures of silver' are rare nowadays."

After a visit to Brierfield "where he found nothing right," Davis decided to proceed with the Andersonville article. But before he could get back to composition another "Yankee" appeared at Beauvoir. Along with his good looks, six-foot length, impeccable manners, Harvard accent, and obvious seriousness, he bore a bombshell.

Alfred Wilkinson, Jr., a twenty-eight-year-old patent attorney, came from Syracuse, New York, where his family was prominent and had once been quite well-to-do. Winnie had first met Wilkinson in 1887 in Syracuse, when she had gone from the Pulitzers in New York to visit at the home of Dr. Thomas Emory, son of her parents' old Washington friends, Federal General and Mrs. William H. Emory. In Syracuse at an evening party when some local people were rather cool to the Confederate President's daughter, a tall, dark-eyed young man had gallantly defended the Southern cause. For both it was love at first sight. Then Winnie learned that ironically Wilkinson was the grandson of one of the North's outstanding Abolitionists and anti-Southerners, the Reverend Mr. Samuel J. May. When she had returned to Beauvoir she had kept her romance secret.

In the summer of 1888 Winnie had again visited the Pulitzers, and Fred Wilkinson had come to New York to see her. The Pulitzers encouraged the match. Winnie was in a dreadful quandary. Now that she was called upon to attend various gatherings of Confederate Veterans as her father's representative and as "The Daughter of the Confederacy," she was torn between love and what she regarded as loyal duty. Since her return home she had gone into a decline. Even a short drive tired her. Her father was distressed and baffled. She seemed to cling to him, and there was something inexplicable in her manner, as if she expected calamity to fall upon the house. Her mother knew that she corresponded with a Northerner, but she did not dream that the attachment was serious.

Then one day in September, 1888, Fred Wilkinson arrived at Beauvoir to ask for Winnie's hand. He said he could be put off no longer. In his first shock, the father said no. He knew that the Southern people, who had suffered so severely under Reconstruction, still felt too outraged to accept such a match. Winnie, "white as death," declared that she would never love anyone else, but that she would dutifully give up Fred if her parents desired.

However, Fred stated his case so well and revealed such sensitivity and cultivation that Mr. Davis invited him to stay on for some days to become better acquainted.

Privately, Varina, with her natural motherly instincts and worldly mind, inquired into Fred's prospects. Though Wilkinson, Sr., had lost most of the family fortune just before his death, Fred assured her that he could maintain Winnie in comfort. The family still owned a handsome mansion in Syracuse. But Fred had two maiden sisters to support and Winnie would apparently have to live in the house with them. Varina was uneasy about such a situation and reserved judgment. She still hoped that Winnie would marry a scion of some wealthy old New Orleans family. For Winnie to live in wintry upstate New York, where a Southerner was rarely seen, did not seem a bright prospect to her mother.

In the meantime, Mr. Davis and the young man got along splendidly together. Fred, a State Rights Democrat, reminded his host that he had had nothing to do with the war. Davis liked both his address and conversation. One night he took him to the pier bathhouse to observe by the light of flares the flounders in the shallow water—a privilege reserved only for the very special. He even invited Fred to accompany him to Brierfield the next month. Though Davis could not yet give his consent, Winnie saw that her suitor had won her father's favor, and hoped "the rest would follow."

But it was a painful crisis to face: the daughter of the Confederate President marrying "a Yankee." Davis doubted if Winnie could endure the opprobrium of Southern disapproval, which he felt would be heaped upon her—as well as upon him. Yet he began to believe that her restoration to health would come only with his blessing on her union with Fred Wilkinson.

One afternoon some months later Winnie in her dark green riding habit rode over to the Hayward estate near-by and announced to the family sitting on the veranda that her father had given his consent to her marriage.* Her sea gray eyes were radiant. But, she said, they were to keep the engagement secret for a while.

Winnie's rapture was short-lived. For the rumor leaked out. Her choice of a husband met with shocked disapproval from some intimate Davis friends. Veterans and complete strangers began writing recriminatory and even threatening letters. Winnie went into another decline. She had a sense of guilt at bringing new trouble upon her father, whose happiness in his last days had been the motivation of her recent years, just as her happiness held first place in his heart.

---

* Mrs. William Fayssoux recalled to the author at her home in New Orleans in 1957 her clear remembrance of that day when she was the little girl Marguerite Hayward and Winnie dashed up and told her news.

CHAPTER XLIX

THE LAST YEAR

---◄◉►---

DAVIS'S WRITING ACTIVITIES helped to ease his disquiet over Winnie's romance. Early in 1889 he sent the finished piece on Andersonville to the *Review* and duly received a check for $250. But because it dealt so frankly with incidents and persons, the editor, Charles Allen Rice, decided to postpone publication.

However, over the protest of Redpath, Rice published in the May issue an article by Viscount Wolseley, Adjutant General of the British Army. On information supplied by the biased Century's *History of the Civil War*, Wolseley wrote an uncomplimentary piece on Davis, questioning his original fitness for the Presidency and picturing him as a man now weighted down with the conviction that he was a failure. He made the ridiculous charge that Davis had believed 10,000 Enfield rifles would overawe the Union forces. Rice, anticipating the reader interest created by such an attack, offered Davis $250 to write a reply. Davis accepted the commission and wrote of Wolseley thus:

I might well be ashamed if I could feel that the opinion of any European stripling, without an earned record of ability either in civil or military life could affect my reputation in America, and therefore I pass unnoticed his personal depreciation.

As to the rest of the Wolseley indictment, Davis vigorously pointed up that every allegation was "either false in direct statement or false by inference." Then he proceeded to answer the particular charges in detail. Davis thought that perhaps Wolseley was taking gratuitous revenge for his having been too busy to receive him when as a youth during the war the Britisher had called at the President's mansion in Richmond.

Redpath, who had resigned his post at the *Review* (presumably because of his resentment over the publication of Wolseley's ignorant attack), now joined forces with the publisher Robert Belford, who was also the editor of *Belford's Magazine*. Belford sent Redpath to Beauvoir to speed the completion of Davis's *Short History of the Confederate States*.

For a few weeks in 1889 Redpath again lived at Beauvoir House, assisting Mr. Davis in readying the history and, as well, getting him started on his autobiography.

In the meantime Rice had died and Lloyd Stephens Bruce had succeeded him as editor of the *North American Review*. He found both Davis's Andersonville article and his reply to Lord Wolseley still unpublished and wanted to print them. But in "Andersonville" he asked Davis to delete his characterization of General Nelson Miles, his jailor at Fort Monroe, as "a heartless vulgarian." Davis requested that the manuscript be returned unless printed without alteration. The reply to Wolseley was published, and the Andersonville article was finally turned over to *Belford's Magazine* and published there.

In his intimate associations with Davis, Redpath had come to admire him more and more. His conception of the public and private man he was to set forth in his own little work *Neither Traitor nor Rebel*. He spoke of Davis as:

A statesman with clean hands and pure heart, who served his people faithfully from budding manhood to hoary age, without thought of self, with unbending integrity and to the best of his great ability.

In *Belford's Magazine* he declared:

Before I had been with Mr. Davis three days every preconceived idea of him utterly and forever disappeared. Nobody doubted Mr. Davis's intellectual capacity, but it was not his mental power that most impressed me. It was his goodness, first of all, and then his intellectual integrity. I never saw an old man whose face bore more emphatic evidences of a gentle, refined, and benignant character. He seemed to me the ideal embodiment of "sweetness and light."

A homely event of the early spring was the arrival of a new suit of clothes, a gift of Jubal Early, who continued to come to Beauvoir. During a brief visit on December 15, 1888, the General had noted that Mr. Davis's best suit was almost threadbare. He wanted to have a new one tailored for him. Davis said he could not accept a whole suit, but finally agreed to accept a gift of some excellent material.

Early had the material sent to Mercier, Davis's New Orleans tailor, who had his measurements. And Early paid the bill for the tailoring (twenty dollars) before his friend could get it. The suit was of Confederate gray. It became him well—both in his last months and in his coffin.

While Mr. Davis was busily engaged in writing in the spring of 1889, he found relaxation in enjoying his three lively grandchildren, whom Maggie Hayes brought to Beauvoir for a long visit. Though he did not suspect it would be the last time he would see them, he devoted a deal of time to keeping them entertained. He took a special interest in his grandson, Addison Jefferson,* who was now four and a half. He would play a card game called "Johnnie Arcoley" with the boy, and help him arrange his lead soldiers in lines of battle. He gave the little fellow a stuffed dog of glazed cloth with bright painted spots. The child loved it above all his possessions. One night when he was in bed, and the rain poured, he realized he had left his dog somewhere in the garden. He began to howl. His mother and grandmother tried desperately to hush him with both promises and threats, but he would not be stilled. In his own words (in 1953) he "screamed like a hawk." The grandfather, who had gone to bed, got up to investigate the commotion. The boy, in sobs, told him about his dog in the rain. Against the women's agitated protestations Mr. Davis, who could never bear to see a child in distress, put on a raincoat over his nightshirt, pulled on boots, and lighting a lantern, went out in the chill, rainy night to search the extensive grounds. Finally he found the toy under a dripping bush. Triumphantly he brought the wet dog to the boy, who cuddled his pet and, satisfied, dropped off to sleep.

When Maggie left for her home a fortnight later, her father missed her and the children more than ever before. He wrote her somewhat poignantly.

The loss of your presence and the absence of the joyous voices of the dear children render this less home than it was when you were here to give it the charm which makes a cot all the heart needs.

God bless and shield you, my beloved child, is the fervent prayer of him to whom you have been a joy and a comfort from your birth.

Shortly after the Hayeses's departure, Davis became ill. He was worried over Winnie's health and the criticism her rumored engage-

* After the death of the ex-President, because there were no heirs through the male line, the boy's name was legally changed to Jefferson Hayes-Davis.

ment to a Northerner was stirring up in the South. The mails continued to bring disapproving letters.

Not able to bear being an added burden to his wife, now without servants, Davis sent for little Bettie Tillman at school in Louisiana. Bettie never failed to brighten the Davis household.

Dearest Bettie:
Come at once, I have been much unwell and need your loving hands and touch to again restore me.

Show this letter to Miss Munro and Mr. Alexander and I am sure they will excuse you.

Bring the "makings" for the delicious herbal tea.

Now for the future, don't worry, dearest little girl, this crisis will pass, and your old Banny will show you several new tricks, maybe sooner.

Since she was really needed at Beauvoir, Bettie stayed on after Mr. Davis recovered, and Mr. and Mrs. Davis would alternate in "hearing her lessons."

Though Davis had marked "Private" his note of June 3, 1888, to the Reverend Mr. Hinsdale, the low state of the Davis finances was widely known. Whenever offers of financial help came, however, Davis would reply that any funds that could be raised should go to disabled veterans or to widows and orphans. Friends tried numerous devices whereby he could be relieved of monetary embarrassment without offending his pride. D. R. Porter, Assistant Secretary of State of Mississippi, knew that Davis owned 5,700 acres of undeveloped land in Arkansas. He proposed to form a corporation entitled the Davis Land Company and sell shares at $10 each. Subscriptions for stock were to be sent to the President of the First National Bank of Jackson, Mississippi.

The prospectus stated with perhaps some exaggeration for quick effect: "It is known that the Hon. Jefferson Davis owes more than $40,000, and that his actual income, over and above the requirements of interest on this debt, does not amount to $200."

Though the prospectus did not mention the considerable amounts of money poured into the levees at Brierfield, it declared that his present financial depletion arose "in great measure from the boundless hospitality made necessary by his exalted position." Many persons felt that Jefferson Davis had for a decade been offering hospitality vicariously in behalf of the South.

For the past two years kind neighbors, among them the A. McL. Kimbroughs, who knew of the enormous drain due to entertaining, had been leaving staple foodstuffs and delicacies on Beauvoir's back veranda in the silence of the night. One friend declared that it would be an everlasting disgrace if a Northern visitor turned up and found the President's pantry bare. Mrs. Davis welcomed these anonymous gifts, but she did not mention them to her proud husband.

The upkeep of Beauvoir was expensive. The grapes had played out, except for personal use. The orange trees had been killed by frosts. There was nothing to bring income. As a rule the Louisiana plantations were leased out at small annual fees and often the lessees could not pay the rent. Brierfield was a perennial headache and in many years showed a considerable debit. But Davis could reflect that he still *possessed* his land, whereas so many of his acquaintances, who had no other income except from crops, had lost their property to banks or private moneylenders. It was the accustomed way of the South to mortgage property; the richest in land were often the poorest in cash. And Davis did have a goodly roof over his head—and always there was the prospect of better times in agriculture.* Fortunately his factor was his lifelong friend, J. U. Payne, who never pressed him.

During the summer of 1889 Mr. Davis had lost interest in going to New Orleans, even though he was ever the welcome guest in a private railroad car maintained by well-off businessmen who commuted from the Mississippi Coast area. When he was not writing, he cared for little but sitting on the veranda in his favorite rocking chair and looking at the sea. However, he enjoyed receiving letters from former associates like John Reagan, now a Senator from Texas, and Burton Harrison, a most successful attorney in New York City, with a summer home in fashionable Bar Harbor. Burton wrote that he often hoped "to treat himself" to a visit to his old Chief at Beauvoir, but that life was "one of work, work every day," and he could join his family in Maine only for short periods. Davis was always interested in news of the beautiful and witty Constance, who had become an author, and of the three handsome Harrison boys.

Davis would answer some of his letters in his own hand, but generally Mrs. Davis, who could imitate his handwriting almost exactly, would reply from his dictation.

Occasionally Mr. Davis would write to his elder grandson in answer to heavy marks the child would make on a sheet of paper

---

* In good crop years without floods, the plantations had made money. In one year the Montgomery Negroes had grossed $18,000 on "Ursino" alone, which they had rented.

and pretend it was a letter. On September 12, 1889, as the boy was approaching his fifth birthday and now had an infant brother, the grandfather sent his last reply.

My darling Son

I was very glad to receive your letter and you were right in supposing your Papa would understand it. It was a full letter to me, for what more did I wish to know beyond the fact that my dear boy was thinking of me, and wished to talk to me. You are now the big boy of the family and will have to teach your little brother some of the many things you have learned. I look hopefully forward to the time when you will all come to see us. Your grandma is well, your Aunt Winnie, who has been ill for some weeks, is now better. Give my love to your parents and sisters and little brother, and take an armful for yourself from your own Papa.

Both Mr. and Mrs. Davis thought it would be well for Winnie to have a complete change and encouraged her to accept the Pulitzers's invitation for an extended stay in Europe. So, on October 23, 1889, Winnie left Beauvoir for New York to sail with them for France. Her father gave her a letter to Dudley Mann in Paris, in which he said that she might "shed a more rose color on the family news" than he himself could give. She was to remain abroad until the following spring, he wrote, when he trusted she would return in good health "and bring back the light which goes out when she goes away."

But before Winnie could deliver her father's letter, Mann had died. Davis got the news of his ever devoted friend's death just as he prepared to start on a business trip to Brierfield in treacherous November weather. On November 8 Mrs. Davis wrote to Maggie Hayes:

Your poor old father went off on a trip to Brierfield positively refusing to let me go, though I urged it very much. . . . I did not so much mind his going alone, as he was well.

Heretofore, in recent years, Mrs. Davis had accompanied him on his periodic trips to the plantation. But as relatives were visiting at Beauvoir, Mr. Davis insisted his wife remain with the guests, assuring her he was quite able to make the journey alone. Although he had been growing frailer, she noted that he still "walked with a firm, light step and held his head erect." While his physicians had warned him to avoid any exercise more strenuous than walks along the beach, the only noticeable sign of his advanced years was a slight deafness.

When Mr. Davis took the train for New Orleans at the flagstop pavilion, he had no reason to suspect that he would never see Beauvoir again. But as his wife said goodbye she could not help ruminating on the sad necessity that the aged father had to be taking a business journey that should have been done by a son.

In a sleety rain in New Orleans Mr. Davis caught a severe cold in the chest. Almost as soon as he boarded the steamer *Laura Lee,* he felt an attack of grippe coming on. When he arrived at the Brierfield landing late in the night he was unable to get up, and let himself be carried on to Vicksburg, where the boat docked in the morning.

That afternoon, with supreme will power, he left Vicksburg for the plantation. Arriving at night, he drove through the chill November air to the bed prepared for him at Brierfield. For four days he continued ill, but refused to have a physician sent for. Finally the young plantation manager was so concerned that, on November 11, he secretly telegraphed Mrs. Davis.

On November 12, 1889, Jefferson Davis wrote his wife what proved to be his last letter. He was so near delirium that he misspelled some words and left out others entirely.

My deerest
    If I can get to the landing I will go down on the heathers [Leathers] to-morrow— Lest you should hear alarming I write say I have suffered much but by the help of the Lord—
    Nothing is as it should be, and I am not able even to look at the place— With best wishes to all the household

                                I am as ever
                                    Your Husband

In the phrase "nothing is as it should be," Davis unconsciously epitomized the frustrations of his last quarter century and the ending of an era.

The next day, while he was being made ready to take the river boat for New Orleans, Alice Desmaris, the little niece of the plantation manager, shyly presented her open album and asked him to write a sentiment for her. Jefferson Davis took the proffered book and wrote the last words he was to write in his own hand, which was now firmer than the day before: "May all your paths be peaceful and pleasant, charged with the best fruit, the doing good to others." He dated it "Brierfield, Nov. 13, 1889." Then he was driven through rain to the landing and was put on the *Leathers* only half-conscious.

CHAPTER L

"JEFFERSON DAVIS AT REST"

———◄◦►———

ON RECEIVING THE telegram from Brierfield reporting Mr. Davis's illness, Mrs. Davis had left by the next train for New Orleans. She had then taken the northbound night steamer, commanded by young Captain Leathers, whom she had known as a boy. In her anxiety, Mrs. Davis did not undress for the night, for she had a feeling that her husband might be already coming downstream. As the *Leathers* approached her ship in the night, the young Captain hailed it to ask news of Mr. Davis. When he learned that the sick man was aboard, he brought his boat alongside his father's and, in midriver, Mrs. Davis was put on the ship headed south. When she entered the stateroom her husband was sleeping. But shortly he awoke and was amazed to find his wife at his side.

At Bayou Sara, Louisiana, two physicians came aboard and examined the patient. They found him suffering from acute bronchitis complicated by a recurrence of the old enemy malaria.

A cold rain was falling when the boat docked in New Orleans. Friends were on hand to receive Mr. Davis; among them Jacob Payne, his lifelong factor, who, though enfeebled by years, had braved the bad weather. With him was his son-in-law, Justice C. S. Fenner, and Dr. Chaillé, Dean of the Medical Faculty of Tulane. Also awaiting Mr. Davis were Edgar H. Farrar and his wife Lucy, daughter of Mary Stamps, now pregnant with her seventh child, which she was expecting in January. Dr. Chaillé saw at once, as he had suspected, that Mr. Davis was too ill to be taken to Beauvoir. Justice Fenner insisted he be brought to the Payne house, which his father-in-law had given him and his wife. An ambulance was standing by, with a soft bed prepared by Mother Superior Agnes herself "as a special privilege." Four young medical students of Tulane, sons of veterans, were on hand to carry the stretcher bed to the ambulance.

The Fenner home, which had been built by Mr. Payne, was a commodious house of brownstone stucco at the corner of First Street and Camp in the Garden District. It was set in a large garden where camellias were now in bloom and oranges hung ripe on the trees. Mr. Davis was taken into the downstairs guest room at the southwest corner of the house. A fire burned brightly. The huge Victorian bed of carved oak had been prepared to receive him.

Almost immediately Dr. C. J. Bickham, one of the city's most noted practitioners, arrived for consultation. His verdict and Dr. Chaillé's varied little from that of the doctors at Bayou Sara: acute bronchitis aggravated by a flare-up of malaria.

Mr. Davis, always averse to giving anyone the slightest trouble, expressed the hope that he might go on to Beauvoir the next morning. But to move him again was out of the question. So he submitted to the solicitude and loving attention of the Fenners. His sickroom was cheery, not only with the warming fire but with four great windows that gave onto the garden; in the morning the winter sunshine streamed into the room.

Mrs. Davis was insistent that she nurse her husband herself, as she now had no household duties, and because he seemed to want her constantly at his side. Sixteen-year-old Bettie Tillman, whom both Mr. and Mrs. Davis loved as a daughter, helped; while a capable practical nurse, an octoroon named Lydia, was engaged for personal services. Nannie Smith, great-niece of Mr. Davis, also came from Beauvoir to assist.

During his illness the patient was never left alone for a minute, "but quiet prevailed." No newspapers, letters, or telegrams were brought into his room. Very little talking was allowed. As florist flowers and bouquets from private gardens arrived, Mrs. Davis would bring them to the bedside for a moment, and then take them into the drawing room. Special fruits, jellies, and molds in profusion came from friends and unknown admirers. But as Mr. Davis could eat little, after three days his wife asked that no more food be sent. The patient's diet consisted almost entirely of crushed ice, milk, and beef tea, and once or twice he was persuaded to eat a broiled lamb chop.

Though he was not despondent, Mr. Davis did not entertain hope for his own recovery. Yet one day he said to Dr. Chaillé with a whimsical smile, "It may seem strange to you that a man of my age should desire to live; but I do. There are still some things that I have to do in this world."

One of the things he had in mind was the completion of the autobiography he had scarcely begun. For he said to his wife one morning: "I have not told what I wish to say of my collegemates, Sidney Johnston and Polk. I have much more to say of them. I shall tell a great deal of West Point, and I seem to remember more every day."

Redpath, the new editor of *Belford's Magazine,* being unaware of the gravity of Mr. Davis's illness, wrote that he was preparing to use the Andersonville article in an early issue of *Belford's* and asked for an introductory statement relating how the author had been treated by the *North American Review* in regard to publication of the piece. To this request Mrs. Davis sent a brief penciled note of explanation on November 28.

Mr. Davis can do absolutely nothing. We sit up with him every night and he is a very ill man. He could not write his name, still less read proof. . . . He is weeks, it may be months, it may be for ever, from being "out." I do not want the household told, but am miserably anxious.

Davis's chief desire now was to have his wife ever near him, or Bettie, when Varina was otherwise occupied. Though he accepted their ministrations with unstinted gratitude, he was often concerned about his hostess. Once, after Mrs. Fenner had brought him some special nourishment she had prepared for him, he spoke to his wife of her charm and grace. "But I am giving her trouble. When can we relieve her and go to our own home?"

Davis would not let his wife send for either of the daughters or even let them know how serious his illness was. Winnie was in Paris with the Pulitzers. Margaret was in Colorado Springs with her husband and four little children. "No," he insisted. "Let our darlings be happy while they can. I may get well."

Though Mrs. Davis tried to minimize the danger, the newspapers strongly hinted at the truth. The Fenner home had become the focus of the city's attention. Outside the gate scores of persons gathered daily, waiting to learn of the ex-President's condition. They watched the physicians entering and leaving, and they saw messenger boys arriving with telegrams and flowers.

During the first week of December, Mrs. Davis, the Fenners, the Farrars, and Mary Stamps alternated between hope and despair of his recovery. Now and again the patient would rally so that an expectation of his recovery seemed justified. Davis's resilient constitution and his good habits caused the doctors to think he had a fair chance of survival.

On the morning of the fifth, Mr. Davis woke at daylight to find his wife sitting beside him. He seemed to have taken a decided turn for the better, though the words he spoke were hardly in accord with his improved condition. "I want to tell you," he said, "I am not afraid to die." She begged him to hush such foreboding talk. He took some nourishment and the whole atmosphere became cheerful.

He continued in what was regarded as a convalescent state into midafternoon. When his old friend Jacob Payne came in to see him and commented sanguinely on the perceptible improvement, Davis said, with something like a twinkle in his eye, "I'm afraid I shall have to agree with the doctors for once and admit I am a little better."

That afternoon of December 5, 1889, Winnie in Paris wrote her father a long letter from the Pulitzers' hotel in Rue Courcelles.

My darling Father:
Today I got Mother's letter saying that you were better, but had been very ill. I am broken hearted to think that you could have had bronchitis and I have been away off here. Had I known, or had an idea of what was the matter, I should have come home immediately, but from the telegrams I concluded it was one of those exaggerated reports so often in the newspapers about prominent men. . . . My dearest, I know now that you were suffering all the time, and I cannot get reconciled to the idea of my having, no matter how unwittingly, left you while you were ill.

I think of you all the time, but every time I eat my breakfast, with a plateful of those little white grapes you used to talk about, I wish, oh how I wish, that any good fairy would lend me his travelling carpet for an hour that I might take them to you. . . .

The other night Kate and I took Ralph to the opera, and you should have seen the grandeur of that little fellow with his miniature beaver and dress suit! He opened the box with an air, and altogether behaved like the fine little gentleman he is.*

I have been thinking for days what I could send you to show you that I had thought about you, and amuse you through Xmas day, which is always, I know, a heavy trial to people after they are grown, and remembering all the pleasure we got out of a bundle of illustrated papers that

* Ralph Pulitzer eventually became editor of his father's New York *World* and married Margaret Leech, the writer.

was once sent to me, I have bought you all the Christmas numbers I could find.

Dearest darling Father, when as now, I want to tell you how much I love you I grow bewildered; what words to choose which are able to express to you the devoted love and tenderness of which my heart is, and always will be, full for you, my darling Father— My pen is the mutest thing about me unfortunately and when I am away from you I can only think, and think, and love you for your goodness and tenderness, with which you covered me as with a cloak, all through my little childhood, screening my faults and answering my unreasonable questions with always an honest reply, the rarest thing given to a child in the world. And so, I will end by saying as I began, My darling Father:

With all the devotion in the world

Your Winnanne

Winnie felt a grateful sense of relief as she posted her letter and the large package of Christmas issues of French magazines for her father's enjoyment.

About four o'clock that same afternoon, Mrs. Davis was so encouraged by her husband's condition that she sent a message to the Farrars and Mary Stamps urging them to attend that evening a special performance at the French Opera House, for which they had long had a grilled box reserved because Lucy Farrar was *enceinte,* and in Catholic New Orleans those boxes for expectant mothers were hard to come by.

When Mr. Davis dropped off into a deep, peaceful sleep, his wife, buoyed up by the happy turn, penned a note to an anxious friend.

Then, a few minutes before six, suddenly, with no preliminary warning, the sleeper awoke from his sound sleep shivering with a congestive chill. Alarmed at the ominous change, as the rigors continued, Mrs. Davis poured out a spoonful of medicine and brought it to his bedside. He smiled wanly and made a slight negative movement with his head. She insisted. With a gentle gesture, he pushed her hand from him and murmured courteously: "Pray excuse me. I cannot take it." They were the last words the ex-President spoke. He closed his eyes and seemed to lose consciousness.

It was seven o'clock before the two physicians arrived. As Mr. Davis became comatose, they agreed that the end would not be long in coming. There was nothing they could do for him. He just lay there peacefully, without a trace of pain, his hand in his wife's.

Twice she looked up to tell the doctors she felt a gentle pressure from his fingers.

About ten o'clock young E. D. Fenner, son of the Justice, went to the Opera to fetch the Farrars and Mary Stamps. Within half an hour they had joined the group clustered about the bed: Mrs. Davis, the physicians, the Fenners, Mr. Payne, Nannie Smith, and Bettie.

When his breathing became a trifle labored, the doctors gently turned the patient on his right side. As they did so, he involuntarily raised his arm and laid his cheek upon his hand like a tired child, while the left hand rested lightly upon his breast.

As midnight approached, the watchers saw the respirations grow weaker and weaker and the calm face become excessively pale. A clock in the hall struck twelve. Time merged into the Friday morning of December 6, 1889. Three quarters of an hour later the faint breathing stopped altogether. The thread of life was broken with the utmost gentleness. The great spirit of Jefferson Davis was no longer connected with his frail mortal body.

Mrs. Davis, who had borne up so valiantly for some three weeks, now gave vent to her grief with uncontrolled, racking sobs. Knowing she had exhausted herself with the strain of watchful nursing and aware of her slight predisposition to heart trouble, one of the physicians led her upstairs, and, as the ladies prepared her for bed, he gave her a strong "composing draft." Just before the sedative took effect, Mrs. Davis said she wished Judge Fenner and her kinsman, Edgar Farrar, to make the decisions on funeral arrangements.

Farrar set off straightway for the Western Union Telegraph office and despatched three death messages: to Winnie in Paris; to Addison Hayes in Colorado; and to Governor Lowry of Mississippi.

Soon the Associated Press and New Orleans representatives of various metropolitan newspapers had messages humming over the wires to New York, Chicago, San Francisco, to all the important dailies in the land and to agencies abroad.

Henry W. Grady, editor of the Atlanta *Constitution,* was awakened at his home shortly after two. Immediately he began to compose an editorial for his paper, beginning "This morning is another page in the history of the world. Jefferson Davis is dead!" One simple declaratory sentence in the finished piece stood out: "Jefferson Davis will be mourned in millions of hearts today."

Before Grady's editorial was quite done, the Mayor of New Orleans, Joseph Shakespeare, prepared a note for the local press inviting certain prominent gentlemen to his office at noon to discuss funeral arrangements. He sent a message to each of the Southern Governors. Then in the darkness between three and four of the December morning he walked to the Fenner residence to offer his services and to learn Mrs. Davis's wishes about the funeral.

A chilly fog hung in dense masses. Familiar shapes along the streets lit by the feeble flames in lampposts fell in distorted shadows. The house was shrouded in near-darkness and intense silence. Young Farrar and old Mr. Payne received the Mayor in the hallway. In a back parlor they sketched a statement for the morning paper. At ten minutes past four the proclamation was handed to a waiting reporter from the *Times Democrat.*

Streamers of heavy crepe were tied to the bell-knob. As the pale gray light of day emerged, some passing workmen wearing overalls and carrying their lunches wrapped in red bandannas were the first to spy the emblem of death hanging near the door. Their low, early-morning talk ceased. Four policemen returning from a night on duty next saw the crepe, paused, and then went on, speaking in undertones. After day broke, early pedestrians took off their hats respectfully.

It was almost eight o'clock before the risen sun dissolved the fog. At ten minutes past eight, although the exhausted household was not yet stirring, the first ladies arrived to pay calls of condolence, their arms full of flowers.

Mrs. Davis slept on until almost noon. When she awoke, she would see no one besides the family except William Preston Johnston, President of Tulane University.

There had been some thought that Mr. Davis might be laid to rest with simple ceremony at Beauvoir. But as a flood of telegrams began to pour in from Governors eager to attend the funeral, from scores of Confederate associations, from Generals, United States Senators, Supreme Court Justice Lamar in Washington, and private citizens in New York, Memphis, St. Louis, and a hundred other places, Judge Fenner and Edgar Farrar agreed that a private funeral would not satisfy those who revered Jefferson Davis.

As telegrams from State capitals and various towns like Memphis and Macon arrived, asking for the President's body, the widow hardly knew what to do. But when Preston Johnston referred to her a note from the President of the Metairie Cemetery Association in New Orleans, she began to make up her mind.

While the entire South claims him as her own, New Orleans asks that
Jefferson Davis be laid to rest within the city where he fell asleep.

New Orleans was convenient and altogether fitting, at least for a
temporary resting place. The tomb of the Army of Northern Virginia at Metairie was selected.

To give delegations from distant states time to arrive on the slow
trains of the period, the funeral was finally set for high noon,
Wednesday, December 11. Arrangements were put in the hands of an
executive committee, with Johnston as chairman. It was decided
that when Mrs. Davis relinquished her husband's body, the ex-
President should lie in state in the City Hall.

By afternoon all the public buildings of New Orleans were draped
with crepe. Most of the shops and private homes, too, had hung
emblems of mourning on their doors and from their balconies.
Throughout the towns and cities of the South flags were set at half-
mast and public buildings were hung with black.

Back in the Fenner drawing room, a photograph was taken of
Jefferson Davis as he lay on a white-sheeted bier, dressed in his suit
of Confederate gray. At his head were two crossed palms and in
the angle of the stems was a sheaf of full-grained golden wheat. A
pillow of roses lay to the side. In his thin hands, which were casually
clasped, someone had put a tiny bunch of white rosebuds.

After the photographer was gone, Mrs. Davis came and sat alone
at her husband's side, just as she had done during his last illness
and during the past decade when she was his amanuensis.

Eight-year-old Anna Farrar, who had adored her great-great-
uncle, had persuaded her grandmother, Mary Stamps, to let her say
goodbye to him before he was put in the casket. They came together, when the room was empty. Little Anna, who was to become
an artist, had never seen her Uncle Jeff without shoes and was
deeply impressed by the beautiful structure of his feet clad in sheer
black silk socks. She was to remember all her life the remarkable
slenderness of those feet and the high aristocratic arches. She was
to remember, too, the grief in the Farrar household: her mother,
Lucy, sitting and weeping uncontrollably, her grandmother standing beside her, "composed as always, but pale as death."

When Anna slipped quietly out of the room, Mary Stamps was
left alone for some minutes with the man she had idolized and who

had found with her a spiritual rapport such as he had perhaps never known with any other human being.

The hall, library, and front veranda of the Fenner home were crowded with friends coming and going, offering service and sympathy; but no one outside the immediate family was permitted in the drawing room. There was one exception made—for an aged Negro named Milo Cooper. He was a former slave of Joseph Davis and had known the ex-President when he was a youth. Cooper had never forgotten his white friends in their adversity; it was he who had sent citrus fruit to Mr. Davis on his eightieth birthday. Reading in a Florida small-town paper of the grave illness, Cooper, full of years and various aches and pains, started for New Orleans. On finally reaching the Fenner home, he was dismayed to find crepe on the front door and sat down on the steps utterly crushed. The household was distressed by his inconsolable grief. When Mrs. Davis was told of the circumstances, she consented to let him look at "Marse Jeff." As he beheld the still face he remembered as a youth, the old Negro broke into heavy weeping. Then he dropped to his unsteady knees and prayed for those left behind.

In midafternoon Mrs. Davis resumed her vigil by the bier. At intervals she would read selected telegrams of condolence, including those from the Governors of the Southern States. Mrs. Davis was particularly moved by the messages from Senator John Reagan of Texas and Fitzhugh Lee, now Governor of Virginia.

The longest telegram was in the form of resolutions drawn up by some prominent Mississippians in Washington, headed by Supreme Court Justice L. Q. C. Lamar. One packed sentence read:

We recall with tender emotion his career as a soldier and civilian, brilliant, eventful, and without parallel in our annals, whether as a soldier pouring out his blood on foreign battlefields, as a statesman in the Cabinet of the nation, as the leader of his party in Congress, as the guiding spirit of the South through the stormiest period of her history, as the vicarious sufferer for us and his people in defeat, he has constantly and fully met the requirements of the most exacting criticism and illustrated in every station and condition the manly courage, the acute intellect, the heroic fortitude, the unfaltering devotion to duty, the constant sacrifice to conviction that won for him our confidence, admiration, love, and reverence.

The phrase "without parallel in our annals" struck the widow forcibly.

As the December light began to dim, two nuns from the St. Alphonsus Convent arrived, with a group of orphan girls in their charge, and earnestly begged to be allowed to pray for the soul of Jefferson Davis. It was such a surprising and touching request that Mrs. Davis granted it, and retired from the room.

As the black-garbed nuns and the little girls knelt around the bier, the pale blue light from the fading afternoon sky filtered through an upper lattice of the window and fell gently upon the serene face of the statesman.

At seven in the evening, a black hearse drawn by white horses arrived with the copper-lined casket covered with black plush. The silver plate on the coffin lid bore the chaste inscription: Jefferson Davis at Rest.

CHAPTER LI

THE SOUTH'S
GREATEST FUNERAL

———◆———

DURING THE AFTERNOON of December 6, while Mrs. Davis sat in solitude by her husband in the Fenner drawing room, carpenters and decorators at the City Hall were feverishly preparing the Council Chamber to receive the body. Outside, the massive granite columns were enshrouded in black cloth and twined with ivy. Within, walls were covered with more black cloth, and the oil portraits of Henry Clay and William Henry Harrison on either side of the Mayor's desk were draped with crepe. High above the desk, an American flag was crossed with a tattered ensign which the Fourth Louisiana had carried through the war. The Mayor's desk was completely concealed by white chrysanthemums.

A catafalque with marble pedestals to support the casket was set up on a two-step dais. From the ceiling above hung strips of crepe wound with ropes of ivy. Inside the railing and pointing at the catafalque stood two twelve-pound howitzers as military insignia.

At half past ten that night the Washington Artillery marched to the City Hall to perform its duty as a guard of honor. When the hearse arrived just before midnight, streets surrounding the City Hall and the building itself were crowded with spectators. At a signal the troops passed through the throng of watchers and set the casket on the catafalque. The upper lid was removed to reveal the pale, chiseled features under glass. On the lower lid was placed a battle flag of the Washington Artillery, a sheaf of wheat, and crossed "Spanish daggers" from the tropical plant of that name.

Though the official lying-in-state was scheduled to begin at ten in the morning, the midnight crowd that had gathered was allowed to look at the ex-President. In the morning at ten, when the doors

517

were opened, a tremendous throng, some of whom had been waiting since daylight, surged forward. In low tones veterans and police
directed a double line that entered from St. Charles Street and
made their exit on the paralleling Lafayette.

A place near the head of the line had been reserved for General
George W. Jones, one-time United States Senator from Iowa and
Davis's collegemate at Transylvania. Jones had made an arduous railroad journey and had arrived a few hours after his friend's death.
Because of his unsteady feet, the handsome old man, with dark
eyes and flowing white beard, was escorted by a soldier to the dais.
For a long time he gazed in silence at the calm face of the man to
whom he had been devoted for more than six decades. Then he bent
over the casket as if to kiss the brow, while tears dropped on the
glass.

Shortly afterwards passed a group of Negroes, who had been
slaves on the Davis plantation. They had come from upriver to pay
their last respects to their one-time master. One of them, William
Sanford, then living at Vicksburg, seemed the most grieved. Gazing
on his old friend, he wept unashamedly. When he left the hall, a
Northern reporter asked him how he felt towards Mr. Davis. Wiping
his eyes, he said, "That I loved him this shows, and I can say that
every colored man he ever owned loved him."

All through the first afternoon and evening, thousands passed
the bier. Many mothers brought little children and lifted them up
to behold Jefferson Davis for an historic memory.

A few minutes before midnight the honor guard was withdrawn
from the Council Chamber. The funeral director and his assistants
unscrewed the glass lid and carefully removed it from the casket.
Then they withdrew, leaving the statesman momentarily alone in
the vast, flower-scented room. While the clock in the City Hall was
striking twelve, Margaret Hayes from Colorado arrived, escorted by
her first cousin, General Joseph R. Davis. "Little Pollie," the child
Jefferson Davis had really loved most, remained in concentrated
silence beside her father for a quarter of an hour.

After she left, Orion Frazee, a sculptor from Atlanta, came in with
Edgar Farrar to make a death mask. The glass was finally replaced
and the guard called to resume its vigil.

For three days and evenings men and women of all degrees
and kinds, from near and far, white, colored, alien, took a farewell
glance at the South's most illustrious son. Some came out of curiosity
and some because they caught the contagion of strange solemnity

in the air. But the majority seemed sincerely moved, and they grieved for what Jefferson Davis had endured.

In viewing the body of Jefferson Davis women found consolation for hurts they had cherished for a quarter century: for husbands, fathers, sons, brothers killed; for homes burned; plantations lost; for all the humiliations and criminal stupidity of Reconstruction. Under glass in this copper-lined box, concentrated in the eighty-one-year-old statesman, lay the epitome of the South's struggle and defeat and endurance. Hearts that had not been at peace since 1865 found relief as people gazed upon the serene face of the fallen leader. Many recalled Shakespeare's line: "After life's fitful fever he sleeps well . . . nothing can touch him further."

Trains from three directions continued to arrive loaded with citizens who had come to pay their respects. The hotels and boarding houses had been filled to overflowing ever since the first night following the ex-President's death. Rooms for rent were offered in a thousand private homes. Some delegations, like one from Kentucky, made their headquarters in chartered sleeping cars.

With each passing day the great chamber in the City Hall had become more overpoweringly sweet with the scent from hundreds of floral offerings. Many arrangements were spectacular in their conception and execution, and the newspapers described scores of them in detail. One of the most magnificent was a tribute from the Confederate Association of Missouri: a cross eight feet tall, made of yellow rosebuds and white camellias. Students of the Jesuit College in New Orleans sent a colossal urn "woven of African immortelles and filled with Duchess roses and calla lilies." "An arch of purple immortelles with a swinging gate of gold-colored chrysanthemums," sent by Sons of Veterans of the Louisiana Artillery, who had fought with the Army of Northern Virginia, bore the inscription "To the hero of our fathers."

But one humble offering arrived that the ex-President would have appreciated more than the magnificent showpieces: two bunches of violets packed in damp sponges in an old shoe box. It came from a rural South Carolina address with a card that merely said "From an old soldier and his son."

It soothed the widow to read telegrams and letters of condolence, especially those from colored persons her husband had been fond of. From Brierfield came a note signed by thirteen Negroes that stirred nostalgic reminiscence.

We, the old servants and tenants of our beloved master, Honorable Jefferson Davis, have cause to mingle our tears over his death, who was always so kind and thoughtful of our peace and happiness. We extend to you our humble sympathy.

Thornton Montgomery, whom Jefferson Davis had helped educate and who had become a man of means in Christine, North Dakota, wrote:

Miss Varina: I have watched with deep interest and solicitude the illness of Mr. Davis at Brierfield, his trip down on the steamer *Leathers,* and your meeting and returning with him to the residence of Mr. Payne in New Orleans, and I had hoped that with his great will power to sustain him he would recover. But, alas for human endeavor! an over-ruling Providence has willed it otherwise. I appreciate your great loss, and my heart goes out to you in this hour of your deepest affliction.

Would that I could help you bear the burden that is yours today. Since I am powerless to do so, I beg you to accept our tenderest sympathy.

Your very obedient servant,
Thornton

The Mayor of New Orleans brought Mrs. Davis a telegram that had been addressed to him from Raleigh, North Carolina, by the disconsolate colored man, James H. Jones, who had accompanied Mrs. Davis on the flight from Richmond and was now employed by the Government in Washington.

As the old body servant of the late Jefferson Davis, my great desire was to be the driver of the remains of my old master to their last resting place. Returning too late to join the State Delegation from this city, I am deprived of the opportunity of showing my lasting appreciation of my best friend.

Newspaper estimates of the number that passed the bier in three days varied widely; one exaggerated report put the figure at 150,000, but none was under 50,000. Because of the clamor of the yet unsatisfied, on December 11, the day of the funeral, set for high noon, the doors of the Council Chamber were opened at seven.

At a quarter to twelve Father Darius Hubert, a Catholic chaplain of the Confederate Army, took his soldierly stand at the head of the coffin. An awesome hush fell upon the room as the detail of honor from the Louisiana Field Artillery, which was to bear the casket to the caisson, entered. At ten minutes to twelve, according to schedule, the funeral director closed the lid, screwed it down tight, just as eight Governors of Southern States appeared in a body. It was too late for a farewell look. The dignitaries merely marched in single file past the bier, as a delegation from the South Carolina Legislature in the charge of Captain Joseph Haskell arrived in breathless haste.

Haskell was given the honor of draping over the coffin a silk Confederate flag from Beauvoir. Then he laid upon it a fresh sheaf of wheat, a badge of the Army of Northern Virginia, and the sword which Jefferson Davis had worn at Buena Vista. Eight soldiers raised the burden to their shoulders and bore it at funereal pace down the long corridor and out upon the great portico where another catafalque had been provided. Bishop Galleher of Louisiana and Bishop Thompson of Mississippi led the procession of clergy that followed. Fifteen other Episcopal ministers were in attendance, including the Reverend Mr. Ebenezer Thompson, the new rector from Biloxi. Then came Rabbi Leucht, several Catholic priests, and chosen ministers of the Presbyterian, Baptist, and Methodist faiths.

In the Mayor's parlor Mrs. Davis, Margaret Hayes, Mary Stamps, and other relatives, together with two daughters of Leonidas Polk and Mrs. Braxton Bragg, were seated behind broad windows which opened directly onto the shaded portico. Mrs. Davis could see a portion of the multitude that jammed Lafayette Square. As the coffin appeared on the portico, a clock struck the hour of noon, cannon boomed, and the great bell in the near-by First Presbyterian Church began to toll. It was a signal for all the bells of New Orleans to sound the call to mourning. Simultaneously, in cities and towns from northern Virginia to San Antonio, Texas, minute guns were fired and bells tolled; and no one anywhere had to ask "For whom does the bell toll?"

Although the season was early December, in New Orleans it was a perfect day. The sun had risen clear and golden, and, now at its zenith, it hung like a benediction over the historic square. As the church bells sounded and cannon boomed at minute intervals, a solemnity settled upon the uncovered crowd standing before the sun-drenched steps of the City Hall. The Rector of the little Church of the Redeemer in Biloxi began the Episcopal burial service: "I am the resurrection and the life—" A surpliced choir made up of boy sopranos sang the anthem "Through the Valley of the Shadow of Death."

Bishop Galleher made a brief address not in the Episcopal liturgy.

The end of a long and lofty life has come. The strange and sudden dignity of death has been added to the fine and resolute dignity of living . . . through every day of his illustrious life he was an incorruptible and impassioned defender of the liberties of men. Greatly and strangely misconceived, he bore injustice with the calmness befitting his place. He suffered many and grievous wrongs, suffered most for the sake of others.

As "Amens" rose from a thousand throats, Father Hubert stepped to the head of the casket and, in a voice unsteady with emotion, uttered a spontaneous prayer:

O God, loving and compassionate Father, in the name of my heartbroken comrades, I beseech thee to behold us in our bereavement, from whom thou hast taken one who was to us a chief, a leader, and a noble and constant exemplar.

Then eight tall artillerymen mounted the steps and took up the casket. The first of seven bands began a funeral march as Jefferson Davis was borne down the steps between military lines and placed on a four-wheeled caisson in a pavilion-like superstructure, supported by six bronze cannon and canopied with heavy black drapery ornamented with silver fringe. Six black horses, with silver-trimmed harness, drew the caisson, a uniformed soldier at each bridle.

Because of the great number of local organizations and out-of-state delegations desiring to follow Jefferson Davis to the cemetery, arbitrary limits had been set: no private carriages were permitted in the cortège and no individuals were admitted without identifying badges. As it was, by newspapermen's timing, it took an hour and twenty minutes for the restricted procession to pass a given spot. Mounted captains of police and walking platoons of policemen, twelve abreast, cleared the way through the crowded thoroughfares "with marvelous military precision." Georgia's General John Gordon, the honorary marshal, was a handsome figure on horseback in black broadcloth with a wide silk sash as his ensign of office. One of the fourteen Confederate Generals among the fifty pallbearers was South Carolina's Thomas F. Drayton, who had been a classmate of Davis at West Point and was now the last surviving member of the class of 1828. Among the other pallbearers were the old riverboat captain, Thomas P. Leathers, a lifetime friend, and E. B. Kruttschnitt, a nephew of the faithful Judah P. Benjamin.

For J. U. Payne was reserved the honor of escorting Mrs. Davis.

They rode in the first of the eight family carriages with Mrs. Hayes and General Joseph Davis. Beside the driver of the span of black horses sat old Robert Brown, the last body servant of Jefferson Davis, wearing a black armband with a crepe rosette.

Because the principal business streets could not accommodate the tremendous concourse of watchers, the procession was routed a roundabout way. The broad sidewalks, the banquettes, the grilled balconies and the front windows of crepe-hung houses and shops were thick with spectators. Through the mist of her heavy mourning veil, the widow could witness that a mighty crowd had come to honor her husband, belying a recent claim in a Northern paper that the Southern people no longer had any interest in Jefferson Davis.

Thousands of marching Confederate veterans from all over the nation were followed by thirty aged men who had fought in the Mexican War. Fifteen Union veterans, now living in Louisiana, were among the walkers. Though the post-meridian sun was hot, only a scattered few of the old soldiers dropped out during the three hours' trek to suburban Metairie.

It was half past three before the vanguard reached the entrance to the cemetery, where an enormous crowd was waiting, some having arrived in midmorning. They had come by horsecar, private carriage, and afoot. Trains had brought four crammed loads of people after the noon services in Lafayette Square. The broad shell-walks, the green turf, even the tops of white sepulchers were spotted with human beings. Some youths seeking places of special vantage had ensconced themselves in trees.

Near the entrance of the cemetery the procession passed the black-draped equestrian statue of Albert Sidney Johnston. Half a mile beyond was the tomb of the Army of Northern Virginia, a great green mound rising in parterres, ornamented with flowering shrubs, and crowned by a statue of Stonewall Jackson atop a fifty-foot column.

It was four o'clock before the caisson arrived at the foot of the monument. Many in the procession who had had nothing to eat since breakfast or even a drink of water were now weary to faintness. Margaret Hayes had lost consciousness twice during the long ride.

Mrs. Davis, leaning on the arm of Mr. Payne, and Mrs. Hayes, escorted by General Joseph Davis, came slowly up the mound. Immediately behind them followed Robert Brown. A stillness fell upon the vast assemblage when Bishop Thompson began to read that part of the Episcopal service reserved for the graveside. The choir chanted the anthem: "I Heard a Voice from Heaven Saying Unto Me, Write: Blessed are the Dead Who Die in the Lord. For They Rest from Their Labors." A soldier sounded "taps." Bishop Galleher consigned the body to the dust: "In the name of God, Amen." Then because of the extraordinary occasion, he added extemporary words, as if briefing the heavenly hosts.

We here consign the body of Jefferson Davis, a servant of his state and country and a soldier in their armies; sometime member of Congress, Senator from Mississippi, and Secretary of War of the United States; the first and only President of the Confederate States of America; born in Kentucky on the third of June, 1808, died in Louisiana on the sixth of December, 1889, and buried here by the reverent hands of his people.

The December sun was sinking behind a bank of cumulus clouds edged with flaming gold as the soldiers once more raised the casket to their shoulders. They marched around the base of the monument to the open doorway leading into the chamber of the dead and descended the stairs. When Mrs. Davis and her escort started down the steps, three volleys from a Louisiana battery rent the air. The soldier's funeral was over.

One sentence in the fourth paragraph of a newspaper editorial the next morning epitomized for the widow the historic passing of Jefferson Davis: "Many millions of people buried yesterday their best beloved."

AFTERWORD

IN MANNER AND setting the death and the funeral of Jefferson Davis had been a decorous and befitting end to a remarkable if tragic life. "Never was a more universal homage rendered a departed chieftain," Professor Dodd of Chicago University was to write. "The North looked on in mute astonishment at the loyalty of the defeated South; for had not the Southern people once blamed Davis for their ruin!"

Far into the night, when the rest of the Fenner household thought her sleeping, Varina Davis read and reread glowing editorial comments in Southern papers. Because of the sincere demonstrations of grief and penitence the widow could absolve the South for once having made Jefferson Davis a sacrificial scapegoat. And a certain vindication in the Northern press was a balm to her sorrow.

During the six climactic days only two things had occurred to add to her grief. One was the attitude of the War Department over which Jefferson Davis had presided with conspicuous success during Franklin Pierce's regime. On the day of the funeral the Department's flag in Washington, which was always set at half-mast when an ex-Secretary died, floated from the top of the flagstaff in a strong southeast breeze. No announcement was made to the army, which Davis had once commanded. Alone among the fifty-eight Secretaries of War, his death passed without official notice.

The other thing that hurt was a venomous editorial in the New York *Tribune*, once edited by the great Greeley, who had esteemed Jefferson Davis and signed his bail bond. In a tissue of misrepresentations, the *Tribune* quoted nothing from admirers but from three of Davis's past political and personal enemies: William Yancey, the disreputable Henry Foote, and the mendacious Pollard.

It ended with its own contemptuous summation of the Confederate President.

But happily and simultaneously, in the New York *Sun* appeared a just and commendatory tribute as a striking variation of the *Tribune*'s denunciation. The editorial was written by Charles A. Dana, who, as Assistant Secretary of War, had been the messenger in transmitting Stanton's permission to General Miles to put Jefferson Davis in chains.

There is no one to revile, and there are many to honor, or at all events to respect, his memory. He has outlived sectional enmity and personal detraction. He has lived long enough to see the political atmosphere purged of prejudice and rancor, and to forecast in the candid attitude of Northern contemporaries the sober and unbiased judgement of posterity. Even among those who looked upon him with least sympathy it was felt that this man bore defeat and humiliation in the high Roman fashion. . . .

The majority of the leading Northern papers, in fact, were not only fair, but admiring in their comments. An editorial in the New York *World* was as understanding as any effusion in the South, and, because it lacked the incandescence of sectional ardor, it was all the more impressive.

The death of Jefferson Davis ends a most remarkable chapter of history. . . . He was the chosen chieftain of the new Republic which strove to establish itself, and whose adherents battled for its existence with a heroism the memory of which is everywhere cherished as one that does honor to the American character and name. . . . He sacrificed all for the cause he cherished, and he alone of all the South has borne the cross of martyrdom.

He was a man of commanding ability, spotless integrity, and controlling conscience. . . . He was proud, sensitive, and honorable in all his dealings and in every relation of life. . . . A great soul has passed.

And a vindication appeared at the end of a New York *Times* editorial.

The South loves his memory as it should love it and as the people of every patriotic country should and ever will respect it. Were the people of the South to forget him, or fail to honor the man who endured so patiently for their sake, they in turn should deserve none of respect or place in the minds of men who have manhood. . . .

Jefferson Davis will live longer in history and better than will any who have ever spoken against him.

When Mrs. Davis returned to Beauvoir a week after the funeral, dreadfully tired and looking considerably older, her Gulf Coast friends commented among themselves that now her life was over. Varina thought so too—then. In the bleak days of despondency that followed she felt terribly alone, though loving relatives were staying with her. Engulfed in a paroxysm of despair and plagued with insomnia, one stormy night she wrote a friend:

I know my life is over, that no one remembers me with any charm and grace & that I am a lame old weary woman to every living soul. The testimonies of my youth are hidden in death, and I with capacity for many things have fallen into desuetude forever— I feel like an executed person swinging in chains on a lonely road.

But "forever" did not last long with the mercurial Varina, who shortly began to sign her letters V. Jefferson-Davis. Out in the cottage-studio she came across some first-draft chapters of the autobiography which her husband had begun at James Redpath's urging. Suddenly she realized she had something to anchor her days to. With the inspiration of a mission to tell the world what sort of a man her husband was, her vitality returned in full force. With terrific energy she began her personal *Memoir*. Before the year 1890 ended, with the help of James Redpath himself, who came down from New York, and two others, she completed a two-volume work that ran to 1,632 large-type pages.

While correcting proofs in New York in the autumn of 1890, Mrs. Davis became diverted by the excitements of the city. And two years later when the Sunday *World* offered her $1,500 a year for a weekly article and a similar correspondent's position to Winnie, she decided to give up Beauvoir. The place was too expensive for her to run on their slender means and too dreary without the ex-President and the guests he attracted. Winnie needed change and the intellectual stimulation New York could provide, for her romance with Fred Wilkinson had been shattered after his mother's handsome mansion in Syracuse had burned and Mrs. Davis had discovered that his modest salary in a law office could hardly support a wife. Like a proper Victorian daughter, Winnie had bowed to her mother's final adverse decision. She never entirely recovered her health, and neither she nor Wilkinson ever married.

Whatever the impulses and motives that really shaped Mrs. Davis's resolve to live in New York, all in all it was a good move. For there she caught the ear and the imagination of the North and served the South as an adroit diplomat-at-large. She was quick to defend her husband's reputation from any false charge, ignorant or malicious. This she could not have done half so effectively under the magnolias and live oaks of the Mississippi Gulf Coast. But in the South she was severely criticized for her removal.

For fifteen years Varina Jefferson-Davis was to live in New York, where she presided over a Sunday salon frequented by literary people and prominent Southerners who had gone East to recoup their vanished fortunes. With her sparkling conversation, she enchanted even Princeton undergraduate comrades of her grandson. She played her role as the Widow of the Confederacy admirably and with great dignity. And never did she let down in her fierce loyalty to her husband. She often changed the attitudes of critical editors and professor-authors, and she did her discreet best to keep the memory of Jefferson Davis green.

In New York she had two disturbing decisions to make: the final resting place of the ex-President and the disposal of Beauvoir after Winnie's death in 1898 (Winnie had rejected as almost sacrilegious a hotel corporation's offer of $90,000 cash for the Beauvoir place.) Mrs. Davis finally accepted a token $10,000 from a Veterans Association, which guaranteed to build, at a respectable distance, a series of apartments for Confederate soldiers and their wives or widows. Beauvoir, she decreed, was to be a perpetual shrine to her husband's memory, as well as a present haven for indigent veterans, whose care had been the ex-President's constant concern.

The decision about the permanent burial place of her husband had caused heart-searching consideration. Mississippi had virtually a lifelong claim. Kentucky begged for the President of the Confederacy because it was his birth state. Even Georgia, which had caused him the most trouble, made attractive overtures. But Virginia had particularly pleased her in its appeals. The most moving and eloquent overtures had come from Governor Fitzhugh Lee and Senator John Daniel. In publicly expressing Virginia's claim, Fitzhugh Lee pointed out the remarkable number of great Americans who were buried in the commonwealth: George Washington, Thomas Jefferson, George Mason, James Madison, Robert E. Lee, Stonewall Jackson. And in Richmond's own Hollywood lay two Presidents, James Monroe and John Tyler, and many gallant soldiers like J. E. B. Stuart, George Pickett, John Pegram, and A. P. Hill.

Virginia holding in her loving embrace the sacred graves of five Presidents of the United States opens wide her arms and asks that she may be permitted to guard the last resting place of the President of the Confederate States. Here let us erect a monument that will stand in lofty and lasting attestation to tell our children's children of our love for the memory of Jefferson Davis!

Mrs. Davis reflected how fitting it would be for Jefferson Davis to have so many first names in American history as neighbors in death. And Virginia had been the battle center; Richmond had been the Confederacy's historic capital, where Jefferson Davis had resided as its chosen head. Senator Daniel, in an eloquent address in which he had brilliantly met every controversial point in the President's executive career, had said better than anyone else what the sometime wavering Southerners needed to hear. He had jolted the literate South with a stark dramatic statement that made even the reluctant and grudging face the truth:

Had a man less sober-minded and less strong than Davis been President, the Confederacy would not only have gone down in material ruin, but it would have been buried in disgrace!

In late May of 1893, Jefferson Davis was removed from the temporary tomb in Metairie and started on his final progress to Richmond. A special train furnished by the L & N Railroad took several days to reach Virginia's capital. It slowed to funereal pace at stations along the way to let the crowds bow their heads in respect. At Beauvoir, where the train first stopped, the tracks for half a mile were strewn with magnolia petals and various white blossoms. At other stations flowers were scattered along the right of way. In Montgomery, where the President had taken the oath of office, the body lay in state at the Capitol for a day. And on the rest of the roundabout route, citizens gathered with offerings of flowers, in the night hours as well as the day.

In Richmond Jefferson Davis was given a full-scale military funeral and laid to rest in an oval-shaped plot of greensward with a prospect of the James River, not far from the tombs of James Madison and John Tyler. The lot was extensive enough to receive his wife, his six children, his son-in-law and several grandchildren, who would eventually be brought there to rest beside him.

In the North, those newspapers that had had little to say about the ex-President's death in 1889 printed columns about his second burial in 1893. As a New Orleans paper commented, "Sensible people of the North now see nothing to criticize in our showing respect, devotion, and admiration for our heroes." Jefferson Davis, it seemed, would be eventually vindicated.

As President of the Confederacy, Davis had suffered agonies in a prolonged *via crucis*. But he had endured, with his integrity intact, his belief in constitutional government unchanged, and his disposition saved from bitterness. So, in the end, despite exhausting labors, the malice of lesser men, grievous family tragedies, he had emerged from the world's great snare uncaught, though cruelly torn. His life would ever offer to future generations of Americans a stellar example of the very finest national qualities.

Acknowledgments
Sources and Notes on Sources
Index

ACKNOWLEDGMENTS

FOR the exclusive use of almost a thousand unpublished Davis letters and documents, I am deeply indebted to Jefferson Hayes-Davis of Colorado Springs, only living grandson of the Confederate President. I am the more grateful because Mr. Davis gave to the University of Alabama in 1962 some six hundred and fifty heretofore unknown letters, so that I could more conveniently work with them here where I live. (I had spent parts of two summers working with the Davis documents in Colorado.) I am most grateful, too, to Mrs. Lucy Hayes Young, only living granddaughter of Jefferson Davis, and to Mrs. John Wolcott Stewart of Santa Barbara, eldest great-granddaughter, for various kinds of help during the last eleven years.

Invaluable assistance has been rendered me by Mrs. Anna Farrar Goldsborough of Newark, New York, a great-grandniece of Jefferson Davis and also a blood relation to Mrs. Davis, and one who knew them both. I am also indebted to other great-grandnieces: the late Mrs. Mary Lucy O'Kelley of Pass Christian, Mrs. Ralph Wood of Biloxi, Maudie Farrar and Sue Brown Hayes of New Orleans, and to Lucinda Ballard Dietz, the stage costume designer of New York, great-great-grandniece, who possesses holograph Davis letters.

To Mrs. Crampton Harris of Birmingham, another great-grandniece, I am grateful for photographs of the cameo portrait of Jefferson Davis which she inherited and which is reproduced on the jacket and used as the frontispiece. My warm thanks to Albert Ganier of Nashville, great-grandnephew of Jefferson Davis, who furnished me with a revised family tree of the Davises and gave me rare photographs of his distinguished relative, as well as copies of his own accounts of Jefferson Davis's plantation life.

For a second time I express gratitude for hospitality, as well as material, to Walter Stauffer of New Orleans, grandson of General Richard Taylor,

533

great-grandson of Zachary Taylor, and great-grandnephew-in-law of Jefferson Davis.

Mrs. Jessie Palfrey Leake, granddaughter of General Josiah Gorgas, Confederate Chief of Ordnance, has provided me not only with her ancestor's private diary, but with numerous personal letters from Mr. Davis to General or Mrs. Gorgas during and after the war, which she copied verbatim.

For help in research in Canada I am deeply indebted to Edgar A. Collard, Editor of the Montreal *Gazette*, and to the Hon. B. N. Holtham, Q.C., of Sherbrooke, Quebec, both collectors of Davis material for more than two decades.

In following Jefferson Davis's 1868 trail through Scotland, I was assisted by Viscount and Lady Weir of Kilwinning, Ayrshire, to whom I express warm gratitude for their gracious, extended hospitality and for taking me by car over much of the Scottish territory Davis covered.

In London, through courtesies and introductions, I was helped in my work by the United States Ambassador, David Bruce, whose great-aunt was the wife of President Davis's Secretary of War, James Seddon of Virginia. I am also grateful to N. C. Bruce, the young son of the Ambassador, an ardent student of Civil War history, who helped me identify places in London where Davis lived on his several sojourns. I express special appreciation for hospitality and kind attentions in London to the late Nancy, Viscountess Astor, to her son David Astor, Editor of *The Observer*, and to my long-time friend Kenneth Harris of *The Observer*. My thanks to Daniel Minchew of St. Johns College, Oxford, Rhodes Scholar from Georgia, who copied Davis letters for me in the Bodleian Library.

On my researches at Karlsruhe, Germany, where Davis sent his younger daughter to school for five years (1876-1881), I was accompanied by Count Lennart Bernadotte of Sweden, whose great-grandmother, the Grand Duchess Luise of Baden, was patroness of the Friedlander School for Young Ladies, which Winnie Davis attended. I am also much indebted to Herr G. Klotz, the Oberbürgermeister of Karlsruhe, for his unearthing material in the city's archives about Winnie Davis's school years in Germany and her parents' separate visits.

To Lee Meriwether of St. Louis, who celebrated his hundred and first birthday on Christmas night, 1963, I am uncommonly indebted for days of talk about Jefferson Davis, whom he knew from the age of seven, and for permission to use his mother's recollections of Davis as well as his own memoirs.

Deserving of special gratitude is the Reverend Mr. Randolph Blackford, Virginia-born Episcopal clergyman, now retired in St. Petersburg, Florida, for his grandmother's manuscript account of Davis's Canadian visits to his great-grandfather, James Murray Mason, and later with her husband, Lancelot Blackford, long-time principal of the Episcopal High School at Alexandria, Virginia.

I am deeply indebted to Hilary Milton of Washington, D.C., who did special research for me and who sent me as a gift a superb full-size reproduction of the Jefferson Davis portrait in oils by Daniel Huntington (1874) which hangs in the Pentagon corridors with the other Secretaries of War.

To Dr. Chester Bradley, Curator of the Jefferson Davis Casemate Museum at Fort Monroe, Virginia, I am grateful for information about Davis's prison life and particularly for his checking the records for dates of visits of prominent persons during the two years' imprisonment.

To Matt Tom Green of New Orleans I am grateful for photostats of original Davis letters to his grandmother, Bettie Tillman, a foster daughter to the Davises.

Frank James, III, of St. Louis searched for me the local St. Louis papers of September, 1875, and the files of the New York *Times* for the data about Davis's numerous speeches given at Missouri fairs that month.

I thank the Hon. Walter Chandler, ex-Mayor of Memphis and ex-United States Representative, for material about Davis inherited from his grandfather, and George Miller of Brewton, Alabama, collateral descendant of George B. McClellan, who gave me access to some family wartime letters from the General.

To Miss Désirée Franklin, Chairman of the Civil War Centennial Commission of New York and Honorary President of the United Daughters of the Confederacy, I am indebted for too many things to enumerate.

Kind, interested strangers from some thirty states have sent me material for this third volume, and some have given me holograph Davis letters. While there is not space to mention them all, I feel especially grateful to Mrs. H. E. Suits, of Kirkwood, Missouri, granddaughter of Judge James D. Halyburton, who administered the oath of office to Jefferson Davis at his inauguration in Richmond. She sent me many original letters, numerous photographs, and an envelope containing immortelles taken from the President's grave in Richmond in 1893. Mrs. R. E. Wilson of Denver also gave me autograph Davis letters, and Mrs. Homer Beckwith of Sewickly, Pennsylvania, whose great-grandfather was Mr. Davis's Rector at the Church of the Redeemer in Biloxi, furnished me with valuable photostats. Judge Leigh M. Clark of Birmingham, Alabama, provided photostats of his grandfather's letters concerning Davis's public appearance in Augusta, Georgia, in October, 1864. Ray D. Smith, Chairman of the Board, Industrial Training Institute, Chicago, furnished me with a most useful Index to the entire output of *The Confederate Veteran Magazine*, with hundreds of references to Jefferson Davis.

Among the persons to whom I express appreciation for special kinds of assistance are: Dr. Rembert Patrick, Professor of History at the University of Florida; Charles G. Dobbins of the American Council on Education, Washington, D.C.; Dr. Charles Summersell, Head of the History Department, University of Alabama; Dr. Dabney Lancaster, President Emeritus of Longwood College, Virginia; Virginius Dabney, Editor of the Richmond *Times-Dispatch;* Frank G. Everett, Jr., lawyer and history enthusiast of Vicksburg, Mississippi; Thomas Hal Phillips, novelist and recent Public Service Commissioner of Mississippi, who helped me with research in the Mississippi Department of Archives in Jackson; Eppa Hunton, IV, of Richmond; Samuel Tilden Moore, Jr., of Richmond; Clyde Strickland of Tuscaloosa, Alabama, collector of documents and rare books on the Civil War; Dr. Stanley Hoole, Librarian of the University of Alabama, author, and Editor-in-Chief of Confederate Centennial Studies; Major General Orlando Ward, Chief of Military History, Washington, D.C.; Dr. Charles Lowry, Head of FRASCO, Washington, D.C.; Brigadier General Donald Armstrong and Brigadier General James E. Morrisette; Mrs. Jean C. Read of Montgomery, Alabama, who knew Jefferson Davis as a little girl; Mrs. Nell Stephens Murfree of Jacksonville, Florida, who possesses a file of pertinent clippings from old papers; Mildred White Wells of Lookout Mountain, Tennessee; Rucker Agee, founder and first President of the Alabama Historical Association; Mrs. M. O. Ross, wife of the President Emeritus of Butler University, Indianapolis; Margaret Gage Bush of Birmingham, whose grandfather, General Wallace, entertained Davis on his retreat through South Carolina; Harriet Owsley, widow of the historian Frank Owsley and his collaborator in the 1959 revised version of *King Cotton Diplomacy.*

I express gratitude for kindly assistance to John McKenzie of the British Museum; to Dr. C. D. Powell of the Manuscript Division of the Congressional Library in Washington, D.C.; Robert W. Hill and Edward R. Morrison of the New York Public Library; to Charlotte Capers, Director of the Department of Archives and History in Jackson, Mississippi, and to Mrs. James Melton, her assistant; to Vivien Lawson, Catherine Jones, Addie Coleman, and Joyce Lamont of the University of Alabama Library; to Eleanor Brockenbrough of the Confederate Museum, Richmond; John Cook Wyllie, Librarian of the University of Virginia; James W. Patton of the University of North Carolina; Mattie Russell of Duke University; the Library staff of Transylvania College; Marguerite Murphy and Salome Brady of Beauvoir, the Jefferson Davis shrine at Biloxi; Ruth Rowell, Regent, and Eltrym Chalker of the First White House of the Confederacy, Montgomery, Alabama; Dr. Dallas Irvine, Chief of the National Archives, Washington, D.C., who was most generous with his suggestions.

Again I express gratitude to the publishers Houghton Mifflin and Appleton-Century for their kindness in permitting me to quote from their respective editions of *A Diary from Dixie* by Mary Boykin Chesnut.

I am indebted to the late De Vane K. Jones of Tuscaloosa for the use of many out-of-print books, to his widow, Katherine Meriwether Jones, for the loan of her great-aunt's scrapbooks, and to Ernest G. Williams for old books from his grandfather's library in Macon, Mississippi.

I thank Thomas King, Director of Maryland Academy of Sciences, for sending me the manuscript of his aunt, Virginia King, who was a young girl in Richmond when Davis was released on bail; Mrs. John R. Crandall of Macon, Georgia, for old newspaper accounts of Davis's exciting last visit to Macon in 1887 and for family reminiscences concerning the occasion.

For various kinds of assistance and the loan of printed documents, manuscripts, or letters, I thank Mrs. Kendall Northup of Asheville, North Carolina; Warren Jefferson Davis of La Jolla, California; Dean Paul Garner of the School of Commerce and Wade Coleman, Professor of Romance Languages, University of Alabama; Professor Johnstone Parr of Kent University, Ohio; Dr. H. Morton Mason of Richmond; Mary Wallace Kirk of Tuscumbia, Alabama; Mrs. Whitefoord Cole of Louisville; Melvin M. Scott of Falls Church, Virginia; M. Clifford Harrison of Blacksburg, Virginia; Lucan D. Phillips of Leesburg, Virginia; Arthur Woolfolk of Pittsburg; Buford Boone, publisher of the Tuscaloosa *News;* John D. Pemberton, III, Wall Street attorney, namesake and grandson of the Confederate General from Philadelphia; Mr. and Mrs. F. G. Strachan of New Orleans, who own and live in the house where Jefferson Davis died.

For personal reminiscences, I thank Duncan Kent of Savannah, Georgia, who, as a pupil of Chatham Academy, threw flowers in Jefferson Davis's path in 1886, and Mrs. Mary Comer Lane of Savannah, who, as a little girl, presented Davis each morning with a fresh boutonniere while he was the family house guest during the same triumphant visit.

I am uncommonly grateful to Palmer Bradley, Houston attorney, deeply versed in Civil War history, for reading the galleys dealing with the years 1864 to 1867 and suggesting helpful emendations. For reading various parts of the manuscript and checking, I am grateful to Lieutenant James E. Fender of the U. S. Air Force Academy, Colorado Springs, and John M. Finlay, graduate student in English at the University of Alabama; and to Dr. Thomas J. Rountree, Assistant Professor of English, for copying the enlightening notations and criticisms in Davis's handwriting from Davis's personal copy of Dr. Craven's *The Prison Life of Jefferson Davis.*

I cannot refrain from expressing appreciation to Allan Nevins and Bruce Catton, two of America's foremost historians, for their stimulating encouragement during the process of writing this biography. Dr. Nevins most generously gave me access to his personal files of years of collateral researches on Jefferson Davis. My thanks to Shelby Foote, author and lifelong student of the War Between the States, for an exchange of pertinent letters during the last decade, and to E. Merton Coulter of the University of Georgia and A. B. Moore, Dean Emeritus of the University of Alabama Graduate School, for help and tokens of approbation.

To Alphaeus P. Cole of New York, who was commissioned by the Trustees of the University of Alabama to paint my portrait in October, 1963, and to Peter A. Juley, photographer, I am grateful for permission to reproduce the picture on the jacket of this book. And I am indebted to Frank Stallworth for diligent assistance in typing.

My warm thanks to Tom Green, Manager of Longfellow House, Pascagoula, Mississippi, for his most thoughtful courtesies during stays in garden guest houses overlooking the Gulf of Mexico, where I began Volume III on New Year's Day, 1959, and where I returned to do the last chapters in the spring of 1964. I am also grateful for special consideration from the management of the Royal Victoria Hotel in Nassau, once headquarters of the Confederate blockade runners, where in its tropical garden I wrote a portion of this biography.

I am grateful to Dr. Frank A. Rose, President of the University of Alabama, and to Dr. Oliver C. Carmichael, former President, for their sustaining and generous interest in my project.

To Naboth Hedin of West Dennis, Massachusetts, Swedish-born retired editor and one-time Director of the American-Swedish News Exchange, I am profoundly grateful for his careful critical reading of my manuscript, for helpful queries, and for editorial emendations.

My bounteous thanks to Jonathan W. Warner, President of the Gulf States Paper Corporation, Tuscaloosa, Alabama, and to Prewitt Semmes, Sr., of Detroit and Prewitt Semmes, Jr., of Charlottesville, Virginia, for foundation grants which made it possible for me to take a two years' leave of absence from professional duties at the University of Alabama, and to travel extensively in this continent and abroad on research missions during the past five years.

Above all, I am grateful to my wife, Thérèse, for her devoted labor in thirteen years of research, for her four typings of this present manuscript, for her astute criticism of my text, and for her remarkable and enduring patience.

SOURCES AND
NOTES ON SOURCES

BEFORE MY BIOGRAPHY of Jefferson Davis, which has appeared in three volumes, 1955, 1959 and 1964 respectively, the last life of the Confederate President was *Jefferson Davis: The Unreal and the Real* by Robert McElroy, Harmsworth Professor of American History, Oxford University, published in 1937. Dr. McElroy is the only biographer who devotes much space to Davis's last twenty-three years. Even Professor Dodd of the University of Chicago, whose *Jefferson Davis* was regarded by Douglas Southall Freeman in 1950 as the best of ten extant biographies, allots less than twenty pages to his career from May, 1865 to his death in 1889. Allen Tate, whose *Jefferson Davis: His Rise and Fall* was published in 1929, eight years before McElroy's two-volume work, gives hardly four pages to the ex-President's last twenty-four years. So in this present volume I have perforce broken much new ground.

For the reader's ease and quick assurance, as in Volumes I and II, I have made considerable use of "internal documentation," quoting my authority directly in the text. When some material appears peculiarly controversial, I have employed footnotes, but as sparingly as possible. Because so many readers are distracted by little numbers identifying sources in the back of the book, I have foregone them, as in the previous two volumes.

Material on the last sixteen months of the war and Davis's post-war life is so voluminous that my task has been chiefly one of elimination and selection. I have had over a thousand letters hitherto unknown to consider. Of surpassing value have been the intimate family letters in the collection of Jefferson Hayes-Davis, the only living grandson. And I have made use of numerous letters belonging to collateral descendants, as well as scores of others privately owned.

In the McElroy collection in the New York Public Library, which embodies the vast quantity of Walter Fleming papers, the majority of items concern the period of this third volume. The manuscript collections in The Library of Congress, which include the Burton Harrison letters, have proved of special value. At Duke University I have consulted the mass of the Clement Clay, Jr., papers and the letters to and from his wife,

539

Virginia Clay, including many holograph Davis letters. At the University of North Carolina are most of the Mary Chesnut letters and the majority of Jefferson Davis letters to his niece-in-law Mary Stamps. At the Confederate Museum in Richmond, the Howard Tilton Library, Tulane University, and the Mississippi Department of Archives and History, are rich collections of Davis documents which I consulted for this present volume.

I shall not again list the extensive sources mentioned in Volumes I and II, though many are made use of in this third volume. But indispensable for the first twenty-four chapters of this volume have been: Jefferson Davis's *The Rise and Fall of the Confederate Government; The War of the Rebellion: A Compilation of the Official Records of the Union and Confederate Armies; A Compilation of the Messages and Papers of the Confederacy, Including Diplomatic Correspondence,* edited by James D. Richardson; Volume IV of *Battles and Leaders of the Civil War,* edited by Robert Underwood Johnson and C. C. Buel; the last four volumes of Dunbar Rowland's ten-volume *Jefferson Davis, Constitutionalist: His Letters, Papers, and Speeches.*

Volume II of Varina Howell Davis's *Jefferson Davis, ex-President of the Confederate States, A Memoir, by His Wife,* has been a constant source of reference, as have been Mary Boykin Chesnut's *A Diary from Dixie,* General Josiah Gorgas's *Diary,* and J. B. Jones's *A Rebel War Clerk's Diary.*

The second edition of Frank Owsley's indispensable *King Cotton Diplomacy,* revised by his widow, Harriet Chappell Owsley, 1959, remains the most thorough single-volume account of Foreign Relations of the Confederate States of America.

The new 1957 edition of *Lee's Dispatches, Unpublished Letters of General Robert E. Lee, C. S. A. to Jefferson Davis,* originally edited by Douglas Southall Freeman, with Additional Dispatches and Foreword by Grady McWhiney, has furnished me with essential material that does not appear in *Official Records.*

I have found of exceeding value *Recollections and Letters of General Robert E. Lee by His Son, Captain Robert E. Lee,* first published in 1904 and reissued in 1924.

I have received special benefits from the following "general" books: E. Merton Coulter's *The Confederate States of America;* J. G. Randall's *The Civil War and Reconstruction;* James Ford Rhodes's *History of the United States,* Vols. V and VI; Edward Channing's *A History of the United States* (Vol. VI, *The War for Southern Independence*); James Truslow Adams's *America's Tragedy;* Stanley Horn's *The Army of Tennessee: A Military History;* Robert Selph Henry's *Story of the Confederacy; The Civil War: The Picture Chronicle* by Ralph Newman and E. B. Long; and Ezra J. Warner's *Generals in Gray.*

Particularly high in my esteem stands Rembert W. Patrick's *Jefferson*

Davis and His Cabinet, the only thorough study of Davis's relations with his official advisers. A new edition was published in 1961.

Among scores of biographies especially consulted for this book, besides the ten of Jefferson Davis, are the last volume of Douglas Southall Freeman's *R. E. Lee;* Rudolph von Abele's *Alexander H. Stephens;* Robert Selph Henry's *"First With the Most" Forrest;* Albert Bushnell Hart's *Salmon Portland Chase;* T. Harry Williams's *P. G. T. Beauregard: Napoleon in Gray;* Vol. IV of Carl Sandburg's *Abraham Lincoln: The War Years;* Benjamin Thomas's *Abraham Lincoln;* J. G. Randall and Richard Current's final volume of Randall's four-volume life of Lincoln, *The Last Full Measure;* James L. Vallandigham's *A Life of Clement L. Vallandigham;* Lloyd Lewis's *Sherman: Fighting Prophet;* Lloyd Paul Stryker's *Andrew Johnson: A Study in Courage;* John W. Thomason's *Jeb Stuart;* and Burke Davis's *Gray Fox: Robert E. Lee and the Civil War.*

The best of the memoirs that refer to Jefferson Davis and his contemporaries, besides the three diaries mentioned above, are: Mrs. Burton Harrison's *Recollections Grave and Gay;* Mrs. Roger A. Pryor's *Reminiscences of Peace and War;* Virginia Clay-Clopton's *A Belle of the Fifties;* Mrs. D. Giraud Wright's *A Southern Girl in '61: War-Time Memories of a Confederate Senator's Daughter; The Private Journal of Georgiana Gholson Walker, 1862-1865,* edited by Dwight Franklin Henderson; John H. Reagan's *Memoirs, With Special References to Secession and the Civil War;* Richard Taylor's *Destruction and Reconstruction;* R. G. H. Kean's *Diary;* John S. Wise's *The End of an Era;* T. C. De Leon's *Belles, Beaux and Brains of the '60s;* George T. Denison's *Soldiering in Canada;* Lee Meriwether's *My First Hundred Years, and a Postscript to My Long Life, 1862-1864;* and James Robert Maxwell's *Autobiography.*

Among the memoirs and diaries by Northerners, I have consulted *Personal Memoirs of Ulysses S. Grant,* edited by E. B. Long; Sherman's *Memoirs;* Gideon Welles's *Diary;* John Bigelow's *Retrospections of an Active Life;* Henry Adams's *The Education of Henry Adams.*

Material on prisons and prison life is voluminous. Perhaps nothing is more vividly revealing and accurate than a book by a Northern prisoner of war: *The True Story of Andersonville Prison, A Defense of Major Henry Wirz* by James Madison Page, Late 2nd Lieutenant, Company A, Sixth Michigan Cavalry. The volumes of *Official Records of the War of the Rebellion,* Series II, deal exhaustively with prison records. One of the best known and most conclusive studies is *The Southern Side: or Andersonville Prison* by R. Randolph Stevenson. Among other works I have consulted are William B. Hesseltine's *Civil War Prisons, A Study in War Psychology;* Albert D. Richardson's *The Secret Service, the Field, the Dungeon and the Escape;* Edward A. Pollard's *Observations in the North: Eight Months in Prison and on Parole;* Ambrose Spencer's *A Narrative of Andersonville;* John W. Urban's *Battlefield and Prison Pen;* W. A.

Wash's *Camp, Field and Prison Life.* Among the most valuable magazine
and newspaper articles are: "Andersonville and other War Prisons" by
Jefferson Davis, in *Belford's Magazine,* January, 1890; "A Yankee in Andersonville" by T. H. Mann, in *Century Magazine,* July, 1890; "The Exchange
of Prisoners" by Robert Ould, in *The Central Presbyterian* of September,
1870.

For detailed facts about the Confederate Navy I have consulted but
little employed in this volume; *Official Records of the Union and Confederate Navies in the War of the Rebellion;* Raphael Semmes's exciting
sea adventures told in *Memoirs of Service Afloat, During the War Between the States;* James D. Bulloch's *The Secret Service of the Confederate States in Europe: or, How the Confederate Cruisers Were Equipped;*
and J. Thomas Scharf's *History of the Confederate Navy from Its Organization to the Surrender of the Last Vessel.*

Recollections of a Rebel Reefer by James Morris Morgan, who was
ordered to accompany Mrs. Davis on her flight from Richmond, furnished me with lively material on the exciting last days of the Confederate
capital and the harried trip to Georgia. There is great merit in A. J.
Hanna's *Flight Into Oblivion,* which traces Davis's movements from April
2, 1865 to his capture and imprisonment. In *The Harrisons of Skimino*
appears Burton Harrison's eye-witness account of the exodus from Richmond and the capture. In *Century Magazine* (November, 1883) appeared
Harrison's article "The Capture of Jefferson Davis." Other sources concerning these episodes include: W. H. Parker's *Recollections of a Naval
Officer;* "The Last Meeting of the Confederate Cabinet" by J. E. Walm-
sley, in the *Mississippi Valley Historical Review,* Vol. VI, pp. 337-338;
Stephen R. Mallory's "The Last Days of the Confederate Government,"
in *McClure's Magazine* in two issues, December, 1900 and January, 1901;
F. R. Lubbock's *Six Decades in Texas;* Basil W. Duke's *Reminiscences;*
The Diary of John Taylor Wood; The Diary of Tench F. Tilghman, the
last being particularly vivid.

For the period of Davis's two years' imprisonment at Fort Monroe, I
have used: Mrs. Davis's letters to her husband and to important Unionists
like Horace Greeley and Senator Reverdy Johnston, Mr. Davis's letters
to his wife, the Reverend Dr. Minnegerode's memoirs, and all important, Dr. John J. Craven's diary incorporated into *The Prison Life of Jefferson Davis. The Trials and Trial of Jefferson Davis* by Charles M. Blackford, published in 1901, is the best compendium on the subject.

For studies of the Reconstruction I recommend the following books,
which have been particularly helpful to me: *The Tragic Era* by Claude
Bowers; *The South During Reconstruction, 1865-1877* by E. Merton Coul-
ter; *The Civil War and Reconstruction* by J. G. Randall; *A History of
Mississippi* by Dunbar Rowland; *Reconstruction in Mississippi* by James
W. Garner; *Documentary History of Reconstruction* by Walter F. Flem-

ing; *A Political History of Virginia During Reconstruction* by H. J. Eckenrode; J. S. McNeilly's *Reconstruction in Mississippi*.

Among various monographs and brochures which I have found enlightening are: *Dr. Craven and the Prison Life of Jefferson Davis* by Chester B. Bradley; *The Confederate Baggage and Treasure Train Ends It's Flight in Florida* by Tench Francis Tilghman; *The Confederacy and Zeb Vance* by Richard E. Yates; *Lincoln's Plan of Reconstruction* by William D. Hesseltine; *"My Ever Dearest Friend": The Letters of A. Dudley Mann to Jefferson Davis, 1869-1889,* edited by John Preston Moore; *The Confederate Rams at Birkenhead* by Wilbur Devereaux Jones; *Ploughshares into Swords: Josiah Gorgas and Confederate Ordnance* by Frank E. Vandiver; *John Slidell and the Confederates in Paris* by Beccles Willson; *Jefferson Davis Lawsuit for Brierfield* by Wirt A. Williams; *The Family Sorrows of Jefferson Davis* by Arthur Marvin Shaw; *History of the Impeachment of Andrew Johnson* by Edmund G. Ross; "Mrs. Greenhow" by Lady Georgiana Fuller in *Temple Bar,* London, November, 1870.

For opinions of Davis's contemporaries the following two thick volumes published in 1890, the year after his death, are essential: *Life and Reminiscences of Jefferson Davis by Distinguished Men of His Time,* with an Introduction by John W. Daniel, United States Senator from Virginia, and *The Davis Memorial Volume and the World's Tribute to His Memory,* edited by J. William Jones, D.D.

I have found most helpful *South of Appomattox* by Nash K. Burger and John K. Bettersworth, containing ten excellent biographical profiles of prominent Confederates and their careers after 1865. In *First Lady of the South,* Ishbel Ross has presented a vivid full length portrait of Varina Howell Davis from her birth to her death in 1906, and her life of Rose Greenhow entitled *Rebel Rose* is the best we have. Harnet Kane's *Spies for the Blue and Gray* makes lively reading.

Among the miscellaneous works that have provided me with interesting material I must mention *Vizetelly Covers the Confederacy* by W. Stanley Hoole, *Pardon and Amnesty under Lincoln and Johnson* by J. T. Dorris, and *The Training of an American: The Earlier Life and Letters of Walter H. Page* by Burton J. Hendrick.

Among the flood of volumes that have been issued during these Centennial years I find of more than special literary and historical interest: *Patriotic Gore* by Edmund Wilson; *Grant Moves South* by Bruce Catton; *The Civil War, a Narrative: From Fredericksburg to Meridian* by Shelby Foote; *Two Roads to Sumter* by Bruce and William Catton.

In the New York Public Library may be found seven brochures of special merit by Walter Fleming, among them: "The Religious Life of Jefferson Davis," "Jefferson Davis, the Negroes and the Negro Problem," and "Jefferson Davis and Andersonville."

Among pertinent magazine and newspaper articles about Jefferson Davis by persons who knew him intimately, I particularly recommend "Jefferson Davis in Private Life," a five-column article by his daughter Winnie in the New York *Herald*, August 11, 1895.

I have found useful The *New-York Historical Society Collections, The Mississippi Valley Historical Review, The Virginia Magazine of History, The Kentucky Historical Review, The Alabama Historical Review,* and *The Missouri Historical Review.*

Newspapers that have yielded material for this third volume include: London *Times*, London *Saturday Review*, Glasgow *Herald*, Montreal *Gazette*, New York *Tribune*, New York *Times*, New York *World*, New York *Herald*, Philadelphia *Press*, Chicago *News*, Washington *Chronicle*, Washington *Post*, Richmond *Dispatch*, Richmond *Examiner*, Richmond *Enquirer*, Montgomery *Advertiser*, Montgomery *Daily Post*, Mobile *Register*, Memphis *Appeal*, Louisville *Courier-Journal*, Charleston *News and Courier*, Macon *Telegraph*.

I have made use of files of the following magazines: *Blackwood's Edinburgh Magazine, The Index, The London Illustrated News, The Atlantic Monthly, Harper's Weekly, Century Magazine, Belford's Magazine, The Southern Bivouac, The Confederate Veteran Magazine, McClure's Magazine,* and *North American Review.*